RealWorld
EVALUATION

RealWorld
EVALUATION

*Working Under **Budget, Time, Data,** and **Political Constraints***

Michael Bamberger
Independent Consultant

Jim Rugh
CARE International

Linda Mabry
Washington State University, Vancouver

SAGE Publications
Thousand Oaks ▪ London ▪ New Delhi

For information:

Sage Publications, Inc.
2455 Teller Road
Thousand Oaks, California 91320
E-mail: order@sagepub.com

Sage Publications Ltd.
1 Oliver's Yard
55 City Road
London EC1Y 1SP
United Kingdom

Sage Publications India Pvt. Ltd.
B-42, Panchsheel Enclave
Post Box 4109
New Delhi 110 017 India

Printed in the United States of America.

Library of Congress Cataloging-in-Publication Data

Bamberger, Michael.
RealWorld evaluation : working under budget, time, data, and political
 constraints / Michael Bamberger, Jim Rugh, Linda Mabry.
       p. cm.
Includes bibliographical references and index.
ISBN 978-1-4129-0946-4 (pbk)
    1. Evaluation research (Social action programs)—Developing countries.
2. Economic development projects—Developing countries—Evaluation.
I. Rugh, Jim. II. Mabry, Linda. III. Title.
H62.5.D44B36 2006
001.4—dc22

                                                    2005023035

This book is printed on acid-free paper.

07   08   09   10   9   8   7   6   5   4   3   2

Acquiring Editor:	Lisa Cuevas Shaw
Project Editor:	Jenn Reese
Copy Editor:	Linda Gray
Typesetter:	C&M Digitals (P) Ltd.
Indexer:	Pamela Van Huss

Contents

List of Figures

List of Tables

List of Boxes

Preface

This book addresses the challenges of conducting evaluations in situations where there is not enough time, not enough money, or not enough data. We also recognize that most evaluators are subject to pressures from many sides concerning the "right" evaluation methods to use, what should be studied (and not studied), who should be involved, and how and to whom the findings should be disseminated. We call this the *RealWorld Evaluation* (RWE) approach because it addresses a set of important issues that affect many evaluations but that are not systematically addressed in most evaluation textbooks.[1]

The RWE approach originally addressed problems of conducting evaluations in developing countries, but it soon became clear that despite the widespread use of evaluation in developed countries such as the United States, Canada, Europe, Australasia, and Japan, many evaluators in these countries faced similar budget, time, data, and political constraints. Consequently, RWE now addresses realities faced by evaluators in both developing and developed countries.

The book is intended for three main audiences. First are the *evaluation practitioners* who design, conduct, and advise on evaluation methodology and use. Second are the *users of evaluation,* including agencies who commission evaluations, the staff of agencies or programs being evaluated, policymakers, academics, groups affected by the programs being evaluated, advocacy groups, public opinion, and the media. The third audience is the *university community* where evaluation methodology is taught and which is one of the main sources of evaluation expertise. Each audience includes both people who are relatively new to the field of evaluation and the "old hands" who have been involved in evaluation for a long time. Of course, there is considerable overlap between the three audiences. For example, many university faculty members also conduct evaluations and advise on their use, and many evaluation practitioners also teach. The introduction includes a reader's guide suggesting the sections of the book likely to be of most interest to each audience.

For people relatively new to the field of evaluation, the book can also be used as an introductory text on the general principles of evaluation, while for experienced evaluators, the book addresses the special issues involved in conducting evaluations under real-world constraints. Our experience from having organized workshops in Canada, Japan, the Philippines, South Africa, Sri Lanka, Russia, the Ukraine, and the United States is that the question of how to conduct adequately rigorous evaluations when it is not possible to follow standard evaluation methodologies is one that most evaluation practitioners and evaluation users have faced at some time. Although most evaluators are familiar with the *fast and dirty* evaluation studies that largely ignore concerns about rigor and validity of conclusions, very few have systematically addressed the challenge of how to ensure maximum methodological rigor under a particular set of real-world constraints. As indicated earlier, to the best of our knowledge no previous evaluation textbook systematically addresses all these questions.

The RWE approach does not claim to have invented any new evaluation methods. What we have done is to show how standard evaluation tools and techniques can be integrated into a seven-step approach for conducting evaluations under real-world constraints. A central premise is the value of mixed-method evaluations that combine quantitative and qualitative approaches and methods so as to draw on the strengths of both approaches while compensating for the weaknesses of either approach if used in isolation. Consequently, the book can also be used as an introductory evaluation text because we draw on and review a broad set of qualitative, quantitative, and mixed-method approaches.

The RWE approach (summarized in Chapter 1 and discussed in more detail in Chapters 2–8) includes the following steps:

1. Scoping the evaluation

2. Addressing budget constraints

3. Addressing time constraints

4. Addressing data constraints

5. Addressing political influences

6. Strengthening the evaluation design and the validity of the conclusions

7. Helping clients and stakeholders use the evaluation

Recognizing that some readers are mainly interested in a relatively nontechnical guide on how to commission, conduct, or use evaluations while others would like to go deeper into the theory and methodology, the book is organized around these different interests. Part I presents a general overview of the RWE approach and should be of interest to all readers. Part II contains seven chapters describing, in a relatively nontechnical way, the seven steps of the RWE approach. Cross-references are given to the more detailed discussions of methodological issues and approaches in Part III. This is intended for evaluation practitioners and users but also provides a useful framework for teaching.

Part III includes more extensive discussion of program theory evaluation; various evaluation designs or scenarios; quantitative, qualitative, and mixed-method approaches and methods for data collection and analysis; and the application of sample design principles to the RWE contexts. These chapters are designed for readers wishing to go into more depth.

Part IV, "Putting It All Together," includes two chapters. Chapter 15 discusses evaluation capacity building for RWE. This covers both the organization of traditional training programs (workshops, courses, etc.) and *interactive evaluation capacity development,* which concerns *learning by doing* during the process of carrying out the design, implementation, analysis, and use of an ongoing evaluation. Chapter 16 shows how to "bring it all together" and how to apply the RWE approach in the field. That summary chapter also describes the main stages in a typical evaluation and shows how the RWE approaches can be used at each stage. This can be used by readers new to the field as a general introduction to the conduct of evaluation. Finally, we provide a guide to evaluation resources available on the Web, which can be informative for those wanting to learn more about evaluation organizations, training resources, and various approaches to and methodologies for conducting and using evaluations.

We wish you success in your evaluation work and hope the book will help you conduct, use, and teach about evaluation in RealWorld contexts.

Note

1. We originally called this the *Shoestring Evaluation* approach (see the Spring 2004 article in the *American Journal of Evaluation*) because we originally focused only on how to conduct evaluations under time and budget constraints. However, it became clear that while these problems affect many evaluations, many other evaluations have reasonably adequate budget and no great time pressure but face problems relating to lack of data (e.g., the evaluation started late and there is no baseline data), while for others, the main problems concern political influences.

Acknowledgments

This book benefited greatly from the advice and encouragement of Lucia Fort, Raymond Gervais, Michael Hendricks, Patrick Leung, Michael Patton, Mike Ponder, Michael Scriven, and Brett S. Sharp. We would also like to thank Susan Kistler and her colleagues in the American Evaluation Association; Karen Ginsberg, Linda Morra, and Ray Rist at the International Program for Development Evaluation Training; Dr. Sivagnanasothy and his colleagues at the Sri Lankan Evaluation Association; Patrick Grasso, Keith MacKay, and Markus Goldberg at the World Bank; Nobuko Fujita at the Foundation for Advanced Studies in International Development in Tokyo; Mary Cole at the Development Bank for Southern Africa; Zenda Ofir of the African Evaluation Association; Alexey Kuzmin of the International Program Evaluation Network; and the Atlanta-Area Evaluation Association, among others, for offering the opportunity to organize workshops and seminars on Shoestring Evaluation and RealWorld Evaluation as the approach developed over the past four years.

We would also like to thank Lisa Cuevas, Karen Wong, Stephanie Adams, Jenn Reese, and Linda Gray of Sage Publications for guiding us through the publication process.

Introduction

The RealWorld
Evaluation Approach

The RealWorld Evaluation (**RWE**) approach was developed to help evaluators who must conduct evaluations when facing budget, time, data, or political constraints. Although originally designed for evaluators working in developing countries, the approach has also attracted the interest of evaluators in developed countries.

Many evaluators have faced the situation in which they are not called in until the project or program they are asked to evaluate is well underway or perhaps nearing completion. Even when the evaluation is commissioned at the start of the project, the evaluation design is often constrained by lack of time or money or by technical difficulties in collecting certain types of data. In many cases, the evaluator is also subject to pressure from clients, stakeholders, or government agencies to adopt certain kinds of evaluation design or to avoid asking certain kinds of questions or interviewing certain groups.

RWE is based on a seven-step approach, summarized in Chapter 1 and described in detail in Chapters 2–8, that includes the following:

- *Step 1: Scoping the evaluation.* Understanding client information needs and the context within which the evaluation is being conducted; defining a program theory that describes the objectives and intended method of operation of the program; and identifying the budget, time, and data constraints and any political factors affecting how the evaluation will be conducted, disseminated, and used
- *Step 2: Strategies for addressing budget constraints.* How to reduce the costs through simplifying the evaluation design, reducing the amounts of data to be collected, using expensive consultants more efficiently, and streamlining data analysis
- *Step 3: Strategies for addressing time constraints.* Rapid data collection methods, planning ahead to avoid delays and bottlenecks—particularly during the often short periods when outside consultants are involved—and using videoconferencing to reduce travel and to permit more frequent interactions between the evaluation team and agency staff

- *Step 4: Strategies for addressing data constraints.* Reconstructing baseline or comparison group data if either of these was not collected, effective use of secondary data, making sure that data are collected from the right people, collecting data on sensitive topics, and how to locate and interview difficult-to-reach groups
- *Step 5: Understanding and coping with political factors influencing how the evaluation is designed, implemented, disseminated, or used.* Identifying the key actors and their political perspectives and understanding how these affect their orientation to the evaluation; developing strategies to address the political realities without compromising the evaluation
- *Step 6: Strengthening the evaluation design and the validity of conclusions.* This involves a checklist to identify threats to the validity and adequacy of the evaluation conclusions and a set of strategies to address the threats and improve the quality of the evaluation
- *Step 7: Helping clients use the evaluation.* Ensuring that clients are actively involved from the start and that they "buy in" to the evaluation; maintaining contact with clients throughout the evaluation and ensuring that by the time the major reports are published they do not contain any surprises for the client; adapting the presentation of findings to the preferred communciation style of different stakeholders

The Organization of the Book

The book is divided into four parts. Part I provides the background to the development and purpose of RWE. Chapter 1 begins by explaining why the RWE approach was developed and the gap it seeks to fill, and then discusses the contexts within which RealWorld evaluations are conducted. Issues covered include (a) the types of constraints facing evaluators, (b) the RWE approach to these constraints and differences and similarities between the RWE context in developing and developed countries, and finally (c) who uses RWE, for what purposes, and when.

Part II, "The Seven Steps of the RealWorld Evaluation Approach," has a chapter devoted to each of the seven steps of the RWE approach. Chapter 2 discusses Step 1, the scoping of the evaluation. Before thinking about the evaluation design, it is important to fully understand the purpose of the evaluation, the information needs and expectations of the clients and stakeholders, and the constraints and pressures under which they are working. What is the client's bottom line? What do different clients really want from the evaluation, and how will the results be used? Clarifying these questions is particularly critical for RWE because difficult choices will often have to be made to accommodate budget and time constraints or to recognize the limitations of the available data. The chapter also introduces *program theory evaluation* (discussed in more detail in Chapter 9), which in addition to clarifying the underlying model on which the program is based, can also help identify the critical hypothesis or the linkages in the program implementation model on which the limited evaluation resource should focus. Step 1 concludes by identifying the different evaluation design strategies available for addressing the cost, time, and data constraints that a particular evaluation will face and then assessing the strengths and weaknesses (threats to validity and adequacy) of each option. The different strategies are then discussed with clients, emphasizing the trade-offs involved in each option, and an agreement is then reached on which options are most acceptable to the client.

Chapters 3 and 4 discuss strategies available for addressing budget (Step 2) and time (Step 3) constraints. How many evaluators have been told by the client, "We really need a rigorous and professional evaluation as it is important to assess impacts, but . . . unfortunately our budget has been cut" or ". . . the evaluation report must be completed in [an incredibly small number of] weeks." Step 2 describes five options for reducing costs, and Step 3 combines these options with four additional options for reducing the time needed to conduct the evaluation.

Chapter 5 (Step 4) discusses ways to address common problems concerning the lack of important data or the quality and reliability of the data. These problems are very commonly encountered in RWEs, particularly when the evaluation is not commissioned until late in the project cycle so that no baseline data have been collected. The chapter introduces a number of approaches for creating (*reconstructing*) baseline data. Many sources of existing documentary data (secondary data) can be used, and guidelines are presented both for identifying documentary sources (e.g., project records, records of public agencies, census and survey data, university research projects, newspapers, photographs) and for assessing their appropriateness for the purposes of the evaluation. Another way to reconstruct baseline data is through the use of *recall* whereby individuals or groups are asked to remember or give their judgment on conditions at the start of the project or how things have changed since then, and guidelines are given for assessing potential biases or limitations of recall. The creation of comparison groups and the reconstruction of information on their baseline conditions are also discussed. In addition, the chapter covers techniques for collecting information on sensitive topics and on difficult-to-reach groups and recognizes the special challenges for the RealWorld evaluator in collecting this information. Many of these groups are the poorest and most vulnerable sectors of the community, and reaching them is often more costly and time-consuming than collecting information on nonsensitive topics from easily identified groups; consequently, there will often be pressures to ignore these difficult questions and inaccessible groups.

Chapter 6 (Step 5) discusses the many ways in which values, ethics, and politics influence how evaluations are designed and implemented and how the findings and recommendations are disseminated and used. We identify common political issues arising at the outset of an evaluation, during implementation, and during reporting and use of the evaluation, and we propose strategies for addressing all these issues. We also discuss some important professional and ethical issues concerning who should be given information on the evaluation and when. Often, the client would like to limit who sees and is invited to comment on the evaluation draft, whereas the evaluator may feel that the report should be given to the mass media and to the different stakeholder groups potentially affected by the project. We will return to these ethical issues throughout the book.

Chapter 7 (Step 6) discusses ways to strengthen the evaluation design and enhance the validity of the conclusions. The purpose of an evaluation is to produce valid conclusions and recommendations based on research methods that conform to accepted professional standards. In all evaluations, many factors can affect the validity of the conclusions. These *threats to the validity and adequacy of the evaluation conclusions* require particular attention in RWE because of the number of compromises that have to be made to accommodate to the budget, time, and data limitations under which most of these evaluations have to be conducted. This chapter presents and illustrates a framework, with supporting checklists and worksheets, for identifying and addressing threats to validity and adequacy. Traditionally, two separate frameworks have been developed for assessing threats to validity of quantitative (QUANT) evaluations and threats to adequacy for qualitative (QUAL) evaluations.[1] In this chapter, we first discuss the validity and adequacy issues for QUANT and QUAL evaluations separately, and we then propose an integrated checklist that can be used to assess all QUANT, QUAL, and mixed-method evaluations. We also identify the points during the RWE cycle when corrective measures can be taken. The chapter concludes by discussing a RealWorld project evaluation worksheet (Appendix 2) that has been developed to assist funding agencies, managers, consultants, and evaluation practitioners who need to assess the strengths and weaknesses of an evaluation. In Appendix 3, we include a worked example illustrating how the worksheet is applied in the field.

Chapter 8 discusses the final step (Step 7) of the RWE approach: helping clients and other stakeholders use the evaluation. The universal concern of evaluators that their findings and recommendations are not used is particularly critical for RWE; many evaluations are conducted under time and budget pressures that may make it even more difficult for the findings to receive due consideration. We discuss some of the reasons that many evaluations are not used and propose practical approaches that can be employed in the field to increase the likelihood that the evaluation findings are useful and that they are actually used.

Part III is titled "A Review of Evaluation Methods and Approaches and Their Applications in RealWorld Evaluation." These chapters reinforce the approach presented in Part II that, wherever possible, mixed-method designs should be used to strengthen the evaluation by combining the strengths and complementarities of QUANT and QUAL evaluation approaches and methods. Chapter 9 reviews program theory evaluation and explains its importance for RWE in helping identify the critical areas and issues on which the limited evaluation resources should focus. Program theory evaluation can overcome one of the major weaknesses of many QUANT pretest-posttest evaluation designs—namely, their failure to explain what goes on during the project implementation process (the *black box,* as this process is often referred to in economic analysis). By combining summative and process evaluation, program theory evaluation opens up the black box and explains the project implementation process and also how the project interacts with the economic, political, institutional, environmental, and cultural context within which it operates. The chapter also discusses the **logical framework analysis** (LFA or logframe) approach used by many international development agencies[2] and national institutions (e.g., the U.S. Centers for Disease Control) to operationalize program theory so that progress and outcomes can be monitored. We also discuss whether and how program theory can contribute to the assessment of causality. This is of particular interest to RWE because budget, time, and data constraints often limit the types of conventional causal analysis that can be used.

Chapter 10 presents seven evaluation designs that among them cover most RWE scenarios. Although these describe general evaluation principles, the designs can more easily be applied in QUANT and mixed-method evaluations. The chapter begins by discussing the randomized design model, considered by most QUANT evaluators to be the strongest impact evaluation design, and then shows different ways in which quasi-experimental designs can be adapted to the budget, time, and data constraints of different RWE scenarios. Significant cost and time savings can be achieved by eliminating one or more data collection points (pretest baseline data collection for the project and control groups and posttest data collection for the same two groups). However, the elimination of any of these observation points weakens the evaluation design and increases the number and seriousness of the threats to validity. Case studies are presented for designs 2 to 7 together with discussion of when each design can be used and the most important threats to validity. Chapter 11 then describes the main QUANT approaches to data collection and analysis and discusses some of the strengths and weaknesses of QUANT methods for impact evaluation.

Chapter 12 describes the main QUAL approaches to data collection and analysis and discusses some of the strengths and weaknesses of QUAL methods for impact evaluation. The chapter explains that most QUAL evaluators approach the assessment of project effects quite differently from their QUANT colleagues, placing much more emphasis on an in-depth analysis of a smaller number of subjects (e.g., classrooms, workplaces, communities, families, or individuals) and adopting a holistic approach to understand the interactions between each subject or project location and the particular setting. Emphasizing the uniqueness of each setting, most QUAL evaluators are cautious about trying to make the kinds of broad generalizations from the cases studied to a wider population that form an integral part of many QUANT evaluations.

Chapter 13 then describes *mixed-methods* designs that seek to combine the strengths of QUANT and QUAL designs for program evaluation. While mixed-method approaches can strengthen most evaluation designs, they are particularly valuable for RWE contexts because they help extract the maximum amount of information and understanding from the more limited amounts of data that can often be collected. There are two main strategies for using mixed methods. One strategy is to use mixed methods to strengthen an evaluation design that has either a *dominant* QUAL or QUANT approach, and the other is to use an *integrated approach* that gives equal weight to QUANT and QUAL approaches where neither is dominant. The chapter discusses some of the different benefits that mixed methods can bring to QUANT and QUAL approaches, including (a) providing different perspectives, (b) conducting analysis on different levels, (c) providing new ways to interpret unanticipated findings, and (d) providing independent sources of data for key indicators and evaluation questions. Implementing a mixed-methods design requires an integrated evaluation strategy that is more than just combining different data collection methods and that has implications for the composition of the research team; the organization of the planning, data collection, and analysis phases; and possibly the cost and duration of the evaluation.

Chapter 14 discusses sampling design for RWE. The approaches to sampling in QUAL and QUANT evaluations are usually quite different. QUAL evaluations usually involve a small number of subjects that are selected *purposively* to represent the different types or issues of interest to the evaluation. Random sample selection is normally not appropriate for the selection of this type of small sample. For QUANT evaluations, on the other hand, the size of the sample is one of the key determinants of the cost and duration of the evaluation. In contrast to QUAL evaluations, random sample selection is essential for most QUANT evaluations because one of the central purposes of the evaluation is to determine whether there is statistically significant evidence that the project has contributed to the intended outputs, outcomes, and impacts. The basic concepts of nonprobability and probability sampling are described, and some of the critical choices in sample design are identified. The concepts of *power analysis* and *effect size* are introduced. These concepts, which may be new to many readers, provide the basis for estimating the required sample size. An understanding of these concepts is critical for RWE because there are often pressures to reduce sample size, but if the sample becomes too small, it will not be possible to identify statistically significant project effects, even if they do exist. Guidelines are presented for estimating the appropriate sample size for QUANT RWEs.

Part IV, "Pulling It All Together," draws together all the material discussed in the previous chapters. Chapter 15 discusses how to strengthen the capacity of evaluation practitioners and users to be more effectively involved in the different stages of evaluation. It suggests ways to design and deliver evaluation capacity building for different audiences, including evaluation users and the agencies that commission evaluations, evaluation practitioners, and community organizations. The chapter also draws on the policy analysis literature to provide pointers on how to plan evaluations and present evaluation findings so as to increase the likelihood that the findings will contribute to the policymaking process.

Chapter 16, "Bringing It All Together: Applying RealWorld Evaluation to Each Step of the Evaluation Process," brings together all the tools and techniques presented step by step in Part II and discussed in more detail in Part III. This concluding chapter takes the reader through the typical stages and decisions in the design and implementation of an evaluation and shows how the different RWE approaches can be used at each stage and how they can be applied in a typical evaluation. This chapter can also be used by readers who are relatively new to the evaluation field as an introduction to the different stages of an evaluation.

How to Use the Book

The book is intended for three main audiences, although many readers may "wear different hats" and be, for example, university faculty members and at the same time evaluation consultants. Under each of these categories, there are persons who have not taken specific courses or had previous experience in evaluation, and there are those who have a long experience in the field. In the remaining sections of this introductory chapter, we address each of these audiences and make suggestions for how each might read this book and/or use it as a reference manual for subjects of particular interest to them.

- *The university community.* This audience includes undergraduates and other groups with only limited background in evaluation as well as graduate students and teaching faculty. The book can be used as an introductory text on the basics of evaluation and also as a more advanced course in practical applications of evaluation theory and methodologies when resources are constrained.
- *Evaluation practitioners.* These include both experienced evaluators, particularly those who have worked mainly on conventional evaluations and who have less experience with real-world constraints, and people who are relatively new to the evaluation field. An important group includes professionals trained in other fields who have little background or training in evaluation but who are assigned responsibility for evaluation, often as an additional task to their main work.
- *Evaluation users.* These include managers of programs being evaluated, the groups affected by the programs, policymakers and planners, funding agencies, civil society, and public opinion, including the mass media. Again, this group includes both experienced evaluators and those with little experience in the commissioning, interpretation, or use of evaluations and their findings.

Each of these audiences includes people from all parts of the world and who work in government, civil society, the private sector, or international development agencies. Recognizing that different readers are likely to use the material in different ways, we designed the book as a reference text where chapters can be read in different orders or where readers can dip into particular sections of a chapter without having to read all the previous chapters. To facilitate this process, we include extensive cross-referencing between chapters. The RWE model as depicted in Figure 1.1 is repeated at the start of each chapter of Part II to show which step of the RWE approach is being discussed. A glossary of terms is included at the end of the book (glossary terms also appear in boldface in each chapter). The following paragraphs suggest how each audience might read the book.

The University Audience

The book provides a rapid review of QUANT and QUAL approaches and the main data collection, analysis and presentation methods used by each approach (Chapters 10–12). It also discusses how mixed-method approaches (Chapter 13) can be used to complement both QUANT and QUAL evaluation designs. These chapters, combined with the chapters on program theory models (Chapter 9) and sampling (Chapter 14), mean that the book can be used as a text for introductory or intermediate evaluation courses. A glossary of technical terms is also a useful reference source. The annotated recommended readings at the end of each chapter will be helpful for introductory courses. For students new to the field, Chapter 16 presents a step-by-step discussion of the stages of a typical evaluation. Some students may wish to read this overview chapter before getting into the more detailed discussion in Chapters 2–8 of how to apply these techniques to RWE constraints.

For graduate students and faculty, Part II presents a framework for conducting evaluations under budget, time, and data constraints and where the evaluation is subject to political pressures. This combination of issues is not specifically addressed in most other textbooks, even though one or more of these factors probably affect most evaluations. Some of the RWE design, data collection, and analysis strategies that are often not discussed in evaluation textbooks include the following:

- *Strategies for reducing cost and time of data collection and analysis.* Although there is a literature on how to conduct rapid and economical evaluations in developing countries, it is difficult to find a similar publication concerning how to conduct evaluations in the United States and other developed countries under similar budget and time constraints. A set of strategies that can be used to address budget and time constraints in both developing and developed countries is discussed.
- *Making the best use of limited data.* This includes a discussion of how to *reconstruct* baseline data and *comparison[3]* groups.
- *Understanding and coping with political influences on the evaluation.* This discusses pressures not only from federal and state government (these have been extensively discussed by Carol Weiss [1993] and others) but pressures from clients (e.g., to not use control groups) and ideological/professional pressures from peers, civil society, and government agencies to use the "right" type of methods. In some cases, right means "scientific" results based on random assignment of subjects to experimental and control groups and the reliance on QUANT indicators, whereas in other cases right means QUAL methods that allow the evaluator to "really understand" the community. Preferences for empowerment and participatory evaluations create another set of pressures on what evaluation approaches should be used.

- *Assessing the potential weaknesses of the evaluation design and how these can affect the validity or adequacy of the conclusions.* Although threats to validity in quasi-experimental designs have been extensively discussed in the QUANT evaluation literature, they tend not to be systematically presented in many evaluation textbooks and are frequently not used in assessing the quality of evaluations—certainly not evaluations conducted under budget and time constraints. QUAL evaluations usually have a different set of criteria for assessing adequacy and validity, and it is only very recently that the application of a standard set of criteria for assessing the adequacy and validity of mixed-method designs has started to be discussed. Drawing on the pioneering work of Lincoln and Guba (1985) and more recent work of writers such as Miles and Huberman (1994) and Yin (2003), we propose a standard checklist that can be used with QUANT, QUAL, or mixed-method designs. Step 6 of the approach also presents pointers on how to address these design weaknesses once they have been identified. Readers familiar with rapid evaluations will appreciate the value of these guidelines because many evaluation practitioners use budget and time constraints as a justification for ignoring the normal standards of evaluation rigor.
- The final step of the model discusses *ways to help clients and other stakeholders to use the findings and recommendations of the evaluation.*

Using the Book as an Introductory Text

The book can be used for two groups of students new to the field of evaluation: undergraduates planning to specialize in evaluation and undergraduate or graduates from other fields (e.g., education, health, political science, and environment and natural resource management) who need a basic understanding of evaluation methods. These groups may wish to read the chapters in the following order:

- Chapter 1: "Overview: RealWorld Evaluation and the Contexts in Which It Is Used". This is a condensed overview of the approach.
- Chapter 16: "Bringing It All Together: Applying RealWorld Evaluation Approaches to Each Stage of the Evaluation Process." This chapter includes a step-by-step discussion of the stages in the design, implementation, analysis, and use of a typical evaluation. It might be helpful to readers who have never conducted an evaluation.
- Chapters 9–14, which provide reviews of evaluation methods. These chapters include an introduction or a review of the basic tools of program evaluation. The chapters are cross-referenced and can be read in any order according to the needs and interests of the reader. People new to the field are encouraged to start with Chapter 9 on program theory evaluation because this discusses how to construct the basic frameworks, models, and hypotheses required for any evaluation. Chapter 10 provides a useful summary of major evaluation designs or scenarios such as before-and-after (pretest + posttest), with-and-without (using a comparison group). Not all readers will need to read all of Chapter 14 (sampling theory), but most will find it helpful to read at least the introduction. Many evaluations either waste time and money by using a sample that is much larger than they need or wrongly conclude that the program did not have any effects because the sample they had selected was too small to detect real but relatively small effects.

- Chapters 1–8, which outline the RWE approach. Having reviewed the evaluation tools, the reader is ready to follow through the seven stages of the RWE approach. It is recommended to start with the overview in Chapter 1 and then strategies for scoping the evaluation (Chapter 2). Readers can then either read Chapters 3 through 8 in order or jump around according to their particular interests and needs.
- Appendix 4, "Resources for Evaluation Capacity Building" and the "Glossary of Terms and Acronyms." Appendix 4 includes useful Web sites and training programs that can be consulted as needed. The glossary is given at the end of the text so that readers can understand and, if necessary, locate definitions of terms discussed in some of the chapters they have not yet read.

Reading Guide for Advanced Students and Faculty

Many advanced readers may wish to use the book as a reference text, focusing only on the chapters of immediate interest. Cross-referencing and a glossary of terms are included to facilitate this process. For readers familiar with evaluation methodology, the newest material will be the summary of the RWE scenarios (Chapter 1) and the step-by-step presentation of the RealWorld approach in Chapters 2 to 8. The discussion of program theory evaluation (Chapter 9) brings together work from a number of different theorists, and Chapter 13 presents some new perspectives of mixed-method approaches. Chapter 15 (on evaluation capacity building) also introduces material not always covered in evaluation texts.

Evaluation Practitioners

The book is designed to provide practical guidance to the people who design, implement, analyze, and disseminate evaluations. The central focus is on "real-world" situations where the evaluation must be conducted with time or budget constraints and where there are limitations on data availability or where there are political pressures on how the evaluation should be designed or disseminated. However, most of the methods and approaches can be applied to almost any evaluation, even when there is an adequate budget, no particular time pressures, and good access to data.

The book will be useful both to practitioners new to the evaluation field and to the "old hands" who have been conducting evaluations for a long time. The RWE workshops that the authors have organized in a number of developing countries as well as in Japan, Canada, and the United States have shown that many people working in evaluation units have been trained in other fields and have only limited formal training in evaluation. Consequently, the book offers a step-by-step guide to the design and conduct of evaluations without requiring extensive training in evaluation. The text contains many practical examples and "how-to" checklists and tables. Part III provides a rapid review of the principal evaluation methodologies for readers wishing to dig a little deeper. At the same time, the book presents an approach and new material that the old hands will find useful.

The authors' goal is to focus on the real-world issues and challenges not covered in many textbooks. Can a useful evaluation be conducted if you only have a few weeks? What can be done if the evaluation budget is much less than what you feel is needed to conduct a good evaluation? How can you estimate impacts if no baseline data have been collected? What should be your strategy if a government agency does not want the study to include a comparison group because this might raise expectations or stir up political sensitivities? How do you respond if the Ministry of Planning wishes you to conduct a "scientific" evaluation based only on sample surveys and not to "waste time collecting the impressions of farmers who do not really understand about irrigation"? However, this is not just a cookbook of recipes for conducting "quick and dirty" evaluations. One of the most important contributions is a set of guidelines for assessing the consequences of the measures taken to cut costs and reduce time on the quality of the evaluation and the validity of the findings and recommendations, and for taking measures to address these threats to validity in order to improve the validity of the findings.

One of the tragedies of the evaluation field is that the findings and recommendations of many methodologically sound evaluations are never used. The final step of the RWE approach, therefore, provides guidelines on ways to help clients and other stakeholders to actually use the findings of the evaluation.

Reading Guide for Practitioners New to the Evaluation Field

Practitioners new to the evaluation field may wish to read the chapters in the following order:

- Chapter 1: "Overview: RealWorld Evaluation and the Contexts in Which It Is Used"
- Chapter 16: "Bringing It All Together: Applying RealWorld Evaluation Approaches to Each Stage of the Evaluation Process." This chapter includes a step-by-step discussion of the stages in the design, implementation, analysis, and use of a typical evaluation. It might be helpful to practitioners who have not yet conducted many evaluations.
- Chapters 9–14, which provide a review of the tools and techniques of QUAL, QUANT, and mixed-method evaluations. These chapters include an introduction to and review of the basic tools of program evaluation. A reader pressed for time should read at least the introductory sections to obtain a basic understanding of these methods. The chapters are cross-referenced and can be read in any order. Practitioners new to the field are encouraged to start with Chapter 9 on program theory evaluation because this discusses how to construct the basic frameworks, models, and hypotheses required for any evaluation. Not everyone will need to read all of Chapter 14 (sampling theory), but most will find it helpful to read at least the introduction. Many evaluations either invest more money and time than is strictly necessary by using a sample that is larger than they need or wrongly conclude that the program did not have any effects because the sample they used was too small to detect potentially important effects (even if they did exist).
- Chapter 10: "The Most Widely Used RealWorld Quantitative Evaluation Designs." This chapter will make more sense and be easier to understand after reading the previously mentioned tools and techniques chapters.
- Chapters 1–8, which outline the RWE approach. Having reviewed the evaluation tools, the reader is ready to follow through the seven stages of the RWE approach. It is recommended to start with discussion of typical evaluation scenarios (Chapter 1) and then strategies for scoping the evaluation (Chapter 2). Readers can then either read Chapters 3 through 8 in order or jump around according to their particular interests and needs.

- Chapter 15: "Learning Together: Building Capacity for RealWorld Evaluation." One of the frustrations of many evaluators is that clients and other users of the evaluation do not understand the basic concepts and principles of an evaluation. Clients will often complain that the evaluation is too expensive, taking too long, or collecting too much data, or they will wish to publish conclusions or make generalizations that cannot be justified by the evaluation design. An important role of the evaluation practitioner, then, is to strengthen the capacity of users to specify their evaluation needs, to understand the trade-offs between different designs, and to interpret and use the findings. Sometimes this will be done through formal training, but often this will be done mostly through informal conversations and regular meetings with staff.
- Appendix 4, "Resources for Evaluation Capacity Building" and "Glossary of Terms and Acronyms." Appendix 4 includes useful Web sites and training programs that can be consulted as needed. The glossary of terms is given at the end of the text so that readers can understand and, if necessary, locate terms discussed in some of the chapters they have not yet read.

Reading Guide for Experienced Evaluation Practitioners (the Old Hands)

Many old hands may wish to use the book as a reference text, focusing only on the chapters of immediate interest. Cross-referencing and a glossary of terms are included to facilitate this process. For readers familiar with evaluation methodology, the newest material will be the discussion of RWE scenarios (Chapter 1) and the step-by-step presentation of the RealWorld approach (Chapters 2–8). The discussion of program theory evaluation (Chapter 9) brings together work from a number of different theorists, and Chapter 13 presents some new perspectives on mixed-method approaches. Chapter 15 (on evaluation capacity building) also introduces material not covered in many evaluation texts. The following is a suggested order of chapters:

- Chapter 1: "Overview: RealWorld Evaluation and the Contexts in Which It Is Used." This chapter summarizes the RWE approach and the typical evaluation scenarios in which these approaches are used.
- Chapter 15: "Learning Together: Building Capacity for RealWorld Evaluation." As indicated above, many clients and other users of the evaluation do not understand the basic concepts and principles of an evaluation. Consequently, an important role of the evaluation practitioner is to strengthen the capacity of users to specify their evaluation needs, to understand the trade-offs between different designs, and to interpret and use the findings. Sometimes this will be done through formal training, but often this will be done mostly through informal conversations and regular meetings with staff.
- Chapters 2–8, which outline the RWE approach. It is recommended to start with strategies for scoping the evaluation (Chapter 2). Readers can then either read Chapters 3 through 8 in order or jump around according to their particular interests and needs.
- Chapters 9–14, which provide a review of evaluation methods. Old hands will be familiar with much of this material, so they should focus on particular areas of interest. Everyone is encouraged to read Chapter 9 (on program theory evaluation) and to at least skim through the chapter on mixed methods (Chapter 13); both chapters synthesize different approaches.

The Users of Evaluation Findings

The book is designed to provide practical guidance to the different groups who commission evaluations and use the findings. This includes program managers, groups affected by the programs, the agencies that commission and fund evaluations, planning ministries, civil society, the mass media, and public opinion. The central focus is on real-world situations where the evaluation must be conducted with time or budget constraints, where there are limitations on data availability, or where there are political pressures on how the evaluation should be designed or disseminated. However, most of the methods and approaches can be applied to almost any evaluation, even when there is an adequate budget, no particular time pressures, and good access to data.

The book will be useful both to people with limited experience in using evaluations and also to the old hands who are experienced in commissioning or using the findings from evaluations.

A number of sections will be particularly useful to evaluation users. First, guidelines are provided for agencies that must commission evaluations when resources are limited or there are time constraints. The book explains the trade-offs between strategies to reduce time or budget on the one hand and ensuring that the evaluation can provide valid and sufficiently precise answers to the key questions that must be addressed in the evaluation on the other hand. It is emphasized that the decision on how to reduce time or budget or address data and political constraints is not a purely "technical" question to be decided by the evaluation specialist but rather a policy decision depending on how the evaluation will be used, the types of evidence required, and the needed precision. Second, guidelines and checklists are provided for assessing the strengths and weaknesses of a proposed evaluation design and the potential threats to the validity of the conclusions. Third, practical guidance is provided on ways to improve the quality of the design and strengthen the validity of the conclusions once the threats to validity have been identified. Finally, the approach focuses on ways to promote the use of the evaluation findings. This covers both improving the use of a particular evaluation and developing an evaluation culture through strengthening the evaluation capacity of the different actors.

The emphasis on addressing threats to validity is essential from the perspective of the users. There are many "cookbooks" for conducting quick-and-dirty evaluations (particularly for developing countries), but very few assess how these approaches affect the validity and credibility of the conclusions. Users will find the discussion of the trade-offs between cost, time, and quality to be particularly helpful when making real-world decisions on which evaluation design to chose in a particular context.

As we said above, the goal of this book is to focus on the real-world issues and challenges not covered in many textbooks. Can a useful evaluation be conducted if you only have a few weeks? What can be done if the evaluation budget is much less than what you feel is needed to conduct a good evaluation? How can impacts be estimated if no baseline data have been collected? How should the evaluation be designed if a government agency does not want the study to include a control group because this might raise expectations or stir up political sensitivities? How do you respond to the preference of certain stakeholders to conduct a "scientific" evaluation based only on sample surveys and not to "waste time collecting the impressions of farmers who do not really understand about irrigation"?

Reading Guide for Inexperienced Evaluation Users

Inexperienced evaluation users may wish to read the chapters in the following order:

- Chapter 1: "Overview: RealWorld Evaluation and the Contexts in Which It Is Used." The chapter summarizes the RWE approach and the typical scenarios in which it is used.
- Chapter 16: "Bringing It All Together: Applying RealWorld Evaluation Approaches to Each Stage of the Evaluation Process." This chapter includes a step-by-step discussion of the stages in the design, implementation, analysis, and use of a typical evaluation. It will be helpful for users who have not been involved in many evaluations.
- Chapter 10: "The Most Widely Used Quantitative RealWorld Evaluation Designs." This chapter briefly summarizes the different QUANT evaluation designs or scenarios in terms of before-after and with-without comparisons. All too often, evaluation users don't take these circumstances into consideration (e.g., expecting an evaluation to measure the impact of a project without baseline or comparison group data).
- Chapters 2–8, which outline the steps of the RWE approach. These chapters introduce the reader to each of the seven steps or elements of the RWE approach. It is recommended to start with strategies for scoping the evaluation (Chapter 2). Readers can then either read Chapters 3 through 8 in order or can jump around according to their particular interests and needs.

Reading Guide for Experienced Evaluation Users

Experienced readers may wish to use the book as a reference text, focusing only on the chapters of immediate interest. Cross-referencing and a glossary of terms are included to facilitate this process. For readers familiar with evaluation methodology, the newest material will be the discussion of RWE scenarios (Chapter 1) and the step-by-step presentation of the RWE approach (Chapters 2–8). The discussion of program theory evaluation (Chapter 9) brings together work from a number of different theorists, and Chapter 13 presents some new perspectives on mixed-method approaches. Chapter 15 (on evaluation capacity building) also introduces material not covered in many evaluation texts. For those not wishing to read the whole book, the following is a suggested reading guide:

- Chapter 1: "Overview: RealWorld Evaluation and the Contexts in Which It Is Used." This chapter summarizes the RWE approach and the typical scenarios in which it is used.
- Chapter 2: "First Clarify the Purpose: Scoping the Evaluation" and Chapter 9: "Applications of Program Theory in RealWorld Evaluation." Step 1 of the RWE approach is critical for evaluation users, and it is important that they be actively involved and do not passively accept the design proposed by the evaluator. It is also argued that all evaluations should be based on a program theory. This defines the sequence of steps through which intended outputs and impacts will be achieved; how implementation and outcomes are likely to be affected by the economic, political, organizational, and environmental context within which each individual program or project operates; and how outcomes are affected by the characteristics of the affected population. The

program theory helps define the critical hypotheses to be tested and provides a framework for assessing the strengths and weaknesses of the different options for addressing the budget, time, data, and political constraints.

- Chapter 7: "Strengthening the Evaluation Design and the Validity of the Conclusions." The guidelines and checklists in this chapter are critical for evaluation users, particularly the agencies commissioning or funding the evaluation.
- Chapter 8: "Making It Useful: Helping Clients and Other Stakeholders Utilize the Evaluation" and Chapter 15: "Learning Together: Building Capacity for RealWorld Evaluation." Promoting evaluation use and creating an evaluation culture are both important roles for many evaluation users.
- Chapter 10: "The Most Widely Used RealWorld Quantitative Evaluation Designs" and Chapter 14: "Sampling for RealWorld Evaluation." These two chapters present some of the important technical issues in evaluation design. Chapter 10 describes the most widely used evaluation designs that can be used in RWE and assesses the strengths and weaknesses of each one. Many evaluation proposals present only one design without explaining why it was chosen, so it is useful for the user to be aware of the range of options. Sample design, particularly the determination of the appropriate sample size, is critical for RWE because the cost of interviews is one of the most expensive items in the evaluation budget. An understanding of the relationship between expected effect size, the power of the test and the required sample size is critical when working under budget constraints. Relaxing requirements concerning the required significance levels can produce important reductions in sample size. On the other hand, if the sample size is too small, there is a danger of overlooking potential project effects.
- Chapter 13: "Mixed-Method Evaluation." This chapter synthesizes material from a number of different authors and may be less familiar to many readers than the chapters on QUAL and QUANT methods.
- Chapters 3–6, which include Steps 2 through 5 of the RWE approach. Although users will often be less involved in these steps, they may want to understand the process and trade-offs involved.
- Chapter 16: "Bringing It All Together: Applying RealWorld Evaluation Approaches to Each Stage of the Evaluation Process," Chapter 12: "Qualitative Evaluation Methods," and Chapter 11: "Quantitative Evaluation Methods." Experienced users may be familiar with most of these methods, although given the wide range of approaches covered, it is likely that most readers will find some techniques with which they are less familiar.

Notes

1. The words *quantitative* and *qualitative* are used so often we'll save space in this book by using the shortened QUANT and QUAL.

2. The term international development agency covers multilateral agencies such as the World Bank and the InterAmerican Development Bank, bilateral agencies such as the U.S. Agency for International Development and the U.K. Department for International Development, and international nongovernmental agencies such as OXFAM and CARE International that finance and/or help implement

social, economic, and other kinds of projects in developing countries. All these agencies are also involved in commissioning and/or conducting evaluations of the projects and programs they support.

3.   Although the term *control group* is used very widely, we will follow the convention of using control group only to refer to evaluation designs in which subjects are *randomly assigned* to the experimental and control situations. In the more common situation where random assignment is not possible, we use the term *comparison group*—which some authors also call a *nonequivalent control group.*

PART I

Overview: RealWorld Evaluation

RealWorld Evaluation and the Contexts in Which It Is Used

The chapter begins with an overview of the RealWorld Evaluation (**RWE**) approach, the contexts in which real-world evaluations are conducted, and the many different constraints, pressures, and influences under which evaluations are formulated, conducted, disseminated, and used. The RWE approach was developed to address four of the most common constraints evaluators face: budget, time, data, and political influences. The two most common RWE scenarios are reviewed. The first is when the evaluator is brought in at the start of the project but with constraints on the types of information that can be collected or the designs that can be used. The second, and probably the more common scenario, is when the evaluator is not called in until the project has been operating for some time and may even be almost completed. In most of these cases, no baseline data have been collected and usually no comparison (control) group has been identified. We compare the similarities and differences between approaches to program evaluation and the potential demand for RWE in developing and developed countries. The chapter concludes by identifying the main groups of users of program evaluation and discusses how and when they use evaluations.

Welcome to RealWorld Evaluation

Most evaluators are familiar with situations in which programs have been underway for some time or perhaps are almost completed before implementing or funding agencies begin to think seriously about evaluating the extent to which the programs are achieving their objectives and producing the intended impacts. Usually, the belated interest in evaluation is motivated by the need for solid **evidence**[1] on which to base decisions about whether the program should be continued or perhaps expanded. When the evaluations do finally get underway, many have to be conducted under budget and time constraints, often with limited access to baseline data and comparison groups. Consequently, it is difficult, if not impossible, to apply many of the methodologically most robust evaluation designs.

Although more resources are allocated to evaluation in developed countries, many evaluators in the United States, Canada, Europe, and Australasia report that they operate under similar, although sometimes less severe, constraints to those faced by their colleagues in developing countries[2]. As if these problems were not enough, many evaluations in both developed and developing countries are often conducted in a *political* environment where funding agencies, clients, and key stakeholders have strongly held views on what are the "right" evaluation methods, what types and amounts of information should be collected, and which groups should and should not be asked to comment on (or even see) the **findings.** New evaluators soon discover that "technical" issues such as whether to use randomized control groups; the choice of qualitative, quantitative, or mixed-method designs; and who to interview and what questions to ask can provoke strong reactions from clients and stakeholders.

Despite the difficult circumstances under which many evaluations have to be conducted, there is a growing demand from funding agencies, governments, civil society, and intended beneficiaries for systematic program evaluations, including whether the program could and/or should be continued or expanded to other communities or locations. Consequently, there is a strong demand from many sides for evaluators to answer basic questions such as these:

- Did the project meet its objectives?
- Did it have an impact?
- Who benefited and who did not?
- Should the program continue?

There is also an increasing awareness that evaluation conclusions need to be supported by sound evidence and not just opinions—although there are often major disagreements as to what constitutes sound evidence.

The pressures of conducting evaluations under budget and time constraints have often resulted in inattention to sound research design or to identifying and addressing factors affecting the validity of the findings. The RWE approach presented in this book was developed in response to the demand for guidance on how to conduct evaluations within budget, time, data, and political constraints while at the same time ensuring maximum possible methodological rigor within the particular evaluation context. RWE is based on the following seven-step approach, summarized more specifically in Figure 1.1 and described in detail in Chapters 2 through 8:

- Step 1: Planning and *scoping the evaluation*. Understanding client information needs and the political context within which the evaluation is being conducted; defining a program theory that describes the objectives and intended method of operation of the program; identifying the budget, time, and data constraints and any political factors affecting how the evaluation will be conducted, disseminated, and used; combining this information with preliminary analysis from Steps 2 to 5 to select the design that best addresses client needs within the **RWE constraints**

- Step 2: *Strategies for addressing budget constraints.* Reducing the costs through simplifying the evaluation design; reducing the amounts of data to be collected; making greater use of secondary data; revising the sample design and streamlining data collection and analysis. Many of the techniques described in Step 3 for using expensive consultants more efficiently can also help reduce costs.
- Step 3: *Strategies for addressing time constraints.* In addition to many of the approaches used in Step 2, strategies include: planning ahead to avoid delays and bottlenecks, particularly during the short periods when outside consultants are involved; building impact-related indicators into routine project monitoring data collection and using videoconferencing to reduce travel and to permit more frequent interactions between the evaluation team and agency staff
- Step 4: *Strategies for addressing data constraints.* Reconstructing baseline or comparison group data if either of these was not collected; making effective use of secondary data; making sure that data are collected from the right people; and time- and cost-effective methods for collecting data on sensitive topics and for locating and interviewing difficult-to-reach groups
- Step 5: *Understanding and coping with political factors influencing how the evaluation is designed, implemented, disseminated, or used.* Identifying the key actors and their political perspectives and understanding how these affect their orientation to the evaluation; developing strategies to address the political realities without compromising the evaluation
- Step 6: *Strengthening the evaluation design and the validity of conclusions.* Creating a checklist to identify threats to the validity and adequacy of the evaluation design and conclusions; creating a set of strategies to address the threats and improve the quality of the evaluation
- Step 7: *Helping clients use the evaluation.* Ensuring that clients are actively involved from the start and that they "buy into" the evaluation; maintaining contact with clients throughout the evaluation and ensuring that by the time the major reports are published, they do not contain any surprises for the client; adapting the presentation of findings to the preferred communcation style of different stakeholders

The RealWorld Evaluation Context

As noted, the RWE approach was developed to assist the many evaluators in both developing and developed countries who must conduct evaluations with budget, time, data, and political constraints. In one common scenario, the client delays contracting an evaluator until late in the project when the funding agency (government, international development agency, foundation, etc.) is about to decide whether to continue to support a project or possibly launch a larger second phase. Such tardiness occurs even when evaluation was built into the original project agreement (see Box 1.1). With the decision point approaching, the funding agency may suddenly realize that it does not have solid information on which to base a decision about future funding of the project, or the project implementing agency may realize it does not have

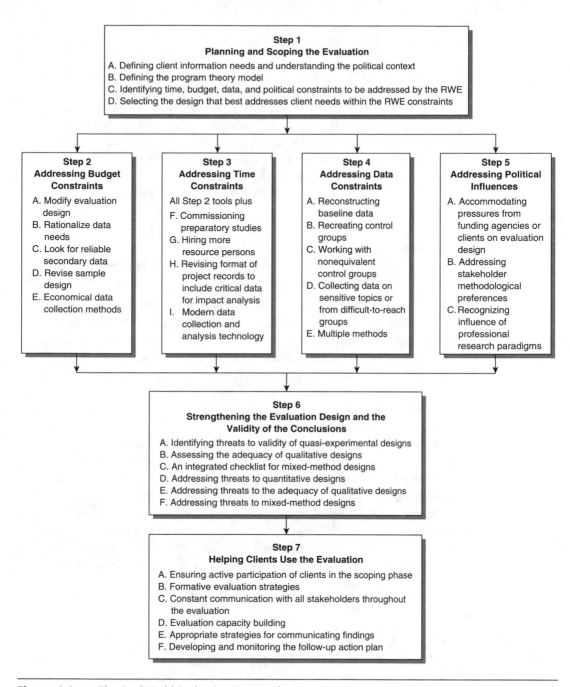

Step 1
Planning and Scoping the Evaluation
A. Defining client information needs and understanding the political context
B. Defining the program theory model
C. Identifying time, budget, data, and political constraints to be addressed by the RWE
D. Selecting the design that best addresses client needs within the RWE constraints

Step 2
Addressing Budget Constraints
A. Modify evaluation design
B. Rationalize data needs
C. Look for reliable secondary data
D. Revise sample design
E. Economical data collection methods

Step 3
Addressing Time Constraints
All Step 2 tools plus
F. Commissioning preparatory studies
G. Hiring more resource persons
H. Revising format of project records to include critical data for impact analysis
I. Modern data collection and analysis technology

Step 4
Addressing Data Constraints
A. Reconstructing baseline data
B. Recreating control groups
C. Working with nonequivalent control groups
D. Collecting data on sensitive topics or from difficult-to-reach groups
E. Multiple methods

Step 5
Addressing Political Influences
A. Accommodating pressures from funding agencies or clients on evaluation design
B. Addressing stakeholder methodological preferences
C. Recognizing influence of professional research paradigms

Step 6
Strengthening the Evaluation Design and the Validity of the Conclusions
A. Identifying threats to validity of quasi-experimental designs
B. Assessing the adequacy of qualitative designs
C. An integrated checklist for mixed-method designs
D. Addressing threats to quantitative designs
E. Addressing threats to the adequacy of qualitative designs
F. Addressing threats to mixed-method designs

Step 7
Helping Clients Use the Evaluation
A. Ensuring active participation of clients in the scoping phase
B. Formative evaluation strategies
C. Constant communication with all stakeholders throughout the evaluation
D. Evaluation capacity building
E. Appropriate strategies for communicating findings
F. Developing and monitoring the follow-up action plan

Figure 1.1   The RealWorld Evaluation Approach

the evidence needed to support its claim that the project is achieving its objectives. An evaluator called in at this point may be told it is essential to conduct the evaluation by a certain date and to produce "rigorous" findings regarding project impact, although unfortunately, very limited funds are available.

Box 1.1　A Familiar Evaluation Story

When a social development fund was launched in an African country a few years ago, it was suggested that a baseline study be conducted as the first phase of a longitudinal impact evaluation study. The project manager asked, "What is the point of spending money and time on a baseline study when we do not know if the project model will work in our country?" He also indicated that staff members were under pressure to launch the project and could not spend time on something that would not be useful until the project was completed. Three years later, when the possibility of a second project was being discussed, consultants were called in to conduct an impact evaluation study. It was agreed that it was unfortunate that no baseline data were available to permit a rigorous measurement of the changes produced by the project. The consultants had to try to reconstruct baseline data using methods described in Chapter 5.

In other scenarios, the evaluator may be called in early but finds that for budget, political, or methodological reasons, it will not be possible to collect data on a comparison group for purposes of determining program impact by comparing participants with nonparticipants. In some cases, it may not even be possible to collect baseline data on the project population for purposes of analyzing progress or impact over time. Data constraints may also result from difficulties of collecting information on sensitive topics such as HIV/AIDS, domestic violence, postconflict reconstruction, or illegal economic activities (e.g., commercial sex workers, narcotics, or political corruption).

Determining the most appropriate evaluation design under these kinds of circumstances can be a complicated juggling act involving a trade-off between available resources and acceptable standards of evaluation practice. Often, the client's concerns are more about budgets and deadlines, and basic principles of evaluation may receive a lower priority. Box 1.2 illustrates this difficult trade-off between budgets and deadlines on the one hand and desired standards of methodological rigor on the other. Failure to reach satisfactory resolution of these trade-offs may also contribute to a much lamented problem: low use of evaluation results (see Chelimsky 1994; Operations Evaluation Department 2005; Patton 1997). RWE is a response to the all-too-real difficulties in the practical world of evaluation.

The Four Types of Constraints Addressed by the RealWorld Approach

Table 1.1 illustrates the different ways in which RWE constraints are combined in the typical contexts in which evaluations are conducted. In some cases, the evaluator faces a single constraint. For example, the budget may be limited, but there is plenty of time. Or the evaluation may begin at the start of the project with no time constraint, but the evaluator is told that for political or ethical reasons, it will not be possible to collect data on a comparison group. Many unlucky evaluators find themselves simultaneously contending with several or all of these constraints!

Box 1.2   RealWorld Evaluation Constraints in the Evaluation of an
Education Project in Egypt

This excerpt from a meta-evaluation (review of evaluation methodologies and practices) by CARE International illustrates the many real-world constraints facing evaluation in the field.

The evaluators mentioned that the methodology they employed had to be more subjective and anecdotal than they would have desired. The decision not to use their preferred (more rigorous) quantitative design was made due to the limited time available (2 weeks for all data-gathering) and the geographic spread, size and diversity of the target population. Although they felt that a random or weighted sampling would lead to statistically significant or statistically representative findings, it was not realistic given time and other limitations. Instead, the team employed other techniques to try to ensure that the information gathered was as comprehensive and thorough and followed as closely as possible accepted approaches to classroom and teacher observation within the very severe time constraints.

The meta-evaluation, recognizing that it is not possible to achieve acceptable standards of evaluation rigor within these time and budget constraints, suggested that CARE may need to re-examine some of its evaluation policies to determine if the desire (or limitations imposed by the donors) to economize on evaluation costs and duration is working at cross-purposes with the level of rigor it hopes to achieve.

SOURCE: Russon (2005:12–13).

Budget Constraints

Sometimes, funds for the evaluation were not included in the original project budget, and the evaluation must be conducted with a much smaller budget than would normally be allocated. As a result, it may not be possible to collect the desirable data or to reconstruct baseline or comparison group data. Lack of funds may create or exacerbate time constraints because researchers may not be able to spend as much time in the field as they consider necessary. Box 1.3 makes the point that it is important to understand whether the main constraint is budget or time (or both), because the best strategy will often be different in each case.

Time Constraints

The most common time constraint is when the evaluator is not called in until the project is already well advanced and the evaluation has to be conducted within a much shorter period of time than the evaluator considers necessary—in terms of a longitudinal perspective over the life of the project, the time allotted for conducting the end-of-project evaluation, or both. Time constraints often make it impossible to conduct a pretest-posttest evaluation design with a baseline study that can be repeated after the project has been implemented. The time available for planning stakeholder consultations, site visits and fieldwork, and data analysis may also have to be drastically reduced to meet the report deadline. These time pressures are

Table 1.1   RealWorld Evaluation Scenarios: Conducting Impact Evaluations with Time, Budget, Data, and Political Constraints

The constraints under which the evaluation must be conducted				Typical Evaluation Scenarios
Time	Budget	Data	Political	
X				The evaluator is called in late in the project and told that the evaluation must be completed by a certain date so that it can be used in a decision-making process or contribute to a report. The budget may be adequate, but it may be difficult to collect or analyze survey data within the time frame.
	X			The evaluation is allocated only a small budget, but there is not necessarily excessive time pressure. However, it will be difficult to collect sample survey data because of the limited budget.
		X		The evaluator is not called in until the project is well advanced. Consequently, no baseline survey has been conducted either on the project population or on a control group. The evaluation does have an adequate scope, either to analyze existing household survey data or to collect additional data. In some cases, the intended project impacts may also concern changes in sensitive areas such as domestic violence, community conflict, women's empowerment, community leadership styles, or corruption on which it is difficult to collect reliable data—even when time and budget are not constraints.
			X	The funding agency or a government regulatory body has requirements concerning acceptable evaluation methods. For example: In the United States, the No Child Left Behind Act of 2001 includes funding preference for certain types of research designs. In other cases, a client or funding agency may specifically request qualitative data, tests of statistical significance regarding measured program effects, or both.
			X	There is overwhelming indication that the evaluation is being commissioned for political purposes. For example, an evaluation of the effects of conservation policy might be commissioned to stall its expansion.
			X	There is reason to suspect that the evaluation will be used for political purposes other than or contrary to those articulated in preliminary discussions. For example, an evaluator might suspect that an evaluation of charter schools might be used (and even misused) by a client with known advocacy for privatization of education.
X	X			The evaluator has to operate under time pressure and with a limited budget. Secondary survey data may be available but there is little time or few resources to analyze them.
X		X		The evaluator has little time and no access to baseline data or a comparison group. Funds are available to collect additional data, but the survey design is constrained by the tight deadlines.
	X	X		The evaluator is called in late and has no access to baseline data or comparison groups. The budget is limited, but time is not a constraint.
X	X	X		The evaluator is called in late, is given a limited budget, and has no access to baseline survey data; and no comparison group has been identified.

NOTE: To simplify the table, the possible combinations of political constraints with the other three factors have not been included in the table.

Box 1.3   Budget and Time Constraints Have Different Implications for the Evaluation Design

---

While budget and time constraints often have similar consequences for the evaluation design, in other cases they can require very different approaches. For example, if an evaluation must be completed by a certain date, the process of data collection can often be speeded up by bringing in consultants, hiring more experienced researchers, or increasing the number of **interviewers**. All these measures may require significant budget increases. If, on the other hand, budget is the main constraint, the decision might be made to contract with a local university that would use cheaper though less experienced graduate students who might require more time for data collection because they cannot work full-time.

---

particularly problematic for an evaluator who is not familiar with the area, or even the country, and who does not have time for familiarization and for building confidence with the communities and the agencies involved with the study. The combination of time and budget constraints frequently means that foreign evaluators (and out-of-town U.S. evaluators) can be in the country or the state for only a short period of time—often requiring them to use shortcuts that they recognize as methodologically questionable.

Data Constraints

When the evaluation does not start until late in the project cycle, there is usually little or no comparable baseline information available on the conditions of the target group before the start of the project. Even if project records are available, they are often not organized in the form needed for comparative before-and-after analysis. Project records and other documentary data often suffer from reporting biases or poor record-keeping standards. Even when secondary data are available for a period close to the project starting date, they usually do not fully match the project populations. For example, employment data may cover only larger companies, whereas many project families work in smaller firms in the informal sector, or school records may cover public schools but not religious and other private schools. In developing countries, survey data are often analyzed and presented only at the household level, even when the data may have been collected on each household member.[3] This is a particular problem for gender analysis.

Most clients are interested in collecting data only on the groups or communities with which they are working. They may also be concerned that collection of information on nonbeneficiaries might create expectations of financial compensation or other benefits (for which the project has no budget), which further discourages the collection of data on a comparison group. Even if funds are available, it is also often difficult to identify a comparison group, because many project areas have unique characteristics. Where intended project impacts concern sensitive topics such as women's empowerment, contraceptive usage, or domestic violence, especially in paternalistic societies, information may be difficult to collect even when funds are available (see Box 1.4). Similar data problems can arise when working with difficult-to-reach groups such as drug addicts, criminals, ethnic minorities, migrants, or illegal residents.

> **Box 1.4**   Problems in Capturing Information from or about Women
>
> - Many household surveys only interview the "household head," who is often considered to be the male. He often does not have all the information on female household members or gives low priority to their concerns. Many men, for example, say their wives are happy to spend several hours per day walking to collect water or fuel because they "sing and chat with their friends as they walk."
> - Women are often interviewed in the presence of other household members where they may not feel free to express their views.
> - Donor agencies often insist that women be invited to attend community meetings to discuss proposed projects. However, the women often do not feel free to speak in public, or they always say they agree with their husbands.
> - In many parts of the world, sexual harassment is one of the main reasons women do not use public transport. However, it is culturally impossible for women to mention this to an outside interviewer, so this major problem is often not captured in surveys.

Political Influences

We use the term *political influences* and constraints in a broad sense to refer not only to pressures from government agencies and politicians but also to include the requirements of funding or regulatory agencies, pressures from stakeholders, and differences of opinion within an evaluation team regarding evaluation approaches or methods.

Evaluations are frequently conducted in contexts where political and ethical issues affect design and use. All programs affect some portion of the public, and most programs consume public funds, always limited and often scarce. Decisions based on evaluation results may intensify competition for funding, expand or terminate programs needed by some and paid for by others, or advance the agenda of a politically oriented group. Box 1.5 gives an example of how political pressures often affect the evaluation design—in this case, forbidding the use of a comparison group.

> **Box 1.5**   Political Influence on the Evaluation of a Power Project in Asia
>
> Consultants were asked to design an evaluation to assess the impacts of a hydroelectric power project in an Asian country that would involve the forced resettlement of a number of villages in the area where the dam was to be constructed. Families who had title to their land would receive compensation. The consultants proposed that the evaluation should include a comparison group of families who did not have land title. They were informed by the power authority that it would not be possible to do this because this would create expectations that these families would also receive compensation for being relocated, and funds for this were not included in the project budget.

While evaluators are always quick to spot the political or ideological biases of their clients and stakeholders, they are often less aware (or open) about their own ideological orientations. Many of the ongoing debates between quantitative and qualitative evaluators are fueled by the search for the "correct" or "best" research paradigm. Let us take, as an example, different approaches to a data set on income and employment in enterprises employing 10 or more people, a common cutoff point in employment surveys. A researcher in an economics department might decide to use econometric analysis to estimate the income and employment characteristics of people working in the smaller enterprises not covered by the data set, whereas a researcher in a sociology department might locate and interview a sample of workers in firms employing fewer than 10 workers.

The RealWorld Approach to Evaluation Challenges

Although RWE does not develop many new data collection or analysis methods, the approach makes several contributions to the conduct of evaluations under real-world budget, time, data, and political constraints. First, it presents ways to draw from a wide range of evaluation approaches and methods to address the four types of constraints described earlier. The systematic use of mixed methods is emphasized throughout. Using mixed-method approaches is considered critical for several reasons: (a) It permits the evaluator to draw on the widest possible range of evaluation methods and tools, (b) it increases the validity of conclusions by providing two or more independent estimates of key indicators (**triangulation**), (c) it permits a deeper and richer analysis and interpretation of the context in which a program operates, and (d) it offers ways to reduce the costs or time of data collection (see Chapters 3 and 4).

Second, RWE's seven-step approach to quality assurance offers corrective measures that can be introduced in different phases of the evaluation process, some even after a draft evaluation report has been produced, helping to enhance the quality of the evaluation. Quality promotes credibility and utility of findings, which, in turn, help ensure that evaluation contributes to the public good.

Third, many quantitative evaluations rely on the pretest-posttest design to estimate the changes and impacts produced by a project or program. This approach, when used in isolation, has two serious limitations: (a) It does not take into account the different socioeconomic and political contexts affecting each project, and (b) it implicitly assumes that each project is implemented as planned and in exactly the same way in each location. One of the contributions of RWE is to look inside the "**black box**" of the project implementation process to examine what actually happens during implementation and how much variation there is between different project sites (see Box 1.6). It also focuses on quality of implementation. This is a critical contribution because in many real-world contexts, some project components are not implemented at all or the quality is so low that it is hardly surprising that the intended impacts were not achieved. In other cases, the intended impacts were achieved, but what went on within the project was quite different from what had been planned!

Box 1.6   Getting inside the "Black Box"

Many impact evaluations assume that projects are implemented exactly as planned and in exactly the same way in each location. In fact, there are often major differences in how each project is implemented depending on local cultural, economic, administrative, and political factors. In some cases, the pretest-posttest evaluation is faithfully conducted without realizing that some of the project components were never implemented at all. Women did not apply for loans because it was too far to travel to the bank in town, teachers did not come to school during the planting season, textbooks never reached many of the schools, and parents in some areas did not send their daughters to school.

Unless the evaluation looks inside the "black box" of the project's implementation process, many of the findings of an impact evaluation can be very misleading and of little practical utility.

Comparing the RealWorld Evaluation Context and Issues in Developing and Developed Countries

The Evolution of Program Evaluation

Discussions regarding how to ensure competent evaluation practice have been underway for more than half a century in the United States, at least since evaluation began to be required on a massive scale with the passage of the Elementary and Secondary Education Act of 1965. In the United States, education continues to be one of the areas in which much of the cutting-edge work on evaluation methodology is conducted. The Great Society programs of the 1960s and 1970s (e.g., Head Start and urban housing programs) were also seen as an opportunity to study scientifically the causes and effectiveness of large-scale programs to eradicate poverty. These produced some of the largest and most carefully designed quantitative program evaluations ever conducted.

Evaluation codes of conduct, especially the *Program Evaluation Standards* (Joint Committee 1994) and the *Guiding Principles for Evaluators* (American Evaluation Association 1995), have been promulgated and periodically reviewed and revised. An increasing number of developing countries have adopted or adapted the *Program Evaluation Standards* (Joint Committee 1994), although there is a continuing debate concerning the applicability of these standards in other countries (Russon and Russon 2005). In the mid-1980s, the Organization for Economic Cooperation and Development (OECD 1986) developed similar guidelines to assist donor countries in the evaluation of their assistance programs to developing countries.

Professional evaluation associations have been active for many years in Western Europe and in Australasia, but an important new development has been the dramatic increase in the number of national and regional evaluation organizations in developing countries. There are now at least 40 national and regional evaluation organizations covering Africa, Latin America, South and East Asia, and the Newly Independent States (see Appendix 4 for a listing with Web sites). In 2004, the International Organization for Cooperation and Evaluation (IOCE)[4] was established to provide a forum and voice for these associations in both developing and industrialized nations.

IDEAS (the International Development Evaluation Association) was also created recently to provide a forum for evaluators who work in developing countries.

Special Evaluation Challenges in Developing Countries

Although the program evaluation tradition is well established in a number of developing countries (e.g., in India, the Program Evaluation Organization has been operating under the Planning Commission for nearly 50 years), in many countries program evaluation systems are not yet well established. Where public resources are desperately scarce, evaluation is often accorded low priority. Key stakeholders may perceive evaluation as impractical, unnecessary, or even threatening and may object to externally imposed monitoring or evaluation systems designed to respond to the information needs of funding agencies rather than to those of the national stakeholders (Bamberger 2001; Horton and Mackay 1999). Yet in countries or regions where it is most difficult to reallocate resources from programming to evaluation, the need for effective and efficient programs and for evaluation to identify and sustain these programs may be greatest.

Lack of support for program evaluation should not be attributed exclusively to a lack of understanding or motivation. Even when local program personnel and other stakeholders are interested in evaluation, formidable challenges can still be encountered, including the following:

- Not enough attention given to evaluation until the program is well advanced, with the consequence that there are no preprogram data (e.g., baseline studies), no defined comparison group, and insufficiently defined program objectives
- Modest budget allocation for evaluation studies
- Pressure to complete the evaluation as quickly as possible
- Cultural and political complexities affecting the conduct and use of evaluations are not easily grasped
- A limited pool of national evaluation expertise

Evaluators from developed nations do not always come prepared for the methodological challenges of working in international development evaluation where data may be more elusive and experienced research collaborators harder to find. Of perhaps even more import, they are often even less prepared for national organizational, institutional, political, and cultural contexts that can complicate an evaluation process. Constraints typically include limited access to data and often the absence of a culture of evaluation among managers, policymakers, and sectors of civil society. As we will see later, these factors should not come as a surprise because they are also operating in the industrialized nations from which many of these evaluators come!

Despite these constraints, demand from policymakers, managers, and civil society for information regarding goal achievement and the impact of projects and policies is increasing. However, many government bodies and international funding agencies do not begin to focus on evaluation until late in the project cycle (Bamberger 2000a), intensifying demand for rapid, cost-effective methodologies for assessing project impact. Unfortunately, enthusiasm for information about impact is usually not matched by adequacy of evaluation resources. Consequently, international and national evaluators are frequently asked to produce methodologically robust impact evaluations under circumstances in which it is impossible to comply fully with conventional evaluation standards.

Similarities and Differences of RealWorld Constraints in Developing and Developed Nations

It would be a mistake to assume that resource and data constraints are always more severe in developing countries and that evaluations in developed countries are always better planned and financed. Although some high-profile evaluations are well funded and the sheer volume of evaluation reports produced by the U.S. General Accounting Office or other federal agencies such as the Department of Education or Health and Human Services is overwhelming, many U.S. state and local agencies and voluntary organizations suffer from serious underfunding, which critically limits their ability to conduct evaluations.

In the United States, Canada, Europe, Australasia, and Japan, evaluation budgets are often just as constrained as in developing countries by low evaluation priority, suspicion, and last-minute requests. While a relatively small number of high-profile evaluations are well funded, many evaluators face budgetary problems similar to those encountered by their colleagues in developing countries, especially during periods in which economic downturns have forced severe financial cuts. Even when expensive and technically sound evaluations are conducted of publicly funded programs in the United States, use of results can be low (e.g., Patton 1997).

It is also important to recall that most of the examples of rigorous, large-scale evaluations are conducted only on government-funded programs or a few large foundation-supported programs. Large numbers of nongovernmental organizations (**NGOs**), community groups, and state and locally funded government programs must conduct evaluations with similar budget, time, and data constraints facing evaluators in developing countries. So while many evaluators in industrialized countries often have greater access to secondary data and longitudinal series from censuses, government surveys, and public records, it is clear that issues addressed by RWE are relevant to many evaluators in the United States, Canada, Europe, and Australasia just as much as to their colleagues in developing countries.

Who Uses RealWorld Evaluation, for What Purposes, and When?

There are two main users of RWE: First, **evaluation practitioners** will find it useful to use RWE for a number of reasons. For example:

- To identify ways to conduct adequately rigorous evaluations given limitations of time and financial resources
- To overcome data constraints, particularly the lack of baseline and comparison data
- To identify and address factors affecting the validity and adequacy of the findings of the evaluation

Second, *government agencies, international development agencies, and foundations* who commission evaluations and/or use evaluation findings will find the RWE approach useful for these reasons:

- To identify ways to reduce the costs and time of evaluations
- To be more fully aware of the various constraints under which an evaluation is to be conducted
- To understand the implications of different RWE strategies on the ability of the evaluation to respond to the purposes for which it was commissioned

Table 1.2 shows that RWE can be conducted at three different points in a project or program: at the start during the planning stage, when the project is already being implemented, or at the end. When the evaluation begins at the start of the project, RWE is used (a) to help identify different options for reducing costs or time of the evaluation, (b) for deciding how to make the best use of available data, (c) to understand client information needs and the political context within which the evaluation will be conducted, (d) for deciding what evaluation design would be appropriate, (e) for deciding what data needs to be collected by the monitoring system during the implementation of the project, and (f) to help identify different options for minimizing costs or time required for evaluation while still providing adequately valid information to meet stakeholders' needs. When the evaluation does not begin until project implementation is already underway, RWE is used to identify and assess the different evaluation design options that can be used within the budget and time constraints and to consider ways to reconstruct baseline data. Attention will be given to assessing the strengths and weaknesses of monitoring and administrative data available from the project and the availability and quality of secondary data from other sources. The feasibility of constructing a comparison group may also be considered. When the evaluation does not begin until toward the end of the project (or when the project has already ended), RWE is used in a similar way to the previous situation except that the design options are more limited because it is no longer possible to directly observe the project implementation process. One of the innovative RWE approaches is to suggest measures that can be taken to strengthen the validity of the findings even up to the point when the draft final evaluation report is being reviewed.

Summary

- Many evaluations are affected by budget, time, and data constraints or by political influences that limit the design options available to the evaluator. We call these the *RWE constraints.*

- RealWorld evaluators most frequently face one of two main scenarios. The first is when the evaluator is called in at the start of the project but the choice of evaluation design is constrained by budget or time pressures, by technical and administrative difficulties in collecting certain kinds of data, or by pressures from clients and stakeholders.

- The second, and probably the most common, scenario is when the evaluator is not called in until the project has been underway some time or may even be nearing completion. Often, the evaluator is again subject to budget and time constraints and political pressures, but even when budget and time are adequate, it is usually the case that no systematic baseline data have been collected and usually no comparison group has been identified.

- Although evaluation constraints such as lack of evaluation expertise, more limited access to secondary data, and often, less of an evaluation culture may be more apparent in developing countries, many evaluations in developed countries also face similar problems. Consequently, the RealWorld approach is applicable to varying degrees in all countries.

Table 1.2 Who Uses RWE, for What Purposes, and When?

When does the evaluation start?	Evaluation practitioners who design or implement the evaluation	Managers and funding agencies
At the beginning of a project (baseline)	• Identify a life-of-project evaluation design that will meet the needs of key stakeholders, given anticipated budget, time, and data constraints • Advise management how to reduce costs and time while achieving evaluation objectives • Negotiate with managers to relax some of the constraints to reduce some of the threats to validity and adequacy • Advise management on plans for a baseline study consistent with evaluation objectives • Identify ways to produce the best evaluation under budget, time, and data constraints	• Seek ways to minimize the costs and time required for the proposed evaluation design, including the baseline study • Assess the relevance, required level of rigor, and quality of the proposed life-of-project evaluation design
During project implementation	• Identify ways for relevant monitoring data to be collected and documented that inform implementers and are relevant for evaluation purposes, given budget, time, and data constraints • If there was no baseline, reconstruct baseline data • Ensure maximum quality under existing constraints	• Identify ways to strengthen the ongoing monitoring and evaluation (these measures may be directly implemented by project management or funding agencies or recommended to the agency conducting the evaluation) • Keep data collection minimized and prioritized on information that informs decision making and learning
At the end of the project	• Identify ways to meet evaluation objectives within limitations of budget, time, political considerations, and data availability • Use the RWE checklist to identify and deal with threats to validity and reliability • Reconstruct baseline data • Ensure maximum quality under existing constraints	• Be clear on the purpose of evaluation and the relevant degree of rigor required • Identify ways to correct weaknesses in the evaluation within the budget and time constraints and/or be willing to allocate more funds and time to achieve required credibility

Further Reading

American Evaluation Association. 1995. "Guiding Principles for Evaluators." Pp. 19–26 in *Guiding Principles for Evaluators*, edited by W. R. Shadish, D. L. Newman, M. A. Scheirer, and C. Wye. New Directions for Program Evaluation, No. 66. San Francisco: Jossey-Bass.

The evaluation guidelines approved by the American Evaluation Association.

Joint Committee on Standards for Educational Evaluation. 1994. *The Program Evaluation Standards: How to Assess Evaluations of Educational Programs.* 2d ed. Thousand Oaks, CA: Sage.

> An essential reference on evaluation standards.

Operations Evaluation Department. 2004. *Influential Evaluations: Evaluations That Improved Performance and Impacts of Development Programs.* Washington, DC: World Bank.

> Case studies of evaluations that had a demonstrable influence on clients and stakeholders and a discussion of the factors determining whether evaluations will be used.

Patton, M. Q. 1997. *Utilization-Focused Evaluation.* 3d ed. Thousand Oaks, CA: Sage.

> One of the most cited texts on how to design evaluations that will be utilized.

Rossi, P., M. Lipsey, and H. Freeman. 2004. *Evaluation: A Systematic Approach.* 7th ed. Thousand Oaks, CA: Sage.

> Chapter 2 introduces the evaluator-stakeholder relationship, and Chapter 12 discusses the social context of evaluation and the ethical issues discussed in this chapter.

Russon, C. and G. Russon, eds. 2005. *International Perspectives on Evaluation Standards.* New Directions for Evaluation, No. 104. San Francisco: Jossey-Bass.

> Discussion of the experiences and issues when other countries in different regions consider adopting and/or adapting U.S. evaluation standards.

Notes

1. **Bold** technical terms are defined in the glossary at the end of this book.

2. One of our colleagues who has worked with major U.S. foundations that support community-level initiatives stated that there is a huge unmet need in the United States for material on how to conduct evaluations when working with very limited financial and professional resources. He stated that his "and other foundations make lots of small grants. There is often not enough money in the grants to hire an external consultant. And the recipients of these small grants don't have the capacity to do internal evaluation. The evaluation work done by these nonprofits is usually pretty bad. I don't really know of any materials targeted to this group."

3. Many surveys include a household roster in which information on age, sex, education, employment status, and the like is collected for each household member. However, even when these data have been collected, analysis is often only conducted at the household level so that many of the data on individual household members are not used.

4. For more information on the IOCE, see http://ioce.net

PART II

The Seven Steps of the RealWorld Evaluation Approach

CHAPTER 2

First Clarify the Purpose

Scoping the Evaluation

This chapter introduces Step 1 of the RealWorld Evaluation (**RWE**) approach—"scoping the evaluation." Figure 2.1 shows the position of this step in the RWE approach. We begin by considering the widely different expectations that **clients** can have about the nature and purpose of evaluation and what they understand by, and expect from, an impact evaluation. It is important to understand client information needs and how clients expect to use the information produced by the evaluation. We then discuss the use of **program theory models** to articulate the assumptions on which the project **design** is based and to ensure that the evaluation focuses on the key issues and hypotheses of concern to stakeholders. Program theory also helps us understand how project implementation, **outcomes**, and impacts are affected by the political, economic, institutional, environmental, and cultural context within which each individual project is implemented. RWEs use both qualitative (**QUAL**) and quantitative (**QUANT**) evaluation methodologies, and there is no a priori preference for either. There are many advantages in using mixed-method designs that draw on the strengths of both QUAL and QUANT methodologies. The chapter concludes by showing how the information collected during the scoping phase is used to identify the cost, time, data, and political constraints that a particular evaluation will face and how this analysis is used to identify and assess the possible RWE designs that could be used for this particular evaluation.

Stakeholder Expectations of Impact Evaluations

There is a wide variety of understandings of what is involved in conducting an impact evaluation and what can be expected from the results. These include those who believe that every impact evaluation must be a sophisticated, "scientific," randomized, or quasi-experimental design.[1] On the other end of the continuum are those who believe that QUAL methods are needed to understand programs and their impacts in the ways in which they are experienced

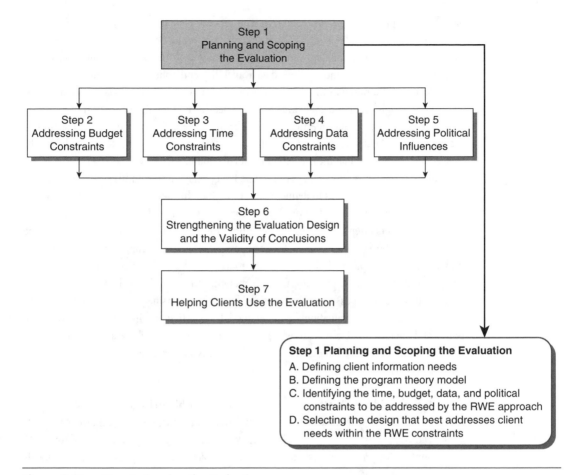

Figure 2.1   Step 1: Scoping the Evaluation

by stakeholders. And there are those who prefer multisite or multiprogram studies of issues or themes to examine broader impact. Although decisions on the choice of evaluation methods are partly based on the methodological preferences of the evaluators and the agencies commissioning the evaluation, they are also influenced by the size and complexity of the **projects** or **programs** (terms that will be used more or less interchangeably in this book) being evaluated and the specific purpose of the evaluation. RWE budget, time, data, and political constraints can also affect the choice of methods.

Understanding Information Needs

Whether plans for evaluating a project[2] begin at the time it is designed or are not thought about until near the end of the life of the project, those responsible for commissioning and conducting the evaluation will need to consider its purpose and therefore what design and methodologies would be appropriate and feasible. Table 1.2 (Chapter 1) shows that RWE can be used at the beginning of a project, during implementation, or at the end; it also describes the purposes for which evaluations are used by **evaluation practitioners** and clients/users at each of these points in the **project cycle.** The process of defining the evaluation purpose begins with a stakeholder analysis conducted by the evaluation team to understand the expectations of key stakeholders and often to negotiate with them what should and can be done, given constraints of money, time, data availability, and political considerations.

A clear understanding of the client's priorities and information needs is an essential first step in the design of a good evaluation and an effective way for the RealWorld evaluator to eliminate unnecessary data collection and analysis, hence reducing cost and time. The timing, focus, and level of detail of the evaluation should be determined by information needs and the types of decisions to which the evaluation must contribute.

While it is usually a simple matter to define the clients (those commissioning the evaluation), a more difficult issue is to define the range of **stakeholders** whose concerns should be taken into account in the evaluation design, implementation, and dissemination. Time and budget constraints often create pressures that limit the range of stakeholders to be consulted and involved. The evaluator should try to assess whether these constraints exclude some important groups—particularly, vulnerable groups who may be difficult to reach and less likely to be included in the planning, implementation, and use of the evaluation.

Meeting as early as possible with clients and key stakeholders helps ensure that the reasons for commissioning the evaluation are understood. It is particularly important to understand policy and operational decisions to which the evaluation will contribute and to agree on the level of **precision** required in making these decisions. Typical questions that decision makers must address include these:

- Is there **evidence** that the project achieved (or will achieve) its objectives? Which objectives were (or will be) achieved and which were not (or will not be) achieved? Why?
- Did the project aim for the right objectives? Were the underlying causes of the problem(s) the project is designed to ameliorate accurately diagnosed and adequately addressed?
- Are outcomes sustainable and benefits likely to continue?
- What internal and/or external contextual factors determine the degree of success or failure?

Many of these questions do not require a high level of statistical precision, but they do require reliable answers to additional questions:

- Are there measurable changes in the characteristics of the **target population** with respect to the impacts the project was intended to produce?
- What impact has the project had on different subsets of the target population, including the poorest and most vulnerable groups? Are there different impacts on men and women? Are there ethnic, religious, or similar groups who do not benefit or who are affected negatively?
- Is it likely the same impacts could be achieved if the project were implemented in a different setting or on a larger scale?

The RealWorld evaluator needs to distinguish between critical issues that must be explored in depth and those that are less critical and can be studied less intensively or eliminated completely. It is also essential to understand when the client needs rigorous statistical or QUANT analysis to legitimize the evaluation **findings** to members of Congress, funding agencies, or those critical of the program and when more general analysis and findings would be acceptable. Answers to such questions can have a major impact on the evaluation design, budget, and time required.

Developing the Program Theory Model[3]

A program theory is "an explicit theory or model of how the program causes the intended or observed outcomes" (Rogers, Petrosino, Huebner, and Hacsi 2000:5). All programs are based on explicit or implicit theory about how intended program **outputs** and **impacts** are to be achieved and the factors constraining or facilitating their achievement. While program theory models can be used in all evaluations, they are particularly useful for RWE to identify critical areas and issues on which limited evaluation resources or time should focus. A program theory model may help explain whether failure to achieve objectives is due to faulty expectations or ineffective project implementation (Lipsey 1993; Weiss 1997).

Program theory is occasionally spelled out in project documents (e.g., a logical framework or flow chart) but more often must be elicited by the evaluator through consultations with program staff members, program participants, and partner agencies. Developing a program theory model is often an iterative process in which an initial model is constructed by the evaluator on the basis of preliminary consultations and then discussed and modified through further consultations.

Figure 2.2 presents a simple program theory model describing seven stages of the project or program cycle:[4]

1. *Design.* How the project was designed (e.g., was it top-down, were there participatory consultations, was a standard "blue-print" used, or was it adapted to the local context)?

2. *Inputs.* The financial, human, material, technological, and information resources used in the project

3. *Implementation process.* The actions taken or work performed through which **inputs,** such as funds, technical assistance, and other types of resources, are mobilized to produce specific outputs; to what extent and how intended beneficiaries were involved

4. *Outputs.* Products and services resulting directly from program activities

5. *Outcomes.* The intended or achieved short- and medium-term effects of an intervention's outputs, usually requiring the collective effort of partners. Outcomes represent changes in development conditions that occur between the completion of outputs and the achievement of impact.

6. *Impacts.* Long-term economic, sociocultural, institutional, environmental, technological, or other effects on identifiable populations or groups produced by a project, directly or indirectly, intended or unintended

7. *Sustainability.* Continuation of benefits after a project has been completed

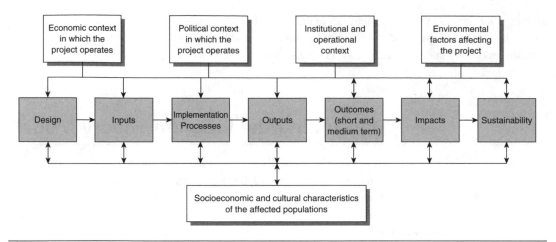

Figure 2.2   A Simple Program Theory Model

Although the first four components of this model—design, inputs, implementation processes, and outputs—may be directly controllable by those managing the project, by contrast, the outcomes, impacts, and **sustainability** depend to a considerable degree on external factors over which the project agency usually has little or no control.

Some of the different ways in which the concept of impact is used in evaluation are described in Box 2.1. There are also a number of agencies that do not use the concept of impact, believing that it is methodologically or philosophically too difficult to define, measure, or interpret. However, because the purpose of most development interventions is to contribute to long-term effects (improvements in the well-being of the target populations) rather than just to produce short-term observable outcomes, we go along with the majority of development practitioners and try to measure impacts—while fully recognizing all the methodological and philosophical limitations on how well impacts can be assessed/inferred, particularly in many RWE contexts.

An **evaluability assessment** may also be conducted during the scoping phase. This is an assessment of the feasibility of assessing project impacts with the available resources and data. While design, inputs, implementation processes, and outputs can be directly observed, measured, and documented by the project's monitoring system, indicators of outcomes and impacts usually require additional data collection (e.g., sample surveys or in-depth QUAL data collection), often using one of the designs discussed in Chapter 10. Whether or not the project makes plausible contributions to such outcomes and impacts must be tested or inferred. And unless there is an ex-post evaluation conducted some time after the project finished operating, sustainable impact can only be inferred and not directly observed. Consequently, one of the purposes of the evaluability assessment (if it is conducted) is to determine whether resources will permit collecting the types of additional data required to assess outcomes and impacts.

Outcomes are the short- and medium-term effects, and impacts are the long-term effects of a project. In other words, these are the changes that can be wholly or partly attributed to the interventions of the project, perhaps by a **counterfactual** that estimates what would have been the economic, sociocultural, institutional, or other conditions of the intended beneficiaries in the absence of the project's interventions. The difference between the observed conditions of

Box 2.1   Defining Impact

In this book we focus on impact evaluations. However, it needs to be recognized that there is a wide variety of definitions of and assumptions related to the meaning of *impact.* In simple terms, impact evaluation goes beyond an examination of outputs produced by a project's interventions, to determine higher-level and longer-term effects.

The definition of impact adopted by the OECD-DAC (2002) is "Positive and negative, primary and secondary long-term effects produced by a development intervention on identifiable population groups, directly or indirectly, intended or unintended. These effects can be economic, socio-cultural, institutional, environmental, technological or of other types."

There are other definitions or nuances, including the following:

- Some writers consider that outcomes are the *observed changes* in the variables the project seeks to affect, whereas impacts are the *proportion of the changes* that can be attributed to the project. Outcomes (changes in conditions) can be observed, whereas impacts (the influence a project had on those changes) can only be inferred through the use of an analytical process such as a quasi-experimental design.
- Some define impact as "higher-level" outcomes (CARE International's definition is "equitable and durable improvements in human wellbeing and social justice"; CARE International 2003) whether or not changes at these levels can be directly attributable to a project. A project can be held accountable for direct attribution to outputs and more immediate outcomes/short-term effects, and thus to their plausible contributions to higher-level sustainable impact, along with other influences that must be identified and acknowledged.
- The dictionary definition of impact refers to *influence,* the effect or impression of one thing on another—for example, what difference did the project make?
- But influence on *what?* A project could have an "impact" on staff paychecks, on direct (but superficial) benefits of services provided to participants, on the capacities of local organizations, on the conditions of the target population, on the empowerment of individuals and community groups, on national policy, on the achievement of the Millennium Development Goals[5] . . . the list could go on. There needs to be agreement among stakeholders (including intended beneficiaries, donors, and partners) on what "success" (and therefore impact) would look like. It depends on their values and expectations—and on what is reasonable to expect from a time- and resource-bound project.
- There are those who refer to impact in terms of *scope* or *scale*—for example, how many people's lives were influenced (impacted) in some way?
- Others refer to it in terms of *degree* or *depth*—that is, whether a project had a minor influence or made a significant difference in the quality of life of beneficiaries in important ways.
- There are also the intended/unintended dimensions of impact, desired/negative impact, and direct/indirect impact (e.g., multiplier effect of people adopting a practice beyond those who participated directly in a project).

And, of course, there is the assumption (that needs to be verified by measurement or projection) that whatever impact there was will be *sustainable*—that is, will continue after the external influence of a project has ended.

the beneficiaries and the counterfactual is the estimated impact of the project. The methodology for assessing project impacts through the use of QUANT quasi-experimental designs is discussed in Chapter 10.

The model in Figure 2.2 also identifies five sets of **contextual variables** that may affect implementation and outcomes. These include the economic, political, organizational, operational, and environmental settings of the project and the socioeconomic and cultural characteristics of the affected populations (Hentschel 1999; Patton 2002). The following are examples of how each of these contextual variables can affect the project and how their analysis can strengthen interpretation of evaluation findings:

- *Economic factors:* In a dynamic economy where jobs are being created and demand for products and services is growing, people are often more willing to invest time or resources in developing marketable skills or in launching small businesses. It is often hypothesized, for example, that parents are more willing to pay for their daughters to stay in school (and to forego the daughter's assistance with domestic and farming activities) if labor market conditions create the expectation that extra education will help them get better jobs.
- *Political factors:* Support from local government agencies (who happen to be from the same political party as the national or state government sponsoring a project) can significantly improve project performance by mobilizing community support or providing free resources such as transport, workers, or buildings. Inversely, politically induced opposition to a project can seriously affect its success or even its ability to operate. Sometimes projects can become affected by political campaigns. In Zambia in the late 1970s, a donor agency was trying to convince the Ministry of Housing to charge full economic rent for low-cost housing. One of the candidates in the municipal election campaign promised families that if he was elected all rents would be subsidized, which contributed to the reluctance of families to pay their rent to the project.
- *Organizational and institutional factors:* Many projects require support from government agencies and other organizations such as **NGOs** (nongovernmental organizations) or religious organizations. The effectiveness of this cooperation can vary considerably from one community, district, or city to another. In some cases, this is due to personalities, in other cases to local politics, but in many cases it is mainly due to differences in staff, financial, or other resources. Sometimes something as basic as that the Ministry of Health in one town has a jeep, whereas in the next it does not, can have a major impact on the level and effectiveness of support.
- *Environmental factors:* Agricultural and rural development projects are directly affected by variations in the local environment. The new grain varieties being introduced may prosper well on flat land but not on hillsides, or they may be very sensitive to variations in seasonal rainfall. Urban development projects may be affected by erosion or flooding. All these factors may produce dramatic differences in crop yield or in the success of water and sanitation projects.
- *Socioeconomic and cultural characteristics of the target communities.* Many countries in Africa and other developing regions have literally hundreds of different tribal groups, each with its own farming practices, rules concerning use of natural resources, marriage practices, and attitudes concerning the mobility and economic participation of women. In one village in Uganda, bicycles proved an effective way to transport water

and reduce women's time burden (because water was carried in square metal jerry cans that could easily be transported on the bicycle's luggage rack), but in a neighboring village, bicycles failed to produce this benefit because water was transported in round clay pots that could not easily be transported on a luggage rack.

An analysis of these contextual factors can often help explain why two identical projects may have very different outcomes in different communities. In one community, the economy may be thriving, whereas in another it is in decline—so parents are more willing to pay for their daughters' continued education in the first than in the second; in one community, most of the farm land is flat and well drained, whereas in the next community, most of the land is hilly and the new variety of grain does not prosper. For these reasons, evaluators are strongly encouraged to incorporate contextual analysis into the evaluation design.

A key element of program theory models is the identification and monitoring of critical assumptions about inputs, implementation processes, and the expected linkages with outcomes. There are two types of assumptions: internal and external. Internal assumptions, or hypotheses, describe the logical cause-and-effect links between interventions and outcomes. External assumptions refer to factors beyond the direct control of a project—for example, whether the project should address policy issues rather than take it for granted that it can have no influence over them. Even those external factors that truly cannot be changed by the project need to be monitored if the success of the project depends on the correctness of those assumptions or on needed adjustments in response to changing external conditions.

Logical Framework Analysis

Logical framework analysis or **logframe** (one form of logic model) is a widely used program theory model that requires the critical assumptions to be identified and their validity assessed at each stage of project implementation (see Chapter 9 for a discussion of logic models). Logframes often follow the stages of the model described in Figure 2.2. One of the important and very useful elements of the logframe is that it identifies some of the critical assumptions about the linkages between the different stages of the model. Table 2.1 illustrates critical assumptions that might be included at each stage of the implementation of a project to strengthen women's economic and social empowerment through **microcredit**. For example, the use of credit as the major input is based on two assumptions: first that lack of access to credit is one of the main constraints on women's ability to start small businesses and second that if women have access to credit, this will significantly improve the number of small businesses they start. Both assumptions can be tested, and their correctness will be an important determinant of the project's success. Similar assumptions can be identified and tested for each stage of the model.

Figure 9.4 (p. 186) shows how these critical assumptions can be expressed in the form of a **results chain** diagram. The left-hand side of the figure shows the intended chain of events (e.g., women will use the loans to create businesses that generate profits that produce improvements in household welfare and are also reinvested to ensure the growth and sustainability of the business). The right-hand (shaded) side of the figure identifies the different reasons why the project might fail to achieve its objectives (e.g., women do not use the loans to create businesses, the profits are taken by the husband or used to pay off debts or to provide dowries, or the businesses fail). Each step can be tested to determine whether the outcomes are positive (as planned) or negative.

Table 2.1   Testing Critical Assumptions in a Logic Model of a Project to Strengthen Women's Economic Empowerment through Microcredit

Stage of Project	Critical Assumptions to Be Tested
Design	• Poor women have the skills needed to operate viable income-generating projects but lack only capital. • Women are able to decide for themselves what business to start/expand. • Women will be able to control how the loan is used, and the money will not be appropriated by the husband.
Inputs	• Access to credit, in a form that women can control, is critical to enhance women's access to economic opportunities.
Implementation process	• The creation of solidarity groups through which loans are approved and technical support provided is essential to enable women to control their use of their loans and to manage their small businesses. • Solidarity groups must select their own members without any outside pressures.
Outputs	• Women will use loans to invest in small businesses (not just to pay off debts or pay for consumption or ceremonial activities). • Women will be able to control the use of the loan (despite cultural traditions that economic resources are controlled by male household members).
Outcomes	• If women produce goods, they will be able to market them. • Their businesses will be profitable. • Women will control or share in the control of the profits.
Impact	• Profits will increase household consumption, women's savings, and quality of life of members of their households.
Sustainability	• The women's solidarity groups will be able to continue providing loans after the project's external credit and support has ended. • Their businesses will continue to operate and to grow.

Identifying the Constraints to Be Addressed by RWE and Determining the Appropriate Evaluation Design

Identifying Budget, Time, Data, and Political Constraints to Be Addressed by the Evaluation Design

The final part of Step 1 of the RWE approach includes preliminary identification of those budget, time, data, and political constraints that can be anticipated. This can lead to a determination of which of the options for Steps 2, 3, 4, and 5 will need to be used. Once the evaluators have identified what they consider to be the best options for addressing these constraints, the proposed strategy will then be discussed with the client and, possibly, key stakeholders. Often, this may involve a period, sometimes quite long, of negotiation and revision of the proposed strategy. In some cases, the evaluation team may try to convince the client that the requested reductions in budget or time are not possible without prejudicing the purposes for which the evaluation is being conducted. If the client is not able or willing to relax the budget or time requirements, the evaluators may in some cases decide to withdraw from the project, but typically some compromise will be reached. However, in these cases it is extremely important for the client to understand the types of information that can and cannot be provided within these constraints and the levels of precision, validity, and adequacy that the evaluation can be expected to achieve.

Chapters 3 through 6 review the options for addressing budget, time, data, and political constraints, respectively.

Developing Designs Suitable for RealWorld Evaluation Conditions

We now address a very important decision that needs to be made by those commissioning and those responsible for conducting an evaluation: What evaluation design would be most appropriate for responding to the priority questions determined during the assessment of client needs, and which design options are even possible, given the constraints and the stage the project has reached? As we saw in Table 1.2 (p. 24), the earlier in the life of the project this decision is made, the more options there are.

A key decision is whether the evaluation will use a QUANT, QUAL, or mixed-method design and methodologies. We emphasize throughout this book that although we see certain advantages to using a combination of methods, both to address RWE constraints and to gain multiple perspectives, there is no "best" evaluation methodology. The choice of research methods is determined by a number of different factors that, in addition to the types of questions to be addressed, include the professional orientation of the client and the evaluation practitioner. The list of questions in the next section can help determine which methods are most suitable for the purposes for an evaluation and the conditions under which it is to be conducted.

Table 2.2 provides a comparison between seven evaluation design models, showing which can be used when the evaluation begins at the start of the project or when it has already been underway for some time. These designs are mainly applicable to QUANT and to mixed-method evaluations. Most QUANT evaluations are based on either an experimental or a quasi-experimental design in that all seek to measure changes in a set of QUANT variables and to assess whether the changes are associated with the project interventions. This makes it possible to identify a limited number of QUANT evaluation designs that cover most RWE **scenarios**. QUAL evaluations, on the other hand, use a wider range of design, data collection, and data analysis approaches, and these cannot be easily summarized into a standard set of designs equivalent to the seven QUANT designs described in Table 2.2 (see Chapter 12 for a discussion of QUAL evaluation designs). Table 2.3 provides a decision tree matrix to help decide which QUANT design is possible under different scenarios. Each of these seven evaluation designs is described in more detail in Chapter 10.

It might be noted that whereas the various quasi-experimental evaluation designs given in Table 2.2 are more commonly associated with QUANT methods, whether or not there can be a before-after and/or a with-without comparison applies to both QUANT and QUAL methodologies. The major differences between these designs have to do with the stage of the project at which the evaluation team collects data (e.g., baseline, midterm, final, ex-post). A separate distinction has to do with whether the data collection methods are QUANT, QUAL, or mixed and whether they also rely on secondary sources or the **recall**[6] perspectives of key informants and participants.

Table 2.2 The Seven Most Widely Used RealWorld Evaluation Quasi-Experimental Designs

Evaluation Design	Start of Project (pretest) T_1	Project Intervention (continues on to end of project)	Midterm Evaluation or Several Observations during Implementation T_2	End of Project (posttest) T_3	Follow-up after Project Operating for Some Time (ex-post) T_4	The Stage of the Project Cycle at which Each Evaluation Design can Begin to be Used
TWO STRONGEST EVALUATION DESIGNS						
1. *Comprehensive longitudinal design with pre-, midterm, post- and ex-post observations on the project and comparison groups.* This is the methodologically strongest design but also the most expensive and time-consuming. Permits assessment of the process of project implementation as well as trend analysis. Random assignment of subjects is rarely possible, so this and following designs normally use comparison groups selected to match the project group as closely as possible.	P_1 C_1	X	P_2 C_2	P_3 C_3	P_4 C_4	Start
2. *Pretest-posttest project and comparison groups.* For most purposes, this is the best available design when the evaluation can begin at the start of the project with a reasonable budget and no particular constraints on access to data or use of a comparison group.	P_1 C_1	X		P_2 C_2		Start
FIVE LESS ROBUST EVALUATION DESIGNS						
3. *Truncated longitudinal pretest-posttest project and comparison group design.* Project and comparison groups observed at two or more points during project implementation, but evaluation does not begin until the project is underway. Evaluation often starts as part of midterm review.		X	P_1 C_1	P_2 C_2		Midterm
4. *Pretest-posttest project group combined with posttest analysis of project and comparison group.* No baseline data collected on comparison group.	P_1	X		P_2 C_1		Start
5. *Posttest project and comparison groups.* No baseline or midterm data collected.		X		P_1 C_1		End
6. *Pretest-posttest project group.* No comparison group.	P_1	X		P_2		Start
7. *Posttest project group only.* No baseline project data or comparison group. This is the weakest QUANT design but very widely used because of limited cost and time requirements.		X		P_1		End

Key

T = time during project cycle
P = project participants
C = comparison group
P_1, P_2, C_1, C_2, etc. = first, second (and in some designs, third and fourth) observations of the project or comparison groups in a particular evaluation design
X = project intervention (a process rather than a discrete event)

Table 2.3   Determining Possible Quantitative Evaluation Designs[a]

Question[b]	If the Answer Is <u>Yes</u>	If the Answer Is <u>No</u>
Was the evaluation pre-planned? That is, was the evaluation design included in the project's monitoring and evaluation plan from the beginning?	Use that preexisting plan as the guide for the project evaluation. The evaluation should include an assessment of the appropriateness of the monitoring and evaluation plan and should acknowledge and use it.	This is going to have to be an ad hoc, one-off evaluation (e.g., Design 5 or 7). This limits the rigor of the evaluation design, but there are things that can be done, even so.
Was there a baseline (pretest)?	That will make a "before and after" (Design 1, 2, 4, or 6) possible—if the baseline was done in a way that can be compared with the posttest (end-of-project evaluation).	Too bad. You'll either have to make do with retrospective analysis, a "with and without" (comparison group at final only, Design 5) or cope with a "one snapshot" limitation.
Was there a comparison group for the baseline?	Recommend Design 1 or 2 *if* there can be the same or a comparable control group for the posttest (see next question).	Too bad. Could still use Design 3 or 4, hoping that the posttest comparison group was similar to the participants at the beginning of the project.
Even if there was no control group in the baseline, can there be a comparison group for the posttest (end-of-project evaluation)?	Design 3, 4, or 5 could be used. Do all possible to verify that the comparison group was similar to the participants at the beginning in all ways except for the intervention.	Consider looking for secondary data that may give general trends in the population to compare with the group that participated in the project.
Was reliable monitoring information collected on effect and/or impact indicators during project implementation?	Very helpful! Quasi-experimental longitudinal Design 1 may be possible, including examining trends over time.	Well, pretest + posttest with comparison group (Design 2) isn't bad. You might still look for secondary data indicating trends.
Will it be possible to conduct an ex-post evaluation some time (e.g., several years) after the end of the project?	An extended longitudinal Design 1 will provide more certain evidence of sustainability (or lack thereof).	Without an ex-post evaluation, predictions about sustainability will have to be made based on the quality of the project's process and intermediary outcomes.

a. These are the kinds of questions that should be asked by an evaluation team when called in to evaluate an ongoing project. Obviously, if these questions are considered at the time a project is designed the evaluation plan can be stronger. Otherwise, the evaluation team will have to cope as well as it can with the given situation.

b. Readers not familiar with any of the terms used in this table are referred to Chapter 10, where all the evaluation designs are discussed.

In the situation depicted by Design 7 (posttest analysis without baseline or **comparison group**[7]), for example, the evaluators would not only want to measure (QUANT approach) or describe (QUAL approach) the present status of the condition the project aimed to change (indicator or other form of evidence), they would also need to find some evidence of how that condition changed over the life of the project and a comparison of how that change may have been different for those participating in the project compared with others under similar conditions who did not. This calls for finding secondary data or collecting the perspectives of knowledgeable people. Whether the evaluator does that by measurement (collecting numbers) or descriptions (words) has to do with methodology. How much of that data is obtained from primary sources (e.g., surveys, observation, key informants) or from secondary sources has to do with evaluation design.

Developing the Terms of Reference for the Evaluation

Those commissioning evaluations may find the following set of questions helpful when preparing the **terms of reference** (ToR) for the evaluation. The evaluators might also find this checklist helpful, particularly for identifying points not covered in the ToR and that must be clarified with the client before the evaluation is designed.

- Who asked for the evaluation? Who are the key stakeholders? Do they have preconceived ideas regarding the purpose for the evaluation and expected findings (political considerations)?
- Who should be involved in planning/implementing the evaluation?
- What are the key questions to be answered?
- Will this be a **formative** or **summative** evaluation? Is its purpose primarily for learning and improving, accountability, or a combination of both?
- Will there be a next phase, or will other projects be designed based on the findings of this evaluation?
- What decisions will be made in response to the findings of this evaluation? By whom?
- What is the appropriate level of rigor needed to collect and analyze the information needed to inform those decisions?
- What is the scope/scale of the evaluation/**evaluand** (program or intervention being evaluated)?
- How much time will be needed/available?
- What financial resources are needed/available?
- What evaluation design would be required/is possible under the circumstances?
- Should the evaluation rely mainly on QUANT methods, QUAL methods, or a combination of the two?
- Should participatory methods be used?
- Can/should there be a survey of individuals, households, or other entities?
- Who should be interviewed?
- What sample design and size are required/feasible?
- What form of analysis will best answer the key questions (see the third question above)?
- Who are the audiences for the report(s)?
- How will the findings be communicated to each audience?

Summary

- Clients and other stakeholders can have widely varying expectations of what an impact evaluation is and what it can produce. These can range from detailed QUANT estimates to case studies on how a program has affected the lives of individual communities, families, or schools.

- An evaluation should be based on a sound understanding of why the evaluation is being commissioned, how the findings will be used, and the political context within which it will be conducted. Understanding the client's *bottom line*—what information and analysis is essential and what would simply be "nice to have"—is critical when decisions have to be made on what can and cannot be cut in the light of budget and time constraints.

- All programs are based on an implicit (or explicit) model of how the program is expected to operate, how the intended program outputs and impacts are to be achieved, and the factors facilitating or constraining achievement. Defining the program theory helps focus the evaluation and identify the key hypotheses and linkages that the evaluation must test.

- The scoping step should end with an agreement between the client and the evaluator on the RWE design that best responds to the purposes for which the evaluation is being commissioned while at the same time adapting to the budget, time, data, and political constraints under which it must be conducted.

Further Reading

Carvalho, S. and H. White. 2004. "Theory Based Evaluation: The Case of Social Funds." *American Journal of Evaluation* 25(2):141–60.

An example of the application of program theory to the evaluation of **social investment funds** (a widely used model for providing health, education, water supply, and other local infrastructure in developing countries). The article illustrates how program theory can be reconstructed during the evaluation when it was not defined in the project documents. The article is also interesting because it presents the concept of an "antitheory" based on the views of critics as to the potential negative outcomes of the project interventions.

Patton, M. Q. 1997. *Utilization-Focused Evaluation.* 3d ed. Thousand Oaks, CA: Sage.

Probably the most widely cited text on how to ensure that evaluations respond to the needs of stakeholders and that findings will be used.

Rogers, P., T. Hacsi, A. Petrosino, and T. Huebner, eds. 2000. *Program Theory in Evaluation: Challenges and Opportunities.* New Directions for Evaluation, No. 87. San Francisco: Jossey-Bass.

One of the most comprehensive overviews of recent developments in program theory evaluation. All the chapters include extensive reference sources.

Rossi, P., M. Lipsey, and H. Freeman. 2004. *Evaluation: A Systematic Approach.* 7th ed. Thousand Oaks, CA: Sage.

A thorough presentation of the design and use of program theory evaluations.

Weiss, C. 2001. "Theory-Based Evaluation: Theories of Change for Poverty Based Programs." Pp. 103–14 in *Evaluation and Poverty Reduction,* edited by O. Feinstein and R. Picciotto. New Brunswick, NJ: Transaction.

A discussion of how program theory models can be applied to the evaluation of poverty reduction programs.

Notes

1. See for example the U.S. Department of Education's preference for randomized experiments as advocated by the Coalition for Evidenced-Based Policy (www.excelgov.org/evidence) and the MIT's Poverty Action Lab (www.povertyactionlab.com).

2. We use the term *project* here, but most of what is addressed can also apply to a program—which can be a longer-term megaproject with a broad goal, plan, and time frame or can consist of a series of projects addressing various aspects of problems affecting a target population, with intended synergy to produce higher-level impact.

3. See Chapter 9 for a more thorough discussion of program theory models.

4. Several of the following definitions are adapted from Organization for Economic Cooperation and Development (2002). This source is widely used by the evaluation departments of international development agencies.

5. See www.un.org/millenniumgoals

6. Recall techniques (see Chapter 5) involve asking individuals or groups to give their recollections of their personal situation or the situation of their community at an earlier point in time. For impact evaluations, the earlier time will usually be the time at which the project was starting.

7. Posttest is the time period after the completion of the project. The comparison group is a group selected to match the project group as closely as possible on a number of key characteristics related to the project and is used to assess what would have been the condition of the project group if the project had not taken place.

CHAPTER 3

Not Enough Money

Addressing Budget Constraints

S tep 2 of the RealWorld Evaluation (**RWE**) approach identifies five strategies for conducting an evaluation on a tight budget (see Figure 3.1). These strategies include simplifying the evaluation **design**, clarifying **client** information needs so as reduce the amount of data to be collected or the types of analysis required, making greater user of secondary data, reducing the sample size, and reducing the costs of data collection. Finally, we identify some of the common threats to validity and adequacy of the evaluation conclusions that occur when measures are taken to reduce costs.

Often, **project** budgets include insufficient funds for evaluation, or by the time managers become concerned with **impact** issues, evaluation funds have been allocated to other activities. This chapter describes five strategies for addressing the budget constraints that evaluators often face (see Box 3.1 and Table 3.1):

1. Simplify the evaluation design (see also Chapter 10).

2. Clarify client information needs, seeking ways to cut out the collection of nonessential information (see also Chapter 2).

3. Look for reliable secondary data (see also Chapter 5).

4. Reduce the sample size (see also Chapter 14).

5. Use more economical data collection methods.

Simplifying the Evaluation Design

One way to significantly reduce the costs and time of the evaluation is to simplify the evaluation design. This will often result in reducing the number of interviews or concentrating the interviews in a smaller number of physical locations so that travel time and cost can be

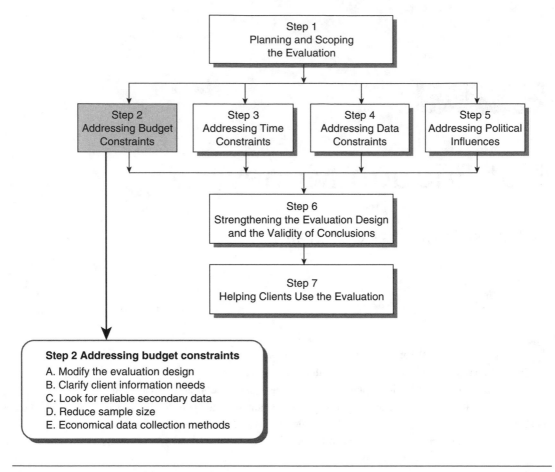

Figure 3.1   Step 2: Addressing Budget Constraints

reduced. The cost and time reduction strategies are easier to define for quantitative (**QUANT**) evaluations because interviews all have a similar duration and there is normally a standard cost for each interview. Consequently, it is easy to estimate the cost savings if the number of interviews are reduced. However, the cost reduction strategies are not so clearly defined for

---

Box 3.1   Five Questions to Help Make the Budget Go Further

1. Can we use a simpler and cheaper evaluation design?

2. Do we really need to collect all of this information?

3. Has someone already collected some of the information that we need?

4. Can we reduce the number of interviews, observations, cases, and so on without sacrificing the necessary precision?

5. Is there a cheaper way to collect the information?

Table 3.1   Reducing Costs of Data Collection and Analysis for Quantitative and Qualitative Evaluations

Quantitative Evaluations	*Qualitative Evaluations*
A. Simplifying the Evaluation Design[a]	
All these designs produce potential cost savings (see Table 3.2) • Truncated longitudinal design (Design 3): study starts at mid-term • Pretest-posttest project group with posttest analysis of project and comparison groups (Design 4)[b]: eliminates baseline comparison group • Posttest comparison of project and control group (Design 5): eliminates baseline • Pretest-posttest comparison of project group (Design 6): eliminates comparison group • Evaluation based on posttest data from project group (Design 7): eliminates comparison group and baseline project group	• Prioritize and focus on critical issues • Reduce the number of site visits or the time period over which observations are made • Reduce the amount and cost of data collection • Reduce the number of persons or groups studied
B. Clarifying Client Information Needs	
Prioritize data needs with the client to eliminate the collection of non-essential data.	
C. Using Existing Data	
• Census or surveys covering project areas • Data from project records • Records from schools, health centers, and other public service agencies	• Newspapers and other mass media • Records from community organizations • Dissertations and other university studies (for both QUAL and QUANT)
D. Reducing Sample Size	
• Lower the level of required precision (lower precision = small sample) • Reduce types of disaggregation required (less disaggregation = smaller sample) • Stratified sample designs (fewer interviews) • Use cluster sampling (lower travel costs)	• Consider critical or quota sampling rather than comprehensive or representative sampling • Reduce the number of persons or groups studied
E. Reducing Costs of Data Collection, Input, and Analysis	
• Self-administered questionnaires (with literate populations) • Direct observation—instead of surveys (sometimes saves money but not always)	• Decrease the number or period of observations • Prioritize informants

(Continued)

Table 3.1 (Continued)

Quantitative Evaluations	Qualitative Evaluations
• Automatic counters and other nonobtrusive methods • Direct inputting of survey data through handheld devices • Optical scanning of survey forms and electronic surveys	• Employ and train university students, student nurses, and community residents to collect data (for both QUAL and QUANT) • Data input through handheld devices

Mixed-method designs
     • Triangulation to compensate for reduced sample size
     • Focus groups and community forums instead of household surveys
     • PRA and other participatory methods	

a. See Chapter 10 for a discussion of the designs.
b. See the seven evaluation design models in Box 3.3 and Table 2.2.

many qualitative (**QUAL**) evaluations because the time required to prepare a case study or conduct **participant observation** can vary greatly.

Simplifying the Evaluation Design for Quantitative Evaluations

RWE approaches are used when the evaluation must be designed and implemented with budget as well as time, data, and political constraints. This means that many of the standard impact evaluation designs cannot be used. Chapter 10 reviews the principles of experimental and quasi-experimental designs and explains why the technically stronger QUANT designs cannot be used in many RWE contexts. Consequently, the RealWorld evaluator must make compromises on elements of the stronger designs because of the budget and other constraints and therefore must recognize the additional threats to the validity of the evaluation conclusions when weaker designs are used. Box 3.2 also points out that technically "robust" designs must be correctly implemented if they are not to lose their methodological strength.

Chapter 10 describes the seven most widely used RWE designs. These designs are summarized in Table 2.2 (p. 46). There is a direct relation between the methodological soundness of the evaluation design and the number of observation points at which surveys are conducted or other forms of data are collected. In the strongest designs (Designs 1 and 2), information is collected on both the project population and a **comparison group** before the project begins (baseline or pretest) and when the project has ended (posttest). If well designed and executed, these designs provide robust estimates of whether there are statistically significant differences between the project and comparison groups with respect to the indicators of project impact. However, these designs are the most expensive because they require that information be collected on two groups (project and comparison group) and at two or more points in time (at least before and after the project's interventions). Each of the cheaper and methodologically weaker designs eliminates collection of data at one or more of these four points. Box 3.3 shows that the seven models include two relatively strong designs and five that are less robust—but that work well enough for most RWE purposes if properly implemented and interpreted.

Box 3.2   "Robust" Designs Require Correct Design and Implementation!

The fact that a "robust" design is selected does not guarantee methodologically sound conclusions unless a study is properly designed, implemented, and analyzed. If the sample is not properly selected, the survey instrument is not properly designed and administered, there is a high nonresponse rate, or if triangulation and other quality control procedures are not used, then the conclusions may be of questionable validity. See Chapter 14 for a discussion of these issues.

However, it is a fact of life that the weakest design (Design 7), in which a posttest analysis of the project group is conducted without baseline data and without a comparison group, is probably also the most widely used!

In addition to cost, the range of available designs is also determined by when the evaluation begins. When the evaluation begins at the start of the project, the choice is among Designs 1, 2, 4, and 6; if the evaluation starts at midterm, then Design 3 is available; and if the evaluation does not begin until toward the end of the project, then the choice is between Designs 5 and 7 (see Table 2.2).

When budget and time are not constraints, most RWEs would use one of the two most robust designs (Designs 1 and 2). However, the RealWorld evaluator must frequently select among the five less robust designs (Designs 3–7), which are less demanding in terms of budget or time. All these less robust designs eliminate one or more of the pretest or posttest observations on the project or **comparison group** and, consequently, increase vulnerability to the four types of "threats to validity" described in Chapter 7. It should be noted, however, that even the two most robust designs (Designs 1 and 2) are subject to a number of threats to validity (see Chapter 10 and Shadish, Cook, and Campbell 2002 for a more extended discussion).

Box 3.3   The Seven Most Widely Used RWE Designs

The two most robust designs

  1. Comprehensive longitudinal design with pre-, post-, and ex-post data collection with comparison group

  2. Pretest-posttest design with comparison group

Five less robust designs

  3. Truncated longitudinal design

  4. No pretest comparison group

  5. No baseline data

  6. No comparison group

  7. Data collected only on the posttest project group with no comparison group

See Chapter 10 for a full discussion of each of these designs.

Design 2 is probably the most widely used quasi-experimental design when budget and time are not major constraints. Interviews or other forms of observation are conducted on a randomly selected sample of project beneficiaries (P_1) and a matched comparison group (C_1) before the project (X) begins. The observations are repeated on both groups (P_2 and C_2) at the completion of the project. The impact of the project intervention X is estimated as the difference of means or proportions between the observed change in the project and comparison groups.[1] It is usually not possible to randomly assign subjects to the project and control groups, so some element of judgment will be involved in selecting the most appropriate "control" or comparison group.

As we mentioned above, each of the five less robust models involves eliminating one or more of the pretest or posttest observations on the control or project groups:

- Truncated longitudinal design (Design 3). The evaluation does not begin until the project has been underway for some time (no baseline data), but several observations are taken during project implementation. This design is most commonly used when the evaluation begins around the time of the project midterm review.
- No pretest comparison group (Design 4). A comparison group is introduced only in the posttest survey.
- Posttest comparison of project and comparison groups (Design 5). No baseline data are collected, and the posttest comparison group is assumed to approximate the pretest conditions of the project population. In most cases, the decision to conduct the evaluation is not made until the project is completed or nearing completion, so the option of collecting baseline data was not available to the evaluators. However, although multivariate analysis can adjust for posttest differences between the two groups, this model cannot address differences between the two groups that existed prior to the project. This model can be strengthened through a **mixed-method** approach to reconstruct baseline data through **recall** or the use of secondary data (see Chapter 5).
- Pretest-posttest comparison of project group (Design 6). A before-and-after comparison is made of the project group through a baseline study and then a similar study at the end of the project. However, no comparison group is used.
- Data collected only on posttest project group (Design 7). There is no comparison group and no baseline data for the project group. In this design (or scenario), the evaluation is a one-off event, conducted only at the end of the project.

Each of Designs 3 through 7 can produce significant cost savings. Table 3.2 presents a rough estimate of the potential cost saving for each of these five weaker designs. It can be seen that the most economical design, Design 7, can potentially reduce data collection costs by as much as 60% to 80%. However, there is a price to pay, because all these designs are less able than the two more robust designs to address threats to validity and are thus more likely to lead to wrong conclusions concerning the contribution of the project intervention to the observed **outcomes**. However, when their strengths and weaknesses are fully understood and addressed, all these designs can provide an acceptable level of **precision** for many if not most management needs at a much-reduced cost.

Table 3.2   Estimated Cost Savings for Less Robust RWE Designs Compared with Design 2

Design		Estimated Cost Saving Compared with Design 2
3	Truncated longitudinal design	5–10%
4	No comparison group baseline study	10–20%
5	No baseline study for either group	30–40%
6	No comparison group	40–50%
7	Only posttest project group	60–80%

NOTE: The estimated cost savings are based on the percentage reduction in the total number of interviews, but take into account that there are fixed costs, such as questionnaire design and training.

Simplifying the Design for Qualitative Evaluations

As indicated earlier, while some QUAL methods follow precise implementation guidelines (e.g., for some focus group techniques or some observation methods), in most cases, the researcher is given much more flexibility in terms of how the methods are applied. In fact, many QUAL evaluators would not accept the concept of standard designs.

Table 3.1 gives examples of how some, but not all, QUAL designs can be simplified to reduce costs. One approach is to identify and prioritize the critical issues that must be addressed, and then to integrate all the tools to focus on the critical questions (Box 3.4). Another option is to use recall to reduce the number of visits or the time period over which the observations are made. For example, respondents can tell the researcher about the time they spent traveling to collect fuel and water without the researcher having to accompany them on the trips. The possibility can also be considered of reducing the number of members of the household or community to be included in the study. Finally, it may be possible to simplify the research hypotheses so as to reduce the amount of data and the collection costs. For example, if the hypothesis concerns only differences of behavior between women of different age groups in the same ethnic group, the study will be simpler (and perhaps cheaper) than if both age and ethnicity are being studied.

Box 3.4   But I Have to Complete This Evaluation in Three Days!

Great! Quick Ethnography [QE] . . . flows out of a theory of culture. QE procedures assume mastery of a wide variety of tools for data collection, data analysis, and the design and management of both. But the efficient collection and analysis of data with high reliability and construct validity come from how you integrate these tools. A theory of culture tells you how to do that quickly and well.

When you have three days to complete your project, you must prioritize extremely tightly.

SOURCE: Handwerker (2001:274–75).

Clarifying Client Information Needs

The costs and time required for data collection can sometimes be significantly reduced through a clearer definition of the information required by the client and the kinds of decisions to which the evaluation will contribute. Some of the ways to elicit this information were discussed in Chapter 2. The approaches and issues in the clarification of information needs are often, but not always, similar for QUANT and QUAL evaluations.

Using Existing Data

Often, secondary data can be identified that obviates or reduces the need for the collection of primary data. Typical examples include the following (also see Table 3.1):

- Census or survey data covering the project and comparison communities. Many governments conduct periodic national household surveys that usually contain information on the socioeconomic conditions of households and communities and include information of interest to the evaluation. If the results can be disaggregated to the specific population reached by a project with adequate statistical validity, such secondary data can be helpful in a project evaluation.
- Data from project monitoring records (e.g., household income, type of housing, school attendance, microloans approved).
- Records from schools (e.g., enrollment, attendance, test scores), health centers (e.g., number of patients, types of illness), and other public service agencies (e.g., water supply and sanitation, public transport).
- Newspapers and other mass media often have extensive coverage on economic and social issues that projects address (e.g., quality and availability of schools, access to health and sanitation facilities, public transport, etc.).
- Records from community organizations (minutes of meetings, photographs, posters, etc.).
- Dissertations and other academic studies.

The identification and evaluation of the validity of secondary data are discussed in Chapter 5.

Reducing Costs by Reducing Sample Size

Adjusting the Sample Size to Client Information Needs

Often, sample sizes are defined by survey researchers without reference to the kinds of decisions to be made by clients and the level of precision[2] actually required. Many clients assume that sample size is a purely technical question and that the evaluator should tell the client what is the "right" sample strategy and size. When sample size is not related to the purpose of the evaluation, how the results are to be used, and the required level of precision, larger and more costly samples may be used than are really necessary. However, in other cases, the sample may not be large enough to support the kinds of analysis required by the client. *It is absolutely essential to involve the client in decisions on the size and structure of the sample.*

The role of the evaluator is to understand the client's information needs and how the evaluation **findings** are to be used. It is critical to understand whether very precise statistical estimates are required or whether this is an exploratory study where only general estimates of potential impacts are required. The evaluator must also present the trade-offs between precision and cost to the client and agree together on the best option to provide the required information within the available budget (and time). In many cases, it is possible to reduce costs by cutting out some kinds of information or analysis included in the initial **terms of reference**, but the decision to do so should be made jointly between the client and the evaluator.

Factors Affecting Sample Size for Quantitative Evaluations

The required sample size can vary greatly according to the characteristics of the population, the nature of the project intervention, and the purpose of the evaluation. Table 3.3 identifies 11 factors that affect the required sample size. All these factors are discussed in more detail in Chapter 14.

The most important concepts in determining sample size are the **effect size** and the **power of the test.** The effect size refers to the size of the change (effect) that the **program** produces. Where possible, use a **standardized effect size**[3] measure so that comparisons can be made between different projects using the same treatment or between projects using different treatments to produce the same effect. To design the evaluation, it is necessary to define the minimum acceptable effect size (**MAES**). This is the minimum change (effect) that the client requires the evaluation to be able to test for. Table 14.1 (Chapter 14) presents eight different criteria that can be used to specify the MAES. In some cases, MAES is simply the expected effect size, whereas in other cases, it is derived from a comparison with other similar programs ("the project must be able to achieve an effect size at least as great as Project X"), or it might be determined by a policy objective ("to reduce the number of families with incomes less than $X"). The MAES is agreed to in consultation between the client and the evaluator. Once MAES and the required power of the test (see below) have been defined, the required sample size can be estimated.

A key determinant of the sample size is that *the smaller the effect size, the larger the required sample.* Because many projects can be expected to produce only a relatively small effect size, the required sample size to test for this effect will often be much larger than clients might have wished. In some cases, it may be concluded that the required sample size cannot be afforded, and a decision may have to be made to revise the objectives of the evaluation or even not to conduct the evaluation. This example emphasizes the importance of conducting an **evaluability assessment** during the scoping phase of the evaluation to ensure that the stated evaluation objectives could be achieved within budget, time, and data constraints (see Chapter 2).

The second key concept is the statistical power of the test (see Chapter 14). Statistical power is defined as "the probability that an estimate will be statistically significant when, in fact it represents a real effect of a given magnitude" (Rossi, Lipsey, and Freeman 2004:309). Figure 14.2 (p. 343) shows that when the effect size is small, there is a high probability that the statistical test may fail to detect the project effect even when it is real. In this figure, the power of the test is only 0.4, meaning that if 100 samples were selected, in 60 of these, the statistical

Table 3.3   Factors Affecting the Sample Size

Factor	Explanation	Influence on Sample Size
1. The purpose of the evaluation	Is this an exploratory study, or are very precise statistical estimates required?	The more precise the required results, the larger the sample.
2. Will a one- or two-tailed test be used? (Is the direction of the expected change known?)	If the purpose of the evaluation is to test whether positive outcomes have increased or negative ones have declined, then a one-tailed test can be used. If the purpose is to test whether there has been "a significant change" without knowing the direction, then a two-tailed test is required (see Chapter 14, pp. 343–344).	The sample size will be approximately 40% larger for a two-tailed test.
3. Is only the project group interviewed?	In some evaluation designs, only subjects from the project group are interviewed. This is the case if information on the total population is available from previous studies or secondary data. In other cases, a comparison group must also be selected and interviewed.	The sample size will be doubled if the same number of people have to be interviewed in both the project and comparison groups.
4. Homogeneity of the group	If there is little variation among the population with respect to the outcome variable, then the standard deviation will be small.	The smaller the standard deviation, the smaller the sample.
5. The effect size	Effect size is the amount of increase the project is expected to produce (see Chapter 14, pp. 337–343).	The smaller the effect size, the larger the sample.
6. The efficiency with which the project is implemented	While some projects are implemented in a very efficient way with all subjects receiving exactly the same package of services, in other cases, the administration is poorer and different subjects receive different combinations of services. The quality of the services can also vary.	The poorer the quality and efficiency of the project, the larger the sample.
7. The required level of disaggregation.	In some cases, the client requires only global estimates of impact for the total project population. In other cases, it is necessary to provide disaggregated results for different project sites, for variations in the package of services provided, or for different socioeconomic groups (sex, age, ethnicity, etc.).	The greater the required disaggregation, the larger the sample.

Factor	Explanation	Influence on Sample Size
8. The sample design	Sampling procedures such as stratification can often reduce the variance of the estimates and increase precision.	Well-designed stratification may reduce sample size.
9. The level of statistical precision	"Beyond a reasonable doubt" is usually defined as meaning there is less than a 1 in 20 possibility that an impact as large as this could have occurred by chance (defined as the "0.05 confidence level"). If less precise results are acceptable, it is possible to reduce sample size by accepting a lower confidence level—for example a 1 in 10 possibility that the result occurred by chance.	The higher the confidence level, the larger the sample.
10. The power of the test	The statistical power of the test refers to the probability that when a project has "real" effect, this will be rejected by the statistical significance test. The conventional power level is 0.8, meaning that there is only a 20% chance that a real effect would be rejected. Where a higher level of precision is required, the power can be raised to 0.9 or higher (see Chapter 14, pp. 341–343).	The higher the power level, the larger the sample.
11. Finite population correction factor	The finite population correction factor reduces the required sample size by the proportion that the sample represents of the population (see Chapter 14, p. 347).	The greater the proportion the sample represents of the total population, the smaller the sample.

test would fail to detect that the project had an effect—even though the effect was real. There are two important rules with respect to sample size:

1. The smaller the effect size, the lower the power of the test.

2. The power of the test can be raised by increasing the sample size.

Table 14.3 (p. 348) illustrates how effect size and the power of the test affect sample size. Using standard assumptions (discussed in Chapter 14), the table shows that if the project was expected to produce a relatively large change (an effect size of 0.5), then a sample of only 22 subjects would be required for both the project and comparison groups (a total of 44 subjects). However, if the project was expected to produce only a small change (an effect size of 0.2), then the sample size for each group would increase to 152 (a total of 304 subjects). In this latter case, if the client indicated that a higher level of statistical significance must be used (setting the power of the test at 0.9 instead of 0.8), the total sample size would increase from 304 to 420.

Impact of the Level of Disaggregation on the Required Sample Size

In many cases, clients require a comparison of project impacts on different sectors of the **target population,** such as different regions, male- and female-headed households, people of different socioeconomic levels, or people who have received different project options or combinations of services. Each additional level or type of disaggregation normally requires a corresponding increase in sample size. Consequently, in cases where some of the levels of disaggregation can be eliminated (e.g., estimating impact on the total project population rather than for each region), it is often possible to achieve significant reductions in sample size. When the levels of disaggregation are reduced because of money constraints, other methods, such as key informant interviews, if representative and reliable, may be used to obtain information on differential impacts on various sectors within the community with at least some degree of validity.

Factors Affecting the Size of Qualitative Samples

Because QUAL sampling has different objectives from QUANT, it is usually not possible to estimate the required sample size with the same degree of statistical exactitude. The following are some of the factors affecting sample size for QUAL evaluations:

- QUAL samples can be considered as having three dimensions: (a) the number of subjects or units of observation (schools, families, drug dealers), (b) the number of physical locations in which observation takes place (the home, the place of work, the street, the bar), and (c) the period of time over which the observations take place. Consequently, sample costs and time can be saved by reducing the number of subjects, reducing the number of physical locations (observe only in the street or only in the school), and the duration of the study or the number of time periods over which observations are made (every day for a week, every day for a month, once a week for a year).
- The required levels of disaggregation must be determined. The more categories (types of schools, ethnic groups, farming systems) that must be compared, the larger the required sample.

The decision on the number of subjects, locations, or duration of the study or units of analysis (communities, schools, prostitutes) usually depends on the professional judgment of the researcher, and there are usually no precise rules as to whether, for example, four or six families would be the appropriate number to study or whether the observations should continue over one week or one month. Researchers are often tempted to increase the number of subjects or the duration because each additional case or observation period offers added dimensions. If pressed, however, it is often (but not always) possible for the evaluator to reduce the number of cases or observations without compromising the purpose of the evaluation.

Reducing Costs of Data Collection and Analysis

Considerable cost savings can often be achieved through reducing the length and complexity of the data collection instruments. The elimination of nonessential information can significantly reduce the length of the data collection instrument or the duration of the observation. Examples of areas in which the amount of information can often be reduced include (a) demographic information on each household member, (b) amount of information on agricultural production and food consumption in a community, and (c) information on urban or rural travel patterns. It is again important to define information requirements with the client and not to arbitrarily eliminate information simply to produce a shorter data collection instrument. For many QUAL studies, the amount and type of information cannot be defined as easily as for QUANT surveys, and consequently, the list of questions or issues cannot be pruned quite so easily. While the original QUAL design—questions, issues, methods, instruments—is available for pruning from the start, the pruning process is more complicated. With emergent designs, issues and questions arise as the research progresses, and often, many of what prove to be the critical issues were not even included on the initial lists of questions. However, the following are examples of ways to reduce the amount of information to be collected:

- The range of topics can be reduced to those of greatest priority.
- The number of interviewees can be reduced.
- The number and types of documents to be analyzed can be reduced.
- The time period studied can be shortened.

A number of alternatives can significantly reduce the costs of data collection for both QUAL and QUANT evaluations (see Table 3.1). Examples include the following:

- Collect information on community attitudes, time use, access to and use of services, and the like through **PRA** (participatory rural appraisal) group interview methods and **focus groups** rather than through household surveys or interviews with individuals. It is important to note, however, that well-designed focus groups are in themselves time-consuming and in some cases can be more costly than surveys. Focus groups require identifying appropriate interviewees, arranging times that all members of the group can get together, preparing and field-testing the interview protocol, transcribing and validating the interview data, and conducting content analysis. In contrast, a survey requires only preparing, field-testing, administering the survey, and aggregating responses to items. The relative costs of the two approaches will, of course, depend on the proposed sample size for the survey.
- Replace surveys with direct observation—for example, to study time use, travel patterns, and use of community facilities. It is again important to note that although some types of observation can be quite rapid and economical (e.g., observation of pedestrian and vehicular travel patterns in areas with relatively few roads), in other cases, observing enough to ensure the validity of observation data and doing content analysis is not necessarily faster than a survey.
- Use key informants to obtain information on community behavior and use of services.

- Use self-administered instruments such as surveys, self-evaluations, reflection or response forms, diaries, and journals to collect data on income and expenditure, travel patterns, or time use.
- Make maximum use of preexisting data, including project records.
- Photography and videotaping can sometimes provide useful and economical documentary **evidence** on the changing quality of houses and roads, as well as on use of public transport services (Heath 2004; Kumar 1993; Patton 2002).

Many of these suggestions involve methodological **triangulation** (Denzin 1989) to obtain confirmational data in two or more ways or from two or more data sources. Triangulation is particularly important for RealWorld evaluators faced by budget and time constraints. The *triangulation by method and source* can help determine the accuracy of information when only limited amounts of data can be collected. Box 3.5 presents three illustrations of reducing the cost and time of data collection.

Box 3.5   Economical Methods of Data Collection

1. In Bulgaria, a rapid midterm assessment was conducted of a project to reduce the environmental contamination produced by a major metallurgical factory. Key informant interviews, review of project records, and direct observation were combined to provide economical ways to assess compliance with safety and environmental regulations and to assess reductions in the level of environmental contamination. A survey of key stakeholders was conducted to obtain independent assessments of the findings reported in the evaluation. The evaluation cost less than $5,000 and was completed in less than two months.

SOURCE: Dimitrov (2005).

2. An evaluation of the impacts of a slum upgrading project in Manila, the Philippines, assessed the impact of the housing investments made by poor families on their consumption of basic necessities. A randomly selected sample of 100 households was asked to keep a daily record of every item of income and expenditure over a period of a year. Households recorded this information themselves in diaries, and the evaluation team of the National Housing Authority made weekly visits to a sample of households to ensure quality control. The only direct cost, other than a small proportion of staff salaries, was the purchase of small gifts for the families each month. Because the study covered only project participants, most of whom were very favorable toward the project, the response rate was maintained at almost 100% throughout the year. This proved to be a very economical way to collect high-quality income and expenditure data and permitted the use of an interrupted time series design with 365 (daily) observation points, although with little analysis of external influences.

SOURCE: Valadez and Bamberger (1994:255–57).

3. An assessment of the impacts of community management on the quality and maintenance of village water supply in Indonesia combined direct observation of the quality and use of water with participatory group assessments of water supply and interviews with key informants. The use of group interviews and direct observation proved a much more economical way to assess project impacts than conventional household sample surveys.

SOURCE: Dayal, van Wijk, and Mukherjee (2000).

Common Threats to Validity
of Budget Constraints

Box 3.6 identifies some of the most common threats to validity and adequacy of evaluation conclusions that must be addressed when assessing the different approaches to budget constraints discussed in this chapter. Similar tables are included for reference in the following two chapters to identify the respective threats to validity when taking measures to reduce time or when working with limited data. It is recommended that readers who are not familiar with the concepts of threats to validity read Chapter 7 and then to return to this section.

Box 3.6   Threats to Adequacy and Validity Relating to Budget Constraints

---

Note. The numbers refer to the RWE "Integrated Checklist for Assessing the Adequacy and Validity of Quantitative, Qualitative, and Mixed-Method Designs" (see Appendix 1). All the concepts are discussed and defined in Chapter 7.

B. Reliability and Dependability

B-2 *Were data collected across the full range of appropriate settings, times, respondents, etc.?* Budget pressures frequently result in the elimination of some groups—often, the most difficult to reach.

C. Internal Validity, Credibility, and Authenticity

C-1 *How context rich and meaningful ("thick") are the descriptions?* Budget pressures often reduce the richness of the data collected.

C-3 *Did triangulation among complementary methods and data sources produce generally converging conclusions?* Budget constraints often reduce the use of triangulation because the application of different data collection methods usually increases costs.

C-5 *Are areas of uncertainty identified? Was negative evidence sought, found?* Budget pressures can reduce the search for negative evidence.

D. External Validity, Transferability, and Fittingness

D-2 *Does the sample design theoretically permit generalization to other populations?* Simplifying sample design to save time can sometimes reduce representativity of the sample.

F. Threats to Statistical Conclusion Validity

F-1 *The sample is too small to detect program effects.* Budget pressures often result in the sample size being reduced below the minimum size required to satisfy power analysis criteria (see Chapter 14).

(Continued)

(Continued)

F-5 and F-10 *Restriction of range and extrapolation from truncated/incomplete database.* Time pressures sometimes result in samples or secondary data with more limited coverage.

G. Threats to Internal Validity

G-3 *History.* Budget pressures often constrain ability to control for historical differences between project and comparison areas.

G-10 *Use of less rigorous designs due to budget and time constraints.*

H. Threats to Construct Validity

H-4 *Use of a single method to measure a construct (monomethod bias).* Budget pressures may limit the number of data collection methods or the number of independent indicators of key variables.

H-12 *Using indicators and constructs developed in other countries without pretesting in the local context.* Budget pressures often result in inadequate testing and customization of instruments.

I. Threats to External Validity

I-7 *Seasonal cycles.* These are often not adequately addressed when budget is a factor.

Summary

- Five strategies can be considered for reducing costs of evaluation planning, data collection, and analysis. (It should be noted that each of these may reduce the validity of results obtained.)

- The first is to simplify the evaluation design, usually by eliminating the collection of data on the project or comparison group before the project begins (pretest) or on the comparison group after the project is implemented (posttest) (see Chapter 10). In the simplest design, when data are collected on only the posttest project group, the data collection budget can be reduced by as much as 80%.

- The second is to agree with clients on the elimination of nonessential information from the data collection instruments.

- The third is to maximize the use of existing documentation (secondary data). See Chapter 5 for more details.

- The fourth is to reduce the sample size. Although this can produce significant savings, if the sample becomes too small, there is the danger of failing to detect statistically significant project effects even when they do exist. See Chapter 14 for more details.

- The fifth is to reduce the costs of data collection through methods such as the use of self-administered questionnaires, direct observation (instead of surveys), automatic counters, inputting data through handheld devices, reducing the number of periods of observation, prioritizing informants, and hiring and training students, nurses, and other more economical data collectors. It should be noted, however, that although these methods may reduce the cost of data collection, they will not necessarily reduce, or may even increase, the costs of data analysis.

- Most of the above strategies for reducing costs involve trade-offs because they pose threats to the validity of the evaluation findings and recommendations. The chapter concludes with a brief introduction to the assessment of threats to validity discussed in more detail in Chapter 7.

Further Reading

Aron, A. and E. Aron. 2002. *Statistics for the Behavioral and Social Sciences: A Brief Course.* 2d ed. Upper Saddle River, NJ: Prentice Hall.

This is a thorough but easily understandable review of all the statistical concepts discussed in the present text. Chapter 7 provides a good overview of statistical power analysis and effect size. There is also a companion study guide and workbook.

Beebe, J. 2001. *Rapid Assessment Process: An Introduction.* Walnut Creek, CA: Altamira.

A clear overview of how to reduce the time required to conduct ethnographic studies of communities, programs, or organizations. Many of the techniques are also useful for reducing costs.

Fink, A. 2003. *How to Sample in Surveys.* Vol. 7, *The Survey Kit.* 2d ed. Thousand Oaks, CA: Sage.

A useful and clear overview of sample design.

Handwerker, W. P. 2001. *Quick Ethnography.* Walnut Creek, CA: Altamira.

Another useful overview of rapid ethnographic methods with applications to cost reduction.

Notes

1. This can be measured either by a test for difference-in-difference (also called double difference) of means or proportions or by using multivariate analysis to examine how attributes such as income, age, education, and family size affect the magnitude and direction of the project effect (see Chapter 11).

2. *Precision* refers to the level of statistical significance used to accept that an observed project effect does not occur by chance (that an effect as strong as the one observed is not due to *pseudo effects* caused by factors unrelated to the project). The convention is to accept a 95% confidence level that the observed effect is not simply due to *statistical noise* (spurious factors). Where a higher level of precision is required, the confidence level can be increased to 99% (or even higher), but this will involve a substantial increase in the size and cost of the sample. See Chapter 14 for more details.

3. The standardized effect size is defined as the mean of the sample minus the population mean divided by the population standard deviation (see Chapter 14, p. 338).

CHAPTER 4

Not Enough Time

*Addressing Scheduling
and Other Time Constraints*

S tep 3 of the RealWorld Evaluation (**RWE**) approach identifies strategies to address time constraints (see Figure 4.1). The first five strategies are similar to those described in Chapter 3 for reducing costs. Additional strategies that can reduce time constraints but that might in some cases increase the cost of the evaluation include reducing time pressures on expensive external (national or international) consultants, hiring more resource people (e.g., interviewers, supervisors, data analysts), and incorporating indicators for future **impact** evaluations into some of the administrative data forms routinely collected by most **projects**. The final option is to use modern technology to speed up data collection, input, and analysis. We conclude by identifying the particular threats to validity and adequacy (see Chapter 7) that arise when time-saving strategies are used.

Similarities and Differences between Time and Budget Constraints

While most cost-saving methods also save time, it is important to clarify in each case whether the main constraint is time or money (or both) because there are some important differences in the approaches to be used. Both budget and time constraints may result from a low priority given to evaluation, but some ways to save time require additional expenditure. Consequently, it is important to clarify with the **client** whether additional resources can be made available to help save time or whether the evaluation is subject to both time and budget constraints.

There are two different ways to think about time saving. The first is a reduction of the *level of effort* (total staff time) required to complete the data collection and analysis period. The second way concerns the total *duration* of data collection or analysis. This distinction is important because the best approach to use will often depend on whether it is more important to reduce the level of effort or the duration of the evaluation. The following paragraph illustrates the differences between these two concepts.

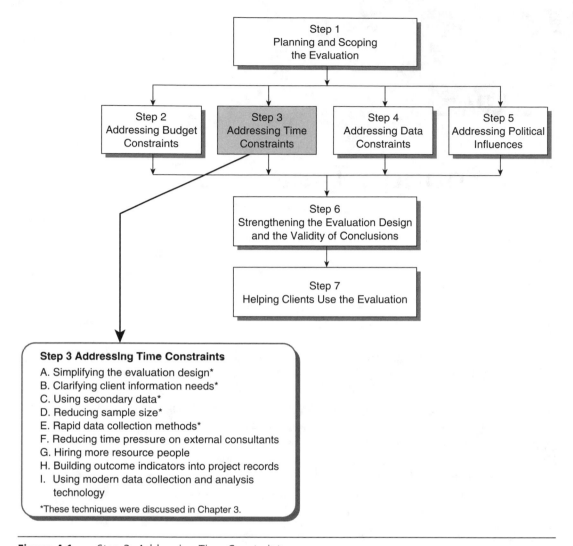

Figure 4.1   Step 3: Addressing Time Constraints

An evaluation of the impacts of a slum upgrading project in Manila, the Philippines, on household expenditures required the collection of household income and expenditure data over a period of one year to observe how expenditures on food and other basic necessities were affected by increased investment in house improvements (see Box 4.1). The original plan was to conduct a panel study in which **interviewers** would visit a sample of households once a week over a 12-month period to record information on all household expenditures and sources of income. However, it was decided instead to ask 100 families to keep daily records of income and expenditure over the year. In return, they would be able to select a small gift at the end of every month. This method of data collection proved successful and saved a considerable amount of *effort* for the evaluation team. However, it did not reduce the *duration* of the study, which still lasted 12 months. In a different situation, the *duration* of a study (not appropriate in this example because it was necessary to collect data over a 12-month period) could be

---

Box 4.1   Two Kinds of Time Saving

It is important to distinguish between approaches that reduce the *duration* of an evaluation (it is completed over a period of six months instead of one year), and those that reduce the *level of effort* (fewer staff weeks required to actually conduct the evaluation). Asking households in Manila (Chapter 3, Box 3.5) to keep a diary of their daily expenditures over one year did not reduce the duration of the evaluation, but it significantly reduced the level of effort of National Housing Authority staff. On the other hand, increasing the size of the field research team can reduce the duration of the data collection and analysis but does not reduce and may even increase the level of effort because larger research teams require more planning and coordination.

SOURCE: Valadez and Bamberger (1994).

---

reduced by increasing the number of interviewers. It is always important when talking about saving time to clarify whether the goal is to reduce effort or duration.

Table 4.1 identifies nine general approaches that can be used to reduce time. The first five approaches are similar to those discussed in Chapter 3 for reducing costs: simplifying the evaluation **design**, clarifying client information needs, using secondary data, reducing sample size, and using cheaper and faster methods of data collection. The final four—reducing time pressures on external consultants, increasing the size of the research team, incorporating indicators for future impact studies into project records, and using modern data collection and analysis technology—do not necessarily reduce costs and may in fact increase them. Each of these nine approaches is discussed in this chapter. The point is made that it is important to clarify whether the constraint facing the evaluation team is to reduce time, reduce costs, or both because the strategies can be different in each case. In particular, there are a number of time-saving strategies that may significantly increase costs.

Box 4.2 illustrates a common situation where it is not possible to complete fieldwork within the very short period of time originally planned (in this case, 10 days) because the data are often more difficult to find or collect than had originally been assumed. This often means that while the team is in the field, a rapid decision has to be made either to limit the scope of the evaluation or to extend the time (and resources) allowed for fieldwork.

Simplifying the Evaluation Design

In Table 2.2 we described the seven evaluation designs commonly used in RWE. In Chapter 3 we pointed out that some of the methodologically weaker designs can cut costs by 50% or more. When these designs are applied to saving time rather than to costs, the distinction between reducing effort and reducing duration is important. The duration of the evaluation can be reduced by selecting any of the designs that collect data only at the end of the project (Designs 5 and 7). In contrast, the level of effort is reduced by selecting designs that do not include a pretest and/or posttest **comparison group** (Designs 4 and 6) as well as those that do not collect baseline data (Designs 5 and 7).

Table 4.1 Options for Reducing the Time Required for Data Collection and Analysis in Quantitative and Qualitative Evaluations

Approaches that reduce both time and costs (see Chapter 3 for description of QUANT and QUAL applications)

1. Simplifying the evaluation design

2. Clarifying and prioritizing client information needs

3. Using existing documentary data

4. Reducing sample size

5. Using cheaper and faster methods of data collection (see also Table 4.2)

Additional approaches that save time but may not save money and often increase costs

	Quantitative	Qualitative
6. Reducing time constraints on external (often foreign) consultants or subcontractors a. Commissioning the advance collection and organization of available data by local consultants b. Commissioning exploratory studies by a local consultant to identify some of the key issues and the characteristics of the population prior to the arrival of the external consultant c. Videoconferences involving external and local consultants prior to the visit of the external consultant to do advance planning and save time	a. Compilation of secondary data and initial assessment of quality and relevance for the study (applicable also to QUAL studies) b. Rapid surveys to obtain demographic, economic, or other relevant data on the target populations to help develop the sample design and the preparation of the sampling frame (list or map with the location of all families or other subjects in the population studied). Rapid studies can also be used to obtain preliminary estimates of, for example, education or literacy scores. c. Establish rapport with the community and local leaders and officials to facilitate the smooth implementation of the study and to avoid bureaucratic delays (e.g., obtaining documents required to start the study).	a. Compilation of research literature and sources such as mass media materials, photographs b. Rapid ethnographic studies, focusing on key concepts and issues to be covered in the study and to lay the groundwork for the external consultants c. Photos, videos, and tape recordings that can be sent to external consultants to document the conditions of the communities during different times of year (e.g., the monsoons and the dry season). This can be important if consultants are not able to visit the region in every season. d. Establish rapport (as for QUANT).

	Quantitative	Qualitative

7. Hiring more data collectors
  a. Increasing the number of interviewers and supervisors
  b. Hiring more experienced interviewers and supervisors can reduce the time required for training and can increase the efficiency and speed of the regular data collectors.
  c. Subcontracting data collection or analysis.
	All these approaches are applicable to QUANT studies.	Some of these approaches can be applied to QUAL studies, but it is often more difficult to recruit more experienced and qualified local researchers.

8. Revising format of project records to include critical data for impact analysis	Include indicators on access and use of services as well as relevant household or individual characteristics—particularly impact indicators.	Encourage/enable project staff to record more than project activities, e.g. to document observations of changes in conditions in beneficiaries' households.
9. Modern data collection and analysis technology	a. Handheld computers for data input b. Optical scanning c. Automatic counters d. QUANT computer software for data analysis and presentation	a. E-mail surveys used for both QUAL and QUANT studies b. Video cameras and tape recorders c. Photography d. GPS mapping and aerial photography to observe demographic patterns, agricultural practices, and condition of infrastructure over a large area, saving considerable amounts of time required to reach remote villages and areas. e. QUAL computer software for data analysis and presentation (does not always save time because the main purpose is to permit more comprehensive analysis)

Box 4.2   Time Constraints Affecting the Evaluation of a Water and
Sanitation Project in Mozambique

The design and implementation of an evaluation of a water and sanitation project
in Mozambique was assessed as part of a **meta-evaluation** of CARE International's approach to the evaluation of its projects. It was assumed that important
data would be easily accessible and that all required fieldwork could be completed
in 10 days. However, the report on the terms of reference for the evaluation found
that the time actually needed for fieldwork was much longer than originally
planned.

"The Terms of Reference (TOR) required a final review of a three year project over a
three week period, with 10 days in the field with the project staff and one week report
writing. The TOR assumed easy access to necessary data, but in the event it has taken
more than four weeks to obtain full details of communities benefiting and construction
details, and also budget and expenditure details. There was no mention of the lack of
any surveys or regular monitoring of impact, which made it necessary to undertake
a full End of Project Survey during the period of the evaluation. This is normally a
separate exercise taking several weeks to design, test, train enumerators, collect field
data and analyze it, and as a result it took up a large proportion of the evaluation time,
but impact could not have been assessed without it."

SOURCE: Russon (2005).

As discussed in Chapter 3, although many of these designs can significantly reduce time or
cost, they do so by relaxing or eliminating many of the quality control and validity measures that
are part of standard evaluation methodology. It is therefore important to assess the trade-offs
between staying within the evaluation time frame and not exposing the evaluation to threats to
quality that may compromise the validity of the conclusions. The general principles for assessing
threats to validity are discussed in Chapter 7, while Chapter 10 applies the threats to validity
framework to assess the strengths and weaknesses of each of the seven RWE designs.

Clarifying Client Information Needs

Because in many cases there is a potential trade-off between reducing the time required for
data collection or analysis and the quality and coverage of the evaluation, it is important to
understand the client's priorities, options, and critical deadlines. The following are typical
options to clarify with the client:

- Is it essential that the evaluation be completed and the full report presented by a certain
  date? *or*
- Would it be acceptable to prepare for this deadline a short summary report outlining
  key **findings** and recommendations? Would this allow more time to complete the full
  final report?

- Is it more important to complete the report by a certain date (even if this will affect quality) or to extend the time period to ensure a better quality report?

It is essential for the evaluator to understand why these deadlines are critical and what kinds of decisions or actions must be taken. Some dates are critical, but the client needs only certain specific information by that date and not the whole report, such as, "Is the project going well?" "Will the evaluation recommend that the project should continue?" "Will additional funds for the evaluation have to be requested in the next budget?" It often takes time to establish exactly what is required, but it may save time later by asking questions such as the following:

- What information is essential and what could be dropped or reduced?
- What level of **precision** and how much detail are required for the essential information? For example, is it necessary to have separate estimates for each subgroup (e.g., male and female beneficiaries, each separate project location), or is a general estimate acceptable? Is it necessary to analyze all project components and services or only the most important?
- Is it possible to obtain additional resources (e.g., money, staff, computer access, vehicles) to speed up data collection and analysis?

Once the deadlines are clearly understood, it is important to establish a cooperative relationship with the client, working together to produce the best report possible by this date. Evaluators can easily find themselves in an adversarial relationship where the client is pressuring them to produce more information by a certain date and the evaluator is seen as obstinately opposing every request. It is important to discuss and agree ahead of time on what can and cannot be produced by a particular date and why.

Then, in negotiating design and methods, it is important that the client understand the trade-offs and potential threats to quality when time-saving approaches are used.

Using Existing Documentary Data

Using preexisting documentary data can be an important time saver if, for example, available surveys or government reports can lessen the need to collect new data. However, preexisting data must always be carefully assessed to determine when and how the data were collected and for what purpose; these characteristics can sometimes limit their usefulness for the current evaluation. This is a particular challenge when there is not sufficient time to fully assess the strengths and limitations of particular documents or data sources because there is a temptation to use them despite potential biases or other problems.

Reducing Sample Size

We saw in Chapter 3 that reducing sample size can potentially save a significant amount of time and money during the data collection phase. However, smaller samples usually increase sampling error and limit the ability of the evaluation to determine whether the project has produced its intended effects. Smaller samples often increase the need to introduce quality controls and to use mixed methods (such as combining sample survey with **participant**

observation, key informant interviews, and **focus group**s) to permit **triangulation**. The use of mixed methods will often increase the duration of data collection and analysis, thus losing some of the time savings from using smaller samples.

However, because many of these mixed methods can, and often should, be conducted at the same time as the survey, the overall time for the evaluation can be significantly reduced if resources are available to hire additional researchers to conduct these additional collections of data for the study—at the same time that other qualitative (QUAL) or quantitative (QUANT) data collection is underway.

Rapid Data Collection Methods

Emphasis in QUAL studies is often placed on iterative learning and understanding through frequent contact, often over a long period of time. Given the need to adapt many of these methods to the time constraints under which most **program** evaluations take place, an international development literature (which is apparently not well known in the United States) has developed where the focus is on rapid methods of data collection (see annotated bibliography at the end of this chapter). Many of these approaches are adapted from traditional ethnographic methods. While many of these approaches can be implemented very rapidly, most of these rapid applications do not systematically address the increased threats to validity to which the findings may be subjected, and there is a need for further work in this area to assess the trade-offs between time, quality, and validity. Box 4.3 gives examples of a number of different methods for rapid data collection. These include participant observation, the use of diaries, group consultations, rapid ethnographic methods, and exit studies as people are leaving a meeting or service facility.

Box 4.3   Examples of Rapid Data Collection Methods

---

1. The cost-saving data collection methods from Bulgaria, the Philippines, and Indonesia described in Box 3.5 also helped save time. The Bulgarian study was completed in less than two months and required only about two weeks of fieldwork. The use of diaries to record expenditures in the Philippines made it necessary for the monitor to visit a subsample of households only once a week for quality control, and the participatory group discussion techniques in Indonesia obviated the necessity for small surveys to obtain information on the use of water and sanitation services and significantly reduced the time required for data collection.

2. Rapid ethnographic methods make it possible to conduct diagnostic studies of communities, programs, or organizations that would traditionally require several months of field research to be completed in one to six weeks (see Box 4.4).

3. Asking people leaving a meeting or the office of a public service agency to answer a single question (such as "Would you recommend a friend or neighbor to use this service?") makes it possible to conduct a very rapid and economical attitude survey.

Box 4.4   Rapid Ethnographic Methods

Beebe states that the *rapid assessment process* means a "minimum of 4 days and, in most situations, a maximum of 6 weeks." He further states that "RAP recognizes that there are times when results are needed almost immediately and that the *rapid* production of results involves compromises and requires special attention to methodology if the results are to be meaningful." He emphasizes that "rapid does not mean rushed, and spending too little time or being rushed during the process can reduce RAP to *research tourism.*" According to Beebe, RAP uses most of the standard ethnographic methods but the defining characteristics of RAP are the following:

- Intensive *team-based* ethnographic enquiry
- Systematic use of triangulation
- Iterative data analysis
- Additional data collection to quickly develop a preliminary understanding of a situation from the insider's perspective

---

SOURCE: Beebe (2001:xvi).

Table 4.2 identifies a number of rapid QUAL and QUANT methods and gives examples of how time requirements can be reduced. The following are some of the ways to reduce time required for applying QUAL methods:

- Focus groups: The selection and recruitment of participants and the conducting and analysis can be subcontracted to specialists such as market research firms. More researchers can be contracted so that several groups can be conducted simultaneously (rather than one at a time as is often done).
- Community interviews, perhaps using **PRA** (participatory rural appraisal) techniques (Kumar 2002) can be used to collect information from groups (e.g., on agricultural practices and crop production, on children's health and nutrition) rather than conducting surveys with households.
- Exit surveys can be used to obtain rapid feedback on meetings and other community activities.
- Community informants or community groups (such as secondary school children or women's organizations) can be trained to collect information or to talk about what they know.

Examples of rapid QUANT methods include these:

- Rapid surveys using very short questionnaires. When only a few questions are asked, the time taken to collect and analyze data is dramatically reduced.
- A number of specialized sampling techniques can significantly reduce the number of interviews required to assess use of, and satisfaction with, public services (see "Lot Quality Acceptance Sampling" in Valadez and Bamberger 1994).

Table 4.2   Rapid Data Collection Methods

	Ways to Reduce Time Requirements	Reducing Duration (elapsed time) or Level of Effort (staff time)	
		Duration	Effort
A. Mainly qualitative methods			
Key informant interviews	Key informants can save time either by providing data (regarding agricultural prices, people leaving and joining the community, school attendance and absenteeism), helping researchers focus on key issues, or pointing out faster ways to obtain information. Ways to reduce time of key informant interviews:		
	• Reduce the number of informants.	✓	✓
	• Limit the number of issues covered.	✓	✓
	• Hire more researchers to conduct the interviews or to tape interviews for the researcher to review. Do this with caution; it is important for the researcher to maintain personal contact with key people in the community.	✓	
Focus groups and community interviews	• Subcontract to focus group specialists such as market research firms.	✓	✓
	• Conduct several focus groups simultaneously instead of sequentially.	✓	
	• Collect information from meetings rather than surveys. Information on topics such as access to and use of water and sanitation, agricultural practices, and gender division of labor in farming can be obtained in group interviews, possibly combined with the distribution of self-administered surveys.	✓	✓
	Note: It is important to use techniques that ensure the views of all participants are captured (time pressures mean that more vulnerable and harder to access groups may be left out).		
Structured observation	• Observation can sometimes, but not always, be faster than surveys—for example, observation of the gender division of labor in different kinds of agricultural production, who attends meetings and participates in discussions, types of conflict observed in public places in the community.	✓	

	Ways to Reduce Time Requirements	Reducing Duration (elapsed time) or Level of Effort (staff time)	
		Duration	Effort
Use of preexisting documents and artifacts	• Many kinds of preexisting data can be collected and reviewed more rapidly than new data can be collected—for example, school attendance records, newspapers and other mass media, minutes of community meetings, health center records, surveys in target communities conducted by research institutions.	✓	✓
Using community groups to collect information	• Organization of rapid community studies (QUAL and QUANT) using community interviewers (local school teachers often cooperate with this).	✓	
Photos and videos	• Giving disposable cameras or camcorders to community informants to take photos (or make videos) illustrating, for example, community problems.	✓	✓
Triangulation	• Having several interviewers simultaneously interview and separately record their observations on the same key respondents rather than having separate interviews. This can save elapsed time if it replaces several separate interviews with the same person.	✓	

B. Mainly quantitative methods

Rapid surveys with short questionnaires and small samples	• Reducing the number of questions and the size of the sample can significantly reduce the time required to conduct a survey. • Increasing the number of interviewers.	✓ ✓	✓
Reduce sample sizes	• There are specialized sampling techniques such as lot quality acceptance sampling (Valadez and Bamberger 1994) designed to provide estimates of the use or quality of public services such as health and education with very small samples. Samples of 14 to 28 households may be sufficient to assess use or quality of a single health center.	✓	✓
Triangulation (used also in QUAL and mixed methods)	• Obtaining independent estimates from different sources (e.g., survey and observation) sometimes makes it possible to obtain estimates from smaller samples, hence saving both elapsed time and effort.	✓	✓

(Continued)

Table 4.2 (Continued)

		Reducing Duration (elapsed time) or Level of Effort (staff time)	
	Ways to Reduce Time Requirements	*Duration*	*Effort*
Rapid exit surveys	• People leaving a meeting or exiting a service facility can be asked to write their views on the meeting or service on an index card. These can then be posted on a wall or notice board to provide rapid feedback to clients.	✓	✓
	• Often only one key question will be asked. For example, "Would you recommend a neighbor to come to the next meeting or use this center?"	✓	✓
Use of preexisting data	• Previous surveys or other data sources may eliminate the need to collect certain data.	✓	✓
	• Previous survey findings can reduce the time required for sample design by providing information on the *standard deviation* (how narrowly or widely subjects are distributed around the mean) of key variables. This may make it possible to reduce sample size or to save time through more efficient stratification or cluster sampling. (These terms are defined in Chapter 14.)	✓	
Observation checklists	• Observation checklists can often eliminate the need for certain surveys (e.g., pedestrian and vehicular traffic flows, use of community facilities, time required to collect water and fuel).	✓	✓
Automatic counters	• Recording people entering buildings or using services such as water.	✓	✓
C. Mixed methods			
Triangulation (used also in QUAL and QUANT methods)	• Triangulating data from several quantitative and qualitative methods may sometimes make it possible to obtain estimates from smaller samples, hence saving effort and elapsed time. This is not always the case because use of several different data collection methods has obvious time/cost implications.	✓	✓
Rapid quantification of *participatory assessment methods* and focus groups	• Short and rapid sample surveys can be combined with numerical estimates obtained from community interviews and focus groups to provide estimates of, for example, service usage, unemployment rates, *time use* for a community or other population group	✓	✓

NOTE: It is often difficult to differentiate between saving time and reducing effort. It is also important to stress that saving time by increasing the size of the team will usually increase the budget. Hence, the need to clarify with the client whether the major constraint is time, budget, or both.

- Observation checklists can be used to collect numerical information on use of community service, transport patterns, or the types of goods on sale in the community or the market.
- Using triangulation to combine QUANT and QUAL estimates of key variables. The use of QUAL indicators to confirm or question QUANT estimates (e.g., of income, proportion of the population with access to public services) can often reduce the required sample size and reduced the time required for data collection.
- Complementing participatory assessments or focus groups with short and rapid surveys can provide rapid QUANT estimates of service usage, unemployment rates, transport patterns, and so on.

Box 4.5 illustrates the use of mixed methods in a study of poverty and survival strategies of poor families in Colombia. The study, which would normally have required two to three months, was completed in four weeks.

Reducing Time Pressure on Outside Consultants

In this discussion, it is helpful to distinguish between the *outside consultant* coming from a different area of the country or from a different country, the *local consultant* who comes from the city or area where the evaluation is being conducted, and the *in-house staff* working with the agency being evaluated or possibly from a planning agency (e.g., the planning department in the Ministry of Health or the national planning agency). Each of these people can play a different role in the evaluation. The issues discussed here are similar for situations in which the external consultant is working in his or her own country (a developed country such as the United States or Europe) or where that person is brought in from another country (e.g., a consultant from France working on an evaluation in Ethiopia). Some of the issues discussed are more relevant to a large country where the national consultant has to travel a long distance so that the timing of the interventions has to be well planned and coordinated.

Many evaluations contract an outside consultant, usually from a different part of the country or from a different country. Although there are well-funded evaluations in which the outside consultant is contracted for long periods of time and may visit the project or program on a regular basis, for RWEs, the outside consultant is usually contracted for a relatively short period of time (often defined in terms of the number of person days) and is seen as an expensive and scarce resource.

The outside consultant(s) may either be responsible for conducting the whole evaluation, with support from local agency staff and local consultants, or he or she may have a specific role to play (e.g., helping with the research design and the development and testing of the data collection instruments). Both because of the high cost and the short time availability of the outside consultant, it is important to ensure that his or her time is used effectively, particularly ensuring that time is not spent on activities that could have been done as well (or better) by local staff and consultants. One way to save time is to collect background data and possibly conduct preliminary exploratory studies prior to the arrival of the outside consultant. A typical exploratory study might involve preparing initial reports on the social and economic characteristics of the target groups or communities and describing key features of the programs or projects to be studied, how they operate, and how they are perceived. In some

---

Box 4.5   Reducing the Time Required to Conduct a Mixed-Method Study
of Survival Strategies of Low-Income Households

A study was conducted in low-income areas of Cartagena, Colombia, to estimate the importance of interhousehold transfers of money and goods as a survival strategy for poor urban households. The study, combining a sample survey of 160 households and the preparation of in-depth case studies on the interhousehold transfer patterns of 5 households, was designed, conducted, and analyzed in only four weeks and used a total of only 40 person days. This was achieved by reducing the number of survey questions to the absolute minimum and planning the timing of the interviews to ensure high response rates. The main time **inputs** were the following:

	Days
Designing and testing the survey instrument	7.5
Sample design	2
Selecting, training, and debriefing interviewers	7
Conducting 160 QUANT interviews	6
Designing QUAL study	8
Developing and testing methodology	2
Conducting case studies	8
Total staff days	40.5 days
Total duration of the study	4 weeks

A study of this size and complexity would normally require at least two to three months to design, implement, and analyze.

SOURCE: Wansbrough, Jones, and Kappaz (2000).

---

cases, a preliminary list of potential key informants and possible participants in focus groups might also be prepared.

Some of this material can be collected by project staff; in other cases, it may be necessary to commission local consultants. Very often, the client or funding agency will have a standard procedure for contracting short-term consultants and perhaps a roster of local consultants from which consultants must be selected based on a description of the work. In other cases, a request for proposals may be sent out in response to a description of the task (this procedure will often significantly increase the timeline). Whichever procedure is used, precise **terms of reference** should be prepared. The contract should also include some time for local consultants, if any, to work with the outside consultant during the evaluation and, ideally, time for follow-up activities after the completion of the evaluation report by the external consultant.

Review of existing data and exploratory studies might be commissioned to collect background information on the program, characteristics of the **target population**, and context or setting. This information is then available when the outside consultant officially starts work.

Box 4.6   Be Considerate of National Staff When Planning "Convenient" Videoconferencing

---

While videoconferencing may seem very convenient and simple for the international consultants, it is important to recognize potential problems for national staff. An obvious point is the difference in time zones. A comfortable 10 a.m. start in Washington or London may be late at night in Asia. One of the authors also discovered later that staff from an Indian agency had to drive for 12 hours (in each direction) to get to the videoconference center in New Delhi. Many local staff may be reluctant to mention these problems when agreeing to participate in the videoconference.

There may be more flexibility concerning the use of local personnel and resources. Videoconferencing is often a useful way to establish contact and rapport with external consultants and to speed up preparatory activities (note the caution in Box 4.6) and reduce time pressures during the external consultant's usually short site visit by developing trust and a good working relationship in advance.

Hiring More Resource People

The time required for data collection can often be significantly reduced by spreading the workload among a greater number of interviewers or other data collectors. However, increasing the number of interviewers will often require additional time for training and may increase the complexity of coordination, so unless it is well planned, the desired time savings may not be achieved. There may also be a risk of reduced quality of information collected. Subcontracting portions of the data collection to private firms with the requisite experience, personnel, and facilities can also help reduce time overall.

Creating an evaluation team that includes both QUAL evaluators and QUANT evaluators may ensure full and appropriate use of both QUANT and QUAL methods of data collection and analysis, but that often considerably increases the time needed for the study because of the number of data collection and analysis methods being used and the need for discussion of their appropriate bundling and balancing. The time required for team building and creating understanding and confidence among professionals from different disciplines or approaches has often resulted in overemphasis of one type of data and relative neglect of another.

Building Outcome Indicators into Project Records

Where evaluation is considered at the time the project implementation is planned and where projects and personnel demonstrate flexibility, it may be possible to modify project monitoring records and forms so that information regarding specific evaluation questions, target populations, and their use of project services can be more easily and rapidly analyzed. Although most project monitoring data reports only on activities and **outputs**, **outcome** indicators can sometimes be built into project monitoring systems and records. Examples include the following:

- Records of use of services by project participants
- Changes in knowledge and attitudes of participants, as in a training course
- Access to and cost of services prior to the start of the project (information on this is often recorded in, for example, housing or **microcredit** projects and sometimes in health programs)
- Socioeconomic conditions of families at the start of the project

However, it is important to identify and evaluate any potential biases in these and all data sources, which may, for example, neglect some groups in the population or fail to include certain critical information. A frequent problem is that quality control standards for completing administrative reports may be lower than for evaluation studies so that the risk of omitted data or careless recording may increase. Another approach is to ensure that information from existing records is organized and recorded in a way that can be easily analyzed. For example:

- Health clinic patient records should be filed by family so that it is possible to estimate how many families have used the clinic.
- Client information should be organized by type of service (e.g., type of training received, individual or communal water collection, type of loan, type of extension services).
- Ensure that client records include information on conditions prior to the project (e.g., type of water supply, whether women were already cultivating vegetables, whether farmers were already using fertilizers, student grades and test scores prior to state accountability).

Data Collection and Analysis Technology

The direct inputting of survey responses to handheld computers can greatly reduce the time required for data processing and analysis. Optical scanning of survey instruments is another time-saving device for data inputting. However, optical scanning sometimes works less well in remote field settings than in the office, so consultation with experts and pilot testing are advisable before relying on such technology.

A wide range of statistical packages for QUANT (see Chapter 11) and QUAL data analysis are available. Statistical packages can save considerable amounts of time during the analysis phase. However, it is not clear whether QUAL data analysis packages can save time for QUAL studies because they take a long time to set up and the purpose is usually to provide more comprehensive analysis rather than to save time. The use of handheld electronic data inputting devices has also created problems in many QUAL evaluation settings because it constrains the use of *emergent designs* where the set of key issues being studied will change (emerge) as the study progresses.

An important new area that is not discussed here are Web-based and electronic surveys that are becoming increasingly important in many developed countries but are used much less frequently in most developing countries due to limited access to technology.[1]

Common Threats to Adequacy and Validity Relating to Time Constraints

Box 4.7 identifies some of the most common threats to validity and adequacy of evaluation conclusions that must be addressed when assessing the different approaches to time constraints discussed in this chapter. Similar tables are included for reference in Chapters 3 and 5 to identify the respective threats to validity when taking measures to reduce costs or when working with limited data. Readers who are not familiar with the concepts of threats to validity are recommended to read Chapter 7 and then to return to this section.

Box 4.7   Threats to Adequacy and Validity Relating to Time Constraints

---

The numbers refer to the sections of the RWE "Integrated Checklist for Assessing the Adequacy and Validity of Quantitative, Qualitative, and Mixed-Method Designs" (see Appendix 1). All the concepts are discussed and defined in Chapter 7.

B. Reliability and Dependability

B-2 *Were data collected across the full range of appropriate settings, times, respondents, etc.?* Time pressures frequently result in the elimination of some groups—often, the most difficult to reach, who tend to be the poorest or most vulnerable sectors of the population.

C. Internal Validity, Credibility, and Authenticity

C-1 *How context rich and meaningful ("thick") are the descriptions?* Time pressures often reduce the richness of the data collected.

C-5 *Are areas of uncertainty identified?* Was negative evidence sought? Time pressures can reduce the search for negative evidence.

D. External Validity, Transferability, and Fittingness

D-2 *Does the sample design theoretically permit generalization to other populations?* Simplifying sample design to save time can sometimes reduce representativity of the sample.

F. Threats to Statistical Conclusion Validity

F-5 and F-10 *Restriction of range and extrapolation from truncated or incomplete database.* Time pressures sometimes result in samples or secondary data with more limited coverage.

G. Threats to Internal Validity

G-3 *History.* Time pressures often constrain ability to control for historical differences between project and control areas.

(Continued)

(Continued)

H. Threats to Construct Validity

H-4 *Use of a single method to measure a construct (monomethod bias).* Time pressures may limit the number of data collection methods or the number of independent indicators of key variables.

H-12 *Using indicators and constructs developed in other countries without pretesting in the local context.* Time pressures often result in inadequate testing and modification of instruments.

I. Threats to External Validity

I-7 *Seasonal and other cycles.* These are often not adequately addressed when time is a factor.

Summary

- When identifying strategies to reduce time, it is important to determine whether there are also budget constraints or whether it is possible to increase expenditures to save time.

- Most of the cost-saving strategies discussed in the previous chapter can also be used to save time.

- Often, the main time pressure is on outside (often foreign) consultants who are available for only a short period of time. Their time can be used more efficiently by commissioning agency staff or a local consultant to prepare background studies or to do preparatory work for developing the methodology. Videoconferencing can also save outside consultant time (and often money). This also means that consultants can contribute to the evaluation design at the critical points when their input is most useful.

- Time can also be saved by increasing the number or raising the professional level of data collectors, field supervisors, and data analysts.

- In cases where the evaluator is involved at the start of the project, it may be possible to incorporate impact indicators into some of the administrative data forms used by the implementing agency to collect information that can later be used in the measurement of impacts.

- Modern handheld computers and similar technology can sometimes be used to reduce the time required for data collection and analysis.

As discussed in the previous chapter with respect to cost-saving strategies, most of the time-saving strategies involve trade-offs because they pose threats to the validity of the evaluation findings and recommendations. The chapter concludes with a brief introduction to the assessment of threats to validity, which is discussed in more detail in Chapter 7.

Further Reading

Bamberger, M., ed. 2000. *Integrating Quantitative and Qualitative Research in Development Projects.* Washington, DC: World Bank.

Case studies on the use of mixed-method approaches to improve quality and often to reduce time.

Beebe, J. 2001. *Rapid Assessment Process: An Introduction.* Walnut Creek, CA: Altamira Press.

A clear overview of how to reduce the time required to conduct ethnographic studies of communities, programs, or organizations. Many of the most widely used qualitative evaluation methods are based on ethnography so the approaches described in this book have a very wide application.

Handwerker, W. P. 2001. *Quick Ethnography.* Walnut Creek, CA: Altamira Press.

Another clear overview of rapid ethnographic approaches.

Scrimshaw, S. and E. Hurtado. 1987. *RAP: Rapid Assessment Procedures for Nutrition and Primary Health Care.* Tokyo: United Nations University.

This short guide is also a useful reference source for rapid assessment in other sectors in addition to health and nutrition.

Note

1. The UNDP (United Nations Development Program) is one of many organizations that regularly uses electronic questionnaires to survey staff located in countries around the world. The survey is sent electronically to offices in well over 100 countries. Most of the questions are multiple choice (although open-ended questions can be included) so that the frequency distribution of responses to each question can be automatically tabulated.

CHAPTER 5

Critical Information Is Missing or Difficult to Collect

Addressing Data Constraints

S tep 4 of the RealWorld Evaluation (**RWE**) approach identifies strategies for making the best use of limited and sometimes biased or misleading data sources (see Figure 5.1). A common RWE scenario is that the evaluation does not begin until the **project** has been underway for some time and no baseline data have been collected. A number of strategies are discussed for re-creating the conditions at the time the project began ("reconstructing" baseline data). A number of additional problems must often be addressed when reconstructing information on comparison groups. A different set of issues faces evaluators in the collection of data on sensitive topics and from groups that are difficult to reach. Addressing these questions, which are of vital importance to the purpose of many evaluations because they concern the most vulnerable groups or most intractable problems, is a particular challenge for the RealWorld evaluator: These kinds of information are often more time-consuming and expensive to collect, so there are often pressures to ignore these groups or issues when time or money is scarce. We conclude by identifying important threats to validity of conclusions when working with limited and often unreliable data.

Data Issues Facing RealWorld Evaluators

Evaluators often face constraints in the real world of practice resulting from the limited availability and accuracy of critical data. Concerns may surface regarding, for example, the following:

- Lack of baseline data on the project
- Selecting a **comparison group**

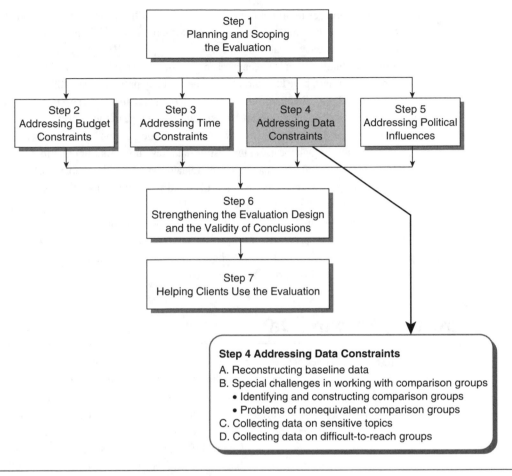

Figure 5.1   Step 4: Addressing Data Constraints

- Identifying a naturally occurring comparison group (i.e., a nonproject group with characteristics that match the project group)
- Collecting data on sensitive topics
- Identifying, locating, and interviewing difficult subjects (e.g., members of illegal or clandestine groups, remote or silenced groups, or participants who are unwilling to be interviewed)

In this chapter, we will propose approaches for addressing each kind of data constraint (see Table 5.1).

Let's consider three different data collection situations, each with its own set of problems. The first relates to project participants from whom data is being collected on their present situation via a baseline survey, end-of-project survey, or other kind of quantitative (QUANT) or qualitative (QUAL) data collection method. In many ways, this is a straightforward situation, provided project participants are easy to identify. Unless the project is going badly, they are usually quite willing to give information. However, if they are involved in activities not authorized by the project (e.g., welfare beneficiaries using project benefits to set up a black market business, housing beneficiaries subletting part of the house provided to them by the project, teachers moonlighting as tutors) or think they might benefit from a misrepresentation of the project (e.g., because they want the service charges to be reduced), there might be reasons for caution about the accuracy of data from them.

In a second situation, people in comparison groups, who would not normally receive any benefit from the project, have little incentive to cooperate by providing data. **Clients** or funding agencies might also discourage interviews of these people to avoid expectations of compensation, benefits, or political pressures to expand the coverage of the project.

A third situation involves the *reconstruction* of baseline data on project participants or comparison groups through the use of preexisting data, key informants, or other indirect techniques. This is often a difficult situation for an evaluator who faces the problem of inaccurate recall (e.g., nostalgia, misremembering) and distorted representations either intentional or unintentional. For example, a community elder might tend to romanticize the "good old days" and underestimate the amount of crime or poverty in the community in the past, or a supporter of an opposition party might downplay the improvements that the present community organization has produced. Let's consider how an evaluator might handle situations where baseline data or comparison groups are unavailable.

Reconstructing Baseline Data

When the evaluation does not begin until midway through, or even toward the end of the project, evaluators all too often find that no baseline data have been collected on the project or on comparison groups or that information was not collected on the access of these groups to the types of services and benefits provided by the project. In most cases, at least some useful data will have been collected on the project population when the project began. Comparable data on potential comparison groups are usually more difficult to find. This section offers some ways to reconstruct baseline data for project participants and then discusses some of the additional challenges regarding comparable data on a comparison group (see Box 5.1).

Reconstructing Baseline Data for Project Populations

Using Existing Documentary Data

Many cultures and organizations are self-documenting. Governments, private enterprises, and many sectors of civil society keep extensive records on their activities. These records may be produced for planning purposes, administrative and financial control, assessing progress, or communicating with different groups, especially those whose authorization, financial support, or general approval are critical to the success of the organization and its activities. Project records, like other documentary sources, should not be considered simply factual representations of "reality," but something more like "social facts . . . produced, shared and used in socially organized ways" (Atkinson and Coffey 2004:58). Project records may provide helpful insights into how an organization operates, its priorities, and how it tries to present itself to stakeholders and external groups. How the records are organized, what they emphasize, what they omit, and to whom they are (and are not) distributed may tell a great deal about an organization in an efficient and unobtrusive manner.

Box 5.1   Examples of Reconstructing Baseline Data

1. In Bangalore, India, in 1999, a sample of households were asked to respond to a "citizen report card" in which they assessed the changes in the quality of delivery of public services (water, sanitation, public hospitals, public transport, electricity, phones, etc.) since the project started in 1993. Families reported that although the quality of services was still low, on average, there had been an improvement in most services with respect to helpfulness of staff and proportion of problems resolved. The use of recall was an economical substitute for a baseline study.

SOURCE: Paul (2002) and Operations Evaluation Department (2005).

2. At the time that an evaluation of the impact of **social funds** in Eritrea was commissioned, the program had already been underway for several years. Baseline conditions for access to health services were estimated by asking families how frequently they had used health services before the village clinic was built, how long it took to reach these facilities, the costs of travel, and the consequences of not having had better access. The information provided by the households was compared with information from health clinic records and key informants (nurses, community leaders, etc.) so as to strengthen the estimates through **triangulation**. While existing documents (secondary data)[1] were useful, it was often found that the records were not organized in the way required to assess changes and impacts. For example, the village clinics kept records on each patient visit but did not keep files on each patient or each family so that it was difficult to determine how many different people used the clinic each month/year and also the proportion of village families who used the clinic. Similar methods were used to reconstruct baseline data on village water supply and rural roads and transport for the evaluation of the water supply and road construction components.

SOURCE: Based on unpublished local consultant impact evaluation report.

3. The Operations Evaluation Department (OED) of the World Bank conducted an ex-post evaluation of the social and economic impacts of a resettlement program in Maharastra State, India. Baseline data had been collected by project administrators on all families eligible to receive financial compensation or new land, but information was not collected on the approximately 45% of families who had been forced to move but who were not entitled to compensation. A **tracer study** was conducted by OED in which families forced to relocate without compensation were identified through neighbors and relatives. A significant proportion of families were traced in this way, and these were found on average to be no worse off as a result of resettlement, but it was not possible to assess how representative they were of all families relocated without compensation.

SOURCE: World Bank (1993).

Using Documents from within the Organization

The following are examples of questions that can be asked to learn about an organization from its own records and documentation:

- What can we infer from the fact that a national poverty reduction strategy contains a detailed analysis of the linkages between economic growth and poverty reduction but only a few paragraphs on the **impacts** of poverty on women?

Table 5.1   Strategies for Addressing Data Constraints

Reconstructing Baseline Data[a]

Approaches	Sources/Methods	Comments/Issues
Using existing documents (secondary data) and assessing their reliability and validity (see Chapter 7 for a discussion of these concepts)	• Project records • Data from public service agencies (health, education, etc.) • Government household and related surveys • School enrollment and attendance records • Patient records in local health centers • Savings and loans cooperatives records of loans and repayment • Vehicle registrations (to estimate changes in the volume of traffic) • Records of local farmers markets (prices and volume of sales)	All data must be assessed to determine their adequacy in terms of • Reference period • Population coverage • Inclusion of required indicators • Documentation on methodologies used • Completeness • Accuracy • Freedom from bias
Using recall: asking people to provide numerical (income, crop production, how many hours a day they spent traveling, school fees) or qualitative data (the level of violence in the community, the level of consultation of local government officials with the community) at the time the project was beginning	• Key informants • PRA (participatory rural appraisal) and other participatory methods	Recall can be used for • School attendance • Sickness/use of health facilities • Income/earnings • Community/individual knowledge and skills • Social cohesion and conflict • Water usage and cost • Major or routine household expenditures • Periods of stress • Travel patterns and transport of produce
Improving the reliability/validity of recall	• Conduct small pretest-posttest studies to compare recall with original information • Identify and try to control for potential bias (underestimation of small expenditures, truncating large expenditures by including some expenditures made before the recall period, distortion to	

Reconstructing Baseline Data[a]

Approaches	Sources/Methods	Comments/Issues
	conform to accepted behavior, intention to mislead)	
	• Clarifying the context (time period, specific types of behavior, reasons for collecting the information)	
	• Link recall to important reference points in community or personal history	
	• Triangulation (key informants, secondary sources, PRA)	
Key informants	• Community leaders • Religious leaders • Teachers • Doctors and nurses • Store owners • Police • Journalists	• Use to triangulate (test for consistency) data from other sources

Special Issues and Challenges When Working with Comparison Groups

Approach	Sources	Comments/Issues
Identifying and reconstructing comparison groups	Government statistics, earlier surveys, records of schools, health centers, and other public service agencies	Challenges and issues include • Political pressures • Ethical issues in using comparison groups • Using previous surveys as sampling frame • Rapid pilot studies to test variance, etc. • Judgmental matching • Use later phase of project as "pipeline" comparison • Internal comparison groups when different participants receive different combinations of services • Appropriateness of potential comparison groups • Statistical matching of samples (e.g., propensity scores)

(Continued)

Table 5.1 (Continued)

Approaches	Sources/Methods	Comments/Issues
Special issues in reconstructing data on comparison groups	• Econometric analysis posttest project and control groups (this design cannot control for historical differences between the two groups—see Chapter 10)	Methodological issues • Self-selection of participants (issues: difficult to match a comparison group on factors such as motivation) • Projects selected to represent either groups with the greatest potential to succeed or the groups facing the greatest challenge (issues: in both cases, difficult to find comparison group with similar characteristics)
Collecting sensitive data (e.g., domestic violence, fertility behavior, household decision making and resource control, information from or about women, and information on the physically or mentally handicapped)	• Participant observation • Focus groups • Unstructured interviews • Observation • PRA techniques • Case studies • Key informants	These issues also exist with project participants, but they tend to be more difficult to address with comparison groups because the researcher does not have the same contacts or access to the community
Collecting data on difficult-to-reach groups (e.g., sex workers, drug or alcohol users, criminals, informal small businesses, squatters and illegal residents, ethnic or religious minorities, and in some cultures, women)	• Observation (participant and nonparticipant) • Informants from the groups • Self-reporting • Tracer studies and snowball samples • Key informants • Existing documents (secondary data) • Symbols of group identification (clothing, tattoos, graffiti)	As for previous point

a. Similar approaches can be used for project and comparison areas, but there is often greater access to information for project populations.

- What can we infer from the fact that evaluation reports on the performance of government **programs** are automatically sent to members of Congress but are available to civil society only "on request"?
- Why was a baseline survey on the socioeconomic conditions of the target communities never conducted but financial reports were produced regularly from the start of the project?
- Why do planning documents for an integrated rural development program not discuss potential impacts on indigenous populations (even though indigenous groups represent a significant proportion of the population in the program areas)?

- Why does the project budget include a detailed analysis of project implementation costs but has little discussion (and less money) for expenditures concerning project **outcomes** and **sustainability**?
- What can we deduce from the fact that planning and evaluation reports from a country in South America are easily available in English, can be found with more difficulty in Spanish, but have never been translated into Aymara or Quechua (the main local languages)?

Documentary data come not only from officially published organizational reports but are also available from other sources within the organization such as computer-based monitoring, evaluation files, accounting records, Web sites, e-mail communications, brochures, personnel records, notice boards and signs, previous reports and evaluations, mission statements, procedures manuals, and policies.

Documentary data may also be available from sources external to the program, such as government statistics agencies, planning departments of ministries or departments, universities, health centers, schools, commercial banks and credit programs, accreditation agencies, professional and licensing agencies, the courts, and the mass media. Demographic data (e.g., enrollments, graduations, educational attainment, salary, births, deaths, marriages) may also be available from records maintained by government, community, or religious institutions.

When using existing data from within the organization, the evaluator must consider the following questions:

- Who collected the data and for what purpose? Were they collected for record-keeping purposes, or were they intended to influence managers or decision makers in some way?
- Were the monitoring data related only to project activities, or did they also measure changes occurring in outcome-related indicators?
- Were the data intended exclusively for internal use? For use by a restricted external audience? Are they publicly available?
- How accurate and complete are the data? Are there any obvious gaps? If so, were these intentional or due to poor record keeping?
- Are there any potential biases with respect to the key indicators required for the impact evaluation baseline or longitudinal data?

Using Records from outside the Organization

Records from other programs or projects in the same area can often provide information on conditions before the current project began. For example, surveys are often conducted to estimate the number of children not attending school, sources and costs of water supply, or availability of **microcredit**. More general statistical data may also be available on, for example, school enrollment rates, infant mortality, agricultural prices, microcredit lending, and transport patterns. However, while these sources can provide a useful (and often the only available) approximation to baseline conditions, it is essential to assess their strengths and weaknesses with respect to the following:

- Time differences between the start of the project (when data are required for the baseline) and the time when the secondary data were collected or reported: Time differences are particularly critical when general economic conditions may have changed between the date of the reports and the project launch.

- Differences in the population covered: For example, did the surveys include employ-ment in the informal as well as the formal sectors? Did it cover pedestrian as well as vehicular means of transport? Did it cover private as well as public schools?
- Was information collected on key project variables and potential impacts?
- Are the secondary data representative of the particular **target population** addressed by the project being evaluated?
- Does information cover both men and women, or was all information obtained from a single person (usually the "household head") and aggregated for all household mem-bers (see Box 5.2)?

Cautionary Tales—and Healthy Skepticism

There are many potential problems with documentary data. Documents may apply to dif-ferent, perhaps not very comparable, time periods. Some sectors of the target population may be neglected. The accuracy of the data or the quality of the data collection and reporting

---

Box 5.2   Examples from Developing Countries of Databases That Do Not Adequately Represent Both Sexes

A common weakness of many secondary data sources that can potentially be used to reconstruct baseline conditions is that they do not provide separate information on both men and women. For example:

- Many household surveys interview only one respondent (usually the "head of household"), who either gives only his or her opinions or presents aggregate data for the whole family. Often, the household head, particularly male heads, do not have full information on all household members.
- Husbands and fathers tend to underestimate the seriousness of problems affecting women (such as the time spent collecting water and fuel and, sometimes, sexual harassment).
- Aggregate data on, for example, consumption and expenditures, mask important differences in how food, medicine, and other goods are divided among different members of the household.
- Household interviews are often conducted in a situation where other household members or neigh-bors can overhear the interview. This will often inhibit spouses from giving information on their true earnings because they may not wish their partner to know how much they earn. It will also make it difficult for women to discuss sensitive topics such as domestic violence, the husband (or mother-in-law's) control over her earnings, or harassment inside or outside the community.
- Women are reluctant to talk about sexual harassment, so many surveys underestimate the serious-ness of harassment in schools, on public transport, or walking around the village. In one survey on public transport, women mentioned "security" as a major problem. This was interpreted in the analysis as referring to problems of bad driving or poor maintenance of the vehicles, whereas in fact women were referring to sexual harassment but were unwilling to be more specific.
- In many cultures, women's participation in community decision making is very limited, so reports on community meetings, while purporting to reflect the views of all the community, in fact often reflect only the opinions of males.
- Many monitoring reports do not even break down attendance at meetings or community activities by gender.

methods may reveal fundamental weaknesses. The skepticism appropriate for documentary sources is like that needed for other data sources; false survey data may be given or recorded, a sufficiently common occurrence in some Latin American countries to have earned the name "*entrevista de cafeteria*" indicating that responses were fabricated while the data collector was sitting alone in the cafeteria. Interviewees may similarly be self-protective or less than fully forthcoming, and test scores can be manipulated by test takers or testing administrators. No data collection method is free from the possibility—even likelihood—of inaccuracy, a main reason why triangulation is so important. Box 5.3 gives three examples of seemingly straight-forward secondary data on girls' education, each of which proved to be completely false.

Using Recall

While most interviews ask people to reflect on or provide information about their past, the term **recall** is used in various research areas such as poverty analysis, demography (Pebley,

---

Box 5.3   Ghost Schools and Missing Girls: Why the Validity of Secondary Data Must Always Be Checked

---

- A donor agency was considering an educational grant to a West African country. One of their concerns was the anticipated difficulty of encouraging girls to continue with secondary education because it was believed that many families pulled their girls out of school once they reached puberty so that they could prepare for marriage. However, an analysis of school attendance reports showed, to the surprise of the donor, that there were no significant gender differences in school attendance rates. However, unannounced follow-up visits to a sample of schools found very few secondary school-age girls actually in the classrooms. It turned out that many traditional families did not wish to send their daughters to secondary school, and because school attendance was compulsory, they were bribing the teacher to report that their daughters were attending, even though they were actually at home.

- In one region of a South Asian country, there were almost no secondary schools for girls. However, exploratory studies funded by a donor had found many families expressing interest in having their daughters continue their education beyond primary school. The enrollment records of a sample of boys' secondary schools were checked to determine whether girls were in fact enrolling in boys' schools; however, the records showed that all the students were boys. A follow-up observation study found that in fact significant numbers of girls were attending the boys' secondary schools but that the headmasters, to avoid possible criticism from their superiors for allowing girls to attend boys' schools, had recorded all the students as being boys.

- Another South Asian country launched a nationwide program to increase girls' enrollment in secondary schools by giving scholarships to girls (but not to boys) and also authorizing special allowances to secondary schools according to the number of female students. Field inspections revealed that significant numbers of schools were claiming allowances for "ghost" girl students not actually attending the school. In a few cases, it was discovered that ghost schools were actually put up in anticipation of the inspector's visits and were then dismantled once the inspection was over.

Noreen, and Choe 1986), and income expenditure surveys (Deaton and Grosh 2000) to refer to techniques used to elicit information on behavior (e.g., contraceptive usage or fertility) or economic status (household income or expenditure) at a particular point in the past (e.g., this time last year, five years ago) or over a particular period of time (e.g., the past seven days, the past month, the past year). Recall is a potentially valuable, although somewhat treacherous, method to retroactively estimate conditions prior to the start of the project and hence to reconstruct or strengthen baseline data. Although the literature on the reliability of recall is quite limited, particularly for developing countries, available **evidence** suggests that although information from recall is frequently biased, the direction, and sometimes the magnitude, of the bias is often predictable (see later in this section) so that usable estimates can often be obtained (see Deaton and Grosh 2000 for a review of the U.S. income and expenditure recall literature). Recall is therefore a potentially useful tool, particularly in the many situations where no other systematic baseline data are available. The utility of recall can often be enhanced through triangulation.

Although recall is generally unreliable for collecting precise numerical data such as income, incidences of diarrhea, or farm prices (particularly in the absence of the kinds of systematic studies referred to in the previous paragraph), it can be used to obtain estimates of major changes in the welfare conditions of the household. For example, families can usually recall which children attended a school outside the community before the village school opened, how children traveled to school, and travel time and cost. Families can also often provide reliable information on access to health facilities, where they previously obtained water, how much water they used, and how much it cost. On the other hand, families might be reluctant to admit that their children had not been attending school or that they had been using traditional medicine. They might also wish to underestimate how much they had spent on water if they are trying to convince planners that they are too poor to pay the water charges proposed in a new project.

Two common sources of bias in recall of expenditure data have been identified. First, the underestimation of small and routine expenditures increases as the recall period increases. Second, there is a "telescoping" of recall concerning major expenditures (such as the purchase of a cow, bicycle, home, car, or item of furniture), so that the time frame of expenditures may be misreported. Although most of the research on recall bias in income and expenditures comes from studies such as the as the Consumer Expenditure Surveys conducted quarterly by the Bureau of Labor Statistics of the U.S. Department of Labor,[2] the general results are potentially relevant to developing countries. The Living Standards Measurement Survey (LSMS) program[3] has conducted some assessments on the use of recall for estimating consumption in developing countries (Deaton and Grosh 2000), which are discussed below.

The most systematic assessments of the accuracy of recall data in developing countries probably come from demographic studies on the reliability of reported information on contraceptive usage and fertility. A number of large-scale comparative studies such as the World Fertility Survey[4] provide national surveys using comparable data collection methods for different points in time. For example, similar surveys were conducted in the Republic of Korea in 1971, 1974, and 1976, each of which obtained detailed information on current contraceptive usage and fertility as well as obtaining detailed historical information based on recall for a number of specific points in the past. This permitted a comparison of recall in 1976 for contraceptive usage and fertility in 1974 and 1971 with exactly the same information collected from surveys in those two earlier years. It was found that recall produced a systematic underreporting, but that the underestimation could be significantly reduced through the careful design and administration of the surveys (Pebley et al. 1986). Similar **findings** are available from demographic analysis in other countries. The conclusion from these studies is that recall can be a useful estimating tool with predictable and, to some extent, controllable errors. Unfortunately, it is possible to estimate the errors only where large-scale comparative survey data are available, and there are few if any other fields for developing countries with a similar wealth of comparative data to that available from demographic studies.

A major challenge in using recall is that estimates are very sensitive to changes in the research **design** methods, particularly the method used for data collection, the period over which estimates are obtained, and how the questions are formulated.[5] The following examples illustrate the design sensitivity. For example, a study in Latvia found that, on average, household expenditures were 46% higher when respondents were asked to keep a record of expenditures in a diary compared with when they were asked to recall expenditures (Scott and Okrasa 1998). In El Salvador, estimated expenditures were 31% higher when respondents were asked to provide detailed expenditure for 75 food categories and 25 nonfood categories compared with when they were asked to provide less detailed information covering 18 food items and 6 nonfood items (Jolliffe 2001). A study in Ghana found that average daily expenditure on a group of frequently purchased items fell by an average of 2.9% for every additional day over which respondents were asked to recall expenditures. The recall error leveled off at about 20% after two weeks (Scott and Amenuvegbe 1991). One of the best-known studies on the sensitivity of expenditure to the recall period comes from India. Between 1989 and 1998, the National Sample Survey in India experimented with different recall periods for measuring expenditure. It was found that when the 30-day recall period for food items was replaced with a 7-day period, the total estimated food expenditures increased by around 30%. When at the same time the 30-day recall period for infrequent expenditures was replaced with a one-year recall, the estimated total expenditure increased by about 17% (Deaton 2005).

Interestingly, a number of studies suggest that recall can provide better estimates of behavioral changes in areas such as primary prevention programs for child abuse, vocational guidance, and programs for delinquents than conventional pre- and posttest comparisons based on self-assessment (Pratt, McGuigan, and Katzev 2000). This is because before entering a program, subjects often overestimate their behavioral skills or knowledge through a lack of understanding of the nature of the tasks being studied and of the required skills. After completing the program, they may have a better understanding of these behaviors and may be able to provide a better assessment of their previous level of competency or knowledge and how much these have changed. Self-assessment of poverty, empowerment, or community organizational capacity in developing countries might all be areas where the *response shift* concept could potentially be applied for reconstruction of baseline data (Schwarz and Oyserman 2001).

Working with Key Informants

Key informants such as community leaders, doctors, teachers, local government agencies, nongovernmental organizations (**NGOs**), and religious organizations may be able to provide useful reference data on baseline conditions. However, these informants like all sources, have potential biases and their own particular agendas. Caldwell (1985), reviewing lessons from the World Fertility Survey, uses these considerations to express reservations about the use of key informants for retrospective analysis in fertility surveys. Box 5.4 illustrates the wide range of key informants that can be used in any given study (in this case, a study of crack cocaine users). When selecting informants, it is important to recognize that people have their own

---

Box 5.4   Selecting a Wide Range of Informants When Studying Sensitive
Topics: Studying Crack Cocaine Addicts in New York

"I spent hundreds of nights on the street and in crackhouses observing dealers and
addicts. . . . Perhaps more important, I also visited their families, attending parties,
and intimate reunions. . . . I interviewed, and in many cases befriended the spouses,
lovers, siblings, mothers, grandmothers and—where possible—the fathers and step-
fathers of the crack dealers."

SOURCE: Bourgois (2002:16).

---

perspective and often their own axe to grind. Consequently, the researcher should try to consult with people likely to have different sources of information (people who know prostitutes
in their family setting or community, as commercial associates or clients), as well as different
perspectives (e.g., the police, neighborhood associations trying to force the prostitutes out of
the community, religious leaders). It is also important not to assume that all informants should
be in positions of authority. The perspective of a child, neighbor, or friend is just as important.

Using Participatory Evaluation Methods

Over the past 30 years, a broad range of participatory research and evaluation techniques has
become widely used in developing countries. These were a reaction against *top-down planning,* in
which surveys were designed, conducted, and interpreted by outside experts who then decided
what a community needed. Participatory research methods—which have a number of different
names, including **PRA** (participatory rural appraisal) and **PLA** (participatory learning and
action) are based on the principle of empowering the community to conduct its own analysis of
its needs and priorities and to translate these into a plan of action. All the approaches have in common that they work through community groups rather than individuals and that they rely heavily on mapping and other graphical techniques, partly to work through group processes and partly
because a high proportion of people in many rural communities is illiterate. These participatory
evaluation approaches have two important attractions for RWE and the present discussion. First,
they have placed a strong emphasis on rapid appraisals (often lasting a maximum of one week)
and second because they have developed a wide range of techniques for reconstructing the history
of the community and for the identification and analysis of critical events in the life of the community. The following is a brief description of some of the techniques. For a fuller description,
with extensive illustrations of the graphical and mapping techniques, the reader is referred to
Somesh Kumar (2002) *Methods for Community Participation: A Complete Guide for Practitioners.*

- *Seasonal calendars.* These are most frequently used in farming studies where farmers
  report for each month factors such as rainfall, planting and harvesting of crops on different types of soil, labor demand, water sources, migration, market prices for agricultural products, and so on (Kumar 2002:148; Theis and Grady 1991). A chart is drawn on
  paper or on the ground marking the months. Participants are then asked to place stones
  or seeds to indicate the months with, for example, the highest incidence of famine,
  out-migration, or expenditures (see Box 5.5).

- *Time trends.* These can be used to study changes over time in farm yields; livestock population; prices; migration; time and distance to collect fuel, fodder, or water; population size and number of households; and malnutrition rates. In most cases, participants are asked to plot changes for each year, but sometimes longer periods may be used (Kumar 2002). A similar type of chart to the seasonal calendar is used, but this time, the spaces refer to years. In some cultures, the concept of a calendar year has no meaning, so reference points such as a major drought, the election of a new president, or the outbreak of a war may be used.

- *Historical profile.* This provides information on historical factors that are important for understanding the present situation in a community or region. This may cover, for example, building of infrastructure, introduction of new crops, epidemics, droughts and famines, foreign and civil war, and major political events (Kumar 2002; Theis and Grady 1991). Information can be collected from historical records as well as from informants. Another approach is to give a tape recorder to different people in the community and ask them to narrate their version of community history. In this case, triangulation is important to reconcile the major discrepancies of interpretation that are often found between the reports of different community members. Often, groups of community elders or senior citizens will be particularly important both because of their direct memory and their role as keepers of tradition.

- *Critical incidents:* This is similar to the historical profile except that the analysis is focused on the stressful events or periods. Sometimes the analysis covers one year (looking at seasonal variations in stress) or it may cover a longer period. Box 5.5 illustrates the application of this technique to the analysis of periods of greatest stress during the past year in a rural community in Kenya.

Special Issues in Reconstructing Comparison Groups

Comparison groups are communities, organizations, or groups selected to match the project communities as closely as possible on social, economic, physical, historical, and other characteristics relevant to the study. The process of selecting well-matched comparison groups is often a challenging task. With few exceptions, project areas are *purposefully* selected to target, for example, the poorest areas or those with the greatest development potential rather than *randomly* selected, increasing the challenge of identifying matched local groups[6]. Whether the match between a project group and a natural comparison group is good enough may be partly a matter of data analysis and partly a judgment call.

Be careful not to make the assumption that a comparison group is matched with the project groups in every respect except participation in the project. Rarely, if ever, in society are all factors equal between any two communities or groups. Many contextual and other factors must be considered in a holistic analysis of results, from which the evaluator should then try to determine the relative influence of the project's interventions compared with different internal and external factors in the project or the comparison group.

> **Box 5.5** Constructing a PRA Seasonal Calendar to Reconstruct Periods of Stress in a Rural Community in Kenya
>
> Families were given small stones or seeds and asked to place them on the months of the year when the following incidents typically occur: light meals (survival foods) during periods of greatest hunger, begging, migration, unemployment, earned income, disease, and rainfall. The chart shows the critical relationships between rainfall and income on the one hand, and disease, migration, begging, and light meals on the other.
>
> *Seasonal Calendar of Poverty Drawn by Villagers in Nyamira Kenya*
>
> | | Jan | Feb | Mar | April | May | June | July | Aug | Sept | Oct | Nov | Dec |
> |---|---|---|---|---|---|---|---|---|---|---|---|---|
> | Light meals | ●●● | ●●● | ● | ● | | | | | | | | ●● |
> | Begging | ●●● ●●● | ●●● ●●● | ● | | | | | | | | | ●●● |
> | Migration | ●●● | ●●● | | ● | ● | ●● | | | | | | |
> | Unemployment | ●●● ●●● | ●●● ●●● | ●● | | | | | | | | | |
> | Income | | | ● | ●● ●● | ●● ●● | ●● ●● | ●●● ●●● | ●●● ●●● | ●●● ●●● | ● | ● ● | |
> | Disease | | | ● | ●● ●● | ●● ●● | ●●● ●● | | ●●● | ●● | | | |
> | Rainfall | | | ●● ●● | ●● ●● | | | | ● | ● | ●●● | ●●● ● | |
>
> SOURCE: Rietberger-McCracken and Napayan (1997).

The following are some of the strategies used for constructing comparison groups:

- It is sometimes possible to construct an *internal* comparison group within the project area. Households or individuals who did not participate in the project or who did not receive a particular service or benefit can be treated as the comparison for the project in general or for a particular service.[7]
- When projects are implemented in phases, it is also possible to use households selected for the second or subsequent phases as the comparison group for the analysis of the impacts of the previous phase. This is sometimes called a pipeline comparison group. For example, the economic status of a new cohort of women about to receive their microfinance loans might serve as a comparison group to compare with the current economic status of women who received loans during the past year. The phased approach was used in the evaluation of the Tondo Foreshore Squatter Upgrading Project in Manila discussed earlier (see Box 3.5).
- When the statistical data are available, cluster analysis can sometimes provide a powerful tool for selecting a comparison group that can be matched on the variables of most interest to the project. (Weitzman, Silver, and Dillman 2002)

Box 5.6 gives examples of potentially strong and weaker comparison groups.

Selection Bias

It is important to check constantly for potential selection bias with respect to the ways that project and comparison group participants were selected or treated or the ways they responded to the project or to the evaluation. It is important to understand and, in the analysis, to take into account potential biases so as to be able to reach reasonable, defensible findings.

Nonparticipants may be different in potentially important ways from those who did participate. In some cases, nonparticipants may have been excluded or discouraged from participation for reasons having little to do with their actual eligibility to participate—reasons that may limit the ability to match project and comparison groups. In other cases, nonparticipants may differ from participants in not having had the motivation or self-confidence to apply.

The following section discusses some of the statistical procedures that may, for QUANT studies, partially address the selection bias issue and improve the comparability of the comparison group. How effective the statistical controls are will depend on the adequacy of the control model and the reliability of the measurement of the control variables (Shadish, Cook, and Campbell 2002:esp.138, 249).

Problems in Working with Comparison Group (Also Referred to as Nonequivalent Control Group) Survey Data

Evaluations frequently compare the project population with comparison areas selected to match the project population as closely as possible. When, as is usually the case, subjects were not randomly assigned to the two groups, this is called a **nonequivalent control group** or comparison group. In some cases, the comparison group may seem to match the project group quite closely on most of the socioeconomic characteristics of the households or individuals, but in other cases, there may be important differences between the two groups (see Box 5.6). When relatively large and reasonably random samples have been interviewed in both groups, it is usually possible to strengthen the analysis by statistically matching subjects from two areas on a number of relevant characteristics such as education, income, and family size. The evaluations of the Ecuador cut flower export industry and the Bangladesh microcredit programs described in Box 5.7 are examples of this approach.

If differences in the dependent variables (the number of hours men and women spend on household tasks, men's and women's savings and expenditure on household consumption goods, etc.) between the project group and the comparison group are still statistically significant after controlling for these household characteristics, this provides preliminary indications that the differences may be due, at least in part, to the project interventions.

Although this type of multivariate analysis is a powerful analytical tool, one important weakness is that, without baseline studies of both groups, the evaluation design does not provide any information on the initial conditions or attributes of the two groups prior to the project intervention. For example, the higher savings rates of women in the communities receiving microcredit in Bangladesh might be due to their having previously received training in financial management or that they already had small business experience. These comparison

---

Box 5.6   Potentially Strong and Weak Comparison Groups

The following three cases are examples of relatively strong comparison groups:

- In a community water supply project in Bolivia, the number of communities who applied to obtain water far exceeded the resources available to construct water systems in that particular year. Successful communities were selected through a lottery so that the process could be seen to be transparent and unbiased.

- In the Tondo Foreshore Slum Upgrading Project in Manila, the project was designed to cover a population of over 100,000 households in several phases over a period of 10 years. The areas to be included in Phase 2 were selected as a comparison group for Phase 1.

- In a low-cost housing project in El Salvador, all the project participants came from one of three distinct types of low-income settlements, and participants represented a relatively small proportion of the population in each of these areas. Although participants were self-selected, so that it was difficult to control for the effect of motivation, it was possible to randomly select a comparison sample from these three low-income settlements. Statistical analysis found the characteristics of the project and comparison groups were similar but not identical.

The following two cases describe situations where it was more difficult to select a strong comparison group:

- An evaluation was conducted in Nairobi to evaluate the impacts of slum upgrading programs that had been operating for a decade or longer. The programs had covered all the major slums that housed well over 75% of the low-income population. The slums not covered by these programs were very small, housing only a few hundred families (compared with some project areas with more than 50,000 households). All the potential comparison areas had special characteristics (such as a unique ethnic group) that distinguished them in potentially important ways from the project areas.

- The project sites to be included in an agricultural extension program in Ethiopia were selected to include the poorest and most remote rural communities and also to include only areas in which no other agencies were working. The selection process also meant that many of the project areas had unique ethnic characteristics. In addition to the difficulties of finding areas with similar characteristics, most other areas had at least one outside agency involved, making it very difficult to find suitable comparison areas.

---

group designs can be strengthened by incorporating some of the methods discussed above for reconstructing baseline data. Using these methods, it is possible to assess the similarities and differences between the two groups at the time the project began. If the two groups are found to be relatively similar on key baseline indicators (socioeconomic characteristics, access to the kinds of services or benefits provided by the project), then this increases the likelihood that statistical differences found in the ex-post comparison are due at least in part to the project. If, on the other hand, there were important initial differences between the two groups in the reconstructed baselines, then it is harder to assume that the posttest differences are necessarily due to the project intervention.

Box 5.7   Working with Comparison Groups in Ex-Post Evaluation Designs

---

1. An evaluation was conducted in Guayaquil, Ecuador, to assess the impact of the cut flower export industry (which employs a high proportion of women and pays women well above average wages) on women's income and employment and on the division of domestic tasks between husband and wife. Families living in another valley about 100 miles away and without access to the cut flower industry were selected as a comparison group. This was a nonequivalent control group because families were not randomly assigned to the project and comparison groups. The project and comparison groups were interviewed after the flower industry had been operating for some time and consequently no baseline data were available. Multivariate analysis was used to determine whether there were differences in the dependent variables (women's employment and earnings and the number of hours spent by husband and wife on domestic chores) in the project and comparison areas after controlling for household attributes such as educational level of both spouses, family size, and so on. Significant differences were found between the two groups on each of these dependent variables, and it was concluded that there was evidence that access to higher paid employment (in the flower industry) did affect the dependent variables (the distribution of domestic chores between men and women and the hours women and men devoted to paid and nonpaid work). Although multivariate analysis matched the project and comparison groups more closely, it was not able to examine differences in the initial conditions of the two groups before the project began. For example, it is possible that the flower industry decided to locate in this particular valley because it was known that a high proportion of women already worked outside the home and that husbands were prepared to assume more household chores thus allowing their wives to work longer hours. The analytical model used in the study was not able to examine this alternative explanation.

SOURCE: Newman (2001).

2. An ex-post evaluation was conducted of the impact of microcredit on women's savings, household consumption and investment, and fertility behavior in Bangladesh. The evaluation used household survey data from communities that did not have access to credit programs as a nonequivalent control group (comparison group). Multivariate analysis was used to control for household attributes, and it was found that women's access to microcredit programs was significantly associated with most of the dependent variables. As in the case of the Ecuador study, this design did not control for preexisting differences between the project and comparison groups with respect to important explanatory variables such as women's participation in small business training programs or prior experience with microcredit.

SOURCE: Khandker (1998).

Collecting Data on Sensitive Topics or from Groups Who Are Difficult to Reach

The collection of data on sensitive topics, such as domestic violence, contraceptive usage, or teenage gangs, or from difficult-to-reach groups, such as sex workers, drug users, ethnic minorities, or the homeless, raises special data-collection issues. These situations require the sensitive use of appropriate QUAL methods such as observation, individual interviews (more sensitive and ethically appropriate than group interviews in many cases), and key informants.

These issues are particularly important for RWE because budget and time constraints may create pressures to ignore these sensitive topics or difficult-to-reach groups.

Addressing Sensitive Topics

At least three strategies are particularly useful for addressing sensitive topics:

1. Identify a wide range of informants who can provide different perspectives.

2. Select a number of culturally appropriate strategies for studying sensitive topics.

3. Systematically triangulate.

Whenever it is necessary to obtain sensitive information, try to identify and talk to as many people as possible who form part of the social network being studied (see Box 5.4, for an example of how this approach was applied in a study of crack-cocaine users). This provides different perspectives, and some respondents may be more willing to discuss the issues than others, in addition to having different experiences and insights to offer.

Some of the culturally appropriate strategies that can be used include the following:

- *Observation.* In some cases, it is possible to use **participant observation** whereas in other cases, such as a study of sex workers or drug users, this will not be possible, and a nonparticipant observation approach will be used. Box 5.8 describes the use of participant observation to observe sexual harassment on public transport in Lima, Peru, and to observe relations between spouses, particular with respect to decisions about use of money in domestic situations in Bangladesh.
- *Focus groups.* Groups of around eight participants are interviewed in a group, using a standard list of questions or topics to be addressed. Again, for sensitivity reasons, in some cases individual interviews may be gentler and more likely to produce information.
- Single-subject or small-scale case studies
- Key informants

Box 5.8 presents three examples of data collection on sensitive topics: (a) assessing the impacts of credit on women's empowerment in Bangladesh, (b) studying the incidence of sexual harassment on public transport in Lima, Peru, and (c) examining the informal operation of rural health clinics in Nepal. Each case demonstrates the need to recognize sensitive topics, the need for development and use of culturally sensitive approaches, and the importance of **mixed methods**. In each of these cases, participant observation or discrete observation was an important way to compare observed behavior with what respondents reported and to collect data on natural, rather than staged, events.

Studying Difficult-to-Reach Groups

Difficult-to-reach or relatively invisible groups include a wide variety: drug or alcohol users, dropouts, criminals, informal and unregistered small businesses, squatters and illegal residents, ethnic or religious minorities, boyfriends or absent fathers, illegal aliens, indentured laborers

---

Box 5.8   Examples of Collecting Data on Sensitive Topics

---

1. In a study in Bangladesh to assess the impact of microcredit on women's empowerment, experience showed that conventional household survey methods would not allow women to speak freely about sensitive issues concerning control of household resources and male authority. Participant observation in subjects' houses and elsewhere was used to observe women's behavior and intrahousehold dynamics over a period of years to study changes in household power relations before and after women had obtained loans from a village bank. Observation was combined with the administration of an empowerment scale based on items identified by the women themselves in group discussions.

SOURCE: Hashemi, Schuler, and Riley (1996).

2. In Lima, Peru, it was believed that one of the reasons women did not use public transport was because of the fear of sexual harassment. However, women were unwilling to mention this in conventional transport surveys. Participant observation, in which researchers spent days traveling on public transport, was able to document the high incidence of harassment. This was confirmed and quantified in focus groups with women, men, and mixed groups stratified by age, conducted by a market research firm in their office in the center of town (i.e., away from the community).

SOURCE: Gomez (2000).

3. Visits by representatives of donor agencies to rural health clinics in Nepal found that all the health diagnosis and prescription of medicines was done by the resident doctors, most of whom had been transferred (against their will) from large towns to the villages. The untrained "peon" recruited from the local community kept the clinic clean, made tea, and the like. However, an anthropologist observed the clinics during normal periods when there were no outside visitors. She found that the doctors were absent for long periods of time and that the peon, who, unlike the doctors, spoke the local language, regularly advised patients and even prescribed medicines during the long absences of the doctor. The donor agency was unwilling to accept this finding because during their visits only the doctor treated patients and the humble peon was very much in the background.

SOURCE: Justice (1986).

---

and slaves, sex trade workers, informal water sellers, girls attending boys schools, migrant workers, and persons with HIV/AIDS, particularly those who have not been tested. Initially, the evaluator may or may not be aware of the existence of these groups. Clients and funding agencies may also be ignorant of their presence vis-à-vis the program. The following are examples of situations in which the researcher was not initially aware of the existence of certain groups:

- In an evaluation of low-cost housing programs in Nairobi, the evaluator was surprised by how many female-headed households had no apparent source of income. A visit to the project early in the morning revealed that many of these women were brewing *buzaa*, the local beer. Because residents were not allowed to establish businesses in the community without special permission, the women were reluctant to tell the evaluator (and, of course, project management) about this source of revenue.

- During the planning of a squatter settlement upgrading project in La Paz, Bolivia, project management was very pleased with the high turnout at community meetings when the willingness of families to pay for water and other services was discussed. Residents enthusiastically endorsed the closing of community hand pumps and wells and their replacement with more expensive individual water connections for each house. The project had been underway for some time before it was discovered (through participant observation) that the community contained a significant proportion of illegal squatters who were paying rent to landowners and who depended on the wells and hand pumps for their water supply. The squatters hid during community meetings with outside agencies, and the project staff members were not aware of their existence until they began finding that the wells that had been sealed because of cholera contamination were being forcibly reopened. The discovery of the large numbers of squatters required a dramatic reassessment of the project's impact because instead of showing that all families were better off because of the improved water supply, it was now realized that a significant number of the poorest families were probably worse off because their access to water for drinking and hygiene had been severely curtailed.
- In a housing project in Guayaquil, Ecuador, it was discovered, again through participant observation, that a clandestine opposition group was pressuring residents not to vote in favor of providing household water connections—arguing that providing water was a trick by the capitalist government and donor agency to deprive the poor of their full rights.

The following are useful techniques for the identification and analysis of difficult-to-reach groups:

- *Participant observation.* This is one of the most common ways to become familiar with and accepted into the milieu where the groups operate or are believed to operate. Often, initial contacts or introductions will be made through friends, family, clients, or in some cases, the official organizations with whom the groups interact. Salmen (1987) lived in low-income housing projects and slum upgrading areas in Guayaquil, Ecuador, and La Paz, Bolivia, for several months until he had sufficiently gained the confidence of the communities that he began to be aware of the presence of illegal squatters and similar difficult-to-reach groups. He made a point of renting rooms in houses of families with children, rather than having his own self-contained house, so that families could help provide him with different entry points to the community.
- *Key informants:* These are identified and used in the ways discussed earlier.
- *Tracer studies:* Neighbors, friends, work colleagues, and so on are used to help locate people who have moved, sometimes a decade or longer ago. Former neighbors and tribal members were used to help locate families in India who had lost their land and been forced to relocate without any compensation more than a decade earlier (World Bank 1993). Because of the close family and tribal networks, it was possible to locate a significant proportion of these households. A study in Brazil used a similar technique to trace the origins of poor Brazilian families who had migrated to the South and who had lost contact with their regions of origin (Perlman 1976, 2002). Carol Stack, an American anthropologist, used an interesting method in one of her early studies to locate African, American men who had moved back to the South after having migrated to the North. She rented a stall in state fairs in some of the Southern States and put up a sign offering a free beer to anyone who had arrived from the North within the past few years (Stack 1996).

- *Snowball samples:* With this technique, efforts are made to locate a few members of the difficult-to-locate group by whatever means available. These members are then asked to identify other members of the group so that if the approach is successful, the size of the sample will increase. This technique is often used in the study of sexually transmitted diseases.
- *Sociometric techniques:* Respondents are asked to identify who they go to for advice or help on particular topics (e.g., advice on family planning, traditional medicine, or for the purchase of illegal substances). A sociometric map is then drawn with arrows linking informants to the opinion leaders, informants, or resource persons.

Common Threats to Adequacy and Validity of an Evaluation Relating to Data Constraints

Box 5.9 identifies some of the most common threats to validity and adequacy of evaluation conclusions that must be addressed when assessing the different approaches to addressing data limitations and reconstructing baseline data and comparison groups. Similar tables are included for reference in Chapters 3 and 4 to identify the respective threats to validity when taking measures to reduce budget or time. Readers who are not familiar with the concepts of threats to validity and adequacy may wish to read Chapter 7 and then return to this section.

Summary

- When evaluations do not begin until after the project has been underway for some time, the evaluator will often find that no baseline data have been collected and that no comparison group has been identified or studied.

- A number of strategies can be used to try to "reconstruct" the baseline conditions that existed at the time the project began. These include the use of documentary (secondary) data sources, interviews with key informants, using participatory methods such as PRA to help the community to re-create historical data and timelines, and the use of recall.

- While documentary (secondary) data are a valuable source of information, they were normally collected for a purpose other than evaluation of a particular project, and it is necessary to identify any biases or other factors that might limit the utility of some secondary sources.

- Additional challenges exist when reconstructing comparison groups because it is necessary to identify a group or community that is comparable to the project population as well as collecting information from this group.

- Many evaluations require the collection of sensitive data or collecting information from difficult-to-reach groups. This is a particular challenge for RWE because this information is often expensive and time-consuming to collect, so there are often pressures to ignore these questions or groups. Some of the techniques for reaching difficult-to-locate groups include participant observation, use of key informants, trace studies, snowball samples, and sociometric techniques.

Box 5.9   Threats to Adequacy and Validity Relating to Data Constraints

---

The numbers refer to the RWE integrated threats to validity and adequacy checklist (see Appendix 1). The concepts are defined and discussed in Chapter 7.

A. Confirmability (and objectivity)

A-2 *Are the conclusions drawn from the available evidence, and is the research relatively free of researcher bias?* Are secondary data biased or in other ways inadequate for use as baseline data?

B. Reliability and Dependability

B-2 *Were data collected across the full range of appropriate settings, times, respondents, etc.?* How well does the comparison group match the project group?

C. Internal Validity, Credibility, and Authenticity

C-2 *Does the account ring true, make sense, seem convincing?* If the comparison group is weak, impacts due to preexisting differences may be wrongly attributed to the project.

C-3 *Did triangulation among complementary methods and data sources produce generally converging conclusions?* In many cases, triangulation is not used.

D. External Validity, Transferability, and Fittingness

D-2 *Does the sample design theoretically permit generalizations to other populations?* Weaknesses in the comparison group design will often invalidate this criterion.

F. Threats to Statistical Conclusion Validity

F-4 *Unreliability of measures of change of outcome indicators.* Particularly a problem when collecting information on sensitive topics.

F-5 *Restriction of range.* Frequent problem when secondary data does not cover the whole project population.

F-10 *Extrapolation from a truncated or incomplete database.* See previous point.

G. Threats to Internal Validity

G-3 *History.* Absence of, or an inadequate, comparison group means that historical factors are not controlled for.

G-9 *Respondent distortion when using recall.* A common problem.

H. Threats to Construct Validity

H-4. *Use of a single method to measure a construct (monomethod bias).* When relying on secondary data, the evaluator has to accept the definitions and methods used in the database—even if there is only a single method or indicator for some key variables.

H-12 *Using indicators and constructs developed in other countries without pretesting in the local context.* Many secondary data sets to which an evaluator may have access were collected for foreign-funded studies, and sometimes the indicators and concepts were not adapted to the local context. Evaluators relying on secondary data usually have little opportunity to adjust or refine the indicators.

I. Threats to External Validity

I-7 *Seasonal and other cycles.* Secondary data are often not available, so the assessment of the validity of recall is critical.

- Like the two previous chapters, the present chapter ends with a discussion of some threats to validity arising from the innovative approaches that have to be used to reconstruct or obtain difficult and sensitive information.

Further Reading

Gubbels, P. and C. Koss. 2000. *From the Roots Up: Strengthening Organizational Capacity through Guided Self-Assessment.* Oklahoma City, OK: World Neighbors.

Useful training and reference manual on how to use PRA techniques, including for reconstruction of baseline data.

Kumar, S. 2002. *Methods for Community Participation: A Complete Guide for Practitioners.* London: ITDG.

Detailed description of all the main PRA techniques that can be used for reconstructing baseline conditions of a community or group or for collecting sensitive data.

Silverman, D. 2004. *Qualitative Research: Theory, Method and Practice.* 2d ed. Thousand Oaks, CA: Sage.

Part III ("Textual Analysis") presents a thorough discussion of ethnographic approaches to the use and assessment of secondary data.

Theis, J. and H. Grady. 1991. *Participatory Rapid Appraisal for Community Development: A Training Manual Based on Experiences in the Middle-East and North Africa Region.* London: Save the Children/ International Institute for Environment and Development.

Useful discussion of PRA techniques that can be used for the reconstruction of baseline data.

Notes

1. The terms *secondary data* and *existing documents* or *existing documentary data* are used by different authors to refer to existing studies, reports, or project documents that can be used to estimate baseline conditions or the characteristics of comparison groups. All the terms are equivalent.

2. The Consumer Expenditure Surveys combine a quarterly survey of expenditures administered to a sample of U.S. households and the completion by a smaller sample of households of a diary in which all expenditures are recorded. The diary is used to check the reliability and sources of bias in the estimates, based on recall obtained from the quarterly surveys. For more information, go to www.bls.gov/cex/home.htm

3. The LSMS (Living Standards Measurement Survey) program was launched in the 1980s by the World Bank to develop standard survey methodologies and questionnaires for comparative analysis of poverty and welfare in developing countries (Grosh and Glewwe 2000).

4. The World Fertility Survey is based on demographic and fertility surveys conducted in 41 developing countries in the 1970s and 1980s by many different agencies. For more information, go to www.pop.psu.edu/data-archive/daman/wfs.htm

5. The references in this and the following paragraph are taken from a chapter by John Gibson in a forthcoming book, *Handbook on Poverty Statistics* (United Nations Department of Economic and Social Affairs).

6. One of the cases in which randomization is used in the selection of projects occurs when demand significantly exceeds supply and some kind of lottery or random selection is used. This sometimes occurs with social funds (see Baker 2000) or with community-supported schools (see Kim, Alderman, and Orazem 1999).

7. For example, subjects may be categorized according to their distance from a road or water source, whether any family member attended literacy classes, the amount of food aid they received, and so on.

CHAPTER 6

Reconciling Different Priorities and Perspectives

Addressing Political Influences

S tep 5 of the RealWorld Evaluation (**RWE**) approach discusses how to reconcile the different priorities and perspectives of clients and stakeholders, and how political factors affect the evaluation (see Figure 6.1). We begin by discussing the interrelated issues of values, ethics, and politics and how they affect the conduct of evaluation. While the politics which affect evaluations can be disturbing, they are a fact of life, and—to take a positive view—indicate the importance of the work and the interests of the stakeholders. Codes of conduct such as the *Program Evaluation Standards* of the Joint Committee on Standards for Educational Evaluation (1994) and the *Guiding Principles for Evaluators* of the American Evaluation Association (1995) provide guidance for the role of the evaluator vis-à-vis stakeholder and other influences. The following sections address political issues that commonly arise at the start of an evaluation, during the conduct of the evaluation, or during reporting and use of the evaluation findings and recommendations. An issue that many evaluators have to address is balancing stakeholders' "right to know" about the progress and findings of an evaluation with the desire of a client to restrict access to potentially sensitive findings. We conclude with a discussion of strategies for addressing political constraints.

Values, Ethics, and Politics

Although the term *evaluation* includes *value* at its etymological core, many evaluation users expect evaluation to be value free so as to be unbiased. They expect programs to be appraised

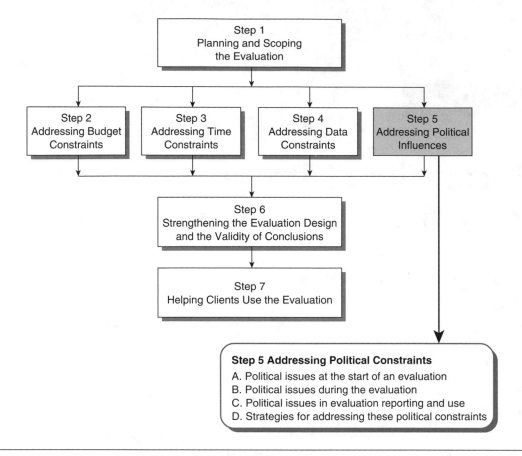

Figure 6.1   Step 5: Addressing Political Constraints

in terms of external standards or progress toward their own goals and objectives and to avoid political maneuvering or pressure; they expect evaluators to adhere to high ethical standards. But in evaluation, values and politics are inescapable. Program goals, manifest values, and implementing programs are ways of pursuing these values. Pursuit of goals through programs is an inherently political enterprise. Programs are part of a political agenda. The result of such activity is that values and politics affect and sometimes constrain the work of the evaluator.

"This is a good program (or not a good program) because . . ." Any ending to this sentence implies values. For example, "This is a good program because it has improved the nutrition of poor children in this community" suggests that proper care of children, including the impoverished, is valued by members of a community working to ensure that funds are allocated to feeding poor children. "This is not a good program because administrative costs divert a large proportion of public funds from job training" suggests that economic capacity building, efficiency, and stewardship are valued and pursued. The following examples illustrate different kinds of political influences on evaluations:

- Public funding for Head Start programs, which provide early childhood education to impoverished children and their families in the United States, comes with a requirement for regular local evaluations and occasional systemwide evaluations. During economic downturns, Head Start's substantial funding generates political debate about the long-term impact of the program, favored by Democrats, and whether tax dollars should be used for this or other educational initiatives such as the No Child Left Behind Act (NCLB 2002), favored by the Republican administration. As part of NCLB, the U.S. Department of Education proposed a "priority [that] makes it possible for any office in the Department to encourage or to require appropriate projects to use scientifically based evaluation strategies" defined as (and in order of priority) experimental design involving random assignment of subjects to treatment and control groups, quasi-experimental design with matched comparison groups, and regression discontinuity designs (U.S. Department of Education 2003). Debate on the appropriateness of requiring particular evaluation designs goes far beyond the technical merits of different evaluation methodologies to concerns about the political motivations underlying the choice of these particular methods.

- Evaluators are sometimes told not to collect baseline data on comparison groups to avoid creating expectations regarding rights to services or compensation. In developing countries, examples might include irrigation, urban renewal, or power projects that involve forced resettlement of large numbers of families or communities. Less common in the United States, examples might include job retraining, allocating limited quantities of influenza vaccine, or providing laptop computers or enrichment programs to students in designated schools.

- In programs involving specific interventions such as new teaching methods, the provision of drinking water, or the introduction of an improved medical treatment, randomly assigning subjects or communities to treatment and control groups is often not possible for ethical or political reasons. For example, a politician might not favor an evaluation design which included selection of his or her constituents for a comparison group because the voters might subsequently clamor for extension of services.

Evaluation is the most challenging of all approaches to inquiry because it often confirms or confronts programs, their underlying values, and their political supporters and opponents. Findings have ramifications for individuals and economic, political, and ethical implications. Throughout the course of a project, evaluators should exercise sharp alertness regarding political and ethical issues.

Societal Politics and Evaluation

Society has a stake in evaluation, so politics writ large sometimes influence evaluation. The *Standards for Program Evaluation* (Joint Committee 1994) and the *Guiding Principles for Evaluators* (AEA 1995) urge evaluators to consider the public good, the societal good—to think in terms of broad stakeholder groups and right-to-know and need-to-know audiences. But, often, the interests of the immediate client, to whom the evaluator reports, take precedence. Evaluators should avoid the assumptions that political influence is either bad or avoidable and that measures should be taken to insulate the evaluation from these pressures. Rather, political maneuvering is natural, inevitable, and a sign that stakeholders care about the results of the evaluation. Box 6.1 illustrates some of the different ways that political pressures can influence an evaluation.

Table 6.1   Some of the Ways That Political Influences Affect Evaluations

	Examples
During evaluation design	
The criteria for selecting evaluators	Evaluators may be selected • For their impartiality or their professional expertise • For their sympathy toward the program • For their known criticisms of the program (in cases where the client wishes to use the evaluation to curtail the program) • For the ease with which they can be controlled • Because of their citizenship in the country or state of the program's funding agency
The choice of evaluation design and data collection methods	The decision to use either a quantitative or qualitative approach or to collect data that can be put into a certain kind of analytical model (e.g., collecting student achievement or econometric data on an education program) can predetermine what the evaluation will and will not address.
Example of a specific design choice: Whether to use control groups (i.e., quasi-experimental design)	Control groups may be excluded for political or ethical rather than methodological reasons such as • To avoid creating expectations of compensation • To avoid denial of needed benefits to parts of a community • To avoid pressures to expand the project to the control areas • To avoid covering politically sensitive or volatile groups On the other hand, evaluators may insist on including control groups in the evaluation design to give an impression of rigor even when they contribute little to addressing evaluation questions.
The choice of indicators and instruments	The decision to only use quantitative indicators can lead (intentionally or otherwise) to certain kinds of findings and exclude the analysis of other, potentially sensitive topics. For example, issues of domestic violence or sexual harassment on public transport will probably not be mentioned if only structured questionnaires are used.
The choice of stakeholders to involve or consult	The design of the evaluation and the issues addressed may be quite different if only government officials are consulted, compared with an evaluation of the same program in which community organizations, male and female household heads, and NGOs are consulted. The evaluator may be formally or informally discouraged from collecting data from certain sensitive groups—for example, by limiting the available time or budget, a subtle way to exclude difficult-to-reach groups.
Professional orientation of the evaluators	The choice of, for example, economists, sociologists, political scientists, or anthropologists to conduct an evaluation will have a major impact on design and outcomes.

Examples

During evaluation design

The selection of internal or external evaluation	Evaluations conducted internally by project or agency staff have a different kind of political dynamic and are subject to different political pressures compared with evaluations conducted by external consultants, generally believed to be more independent.
	Outside the United States, the use of national versus international evaluators also changes the dynamic of the evaluation. For example, although national evaluators are likely to be more familiar with the history and context of the program, they may be less willing to be critical of programs administered by their regular clients.
Allocations of budget and time	While budget and time constraints are beyond the total control of some clients, others may try to limit time and resources to discourage addressing certain issues or to preclude thorough, critical analysis.

During implementation

The changing role of the evaluator	The evaluator may have to negotiate between the roles of guide, publicist, advocate, confidante, hanging judge, and critical friend.
The selection of audiences for progress reports and initial findings	A subtle way for a client to avoid criticism is to exclude potential critics from the distribution list for progress reports. Distribution to managers only, excluding program staff, or to engineers and architects, excluding social workers and extension agents, will shape the nature of findings and the kinds of feedback to which the evaluation is exposed.
Evolving social dynamics	Often, at the start of the evaluation, relations are cordial, but they can quickly sour when negative findings begin to emerge or the evaluator does not follow the client's advice on how to conduct the evaluation (e.g., from whom to collect data).

Dissemination and use

Selection of reviewers	If only people with a stake in the continuation of the project are asked to review the evaluation, the feedback is likely to be more positive than if known critics are involved. Short deadlines, innocent or not, may leave insufficient time for some groups to make any significant comments or to include their perspectives, introducing a systematic bias against these groups.
Choice of language	In developing countries, few evaluation reports are translated into local languages, excluding significant stakeholders. Budget is usually given as the reason, suggesting that informing stakeholders is not what the client considers valuable and needed. Language is also an issue in the United States, Canada, and Europe where many evaluations concern immigrant populations.
Report distribution	Often, an effective way to avoid criticism is to not share the report with critics. Public interest may be at stake, as when clients have a clear and narrow view of how the evaluation results should be disseminated or used and will not consider other possible uses.

Box 6.1   Political Influences Can Affect Evaluations in Many Ways

The following are a sampling of the many ways that political factors can affect an evaluation:

- Many evaluators are reluctant to "bite the hand that feeds them," reluctant to express strong criticisms of clients from whom they hope to receive future contracts.
- In developing countries, major irrigation, power, and urban development programs often involve the forced resettlement of large numbers of people. Most families with clear land or property titles receive compensation, but many other families who do not have clear title are not eligible for compensation. Consequently, clients may be reluctant for evaluators to interview these people or to select them for control groups because of their basis for complaint or because of raising expectations of compensation. In developing countries, many agriculture, rural roads, or rural development projects include areas inhabited by indigenous peoples. Project managers are sometimes reluctant to allow an evaluation to address the indigenous communities because "we will never get the project started if we have to set up special culturally sensitive consultative mechanisms."
- More than one evaluation containing critical assessments of government policies or programs has somehow not got published or released to the public until a local or national election has taken place.

Societal politics have proved critical at times in the history of evaluation. The modern period in evaluation is often dated to the U.S. response to the U.S.S.R.'s successful launch of the first spacecraft, Sputnik I, in 1957, when the Kennedy administration funded new educational programs and evaluations to determine which programs worked best. The Great Society programs of the 1960s and 1970s (e.g., Head Start, urban housing programs) also gave an impetus to program evaluation in the United States. Evaluations were undertaken to study which attempts to improve education and to eradicate poverty merited government funding. During the Reagan presidency, 1981 to 1989, evaluation findings were cited as rationales to cut and close social programs (Stake 1986). During the first term of George W. Bush, 2001 to 2005, the U.S. Department of Education proposed to prefer certain quantitative evaluation designs over all other quantitative and qualitative approaches to program evaluation in determining which programs to fund (U.S. Department of Education 2003).

In Europe, funding from the European Union in support of economic and social development programs for the economically less developed regions of Europe has resulted in similar recent growth in the demand for systematic evaluation, although not so far on the scale found in the United States. While the early European evaluations were mainly financial and quantitative, the past decade has seen an increasing emphasis on participatory evaluation and the involvement of a broad range of stakeholders. This trend mirrors the evolution of evaluation approaches in the United States and, more recently, in developing countries, where national and multilateral funding agencies seek assessments of the effectiveness of their development assistance activities. Here, too, a shift toward human development and poverty reduction, together with strong pressures from nongovernmental organizations (**NGOs**), has resulted in an increasing use of participatory and qualitative evaluation approaches.

Clearly, then, national, regional, and international policy can either catalyze or constrain evaluation. When a program draws from public funds, all members of society are stakeholders in its evaluation. Some people are directly affected and constitute right-to-know or need-to-know audiences, while others are distant stakeholders. In some cases, public reporting is appropriate, even over the objections of the clients who are financing the program and the evaluation. For example, in 1990 evaluators publicly reported that the standards-setting procedures for the National Assessment of Educational Progress (NAEP) were flawed despite strong governmental efforts to suppress and contradict this finding, which was upheld in subsequent evaluations (Mabry et al. 2000). This instance illustrates how a national government can act to obstruct, discontinue, or discredit an evaluation.

Stakeholder Politics

Diverse stakeholder values ensure that politics writ small always plays a role in evaluation. In urging propriety, the *Program Evaluation Standards* assert that "Evaluations should be designed to assist organizations to address and effectively serve the needs of the full range of targeted participants" (Joint Committee 1994). But it is not easy to identify the multiplicity of stakeholder values and much more difficult to prioritize their interests appropriately.

Some stakeholders wield more influence than others and are in a stronger position to affect an evaluation's focus, criteria, and methods and to ease or obstruct access to data. Other stakeholders may be harder to identify, harder to contact, and harder to understand for cultural or other reasons, and their interests may be harder to incorporate in the political swirls of an evaluation. Although developing consensus among stakeholders is often urged on evaluators—for example, during the process of determining evaluation focus and criteria for judging program quality—dissension among diverse stakeholder groups may be more natural and more common. These differences are often intractable and appropriate for representation in the design and report, although it may be neither feasible nor appropriate for the evaluator to try to resolve them.

Program managers are generally an evaluator's main contacts. Clients are almost always what Patton (1997) calls "primary users." These stakeholders make program decisions, formalize procedures, and allocate resources. To promote use of evaluation for program

---

Box 6.2 Institutionalizing Stakeholder Consultations in U.S. Public Transportation Programs

When public transportation programs (e.g., road construction, a new subway station) are being planned, many states require that all affected groups be identified and that public hearings be held in which these groups are invited to express their views. While agreeing with the principle of democratic participation, some agencies feel that public hearings may not be the most equitable way to obtain stakeholder feedback; it is relatively easy for a small, well-organized group to manipulate the public meetings to their advantage.

improvement, some approaches explicitly prioritize the provision of data and findings to assist these stakeholders with programmatic decision making (e.g., Stufflebeam 1987). Although other approaches to evaluation explicitly prioritize either a broader spectrum of stakeholders or the historically underserved, the interests of managers, who are often concerned with financial bottom lines and outcome statistics, often dominate. Their values are not easily melded with the values of beneficiaries who are more likely to be concerned with the availability and quality of the medical, social, or educational services to which they are (or feel) entitled. In actuality, because evaluation clients are often managers or directors, their interests often supersede those of other stakeholders.

Such *managerial bias* is compounded by **clientism,** evaluators' desires to please their clients and to secure future contracts (Scriven 1991). It has been suggested that, as more women become evaluators, their inclination toward relational ethics may promote a *positive bias* toward increasing a broader range of stakeholders in evaluations compared with the male inclination toward utilitarian ethics. The manner in which evaluators should respond to clients and other stakeholders is not a settled issue but, rather, contributes to yet another type of evaluation politics—professional politics.

Professional Politics

Just as there is a variety of approaches to inquiry in general, there is a variety of approaches to evaluation as a specialized form of inquiry (e.g., Madaus, Scriven, and Stufflebeam 1987; Stufflebeam 2001a). Individual evaluators have not only developed approaches that resonate with their personal views as to what constitutes competent, appropriate practice but have also publicly argued for their own approaches and against the approaches of others (e.g., Scriven 1998; Stufflebeam 1994; Stufflebeam et al. 2001). These arguments indicate the presence of diverse professional values in the field of evaluation, as in society, and professional politics among evaluators based on the pursuit of values.

Evaluators who continue their work beyond delivery of findings to assist with **utilization** of results (Patton 1997) or the empowerment of stakeholders (Fetterman 1996), for example, have been described by some authors as *consultants* rather than *evaluators* for exceeding the scope and purpose of evaluation (Scriven 1998). Ideologues pressing for evaluation in the service of social justice (House 1993) or for evaluation focused on improving working relationships within programs (Greene 1997) can find themselves at odds with colleagues who urge rational, dispassionate efforts (Chelimsky 1997; Scriven 1997). At times, the differing values that underlie differing evaluation approaches have created arenas of heated professional politics.

Divergent views about professional practice have obstructed sporadic initiatives in the United States to ensure competence through accreditation or licensing. After consideration, many evaluators have realized that trying to resolve some of the unresolved and probably irresolvable differences of approach and philosophy within an evaluation code of practice would further politicize evaluation.

On a smaller scale, within an evaluation team, as within the professional field, different opinions may arise when questions such as these must be collectively considered:

- We were contracted to evaluate the cost-effectiveness of the program's service delivery, but should we also consider the quality of the services?

- Should we check to see why Native Americans are underrepresented among the program's beneficiaries even though we were not asked to do so?
- Should we follow up our suspicion that the agency funding the evaluation is merely a front for a corporation manipulating its regulatory agency at the expense of the public?
- Should we release our findings to the media?

Different evaluators, even those who have chosen to work together on a project, may naturally take different stances regarding their public and ethical responsibilities. In vigorous exercise of their differing opinions regarding professional responsibilities, an evaluation can become subject to acrimonious team politics.

Individual Advocacy

Evaluators charged with making determinations of program merit or quality, have, like everyone else, their own personal values. However, for many evaluators, it may be more comfortable to think of the work of evaluation not as an imposition of the evaluator's values but, rather, as a data-based judgment about program merit, shortcoming, effectiveness, efficiency, and goal achievement. That individual values are influential in evaluation has been recognized in the *Guiding Principles for Evaluators* (AEA 1995, 2004).

Even what the evaluator regards as data is influenced by perspective and values. This was demonstrated in a brief volume in which several prominent evaluators each authored a chapter reporting their various methods and wildly different findings for the same program (Brandt 1981). Best, in his discussion of how politicians, the media, and advocates for particular causes misunderstand or deliberately distort statistics, points out that "all statistics are products of social activity, the process sociologists call social construction" (Best 2004, p. xiii), adding this:

> We usually envision statistics as a branch of mathematics, a view reinforced by high school and college statistics courses, which begin by introducing probability theory as a foundation for statistical thinking, a foundation on which is assembled a structure of increasingly sophisticated statistical measures.

Many people have similar faith in the findings of what are believed to be rigorous, scientific evaluations. Many evaluation users fail to appreciate how much personal judgment, which always involves bias, inevitably goes into the formulation of evaluation questions and design. Whether or not evaluators explicitly advocate for their own values in their professional endeavors, their values—those they recognize and those they do not—inevitably affect what they see and interpret. All these intrusions might be considered advocacies of a sort, sometimes subtle and unrecognized, other times clear; sometimes unintentional and other times deliberate and proactive.

Is advocacy an improper intrusion of the evaluator's individual values? For those who seek to improve social conditions through evaluation, the answer to this question may be an unequivocal "yes." Among those who object to advocacy, the answer may depend on contingencies such as who or what is threatened, the magnitude of the threat, and the consequences if the evaluator failed to speak up. Still others might say the evaluator should argue for the data, which might lead to entering the fray.

Codes of Conduct

Codes of professional conduct, such as the *Program Evaluation Standards* (Joint Committee 1994) and the AEA *Guiding Principles for Evaluators* (AEA 1995, 2004), can be helpful in clarifying potential responses to political situations or moves. They may also be helpful in supporting those choices when they are presented to clients and stakeholders. If the political constraints on an evaluation overwhelm the possibility of competent practice, adherence to the *Standards* and *Principles* may result in refusing or discontinuing the work.

However, it is also possible that the *Standards* and *Principles* may not clarify the appropriate course of action or that they may complicate decisions. It may not be clear, for example, how to ensure the following:

- That an evaluation is "conducted to respect and protect the rights and welfare of human subjects," as Standard P3 prescribes (Joint Committee 1994:93)
- That the evaluation supports their "security, dignity, and self-worth," as Principle D directs (Joint Committee 1994:24)
- And simultaneously to "ensure that the full set of evaluation findings along with pertinent limitations are made accessible to the persons affected by the evaluation and any others with expressed legal rights," as Standard P6 requires (Joint Committee 1994:109)

It may be impossible to provide full reporting and full protection simultaneously. The codes of evaluation conduct do not explain how to prioritize directives; all are clearly important.

Codes of conduct also cannot anticipate the many types of difficulties evaluators face. At best, they must be interpreted and adapted for specific situations, where there may be many conflicting values. Application of professional standards is a matter of judgment, which is fallible (Mabry 1999; see also Newman and Brown 1996). The role of individual judgment and personal values is explicitly recognized in the *Guiding Principles:*

> [E]valuators must use their own values and knowledge of the setting to determine the appropriate response. Whenever a course of action is unclear, evaluators should solicit the advice of fellow evaluators about how to resolve the problem before deciding how to proceed (AEA 2001:21).

Establishing advisory panels (if budgets allow) and seeking the advice of colleagues may help evaluators find paths through political quagmires. Still, because perfect and win-win decisions are often elusive, the paths available may not be entirely comfortable.

Political Issues at the Outset of an Evaluation

Just as programs reflect values advanced through policy and politics, program evaluations are often commissioned with political motives. These motives may or may not be clear to an evaluator at the outset. Even if political intent is clear, how best to respond may not be. Table 6.1 illustrates some of the many ways that the political context can affect how an evaluation is designed, implemented, disseminated, and used.

Hidden Agendas and Pseudoevaluation

A client, sure that the findings of an evaluation of his or her program will be strongly positive, may commission an evaluation in hopes that it will serve a public relations function. She or he may mount strong opposition to any other result and may insist that the evaluation look only at the aspects of the program that are likely to be judged positive. When evaluators capitulate to these demands, they may be said to conduct **pseudoevaluations** (Scriven 1991; Stufflebeam 2001a). Other political agendas, often hidden, can be even more problematic. When elections alter the composition of government and the enforcement of policies, evaluations may be commissioned with the idea that data-based judgments of the inadequacies of previous initiatives may fuel their termination or the ouster of lingering personnel committed to different social ideologies. Evaluations may also be used as delaying tactics to stall changes in policy, to reallocate funding, to downsize personnel, or for many other politically charged motives.

Clients may be influenced by political intentions when they select evaluators. Evaluators may be selected because their reputation for uncompromising honesty ensures the credibility and acceptance of findings, because they have taken ideological stances in agreement with the client, or because the client expects they can be persuaded. These manipulations, too, may be so understated as to go unnoticed initially in friendly negotiations, generous travel allowances, and enthusiastic statements about the importance of getting the word out.

Sometimes political constraints can be avoided by being selective about the work an evaluator agrees to perform or diminished through negotiation. For example, where there is a suggestion of conflict of interest because of a preexisting relationship, an evaluation contract can be refused. In developing a contract, an evaluator might specify the client's obligation to ensure access to crucial or sensitive data as a condition of performance. In discussions or in the response to a sample of previous reports, an evaluator might attempt to judge the client's openness to methodological comprehensiveness and findings, both positive and negative. Questions about previous evaluations of the program and management's reaction, about how the program is responding to the legal and regulatory requirements to which it may be subject, about the existence of internal and external conflicts, about personnel cohesiveness or divisiveness, and about management style and its impact may be revealing and helpful.

Unfortunately, the obvious benefits of avoiding difficulty by refusing work with heated political implications or by negotiating them away is not matched by opportunity to do so. Political entrenchments or obstacles may not be initially clear, although later pressure may make them all too obvious—threats to cancel the contract or to deny future work, or bringing in other analysts likely to reach contrary conclusions and to discredit the work. Learning enough in advance of contractual agreements to identify difficulties and to estimate the degree to which they might obstruct the work may require background research tantamount to conducting the evaluation—or luck!

In international evaluations, understanding is often further complicated by subcontracting that leaves the evaluator hierarchically as well as geographically remote from clients and program managers. There may even be a series of subcontracts—for example, an evaluation managed by the country office of an international aid agency on the other side of the world may be working with a government agency to evaluate a program being implemented by another international aid agency. Even greater complications arise when the evaluation is cofinanced by two or more agencies, each with its own agenda. When a rapid evaluation is being conducted in which the evaluator is on site for only a few weeks, she or he may never meet some of the key stakeholders, and the evaluation may be almost completed before some of the hidden agendas of the key agencies start to be revealed.

In the design phase, evaluation clients have a strong voice in determining the focus of the evaluation, the program aspects to be scrutinized, and even the methods to be used. Their efforts may represent diligence in ensuring that they obtain the information they need or crass self-protection. Sometimes their narrow focus constrains the comprehensiveness of an evaluation as, for example, when an agency such as the World Bank requires an econometric rather than an educational emphasis in evaluations of schooling or training in developing countries. Professional ethics suggest that where clients adamantly stipulate inappropriate or improperly constrained designs and methods, contracts should be refused.

Differences among Stakeholders

Preexisting differences among stakeholders can immerse evaluations in political turmoil. Policymakers, managers, or implementation personnel may be at odds about the value of or approach to implementing of a program, rendering some of them naturally opposed to an evaluation. Affected communities or members of communities may hold strongly divergent opinions about a program, its execution, its motives, its leaders, and its evaluation. Evaluation opponents may be able to preempt an evaluation or obstruct access to data, acceptance of evaluation results, or continuation of an evaluation contract.

Where time and budgets permit, reconnoitering in advance to try to identify sources of support and opposition may be useful. However, in the real world, time and budgets often do not make this practical, at least not as thoroughly as may be needed.

Political Issues during the Conduct of an Evaluation

Evaluations can make explicit a variety of underlying assumptions and perspectives held by a variety of stakeholders. The increased visibility of potentially divisive issues can raise pressure on evaluators and the stakes associated with evaluation findings.

Shifting Roles: The Evaluator as Guide, Publicist, Friend, Critic

The function of the evaluator, from the perspective of clients and other stakeholders, often tends to shift and overlap—guide, publicist, critical friend, hanging judge. Clients who initially see evaluators as partners helping them identify areas for potential improvement may feel stung when midcourse formative reporting is shared, as may be required, with funding agencies. Cooperation may decline as project managers and personnel realize that evaluators might endanger their programs.

Data Access

Ensuring access to data by maintaining rapport and good working relationships can be challenging. Observers may be suspected as management spies and interviewers as

---

Box 6.3   Making Sure Foreign Consultants See What Agencies Want Them to See

---

Many international funding agencies are concerned to ensure that women are actively involved in project planning, and their participation may be a condition for continued funding. When given advanced warning, most agencies are able to arrange for a sufficient number of women to attend the meeting during the funding agency visit—even if none of them participate in the discussion.

Robert Chambers (1983) in his discussion of "Rural Development Tourism" describes many examples of how foreign staff going on rapid visits to the projects they are funding always seem to end up in the model project where everything is going well and everyone is very happy with the project.

---

interrogators, complicit or unwitting pawns in power plays orchestrated by clients. Maintaining professional neutrality visible to all parties is advisable but not always easy, not always possible, not always ethical. Some grievances are real and should be strongly investigated and reported. In some instances, evaluators may feel that action as well as reporting is required to discharge their public responsibilities fully or appropriately. While the mere presence of evaluators may intensify the political swirl, evaluators' proactive engagement in it will certainly raise the stakes.

Because evaluation can threaten programs and personnel, some people who are important data sources may take protective measures by limiting or denying access to information. Documents and records can be delivered slowly, partially, illegibly, or not at all. Observable events can be staged (see Box 6.3) or unannounced until after they have happened. Interviewees can be less than forthcoming. Survey instruments can be ignored or their distribution and collection by program personnel can be faulty.

Limited access sometimes results from cultural barriers rather than obstructionism. For example, in paternalistic societies, where outside visitors are expected to meet only with male community leaders and male household heads, determining whether women or girls are benefiting from initiatives undertaken in their behalf can be difficult. Where the evaluator does not share the language, dialect, or street vernacular of interviewees, dependence on a translator or the extrapolation of meanings can be problematic. For these and for ethical reasons, there have been increasing calls for cultural competence in evaluation in recent years.

Political Issues in Evaluation Reporting and Use

Most—perhaps all—competent evaluations end with mixed results to report because programs, like all human endeavors, are imperfect. Consensus is often needed to implement results and recommendations, but evaluations sometimes reveal discord more clearly than stakeholders previously realized, and the revelation may serve to entrench disagreement.

Evaluation Reporting: Clientism and Positive Bias

The professional evaluation community has often expressed concern that evaluators may be tempted to provide overly positive findings to avoid conflict with clients and ensure future work. The temptations toward clientism and positive bias may fall heavily on private evaluation firms and independent consultants, whose livelihoods and that of their staff associates may depend on continuing and future contracts, and on internal evaluators, whose jobs may be threatened by their immediate superiors. Developing a reputation for unswerving honesty and competence as a long-term professional goal, which may ultimately ensure future work, may be threatened by the need to maintain short-term relationships with current clients and stakeholders.

Maintaining the interests of stakeholders groups may be needed to preserve the opportunity to conduct good evaluation. Timely provisions of data to support program decisions through focused discussions, for example, can help to build confidence in the work and its usefulness. Appropriate assistance, consistent care regarding confidentiality, and professional demeanor can also help. Perhaps most important are the accuracy and comprehensiveness of data and the validity of findings. Where evaluators have earned reputations for competence and honesty under pressure, stakeholders may feel confident about an evaluation and the implementation of its results (see Chelimsky 1994).

Evaluation Use: Neglect and Suppression, Distortion and Misuse, Discrediting

The possibilities for disagreement related to evaluation results and their dissemination are limitless. Members of an evaluation team may disagree about findings and recommendations—or even whether they should make recommendations—and either find consensus or dissociate themselves from the evaluation. Meta-evaluators may disagree with evaluators. Stakeholders, faced with a combination of positive and negative findings, may hold quite different ideas regarding what constitutes an appropriate response to an evaluation report. Box 6.4 describes the manipulation of the findings from an international commission on alleged atrocities in the Belgian Congo in the early 20th century to illustrate that the art of putting a positive "spin" on evaluation findings is not new.

Box 6.4   Spinning the Findings: An Old Artform

Due to increasing concerns about the alleged atrocities in the Belgian Congo in the late 19th and early 20th centuries, King Leopold of Belgium found himself forced to create an independent commission to assess his policies in the Congo. The commission produced a long and very damning report on Belgian policies. However, before the report was issued, Leopold was able to arrange for a "summary" report exonerating the King's policies to be circulated, and for the full report to vanish quietly into the archives. The "summary" was largely accepted by the public, and Leopold continued to receive awards as a protector of Africans from the Arab slave traders.

SOURCE: Hochschild (1998).

Powerful stakeholders are not helpless. In the field of evaluation, enduring issues across time include failure to utilize evaluation results and, more ominously, misuse of evaluation results. Clients can and do neglect evaluation reports, relegating them shelf space among unused volumes. Clients can and do suppress distribution by only circulating to carefully selected readers, by circulating only abbreviated and softened summaries, by taking responsibility for presenting reports to funding agencies and then acting on that responsibility in manipulative ways. Clients can and do give oral presentations and even testimony that distorts evaluation findings. Clients can and do cite evaluation reports to engage in follow-up activities not suggested and even contraindicated by evaluation reports. Clients can and do attempt to discredit evaluations and evaluators who threaten their programs and prestige. When clients choose to employ this formidable arsenal, evaluators often find themselves blindsided and their response options weaker than the clients' offensives.

The *Program Evaluation Standards* require that "the full set of evaluation findings along with pertinent limitations are made accessible to the persons affected by the evaluation and any others with expressed legal rights to receive the results" (Joint Committee 1994:109). Doing so may pit evaluators and their professional standards against clients and their efforts to protect themselves and their programs. If the evaluators perceive that their responsibility also requires that they argue for the data or attempt to set the record straight, they may find themselves engaged in advocacy, labeled political instigators, and in other ways embroiled in politics they did not seek.

In a series of programs and evaluations, evaluators may detect a larger agenda. If this agenda opposes prevailing social values or their own values, evaluators may face the decision of whether or not to speak out. For example, if they see that evaluation is being used to undermine social programs or to force unfamiliar Western values and cultural institutions on poor countries, evaluators may consider it ethically and professionally obligatory to notify the media and the public. In these circumstances, evaluators may find themselves in uncomfortable positions on grand policy stages.

RealWorld Strategies for Addressing Political Constraints

Addressing Political Constraints during the Evaluation Design

Understanding the Political Environment

The many dimensions of political positions—economic, institutional, environmental, and sociocultural—influence the way that politically concerned groups will view a project and its evaluation. Evaluation may create pressure for job creation, welfare support, alternative program delivery, protection against deforestation and water contamination, and protection of programs by (or from) government. Working to understand stakeholder concerns may help an evaluator identify ways to address the pressures from them on the evaluation.

Conducting a Stakeholder Analysis

As a part of scoping the evaluation (see Chapter 2), a stakeholder analysis should be conducted to identify the priorities, concerns, and constraints of different stakeholders. In identifying and seeking solutions to potential political constraints, stakeholders might be asked the following questions:

- Is there anything in the context of the program that helps or hinders it?
- Is there anything that helps or hinders the access of different stakeholders to program benefits?
- Which of these factors do they consider particularly critical?
- What are the key problems and challenges facing the project?
- What are the critical questions the evaluation should address? Are there any politically sensitive issues that might be difficult to address in the evaluation? Are there any questions that it would be better not to include in the evaluation at this point?
- How should the evaluation be designed and conducted, and what data collection and analysis methods should be used?
- Is there anyone who may try to bias or manipulate the evaluation or insist on approaches that are not appropriate?

Participatory Planning and Consultation

As the concerns of stakeholders are discussed and potential areas of disagreement and conflict identified, a meeting with all stakeholders may help create shared investment in the evaluation and establish common ground. A purpose of such a discussion is to distinguish between various information requirements and actual disagreements as to how the evaluation should be conducted and what it should and should not address.

Addressing Political Constraints during the Implementation of the Evaluation

Ensuring Access to Information during the Implementation of the Evaluation

Access to information during the implementation of the evaluation is sometimes affected by cultural barriers as much as by deliberate intention to withhold information. In many countries, officials assume that visitors wish to meet only with "important" people and find it difficult to understand desires to see the poorer sections of the community or to meet with poor or low-status people. Often, an explanation ahead of time can broaden the range of meetings, although it is unlikely that meetings with government critics or with groups not benefiting from projects will be easily forthcoming. Meetings can often be more easily arranged by local intermediaries on whom the external evaluator may often need to rely for making contact with some difficult-to-reach groups.

Providing Feedback to Allay Suspicion and Demonstrate the Value of the Evaluation

Keeping stakeholders informed of the progress can sometimes reduce opposition to an evaluation, particularly if it can be shown that the evaluation is less negative than had been feared or that useful information is being produced. Feedback can also demonstrate the practical utility of either the quantitative or qualitative methods about which stakeholders may have had reservations.

Politicians and managers are often concerned that community reactions will be negative. Showing that attitudes are mixed and that residents often have constructive suggestions to make can help gain at least cautious support for the evaluation. In some cases, arranging meetings for politicians with community residents can have a positive effect.

Addressing Political Constraints in the Presentation and Use of the Evaluation Findings

As indicated earlier in this chapter, evaluators encounter clients who do not intend to publish or use findings. This presents a not uncommon dilemma as to whether and when it is appropriate for the evaluator to take actions to ensure the evaluation findings are made available to the public or to right-to-know stakeholder groups. Conflicts between the evaluator's professional responsibilities to the client, which would normally preclude independent actions to disseminate the findings, and the evaluator's values and commitments to broader social concerns, are not easily decided.

One of the most effective ways to increase the likelihood that evaluation findings are used is to ensure that the findings are of direct practical utility to the different stakeholders. Some of the factors affecting utilization include the following:

- Timing of the evaluation
- Recognizing that the evaluation is only one of several sources of information and influence on decision makers and ensuring that the evaluation complements these other sources.
- Building an ongoing relationship with key stakeholders, listening carefully to their needs, understanding their perception of the political context, and keeping them informed of the progress of the evaluation.

Summary

- In evaluation, values and politics are inescapable, and no evaluation can ever be value free and completely objective. Decisions as to what to study, which methods to prefer, and whose criteria to use in determining program success all involve human judgment.

- A recent example of political influences on evaluation and the role of values is the debate over the use of **evidence-based evaluation** and the recommendation that randomized experiments and other quantitative approaches should be the preferred evaluation methodologies.

- The *Program Evaluation Standards* (Joint Committee 1994) and other codes of conduct for evaluators provide guidance on issues such as the identification of stakeholders and their values, the appropriate prioritization of their interests in the evaluation, and balancing the "right to know" with client concerns to restrict access to sensitive ongoing evaluations and to the findings and recommendations.

- A number of political issues can arise at the outset of an evaluation. These include efforts to select an evaluator favorable to the client's perspective on the project, ensuring that potentially sensitive issues such as access to data or dissemination of findings are discussed and spelled out in the **terms of reference**, and understanding the political context within which the evaluation will be conducted.

- Some of the issues that may arise during the conduct of the evaluation include (a) shifting roles of the evaluator (particularly the shift from being a friend to becoming a critic), (b) access to data (both because of political sensitivities but also because of the time and cost required to produce the data), (c) difficulties of access to certain communities or groups, and (d) in some instances, the language and communication barriers of working with other cultures.

- During the reporting and use phase, issues include (a) pressures or temptations to produce overly positive findings, (b) selective use and citation of findings by clients and other stakeholders, and (c) the decision on who has access to the reports and is asked to comment on the findings.

- The chapter concludes with recommendations on how to address political issues at the different stages of the evaluation.

Further Reading

American Evaluation Association. 1995. "Guiding Principles for Evaluators." Pp. 19–26 in *Guiding Principles for Evaluators*, edited by W. R. Shadish, D. L. Newman, M. A. Scheirer, and C. Wye. New Directions for Program Evaluation, No. 66. San Francisco: Jossey-Bass.

An example of a widely used set of evaluation standards.

American Evaluation Association. 2003. "Response to U.S. Department of Education notice of proposed priority, 'Scientifically Based Evaluation Methods.'" *Federal Register*, November 4, RIN 1890-ZA00.

A recent example of a very heated debate on the appropriateness of the evaluation standards being proposed by the Department of Education. The debate reflects concerns about both the methodological and political dimensions of the standards.

American Journal of Evaluation.

The section on Ethical Challenges that appears in most issues of the journal since at least 1999 discusses a wide range of ethical issues and dilemmas relevant to the present chapter.

Best, J. 2001. *Damned Lies and Statistics: Untangling Numbers from the Media, Politicians and Activists.* Los Angeles: University of California Press.

Best, J. 2004. *More Damned Lies and Statistics: How Numbers Confuse Public Issues.* Los Angeles: University of California Press.

Two nontechnical books showing the many political influences on how evaluation and other forms of research are commissioned, conducted, and used.

Chelimsky, E. and W. R. Shadish, eds. 1997. *Evaluation for the 21st Century: A Handbook.* Thousand Oaks, CA: Sage.

Different chapters of this handbook provide a wide range of perspectives on the political context of evaluation. See particularly Chapter 3, "The Political Environment of Evaluation and What It Means for the Development of the Field" by Eleanor Chelimsky, Chapter 16 ("Lessons from Immigration Policy" by John Niewenhuysen), Chapter 32 ("Advocacy in Evaluation" by Robert Stake), and Chapter 33 ("Truth and Objectivity in Evaluation" by Michael Scriven).

Joint Committee on Standards for Educational Evaluation. 1994. *The Program Evaluation Standards: How to Assess Evaluations of Educational Programs.* 2d ed. Thousand Oaks, CA: Sage.

Probably the most widely used evaluation standards. Many developing countries have adopted or adapted these standards.

Patton, M. Q. 1997. *Utilization-Focused Evaluation.* 3d ed. Thousand Oaks, CA: Sage.

A comprehensive discussion of many of the issues covered in this chapter.

Rossi, P., M. Lipsey, and H. Freeman. 2004. *Evaluation: A Systematic Approach.* 7th ed. Thousand Oaks, CA: Sage.

See particularly the discussion in Chapter 2, "Tailoring Evaluations," including the discussion of evaluator-stakeholder relationships, and Chapter 12, "The Social Context of Evaluation."

Vaughan, R. J. and T. F. Buss. 1998. *Communicating Social Science Research to Policymakers.* Applied Social Research Methods Series, No. 48. Thousand Oaks, CA: Sage.

The authors discuss the reality of the policy-making process and show the many different ways that evaluation studies and findings fit into this process.

CHAPTER 7

Strengthening the Evaluation Design and the Validity of the Conclusions

S tep 6 of the RealWorld Evaluation (**RWE)** approach identifies threats to the validity of evaluation conclusions and proposes strategies for correcting the threats once they have been identified. The concepts of validity as used in quantitative (**QUANT**) and qualitative (**QUAL**) evaluation traditions are compared, and factors affecting validity are discussed. We then discuss ways to assess threats to the validity of QUANT evaluation **designs** and strategies for correcting the threats once they have been identified. Recommendations are offered on how to strengthen the design of QUANT evaluations so as to reduce potential threats to validity. The subsequent sections cover the same ground for QUAL evaluation designs. The final section identifies points in the evaluation cycle when corrective measures can be taken.

Appendixes 1, 2, and 3 at the end of the text present a checklist for identifying threats to validity of QUANT, QUAL, and **mixed-methods** designs; a worksheet for assessing threats to validity of an evaluation; and a completed example of how to use the worksheet.

Validity in Evaluation

In common terms, *validity* has a meaning roughly similar to *accuracy.* Evaluation data may be described as *valid* if actual conditions are accurately represented. For example, survey or interview data recording that teachers are satisfied with a new curriculum but parents are not could be described as valid only if a majority of teachers are, in fact, satisfied with a new curriculum and a majority of parents are not. Data that recorded that borrowers from a **microcredit program** established small businesses lasting more than two years would be less than entirely valid if, in fact, only the better-off borrowers who were able to take out larger loans established small business that lasted more than two years. In QUANT methodology, the accuracy of the

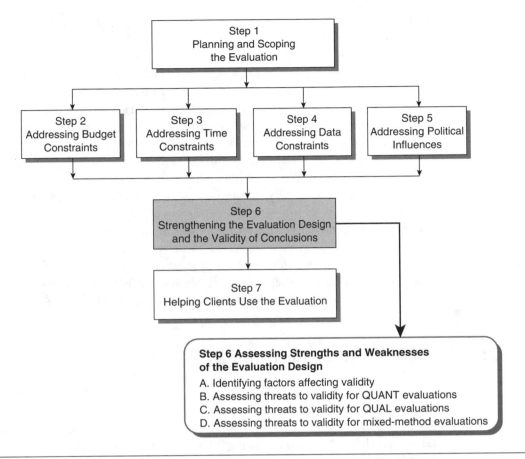

Figure 7.1   Step 6: Strengthening the Evaluation Design and the Validity of Conclusions

data is referred to as **internal validity** (Shadish, Cook, and Campbell 2002) and, in QUAL methodology, as *descriptive validity* (Maxwell 1992) or **credibility** (Lincoln and Guba 1985).

Findings as well as data need to be valid. Findings are judgments, interpretations, and inferences of program quality. To be valid, findings need to be adequately and appropriately based on valid and comprehensive data. Findings based on hopelessly limited, inaccurate, or falsified data are certain to be *invalid*. Invalid data obstruct the validity of the findings based on the data.

Invalid findings may also result from failure to understand the meaning of the data. For example, data from a criminal justice program indicated that recidivism rates (i.e., repeated offenses by convicted criminals) were identical for serious offenders sentenced to ten years in prison and for those sentenced to ten days in the local jail. But it would have been erroneous to infer that the enormous public expense of prison could be dramatically reduced by incarcerating serious offenders for 10 days rather than 10 years. What the data do not show is whether offenders "went straight" after 10 days because of the threat that, if they were convicted a second time, they would probably be sentenced to 10 years. If an evaluator had recommended the establishment of a 10-day jail time program for these offenders, failing to attribute its success to the potent implications of longer sentencing, public safety might well have been undermined.

The sensitivity of the methods to define and measure actual program **outcomes** is crucial for ensuring the validity of findings. For example, in the 1980s, in the United States, an evaluation of a multistate program to meld school and social services for at-risk urban youth reported the program had no substantial **impact**, a finding that led to funding cuts for many federally supported social programs. This occurred despite a **meta-evaluation** (evaluation of the technical quality and adequacy of the evaluation design) indicating that the data were collected at too broad a level to detect impacts that were well-known to program personnel and beneficiaries—a failure of the evaluation rather than of the program.

Invalid findings do occur. Every evaluator is capable of design flaws, off-target data collection, failures to restrain subjective tendencies, and errors of judgment. All evaluators need to work hard to ensure that their designs are well focused, methodologically strong, and capable of generating accurate data from which valid findings may be constructed. In this chapter, we will consider how evaluators may strengthen their designs to ensure the validity, **trustworthiness** (Lincoln and Guba 1985), or adequacy of their data and of the findings based on the data—in QUAL terms, the *interpretive validity* or *evaluative validity* (Maxwell 1992).

Factors Affecting Adequacy and Validity

In evaluation, validity and feasibility often demand different courses of action. For validity, the most skillful team operating with unlimited time, budget, and access to data is desirable. Rarely, if ever, are such perfect conditions available. Budget is limited; time is limited; personnel are limited; not all the data needed may be available or, if available, easily accessed. For feasibility, evaluators must consider what can be competently done within such limitations. To avoid having to refuse potential clients, evaluators have sometimes overestimated whether good evaluations could be accomplished. Sometimes designs and methods have been so minimized that it becomes impossible to produce valid findings. Methodological weaknesses owing to real-world constraints can threaten the validity of evaluation findings.

Box 7.1 illustrates how the concept of threats to validity is used in the field to assess factors affecting the validity of evaluation conclusions. The case is extracted from a meta-evaluation of CARE International evaluation methodologies that identified four main factors affecting the validity of the evaluations. It is emphasized that the evaluations were conducted under very difficult circumstances, often at great personal risk to the evaluators, and the threats to validity were largely due to factors beyond the control of the evaluation team.

The adequacy of an evaluation design and of the findings based on subsequent data collection is contingent on a number of important factors (see Table 7.1):

- How well suited the evaluation focus, approach, and methods are for obtaining the types of information needed, for example
  - Information needs regarding managerial decision making. Does the evaluation focus on program procedures, personnel, and product quality? Does the evaluation design take into consideration infrastructure, resources, training, safety, and access as well as outcomes?

Box 7.1   Factors Affecting the Validity of CARE International's Program
Evaluation Methodology

A meta-evaluation of recent evaluations of CARE International projects and programs identified four common threats to validity of the evaluation findings and conclusions. Historical factors affected the validity of more than half of the evaluations, and problems with the measurement instruments (testing) and bias in terms of who was interviewed affected nearly half of the evaluations; problems of experimental mortality affected nearly 20%. The report commented, "CARE evaluators conduct their work under very difficult circumstances and sometimes at great personal risk. Considering all of these challenges, it is often amazing that any evaluation could be conducted at all."

Threat to validity	Responses	% of evaluations affected
History	17	53.1%
Testing	15	46.9%
Bias	13	40.6%
Experimental mortality	6	18.8%
Total	51	

Definitions: *History:* changes to an area's security status between evaluator visits, civil unrest, invasions, de-escalation of conflicts, weather, changes in a country's economic status, elections, and international terrorism. *Testing:* changing evaluation questionnaires in midproject, changing indicators between baseline and final surveys, delays in establishing a baseline, poor record keeping, and badly formed questions. *Bias:* in Muslim countries, male evaluators did not have access to female translators, so they were unable to interview female subjects, and the unavailability of some subject groups. *Experimental mortality:* CARE and government staff turnover, out-migration in response to crises, sites being replaced because wells went dry, and budget cuts that closed project sites.

SOURCE: Russon (2005).

  – Information needs regarding stakeholder perspectives of program adequacy. Does the evaluation design include procedures for understanding the experiences and perceptions of intended beneficiaries? Are the methods to be used sensitive to the gender, cultural, and linguistic characteristics of stakeholders?

- Availability of data and data sources, for example:
  – Whether appropriate data exist or can be generated to address information needs. Do records provide accurate information about how, when, and to whom program services and benefits are delivered? Are financial records available and accurate, and have they been audited?
  – Whether stakeholders are accessible to evaluators. Can stakeholders be identified and located? Are they willing and able to provide data? Are there language, cultural, political, or other barriers to their provision of information?

- How well the data collected will support valid interpretations about the program, for example:
  - Findings regarding achievement of program goals. Which program objectives accomplished, and how well? Did some intended beneficiaries fare better than others? Which factors, if any, proved critical to program success? What, if anything, hindered or undermined goal attainment?
  - Findings regarding the cost-effectiveness of the program. How accurate and comprehensive are the program's financial records? What was the cost of program delivery per beneficiary (or other unit of analysis)? Did benefits justify the cost of the program? How do the costs and benefits of this program compare with similar programs?
  - Findings regarding the extent of delivery of program benefits. Did all intended beneficiaries benefit as planned? Did all appropriate stakeholders enjoy sufficient and equal access to program benefits or services? Should benefits or services have been accessible to a larger group than those defined by the program? Was there any significant "leakage" of benefits to groups not entitled to receive them? Were the benefits readily available or hard to obtain?
  - Findings regarding the adequacy of resources affecting goal attainment. Were funding, personnel, and other resources sufficient for satisfactory program implementation? Where funding was authorized, were needed resources actually available within the program's context?
  - Findings regarding unintended consequences. Were there unexpected benefits resulting because of the program? How important were they? Were there negative side effects? To what extent did they undermine or counteract benefits?

- The professional expertise and knowledge of the evaluation team are in terms of both evaluation methodology and the specific sector or field of the program, for example:
  - Expertise in terms of evaluation methodology. If content analysis of QUAL data is part of the design, does the team include specialists in QUAL methodology? If a cost-effectiveness analysis is part of the design, does the team include financial analysts?
  - Expertise in terms of the specific field of the program. If evaluating a well-child program, does the team include medical and public health specialists? If evaluating an adult literacy program, does the team include specialists in reading curriculum and pedagogy for adult education?
  - Capacity of evaluation resources for the scope of the program. Are there enough interviewers to collect the interview data? Are they sufficiently trained, or are there sufficient resources (expertise and budget) to provide training? Is there sufficient evaluation capacity in terms of database development and capacity, statistical analysis of QUANT data? Are there adequate logistical resources for communication, transportation, and other needs?

Because the adequacy and appropriateness of an evaluation design are fundamentally connected to the specific program to be evaluated and the information needs of clients and other stakeholders, general discussion of how to strengthen design is necessarily somewhat abstract. The judgment of the evaluator in applying and adapting advice and guidelines to particular programs and circumstances will be the crux on which quality and validity ultimately depend.

Table 7.1 Factors Determining the Adequacy of the Evaluation Design and of the Findings

---

1. **How well suited are the evaluation focus, approach, and methods for obtaining the information needed regarding, for example:**
   a. Managerial decisions
   b. Stakeholder perspectives on program adequacy

2. **How available are data and data sources, for example:**
   a. Whether appropriate data exist or can be generated to address information needs
   b. Whether stakeholders and documentary data sources are accessible to evaluators

3. **How well the data will support valid interpretations about the program regarding, for example:**
   a. Achievement of program goals, extent of delivery of program benefits
   b. Cost-effectiveness of the program
   d. The adequacy of resources affecting goal attainment
   e. Unintended consequences

4. **How adequate the evaluation team is, for example in terms of:**
   a. Evaluation methodology
   b. The specific field of the program
   c. Sufficiency of evaluation resources for the scope of the program

---

Assessing the Adequacy of Quantitative Evaluation Designs

One approach to fostering validity in QUANT evaluations is to address potential threats to the validity of conclusions drawn from the evaluation. Four categories of threats have been recognized (Shadish, Cook, and Campbell 2002, after Cook and Campbell 1979):

1. *Statistical conclusion validity*—incorrect inferences about covariation between two variables. QUANT evaluations involve the use of statistical tests to determine whether there are statistically significant differences between, for example, the **project** and **comparison groups** or a statistically significant association between observed outcomes and the project or one or more of its components. Consequently, it is important to ensure that the procedures for selecting the project and comparison group samples, and the choice and application of statistical tests, follow accepted procedures and permit statistical interpretations to be made of the findings. Section F of Table 7.2 shows the main ways in which statistical procedures can be violated, particularly when operating under RWE constraints (these are explained in Appendix 1, Part F). When this occurs, some of the statistical findings and interpretations may not be valid. For example, later in this chapter we cite an example of an evaluation of a housing program that assumed that an increase of 70% in the average income of program beneficiaries was **evidence** of the positive impact of improved housing on income. In fact, a slightly higher increase was found in the comparison group—suggesting the increase in income was the result of a general improvement in the economic climate of the city.

2. *Internal validity*—incorrectly inferring that the relationship between two variables is causal. Most statistical tests assume that the data have been collected from samples randomly selected from the populations being compared and that the data collection instruments adequately measure the constructs being studied. Frequently, these assumptions are not met so that the conclusions from the statistical analysis are not completely valid. Table 7.2 Section G shows that many internal validity problems arise from the way in which project participants were selected (they are different in important ways from the comparison group), because the characteristics of the project group have changed due to people dropping out, or because experiences during the project influence the way they respond. There may also be problems in determining whether the effects being measured did in fact occur after (rather than before) the presumed causes—the project interventions. For example, let us assume that women who participate in entrepreneurial development training and who then obtain a loan to start a small business on average experience an increase in their income. Program managers will usually assume that the increased income is a result of the program. While this may be true, it might also be the case that most of the women who join the program already have experience with small businesses and also tend to be the most enterprising women from their communities. So perhaps their incomes would have increased even without the program.

3. *Construct validity*—incorrect inferences about the constructs of interest, what it is the program is trying to achieve. Many of the key constructs being studied and measured are difficult to define (for example poverty, vulnerability, well-being, hostile work environment) and even harder to measure. Consequently, there may be ambiguity as to exactly what is being measured and how closely the operational definitions really reflect the underlying constructs. For example, if an educational program is trying to raise student achievement, *achievement* is the construct. How can achievement be determined? Do test scores, grades, teacher judgments, or some combination of these provide adequate ways of understanding changes in the construct—whether students in the program have achieved more? Inferring achievement from test scores can be hazardous because of test bias and measurement error.

4. *External validity*—incorrect inferences about whether study results would apply to different persons, times, or settings. One of the purposes of most QUANT evaluations is to determine the extent to which the findings of the evaluation can be generalized to a broader population (e.g., all low-income communities, all unskilled women workers, all secondary school children). Table 7.2 Section I identifies a number of ways in which the characteristics of the project population may not be very typical of the broader populations so that generalization of findings may be misleading. For example, an adult literacy program may have been successful, at least in part, due to the enthusiastic support of the director of the local high school and also the local Chamber of Commerce who provided free exercise books and snacks for the participants. Consequently, the fact that the program was successful does not justify the conclusion that it would be similarly successful in other cities where it might not enjoy this strong support.

Table 7.2 presents a checklist including the most common threats to validity under each of these four categories. All these categories are explained in Parts F, G, H, and I of Appendix 1 (“**Integrated Checklist for Assessing the Adequacy and Validity of Quantitative, Qualitative, and Mixed-Method Designs**”). These sections of the checklist can be used to identify and assess potential weaknesses in QUANT evaluation designs, including all the seven quasi-experimental designs most frequently used in RWE (see Chapters 2 and 10). Many readers who are not specialists in statistical analysis and QUANT evaluation may find some of the categories in these sections of the checklist difficult to follow. While it is worth reviewing these

Table 7.2   Threats to Validity of Quantitative (Quasi-Experimental) Evaluation Designs[a]

F. Threats to Statistical Conclusion Validity. *Reasons why inferences about covariation between two variables may be incorrect*

1. The sample is too small to detect program effects
2. Violated assumptions of statistical tests
3. Fishing for statistically significant results
4. Unreliability of measures of change of outcome indicators
5. Restriction of range
6. Unreliability of treatment implementation
7. External events influence outcomes

8. Diversity of the population
9. Inaccurate effect size estimation
10. *Extrapolation from a truncated or incomplete database*
11. *Project and comparison group samples do not cover the same populations*
12. *Information is not collected from the right people, or some categories of informants not interviewed*

G. Threats to Internal Validity. *Reasons why inferences that the relationships between two variables is causal may be incorrect*

1. Unclear whether project intervention actually occurs before presumed effect
2. Selection
3. History
4. Maturation
5. Regression toward the mean
6. Attrition

7. Testing
8. Researchers may alter how they describe/interpret data as they gain more experience
9. *Respondent distortion when using recall*
10. *Use of less rigorous designs due to budget and time constraints*

H. Threats to Construct Validity. *Reasons why inferences about the constructs of interest, in particular what it is the program is trying to achieve, may be incorrect*

1. Inadequate explanation of constructs
2. Indicators do not adequately measure constructs
3. Use of single indicator to measure a complex construct
4. Use of a single method to measure a construct
5. Only one level of the treatment is studied
6. Program participants and comparison group respond differently to some questions

7. Participants assess themselves and their situation differently than comparison group
8. Reactivity to the experimental situation
9. Experimenter expectancies
10. Novelty and disruption effects
11. Compensatory effects and rivalry
12. *Using indicators and constructs developed in other countries without pretesting in the local context*

I. Threats to External Validity. *Reasons why inferences about how study designs would apply to different persons, times or settings may be incorrect*

1. Sample does not cover the whole population of interest
2. Different settings affect program outcomes
3. Different outcome measures give different assessments of project effectiveness

4. Program outcomes vary in different settings
5. Programs operate differently in different settings
6. *The attitude of policymakers and politicians to the program*
7. *Seasonal and other cycles*

SOURCE: From Shadish, W., T. Cook, and D. Campbell, *Experimental and Quasi-Experimental Designs for Generalized Causal Inference.* Copyright © 2002 by Houghton Mifflin Company Adapted with permission, Tables 2.2, 2.4, 3.1, and 3.2, respectively. *The subcategories in italics were added by the present authors as being particularly relevant for RWE evaluations.*

a. Numbering corresponds to Appendix 1. For an explanation of categories, see Appendix 1.

categories to get an idea of the broad range of factors that can affect the validity of QUANT evaluation designs, it is always possible to ask the advice of a specialist when rigorous QUANT evaluations must be designed and assessed.

Strengthening Validity in Quantitative Evaluations

Strengthening the Evaluation Design

Random Sampling

QUANT evaluators are concerned to ensure that the sample of subjects to be surveyed or tested is randomly selected and sufficiently large to permit the use of statistical analysis and significance testing procedures. One of the key questions in sample design is, "Was the sample selected in such a way as to permit statistically valid generalizations to be drawn from the analysis of the data?" For readers who are interested in sample design, Chapter 14 identifies key design and analysis decisions that must be made before the sample is designed, during the process of sample selection, and after the survey has been administered. If the right decisions are not made before the sample is designed and selected, there is little that can be done to rectify the problems during the postsurvey analysis phase.

One of the main messages is that management and administration of the actual sample selection process in the field is as important as the theoretical sampling design in ensuring the validity of the findings. For example, the sample design may include precise instructions as to what procedure to follow if the person to be interviewed is not at home when the interviewer comes to the house. Perhaps the instruction is that the interviewer must return once more to try to locate this person, before selecting a replacement family. However, if the interviewer ignores this instruction and either interviews a different member of the family (who happens to be present) or immediately selects another family, then the theoretical sample design will not actually have been implemented. In a well-managed survey, a supervisor would detect most of these selection errors either by debriefing the interviewer at the end of the day, or by randomly revisiting a sample of households to check that the correct procedures were followed. These issues are particularly critical for the RealWorld evaluator because decisions often have to be made as to how to invest limited budget resources to ensure the quality of the sample and of the survey data. Is it more important to invest resources to improve the sample frame (e.g., by preparing community maps locating all houses—if such a map does not exist), to increase the sample size, or to carefully monitor the implementation of the survey? Unfortunately, the answer is usually that all these are important, so careful thought must be given as to how to use the limited budget.

A critical issue for **statistical conclusion validity** is sample size. The sample needs to be large enough to detect whether the project has contributed to producing the intended effects (impacts) without wasting resources by having a sample larger than necessary. Reducing sample size is often an important option for reducing costs, so it is essential to strike the right balance between saving money and ensuring that the sample is still large enough to detect project impacts. The factors determining the appropriate sample size for a given evaluation are discussed in Chapter 14.

Triangulation

One of the advantages of mixed-method approaches is that they provide two or more independent measures of key variables (e.g., household income, school enrollment and absentee rates, main sources of economic activity—particularly in the informal sector—changes in crime rates, and community violence over time). This makes it possible to use data **triangulation,** to collect data at different points in time and from different sources to compare information from different sources to check whether the information is consistent. Chapter 10 gives an example where three different sources are used to obtain independent estimates of changes in household income: a household survey, observation, and interviews with key informants. In one example, the estimates from the three sources are consistent with each other (*converging*), whereas in the second case they are inconsistent (*diverging*)—with the survey suggesting that, on average, household income has increased while at the same time observation and key informants both suggest that, on average, income has declined. In addition to checking for consistency of information and estimates, using both QUANT and QUAL sources of data on key variables also provides a broader understanding of the multidimensionality of concepts such as poverty, vulnerability, and attitudes to public services.

An important aspect of triangulation is to plan ahead what will be done if triangulation reveals inconsistencies among measures made by different methods. While many QUAL approaches expect that inconsistencies will be revealed and consider this as adding to the richness of the data and something that will be addressed during the interpretation phase, most QUANT approaches try to obtain consistent and uniform responses. Ideally, the QUANT evaluation design should allow time and resources to return to the field (as is common practice in much QUAL research using, for example, constant comparative methods) to follow up when inconsistencies are discovered, either during the interview supervision phase or during the analysis phase (when the discrepancies tend to be discovered). Unfortunately, this is usually not possible, particularly on the RWE budget, so other options should be considered. These include the following:

- Those who conduct evaluator-administered surveys should be instructed to note inconsistencies between interviewee-reported information and their direct observation. They should indicate how they interpret the discrepancies and possibly what they think is the best estimate of the truth. They may also be instructed to ask some follow-up questions such as, "Why do you think that so many residents say they are dissatisfied with the health clinic?" "Could you explain what you mean by that?"
- Identify as many as possible of the inconsistencies during the interview supervision phase and follow up through postinterview discussion with interviewers and possibly revisits to a sample of respondents. The purpose is to understand the reasons for the discrepancies and to provide guidance to the interviewers on what to do when similar discrepancies are detected in future interviews.
- Define rules for interview coding and analysis of how to address inconsistencies (e.g., whether more weight be given to one source of data, whether QUANT estimates should be adjusted in a certain defined way—when, for example, one family in the community is reported as having an income far in excess of any other family or when reported expenditures are far greater than reported income). These rules should take into account feedback received during the interview process (another reason for the

importance of the postinterview debriefing sessions). However, such rules rarely anticipate all the judgments that were made in the field, which is one of the major benefits of mixed-method designs, where QUANT analysis can be combined with emergent QUAL designs that can help interpret these kinds of questions.

- For critical indicators in QUANT analysis, it is possible to create during the analysis phase two different variables giving upper and lower estimates (e.g., income, school enrollment, unemployment). One estimate is derived from the survey information and is not adjusted, whereas the other is adjusted up or down to take into account the estimates obtained from other data collection methods (e.g., observation, key informants). Statistical tests can then be used to examine whether the two estimates are associated in a consistent way and also how each is affected by household attributes (e.g., income, size, education) and by **contextual variables**. This is an example of the practical utility of mixed-method approaches allowing a number of different explanations of the discrepancies to be compared.

Selection of Statistical Procedures

One important aspect of statistical procedures for RWEs is the decision on sample size. A trade-off often has to be made between the level of **precision** that is required and the available resources. A common threat to statistical validity is the lower **power of the test,** and the resulting inability to test for small **effect sizes** when the sample is too small. This important question is discussed in Chapter 14 where guidelines are given for determining the appropriate sample size for typical RWE contexts where the budget is tight. When mixed-method evaluations are used, it will usually be necessary to select different statistical procedures for the analysis of *interval variables* (such as weight, age, and number of children), *ordinal variables* (e.g., satisfaction with school, level of agreement or disagreement with statements concerning local health facilities), and *nominal variables* (e.g., economic sector in which a person works, region of origin, reasons for migrating to the city). As we will see later in this chapter, several of the factors affecting statistical conclusion validity are related to the use of an inappropriate statistical test.

Peer Review and Meta-Evaluation

The evaluator's peers and professional colleagues are often the group best qualified for assessing the strengths and weaknesses of the evaluation design. An effort should always be made to solicit either formal or informal peer review of the evaluation design and later the analysis.

If resources permit, it is also extremely useful to commission a meta-evaluation in which an evaluation specialist is commissioned to critique the evaluation methodology. The meta-evaluation will often address most of the questions included in the checklists in Table 7.2 and should include an assessment of the potential threats to validity and adequacy of the evaluation design, data analysis, and presentation of findings.

Taking Corrective Actions When Threats to Validity Have Been Identified

The application of the "Integrated Checklist for Assessing the Adequacy and Validity of Quantitative, Qualitative, and Mixed-Method Designs" (the Integrated Checklist), shown in Appendix 1, will usually identify a number of potential threats to the validity of the methodology or conclusions of QUANT evaluations in one or more of the four categories: statistical conclusion validity, internal validity, **construct validity**, and **external validity** (discussed later in the chapter). The next step is to assess the seriousness of each potential threat with reference to the purpose of this particular evaluation. For example, many of the threats to statistical conclusion validity (see Table 7.2) such as the sample size being too small, the use of the wrong statistical test, and using data from surveys that do not cover all the population, will be of great concern if the purpose of the evaluation is to produce rigorous estimates of the statistical significance of different project interventions. However, these statistical threats to validity may be less important in an exploratory evaluation where the purpose is to assess whether an innovative approach (such as a new system for reducing postharvest crop loss by protecting stored grain from rats and mold) is being adopted by significant numbers of farmers.

Readers who are interested might like to refer to the Project Evaluation Worksheet in Appendix 3. This illustrates how threats to validity are identified and their importance assessed in a typical evaluation (the impacts of a low-cost housing program on family income). Several common threats to validity are discussed in this example. In the following paragraphs, we present one example to illustrate the process of identifying potential threats to validity, deciding how important they are, and then deciding what actions to take to try to correct or reduce the threat.

We take the example of one of the most common threats to internal validity—namely, history (Threat G.3 in the checklist in Table 7.2). *History* refers to the fact that external events unrelated to the project but that affect outcomes might have occurred during the period in which the project is being implemented. For example, drought, changes in the demand for agricultural produce, or the construction of a new road might all have affected farm income, or a school-feeding program started by a nongovernmental organization (**NGO**) might have affected school enrollment or attendance rates. If the effects of these external events are not taken into account, it may be wrongly assumed that the observed changes in farmers' income or school enrollment are due to the projects when in fact they may be at least partly due to these external history factors.

In the example in Appendix 3, it was found that household income had increased by an average of 70% over the three years since the start of the housing project. The evaluation report assumed that the increase in income could be attributed to the benefits of improved housing. However, the lack of a comparison group meant that the analysis did not take into account general changes in wage levels and income that might have affected all the low-income population. This threat was considered very serious because it could lead to completely wrong conclusions about the impacts of the project.

Several possible actions are proposed to rectify the problem. The first option was to reconstruct a comparison group through the use of secondary data or through information provided by key informants such as the Chamber of Commerce, Ministry of Planning, local industries, community leaders, or NGOs. The second option was to identify areas of the city with similar characteristics that could be used as a comparison group. Ideally, a rapid survey would be conducted to obtain information on current and past economic conditions, or if this is not possible, qualitative interviews could be conducted with people who have lived in the comparison areas for a number of years and who can provide information on the changes that have occurred. The cheapest option would be to use direct observation to compare the physical and economic conditions of the project and comparison areas.

It was concluded that the proposed actions could identify potentially important external factors and provide a rough estimate of their importance. This could significantly reduce, but not eliminate, the problem.

Box 7.2 provides additional examples of how to identify and address typical problems affecting each of the four types of threat to validity of QUANT evaluation designs.

Box 7.2   Examples of the Identification and Ways to Address Typical Threats to Statistical, Internal, Construct, and External Validity

---

- *Unreliability of measures of change of outcome indicators* (threats to statistical conclusion validity—Threat F.4). Unreliable measures of the rate of change in, for example, income, literacy, or infant mortality reduce the likelihood of finding a statistically significant effect. The problem may be that the concepts are multidimensional (such as income) so that a single indicator can never fully capture all the dimensions, or it may be that different organizations use different definitions (e.g., literacy).

Possible corrective measures: Two approaches can be considered to address this threat. First, ensure that sufficient time and resources are allocated to develop and field-test the data collection instruments; second, incorporate multimethod data collection approaches so that at least two independent measures are used for all key variables, and use triangulation to check on the reliability and consistency of the different estimates. Where estimates are *convergent* (consistent), the evaluator can feel more confident of the findings. However, when estimates are *divergent* (not consistent), a decision must be made as to how to interpret the inconsistencies. A first step is to consult with the team members who have been using QUAL methods to discuss what these studies have to say. Resources permitting, it may be possible to explore these issues further, either through the ongoing QUAL studies or by conducting a rapid follow-up survey.

- *Selection (bias)* (threats to internal conclusion validity—Threat G.2). Project participants are often different from comparison groups in important ways. Participants may be self-selected, as when people apply to participate in the program, or the project may deliberately target groups with special characteristics, such as the poorest communities or those with the most dynamic community organizations. In either case, it is difficult to find comparison groups that match these characteristics.

Possible corrective measures: Four possible measures are proposed. First, compare characteristics of participants and comparison groups, and identify important differences. Try to find ways to produce a better match, but even if this is not possible, it is useful to understand what the differences are so these can be taken into account in the analysis and preparation of recommendations. Second, statistically control for differences in participant characteristics in the two groups (see Chapter 10, pp. 207–208, for a discussion of the use of multivariate analysis for this purpose). Third, use key informants (particularly if no comparison group is used) to compare participants with the total population. Fourth, use focus groups or direct observation of other group settings to assess psychological characteristics such as self-confidence and motivation.

- *Reactivity to the experimental situation* (threats to construct validity—Threat H.8). Often, project participants try to interpret the project situation, and this may affect their behavior. For example, if participants think the program is being run by a religious group, they may react differently than if they think it is organized by a political organization.

Possible corrective measures: Use exploratory studies and observations to understand respondent expectations and to identify potential response bias. Of course, these studies, too, would have observer effects.

- *The attitude of policymakers and politicians to the program (and how this may affect the success of the program and estimates of its replicability in other locations)* (threats to external validity—Threat I.6). Identical programs may have different outcomes depending on the level and type of support or opposition of policymakers and politicians.

Possible corrective measures: If a project is implemented in different locations, identify differences in the attitudes of policymakers and politicians in each location (through interviews, secondary sources such as newspapers and radio, or key informants) and assess how these differences appear to affect the project.

Assessing the Adequacy of Qualitative Evaluation Designs

As with any design, the adequacy of QUAL designs rests on the match with information needs and resources, including evaluator expertise. With QUAL designs, adequacy also requires safeguards against the undue intrusion of subjectivity and care in selecting where and by whom this methodology's more time-consuming ethnographic methods will be implemented. Building triangulation, validation, and **purposive** or *purposeful* **sampling** strategies into QUAL designs helps promote valid data and findings.

Approaches to Validity in Qualitative Evaluations

The inductive, intuitive nature of findings in QUAL evaluation makes enormous demands on the judgment capacity of the QUAL evaluator (see Chapter 12). It has been noted on more than one occasion that the analytic skills needed for this type of work are difficult to teach or acquire. As examples earlier in this chapter illustrate, for any program or data set, there may be a variety of interpretive possibilities. This raises special issues of validity and credibility in QUAL evaluations.

The implications for accuracy and bias have often generated concerns among QUANT evaluators about the potential mischief of the subjective judgments of their QUAL colleagues. In response, QUAL practitioners have sometimes responded that all human ways of knowing are necessarily subjective, including QUANT ways, that subjective minds are all evaluators have, and that what is important in evaluation is *trustworthiness* (Guba and Lincoln 1989).

More familiar than their QUANT colleagues with the notion of researcher-as-instrument and the vulnerability of interpretive findings, QUAL practitioners more readily accept that "there are *no* procedures that will regularly (or always) yield either sound data or true conclusions" (Phillips 1987:21, emphasis in the original). All data sets are biased by decisions about what to observe, how to categorize, what to record, and how to interpret. Not only because of acknowledged subjectivity in QUAL methodology but also because of the more personal interactions between data collectors and data providers, QUAL reports may be especially endangered. Methodological bias in the form of *social response set*, the desire of informants to please researchers or to give the *right* answers, may also be greater with QUAL methods.

Box 7.3   Qualitative Approaches for Promoting Validity

The following are some of the approaches used by QUAL evaluators for promoting the validity and credibility of their data and findings:

Triangulation. Confirming and disconfirming facts and interpretations through reference to multiple sources, multiple methods, multiple observers, and across multiple times

Validation. Checking with informants on the accuracy of recorded data and the reasonableness of interpretations

Meta-evaluation and peer review. Critical review of the evaluation methods, sources, and findings by evaluation colleagues and external experts

Noting that, in evaluation, "judgments often involve multidimensional criteria and conflicting interests," House (1994), among others, has advised that "the evaluator should strive to reduce biases in making such judgments" (p. 15). But one's own biases can be difficult to recognize, especially because they are multidimensional. Naturally occurring diversity in values, in standards of quality, in experiential understandings, and in theoretical perspectives offer many types of subjective bias. Having accepted that objectivity is unattainable, QUAL practitioners try hard to discipline their subjectivity so that it does not undermine accuracy. In this effort, triangulation, validation, and meta-evaluation are strong allies.

One approach to assessing the capacity of QUAL evaluation designs to support valid conclusions involves applying validity criteria of different types or at different stages of the evaluation process (Maxwell 1992), as follows (see also Box 7.3):

- *Descriptive validity*—whether the data accurately and comprehensively portray the actual events observed, the reported experiences and perceptions of interviewees, and the content of documents reviewed
- *Interpretive validity*—whether the interpretations adequately represent the program and are warranted by the data
- *Evaluative validity*—whether evaluative judgments are warranted and appropriate

Ethical Considerations

The interactive nature of QUAL fieldwork opens myriad opportunities for micropolitics and for personal sympathy and persuasion, not always at a conscious level, raising special issues related to bias and ethics (Newman and Brown 1996). An evaluator using highly interactive QUAL strategies must plan for and be alert to potential stakeholder vulnerability. For example, interviewing tends to elicit more detailed, more personal, more revealing, more potentially injurious information about the respondent than does the administration of a self-administered survey. Even when vulnerable respondents are treated confidentially, sometimes interviewees are recognizable in text to colleagues and superiors because of their positions, knowledge of certain program activities, or speech patterns. Accuracy in reporting the perceptions and experiences of stakeholders may include embarrassing or threatening revelation, leaving the evaluator with the difficult task of balancing the accuracy and integrity of the evaluation against the rights, risks, and interests of informants.

Strengthening Validity in Qualitative Evaluations

Strengthening the Evaluation Design

Purposeful (Purposive) Sampling

The sampling strategies useful and appropriate for QUAL evaluation differ markedly from those appropriate for QUANT evaluation. QUAL methods, concentrating on depth rather than breadth, require understanding at the level of the individual participant—*phenomenological* understanding, or understanding from the participant's insider perspective. Because it takes longer to interview a person and to transcribe or write up the interview data, for example, than it does to hand him or her a self-administered survey, or even to administer a closed-question questionnaire, fewer persons can be interviewed than can be surveyed. When relatively few participants in a program can be interviewed, selection of interviewees must be very careful—not random, but *purposive* or *purposeful.*

The QUAL evaluator may choose from a variety of selection criteria in determining a sample. For example:

- *Typical case sampling.* Subjects are selected who are likely to behave as most of their counterparts would. *Example:* Villagers with a demographic profile like that of the larger population are selected.
- *Unique case sampling.* Subjects are selected who display unique or rare attributes. *Example:* Chess prodigies are selected.
- *Extreme or deviant case sampling.* Subjects who are particularly troublesome or particularly competent are selected. *Example:* Exceptionally high- or low-achieving students are selected.
- *Critical case sampling.* Subjects are selected because information obtained about them is likely to be revealing generally or true of others. *Example:* Low-performing fourth graders at an otherwise high-achieving school are selected because it is believed that, if they can grasp the math curriculum, the other fourth graders are sure to be able to do so.
- *Reputational case sampling.* Subjects are selected on the recommendation of experts. *Example:* The floor manager recommends those workers who have demonstrated leadership.
- *Comparable case sampling.* Subjects are selected to provide a basis for comparison with other subjects. *Example:* English-speaking girls are selected for comparison with Spanish-speaking immigrant girls to help understand whether the latter's difficulties in school are language or gender related.
- *Comprehensive sampling*: All members of a particular population are selected. *Example:* Not every trainee but every trainer in the program is selected.
- *Range, maximum variation, or quota sampling.* Subjects are selected to represent the range of known differences. *Example:* Participants are selected who represent each ethnic group in the community, each religious affiliation, the various levels of affluence, both genders, and geographic diversity.

Determinations as to which of these sampling strategies (or others) is appropriate depend on the evaluation questions and the information needs of stakeholders.

Triangulation

Program quality should not, of course, be based on unsubstantiated opinion or a few site visits where the evaluator may observe nonrepresentative interactions, either innocent or planned. Triangulation, crucial to protecting against invalidity, involves deliberate attempts to confirm, elaborate, and disconfirm facts and interpretations through reference to the following:

- Multiple data sources
- Multiple methods of data collection
- Multiple evaluators or data collectors

- Repeated observations over time
- Multiple analytic perspectives

For example, the evaluator will need to confirm the information from an interview through direct observation of the events described by the interviewee, through interviews of others, through documentary evidence of the events, and through patterns of their occurrence. In this way, the *descriptive validity* of the interview data can be assessed, answering the question, Is the program fully and accurately represented by the data? Through consideration of the events' meaning and implications from perspectives other than those of the interviewee—including those from other program participants, different members of the evaluation team, and relevant literature—the *interpretive validity* can also be strengthened, answering the question, Are the interpretations of program aspects or program quality overall warranted (supported) by the data?

Validation

Validation is also used to strengthen the accuracy of the data set and the reasonableness of interpretations. Validation involves checking with informants about the accuracy of the recorded data and the reasonableness of the interpretations drawn from it. The best known validation techniques are these:

- *Member checking*—the review of data and interpretations by a gathering of persons representing relevant stakeholders (Lincoln and Guba 1985)
- *Comprehensive individual validation*—individual validation of data and findings, with each informant provided an opportunity to review, first, the relatively uninterpreted data that he or she provided (such as an interview transcript or an observation write-up) and, later, a draft of the report that includes the selected presentation and interpretation of data, for validation of both data and interpretations (Mabry 1998)

In addition, drafts of reports may be submitted to diverse audiences, selected on the bases of expertise and confidentiality, to try to ensure "getting it right" (Geertz 1973:29). The scope of distribution of the draft should reflect sensitivity to ethics and politics, including matters such as possible need to protect informants' identities or to avoid premature distribution of tentative interpretations that might be either wrong or damaging. Also, validation may occur informally by opening conversational opportunities for participants to react to some data or to ideas about its meaning.

Meta-Evaluation and Peer Review

Meta-evaluation, the evaluation of an evaluation, is advisable especially for expensive and high-impact evaluations. Where full-scale meta-evaluation would strain fiscal resources, less formal collegial review may help to discipline the subjectivity of the evaluator, enhance analysis, and bolster the validity of findings.

Critical review by evaluation colleagues and external substantive experts, either individually or as professional panels, may promote both validity and credibility. Technical advisory panels may monitor and assess an evaluation's quality, providing ongoing checks and critique during report drafting. Informally, too, colleagues may listen, read, comment, argue, suggest, and advise. In addition to review by program participants and other stakeholders, internal review by the evaluation team may be either informal and ongoing, formal and undertaken at critical junctures, or both.

Addressing Threats to Validity in Qualitative Evaluations

To help ensure the validity of findings in QUAL evaluations, the following suggestions regarding comprehensiveness of data, sensitivity to informants, opportunity for analysis, and observer effects are offered.

Collecting Data across the Full Range of Appropriate Settings, Times, and Respondents

Consider whether a sufficient number and type of observations and interviews have been planned or conducted to ensure thorough understanding and the validity of findings. If not, and if the study has not yet been conducted, discuss ways to revise the evaluation design. If data collection has already been undertaken, consider the possibility of re-interviewing key informants or others or revisiting a site to fill in some of the gaps.

If stakeholders engaged in review of data and findings consider the report's representation of the program faulty, consider seeking out key informants or organizing meetings to determine whether the problems concern missing information (e.g., only men were interviewed), whether there are factual errors, or whether the problem concerns how the material was interpreted by the evaluator. Based on the types of problem identified, consider revising the report or returning to the field for further interviews, observations, or review of documents.

Inappropriate Subject Selection

If important program participants have inadvertently been neglected and if the fieldwork has not yet been completed, include them in the sample to make the evaluation data more representative of the total population. If fieldwork has already been conducted, consider individual or group interviews with some members of the missing population groups. In areas where subjects have access to these technologies, telephone or e-mail interviews may be needed if the evaluator is not able to return to the program site. If this is not possible, try to identify and review information about the missing groups or to observe them (or arrange for them to be observed by local team members) to obtain missing information.

Insufficient Language or Cultural Skills to Ensure Sensitivity to Informants

If, in negotiating the evaluation design, it becomes apparent that specific cultural competencies are needed to collect valid data, consider hiring experts in the competencies needed or hiring (and perhaps training) local persons for additional data collection. If the need for specific skills has become apparent as data have been collected, consider bringing in experts or representatives of the community to help with the analysis to ensure appropriate cultural and linguistic sensitivity.

Insufficient Opportunity for Ongoing Analysis by the Team

If periodic analytic discussion by evaluation team members is precluded by the timeline of the evaluation or the geographic remoteness of program sites, consider electronic means of sharing. For example, debriefing updates may be faxed or e-mailed to all team members, or report-and-respond forms (see Chapter 12) may be adapted for internal use to spur interpretation toward collective preliminary findings.

Minimizing Observer Effects

Threats to validity from observer effects can be minimized by building triangulation and validation into the design—checking impressions from observations by interviewing those observed or by conferring with other observers, checking the validity of data from interviews against first-hand observations and documents. Validation of data write-ups through requests for additions and corrections from those observed and interviewed can guard against misinterpretation. Discussions within the evaluation team, with selected clients, review panels, or technical advisory panels or meta-evaluators can also bring balance to individual impressions.

Supporting Future Action

Interpretive findings do not necessarily imply specific corrective actions. Many well-known evaluators advise against making recommendations or consider the program personnel better able than evaluators to devise action plans because of their more intimate knowledge of their program and participants. Evaluators could meet with key stakeholders to discuss or brainstorm plans for program improvement, although some evaluators would consider this a threatening move beyond evaluation into consultancy.

Points during the RWE Cycle When Corrective Measures Can Be Taken

The RWE Integrated Checklist and other similar checklists can help identify threats to validity and adequacy of designs, as well as strategies for addressing the threats once they have been identified. Threats can be addressed at three points in the evaluation: during design, during implementation, and during report preparation. Some of the questions to be addressed when assessing the adequacy and validity of evaluation designs include the following:

- Are methods appropriate for information needs? For example, is the evaluation question to be addressed in data collection one of meaning, understanding, or process? Will the methods generate data that will help the client and other stakeholders address their information needs?
- Is there a clear, positive relationship of the methodology to the evaluation focus or questions?
- Are the evaluation team's expertise and capacity sufficient for the approach and methods?

- Are strategies to ensure validity, trustworthiness, and confirmability adequate and appropriate?
- Using this design, are the data to be collected likely to be relevant, comprehensive, and representative of the program?
- Are adequate and appropriate technical and ethical safeguards in place?
- Are there procedures to ensure cultural sensitivity, competence, and capacity?

Increasing the comprehensiveness of the methods would improve many evaluations. For example, increasing the period and number of observations or increasing the number of stakeholders and stakeholder groups interviewed or surveyed. Adding experts in the application of these methods (e.g., sociologists, statisticians) or in the type of program to be evaluated (e.g., economists to study a microcredit program, civil engineers to study a clean water program) can also strengthen evaluation designs. However, in many RWE contexts, budget and time constraints limit the ability of the evaluation team to take these additions.

Strengthening the Design

The Integrated Checklist (see Appendix 1) can be used to review a proposed evaluation design and make corrections before the evaluation begins. If analysis by an evaluator, evaluation team, or technical advisory panel determines that an evaluation design is weak, steps may be taken to improve the design, protecting the quality of the evaluation before data collection begins. The specific improvements needed vary from design to design, of course, but some general advice may be helpful.

Strengthening Data Collection Methods

As the evaluation focus, questions, and information needs are considered with reference to the planned methods, it may become clear that the methods may not elicit adequate or strong enough data to provide sufficient evidence of program quality. The substitution of more appropriate methods or addition of complementary methods may be needed.

For example, in an evaluation of state assessment programs in education, an examination of methods may suggest that the evaluation will generate data describing the types of achievement testing used by the state, the types of items on the tests, whether the tests are standards based or norm referenced, how they are scored, how scores are reported, and the proportions of students across time who are passing and failing the tests. Such information can be obtained from state documents and online sources, perhaps supplemented by interviews with state education agency personnel. The combined use of several or all these methods would provide extremely useful data for judging the quality of the state assessment system.

But these data would not be sufficient to determine how much measurement error is included in the tests, whether the tests are well aligned with state content standards and state curriculum guides such that teaching is likely to provide appropriate preparation for test takers, and whether failure rates impose inappropriate negative consequences on students and educators. For information of this type, more detailed study of the test content, content standards, and standards-based curricula are needed. Interviews with a representative sample of teachers, school administrators, students, and parents are needed to provide the perspectives of critical stakeholders regarding whether the state testing program is strengthening or corrupting educational practices and outcomes—and these interviews need to be followed up with surveys to determine how widespread the experiences of those interviewed are in the affected population. Observations in classrooms are needed to determine whether standards-based curricula are integral to learning opportunities and, therefore, aligned to standards-based tests. The design needs to expand from review of documents and state-level interviews to classroom-level observation, interviews of a variety of stakeholder groups, and general surveys.

In such a case, a wider range of methods and data sources would often provide triangulation, strengthening the validity protections in the evaluation design. More carefully focused methods—in this case, getting into the details of test content, measurement soundness, and the appropriateness of score-based consequences—allow for the refinement and validity of findings. Such findings would be more informative, better supported by the data, and more useful for state assessment directors who may be hoping to improve their systems on the basis of evaluation data and findings.

Strengthening Capacity of the Evaluation Team

So that the benefits of different types of methodological approaches and techniques can help protect the soundness of the evaluation and the validity of its interpretations, specialized types of methodological expertise may be needed on the evaluation team. QUANT team members may be needed to ensure appropriate sample sizes for data to be used in representing populations or determining statistical significance, comparable experimental groupings, and selection and use of statistical tests and procedures. QUAL team members may be needed to ensure fine-grained focus on individually and socially constructed meaning, the human implications of program effects, the identification and magnitude of unintended consequences.

The complementarity of these approaches—that is, using mixed methods—can be extraordinarily useful in producing high-quality evaluation. It takes considerable open-mindedness and managerial expertise, however, to find working consensus among disparate points of view. A positional stance that privileges macrolevel descriptors of the program, the population overall, or aggregated results and costs may be dismissive of microlevel effects on individuals, their experiences, and their perspectives of program quality. From an opposing positional stance, macrolevel indicators and trends may be accorded little meaning if intended beneficiaries disagree with numbers that suggest they should be satisfied with program outcomes they may actually find unsatisfactory. Working consensus, rather than melding or integration, may be useful for preserving the benefits of different methodological perspectives and expertise.

Often, an evaluation benefits from more than a variety of methodological specialties. Professionals in the field of the program who are familiar with relevant theory, professional literature, and best practices are as critical to the strength of data analysis as evaluators trained and experienced with inquiry procedures, including different strategies of data analysis. The situation is analogous to that in critical thinking: General critical-thinking strategies can be taught, but one must be able to think critically within a content area, where general strategies may be greatly differentiated and augmented. Analysis attentive to the literature in the field of the program (e.g., the field of epidemiology in programs intended to combat HIV/AIDS or the field of early childhood education in programs intended to reduce school dropout rates through early intervention) is as important as methodological strength.

For example, survey data in an evaluation of a state grant program to support the inclusion of children with disabilities suggested that all the 150 or so grantees had included, as intended, children with disabilities in prekindergarten, kindergarten, and first-grade classrooms of typically developing peers. Telephone interview data, however, suggested that some of the grant programs provided more inclusion than others. Observations and interviews at daylong site visits and a few weeklong case studies indicated that, at some sites, no inclusion was practiced. While all members of the evaluation team were able to recognize when programs segregated special education from regular education classrooms, initially only the special education members of the evaluation team were able to distinguish whether classrooms with mixed populations met the definition of *inclusion* or segregated regular education from special education students within the same physical spaces. Only the trained special education eyes perceived whether instruction was differentiated and developmentally appropriate.

Determining the point of entry of such content specialists in the evaluation of a program and the scope of the role they might play is a consideration in strengthening evaluation design and conclusions. In the ideal world, of course, such resources would be abundant for an evaluation. However, in the real world, balancing the costs of differentiated expertise (feasibility) with the value to the evaluation (quality, validity, credibility) is almost always necessary.

Strengthening the Implementation of the Evaluation

The RealWorld evaluator is always encouraged to consider the use of mixed-method approaches. One of the strengths of these approaches is that QUAL methods can be used in parallel with QUANT data collection methods in a compensatory manner. For example, in the evaluation of a community water supply project, surveys may not reveal that residents have to pay bribes to local leaders to obtain water, information more likely to be revealed through ethnographic observation.

Strengthening Data Analysis Procedures

Too often, data analysis progresses no farther than trends or correlations, sometimes in combination with calculations of statistical significance. Consider a trend toward increased numbers of children from an indigenous population in the highlands of Papua New Guinea in English-speaking primary schools. The trend itself is not a finding; it must be interpreted. Should the interpretation be that education is improving for indigenous children living in the highlands of Papua New Guinea? If analysis ventures no further than enrollment figures, using easy-to-analyze simple QUANT procedures, important underlying explanations may be missed.

On the other hand, analysis complicated by both QUANT and QUAL data, including ethnographic observations and systematic interviews, requires more complex analysis. Content analysis may, for example, make it much less clear whether education in English language primary schools is beneficial for children in Papua New Guinea. While English language primary schools may improve children's chances to succeed in higher education, those chances may come at the risk of extinguishing the indigenous language and culture. Records kept by state officials are unlikely to include such data and important stakeholder considerations, while sensitive inquiry—in this case, such as that by Malone (1997)—can offer more comprehensive and informative analysis.

Strengthening the Evaluation
When Preparing to Report

Many evaluators submit draft reports to clients for review, comment, and correction prior to finalization. This practice is sometimes referred to as *negotiation drafts*. Feedback from clients may identify issues or gaps needing attention. Some time and budget should be reserved to permit additional fieldwork or analysis, if called for. These may incluse follow-up clarification interviews with key informants, focus groups interviews with newly identified groups of stakeholders or site visits to newly identified natural comparison groups.

Summary

- When referring to data the term *validity* is roughly similar to *accuracy.* It is a criterion used to assess whether data adequately and accurately represent actual conditions.

- The validity and adequacy of an evaluation are affected by (a) the appropriateness of the evaluation focus, approach, and methods; (b) the availability of data; (c) how well the data support valid findings; and (d) the adequacy of the evaluation team in terms of methodology, the specific field of the program, and the available resources.

- The validity of QUANT evaluations is usually assessed in terms of statistical conclusion validity, internal validity, construct validity, and external validity.

- QUANT evaluation designs can often be strengthened by (a) ensuring that random sample selection has been properly applied, (b) using triangulation to obtain independent estimates of key indicators, (c) correct selection of statistical procedures, and (d) using peer review and meta-evaluation.

- Once threats to QUANT validity have been detected, measures can be taken to correct or reduce their effects.

- The capacity of a QUAL design to support valid conclusions can be considered in terms of descriptive validity, interpretive validity, and evaluative validity.

- The Integrated Checklist for assessing evaluation validity and adequacy assesses QUAL and mixed-method evaluations in terms of confirmability, reliability, and **dependability**; credibility and **authenticity**; **transferability** and fittingness; and use, application, and action orientation.

- QUAL evaluation designs are strengthened through triangulation, validation, meta-evaluation, and peer review.

- Once threats to the validity of QUAL, QUANT, or mixed-method evaluations have been identified, measures can be taken to correct or reduce their effects.

- Measures can be taken to improve the validity of evaluations during the design stage, during implementation, or when preparing and reviewing the report on evaluation findings and conclusions.

Further Reading

American Evaluation Association. 1995. "Guiding Principles for Evaluators." Pp. 19–26 in *Guiding Principles for Evaluators*, edited by W. R. Shadish, D. L. Newman, M. A. Scheirer, and C. Wye. New Directions for Program Evaluation, No. 66. San Francisco: Jossey-Bass.

Guidelines for competent and ethical evaluation practice developed and periodically revised by the largest professional evaluation association.

Beebe, J. 2001. *Rapid Assessment Process: An Introduction*. Walnut Creek, CA: Altamira Press.

Discussion of the different ways to use triangulation in rapid evaluations.

Campbell, D. T. and J. C. Stanley. 1963. *Experimental and Quasi-Experimental Designs for Research*. Boston: Houghton-Mifflin.

The classic reference for explaining different types and advantages of quantitative designs and for terms such as internal and external validity.

Denzin, N. K. 1989. *The Research Act: A Theoretical Introduction to Sociological Methods*. 3d ed. Englewood Cliffs, NJ: Prentice Hall.

Thorough and classic reference for the types and purposes of triangulation.

Handwerker, W. P. 2001. *Quick Ethnography: A Guide to Rapid Multi-Method Research*. Walnut Creek, CA: Altamira Press.

Illustrations of how to incorporate triangulation into rapid evaluation studies. Also a nontechnical chapter on how to apply the difficult concept of construct validity to the analysis of culture.

Joint Committee on Standards for Educational Evaluation. 1994. *The Program Evaluation Standards: How to Assess Evaluations of Educational Programs*. 2d ed. Thousand Oaks, CA: Sage.

Guidelines for competent and ethical evaluation practice developed and periodically revised by a collaborative group of professional associations with interests in evaluation.

Lincoln, Y. S. and E. G. Guba. 1985. *Naturalistic Inquiry*. Beverly Hills, CA: Sage.

A classic reference across fields and the source for the most common terms and explanations of validity and reliability in qualitative work. This is also the source for member checking as a validation technique.

Newman, D. L. and R. D. Brown. 1996. *Applied Ethics for Program Evaluation*. Thousand Oaks, CA: Sage.

An important source of information regarding ethical practice in evaluation.

Shadish, W., T. Cook, and D. Campbell. 2002. *Experimental and Quasi-Experimental Designs for Generalized Causal Inference*. Boston: Houghton Mifflin.

Probably the most comprehensive reference on threats to validity in quantitative evaluation designs. Quite technical and long, but provides an excellent overview of the philosophy, theory, and methodology of quasi-experimental designs.

CHAPTER 8

Making It Useful

Helping Clients and Other Stakeholders Utilize the Evaluation

T his chapter presents the final step of the RealWorld Evaluation (**RWE**) approach, in which guidelines are presented for increasing the likelihood that the evaluation **findings** will be used (see Figure 8.1). We begin by discussing some of the reasons why evaluation findings are frequently underused and by stressing the importance of the scoping phase in ensuring that the evaluation is focusing on the right issues and is involving **clients** and **stakeholders**. We then describe **formative evaluation** strategies that provide constant feedback of findings to managers and planners so that they can be used to improve performance of the ongoing **project**, and we suggest ways to ensure constant communication with clients and stakeholders. We then discuss building evaluation capacity as a way to strengthen use and provide pointers on effective communication of evaluation findings. Finally, we suggest ways to develop a follow-up action plan to ensure that evaluation findings are put into practice.

The Underutilization of Evaluation Studies

Evaluations Are Underutilized in Both Developing and Developed Countries

There is widespread concern that despite the significant resources devoted to **program** evaluation and its importance in both industrial and developing countries, the use of evaluation findings is disappointingly low (Patton 1997, chap. 1). This holds true even for evaluations that are methodologically sound. In 1995, the U.S. General Accounting Office conducted follow-up case studies on three major federal program evaluations: the Comprehensive Child Development Program, the Community Health Centers program, and Title 1 Elementary and

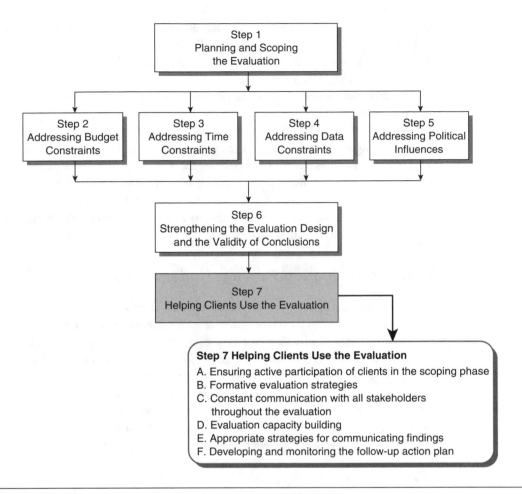

Figure 8.1   Step 7: Helping Clients Use the Evaluation

Secondary Education Act aimed at providing compensatory education services to low-income students. The GAO came to the following conclusion:

> Lack of information does not appear to be the main problem. Rather, the problem seems to be that available information is not organized and communicated effectively. Much of the available information did not reach the [appropriate Senate] Committee, or reached it in a form that was too highly aggregated to be useful or that was difficult to digest. (General Accounting Office [GAO] 1995:39)

The GAO's report helped to explain why "the recent literature is unanimous in announcing the general failure of evaluation to affect decision-making in a significant way" (Wholey et al. 1970:46) and confirmed that "producing data is one thing. Getting it used is quite another" (House 1972:412)[1]. Evaluators are also concerned about the related issue of *misuse* of evaluation findings. House (1990) observed, "Results from poorly conceived studies have frequently been given wide publicity, and findings from good studies have been improperly used" (p. 26).

In some cases, the misuse might be intentional, but in other cases it results from a lack of understanding of how to interpret and use evaluation findings (Best 2001, 2004). We will return to these issues in Chapter 16 (pp. 374–376), particularly with respect to the many ways in which evaluation findings can be misused.

Regarding evaluations of development programs, the World Bank Operations Evaluation Department (OED) recently concluded that "for all development agencies, monitoring and evaluation remains the weakest link in the risk management chain."[2] The Swedish International Development Agency (SIDA), in a recent assessment of its evaluation practices, found disappointingly that most stakeholders never even saw the findings and that few of those who did found nothing very new or useful and concluded that "for the majority of stakeholders evaluation could just as well have been left undone" (Carlsson et al. 1999). A former Director General of OED observed that the "prerequisite of **credibility** is missing in the evaluation systems used by most governments, companies and development agencies" (Picciotto 2002:14).

Why Are Evaluation Findings Underutilized?

Lack of ownership or investment in evaluation may be an inevitable result when, as is often the case, many stakeholders are never consulted about the objectives or design of the evaluation, are not involved in the implementation, and have no opportunity to comment on the findings. This is as true in the United States as in many developing countries. Many stakeholders never even get to see the report. For evaluations in developing countries, access and use are further limited because relatively few reports are translated into the national language of the country studied, and even fewer are available in the local languages spoken by many stakeholders. Civil society also frequently shows its frustration at the lack of involvement in the evaluation process.

There are a number of reasons why evaluation findings are underused:

- *Bad timing:* The findings are often not available when they are needed, making them largely irrelevant by the time they are available. At the other end of the **project cycle**, evaluators often wish to discuss baseline studies and evaluation design at the start of the project at a time when program management is still struggling to launch the project and when it is far too early for them to have any interest in thinking about results that will not become available for perhaps five years (see Box 1.1, p. 22).
- *Lack of flexibility and responsiveness to the information needs of key stakeholders:* Evaluations are normally conducted according to their own administrative logic and frequently cannot respond to the information needs and deadlines of the stakeholders.
- *Wrong question and irrelevant findings:* Many evaluations do not ask the questions of concern to stakeholders and instead provide extensive information on topics that are of little interest.
- *Weak methodology:* The complexities of attributing causality for complex programs operating in a context with many other actors and many exogenous factors, combined with time and budget pressures, and a lack of comparative data, frequently make it impossible to produce very precise and conclusive evaluation findings.
- *Many evaluations are expensive and make too many demands on overtaxed program staff:* Even many potential supporters of evaluation may complain that the exercise requires more resources in terms of funds, staff time, and effort than they feel are justified in terms of added value.

- *Lack of local expertise to conduct, review, and use evaluations:* The lack of familiarity with evaluation methods on the part of client agencies also limits their potential usefulness.

The Challenge of Utilization in RealWorld Evaluation

Ensuring that the findings of RWE are used offers additional challenges. First, many of the time and budget constraints that affect the conducting of the evaluation also affect the ability of the program staff to use the findings. The implementing agency is often understaffed, and clients often do not have time to attend briefing meetings on the evaluation or even to read the report. Funds may not be available to bring key staff members together for briefing meetings, and budget constraints limit the organization's ability to follow up on many of the recommendations. Time constraints may also make it particularly difficult to deliver the report in time for it to contribute to the decision-making process. The loss of even a few days can be critical in situations where the evaluation team is given only a few weeks to conduct the evaluation and present the findings.

Many of the political constraints discussed in Chapter 6 affect the acceptance or implementation of RWE recommendations. As any experienced evaluator will tell you, if stakeholders agree with the findings, there are rarely any questions about the methodology, but if the findings are negative, claiming that the evaluation methodology was unscientific can be a convenient excuse for ignoring findings. RWE constraints may also affect the quality of the evaluation and consequently its credibility. Even if the **mixed-method** approach is able to provide reliable answers to the key questions of concern to the client, the lack of large sample surveys may affect the credibility of the findings in the eyes of some important stakeholders such as project management, the donor agency, or the Ministry of Planning or Finance. Consequently, it is very important to encourage the active involvement of the client right from the start to ensure that she or he understands and accepts the strengths and the limitations of the proposed methodology.

The Importance of the RealWorld Evaluation Scoping Phase for Promoting Utilization

One of the key determinants of whether the evaluation will be useful and whether the findings will be used is the extent to which the clients are involved in all stages of the evaluation process (see Chapter 2 for a discussion of Step 1: Scoping the Evaluation). Do the clients feel that they "own" the evaluation, or do they not really know what the evaluation will produce until they receive the final report? How many times have evaluators felt frustrated when the main reaction from the client to a beautifully prepared report is, "This is not what we wanted or expected"? Table 8.1 summarizes guidelines for helping clients to use the evaluation, and Box 8.1 lists lessons learned from a recent study on ways to enhance evaluation use. The following guidelines for the scoping phase will help increase the likelihood that the evaluation will be useful:

1. Understand the client's information needs (see Chapter 2). Some of the critical questions to determine include the following:

- *What do the clients "need to know," and what would they simply "like to know"?* This distinction is critical when deciding whether the data collection instruments can be simplified and information cut.
- *How will the evaluation findings be used?* To defend the program from its critics? As an initial exploration of whether a new approach seems to work? To present statistically precise estimates of whether the program has achieved quantitative goals? To estimate the cost-effectiveness of the program compared with competing programs?
- *How precise and rigorous do the findings need to be?* As we have emphasized earlier, some digging may be required to determine this. Sometimes the client will state that "a rigorous scientific evaluation" is required. The evaluator may assume this means that a large sample survey is needed to a support pretest/posttest evaluation design with a **comparison group**, when in fact the client means only that the report must be considered by parliament or the funding agency to have been professionally conducted.

2.   Understand the dynamics of the decision-making process and the timing of the different steps. Many evaluations had little practical utility because they missed some critical deadlines or did not understand who the key actors in the decision-making process were. A report delivered on March 4 may be of no practical use if the Ministry of Finance had already made decisions on future funding on March 3! Similarly, utility will be reduced if the preliminary findings did not reach some of the key decision makers on time (or at all).

3.   Define the program theory on which the program is based in close collaboration with key stakeholders (see Chapter 9). It is essential to ensure that the clients and stakeholders and the evaluator are "on the same page" with respect to the understanding of the problem the program is addressing, what its objectives are, how it is expected to achieve these objectives, and what criteria the clients will use in assessing success. In some cases, it is necessary to formulate two or more **program theory models** to reflect the views of different stakeholder groups. This can be particularly important if the evaluation needs to acknowledge and address the views of important critics of the program. Even when conducting an evaluation under extreme time pressure, it is essential to find time to involve clients in this process so as to give them ownership and so they have a stake in the evaluation **outcomes**. There is a great temptation for the evaluators to prepare a model describing what they understand the model to be, and then to present this briefly to the client. Silence or unenthusiastic nods of the head are taken to signal full understanding and agreement.

4.   Identify budget, time, and data constraints and prioritize their importance and the client's flexibility (see Chapter 2). The constraints will be assessed by the evaluator, but their importance and the client's flexibility (e.g., to delay submission of the report or obtain additional funds) must be discussed and agreed to with the client. It will sometimes be found, for example, that the "deadline" for presenting the report is in fact only a deadline for the preparation of an informal status report. Similarly, there may be some flexibility in the evaluation budget. However, these constraints and priorities must be fully discussed in a strategy session with the client, and the evaluator must never assume, for example, that "the client would not mind waiting a few more weeks to get a better report."

5.   Understand the political context (see Chapter 6). It is essential for the evaluator to understand as fully as possible the political context of the evaluation. The evaluation may often

address sensitive or even confidential issues, so a great deal of sensitivity and tact is required. Some of the questions include the following:

- Who are the key stakeholders, and what is their interest in the evaluation?
- Who are the main critics of the program, what are their concerns/criticisms, and what would they like to happen? What kinds of **evidence** would they find most convincing? How can each critic influence the future direction of the program (or even its continuance)?
- What are the main concerns of different stakeholders with respect to the methodology? Are there sensitivities concerning the choice of quantitative (**QUANT**) or qualitative (**QUAL**) methodologies? How important are large sample surveys to the credibility of the evaluation?

In addition to the sensitivity of the questions, the relationship with the client on these issues must also be treated carefully. Although it is important to gain the confidence of the client, it is essential for the evaluator to maintain objectivity and not to be seen as an ally of program management against their critics.

6. Prepare a set of RWE design options to address the constraints and strategize with the client to assess which option is most acceptable. A chart or similar format should be prepared describing several possible design options that can address the budget, time, and other constraints and highlighting the strengths and weaknesses of each one. It is particularly important that the client understands the trade-offs and how the validity of the conclusions can be affected by the different options. It is essential that clients see this as a strategy session in which they have a major role in making the final decision on the option to choose. The role of the evaluator is to advise on the consequences of each option and *not* to tell the client which is the "best" or the "correct" option. This is usually the most critical stage at which the client either buys into the evaluation or abdicates responsibility and ownership.

Formative Evaluation Strategies

An evaluation intended to furnish information for guiding program improvement is called a formative evaluation (Scriven 1991) because its purpose is to help form or shape the program to perform better (Rossi, Lipsey, and Freeman 2004:34). A central element of the RWE approach, particularly for QUANT evaluations, is that, even when the primary objective is to assess program outcomes and **impacts**, it is important to "open up the **black box**" and to study the process of program implementation.[3] This is important for the following reasons:

- To explain why certain expected outcomes have or have not been achieved
- To explain why certain groups may have benefited from the program while others have not
- To identify and assess the *causes* of outcomes and impacts. These may be planned or unanticipated, positive or negative.
- To provide a framework for assessing whether a program that has not achieved its objectives is fundamentally sound and should be continued or expanded (with certain modifications) or whether the program model has proved not to work—at least not in the contexts where it has been tried so far.

Box 8.1   Enhancing Evaluation Utilization: Lessons Learned

The Operations Evaluation Department of the World Bank prepared case studies on evaluations in seven different countries that had a significant influence on the client agencies and on the design or implementation of future policies or programs. The following factors affected the likelihood that evaluation findings would be used:

- *The importance of a conducive policy environment:* The findings of the evaluation are much more likely to be used if they address current policy concerns and if policymakers are committed to accepting the political consequences of implementing the findings.
- *The timing of the evaluation:* The evaluation should be launched when decision makers have clearly defined information needs. The findings must be delivered in time to affect decisions, and key results must often be communicated informally before the final report is completed.
- *The role of the evaluation:* The evaluation is rarely the only, or even the most important, source of information or influence for policymakers and managers. A successful evaluation must adapt to the context within which it will be used, and the evaluator must understand when and how the findings can most effectively be used.
- *Building a relationship with the client and effective communication of the evaluation findings:* It is essential to establish a good relationship with key stakeholders, listen carefully to their needs, understand their perception of the political context, and keep them informed of the progress of the evaluation. There should be "no surprises" when the evaluation findings are presented.
- *Defining who should conduct the evaluation:* There are pros and cons of conducting an evaluation internally or of commissioning an independent external evaluation. It is important to determine the most appropriate arrangement for each evaluation. Sometimes a combination of internal and external evaluators can be a good compromise.
- *Adapting the scope and methodology of the evaluation to the client's needs and local context:* Sometimes use can be enhanced if the scope of the evaluation can be broadened or the methodology modified in response to a better understanding of client needs.

SOURCE: Operations Evaluation Department, World Bank (2005).

In addition to the preceding reasons, the analysis of the program **implementation process** also means that the evaluation can contribute to improving the performance of the ongoing program (formative evaluation). The first way to do this is by the evaluator's providing regular feedback and suggestions to program management and other key stakeholders. The second way is by involving program staff and other stakeholders in the evaluation so that they learn for themselves what is working and what is not. Box 8.2 gives several examples of ways in which rapid feedback from the evaluation can help improve the operation of a project.

Many, but not all, formative evaluation strategies help promote evaluation **utilization** as stakeholders start to use the findings of the **process evaluation** long before even the draft final evaluation reports have been produced. Involving the clients at this early stage also means they are more likely to review the final reports and consider how to use the recommendations.

Table 8.1   Guidelines for Helping Clients Use the Evaluation

1. **Scoping the evaluation**
   a. Understand the client's information needs.
   b. Understand the dynamics and timetable of the decision-making process.
   c. Define the program theory on which the program is based in close collaboration with key stakeholders.
   d. Identify budget, time, and data constraints and prioritize their importance.
   e. Understand the political context.
   f. Prepare a set of RWE options to address the constraints and strategize with the client to assess which option is most acceptable.

2. **Formative evaluation strategies**
   Try to incorporate *process evaluation* and other methods that provide periodic feedback to clients on ways to improve project implementation.

3. **Constant communication with clients throughout the evaluation**
   a. Keep clients informed about the progress of the evaluation and the preliminary findings and hypotheses.
   b. Ensure there are "no surprises" for clients in the main evaluation reports.

4. **Evaluation capacity building**
   a. Actively involve clients and users in the scoping phase.
   b. Ensure that the program theory model is developed in a participatory way.
   c. Ensure that users understand the trade-offs in the choice between RWE designs.
   d. Invite users to participate in the evaluation training programs for practitioners.
   e. Encourage users to participate in the periodic progress briefings on the evaluation.
   f. Involve users as resource people in briefings for other organizations that are planning evaluations.

5. **Communicating the findings of the evaluation**
   a. Understand what users want to know.
   b. Understand how different users like to receive information.
   c. Understand the kinds of evidence users want (statistics, case studies, photos, etc.).
   d. Ensure that presentations are pitched at the right technical level.
   e. Consider separate customized presentations targeted for different audiences.
   f. Ensure that reports are available in the user's language.

6. **Developing a follow-up action plan**
   a. Ensure that there is user buy-in to the evaluation so users are prepared to consider using relevant findings and recommendations.
   b. Identify options, but where possible let users decide the actions to be taken.
   c. The role of the evaluator in the preparation of the action plan should be as a low-key technical resource and facilitator. Sometimes it's better not to attend all action planning meetings to allow more freedom to clients and other users.
   d. A key role for the evaluator is to ensure that an action plan is prepared. As far as possible, the content should be left to the users to define and follow up.

Box 8.2   Using Feedback from Process Evaluation to Improve Project
Performance (Formative Evaluation)

The following are examples of feedback for **process evaluations**:

- The material supply stores (for a self-help housing program) need to stay open later in the evening so that people can go there after work.
- Less educated people are discouraged from applying for small loans because the forms are too difficult for them.
- There are frequent complaints that bribes must be paid to staff in the health clinics.
- Absentee rates for girls in high school increase because many girls are teased when they walk through the village to school.

Communication with Clients throughout the Evaluation

Promoting a positive attitude toward evaluation findings often involves ensuring that clients face no surprises (Operations Evaluation Department 2004, 2005). The client should be kept informed of the progress of the evaluation and of preliminary findings as they emerge. In particular, the client should be fully briefed on, and should have a chance to react to, the final conclusions and recommendations before they are presented or made available to others. Clients tend to react more defensively to negative findings if they are sprung on them in a formal meeting with other agencies or, even worse, if they learn the findings from the press or another agency.

As always, there is the need to involve clients while maintaining neutrality. This is particularly the case where some negative or sensitive results are coming out that the client may wish to suppress.

Evaluation Capacity Building

Although some evaluations are one-time activities that will probably not be repeated, others are likely to continue over a number of years, over different phases, or over subsequent programs. In such instances, **evaluation capacity building** (strengthening the capacity of stakeholders to commission, design, implement, interpret, and use evaluations) can be viewed both as an enhancement of the quality and utility of the ongoing evaluation and as an investment in strengthening the use of findings (see Chapter 15).

We use the term *evaluation capacity building* to include strengthening both the technical capacity of evaluators to conduct evaluations and the capacity of clients and stakeholders to interpret and use the findings of the evaluation. Although evaluation capacity building is often limited to working with **evaluation practitioners,** in fact one of the most important components is strengthening the motivation and capacity of managers, planners, policymakers, legislators, funding agencies, and public opinion to commission, assess, and/or use the findings of evaluations. In many cases, when agencies do not use evaluation findings, one of the contributing factors is often the lack of evaluation capacity in one of the areas described above.

From the perspective of enhancing evaluation utilization, the following are some of the key activities with **evaluation users** (in addition to the client actually commissioning the evaluation):

- Involve key stakeholders and other potential users in the scoping and design phase. The construction of the program theory model is an important opportunity for capacity building. This is an opportunity to discuss important concepts such as **input**, **process**, and **output** indicators and the definition and measurement of **impacts**.
- Help users understand the logic of the evaluation design and the trade-offs between the different possible designs in terms of how the evaluation will be used.
- Invite interested stakeholders to participate in some of the evaluation training programs or workshops that might be organized primarily for the evaluation practitioners.
- Try to involve all key user audiences in the periodic briefings on the progress of the evaluation.
- Employ users as resource persons if evaluations are organized with other agencies.

Communicating Findings

Many potentially useful evaluations have little impact because the findings are not communicated to potential users in a way that they find useful or comprehensible or, even worse, because the findings never ever reached important sections of the user community. The following are some guidelines for communicating evaluation findings to enhance utilization (see Chapter 15):

- Clarify what each user wants to know and the amount of detail required. Do specific users want a long report with lots of tables and charts or a brief overview? Do they want many details on each project site, school, region, or just a summary of the general findings?
- Understand how different users like to receive information. In a written report? In a group meeting with slides or a PowerPoint presentation? In an informal personal briefing?
- Clarify whether users want "hard facts" (statistics) or whether they prefer narratives supported by photos and video. Do they want a global overview, or do they want to understand how the program affects individual people and communities?
- Be prepared to use different communication strategies for different users. One size does usually not fit all.
- Ensure that presentations are pitched on the right level of detail or technicality. Do not overwhelm managers with statistical analysis or detailed discussion of sample design, but do not insult professional audiences by implying that they could not understand the technicalities.
- Ascertain the preferred medium for presenting the findings. A written report is not the only way to communicate findings. Other options include verbal presentations to groups, video, photographs, meetings with program beneficiaries, or visits to program locations. Sometimes attending a meeting in the community in which residents talk about the program can have much more impact than a written report.
- Make sure the communication is in the right language(s) when conducting evaluation in multilingual communities or countries.

Developing a Follow-up Action Plan

Many evaluations present detailed recommendations but then have very little practical utility because the recommendations are never put into practice—even though all groups might have expressed agreement. What is needed is an agreed action plan with specific, time-bound actions, clear definition of responsibility, and procedures for monitoring compliance. Many government and international agencies have standard procedures to monitor the implementation of evaluation recommendations, but such systems are used much less frequently for RWE-type evaluations. For example, the World Bank Operations Evaluation Department and the Department of Budget (DIPRES) of the Ministry of Finance in Chile among many other agencies keep a log of all recommendations included in their evaluations, management response to these recommendations and the agreed actions, and periodic follow-ups to report on the status of the agreed actions.

For RWE, as for many other evaluations, the definition of a follow-up action plan is an effective way to promote utilization of the evaluation findings. Some of the steps include the following:

- As we stressed earlier, a key strategy involves ensuring client and stakeholder "buy-in" to the evaluation process so that there is willingness to review and, where there is agreement, implement the evaluation findings.
- The evaluation report must identify the key issues on which decisions must be made and follow-up actions agreed. However, the external evaluator needs to be cautious about presenting specific recommendations so as to not discourage users from taking ownership of the action plan. In preparing the report, the evaluator, in consultation with the clients, must decide which of the following is best:
  - Present a list of issues but not propose specific actions
  - Present a number of follow-up options but not recommend which one is best
  - Present specific recommendations on follow-up actions. This may be appropriate when discussing technical issues (e.g., which financial management package is compatible with the computer systems used by the agency)
- The action plan must be developed by the interested organizations with the evaluator as a technical resource and, possibly, facilitator. It is sometimes better for the evaluator not to participate in the action planning meetings so as to give more feeling of ownership and freedom of action to the agencies themselves.
- Often, the evaluator can help develop measurable indicators and timetables to monitor progress. One of the evaluator's key contributions is to ensure that the action plan is actually developed before she or he leaves.

Summary

- Evaluation findings from both developed and developing countries are frequently underutilized. Reasons include (a) bad timing, (b) lack of responsiveness to stakeholder information needs, (c) the right questions are not addressed, (d) weak methodology, (e) the evaluations are too expensive or make too many demands on busy managers, and (f) a lack of local expertise to conduct, review, and use evaluation.

- The scoping phase is critical to ensure that the right questions are included in the evaluation to secure commitments and involvement by key stakeholders.

- Impact (summative) evaluation should be combined with formative evaluation so that clients see constant feedback and benefits from the evaluation.

- Building evaluation capacity among stakeholders, including evaluation practitioners, users, and teachers, is essential to increase the agency's or national capacity to commission, implement, and use evaluations. Evaluation capacity building is a process that can continue over many years.

- A communication strategy is required to ensure that the findings and recommendations reach all the right audiences and that they are presented in a way that is understandable and acceptable to different audiences. Ensuring that the findings are available in the right languages is an important, but often overlooked, point.

- Finally, stakeholders often agree with evaluation findings and plan to implement them, but the good intentions are forgotten in the pressure of other activities. Consequently, it is important to work with clients and stakeholders to develop a follow-up action plan and to put in place mechanisms, such as periodic meetings or the preparation of regular reports, to monitor progress.

Further Reading

Gray, D. 2004. *Doing Research in the Real World.* Thousand Oaks, CA: Sage.

Chapter 14 provides a useful discussion of action research—one of the important utilization-focused approaches to evaluation.

Operations Evaluation Department. 2004, 2005. *Influential Evaluations: Evaluations That Improved Performance and Impacts of Development Programs.* Washington, DC: World Bank. Available at www.worldbank.org/oed/ecd

This describes eight evaluations from countries in Africa, South and East Asia, and Eastern Europe that had a significant impact on the future directions of the programs or policies evaluated. A set of criteria is applied for determining whether observed changed could be attributed to the evaluation and where possible cost-effectiveness analysis was applied to demonstrate that evaluation can be an effective management tool. The final chapter includes lessons on how to design and implement useful evaluations. The summary (2004) report is available in English, Spanish, French, Portuguese, Arabic, and Russian. The 2005 report provides more detailed information on each case study.

Patton, M. Q. 1997. *Utilization-Focused Evaluation.* 3d ed. Thousand Oaks, CA: Sage.

This is one of the most comprehensive and widely used texts on evaluation utilization.

Rossi, P., M. Lipsey, and H. Freeman. 2004. *Evaluation: A Systematic Approach.* 7th ed. Thousand Oaks, CA: Sage.

Chapters 2 and 12 (pp. 411–18) are particularly useful with respect to stakeholder analysis and the social and political context of evaluation.

Notes

1. Several of the examples and citations in this paragraph are taken from Patton (1997, chap. 1).

2. Operations Evaluation Department Memorandum to the Executive Directors and the President on the Annual Report on Operations Evaluation 2002 (June 10, 2002).

3. The issue of the "black box" (a term widely used in economic analysis) concerns only QUANT pretest/posttest evaluation designs where data are collected only at the start and the end of the project and the project implementation process is not studied. Many authors—including Stufflebeam's (1987) CIPP, Greene's (1997) participatory, Stake's (1975) responsive, Patton's (1997) utilization, Fetterman's (1996) empowerment, Scriven's (1991) goal-free, House's (House 1993; House and Howe 1999) democratic approaches—do not treat implementation or process as a black box.

PART III

A Review of Evaluation Methods and Approaches and Their Applications in RealWorld Evaluation

CHAPTER 9

Applications of Program Theory in RealWorld Evaluation

T his chapter discusses program theory evaluation and some of its main applications. Program theory is particularly useful for RealWorld Evaluation (**RWE**) because it helps identify the critical issues on which scarce evaluation resources should focus, and where possible a **program theory model**[1] should be developed during Step 1 (scoping the evaluation) of the evaluation. Two submodels are frequently combined in program theory: the *impact model* (sometimes called the change model) and the *implementation model* (sometimes called the action model). The construction of these two submodels and their main components are discussed together with the ways in which each is used. Although all **programs** are based on a set of ideas and assumptions about the problems being addressed, how the program will work, and what it will achieve, these assumptions have often not been made explicit, and often, one of the tasks of the evaluator is to work with the **client** and other **stakeholders** to elicit and formulate the underlying program theory model. We then discuss logical framework analysis (logframe), a form of program theory used by many agencies to monitor program performance. The chapter concludes with a review of some of the different perspectives on the extent to which program theory can help explain causality.

Defining Program Theory Evaluation

Program theory evaluation "consists of an explicit theory or model of how the program causes the intended or observed **outcomes** and an evaluation that is at least partly guided by this model" (Rogers, Petrosino et al. 2000:5). Program theory "identifies program resources, program activities, and intended program outcomes, and specifies a chain of causal assumptions linking program resources, activities and intermediate outcomes and ultimate program goals" (Wholey 1987:78). Also known as program theory (Bickman 1987), theory-based evaluation (Weiss 1995, 1997), and program logic (Funnell 1997, 2000; Lenne and Cleland 1987), program theory evaluation has been gaining in popularity due to the recognition that a program's success or failure can be assessed only with a clear understanding of the problem it was intended to address, the rationale for choosing a particular approach, and how the program was expected to operate.

Program theory can significantly strengthen quantitative pretest-posttest evaluation designs. Critics of these designs often refer to them as "**black-box**" evaluations (see Figure 9.1) because no information is collected on what actually happens inside the **project** while it is being designed and implemented. If a project fails to produce the intended changes or impacts, this type of pretest-posttest evaluation is not able to judge whether the failure was due to a weakness in the analysis and theory on which the project was based, weaknesses in how the project was implemented, or the effects of a particular set of contextual factors such as a weak economy, political opposition, lack of support from partner agencies, or environmental and climatic factors.

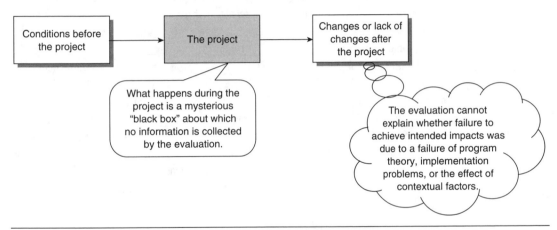

Figure 9.1   Weaknesses of the "Black Box" Approach to Evaluation

The purpose of program theory evaluation is to help explain why expected impacts were or were not achieved by assessing the following:

- The strengths and weaknesses on the program theory underlying the program design
- The strengths and weaknesses of how the program was implemented
- How contextual factors contributed to, or militated against, the achievement of intended impacts.

In this way, program theory can both contribute to improving the design and implementation of ongoing programs (**formative evaluation**) and also recommend whether, where, and how the program could be scaled up or applied in other settings.

Applications of Program Theory in Evaluation

The Increasing Use of Program Theory in Evaluation

Program theory in evaluation is now used extensively by government agencies, not-for-profit organizations, and discipline-specific research journals in many fields including education, criminology, and sociology (Rogers, Petrosino, et al. 2000). For example, the U.S. National

Institutes of Health now require the discussion of program theory in all research proposals, and the Centers for Disease Control and Prevention has developed extensive training material to assist the organizations with whom it works to strengthen their capacity in the use of logic models (Centers for Disease Control 1999). Three separate volumes of *New Directions for Evaluation,* a periodical published by the American Evaluation Association, have been devoted to program theory evaluation, and many evaluation textbooks (e.g., Chen 2005; Creswell 2003; Rossi, Lipsey, and Freeman 2004) include chapters on program theory. In the United States many nongovernmental organizations (**NGOs**) (e.g., Community Tool Box 2005) and the organizations that fund them (e.g., W. K. Kellogg Foundation 1998) also provide extensive guidance on the use of **logic models.**

Logical framework analysis or one of its variants (see later in this chapter), one of the most common ways to translate program theory into monitorable performance indicators, is now required by many national and international development agencies, including the World Bank, the U.S. Agency for International Development, and the U.K. Department for International Development.

By identifying critical assumptions and issues in program design, program theory can contribute to improving the way in which the program is managed and implemented by ensuring that the monitoring system provides feedback on issues affecting performance (see Box 9.1). By pointing out where to look, a program theory can increase the practical utility of monitoring and rapid assessment studies. For example, a program theory that anticipates different ways that men and women are likely to participate in and be affected by the project can help ensure that sex-disaggregated monitoring and performance indicators are used.

Developing a program theory can assist evaluation design in the following ways (see also Chen 2005:74):

- *Defining the program rationale.* What problem is the program trying to alleviate or resolve? On which target groups does it focus? Which interventions are used to affect

---

Box 9.1   Applying Program Theory to Evaluate the Family Empowerment
Project

Bickman and his colleagues conducted an experimental test of the effects of a program that trained parents to be stronger advocates for children in the mental health system. They articulated a model of how the program was assumed to work. First, parent training would increase the parent's knowledge, self-efficacy, and advocacy skills. Second, parents would then become more involved in their child's mental health care. Finally, this collaboration would lead to the child's improved mental health outcomes. They also constructed measures, collected data, and then analyzed them to test these underlying assumptions. The program was able to achieve statistically significant effects on parental knowledge and self-efficacy, but no useful measures for testing advocacy skills could be found. Based on this model, it was found that the intervention had no apparent effect on caregiver involvement in treatment or service use and ultimately had no impact on the eventual mental health status of the children.

SOURCE: Bickman (1987).

program implementation and outcomes? On which determinants should the evaluation focus? What program goals or outcomes are to be achieved?

- *Clarifying stakeholders' implicit program theories.* Program planners and implementers almost always have assumptions about why this program approach is better than other options and how it is expected to work and produce the desired results. Frequently, these assumptions have not been written down or clearly articulated in a manner that can be used for developing the program theory. Sometimes, different staff members or stakeholders have different assumptions that may be tested. For example, some staff members may feel that the inculcation of moral values is a key factor in determining success of programs for youth, whereas others may feel that the organization of sports and other group activities is more important.

- *Articulating program rationale.* Programs are often based on explicit or implicit assumptions about the needs that should be addressed. If a social and economic study or needs assessment has not been conducted, one may be helpful for answering such questions as these: What are the most important social, economic, cultural, psychological, and security problems affecting the community? How could the program address them? This information might be obtained through interviews with community leaders and other key informants, **focus groups,** and rapid socioeconomic surveys.

- *Choosing interventions/treatments that affect the problems the program is designed to address.* Usually, a number of different interventions can be used to address the problems on which the program is focused. These options should be identified (e.g., a review of the literature, experience from earlier programs, consultation with specialists in the field) and the strengths and weaknesses of each approach assessed.

- *Identification and analysis of unintended effects.* Many programs have unanticipated effects, some of which may be positive (e.g., when the experience gained in this project encourages a community council to launch other programs) or negative (e.g., if the project creates conflicts between different groups in the community or the construction of a road leads to an increase in robberies and violence by outsiders who can now more easily visit the community). Sometimes the program theory will be able to specify some of the effects (see Figure 9.4 for an example of how potential negative effects were identified for a **microcredit** program from women). In many cases, a program theory will be able to alert evaluators and staff to some of the areas where such effects might occur.

- *Identifying the critical areas or linkages of the program to evaluate.* Figure 9.4 also illustrates how program theory can identify critical areas or linkages. For example, once new businesses established by women drawing on a microcredit program begin to generate profits, it is possible that these profits will not be reinvested in the business (as intended in the program design) but instead taken by the husband or used by the woman to provide her daughter with a dowry or to pay off debts. A program theory might be helpful in identifying this as one of the critical issues to be assessed in an evaluation.

- *Using program theory to help scale up successful programs.* By identifying and then assessing the critical assumptions on which the program was based, program theory can help assess the likely success of expanding the program to benefit larger numbers of stakeholders. It can also help identify the elements of program design that will require particular attention if it is expanded.

Utility of Program Theory for RealWorld Evaluation

Program theory can be particularly valuable for RWE in helping to identify priority issues on which to concentrate when working under time, budget, and possibly data constraints. For example:

- What are the critical links and assumptions on which the success of the program depends? Do the key issues address whether the program will be able to reach all the target groups (e.g., ethnic minorities, landless laborers)? Will the program's inputs (e.g., training, technical assistance, mentoring) be sufficient to produce the desired effects? Will the effects be sustainable over time?

- What are the critical links and assumptions for which additional information is needed? An analysis of the literature, consultation with experts, or a review of earlier project evaluations may be able to help determine which links in the program theory model are supported by existing data and which have very little support.

- Which are the key issues or areas of concern to program managers and other key stakeholders? Consultations with managers and stakeholders as the program theory is developed will help identify priority issues for management. Often, the realization that there is no firm **evidence** to support some assumptions may also highlight the importance of new questions.

- Which links or assumptions are most critical for assessing the potential expansion of the program? When evaluation resources are tight, program theory can help identify the questions that are critical. For example, a pilot job training program to help young men move from welfare to work may include subsidies (e.g., travel vouchers, help with car payments) that would not be included in a large-scale replication of the program. Consequently, a critical question for replicability might be whether the kinds of jobs that the young men are able to get pay enough for them to stay at work without these subsidies.

- What initial indicators of program success can be used? Using a **results chain** model similar to the one in Figure 9.4 can often identify economical and easy-to-measure indicators showing that the program is on the right track. These can be very useful for RWE if resources are not available to conduct a full evaluation covering all stages of the program (i.e., long-term economic impact or effects on school enrollment).

- Can program theory suggest some simple and economic ways to determine program impact? Our view is that, when used with the appropriate caveats, program theory can suggest some useful tentative indications of potential impacts. However, readers should read the section of this chapter presenting both sides of the argument and decide for themselves.

- Can program theory help distinguish between theory failure and implementation failure (Chen 2005; Lipsey 1993)? In cases where the intended program effects have not been achieved, program theory can help determine whether the program model does not work or whether it is a potentially good model requiring fine-tuning.

Constructing Program Theory Models

Program Impact and Implementation Models[2]

A program theory includes both descriptive assumptions about the causal processes explaining the social problems a program is trying to address and prescriptive assumptions about the components and activities that program designers and other stakeholders consider necessary to a program's success. *Descriptive assumptions* are generally based, at least in part, on an analysis of available research and evidence from other programs and often include a needs assessment or rapid diagnostic study of the social, economic, cultural, security, and other characteristics of the subjects or communities that the program is intended to affect. *Prescriptive assumptions,* on the other hand, are based on judgments and values about which intervention strategy should be selected. These assumptions may be based on a review of earlier projects or consultation with specialists, or they may be largely based on personal values concerning what is the "right" way to address the problems.

The descriptive assumptions are translated into a *program impact model* (Donaldson 2003) articulating the assumptions about the causal processes underlying the decisions to use certain program strategies.[3] Some program theories also develop a *program implementation model* describing how the program will be organized to achieve the intended outcomes and impacts. Depending on the focus of the evaluation, it may be that only one of these two models will suffice, often the case for RWE operating with budget and time constraints. If the purpose of the evaluation is to assess the achievement of goals and the impacts and **outputs**, then the impact model will probably be sufficient. If, on the other hand, the purpose is to assess effective implementation and help improve performance (formative evaluation), then the implementation model may be preferred. In some cases, and resources permitting, it may be useful to use both models.

Program Impact Model

Different terminology has been used to describe the components of an *impact model* (Bamberger et al. 2004; Chen 2005; Creswell et al. 2003; Donaldson 2003; Rossi et al. 2004), sometimes indicated by terms such as *change model.* Figure 9.2 illustrates a program impact model for a women's microcredit project. This model integrates the following components:

Contextual Variables (the setting).[4] A contextual analysis is conducted to identify and understand the social, economic, psychological, security, and environmental setting within which the project operates and the problems, needs, priorities, and constraints of the intended project beneficiaries and the different stakeholders. Projects implemented in the same way in different communities, schools, or regions can have very different outcomes because of differences in these **contextual variables**. This analysis may cover the following:

- *The economic climate.* Are economic conditions getting better, remaining constant, or getting worse? This will influence the decision of families to participate in any project that either requires payments or that promotes present or future income-generating activities.

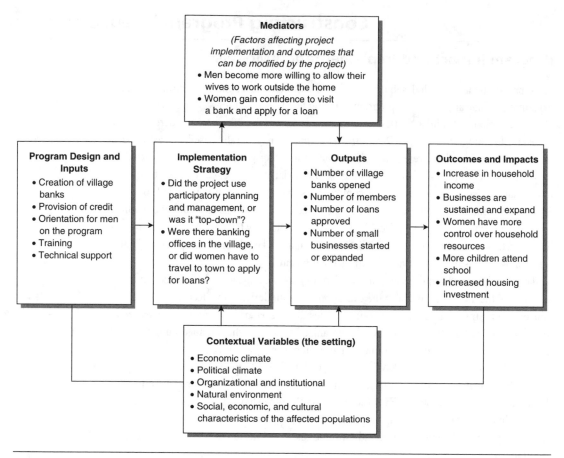

Figure 9.2 An Impact Model for a Women's Small Business Development Program

- *The political climate.* Is the local political climate likely to support or undermine the project?
- *Organizational and institutional factors.* To what extent do local organizations (government, NGOs, and private sector) support or hinder the project?
- *Natural environmental factors.* Do environmental factors influence the project?
- *The characteristics of the communities affected by the project.* How do social, cultural, economic, and other characteristics influence how different groups respond to the project or are affected by it? How might the needs, problems, constraints, and expectations of the different groups affect the project?

The contextual analysis can be derived from a review of the literature, the opinions of stakeholders, a rapid assessment study, or a needs assessment during which the target group is consulted. The needs assessment might use a market research approach in which a target group is surveyed and asked to select among a set of options relating to the planned program strategies, or it might use a participatory assessment method in which families identify their concerns, needs, and proposed solutions. In a microcredit example (see Figure 9.2), a contextual analysis identified a number of constraints on women's access to economic opportunities, including labor laws, labor union protection of male workers, and women's difficulties in obtaining bank loans.

Program Design and Inputs. **Inputs** refer to resources allocated to program efforts to achieve desired outcomes and goals (e.g., money, staff, materials, trainers, vehicles, teaching materials).[5] This includes what some authors call *interventions.* Although some interventions are intended to directly achieve program goals (for example, emergency food or medical supplies), in most cases, programs are designed to influence **mediators** (see below) through changing knowledge, attitudes, or practices. In the case of the women's small business development project, interventions might include the organization of women's banking groups, orientation sessions to reduce the opposition of men to their wives starting their own business, and the provision of credit.

Implementation Strategy. The implementation strategy refers to the way in which inputs are used to achieve the desired effects. Two programs using the same inputs might achieve different results depending on their implementation strategies. For example, one project may use participatory planning and management in which stakeholders were actively involved in program design, implementation, and monitoring, while another uses top-down planning with design and management by client or funding agency. Similarly, one microcredit project might open an office in a community, while another might require women to travel to the nearest town to apply for loans.

Mediators.[6] Mediators are **intervening variables** potentially affecting project performance and that the project may be able to influence (Donaldson 2003). Most programs are influenced by many factors that exert influence on program outcomes. For example, in the case of a health program, mediators might include how a person's course of action is influenced by his or her perceived susceptibility to illness, perceived seriousness of the problem's consequences, perceived benefits of a specific action, and perceived barriers to taking action (Strecher and Rosenstock 1997, cited in Chen 2005:21). For the microcredit program, mediators could be the willingness of husbands to allow their wives to work outside the home following an orientation session on the program or poor rural women gaining sufficient confidence, after joining a village banking group, to visit the local bank to apply for a loan.

Outputs. Outputs are the immediate results that a project seeks to achieve. In the case of the small business development project, these might include the creation of a certain number of village banks with a certain number of members and the authorization and repayment of a certain number of loans. Outputs are immediate results that the project is able to directly influence, although contextual factors will always have an effect.

Outcomes and Impacts. These are the short-, medium-, and long-term changes that the project hopes to affect. Again referring to the microcredit example, outcomes and impacts might include the number of businesses started or expanded, the additional income earned, the increase in women's control over family resources and role in family decision making, and the improvements in family living conditions, such as increased school attendance, better health, and increased investment in housing.

Program Implementation Model

A *program implementation model* describes how staff and resources are to be used to deliver the program services to the **target population**. It also identifies the support components, including organizations with whom the program will interact, and the context within which the program will operate. A program implementation model also explains "how and why the intended beneficiaries will actually become engaged with the program and follow-through to the point of receiving sufficient services to initiate the change process" (Rossi et al. 2004:142.) An implementation model[7] usually includes most of the following components, although sometimes with different names (Bamberger et al. 2004; Chen 2005; Donaldson 2003; Rossi et al. 2004):

Program Design and Operational Plan. An operational manual may be the means of describing program content and activities in the intervention and operating procedures. Often, this manual will cover topics such as program objectives, the service lines to be provided, the program implementation calendar, and the program budget. Many programs spell out the activities in a logical framework (see later in this chapter). Some programs also have a *service delivery protocol* that spells out the steps to be taken to deliver the intervention in the field (Chen 2005). This protocol will normally cover (a) client processing procedures (how clients move through the system), (b) division of labor in service delivery (who is responsible for what), (c) settings (where services are provided), and (d) communication channels (how the agency communicates with its staff and clients and with the other agencies with which it is working).

Implementing Organizations. The implementing organizations component of the model identifies the organizations that will be responsible for implementing different components of the program and describes their responsibilities and, where appropriate, the coordinating mechanisms among them.

Staff Recruitment and Human Resource Development Goals. These goals describe the process of recruiting and training staff, defining their functions, communication mechanisms, and performance monitoring and feedback mechanisms. Social objectives, such as promoting gender equality or ensuring the equitable treatment of ethnic minorities, may be included as goals.[8]

Partner Organizations. This component describes the responsibilities of the different organizations and the coordination mechanisms among them. The model may include indicators for assessing the effectiveness of different cooperation mechanisms.[9]

Contextual Variables. The degree to which a program is able to achieve its goals and impacts is determined to a considerable degree by contextual variables described in the previous section. When projects with the same design and inputs are implemented in different locations, the outputs and impacts are often significantly different because of the operation of these contextual variables. As a result, **findings** related to generalizability are always somewhat speculative, and a situation analysis should include these variables and their effects on program performance.

Target Population. Useful information for a program implementation model includes whether there are clearly defined eligibility criteria for prospective beneficiaries, the feasibility of reaching and effectively serving them, and the willingness of potential clients to participate in the

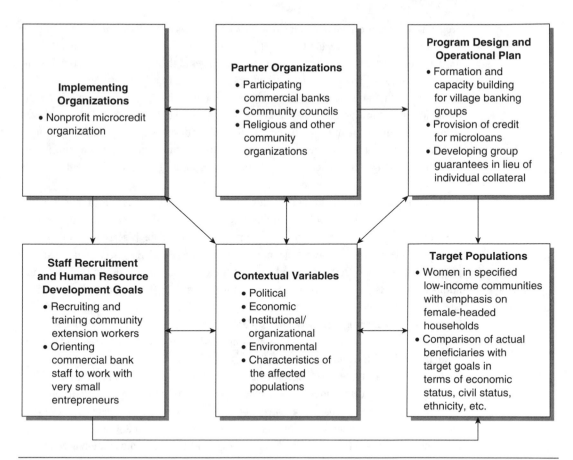

Figure 9.3   Applying the Implementation Model to a Women's Small Business Development Program

SOURCE: Adapted from Chen (2005, chap. 2). Example developed by the present authors.

program. Eligibility criteria and how they are applied often require careful scrutiny because, for example, one race or sex or age group may be excluded from benefits in practice, despite their formal eligibility. It is generally necessary to compare the characteristics of the actual beneficiaries with specified eligibility criteria, for example, to determine how intended and actual participants compare in terms of age, economic characteristics, sex, ethnicity, or occupation. Comparing at different points in the **project cycle** may show improvements in breadth of coverage over time or not.

Figure 9.3 illustrates how the implementation model could be used to describe the women's small business development program discussed earlier in this section.

Articulating Program Theory

Social science literature relevant to the type of program to be evaluated and the beliefs of stakeholders concerning the nature, causes, and possible remedies for the problems the program should address are important sources of information for developing a theory of the program. A literature review may help in developing a *theory-driven evaluation* approach focused on the problems facing the target population and the causal chains through which impacts are expected to be achieved. One of the challenges of theory-driven evaluation is identifying and accounting for unanticipated effects not specified in the model. Especially when programs are based on the beliefs of stakeholders or the lessons drawn from experience, the theoretical basis for a program may not be clearly articulated. In these cases, theory-driven evaluation design will require articulating the theory. For developing program theory, evaluators may review material produced by the program (e.g., funding proposal, program implementation plan, reports, publicity materials, brochures, posters) and interview (individual or focus group) program staff members.

Different people may hold significantly different opinions about the problems to be addressed and how they should be approached. Evaluations done without agreement on the program definition are likely to be of limited use (Centers for Disease Control 1999:3). Different models reflecting these different views can be presented, discussed, compared, and perhaps tested. Weiss (2000) recommends that three or four is realistically the maximum number of models that can be compared. Sometimes, negotiating with stakeholders to formulate a clear and logical description of the program will bring benefits before data are even available to evaluate program effectiveness (Centers for Disease Control 1999:3). Box 9.2 illustrates an example of two alternative theories formulated to evaluate the outcomes and impacts of **social funds** in developing countries.

There are at least three ways to reconstruct a program's theory. The *strategic approach* identifies, through group discussions with key stakeholders, the means through which the program is expected to achieve its goals. In an *elicitation approach,* strategic documents are reviewed, managers are consulted, and decision-making processes are observed, from which the program theory is derived (Leeuw 2003). Field studies can also provide information used to construct program theories with, for example, the evaluator observing how the program is explained to clients and other stakeholders by program staff and whether staff members encourage or discourage different groups of potential beneficiaries.

Box 9.2   Formulating and Testing Two Rival Program Theories

Social funds are widely used programs in developing countries in which local communities are invited to identify social infrastructure projects (water supply, schools, roads, health centers, etc.). The projects are then funded and usually constructed by local government agencies with a high level of community involvement. In their evaluation of more than 50 social funds, Carvalho and White (2004) identified two alternative theories of potential outcomes and impacts of the social funds. Critics argued that the social funds would be captured by the local elites and would also undermine local government by creating parallel social service implementing agencies. In contrast, supporters argued that the social funds would strengthen community-level institutions while at the same time providing a cost-effective delivery system for the provision of social services. Two social program models were formulated to test these two alternative theories.

A *conceptualization facilitation* approach to formulating program theories (Chen 2005) draws on program planners and stakeholders, who often have plenty of ideas about their program's rationale, but often do not know how to clarify their thoughts and connect them systematically. An evaluator may facilitate this process by helping them either through *forward reasoning* (working from a prospective intervention to predicting its outcomes) or *backward reasoning* (starting from the desired outcomes and working backward to identify determinants and intervening factors). In intensive interviews or working groups, they may identify the problem, target population, final goals and measurable outcomes, and critical influences on outcomes. Backward reasoning may permit greater flexibility, but whether or not the group has already decided on the program's intervention may determine whether forward or backward reasoning is appropriate.

Weiss (2000) proposed criteria for helping identify research findings that can contribute to the program theory. First, study the beliefs of implementers, sponsors, and other people associated with the program. What these people deeply believe to be critical is likely to determine their actions with respect to the program. Second, assess plausibility. Can the program actually do the things the theory assumes? Some indicators of plausibility include the following:

- *How funds have been allocated.* If people talk a lot about the importance of something but no funds have been allocated, this is an indication that the program component or process is not a high priority.
- *The topics on which information is and is not available.* A lack of available information often (but not always) suggests an aspect that is not a high priority.
- *What staff members actually do.* How people spend their time is another good indicator of priorities.

A third factor is the *centrality of the theory* to program activities. Some theories are interesting but not essential to a program's effectiveness, whereas others address critical issues that affect program success. This distinction is particularly important for RWE because the evaluator must decide which are the critical theories to test when resources are limited. If a program provides resources to community groups to allow them to select from an array of available services, then understanding how the provision of funds works and how well communities use them is likely to be critical to the program theory and success. In another example, if the program makes very little use of the mass media as a way of informing community groups about available options, a theory of how mass media would affect program outcomes may be of little importance.

Weiss (2000) also points out that cost and time constraints usually make it impossible or unnecessary to study all aspects of program change, as might be articulated in theories of change or theories of action, and proposes the following guidelines for selecting the critical program links on which an evaluation should focus.

- *When in the program timeline the evaluator is engaged.* Some kinds of issues are important to study at the start of a program (e.g., the criteria for defining the target group and participant selection) but less important at a later point in the project. When an evaluation begins long after the start of the program, early documents may no longer represent actual components on which the evaluation should focus its attention and resources.
- *Funds and time available for the evaluation.* Some issues may be important but be so expensive and time-consuming to study that they may have to be excluded from the evaluation.

- *How easy it is to collect different kinds of information.* Some kinds of information are more difficult to collect than others; importance and availability need to be balanced.
- *Priority concerns of program staff.* Special attention must usually be given to the issues of concern to staff. However, this is not the only criterion for determining evaluation priority; there may be issues that staff members do not consider important but might nevertheless appreciate after valuable information has been collected.
- *Psychosocial linkages (the why of social change) underlying the program.* Why should developing countries give priority to getting more girls into school? Why do trainees remain in programs? Understanding the justification for the beliefs that underlie program goals and strategies often helps identify critical issues and assumptions that an evaluation might usefully address.
- *The links most critical to program success.* Some assumptions about linkages between inputs, implementation strategies, mediators, contextual factors, and outcomes may be critical to the success of the program and receive priority.
- *The degree of uncertainty.* Some information is likely to be already known reasonably well (e.g., the proportion of children enrolled in school), whereas information on other topics may be scarce (e.g., the reasons why certain groups of children drop out of school or perform poorly). Often (but not always) there is a higher payoff on collecting data to fill bigger information gaps than to add small details.

Logical Framework Analysis and Results Chains

Logical framework analysis (LFA or logframe) translates program theory into a series of monitorable indicators so that progress can be tracked and factors determining achievement or nonachievement of outputs and impacts can be assessed. Logframes or variants thereof are widely used as a program monitoring and evaluation tool by international development agencies (e.g., World Bank, U.S. Agency for International Development, and the U.K. Department for International Development) and agencies such as the Department of Education and the Centers for Disease Control and Prevention in the United States.

Let's consider an example in depth. Table 9.1 illustrates a typical logframe matrix used to monitor a large development program for flood-affected areas in a south Asian country. The purpose of the program was to improve the provision of public services such as health and education and to provide increased economic opportunities through markets, transportation, and small business development. The left-hand column of the table shows the levels of analysis, starting at the top with the broad objectives (*goal*) and moving downward through *purpose* and then *components,* each with a number of activities to be conducted under each component. In this case, the broad goal of the program is to halve the proportion of the population living below the poverty line. The purpose of the program that will be undertaken to achieve the goal is the improved livelihood security and reduced natural environmental and economic vulnerability of residents. The program had a number of components, only two of which are listed in this illustration.

Component 1: *reduced vulnerability through the targeted provision of infrastructure (water supply, roads, flood-proofing of houses) and services (primary health services and education).* The table lists the *activities* to be carried out in implementation of this component. For purposes of illustration, only two of the program's 10 activities are listed: (a) the selecting and

Table 9.1 Illustration of Part of a Typical Logical Framework Analysis Matrix[a]

Level	Operationally Verifiable Indicator (OVI)	Method of Verification (MOV)	Assumptions and Risk
Goal			
To halve the proportion of the population living below the poverty line			
Purpose			
Improved livelihood security and reduced vulnerability for men and women in the project area			
Component 1:	75% of communities have an improved infrastructure or service	1. Minutes of community meetings	1. The government will continue to make resources available for the project.
Reduced vulnerability through targeted provision of infrastructure and services		2. Citizen satisfaction surveys	2. Communities will demonstrate capacity and willingness to participate in planning activities
		3. Feedback from PRA studies	
Activity 1.1 Select and contract local companies that can construct infrastructure			
Activity 1.2 Existing social protection schemes are extended and improved			
[Other activities for Component 1]			
Component 2:			
Poor men and women have sustainable livelihoods and greater participation in the local economy			
Activity 2.1 Identify and contract agencies that can work on livelihood development			
Activity 2.2 Develop communication channels to ensure flow of market information between community groups and contractors			
[Other components and activities]			

a. Only a few cells have been filled in for illustration.

contracting of local contractors to work on infrastructure and (b) extension and improvement of existing social protection programs.

Component 2: *that poor men and women have sustainable livelihoods and greater participation in the local economy.* This component also has a list of corresponding program activities. Each row of the table contains columns defining how progress will be monitored and identifying some critical assumptions about the goals, purposes, components, or activities. For purposes of illustration, only the row for Component 1, *Reduced vulnerability through targeted provision of infrastructure and services,* is listed, showing the following in the cells of the table:

- *Operationally verifiable indicators* (OVI) to assess progress and achievements toward the respective goals, purposes, or components. In this case, the indicator of success is that 75% of communities have at least one improved infrastructure (e.g., road, well, houses raised to increase protection from flooding) or service (e.g., a school or clinic built or improved). Since about 2 million people live in the flood-prone areas and the program has to operate within a fixed budget, the target for each community is quite modest—only one infrastructure or service provided or improved per community.
- *Method of verification* (MOV) to specify where and how data will be obtained to evaluate the OVIs. In this case, three sources of information will be used: minutes from community meetings in which the progress of projects are discussed, a brief citizen satisfaction survey administrated to a small sample of households, and feedback from participatory appraisal (**PRA**) studies (see Chapter 5).
- *Assumptions and risks affecting the achievement of the component.* In this case, the two critical assumptions are that the government will continue to make counterpart national resources available for the project and that communities will demonstrate capacity and willingness to participate in the planning of activities. Both assumptions reflect real risks that could seriously affect the success of the component.

Sometimes a process model describing the project cycle (see Chapter 2) will be developed to help define stages in the logframe. Some program staff may find it easier to visualize the stages of a project when they are presented graphically (see Chapter 2, Figure 2.2). The typical stages in a project cycle are these:

- Design
- Inputs
- Implementation process
- Outputs
- Outcomes
- Impact
- Sustainability

Some of the stages of the project cycle are then translated into the left-hand categories in the matrix (e.g., the *Levels* of *Goal, Purpose,* and *Component*). For example:

- *Sustainability* in the process model becomes *goal* in the logframe.
- *Impacts* in the process model become *purpose.*
- *Outcomes* become *components.*
- *Implementation* process and inputs become *activities.*

Some of the **contextual variables** (political, economic, institutional, and environmental factors and the socioeconomic characteristics of the target communities) may also be incorporated into the *Assumptions and Risk* column. For example, the continued financial support from government is an *institutional* factor, and the capacity and willingness of communities to participate in planning activities relate to the socioeconomic characteristics of different sectors of the target population.

A logframe and other types of program theory models identify for monitoring the critical assumptions on which the choice of inputs, the selection of **implementation processes**, and the expected linkages between the different stages of the program cycle are based. One of the important and very useful elements of the logframe is that it identifies some of the critical assumptions about the linkages between the different stages of the model. Table 9.2 illustrates critical assumptions that might be included at each stage of a logframe of a project to strengthen women's economic and social empowerment through microcredit. For example, the use of credit as the major input is based on two assumptions: first that lack of access to credit

Table 9.2   Testing Critical Assumptions in a Logic Model of a Project to Strengthen Women's Economic Empowerment through Microcredit

Stage of Project	*Critical Assumptions to Be Tested*
Design	• Poor women have the skills needed to operate viable income-generating projects but lack only capital. • Women are able to decide what business to start/expand. • Women will be able to control how the loan is used, and the money will not be appropriated by the husband.
Inputs	• Access to credit, in a form that the woman can control, is critical to enhance women's access to economic opportunities.
Implementation process	• The creation of solidarity groups through which loans are approved and technical support provided is essential to enable women to control their use of their loans and to manage their small businesses. • Solidarity groups must select their own members without any outside pressures.
Outputs	• Women will use loans to invest in small businesses (not just to pay off debts or pay for consumption or ceremonial activities). • Women will be able to control the use of the loan (despite cultural traditions that economic resources are controlled by male household members).
Outcomes	• If women produce goods, they will be able to market them. • Their businesses will be profitable. • Women will control, or share in the control of, the profits.
Impact	• Profits will increase household consumption, women's savings, and quality of life of members of their households.
Sustainability	• The women's solidarity groups will be able to continue providing loans after the project's external credit and support has ended. • Their businesses will continue to operate and to grow.

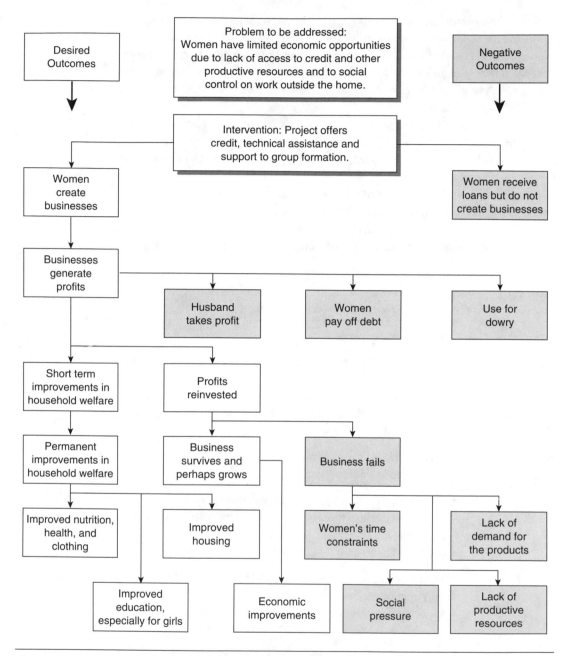

Figure 9.4 A Results Chain Model of the Women's Microcredit Project

is one of the main constraints on women's ability to start a small business and second that if women have access to credit, this will significantly increase the number and **sustainability** of small businesses they start. Both of these assumptions can be tested, and their correctness will be an important determinant of the project's success. Similar assumptions can be identified and tested for each stage of the model.

Figure 9.4 shows how these critical assumptions can be expressed in the form of a results chain diagram. The left-hand side of the figure shows the intended chain of events (women use the loans to create businesses that generate profits that produce improvements in household welfare and that are also reinvested to ensure the growth and sustainability of the business). The right-hand (shaded) side of the figure identifies the different reasons why the project might fail to achieve its objectives (women do not use the loans to create businesses, the profits are taken by the husband or used to pay off debts or to provide dowries, or the businesses fail). Each step can be tested to determine whether the outcomes are positive (as planned) or negative.

Program Theory Evaluation and Causality

Arguments for and against the Use of Program Theory to Help Explain Causality

Some quantitative evaluators have argued that a carefully designed program theory can provide *operationally useful* estimates of program impacts in situations in which it is not possible to implement one or more of the quantitative (**QUANT**) evaluation designs discussed in Chapter 10. As noted earlier in this chapter, many QUANT pretest-posttest evaluation designs do not address one of the key questions of interest to many stakeholders—namely, Do disappointing statistical results mean that the underlying theory is wrong and the program should be scrapped, or is the theory potentially sound but with some weaknesses in its design or implementation? Both program theory impact models and implementation models provide frameworks for assessing the effectiveness of project implementation that can help address this question.

Davidson (2000) identifies nine potential types of evidence for inferring causality (Box 9.3) that can be obtained from program theory models. These are based on different kinds of logical inference. For example, the first type of evidence (causal list inference) states that if a number of different causes of an Event B have been hypothesized, but if A is the only one that

---

Box 9.3   Nine Potential Types of Evidence for Inferring Causality

1. *Causal list inference*: Almost all Bs are caused by As. If there is a list of possible causes (As) and only one is systematically present when B occurs, this can infer that this A is the cause.

2. *Modus operandi influence*: Establish causal chain/modus operandi and use all available sources of evidence to systematically eliminate other possible causes.

3. *Temporal precedence*: A happens before B is seen.

4. *Constant conjunction*: When A is present, there is always B.

5. *Contiguity of influence*: A plausible mechanism links A and B.

6. *Strength of association*: Much more B with A than other possible causes.

7. *Biological gradient*: If more A, then more B.

8. *Coherence*: The A-B relationship fits with what else we know about A and B.

9. *Analogy*: The relationship between A and B resembles the well-established pattern documented between C and D.

SOURCE: Adapted from Davidson (2000:21–22).

is systematically present when B occurs, then this is evidence for inferring that A may have caused B. Similarly, Type 3 (temporal precedence) states that if A is always observed to occur before B, then this (in conjunction with other evidence) supports the possibility that A is a cause of B. None of these types of evidence in isolation is very convincing as an explanation of causality, but if several of the types are all found to be present, then the case for a causal relationship becomes more plausible.

Other writers argue that there are a number of fundamental methodological reasons why program theory is not able to provide sound estimates of causality and cannot be considered a satisfactory alternative to randomized experiments. Cook (2000) argues that program theory is often used as an excuse for not conducting appropriate experimentation and that the design of a program theory can be manipulated and the findings interpreted to justify a program or protect it from criticism. Disappointing results may also be dismissed by arguing that it was too early to expect results or that the indicators did not adequately capture many important program outcomes. The following are Cook's (pp. 29–32) main criticisms of program theory as a tool for assessing program impact and causality:

- The formulation of program theory is not sufficiently explicit to permit testing or refutation.
- The formulation of most program theories is linear (i.e., if *X*, then *Y*) and does not capture feedback loops or the effects of external contingencies.
- Most program theories do not specify time periods over which effects are expected to be achieved. Consequently, it is not possible to assess whether negative results show a program does not work or that it is too early to judge.[10]
- Program theory often does not provide sufficient guidance on what to measure and how.
- Most program theories do not identify alternative models for examination. Consequently, even if observed outcomes fit the theory, it is impossible to know whether there are other theories that might equally well explain the facts.
- Another major weakness is the lack of a **counterfactual,** a comparison that provides a way to know whether the observed changes might have been caused by other factors unrelated to the project.

For quantitative evaluations, even without strong supporting quantitative data, some of the program theory approaches discussed earlier can provide useful preliminary indicators of possible program effects. Defenders of program theory can also point out that the explanatory value of most experimental and quasi-experimental designs is limited to estimating a statistical association, but they do not help clients to understand *why* the association exists. Also, as we indicated earlier in this section, experimental designs are particularly limited in their ability to provide guidance to clients on how to interpret negative results that did not find any statistical association between project interventions and intended outcomes and impacts.

Using Program Theory to Help Explain Causality in Mixed-Method Evaluations

While program theory cannot provide the precise statistical estimates of causality that can be obtained from experimental and strong quasi-experimental designs, theory models can provide a useful way to support or challenge evidence of causality obtained through **mixed-method** evaluation designs. A program theory model can sometimes provide useful indicators of *probable causal linkages*. The following guidelines can be applied:

Step 1: Construct an impact model (see p. 176). This should include a contextual analysis of the underlying rationale of the program based on the analysis of the situation and a review of the literature, definition of the proposed interventions and intended outputs, and an identification of potentially important **moderators** and **mediators**. The model should also recognize the likelihood of multiple causality and that different people may respond differently to the same set of program services. The model should also include the feedback loops found in interactions between the project and its environment.

Step 2: Identify some of the alternative hypotheses/explanations concerning the causes of change and the expected outcomes/impacts. Obtain alternative explanations for causal links through, for example, a review of the research literature, evaluations of similar programs, discussions with program staff and other stakeholders, soliciting the views of program critics, and exploratory fieldwork. Defining at least one alternative model to test alternative outcomes, perhaps using qualitative approaches, can be useful for understanding actual effects.

Step 3: Define operationally measurable input, outcome, and process indicators. Define indicators with sufficient **precision** to permit them to be measured and quantified.

Step 4: Define the time period over which outcomes and impacts are expected to occur and the intensity of inputs required to achieve outcomes. The time period selected to measure project effects can have a significant impact on the estimated magnitude of the effects. Table 9.3 illustrates three ways in which the effects of a project could vary over time. In Scenario 1, the maximum effects could be achieved immediately; for example, all the health benefits (e.g., reduced intestinal infections) could be achieved as soon as drinking water is available, and could be sustained with no decrease over time. In Scenario 2, the effects gradually increase, not reaching their maximum level for about nine years. In Scenario 3, the effects gradually increase until about Year 5, after which they steadily decrease. It can be seen from this example that a posttest measurement taken in Year 3 would find a high level of effect in the first **scenario**, a low level in the second, and a medium level in the third. On the other hand, observations in Year 5 would find high effects in the first and third scenarios, with medium effects for the second (see Figure 9.5). These variations show that the program theory model should specify the expected time period for producing effects and whether the effects are expected to be sustained or to decrease over time. If the time dimension is not specified, then it is impossible to tell whether low effects show that the program theory model is invalid or whether the measurements were taken at the wrong time.

Table 9.3   Variations in the Estimated Level of Effects Depending on the Year in Which the Posttest Study Is Conducted

Scenario	Year 3	Year 5	Year 8
1	High	High	High
2	Low	Medium	High
3	Low	High	Low

Step 5: Using PRA and other qualitative methods to identify causality. Participatory appraisal (variously known as RRA, PRA, and PLA),[11] which was discussed in Chapter 5, has developed a variety of tools for working with community groups to identify causality. Some of the *time-related methods* include timelines, trend analysis, historical transects (used to explore and represent the temporal dimension of people's reality[12]), and seasonal diagrams; *relational methods* include cause-effect diagrams, impact diagrams, systems diagrams, network

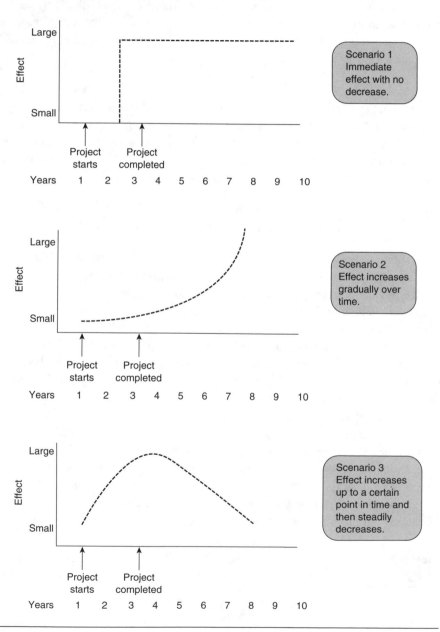

Figure 9.5   Different Scenarios for the Variation of Project Effects over Time

SOURCE: Adapted by the authors with permission from Lipsey (1990:149).

diagrams, and process maps. All these techniques are based on working with stakeholders in facilitated discussions and exercises to construct maps, timelines, or causal chains defining the natural, political, and sociocultural factors relevant to the program (see Kumar 2002 for a detailed explanation of these techniques). For example, in a recent evaluation in the Philippines using PRA techniques, facilitated community meetings identified the impacts of constructing a water supply system, and **triangulation** through site visits, observations, and interviews confirmed the identified impacts.

Step 6: Define and combine all available evidence for inferring causality. When operating with budget, time, and data constraints, the evaluator will often collect a number of different types of data that provide evidence on how the project has performed, what types of effects it has produced, and which groups have benefited most and least. Often, none of these sources of information are completely convincing when taken in isolation, but when they are combined and their consistency checked through triangulation, the evidence base becomes stronger. Table 9.3 describes different strategies that can be used to incorporate different kinds of logical analysis that can provide additional support for an association between the project interventions and the intended effects.

Summary

- A program theory is an explicit theory or model of how a program is intended to produce the intended outputs, outcomes, and impacts and the factors affecting or determining its success.

- A program theory is particularly helpful in planning an evaluation under RWE constraints because it helps identify the critical issues or hypotheses on which scarce evaluation resources should focus.

- Evaluators often have to work with clients and stakeholders to construct the implicit program theory because it has often not been formally articulated in project documents.

- Program theories often combine an impact model and an implementation model.

- The impact (change) model describes the linkages between project inputs, the implementation strategy, and the intended outputs, outcomes, and impacts. It also examines how performance is affected by *mediators*—factors affecting performance that can be modified by the project (e.g., willingness of different groups to support the project or to change their behavior)—and by *contextual factors* (such as the economic, political, organizational, natural environment, and characteristics of the affected populations) that affect performance but over which project managers have little control.

- The implementation (action) model describes how staff and resources are to be used to deliver the program services to the target population.

- Logical framework analysis (logframe) is a form of program theory used by many agencies to monitor program performance against a set of measurable indicators. Logframes also identify and test critical assumptions (e.g., actions that the government must take, the stability of the local and national economy, the willingness of communities or individuals to change traditional forms of behavior) about conditions that will affect program success.

- Some, but not all, program theory practitioners believe that program theory can be used to help explain causality in situations where it is not possible to use **randomization** or quasi-experimental designs.

Further Reading

Centers for Disease Control and Prevention. 1999. Summary of the Framework for Program Evaluation in Public Health. *Morbidity and Mortality Weekly Report* 48(No. RR-11):1–43. Retrieved August 10, 2005 (www.cdc.gov/eval/framework.htm).

Extensive reference material on logic models presented in a user-friendly format and including material prepared for use by community groups. Portal to other Web sites.

Community Tool Box. 2005. *Developing a Framework or Model of Change: Part J. Evaluating Community Programs and Initiatives.* Available at http://ctb.ku.edu/tools/en/chapter_1036.htm

The referenced section explains how to use program theory in the evaluation of community health and development programs. Other sections of the handbook provide guidelines for other stages of the evaluation process.

Chen, H. T. 2005. *Practical Program Evaluation: Assessing and Improving Planning, Implementation, and Effectiveness.* Thousand Oaks, CA: Sage.

A thorough, clear introduction to the design and use of program theory evaluation.

International Program for Development Evaluation Training. 2004. *Evaluation Models.* Retrieved August 10, 2005 (www.worldbank.org/oed/ipdet/Modules/M_02-na.pdf).

This is Module 2 of the core IDPET international evaluation training program. This module, which is available in both PowerPoint and text form, presents an overview of program theory and logic models.

Rogers, P., T. Hacsi, A. Petrosino, and T. Huebner, eds. 2000. *Program Theory in Evaluation: Challenges and Opportunities.* New Directions for Evaluation, No. 87. San Francisco: Jossey-Bass.

One of the most comprehensive overviews of recent developments in program theory evaluation.

Rossi, P., M. Lipsey, and H. Freeman. 2004. *Evaluation: A Systematic Approach.* 7th ed. Thousand Oaks, CA: Sage.

A thorough presentation of the design and use of program theory evaluations.

United Way. 2005. *Connecting Program Outcome Measurement to Community Impact.* Available at http://national.unitedway.org/files/pdf/outcomes/ConnectingPOM_toCI%20Final.pdf

Another set of guidelines for applying program theory to community development programs.

Notes

1. There is often overlap and confusion between the terms *model* and *design*. We define model as "different approaches to evaluation" (see Note 2) and design as the methodologies used to determine whether a project or program has produced the desired outcomes and impacts.

2. Evaluation models are different approaches to evaluation. Stufflebeam (2001) identifies 22 evaluation models that he categorizes into four groups: pseudoevaluation, quasi-evaluation studies, improvement or accountability oriented, and social agenda or advocacy. Various other classifications describe models in terms of purpose, assumptions, organization, questions asked, strengths and weaknesses, intended users, primary methodology, proponents of the model, epistemology, and ethics (Mathison 2005:256–68). In this book, we distinguish between quantitative, qualitative, and mixed-method models or approaches.

3. Chen (2005) uses the term "change model."

4. This component is not included in the Chen (2005) and Donaldson (2003) models. However, conceptual factors are similar to what Donaldson (2003) defines as moderators.

5. Some authors, for example Chen (2005) use the term *interventions* to cover both the resources (what we call inputs) and the way the resources are used (what we call the implementation strategy). However, we consider it helpful to distinguish between the two because the same inputs can have very different effects depending on the implementation strategy.

6. Chen (2005) combines moderators and mediators into a single category, "determinants," but the present authors consider it is better to separate the two because they operate in different ways (see Donaldson 2003).

7. Chen (2005) calls this an action model.

8. Many aid organizations, such as the U.N. Development Program and multilateral and bilateral aid agencies, require gender analysis incorporated into project selection and design to ensure that factors affecting the equal participation of women and men are identified and addressed. Managers and staff are assessed, in part, in terms of their compliance with these guidelines.

9. The *Community Tool Box* provides detailed guidelines and case studies on how to plan and assess the participation of community level organizations in the United States. See, for example, Chapter 36 of the tool box (available free online at http://ctb.ku.edu/tools/en/chapter_1036.htm).

10. For a discussion of the importance of defining how effects are expected to evolve over time, see Lipsey's (1990) *Design Sensitivity*, Chapter 7.

11. See Chapter 5 for a discussion of PRA approaches.

12. For example, farmers in a PRA session might be asked to draw pictures for different periods in the past, the present, and the future of the seed varieties they use; access to water, forest cover, food availability, and agricultural productivity (Kumar 2002: 143–48).

CHAPTER 10

The Most Widely Used RealWorld Quantitative Evaluation Designs

D rawing on the pioneering work of Campbell, Stanley, and Cook and the recent work of Shadish, Cook, and Campbell (Campbell and Stanley 1963; Cook and Campbell 1979; Shadish, Cook, and Campbell 2002), this chapter describes seven quasi-experimental designs (**QEDs**), ranging from longitudinal QEDs with multiple measurement events to a one-off, end-of-project evaluation without a baseline or **comparison group**. Although it is preferable to use one of the more robust **designs** described in this chapter, under RealWorld budget and time constraints, it is often necessary to use a design without a before-and-after comparison or without a control or comparison group. We begin by describing **randomized** evaluation designs, considered by most QUANT evaluators to be the strongest evaluation designs for assessing project **impacts**, and then discuss the reasons why these designs are not more widely used under real-world conditions, particularly in developing countries. We then discuss factors affecting the choice of the best evaluation design under different RealWorld Evaluation (**RWE**) scenarios. The seven designs are then described: (a) when they can be used, (b) how to identify and address the principal threats to validity for each, and (c) how **mixed-method** approaches can be incorporated among a number of strategies that can be used to strengthen the evaluation designs. We include case studies from different countries and sectors and from small and large evaluations to illustrate the designs.

Randomized and Quasi-Experimental Evaluation Designs

The Limited Use of Randomized Evaluation Designs in Development Evaluation

In a true randomized experimental design,[1] subjects or units (e.g., individuals, rats, agricultural plots) are randomly assigned to the experimental and control groups. If the sample is reasonably large, the two groups can be assumed to be very similar at the start of the experiment. The two groups are measured on indicators of the **output** or **outcome** that the experiment is seeking to produce. The treatment (e.g., teaching method, drug, fertilizer) is administered to the experimental group and not to the control group, but otherwise the conditions of the two groups are kept the same until the posttest measurements are taken. If there is a significant difference in the posttest measures for the two groups (after controlling for any pretest differences[2]), this is taken as an indication that the experimental treatment had an effect. Ideally, the experiment should be repeated several times under slightly different conditions (such as duration or intensity of the treatment and how it is administered) before any conclusions are drawn about a causal relation between the treatment and the observed outcomes.

Box 10.1 gives examples of randomized evaluation studies conducted by the MIT (Massachusetts Institute of Technology) Poverty Action Lab. The examples cover education, nutrition, labor market, health, and **microcredit** projects in India, Kenya, South Africa, and the

---

Box 10.1   Examples of Randomized Program Evaluation: The MIT Poverty Action Lab Research Program

---

In June 2003 the Massachusetts Institute of Technology (MIT) launched a program of **randomized trials** to assess the impacts of development programs in developing countries and the United States. The main justification for doing this was the belief that nonrandomized, quasi-experimental evaluation designs can often come to erroneous conclusions about program effectiveness because of the "omitted variable" problem (important factors that might explain apparent program effects have been excluded from the analysis). Some of the randomized evaluations have included the following:

- Women as policymakers—the impact of female political leaders on policy decisions
- The Balsakhi (Mumbai, India) Program—charting the effects of remedial education programs on school quality and test scores
- Measuring the impacts of school inputs in Kenya—the case of flip charts (see next page)
- Primary school deworming project (Kenya)—the impacts of child health gains due to preschool health and nutrition projects on preschool participation
- Incentives to learn—the impacts of scholarships for girls in Kenya
- School choice in Colombia—measuring the impacts of vouchers for private schooling
- Peer effects, alcohol, and college roommates in the United States—the impact of randomly assigned college roommates on drinking behavior
- A study of racial discrimination in the job market in Chicago and Boston
- The Balwadi health program (New Delhi, India)—the impacts of child health gains due to preschool health and nutrition project on preschool participation
- Interest rate and consumer credit in South Africa—the effect of changing interest rates on loan acceptance
- Understanding technology adoption—fertilizers in Western Kenya: Why do farmers not use fertilizer even though it appears to have the potential to increase yields considerably?

SOURCE: Adapted by the authors from MIT Poverty Action Lab (www.povertyactionlab.org).

United States. These examples show that it is possible to conduct randomized evaluation designs in developing countries as well as in countries such as the United States. One of the situations in which randomization is used, particularly in developing countries, is when demand for a particular service (e.g., improved water supply or sanitation or self-help housing) exceeds the supply of the service that an agency can provide in a given year. Under these circumstances, a lottery is sometimes used to select the families or communities who will receive the services, and the unsuccessful applicants can be used as a control group (Carvalho and White 2004).[3]

Although there are serious questions related to the ethics of using randomized designs under real-world conditions, and also concerns that the lack of control over the process of project implementation makes it difficult to isolate project effects from extraneous factors, there are those who feel that in situations where only a subset of the population can be reached by a planned intervention anyway, randomized trials to test the efficacy of a specific experimental intervention may be justified.

An example of the MIT Poverty Action Lab approach was an evaluation in Kenya to assess the impacts of flip charts (i.e., hand drawn or preprinted charts that can be presented on an easel) on student test scores on various school subjects. Of a total of 178 schools, 89 were randomly assigned (by listing schools alphabetically and then randomly allocating alternate schools to the project and comparison groups) to receive the flip charts and the other 89 formed the comparison group. Test scores were measured at the start of the school year (before the flip charts were introduced) and again at the end of the year. A statistical analysis found no significant differences between the two groups (Glewwe et al. 2004). This example is interesting because an earlier *retrospective evaluation,* in which test scores were compared for the project and comparison groups after the flip charts had been introduced into the schools, found a significant test score improvement in the project scores. Glewwe and his colleagues argued that this apparent project effect was due to the **omitted variable problem**—in this case, that the analysis did not control for the level of parental participation in their children's education. The authors argue that schools with a higher level of parental involvement showed significant improvements in test scores and that when the analysis controls for the level of parental involvement, flip charts are no longer positively associated with test score improvement. This example shows that the omitted variable problem is one of the reasons for preferring randomized designs and one of the potentially serious threats to validity presented by *omitted variables* in QEDs.

The implementation of randomized designs in real-world field settings offers many challenges. Although it is possible in a number of situations to achieve or approximate a randomized allocation of communities, schools, or other units to project and control groups, most of these designs have found it much more difficult to ensure a standardized implementation of the project in all sites or to control for differences between the project and control sites during the **implementation process**. In the case of an education project, for example, there will often be differences in the extent to which different schools are able to comply with the proposed project design. The quality of teachers may vary; the ability of schools to provide the required administrative and other support may also vary, as well as the physical conditions of the schools and the class sizes. In the case of health programs, not all health centers may have adequate supplies of the medicines, or pressures on staff may mean that not all patients receive advice on how to use the medicine or the necessary follow-up support. In many cases, these variations will not be well monitored, so the extent of the variations in the treatment may not be known.

Another set of issues has to do differences that will often develop between the project and control groups during the implementation period. The fact that an international donor agency is supporting a project may raise the profile of the project and draw in other sources of support (particularly when the implementing ministry or agency wants the project to work well in the hope that additional funding will be received for a future expansion). On the other hand, staff members working on similar projects in control areas may become discouraged, or they begin lobbying local politicians hoping that their communities will also receive some of the same benefits.

Given the complex interactions among all these factors, if a randomized design does not find statistically significant project impacts, it is difficult to assess to what extent this is due to weaknesses in the project design concept (*design failure*) or to problems that arose during implementation (*implementation failure*). Similarly, it may also be difficult to assess to what extent statistically significant project impacts are due to the project and not to the effect of these other factors. The lack of attention to process analysis (*implementation monitoring*) in many randomized designs makes it even more difficult to address these questions.

Although randomized evaluation designs offer many methodological advantages, in most evaluations conducted in the field (in contrast to research conducted in laboratories), it is not possible to use these designs due to a combination of cost, logistical, and methodological issues. Even if budget is not an issue, there are a number of methodological reasons why random assignment is not possible in most real-world situations. One of the most common situations for RWE is that the evaluation does not begin until the project has already been implemented, so there is obviously no way to influence who does and who does not benefit from the project. Even when the evaluation begins at the start of the project, in many cases the choice of project locations is based on political considerations (e.g., one school must be included in each district) or technical factors (e.g., it must be possible to link the water and sanitation system or the feeder roads to the main infrastructure). In other cases, the project is designed to cover communities or groups with certain unique characteristics (e.g., the largest or the poorest urban slums or the communities with the most dynamic community leadership) that make it difficult to use a random allocation of subjects to a control group. In yet other cases, participants are self-selected (e.g., communities apply to participate in a water supply project or entrepreneurs decide to apply for small business loans).

There are also important ethical concerns about withholding services and benefits from people in the control group. These are particularly critical with respect to drugs or other medical services that can potentially save lives or protect people from serious illness, but there are also important concerns if improved educational opportunities or better housing or infrastructure is being withheld. These are important issues that must be seriously addressed, in consultation with all major **stakeholders,** whenever the possibility of using a randomized design is being considered. In many cases, political pressures—some of which reflect the ethical concerns discussed above, others of which are less idealistic—may make it impossible to ensure that services are not provided to the constituents of local politicians, whether or not they were in the comparison group.

Despite the limited use of randomized designs in most evaluations in the field, the randomized design serves as a reference point for assessing the strengths and weaknesses of the different QEDs (nonrandomized) used in most quantitative (QUANT) RWE evaluations.

Quasi-Experimental Designs: Adapting Randomized Designs to RealWorld Quantitative Program Evaluation

When using QUANT designs to evaluate the impacts of development projects and service provision (e.g., water supply, road construction, microcredit, teacher training, and provision of teaching materials), there are very few situations in which randomized designs can be applied. For example it is rarely possible, and in many cases not ethical, to randomly assign community residents or whole villages to treatment and control groups. In response to these constraints, a variety of QEDs, inspired by the pioneering work of Campbell and Stanley (1963) and Cook and Campbell (1979) have been developed (see Shadish et al. 2002 for an update and expansion of the original approach). As we will see in Chapter 12, for qualitative (QUAL) practitioners, laboratory settings and controlled randomization, even if they were possible, are not as helpful as naturalistic settings. Just because something has a certain effect in controlled conditions doesn't mean the effect can be achieved in natural settings.

QEDs seek to approximate as closely as possible the randomized evaluation design under real-world conditions in order to accomplish the following:

- Make the best possible estimate of the extent to which a **project, program,** or policy has produced its intended impacts
- Identify the factors that positively or negatively influence the magnitude and direction of the impacts

Different QEDs can be used to address RWE constraints. In the real world, evaluators trying to approximate a randomized design typically face one or more of the following problems:

- It is almost never possible to randomly assign subjects to experimental and control groups. For logistical, administrative, political, and sometimes ethical reasons, most projects are accessible to or affect everyone in a given community or area. For example, a school, water supply system, or road will usually be accessible to all families in the community, and it is difficult to tell some families they cannot send their children to the school or use the water (assuming they are willing to pay or that they have participated in the construction of the water system).
- Some projects use a self-selection process, when, for example, people decide if they wish to apply for microcredits, enroll in a literacy class, or plant new varieties of seed. In these cases, it is likely that the people who do decide to participate will be different in important ways from those who do not participate. Typically, people who take the initiative to participate are economically better off, better educated, and have more self-confidence. Consequently, it is difficult to know whether observed changes in income, reading skills, health, and so on are due to the effects of the project or to the differences in initial conditions and capabilities of participants and nonparticipants.
- It is very difficult to find a comparison group closely matching the experimental group on the key indicators. Project communities are often selected because of special characteristics. In some cases, project planners choose the poorest communities; in other cases they choose communities that have the greatest likelihood of success. In either case, it will be difficult to find a comparison group that closely matches the project population.

- In many cases, it is difficult to use any kind of comparison group at all for political or ethical reasons. Frequently, politicians and community leaders in a designated comparison group area will pressure for their community to be included in the project. From the ethical perspective, one would not want to withhold a service (such as oral rehydration treatment for severely malnourished children) just to prove the efficacy of the treatment. Another ethical (or practical) consideration is that it is often considered inappropriate to ask families in comparison communities to spend a long time responding to surveys if they will not receive any benefit. In some cases, the fact that families are being interviewed creates false expectations that they will be eligible to participate in a later phase of the project.
- It is also difficult to ensure that treatments (services) are administered in exactly the same way to all project sites and families. Sometimes, the delivery of materials and equipment is delayed; in other cases, there are major differences with respect to the organization of the project and delivery of services in different sites. In one microcredit program, the local administrator may speak the local language and may create a welcoming atmosphere that encourages families to visit the project to discuss loans. In another site, the administrator may not speak the local language and the project may be seen as hostile to the community so that fewer people visit the center. For all these reasons, it is difficult to determine whether differences in project performance are due to differences in the responsiveness of different communities or whether the differences are due to the way the project was administered in different sites.
- Finally, each project operates within a unique economic and political context and must interact with a number of government or nongovernmental organizations (**NGOs**), each of which has its own particular characteristics. Also the social, economic, and cultural characteristics of the **target population** may vary significantly among project sites. All these **contextual factors** can have an important influence on the outcome of the project. Consequently, even when a project is administered in exactly the same way in each site, there may be significant differences in the outcomes as a result of these contextual factors.

These issues stress the need to understand fully the problems facing a particular evaluation and to select the methodologically strongest design possible under the particular circumstances. The strengths and weaknesses of each evaluation design should be carefully analyzed and the implications for the interpretation of **findings** and the presentation of conclusions assessed. In some cases, the methodological weaknesses may not seriously affect the kinds of recommendations to be prepared, whereas in other cases they may be very serious. For example:

- The lack of a comparison group may not be very important if the purpose of the evaluation is to assess whether indigenous communities participating in pilot projects are able to manage and sustain community water supply projects or whether women will apply for small loans if a loan office, staffed by local-language speakers, is established in the community.
- On the other hand, if the purpose of the evaluation is to estimate whether a pilot project could be replicated on a national scale and if it would offer a more cost-effective way to deliver a particular service, then the lack of a comparison group might be a serious problem.

The Most Widely Used
Quantitative Evaluation Designs

Determining Which Quasi-Experimental Design
to Use in Different RealWorld Evaluation Contexts

QUANT evaluation designs can be used at different points in the program cycle. They can be used at the start of a project, when the project has been underway for some time, or after the project has ended. In some cases, the design may involve a comparison group, whereas in others it does not. Lack of a life-of-project (e.g., longitudinal or at least pretest-posttest) evaluation plan, budget and/or time limitations, or political constraints can limit the options for evaluation design and the kinds of information that can be collected. Taking into account these and other factors, the choice of the best QED to use for a particular RWE will be determined by the following factors:

- *When did the evaluation begin?* At the start of the project, while the project was being implemented, just before the end, or after the project had ended?
- *When will the evaluation end?* Will it be a one-time evaluation conducted while the project is being implemented (most commonly for the midterm review), will it end at approximately the same time as the project (end-of-project report), or will it continue after the project ends (ex-post evaluation)?
- *What type of control or comparison was or can be used?* There are three main options: First, a randomized design in which individuals, families, groups, or communities are randomly assigned to the project and control groups. As indicated earlier, this design can rarely be used for RWE. Second, a comparison group (sometimes called a **nonequivalent control group**) design in which a group of subjects (e.g., people, families, schools, communities) are selected who are similar in as many relevant ways as possible to the project group except that they were not affected by the project. Depending on the context and resources, the comparison group may match quite closely the characteristics of the project group, or it might be quite dissimilar in many important ways. Third, no type of control group is used.
- *Does the design include process evaluation?* Is the purpose of the evaluation to assess only QUANT impact indicators (and only use a pretest-posttest design) or to also assess the project implementation process and to analyze how this affects the quality of outputs and their accessibility to different sectors of the target population?
- *Will the evaluation use a predominantly QUANT design, or will it also incorporate a mixed-method design?* Some evaluation designs rely almost exclusively on the administration of a structured survey or similar QUANT data collection method, whereas other predominantly QUANT designs also incorporate a mixed-methods design that includes a number of QUAL methods to triangulate or add different perspectives. RWE recommends that where the original design is exclusively QUANT, the benefits of incorporating a mixed-method design be considered.

The answers to these questions will help define which of the seven QEDs described in Table 10.1 will be the most appropriate (or even possible) for quantitatively oriented designs in different RWE contexts. For example, if the purpose of the evaluation is to assess both the QUANT effects as well as how the process of project implementation affects outcomes, then

Table 10.1 The Seven Evaluation Designs Most Widely Used in Quantitatively Oriented RealWorld Evaluations

Evaluation Design	Start of Project (pretest) T_1	Project Intervention (continues on to end of project)	Midterm Evaluation or Several Observations during Implementation T_2	End of Project (posttest) T_3	Follow-up after Project Operating for Some Time (ex-post) T_4	The Stage of the Project Cycle at which Each Evaluation Design can Begin to be Used
TWO STRONGEST EVALUATION DESIGNS						
1. *Comprehensive longitudinal design with pre-, midterm, post- and ex-post observations on the project and comparison groups.* This is the methodologically strongest design but also the most expensive and time-consuming. Permits assessment of the process of project implementation as well as trend analysis. Random assignment of subjects is rarely possible, so this and following designs normally use comparison groups selected to match the project group as closely as possible.	P_1 C_1	X	P_2 C_2	P_3 C_3	P_4 C_4	Start
2. *Pretest-posttest project and comparison groups.* For most purposes, this is the best available design when the evaluation can begin at the start of the project with a reasonable budget and no particular constraints on access to data or use of a comparison group.	P_1 C_1	X		P_2 C_2		Start
FIVE LESS ROBUST EVALUATION DESIGNS						
3. *Truncated longitudinal pretest-posttest project and comparison group design.* Project and comparison groups observed at two or more points during project implementation, but evaluation does not begin until the project is underway. Evaluation often starts as part of midterm review.		X	P_1 C_1	P_2 C_2		Midterm
4. *Pretest-posttest project group combined with posttest analysis of project and comparison group.* No baseline data collected on comparison group.	P_1	X		P_2 C_1		Start
5. *Posttest project and comparison groups.* No baseline or midterm data collected.		X		P_1 C_1		End
6. *Pretest-posttest project group.* No comparison group.	P_1	X		P_2		Start
7. *Posttest project group only.* No baseline project data or comparison group. This is the weakest QUANT design but very widely used because of limited cost and time requirements.		X		P_1		End

Key

T = time during project cycle

P = project participants

C = comparison group

P_1, P_2, C_1, C_2, etc. = first, second (and in some designs, third and fourth) observations of the project or comparison groups in a particular evaluation design

X = project intervention (a process rather than a discrete event)

Designs 1 or 3 would be considered (with the choice depending on whether the evaluation begins at the start of the project or when it has already been underway for some time). If, on the other hand, the evaluation does not begin until toward the end of the project then the choice would be limited to Designs 5 or 7.

The Seven Quasi-Experimental Designs Most Frequently Used in Quantitatively Oriented RealWorld Evaluation

Based on the first three factors identified in the previous section, seven widely used QEDs can be identified that are applicable to many quantitatively oriented RWE evaluations. These are summarized in Table 10.1. These seven designs include two methodologically robust designs, and five less robust, but widely used, designs (see Box 10.2). There are many situations in which it is not possible to use Designs 1 and 2. In some cases, this is due to time and budget constraints that do not permit the use of a comparison group. In many other cases, the evaluator is not called in until the project is almost ended, so it is not possible to go back in time and collect baseline data. In these situations, one of the simpler and more economical designs (Designs 3–7) can be used. However, Designs 3 through 7 all sacrifice one or more essential elements of a sound evaluation design and consequently become vulnerable to a wider range of methodological problems. Each of the seven designs is described in the following sections.

Box 10.2   Seven QEDs That Can Be Applied in RealWorld Evaluation Scenarios

The two most robust designs:

1. Comprehensive longitudinal design with pre-, midterm, post- and ex-post observations on the project and comparison groups

2. Pretest-posttest project and comparison groups

Five less robust designs:

3. Truncated longitudinal pretest-posttest project and comparison group design

4. Pretest-posttest project group combined with posttest analysis of project and comparison group

5. Posttest project and comparison groups

6. Pretest-posttest project group

7. Posttest data collected only on the project group with no comparison group (the least methodologically robust but perhaps, unfortunately, the most widely used design)

Although these evaluation designs apply most directly to QUANT methods, it should be noted that even when using QUAL methods under the Design 7 scenario (a one-off study) the evaluator, directly or indirectly, seeks respondent's own perspectives on how things have changed during the life of the project or how things would have been without the project's interventions. Thus, one of the main differences has to do with whether the evaluators collect primary data at the different times depicted by these designs (T_1, T_2, etc.) or ask participants to **recall** how things were at those times (i.e., before and after) and make comparisons (with and without).

Box 10.3 presents the results of a **meta-evaluation** of 67 evaluations conducted by CARE International over the past two years on their relief and development projects in different countries. It was found that 50 of the 67 projects on which information was available used an evaluation design in which information was collected only after the project had been operating for some time and collected information only from the project communities. In other words, no baseline data were collected before the project began and no information was collected on a comparison group. This is Design 7 of the RWE evaluation designs that we describe in this chapter. From the methodological point of view, this is the weakest design and the one most open to a wide range of threats to validity of the conclusions of the evaluation. In many situations, the evaluation design could have been strengthened had project management begun the evaluation process from the beginning of the project and conducted a baseline study on at least the target population. However, in many real-world situations, this is the only design possible within the time and budget constraints and within the local political and security context in which the evaluation must be conducted.

Box 10.3   The Widespread Use of Design 7 (the Methodologically Weakest Evaluation Design)

Of the 67 projects included in the meta-evaluation by CARE International, 50 used a posttest-only design without a comparison group (Design 7). However, there actually had been baseline studies conducted for 19 of the projects where posttest-only evaluations were conducted. Among the reasons the baselines were not used included accessibility of the baseline data to the evaluators, comparability (in terms of indicators and methodologies), questions regarding the quality of the baseline studies, and/or oversight by those conducting the evaluations.

Evaluation Design	Design Number	Frequency	%
Longitudinal design	1	1	1.5
Pretest-posttest project and comparison group	2	1	1.5
Truncated longitudinal design	3	1	1.5
Pretest-posttest project group and posttest comparison group	4	2	3.0
Posttest project and comparison	5	4	6.0
Pretest-posttest project group	6	8	11.9
Posttest project group without comparison	7	50	74.6
Total		67	100

SOURCE: Russon (2005).

Ways to Strengthen Quantitative RealWorld Evaluation Designs

Because of the real-world constraints under which evaluations are designed and implemented, the conventional QEDs described below (pp. **206–225**) are subject to a number of threats to validity likely to weaken the quality of the data and the validity of the conclusions. These include the following:

- Problems concerning the reliability and/or validity of measurement of key indicators, particularly when these relate to sensitive issues such as household income, control of household resources, domestic violence, and social constraints on women's economic activities or mobility.
- Variations in the way the project is implemented, in the quality of services, and in the differential access of different groups to the services and benefits.
- Contextual factors affecting the outcomes and impacts of the project even when it is implemented in exactly the same way in each community/site.
- Important differences (nonequivalency) between the project and comparison groups, particularly those that are difficult to quantify (e.g., motivation, community organization, etc.). This includes the omitted variable problem (see the earlier discussion of the Kenya flip chart evaluation).

The following sections describe a number of procedures that can be used to strengthen these QUANT designs.

Basing the Evaluation Design on a Program Theory Model

A **program theory model** defines the steps through which a program is intended to achieve its objectives and identifies and tests some of the critical assumptions on which the success of the program will depend (see Chapters 2 and 9). Program theory also helps identify the contextual factors (economic, political, organizational, environmental, and sociocultural) likely to affect implementation and outcomes of the project and that can help explain why the same project implemented in the same way can have very different outcomes in different locations. The formulation of this model helps identify the concepts and issues that should be examined by the evaluation and the hypotheses that should be tested. The theory model is also very helpful in the interpretation of the findings and in the assessment of whether or not a project should continue or be replicated.

Program theory is particularly valuable in many RWE settings because it helps identify the key assumptions and hypotheses on which the limited evaluation resources should focus.

The following examples illustrate how program theory could be used to strengthen two of the case studies used in this chapter to illustrate the different evaluation designs:

- *Design 2: the impacts of housing on family income* (see Box 10.6). The pretest-posttest evaluation design could have been strengthened by using program theory to formulate the processes through which the intended outputs were expected to be produced. This would have made it possible to identify and test some of the key assumptions about how improved housing was expected to increase employment and household income. **Contextual analysis** would also have helped identify local political, economic, institutional, environmental, and cultural factors explaining why the same housing designs, implemented in the same way, had different outcomes in different locations. For example, Box 10.6 indicates that local economic conditions might have contributed as much as improved housing to influence changes in household income.

- *Design 4: the effects of resettlement on project beneficiaries and nonbeneficiaries in an irrigation project in India* (see Box 10.10). The evaluation found that the differences in the social and economic conditions of families who had received land and support to resettle and those who were forced to resettle without any compensation were much less than expected. The evaluation was not able to explain why the differences were so small and why the project seemed to have produced so little benefit for participants. A program theory model could have helped define the process of resettlement and could have identified and suggested ways to test hypotheses about how project beneficiaries were expected to benefit from the provision of land and other services. Designing the evaluation to test these hypotheses would probably have helped to explain why these benefits did not occur.

Complementing the Pretest-Posttest Quantitative Evaluation with Process Analysis

Many QUANT evaluations use a pretest-posttest design where the purpose is to assess the QUANT effects of the project (**summative evaluation**). With many of these designs, data are collected only at the start of the project (pretest baseline data) and at the end of the project (posttest) and no information is collected during the process of project implementation. The limitation of these designs is that they do not study how well the project was implemented or how the implementation process affected outcomes or the accessibility of the project to different sectors of the target population. This lack of understanding of the implementation process can be a particular problem in situations where the project does not achieve its intended outcomes or impacts. Without a process analysis, it is difficult to know whether the lack of observed impacts is because the program is not a good model to achieve the intended impacts or whether the program is potentially good but the problem had to do with the way it was implemented.

The incorporation of process analysis also strengthens the ability of the evaluation to provide guidance on ways to improve program effectiveness (**formative evaluation**). Process analysis can assess, for example, whether participatory planning does in fact involve all the intended sectors of the community and whether the benefits reach all the intended groups. Depending on the scale of the project and the types of questions being addressed, process analysis can use QUANT, QUAL, or mixed-method designs. The following are some of the questions typically addressed:

- How were the different components of the project implemented and how closely did this conform to the project plan, operations manual, or relevant sectoral good practice standards?
- How can the quality of the services be assessed?
- Who had access to and/or used the services and who did not? Why did certain groups not use the services?

- Was the organization of the project participatory, managed by a small group, or top-down?
- What proportion of the community (intended beneficiaries) know about the project, is their information correct, and what do they think about the project?
- What are the relations between the project organizers and the community?

Incorporating Contextual Analysis

While contextual analysis is a standard part of many QUAL evaluations, it is frequently not included in QUANT evaluations (see Chapters 2 and Chapter 9). However, because an understanding of the influence of contextual factors can greatly enrich the interpretation of QUANT analysis, RWE evaluators are always encouraged to consider the utility and feasibility of incorporating contextual analysis into their evaluation design. Contextual analysis assesses the influence of economic, political, organizational, and environmental factors on the implementation and outcome of projects. These factors are defined in some program theory models as **mediators** (see Chapter 9). Contextual analysis also examines the influence of the preexisting sociocultural characteristics of the target populations on how different groups respond to the project. These are described in some program theory models as **moderators**.

Most contextual analysis is descriptive—for example, using interviews with key informants, review of project and non-project documents for context, and **participant observation**. However, it may also use quantitative data from surveys of, for example, households, students, factory workers, or farmers.

Complementing Quantitative Data Collection and Analysis with Mixed-Method Designs

Many QED designs can be strengthened by incorporating mixed-method approaches in the evaluation design, data collection, or analysis stages through, for example, the following:

- Exploratory studies to understand the context and to identify key issues and hypotheses to be tested. This is particularly important in the construction of the program theory model (see Chapter 9).
- Analysis of the quality of the services provided by the project and the accessibility of these services to different sectors of the target population
- Analysis of the contextual factors (the economic, political, organizational, and natural environmental conditions) within which each project site operates
- Understanding the cultural characteristics of the affected populations and how these affect project implementation and outcomes
- Using **triangulation** to provide one or more independent estimates of key process and outcome indicators (see below)

Estimates obtained from a single data collection method can often be strengthened if they can be independently confirmed from two or more independent sources. This can be done in any of the following ways:

- Getting independent estimates of the magnitude or direction of change in variables (such as income, school enrollment and absentee rates, proportion of households using the village health center) obtained from surveys, observation, **focus groups,** secondary data, and so on

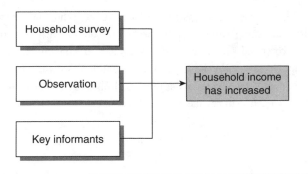

Figure 10.1   Converging Estimates of Household Income

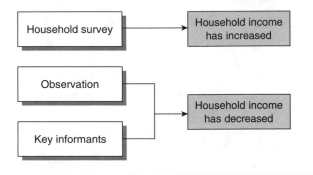

Figure 10.2   Diverging Estimates of Household Income

- Comparing the estimates through triangulation. If estimates using different methods are consistent, there can be greater confidence in the findings.
- If estimates are inconsistent, follow-up is required to determine reasons and make adjustments to the estimates.

In Figure 10.1 three independent estimates all provide consistent ("converging") estimates that household income has increased.

In contrast to the converging estimates in Figure 10.1, in Figure 10.2, the household survey estimates that household income has increased, but direct observation and interviews with key informants suggests that it has decreased ("diverging" estimates). In situations such as this, further analysis is required to determine the reason for the diverging estimates.

Adjusting for Differences in the Characteristics of the Project and Comparison Groups

Multivariate Analysis

When large sample surveys are conducted, multivariate analysis is often used to statistically control for differences between the project and comparison groups to improve the estimates of project impact. For example, assume that a study is being conducted to assess the impact on school attendance of the construction of a primary school in the project community. Assume also that a comparison group is selected that does not have a primary school in or very near to the community but that has similar social and economic characteristics to the project area. A sample survey is conducted in both communities with questions on school attendance and the social and economic conditions of the household. The following multivariate analysis is conducted to estimate the impact of the school:

$$Y_1 = f(d_1, x_1, x_2, \ldots x_n)$$

Where:

Y_1 = proportion of children attending primary school

d_1 = **dummy variable** for project and comparison group (d_1 = family in project, d_2 = family in comparison area)

$x_1, x_2, \ldots x_n$ = household attributes (size, income, parents' educational level, etc.)

If the regression coefficient of d_1 is statistically significant, this means that there is a statistically significant difference in school attendance rates between the project and comparison areas after controlling for household size, income, parents' education, and so on. This does not, of course, mean that the difference in school attendance rates is necessarily due to the existence of a school in the project community, because differences could also be due to other factors not controlled for in the analysis.

Elsewhere in this book (Box 5.7, p. 105), we refer to two examples of the use of multivariate analysis in ex-post comparisons of project and nonequivalent control groups:

- Assessing the impacts of employment in the cut flower industry in Ecuador on male and female domestic time allocation (Newman 2001)
- Assessing the impacts of microcredit on household savings and consumption and fertility behavior in Bangladesh (Khandker 1998)

Using Mixed Methods to Analyze Differences between Project and Comparison Groups

Key informants, focus groups, and participant observation are some of the QUAL methods that can be used to identify potentially important differences between project and comparison groups and to assess how they might affect project outcomes and the estimation of project impacts (see Chapter 12).

Identifying and Addressing Threats to Validity and Adequacy

A key component of the RWE approach is the application of a checklist to assess the methodological quality of the evaluation design and to identify potential threats to the validity and adequacy of the conclusions. The "Integrated Checklist for Assessing the Adequacy and Validity of Quantitative, Qualitative, and Mixed-Method Designs" (see Chapter 7 and Appendix 1) should be used with all the designs, and appropriate measures should be taken to address problems once they have been identified.

Seven Quasi-Experimental Designs That Cover Most RealWorld Evaluation Scenarios

All the following designs can be strengthened if used in combination with the methods described in the previous section. Design 1 is discussed in more detail to explain some of the basic procedures used in all the subsequent designs. Table 10.3 (at the end of the chapter) summarizes some of the strengths and weaknesses of each of these designs.

Design 1: Comprehensive Longitudinal Design with Pre-, Midterm, Post- and Ex-Post Observations on the Project and Comparison Groups

When to Use

This design is the most rigorous of the seven RWE evaluation designs. Although it does not involve randomly assigning units into experimental and control groups, it comes closest to the "scientific" experimental design. Longitudinal QED requires collecting data on both the project and comparison groups during at least four different points in time. It also requires the evaluation to continue throughout and even after the life of a project. The first round of data is collected at the start of the project (baseline), and the final round of data is not collected until some time after the project has ended (ex-post). The advantages of this design are that it provides the most comprehensive and methodologically robust assessment of project impacts and **sustainability** as well as getting "inside the **black box**" to describe the process of project implementation. Although more expensive than other RWE designs, this design is recommended for projects that have an important research function, to thoroughly test an experimental strategy or approach and where the evaluation will be used to guide future decisions on the continuation, modification, or expansion of a major project. The design can be used only when the evaluation begins at the start of the project so that baseline data can be collected. It also requires the evaluation to continue over a relatively stable environment in which the project is expected to continue to operate more or less as planned and where it will be possible to revisit the comparison groups over a number of years. It may be difficult to apply the design to a large-scale, low-income urban development project because it is likely that the housing of many of the comparison groups will be demolished or dramatically restructured over the life of the project (even though the comparison groups are expected to remain largely intact during the period of project implementation).

Description of the Design

As for all designs, the design should be based on a program theory model (see Chapter 9). Design 1 compares the project and a comparison group at the start of the project (T_1), at midterm or even more frequently during the life of the project (T_2), at project completion (T_3), and some time (preferably several years) after the project has ended (T_4) to assess sustainability (see Box 10.4). Among the advantages of having multiple observations made during the life of project implementation are to be able to describe and assess the implementation process and to identify trends in outcome indicators over time.

A comparison or nonequivalent control group (C) is selected at the start of the project to approximate as closely as possible the project beneficiary group (P). The observations from the comparison group represent the **counterfactual,** or what the conditions of the project group would have been like if the project had not taken place. In other words, if the average household income of the comparison group increases by 5% between T_1 and T_3, it is assumed that there would have been a similar increase in the project group if the project intervention had not taken place.

Our use of the term *comparison* group, rather than *control* group, reminds us that it is rarely possible to assign subjects randomly to the project and control groups, so differences may exist between the characteristics of the two groups that could distort the interpretation of the findings. It also acknowledges that in the real world, communities not participating in our project cannot be "controlled" in terms of external factors or alternative developmental activities undertaken in those communities by other agencies.

Both groups are interviewed at Time 1 (T_1) before the project begins, and information is obtained on a set of indicators ($I_1, I_2 \ldots I_n$), measuring the variables that the project is

---

Box 10.4   Design 1: Comprehensive Longitudinal Design

Time	T_1 *(baseline)*	Project Intervention *(over time)*	T_2 *(midterm)*	T_3 *(end of project)*	T_4 *(after project)*
Project group	P_1	X	$P_{2(n)}$	P_3	P_4
Comparison group	C_1		$C_{2(n)}$	C_3	C_4

T_1 = preproject observation

T_2 = observation(s) during project implementation period

T_3 = project completion (when project funding ends)

T_4 = ex-post follow-up evaluation some time after project completion to determine sustainability

P_1 and C_1 = baseline observations on the project and comparison groups before start of the project

$P_{2(n)}$ and $C_{2(n)}$ = periodic (longitudinal) observations on both groups during project implementation to observe the processes of change; (n) indicates the number of observation points during implementation. Some evaluation designs use panel informants (a small subsample of the participants and perhaps comparison groups) to track trends over time. If only one observation is made at the midterm review, this would be simplified to P_2 and C_2

X = implementation of the project (construction of schools, water system, etc.). It is important to remember that project implementation is a process that continues over time and is not a finite event occurring at a specific point in time

intended to affect (e.g., increase in household income, reduced daily travel time, number of children attending school).

Information is also collected on the social and economic characteristics of the individuals or families ($x_1, x_2, \ldots x_n$), called **intervening variables**, that might affect project outcomes. Data collection is repeated at Time 3 (T_3) at the completion of project implementation (e.g., occupation of new houses, turning on the water supply, completion of the rural roads) and again after the project has been in operation long enough to have produced its intended impacts (T_4). Ideally, the analysis should also include the contextual factors discussed in the previous section.

If the observations P_1, P_3, C_1, and C_3 refer to the mean scores for each group (e.g., average income, average educational test scores, or average anthropometric scores) before and after, and with and without, project implementation, then a statistical test such as the t test for the difference of means is used to determine whether the observed difference is statistically significant. If, on the other hand, the values refer to proportions (e.g., the proportion of children attending school or the proportion correctly answering a test question), then the appropriate statistical test would be a measure such as the Z score, for difference of proportions (Moore and McCabe 1999, chap 8; see also Chapter 14 of the present book).

The advantages of this design are that it examines the processes of project implementation over time, as well as the outcomes, and it addresses the important issues of sustainability, which are ignored in many evaluations. This is the design that most closely approximates the program theory model presented in Chapter 2 and discussed in more detail in Chapter 9. Design 1 is a very robust design that can address many of the "threats to validity" discussed in Chapter 7. However, it is also expensive because the survey questionnaire, or similar data collection instrument, is administered at four or more points in time.

In the great majority of cases, it is not possible to randomly allocate subjects to the project or control groups. In these cases, multivariate analysis can be used to statistically control for differences between the project and comparison groups. Many refinements can be introduced into the basic design to assess multiple treatments or to capture impacts that evolve gradually over time (Shadish et al. 2002; Valadez and Bamberger 1994).

Incorporating Mixed-Method Approaches into the Design

Design 1 is usually described as a quantitative QED relying exclusively on QUANT statistical analysis to estimate project impacts. However, the analysis and interpretation of the findings can be greatly enhanced either by conducting complementary QUAL studies or by using an integrated mixed-method design. These methods are used both to strengthen the design of the evaluation and the interpretation of the findings and to strengthen the reliability and validity of the indicators through triangulation.

Threats to Validity and Adequacy of the Conclusions

This is the methodologically strongest RWE design, so if it is applied appropriately, most threats to validity and adequacy (see Chapter 7 and Appendix 1) should be less serious than for most of the subsequent designs. However, under real-world conditions, it is never possible to design a perfect evaluation, so it is always important to review the Integrated Checklist (Appendix 1) to identify potential problems. Table 10.2 identifies from this checklist some of

Table 10.2   Some Threats to Validity That Must be Checked for Designs 1 and 2

	Threats to Validity[a]
F. Threats to statistical conclusion validity	
1. *Low statistical power*	The sample is too small to be able to detect statistically significant effects (see Chapter 14).
4. *Unreliability of measures*	The indicators do not adequately measure key variables.
5. *Restriction of range*	The sample does not cover the whole population. For example, the lowest- or highest-income groups are excluded, or the sample covers only enterprises employing more than 10 people.
6. *Unreliability of treatment implementation*	The treatments were not applied uniformly to all subjects, and often there is no documentation of the differences in application. For example, some mothers received malaria tablets and guidance from the nurse, but others received only the tablets.
G. Threats to internal validity	
2. *Selection bias*	Differences between project and comparison groups with respect to factors affecting outcomes.
6. *Attrition*	While the project group is initially representative of the total population, certain subgroups (e.g., the less educated, women with small children, the self-employed) have higher dropout rates, so the people who are actually exposed to the project are no longer representative of the whole population.
H. Threats to construct validity	
1. *Inadequate explanation of constructs and program theory model*	The basic concepts of the model are not clearly explained or defined.
8. *Reactivity to the data collection instruments*	Responses may be affected by how subjects react to the interview or other data collection methods. For example, respondents may report that they are poorer than they really are or that the project has not produced benefits because they are hoping the agency will provide new services or reduce the cost of current services.
I. Threats to external validity	
6. *Influence of policymakers on program outcomes*	Support or opposition of policymakers in particular locations may affect program outcomes in ways that might be difficult to assess.
7. *Seasonal cycles*	Many surveys are conducted at only one time in the year and may not adequately capture important seasonal variations.

a. See Integrated Checklist for Assessing the Adequacy and Validity of Quantitative, Qualitative, and Mixed-Method Designs (Appendix 1) for the full list of threats. The numbers in the left column correspond to that checklist.

the potentially important threats to conclusion validity affecting this design to which particular attention should be paid.

These potential threats should be examined during the design phase and at later points in the evaluation. Where possible, corrective measures (see Chapter 7) should be taken. If this is not possible the evaluation reports must clearly identify the existence of these threats and how they affect the findings and conclusions.

Design 2: Pretest-Posttest Project and Comparison Groups: The Strongest General-Purpose RealWorld Evaluation Design

When to Use

This design is used under similar conditions to Design 1, but it is used more frequently because it covers a shorter time period (ending around the same time as the project) and is also cheaper than Design 1 (although still more expensive than the less robust designs) because data are collected at only two points in time rather than four. This design is still quite robust and is often the design of choice for RWE when the evaluation starts at the same time as the project and when a fairly rigorous evaluation is justified (and, of course, when the resources are available).

Description of the Design

This design represents a simplified version of Design 1. It involves comparison of the project and nonequivalent control groups at the start of the project (T_1) and again at project completion (T_3). For most purposes, this is the most useful, general-purpose RWE design when the evaluator is brought in at the start of the project and has access to a reasonable budget.

As always, it is recommended that the design should be based on a program theory model and should be combined with a **process evaluation** to analyze the project implementation process and a contextual analysis to assess the influence of the economic, political, organizational, and natural environment within which the different project sites operate and to study the influence of cultural characteristics of the affected populations on program outcomes.

Box 10.5   Design 2: The Strongest General-Purpose Quasi-Experimental Design

Time	T_1 (baseline)	Project Intervention	T_2 (midterm)	T_3 (end of project)	T_4 (after project)
Project group	P_1	X		P_2	
Comparison group	C_1			C_2	

Refinements to the Design

The design presented in this section is in fact the most basic QED for pretest-posttest comparison group designs. Although cost and time constraints mean that this is the form in which the design is most frequently used in RWE applications, a number of refinements can significantly strengthen the design (Shadish et al. 2002, chap. 5). Several of the refinements increase the number of pretest or posttest observation points, whereas others reverse the treatment between the project and comparison groups at different points. It is also possible to use **cohort analysis** in which successive groups passing through the same cycle (e.g., third-grade students, medical trainees, families who will receive houses or public services in different phases of a project) are compared. One variant of this is to use subjects who will receive services or benefits in later phases of a project as a comparison group for subjects who received the services in an earlier phase.

Incorporating Mixed-Method Approaches into the Design

These can be incorporated in the same way as for Design 1. Box 10.6 describes how QUAL methods were integrated into this design in an evaluation of a low-cost housing program in El Salvador. These methods were helpful in documenting the project implementation

---

Box 10.6 Case Study for Design 2: Evaluating the Impacts of Improved Housing on Household Income in El Salvador

---

A four-year evaluation was conducted in El Salvador between 1976 and 1980 to assess the impacts of improved housing on poor households in San Salvador, the capital. In 1976, a randomly selected sample of households was interviewed shortly before they entered a self-help housing construction project. A comparison group was selected by combining samples of randomly selected families from the three main types of inner-city housing from which project participants were selected. The samples were repeated in 1980. The survey was combined with various QUAL methods such as participant observation during project workdays and in comparison group communities, case studies of individual families, and interviews with key informants. These assessed the quality of implementation, examined factors affecting the participation of particular groups such as female-headed households and the self-employed, and also documented the influence of certain contextual variables such as the local economy and the involvement of government housing agencies.

It was found that between T_1 and T_3 the average household income for project participants had increased by 70.0% compared with an increase of 74.6% for the comparison group. This showed that there was no evidence that improved housing had a positive impact on income, and in fact, the income of the comparison group rose slightly faster. This illustrates the importance of a carefully selected comparison group. If only project participants had been studied, one might have concluded that "*improved housing has a significant impact on household income because the income of participants in the low-cost housing project increased by 70% in four years.*"

SOURCE: Unpublished national consultant report.

process and the quality of the project services. They were also helpful in understanding the particular problems of female-headed households and the self-employed to participate in the project.

Threats to Validity and Adequacy of the Conclusions

The approach for Design 2 is similar to that of Design 1 (see Table 10.2).

Design 3: Truncated Pretest-Posttest Project and Comparison Group Longitudinal Design

When to Use

This design is used when an adequate budget is available but the major constraint is that the evaluation does not begin until the project has been underway for some time. Often, the evaluation will be required in time to produce an initial evaluation report for the midterm project review, which is often commissioned between two and three years after the start of a five-year project. The size of the sample and the complexity of the design can be adapted according to whether this is a pilot project or a well-tested program and according to the types of decisions to which the evaluation will contribute. Like Design 1, this design should complement the pretest-posttest impact assessment with a process evaluation.

Description of the Design

The truncated longitudinal design is used when the evaluation cannot begin until around midterm when the project has already been operating for some time but where at least another 18 months remain in its operational cycle. The first observation is considered to be a proxy baseline, while recognizing that the project has already been underway for some time. Observations are then repeated at several points in time to observe the process of project implementation. The final observation is then made at T_3 around the time of project completion. Another difference between Design 1 and Design 3 is that there are no plans for conducting an ex-post evaluation.

As always, it is recommended that the design be based on a program theory model and should include a contextual analysis to assess the influence of the economic, political,

---

Box 10.7   Design 3: Truncated Pretest-Posttest Project and Comparison Group Longitudinal Design Starting at the Time of the Midterm Review

Time	T_1 (baseline)	Project Intervention (continues past midterm)	T_2 (midterm)	T_3 (end of project)	T_4 (after project)
Project group		X	$P_{1(n)}$	P_2	
Comparison group			$C_{1(n)}$	C_3	

organizational, and natural environment within which the different project sites operate and to study the influence of cultural characteristics of the affected populations on program outcomes.

Incorporating Mixed-Method Approaches into the Design

Box 10.8 illustrates how QUAL and mixed methods were incorporated into the design of an evaluation of a feeder roads project (rural roads connecting villages to the main road network) in Eritrea. These were used for purposes of triangulation (comparing secondary sources with observational estimates of the volume and types of road transport), conducting a process analysis of project implementation and evaluating the quality of road construction and maintenance. Observational techniques were also used to reduce the costs of obtaining data on vehicular and pedestrian traffic.

Threats to Validity and Adequacy of the Conclusions

Although all the threats to validity must be reviewed, the nature of Design 3 means that several potential threats require particular attention.

- The feeder roads evaluation described in Box 10.8 is an example of Design 3 that does not include a comparison group. In these cases, particular attention must be given to how this affects internal threats to validity (see Appendix 1, G-3, controlling for history) and external threats to validity (see Appendix 1, I-7, seasonal and other cyclical variations).
- The absence of baseline data makes it more difficult to measure change between T_1 and T_3 because inferences have to be made about how much change has already taken place between T_1 and the midterm review (T_2) when the first measurement was made.

Box 10.8   Case Study for Design 3: Assessing the Social and Economic
Impacts of the Feeder Roads Component of the Eritrea Social Fund

---

This evaluation did not begin until the project had reached midterm. It combined an end-of-project survey of the project areas combined with a simple longitudinal study to observe the process of change. In this case (deviating from the full Design 3), no comparison group was used. Observations were made at three points in time during the approximately nine-month period of road construction to document changes such as the number of small businesses operating along the route of the future road, the number of pedestrians, the number of trucks and buses, and the number of people visiting the health clinic. Observation was also used during road construction workdays to assess the efficiency of organization and the quality of construction and maintenance. Data reliability was strengthened through triangulation of findings from focus groups, key informant interviews, and direct observation. Baseline conditions were reconstructed through recall, and secondary data compensated for the lack of a comparison group.

SOURCE: Unpublished national consultant report.

- Reliance on respondent memory and key informants to recall the situation at the start of the project is another potentially important source of bias.
- Many Design 3 evaluations also use secondary data to reconstruct baseline data and, as in this example, comparison group data. These introduce other potential sources of bias.

Design 4: Elimination of the Baseline Comparison Group (Pretest-Posttest Project Group Combined with Posttest Analysis of Project and Comparison Groups)

When to Use

This design is used either when the evaluation begins at the start of the project or when the evaluation starts later but previously collected baseline data are available on the project group. Baseline data are not collected on comparison groups for one of a number of reasons: to save money, because of technical or ethical difficulties in collecting the data, or because management does not consider this necessary. It is quite common that when the project begins, management does not feel it is necessary to include a comparison group because they feel the purpose of the evaluation is simply to compare the project group before and after the project intervention. However, as the project evolves and the need to justify an extension or the launch of a new project, the need for a comparison group is understood. Consequently, it is not uncommon for the evaluator to be asked to create a comparison group for the end-of-project evaluation.

Description of the Design

In this design, a baseline survey is conducted with the intended project beneficiaries before the project begins, but no comparison group is used at this stage. Only at the time of the final project evaluation (in T_3) is a survey conducted that includes both project and comparison groups. This design works reasonably well for assessing how a project is being implemented and whether it is able to produce the intended outputs. It is also able to compare the characteristics of the project group and the comparison group at the time the project completes its work. If, retrospectively, it can be adequately documented that the comparison group was essentially the same as the project group at the time the project started (T_1), this design may be sufficient to demonstrate project effects.

For example, with a rural road construction project, surveys and participatory consultations with the community may have identified a number of factors affecting the willingness of the community to participate in the project and the benefits they obtain from the road. These factors might include whether local culture permits women to participate in road construction and to travel to the market, the distance from the local market, and the agricultural surplus available to sell. A comparison group, if it is well selected, could rate other local communities on these variables and hence determine the likelihood that the project would be well received and would have an impact in other areas. The project and comparison groups could also be compared on indicators such as amount of produce sold in the local markets, average number of trips and distance traveled, and kinds of consumer goods available in community shops.

As always, the design should be based on a program theory model and should be combined with a process evaluation and a contextual analysis.

Box 10.9 Design 4: Elimination of the Baseline Comparison Group (Pretest-Posttest Project Group Combined with Posttest Analysis of Project and Comparison Groups)

Time	T_1 (baseline)	Project Intervention	T_2 (midterm)	T_3 (end of project)	T_4 (after project)
Project group	P_1	X		P_2	
Comparison group				C_1	

Incorporating Mixed-Method Approaches into the Design

In addition to the incorporation of a process and contextual analysis, a mixed-method approach can be very helpful for reconstructing the baseline conditions of the comparison group. For the interpretation of the findings, it is important to have the best information possible on how similar the characteristics of the project and comparison groups were at the time the project started. In the case of the Maharashtra irrigation project (see Box 10.10), QUAL methods (informal conversations with neighbors and key informants) were used to identify former residents who had not been eligible for compensation or new land and who had moved·

Box 10.10 Case Study for Design 4: Comparing the Effects of Resettlement on Project Beneficiaries and Nonbeneficiaries in the Second Maharashtra Irrigation Project, India

Sample surveys were conducted periodically between 1978 and 1985 in areas from which families were to be resettled as a consequence of a large-scale irrigation project. The study covered only families who were eligible to receive land or housing plots in the relocation areas. The surveys were repeated in 1990 after project families had been relocated. An ex-post comparison group survey was conducted in 1990 with a sample of families who had remained in the command area of the irrigation project. This was not an ideal comparison as many of the sample households forced to move as a result of the dam had remained in the project, so their situation did not really represent families not affected by the dam. Recognizing that no information was available on the approximately 45% of families who were forced to relocate but who were not eligible for compensation, a tracer study was conducted in 1990 to try to identify these families. The study found that the economic conditions of most families receiving compensation had improved. The situation concerning the families who had not received compensation was more mixed, but in general, forced resettlement appeared to have had less negative consequences than had been expected.

SOURCE: Valadez and Bamberger (1994:264–66, summarizing World Bank 1993).

out of the area. A **tracer study** was then conducted with these families to compare their situation with the project families who had received compensation.

Threats to Validity and Adequacy of the Conclusions

This design has some important weaknesses that require special attention when assessing potential threats to validity and adequacy:

- The lack of comparison group baseline data means that it is not possible to determine whether observed differences between the project and comparison groups in T_3 are due to the project or to differences that already existed between the groups before the project began. These threaten **internal validity** (G-3, controlling for history) and **external validity** (I-7, seasonal and other cyclical variations).
- Another weakness is that we cannot control for *local history,* which might have affected outcomes. This is particularly important for projects seeking to increase agricultural output or sales. Sales of maize or wheat may have increased because of the good rains and not because of the project. The end-of-project comparison group can provide some information on this but the analysis is obviously much stronger if changes in the project and control areas can be compared over time. This again concerns threats to external validity (I-7, seasonal and other cyclical variations).

Design 5: Posttest Comparison of Project and Comparison Groups

When to Use

This design is used when the evaluation does not begin until project implementation has been underway for some time or has been completed. Despite the late start, evaluations using this design are often quite well funded, and it is often possible to administer surveys to quite large samples of subjects in both the project and comparison groups. In other cases, the evaluation is based on secondary data from household, agricultural, labor force, and other surveys that had been collected for some other purpose.

Description of the Design[4]

This design relies entirely on an end-of-project comparison between the project group and a nonequivalent control group (comparison group), and no baseline data were collected on either the project or comparison areas. It can be used to obtain an approximate estimate of project impacts. The design works better in isolated communities where the project is the only major outside intervention so that it is less important to isolate the effects of other interventions taking place at the same time. It can also be used to compare the characteristics of project participants with people from other similar communities. If project households have similar characteristics to other communities, then it is more likely that the results of the pilot project can be generalized. If, on the other hand, there are significant differences between the two groups, it will be more difficult to generalize.

Box 10.11 Design 5: No Baseline Data (Posttest Project and Comparison Groups)

Time	T_1 (baseline)	Project Intervention	T_2 (midterm)	T_3 (end of project)	T_4 (after project)
Project group		X		P_1	
Comparison group				C_1	

The fact that large, carefully selected samples are often used means that the analytical **power** of the design can be strengthened through the use of multivariate analysis to statistically control for differences between the two groups (see Box 10.12).

Incorporating Mixed-Method Approaches into the Design

Often, this design relies exclusively on QUANT data collection and analysis, particularly when the evaluation is based on survey data collected for some other purpose. A fundamental weakness of the design is that it does not control for historical events or for preexisting differences between the project and comparison groups. Mixed methods can significantly strengthen the design by obtaining information on the characteristics of the two groups at the time the project began. This can be obtained through focus groups, participatory appraisal (**PRA**) techniques (see Chapter 5), or interviews with key informants. For example, in the evaluation of the impacts of microcredit programs in Bangladesh (Box 10.12), the analysis found

Box 10.12 Case Study for Design 5: Assessing the Impacts of Microcredit on the Social and Economic Conditions of Women and Families in Bangladesh

In 1991–92, a random sample of households was interviewed in a sample of villages where some of the leading village bank programs were operating in rural Bangladesh. A comparison group was interviewed in villages where none of these village bank programs were operating. The surveys were conducted ex-post when the village banks had already been operating for several years. No baseline information had been collected on the condition of families before the banks began to operate. It was found that borrowing from a village bank had much greater impact on women than on men (although the latter also benefited). Per capita household expenditures increased almost twice as fast when women received loans rather than men, housing conditions improved, and personal savings increased. Interestingly, it was found that contraceptive usage declined for women borrowers and their fertility increased. The lack of baseline data made it difficult to determine to what extent the observed differences between the project and comparison groups were due to the effects of the project or whether they were due, at least in part, to differences that already existed before the project began.

SOURCES: Khandker (1998), Baker (2000, Annex 1.2), and World Bank (2001).

that when women obtained loans, this had a greater impact on household expenditures, investment in housing, and children's school enrollment, than when men obtained loans. It was assumed that the difference was due to the strong emphasis of the credit groups on group development and strengthening women's self-confidence. However, an alternative hypothesis, which could not be tested on the basis of the survey data, would be that the women who decided to apply for loans already had more self-confidence and perhaps entrepreneurial experience. This hypothesis could have been tested through some of the mixed-method approaches described above. This assumes, of course, that it would be possible for the researchers to go to the field to apply these techniques.

Threats to Validity and Adequacy of the Conclusions

This design does not control for historical events that may have affected outcomes and has the same weaknesses as Designs 3 and 7, which also do not collect any baseline data. The simple QUANT model described above also does not evaluate the project implementation process. Some of the specific threats to consider include the following:

F-4: Unreliability of indicators. Does the secondary data set accurately measure the critical variables?

F-5 and F-10: Restriction of range and extrapolation from a restricted or incomplete database.

G-3: History: The design is not able to control for economic, political, or other events occurring during the life of the project that might have had different effects on the project and comparison groups.

H-1: Inadequate explanation of constructs. The program theory model is not sufficiently precise or key variables or steps are missing.

H-2: Indicators do not adequately measure constructs. When using secondary data, it is often necessary to rely on surveys that were formulated for different purposes, and the indicators may not adequately capture the key constructs and concepts—particularly when these concern complex ideas such as motivations affecting fertility behavior or control of different household members over economic resources.

Design 6: No Comparison Group (Pretest-Posttest Project Group)

When to Use

This design is used under similar conditions to Design 4. The evaluation begins at the start of the project, but again, for budget, technical, or political reasons, baseline data are collected only on the project group, and there is no comparison group, either at the beginning or at the end of the project.

Description of the Design

This design completely eliminates the comparison group, and the analysis is based on a comparison of the project group before and after implementation. The design works reasonably well for projects using "best practice" interventions that have been previously proven to work under very similar conditions—for example, the construction of a village school or clinic where there was previously no such facility within easy access. It can also work well when the purpose of the evaluation is to understand the project implementation process and where QUANT assessment of impacts is less important.

As always, the design should be based on a program theory model and should be combined with a process evaluation and a contextual analysis.

Incorporating Mixed-Method Approaches into the Design

One of the main contributions of mixed-method approaches for this design is to reconstruct a comparison group for both the baseline and the posttest situations. Some of the methods that can be used include use of secondary data, consultations with community groups

---

Box 10.13   Design 6: Pretest-Posttest Project Group with No Comparison Group

Time	T_1 (baseline)	Project Intervention	T_2 (midterm)	T_3 (end of project)	T^4 (after project)
Project group	P_1	X		P_2	
Comparison group					

Box 10.14   Case Study for Design 6: Using a Before-and-After Survey of Resettled Households to Evaluate the Impact of the Khao Laem Hydroelectric Project in Thailand

The project called for the involuntary resettlement of 41 affected villages with a total of 1,800 families. A survey of 50% of the intended beneficiaries was conducted in 1978–79 prior to the start of the project, and a follow-up survey was conducted in 1989–90 with 200 resettled families. No formal comparison group was used either before or after resettlement, although the research team consulted available secondary sources. While the comparison of quantitative surveys conducted before and after resettlement showed that families were better off on the basis of a set of economic indicators, a qualitative survey found that the majority of families considered themselves to be worse off. No information was available on the families who did not move to resettlement areas or on the 30% who did not remain in the project.

SOURCE: Valadez and Bamberger (1994:259–61).

through PRA or similar techniques to obtain opinions on how the project compares with other communities, rapid observation studies, and consultation with knowledgeable key informants.

Threats to Validity and Adequacy of the Conclusions

This design does not work well when precise estimates of the magnitude of project impacts are required. It also does not control for the influence of local history (internal validity G-3). The lack of comparative data on the project and other communities also means that it is difficult to assess the potential for replicating the project on a larger scale (Section I. external validity—various categories). For example, if the project was successful because it had selected communities with higher than average levels of education and income, it would be difficult to assess how successful a larger project would be if it was extended to more typical communities with lower education and income.

Design 7: Data Collected Only on Posttest Project Group

When to Use

This is technically the weakest RWE design because it does not control for most of the threats to validity and, consequently, the conclusions and recommendations must be treated with caution. The absence of a pretest makes it difficult to know if a change has occurred, and the absence of a no-treatment comparison group makes it difficult to know what would have happened without the project treatment (Shadish et al. 2002:106). It is also not possible to obtain precise QUANT estimates of project outcomes or impacts. Despite these limitations, Design 7 is probably the most widely used RWE evaluation design—particularly for small projects or those working on a very tight evaluation budget. This design is used when the evaluator has very little time (sometimes as little as one or two weeks) and a very limited budget (sometimes as little as a few thousand dollars).

There are two main situations in which this design is used. The first is where the project being evaluated is very small, perhaps operating in only one location, or where this is an exploratory study where the main purpose is to obtain an initial assessment of whether the project "works" and whether it seems potentially able to achieve its stated objectives. In this context, "works" might mean any of the following:

- Are women able and willing to apply for loans and invest the proceeds in a small business?
- Do most residents use the community toilets, and are they maintained in good working order?
- Are teachers able to apply the new teaching tools and methods, and are there preliminary indications that they affect students' behavior and performance?

The second situation is where the project is quite large and **clients** are interested in obtaining estimates of outcomes and impacts, but there was no life-of-project evaluation plan, or even baseline. In this context, the evaluators are aware that they have to do the best they can with a methodologically weak evaluation design.

When using this design, the scoping of the evaluation (Step 1, see Chapter 2) is particularly important to fully understand the client's information needs and how the evaluation results will be used.

Description of the Design

In this design, only the project population is studied, and they are surveyed only after the project has been implemented. Data may be collected from a small, rapid sample survey; from QUAL methods (PRA, focus groups, secondary sources, key informants, etc.); or from a mixed-method design combining QUANT and QUAL methods.

Strengthening the Design

Given its methodological weaknesses, it is important to strengthen the design by using some of the approaches described earlier in the chapter. Maximum use should be made of mixed-method approaces (see Chapter 13). Even when operating under time pressures, efforts should be made to construct at least a simple program theory model using the techniques described in Chapter 9 to obtain an approximate estimate of causality. This permits the use of logical deduction through techniques such as pattern matching (Campbell 1966) or coherence (Rosenbaum 1995) and through the nine strategies proposed by Davidson (2000:21–22), described in the previous chapter (p. 187). Some of these approaches have been described as being analogous to detective work in which a causal sequence is deduced from observing all the clues, and alternative explanations are eliminated through **evidence**. Readers should also be aware of the criticisms of the use of program theory to estimate causality (Cook 2000:29–32).

Incorporating Mixed-Methods Approaches into the Design

The evaluation of village schools in Eritrea (Box 10.16) illustrates the use of a mixed-method approach. To try to make up for the lack of pretest and comparison data, **recall** was used to assess school attendance prior to the construction of the school, and these estimates were triangulated with key informant interviews and a review of school attendance records.

Box 10.15 Design 7: Data Collected Only on Posttest Project Group

Time	T_1 (baseline)	Project Intervention	T_2 (midterm)	T_3 (end of project)	T_4 (after project)
Project group		X		P_1	
Comparison group					

Box 10.16   Case Study for Design 7: Assessing the Impacts of the
Construction of Village Schools in Eritrea

In the evaluation of the Eritrea Social Fund, an end-of-project survey was conducted in 48 communities representing the catchment area for 10 newly constructed primary schools. No comparison group was used. Baseline data on school attendance prior to the construction of the schools were estimated by asking families to recall the situation before the schools were built. Recall data seem to have been reliable because it was easy for families to recall whether their children attended school before the village school was built and also because they did not have any incentive to give wrong information. Triangulation was used to compare estimates from recall with key informant interviews and a review of school attendance records. The analysis focused on the following topics:

- *Process evaluation:* More than 90% confirmed that the school was a high priority, but only 37% had attended meetings to participate in planning the project.
- *Accessibility, impact, and gender:* The schools were successful in reaching the poorest sectors of the community; it was more difficult to involve recently returned refugees because they were still unsettled and not motivated to send their children to school; families are equally motivated to send boys and girls to school, but if they have to choose for economic reasons, they normally give priority to a boy.
- *Social impact:* School construction reduced travel time for students by one-half to two-thirds.
- *Sustainability:* Despite extreme poverty, almost all households contributed the required 10% of the cost of the school in cash, labor, or materials.

SOURCE: Unpublished national consultant report.

Threats to Validity and Adequacy of the Conclusions

The fact that data are collected only on the project group and only after the project has been implemented makes the conclusions vulnerable to most of the threats to validity listed in Table 10.2. The design cannot be used to obtain reasonably precise estimates of impact. It cannot control for local history events that might affect outcomes, and it does not provide any comparative data on the characteristics of the project population, so it is not possible to generalize to a wider population.

Summary

- Randomized experimental designs can be considered the methodologically strongest QUANT designs for impact assessment. However, the appropriate role for randomized designs for the evaluation of education and other social programs is hotly debated in both the United States and developing countries. Even without these debates, the application of randomized designs—particularly for RWE scenarios—is limited by the technical, budgetary, ethical, and political difficulties in using a randomly selected control group that will be excluded from receiving the services being offered to the project group.

- Quasi-experimental designs (QEDs) seek to approximate as closely as possible to the experimental design while adapting to realities of the real-world social context. One of the most robust QEDs involves pretest-posttest comparisons of the project group and a comparison group selected to approximate as closely as possible relevant characteristics of the project group.

- Even under the most favorable conditions, experimental designs or even QEDs, when used in isolation, have a number of limitations for impact assessment. A purely QUANT pretest-posttest design does not examine the project implementation process or the contextual factors (economic, political, organizational, environmental, and the characteristics of the affected populations) affecting project performance. It is also difficult to quantify many important **input**, process, and outcome indicators, and the rigidity of the design makes it difficult to adapt to changes in the project design and or the evolution of the internal and external contexts over time.

- Seven variations of the basic QED are described that can be applied in RWE contexts. The different designs adapt to cost and time constraints and to the fact that many evaluations do not start until the project has been underway for some time and, consequently, no baseline data were collected. Some of these designs save cost or time by eliminating one or more of the four major data collection points (pretest-posttest of project and comparison groups).

- The less robust designs involve trade-offs as the elimination of data collection points increases vulnerability to different threats to validity of the conclusions. A number of strategies can be used to strengthen all these designs, including (a) the use of mixed-method designs, (b) using a program theory model, (c) incorporating process analysis, and (d) using multivariate analysis to more closely match the project and comparison groups.

Further Reading

Gray, D. 2004. *Doing Research in the Real World.* Thousand Oaks, CA: Sage.

Chapter 4 provides a simple introduction to quasi-experimental designs.

Reichardt, C. 2005. "Quasi-Experimental Designs." Pp. 351–355 in *Encyclopedia of Evaluation,* edited by S. Mathison. Thousand Oaks, CA: Sage.

Provides a five-page overview of the principles of quasi-experimental designs.

Rossi, P., M. Lipsey, and H. Freeman. 2004. *Evaluation: A Systematic Approach.* 7th ed. Thousand Oaks, CA: Sage.

Chapters 8 and 9 review randomized field experiments and quasi-experimental designs and also discuss limitations of quasi-experimental designs for impact assessment.

Table 10.3 The Strengths and Weaknesses of the Seven Most Frequently Used Quasi-Experimental Designs

Design	Advantages	Disadvantages
1. Comprehensive longitudinal design with pre-, midterm, post-, and ex-post observations on the project and comparison groups	This is the strongest design, studying both the implementation process and sustainability. May be required for research testing new project innovation that, if impact can be proven, will be expanded to much greater scale.	• The disadvantage is that it is the most expensive, the most time-consuming, and the most difficult to implement.
2. Pretest-posttest project and comparison groups	This is the strongest general-purpose QED. With a well-selected comparison group it provides good estimates of project impacts.	• Assumes the comparison group is reasonably similar to project group and willing to participate in two surveys even though they receive no benefits. • Does not assess project implementation
3. Truncated longitudinal pretest-posttest project and comparison group design	• Observes implementation process as well as impacts • Reasonably robust model, particularly for projects where implementation begins slowly so that not too much is missed by starting the evaluation late	• Does not begin until around project midterm, so the project startup and initial implementation period are not captured.
4. Pretest-posttest project group combined with posttest analysis of project and comparison groups	• Assesses if the project model works and produces the intended outputs • Assesses similarities and differences between project and comparison areas • Assesses the extent to which the project could potentially be replicated.	• Does not assess whether observed end-of-project differences between the project and comparison groups are due to the project or to preexisting differences between the two groups • Does not control for local history that might affect outcomes
5. Posttest project and comparison groups	• Evaluates projects that implement well-tested interventions or that operate in isolated areas where there is no interference from other outside interventions	• Does not estimate the exact magnitude of project impacts • Does not control for local history • Does not assess potential for replication on a larger scale • Does not study project implementation process

(Continued)

Table 10.3 (Continued)

Design	Advantages	Disadvantages
6. Pretest-posttest project group	• Provides an approximate estimate of project impacts, particularly in small or isolated communities	• Does not estimate the exact magnitude of project impacts • Does not control for local history • Does not compare project with other communities • Does not control for the effect of intervening variables through the use of multivariate analysis
7. Posttest project group only	• Useful for exploratory studies to get a general idea of how well the project model works • Provides a first, approximate estimate of results, particularly for small or isolated projects.	• Does not obtain reasonably precise estimates of project impact • Hard to feel confident that the observed changes are due to the project and not to other factors or interventions • Does not control for external events • Does not obtain comparative data to estimate potential replicability

NOTE: The strength of all of these models can be increased by combining them with the impact evaluation framework and analysis of contextual factors discussed in Chapter 9 (pp. **175–177**) and with some of the RWE techniques discussed earlier in this chapter. For Designs 1, 2, 3, 4, and 5, which use comparison groups, the analysis can be greatly strengthened by using multiple regression analysis to statistically control for differences in the characteristics of the project and control groups. Where appropriate secondary data is available, these designs can also be strengthened through statistical matching techniques such as **propensity scores** and **instrumental variables**.

Shadish, W., T. Cook, and D. Campbell. 2002. *Experimental and Quasi-Experimental Designs for Generalized Causal Inference*. Boston: Houghton Mifflin.

The most comprehensive reference on quasi-experimental designs and threats to validity. However, many readers may find this too detailed (600 pages) and technical for their needs.

Notes

1. See Shadish, Cook, and Campbell (2002, chap. 1) for a discussion of experiments and the analysis of causation.

2. Even with relatively large samples, sampling variation will normally produce differences between the project and control groups with respect to, for example, average weight, crop yield, family demographic characteristics, or pretest performance scores.

3. This does not, of course, mean that ethical issues are not important, but it does show that a number of research institutions and development agencies have felt that there are acceptable ways to address these issues.

4. It should be noted that this design can be strengthened when secondary data is available, particularly when this covers the baseline period. This permits the use of statistical matching techniques such as propensity scores and instrumental variables (see Baker 2000:50–51).

CHAPTER 11

Quantitative Evaluation Methods

T his chapter discusses QUANT data collection and analysis methods, and the following two chapters cover similar ground for QUAL and mixed-method evaluations. We begin with an overview of QUANT and QUAL traditions in evaluation research and discuss some of the common applications of QUANT evaluation methodologies. We then review QUANT data collection methods and the management of data collection for QUANT studies, with emphasis on the data management challenges for RealWorld Evaluation (**RWE**). The chapter concludes with a discussion of QUANT data analysis.

The Quantitative and Qualitative Traditions in Evaluation Research

Social science research has, since its earliest days, had two distinct and often competing traditions. One of these traditions, influenced by the natural sciences, has viewed the world as a set of objective phenomena that can be observed, measured, and analyzed in much the same way that natural scientists can study chemicals and medical researchers can study the human body. In this tradition, the social world consists of "social facts" that the social science researcher can study in a detached and objective way. In principle, these social facts can be defined and measured in a precise way so that other researchers should be able to measure the social phenomena in exactly the same way. In the social sciences, much of conventional economics and demography, for example, subscribes to this view of the social world. This is what is commonly defined as the *quantitative* (**QUANT**) research tradition.

In the interpretivist or *qualitative* (**QUAL**) tradition, social research is seen in a fundamentally different way, with the researcher's perspective acknowledged as an integral part of what is recorded about the social world that she or he is studying. Consequently, it is neither possible nor appropriate to assume the kind of scientific detachment from the phenomena being studied to which the quantitative researcher aspires.[1] The *meanings* given to social phenomena and social situations by the individuals and groups who are experiencing them must be understood for social behavior to be interpreted accurately. Different individuals and groups can give different meanings to the same phenomenon, all of which contribute to its meaning. That meaning is both *individually* and *socially constructed.*[2] Social phenomena are socially constructed—community norms and expectations, legal and governmental systems, policies and implementations for allocating resources—are all aspects of the **programs** to be evaluated. The task of the social researcher is to find ways to enter into the worlds of the different participants or **stakeholders** to try to capture and understand the meanings that they give, since what they believe affects what they do, and what they do affects the nature of the phenomenon of study. QUAL researchers, like their human subjects and even their QUANT counterparts, must also construct their own meanings and interpretations of what they study. Acknowledging that there is no single "correct" interpretation of the phenomena of the social world, QUAL researchers are obliged to collect enormous amounts of detailed information over time in order to warrant their interpretations.

QUAL researchers are also obliged to study phenomena naturalistically—in their natural settings. They recognize that social phenomena, even on a small scale, exist within many overlapping contexts, such as ideological, legal, political, historical, economic, psychological, and physical contexts. These contexts and many other dynamic influences affect the phenomena of study, continuously shaping and reshaping them. QUAL researchers engage in sensitive, nuanced studies to develop complex understandings—not simple bottom lines or correlations—of complex phenomena.

In **mixed-method** evaluation, both QUAL and QUANT methods are combined. When the mix is well designed and well implemented, the resulting evaluation often benefits enormously from the strengths of both traditions. QUANT approaches may provide a broad, big-picture view of the extent of a phenomenon or program, numerical measurements and correlations of measurable aspects, and analyses of statistically significant differences between program beneficiaries and nonbeneficiaries or between before-and-after conditions. QUAL approaches may provide the detail necessary to understand why, for whom, how much, and under which circumstances stakeholders experienced *real* significance, not just whether measurable differences are statistically significant. Both QUAL and QUANT approaches offer distinct advantages that complement each other when used well together.

Often, the discussion of these two approaches and their differences are conducted in specialized academic journals, which may at first glance appear to have little relevance to the real world of evaluation practice and use. However, it is useful for **evaluation practitioners, clients,** and **users** to have a basic understanding of the two approaches for several reasons.

First, many social scientists have a professional or personal preference for either QUANT or QUAL, even though they frequently use mixed methods to a greater or lesser extent. Because of individual practitioner preferences, if an agency commissions a quantitatively oriented researcher to conduct an evaluation of their program, it is likely to receive a different product than if it had given the same terms of reference to a qualitatively oriented evaluator. Thus, having a basic understanding of the two orientations will help a client anticipate some of the approaches and methods that QUANT or QUAL evaluators are likely to use.

Second, clients are well-advised to assess the information needs and expectations of different audiences for an evaluation report and to consider whether one evaluator or another is more likely to produce the types of **evidence** that stakeholders will find convincing. However, the caution about personal preferences regarding different approaches applies to clients as well as to evaluators. Clients too have preferences, sometimes without realizing them, and may be unaware of the benefits of data they fail to anticipate or appreciate. Consequently, clients and stakeholders oriented toward just one approach (QUANT or QUAL) may especially benefit from mixed methods and from what evaluators call *client education* about evaluation practice. Otherwise, clients are likely to select evaluators who will provide only the kinds of evidence and arguments to support **findings** about a program and its effectiveness that clients are most likely to find accessible—not necessarily those that might provide the most useful information.

Clearly, then, QUANT and QUAL orientations have different advantages and disadvantages that the client, user, and practitioner should recognize. A central tenet of RWE is the importance of mixed methods to use the unique strengths and to compensate for the weaknesses of both QUANT and QUAL orientations. It is also helpful to recognize that the effective use of mixed methods is more complex than exclusive reliance on either QUANT or QUAL approaches. The successful use of mixed methods requires an understanding of both orientations and the particular challenges of getting evaluators from both disciplines to work together.

Quantitative Methodologies

A key characteristic of most QUANT methodologies is that standardized indicators are defined and standardized data collection procedures are used throughout the evaluation to ensure comparability. Most QUANT program evaluation is based on one of two types of experiments to estimate the effects of treatments and interventions: randomized experiments and quasi-experiments (Reichardt 2005:351). Both **designs** involve the collection of quantitative data that can be represented in numerical form (e.g., age, number of people living in the household, income, percentage of students passing a standardized test) and that can be analyzed with statistics, both descriptive and inferential. The data can be used to test hypotheses or to determine the statistical difference between observations made at two points in time (e.g., student test scores before and after the introduction of new teaching methods) or between two or more groups (e.g., families who received technical assistance and small-business loans and a comparable group who did not). Many QUANT methodologies are *deductive* in that they begin with a theory or hypothesis and then develop a research design to test it. In this section, we describe some of the features of QUANT methodologies.

Experimental Designs

A **randomized** or experimental evaluation design involves the random assignment of subjects (e.g., individuals, families, schools, communities) to the treatment (**project**) group and to a control group that does not receive the treatment. The two groups are compared at the start of the experiment and then the experimental treatment (e.g., drug, nutritional supplement, new teaching method) is administered to the treatment group but not to the control group while all other conditions are carefully regulated and kept constant for both groups. The two groups are again compared at an appropriate point in time after the treatment. If a statistically significant posttest difference is found between the two groups, this is considered as a preliminary indication of a project effect. Ideally, the experiment would be repeated a number of times to determine whether the effect is still found when conditions such as intensity of the treatment or the point at which the posttest comparisons are varied.

Although precisely controlled randomized **experimental designs** are often used in areas such as medical research, animal behavior, and some areas of psychological investigation, it is normally not possible to ensure the same degree of control when randomized experiments are used in field settings. Although randomized allocation of subjects to treatment (project) and control groups can be used in program evaluation, it is rarely possible to control the conditions of the two groups in the period during which the project (treatment) is being implemented (which can be a period of several months or even several years), and consequently, there is always the problem of determining how much of any observed difference is due to the effect of the project and how much is due to other differences, unrelated to the project, in the situation of the two groups during the project implementation period.

In Chapter 10, we gave a number of examples of randomized evaluations in the fields of education, primary health, and agricultural extension in developing countries such as Kenya, India, Colombia, and the United States (see Box 10.1). A high proportion of the reported randomized experiments in developing countries is in the field of education and involves the random assignment of school classes to receive educational TV programs or special textbooks, or to have teachers who have received special training. Many of these designs provide different classes with different combinations of treatments so that interactions can be studied.

Shadish, Cook, and Campbell identify the following conditions most favorable to random assignment (Shadish et al. 2002:269–75):

- When demand outstrips supply
- When an innovation cannot be delivered to all units at once
- When experimental units can be temporally isolated
- When experimental units are spatially separated or interunit communication is low
- When change is mandated and solutions are acknowledged to be unknown
- When some persons express no preference among alternatives
- When you can create your own organization
- When you have control over experimental units
- When lotteries are expected

An example where demand outstrips supply are **social investment funds** (Carvalho and White 2004) that allow poor communities in many developing countries to select to receive one service (e.g., water, sanitation, health centers) from a menu of services. The demand for services is often very high, and the lottery system has been used in a number of countries such as Bolivia to select the communities that will receive the service. This example of randomized assignment has worked well, both because it is completely transparent and because communities that are not selected to receive the service one year have the opportunity to apply again in future years.

There are, however, a number of practical, ethical, and political problems that limit the use of randomization. Some of these problems relate to costs or to the logistical difficulties of administering a random allocation (including problems relating to how participants are recruited), and others are ethical (e.g., withholding medicines or beneficial services from the control groups) or political (pressures from local politicians to extend coverage to the whole population). Many educators and evaluators of educational programs would object on ethical grounds to depriving some students—those who might be assigned to control groups—of promising educational TV programs, special textbooks, or teachers who have received special training. Ethical issues in evaluation design, including the question of randomization, are discussed in Chapters 6 and 10.

Another set of problems concerns the difficulties of ensuring that the project is administered uniformly so that all subjects receive exactly the same set of services delivered in exactly the same way. A final set of problems relates to participant attrition as when, for example, the poorer, less educated, or less motivated participants drop out of the project more rapidly. The combination of these factors often makes it extremely difficult to approximate an experimental design even when it is initially possible to use random assignment of subjects to the treatment and control groups.

Although there are examples where a specific intervention needs to be tested using a randomized experimental design to test the correlation between intervention and effect, in most development programs we are evaluating much more complex and multifaceted phenomena so that there are limitations on the utility of randomized designs, even when resources are available.

Quasi-Experimental Designs (QEDs)[3]

Much more commonly, the evaluator has no control over the individuals or groups who participate in programs or receive services. In many cases, the individuals, families, communities, organizations, or regions who will receive services such as educational programs, roads, water supply, soil conservation, or public transportation are selected on the basis of administrative or political criteria, and the evaluator has no influence over the allocation process. In other cases, beneficiaries are self-selected, as when individuals apply for small-business loans or mothers enroll children in an education or health program. In both cases, if the evaluator wishes to compare project beneficiaries to a group that did not receive these services, the evaluator must attempt to identify a comparison or matched group in which the individuals resemble the beneficiary group as closely as possible. Box 11.1 clarifies that technically the term *control group* should be used only when subjects have been randomly assigned to the treat (project) and no-treatment groups. When the no-treatment group has to be selected independently, then this should be referred to as the comparison group.

Comparison groups may be selected in one of the following ways:

- An external comparison group may be selected from, for example, different communities or schools.
- An internal comparison group can be used where projects are implemented in phases. For example, families who will receive the services in Phase 2 can be used as a comparison to assess the **impacts** of the program on Phase 1 families. This is sometimes referred to as a "rolling baseline," or a "pipeline" comparison group, where the baseline for the second cohort can be used to serve as the comparison group for the achievements of the first cohort.
- Both QUANT and QUAL evaluations make use of naturally occurring comparison groups. For example, one of the authors was involved in an evaluation of the impacts of a program to improve access to infrastructure and public service of communities living on islands (*chars*) in the main rivers in Bangladesh. These islands are flooded every monsoon season, and many of them completely vanish each year while new islands constantly emerge from the river. The variable duration of the islands provides

---

Box 11.1   Control Groups and Comparison Groups

Although the term *control group* is often used quite broadly, we follow the widely accepted practice of using control group to refer only to the group in a randomized experimental design that does not receive the experimental treatment. We use the term *comparison group* to refer to a group that is selected independently and by a different procedure in a quasi-experimental design to match as closely as possible some important characteristics of the project group. The distinction is important because the comparison group will often differ from the project group in ways that can significantly affect the interpretation of the evaluation findings. For example, if families enrolled in a children's nutrition program turn out to be on average better educated and to have higher incomes, some of the differences in **outcomes** between the project and comparison groups may be due to these initial differences—rather than to the effects of the program per se.

(unfortunately, for the inhabitants) a natural experiment in which the conditions of communities on islands that have survived for different periods of time can be compared.

- Documentary data (e.g., census data, household surveys, records of agricultural sales, and data from local health centers) can be used to compare the project group with the larger population of which it is a part.

One of the biggest challenges for **QED** is to understand how differences between the project and comparison groups might affect the interpretation of findings and the assessment of project impacts. For example, when participants are self-selected, it is likely that the individuals or groups that decide to participate will differ in some important ways from those who do not. Participants may differ from nonparticipants in terms of their economic status, political or religious affiliation, education, or household composition. While some of these characteristics may be relatively easy to identify, other potentially important factors such as motivation, self-confidence, teaching styles, or a woman's role in control over household resources are much more difficult to identify and assess.

On the other hand, when beneficiaries are selected on administrative grounds, it is likely that selection criteria will be used that will be difficult to match in the selection of a comparison group. For example, project groups may be selected because they are the poorest or the largest communities, because they are considered to have the highest probability of success, or because of their political affiliation or ethnic characteristics. These criteria will be difficult to match, as when, for example, the project includes all the largest urban slums.

Use of Program Theory in Quantitative Evaluations

Program theory can be defined as an explicit theory or model of how the program causes the intended or observed outcomes. Program theory is useful in QUANT, QUAL, and mixed-methods evaluation designs, although used differently in each case. A central element of many QUANT methodologies is the specification of hypotheses that can be tested through experimental or quasi-experimental designs. Sometimes an evaluation will test a single hypothesis, such as, "School attendance rates will be higher for children who receive free school meals." However, in many cases, a **program theory model** is developed in which a causal chain of interlinked hypotheses is specified and tested. For example, Carvalho and White (2004) develop a program theory model to describe the process through which social investment funds[4] are intended to improve the welfare of low-income populations in developing countries, and how the participatory mechanisms built into these programs help ensure **sustainability** of the programs. The following chapter describes how program theory is used in QUAL evaluation. There are also a number of important applications of program theory in mixed-method evaluations, including, for example, the incorporation of QUAL contextual analysis (assessing the influence of local economic, political, institutional, and environment factors on program outcomes) into QUANT survey designs.

Data Collection Methods

Two of the distinguishing characteristics of QUANT data collection methods are that data are collected in the form of numbers that can be manipulated statistically and that indicators and data collection methods are standardized throughout the evaluation to permit comparability between, for example, pretest and posttest or between project and comparison groups. A consequence of these requirements is that complex phenomena must be broken down into a set of simpler numerical indicators. Another is that QUANT studies tend to focus on what can be described in numerical terms so that opinions, meanings, social interactions, and ongoing processes are either ignored or treated in very simplified ways. The following chapter shows that QUAL evaluators adopt a very different approach to all these questions.

Later in this chapter, we describe the most widely used methods for QUANT data collection, including questionnaires and other closed or semiclosed survey instruments, structured observation, **focus groups,** self-reporting methods, unobtrusive measures, tests, anthropometric measures, and other physical tests. Several of these methods, such as observation and focus groups, are generally considered to be QUAL data collection methods, and they are discussed in more detail in the following chapter, but there are also a number of QUANT applications.

Sampling

Sampling procedures for QUANT surveys are intended to ensure (a) that the subjects sampled are representative of the whole population so that generalizations about the population may be made confidently and (b) that the sample is sufficiently large so that statistical differences between groups can be estimated. Much of the discussion of QUANT sampling focuses on the estimation of sample size, although as we will see in Chapter 14, the effectiveness of the sample also depends on the adequacy of the **sampling frame**, policies for addressing nonresponse, and how carefully the implementation of the sample design is managed. Sampling procedures, discussed in Chapter 14, are particularly important for quantitative RWE, because one of the most common ways to save cost and time is by reducing the size of samples. When reducing sample size, it becomes critical to ensure that samples are still sufficiently large to allow for statistical analysis and appropriate generalizations.

Most QUAL evaluations adopt an approach to sample selection that is very different from that described for QUANT evaluations. A great deal of time and effort is invested in the careful selection of what is normally a fairly small number of subjects that between them represent the main types of subjects, issues, or processes of concern to the evaluation. The goal is to select a sample that can provide the maximum depth and understanding of the issues being studied. The selection process may continue over time, and the selection criteria may be revised as the researchers learn more about the issues. Most QUAL samples do not claim to be statistically representative, and in fact statistical sampling procedures would not work with such small samples, but the samples are considered to be representative in a substantive sense in that all important issues are addressed.

When mixed-method evaluation approaches are used (see Chapter 13), one of the important design issues is how to ensure that the QUANT and QUAL data refer to comparable populations. One of the challenges facing many mixed-method designs is that sometimes the QUANT and QUAL components of a study produce what seems to be conflicting information, and it is often difficult to judge whether this reflects real differences or whether the differences are due, at least in part, to the way the samples were selected. For example, the QUANT survey may suggest that the proportion of the population living below the poverty line has decreased, whereas the QUAL studies reveal that most of the people studied feel they are worse off. In another example, the QUANT survey may find that a majority of families in the **target population** report that they are using the local health services and are satisfied with the services, but the QUAL studies report that many people do not like to use these services or are dissatisfied with them because of corruption, absence of staff or medicines, or concerns about sexual harassment. It is important in cases such as these to agree at the start of the study on the procedures that will be used for the selection of the villages or households to be included in both the QUANT and QUAL studies to ensure comparability. This is particularly important in cases where the QUAL findings reveal weaknesses or problems in programs and services that were not found in the QUANT surveys and where the agencies being evaluated may try to dismiss the criticisms by claiming that the QUAL findings are not representative because of the way in which the cases were selected. A key challenge for mixed-method designs is to ensure comparability of QUANT and QUAL samples while respecting the iterative and flexible procedures by which QUAL cases are selected and data are collected on them.

Applications of Quantitative Methodologies in Program Evaluation

Strengths and Weaknesses of Quantitative Evaluation Methodologies

Table 11.1 summarizes some of the frequently stated strengths and weaknesses of QUANT evaluation methods. A well-selected sample is representative of the total population so that findings can be generalized to a broader population, such as all program beneficiaries or members of a community, city, country, or particular socioeconomic group of interest (e.g., the poor, agricultural laborers, secondary school students). Another advantage is that systematic statistical comparisons can be made among groups. QUANT evaluations also offer means to quantify the influence of **intervening variables** such as age, sex, class, or type of school on program outcomes. The QUANT approach also allows the specification and testing of hypotheses. Standardized research instruments and methods also mean that if the study is replicated

Table 11.1   Frequently Cited Strengths and Weaknesses of QUANT Evaluation Approaches

Strengths	*Weaknesses*
• Study findings can be generalized to the population about which information is required.	• Many kinds of information are difficult to obtain through structured data collection instruments, particularly on sensitive topics such as domestic violence or income.
• Samples of individuals, communities, or organizations can be selected to ensure that the results will be representative of the population studied.	• Many groups such as sex workers, drug users, illegal immigrants, or squatters and ethnic minorities are always difficult to reach, but the problems are often greater for QUANT data collection methods.
• Structural factors that determine how inequalities (such as gender inequalities) are produced and reproduced can be analyzed.	• Self-report information obtained from questionnaires may be inaccurate or incomplete.
• Quantitative estimates can be obtained of the magnitude and distribution of impacts.	• There is often no information on contextual factors to help interpret the results or to explain variations in behavior between households with similar economic and demographic characteristics.
• Quantitative estimates can be obtained of the costs and benefits of interventions.	• The administration of a structured questionnaire creates an unnatural situation that may alienate respondents.
• Clear documentation can be provided regarding the content and application of the survey instruments so that other researchers can assess the validity of the findings.	• Studies are expensive and time-consuming, and even the preliminary results are usually not available for a long period of time.
• Standardized approaches permit the study to be replicated in different areas or over time with the production of comparable findings.	• Research methods are inflexible because the instruments cannot be modified once the study begins.
• It is possible to control for the effects of extraneous variables that might result in misleading interpretations of causality (although this can be challenging in the natural settings of evaluations).	• Reduction of data to numbers results in lost information.
	• The correlations produced (e.g., between costs and benefits, gender, and access to services or benefits) may mask or ignore underlying causes or realities.
	• Untested variables may account for program impacts.
	• Errors in the hypotheses tested may yield misimpressions of program quality or influential factors.
	• Errors in the selection of procedures for determining statistical significance can result in erroneous findings regarding impact.

in other areas, it will be possible to compare the findings. Finally, QUANT approaches require that the study instruments and procedures are carefully documented so that other researchers can assess the methodology, the analytical procedures, and the validity of the findings.

On the other hand, many of the criticisms of the QUANT approach concern the reduction of detailed data into numbers, inattention to **contextual variables**, and the rigidity of procedures that prevent refinements of focus based on increasingly sophisticated understanding of the program. The standardized categories found, for example, in questionnaires and QUANT data coding schemes often fail to capture variations and nuances within the groups or communities studied, and the analysis often lacks the depth and detail of QUAL methods. QUANT evaluation risks becoming *decontextualized,* ignoring how programs are affected by the economic, political, institutional, and sociocultural characteristics of the populations studied. The RWE approach fully recognizes all the strengths and weaknesses of QUANT and QUAL approaches, which is why mixed-method designs are frequently preferable.

Analysis of Population Characteristics

QUANT methods can be used to produce descriptive quantitative analysis of the characteristics of the project and comparison populations. Understanding the size and characteristics of a population is often an important preparatory stage in evaluation design and also for sample strategies. For example, if a population is made up of a number of different or widely dispersed subgroups (e.g., communities producing different types of crops or urban communities of different economic levels), *stratified sampling* may be needed to ensure that all the different kinds of communities or groups are adequately represented in the sample. This will make it possible to conduct *disaggregated analysis* in which the characteristics of the different groups or strata are compared. However, disaggregation can significantly increase the size and cost of the sample, so a preliminary analysis can help decide whether disaggregated analysis and a larger sample are really necessary.

Hypothesis Testing and the Analysis of Causality

QUANT evaluations often use a deductive approach based on a set of hypotheses about how the project communities or groups are likely to respond to the program treatments (e.g., new varieties of seed, access to **microcredit**, new teaching materials, or teaching methods). Hypotheses may also link treatments and implementation methods with a program's goals and the intermediate steps and intervening variables expected to influence the magnitude and direction of change and which groups benefit least and most.

Programs often begin with a hypothesis about how a desired outcome might be achieved—for example, that education in rural areas might be improved by the use of interactive video programs. Among the intervening variables influencing whether an educational video outreach program might actually improve rural education might be the availability of video technology at the project sites, personnel with sufficient technological expertise, the quality and relevance of the programs made available to rural schools, and the willingness and ability of teachers to embed the programs usefully in their curricula. Deductive analysis would involve discovery of whether the data do, in fact, indicate that these intervening variable are important to achieving the desired outcome—that is, whether having technology, technology personnel, good programs, and capable willing teachers *caused* an improvement in rural education. When a study begins with the hypothesis of such a *causal chain* and data are collected and analyzed in order to confirm or disconfirm it, then the analysis is said to be deductive.

While the purpose of an evaluation is normally to test whether a program or intervention has had an effect, the statistical analysis will often use a **null hypothesis** (see Chapter 14). The simplest form of a null hypothesis is to state that outcomes for an experimental group (those participating in the program) will not differ significantly from those of the comparison group. If there is a statistically significant difference between the two groups, then the null hypotheses will be rejected "beyond any reasonable doubt." The null hypothesis can be formulated in terms of mean scores or other appropriate measures. Following the example above, the state test scores of students in rural schools participating in the educational video outreach program might be compared with the state test scores of students in nonparticipating rural schools at the end of the academic year in which the treatments were introduced (see Evaluation Design 5 in Chapter 10). In that case, P_1 might be the average test score of students in participating schools, and C_1 might be the average test score of students in nonparticipating rural schools. If P_1 were higher than C_1 to a statistically significant degree, this could be considered evidence that the video outreach program was having a positive educational impact and the null hypothesis would be rejected. There are statistical procedures for calculating whether an observed difference between groups is statistically significant.

Cost-Effectiveness Analysis

QUANT methods may be used to estimate program costs, outputs, and benefits, including the cost of delivering each service provided by the program. Comparisons of costs against the outputs or benefits provided by the program is the approach taken in a cost-effectiveness analysis. While it is important to policymakers to know whether a program had a statistically and practically significant effect on outputs or benefits, it is also generally necessary to know what the cost of achieving the outputs or benefits was. This may include an estimation of the cost per participant of providing the service (the unit cost) or how the unit cost compares with that of alternative (and often competing) programs. Note that, in contrast to cost-benefit analysis, cost-effectiveness does not (necessarily) attach a monetary value to the outputs or benefits achieved, which is hard to do in social contexts—for example, the value of a healthier child or lives saved.

Quantitative Methods for Data Collection

This section describes some of the most common QUANT methods for data collection. We also discuss some areas of overlap with QUAL data collection methods, although the methods for recording data tend to be different when used by QUANT and QUAL researchers. QUANT evaluation records information into precoded categories that can be converted to numerical form, whereas QUAL approaches favor open-ended and less structured formats.

Questionnaires[5]

Questionnaires are research instruments through which people are asked to respond to the same set of questions in a predetermined order. The potential advantages of questionnaires are that comparable data can often be collected from large numbers of people much more quickly

> **Box 11.2** Beware of Producing Reports Based on Spurious Data!
>
> Many people in the business and education worlds have had experience in data gathering using questionnaires, but fewer are knowledgeable about how difficult it is to construct questionnaires that are valid, reliable, and objective. It is thus relatively easy to produce reports and recommendations based upon the most spurious of data.
>
> SOURCE: Gray (2004:187).

than if they were interviewed or observed using in-depth QUAL methods; responses to closed items can be obtained in numerical form so that statistical analysis is possible, and the sample can be selected to avoid statistical bias and to permit calculations of the statistical significance of the association between the program intervention and the desired outcomes. The order in which questions are asked, and the way in which they are asked, can also be controlled.

Although most researchers have some familiarity with questionnaires, skill is needed to design a questionnaire that produces reliable responses that support valid findings (see Box 11.2). There are many ways in which questionnaires can produce misleading responses. For example, the meaning of questions may be unclear, or the way in which the question is phrased may influence how people respond (e.g., "Do you agree that school fees should be increased?" may incline people to respond affirmatively, whereas the wording "Do you think that school fees should be increased, stay the same, or be reduced?" is more neutral).

One of the disadvantages of a questionnaire is that this is not a natural way for people to communicate. Many people would rather talk informally than answer survey questions—particularly when they feel the questions are forcing them to give answers that do not fully capture how they feel or what they did. Also in many field surveys, the longer the questionnaire, the less reliable the information becomes as people either become fatigued, annoyed, or try to answer as quickly as possible to get rid of the **interviewer**. Box 11.3 reminds us that the person analyzing the data collected with a structured questionnaire often has very little knowledge of exactly how the information was collected in the field.

> **Box 11.3** The Statistician and the Village Watchman
>
> The noted British statistician Sir Josiah Stamp commented that whatever wonders experts performed with statistics, one must not forget that the figures came initially from someone like a village watchman, who recorded what he pleased.
>
> SOURCE: Vaughn and Buss (1998:20).

Types of Questions

The following are commonly used types of question (adapted from Gray 2004:191–198). It should be noted that some of the categories, such as open questions, are normally considered as qualitative approaches, but questions of this type are frequently included in quantitative surveys as probes or for clarification, so they are discussed here.

- *Classification questions* collect information on the age, sex, education, and other relevant characteristics of individuals, communities, or groups. In household surveys, a *household roster* will often compile information on each household member.
- *Open questions* do not present a predefined menu or list of options. The responses should be recorded in full. Examples include, "Why did you move to this community?" "How do you feel about . . .?" "What do parents think about the new teaching programs introduced into the school this year?"
- *Closed questions* can ask for Yes/No answers or can ask respondents to choose one answer from a multiple-choice menu.
- *Lists.* Respondents can select as many responses as they wish from a list.
- *Category questions.* These are a variety of closed questions where numerical information is put into a series of categories. Instead of asking an open question such as, "How much did you earn last month?" or "How frequently do you and your spouse go out together?" the question is asked in the form:
  - Several times a week
  - Once a week
  - Once a month
  - At least once a year
  - Never

Although category questions can simplify the analysis and appear easy to use, they must be designed with care and require careful field testing. One danger if there is insufficient pretesting is that the wrong range of categories may be selected and everyone may select the same response category (e.g., all spouses go out together several times a week, or everyone falls into the lowest or highest income category) making the information of very little use. There is also evidence that the range of categories can influence the response. For example, if the questions asks, "How many times did you and your husband have an argument during the past week?" some respondents will consider this includes minor arguments, such as which TV program to watch. However, if the question uses the same wording but asks "during the past year" many respondents will only report on major family disputes, perhaps mentioning only one or two.

- *Ranking questions* ask respondents to rank a set of options in order of their importance, seriousness, and the like. Questions may cover what they like or do not like about the local school or a community organization, the main causes of worker absenteeism, important features of a public transport system, and so on.
- *Scales.* Scales are designed to measure the degree or intensity of opinion or experience on a particular topic. The following example illustrates one of the many ways in which scales can be presented. Respondents are asked to indicate how strongly they agree or disagree with a statement such as, "The community has become a much safer place since the police post was opened last year."
  - Agree strongly (or very satisfied)
  - Agree (or satisfied)
  - Neither agree nor disagree (or neither satisfied or dissatisfied)
  - Disagree (or dissatisfied)
  - Strongly disagree (or very dissatisfied)

A common form of a scaled question is one that asks the respondent to rate his or her judgment of or opinion on something on a scale like the Likert scale, where responses are recorded somewhere between *poor or not at all* (1) to *excellent or always* (5). Although scales are a useful way to measure how people feel about, for example, community organizations or public service agencies that affect their lives, the development and testing of scale items and the structure of the whole scale is a time-consuming and specialized skill. Consequently, when scales are constructed rapidly and items are not carefully selected or pretested, there is a danger that the results will be either meaningless or very misleading. Even when scales are carefully designed, there is still the danger that they may provide distorted or misleading information that leads to invalid findings.

Most scales are also based on the assumption (sometimes not explicitly stated) that attitudes are unidimensional. Respondents either like everything about the school or they don't like anything. They find that everyone in the government agency is helpful or that everyone is unhelpful. Unfortunately, life is rarely so simple. If, instead of using a scale, respondents had been asked an open question—"What do you like and dislike about the school?"—it would probably have been found that there are some aspects of the new programs that they like and other aspects that they do not like, some teachers and administrators that they like and others that they do not.

Interviewing

An interview is a focused conversation between people in which one person has the role of researcher. Interviews can be effectively combined with QUANT evaluations through the use of the mixed-method approaches discussed in Chapter 13. For example, follow-up questions can be included in a closed interview to clarify answers or to ask for details. Closed questions often include an "Other" category, and when respondents use this category, the survey administrator is often asked to write in the answer. Interviewing techniques are discussed in the next chapter.

Observation

Observation is normally considered a QUAL technique (see Chapter 12), but there are a number of applications in QUANT evaluations. The purposes of observation in QUANT evaluation include its use as a principal data collection method and also as a complement to other methods as part of a **triangulation** strategy to confirm data collected by other methods. For example, when informants are asked about their economic status, it is useful to observe the quality of house construction, the type of furniture, and possession of durable consumer goods to determine whether these seem consistent with what the respondent has reported about household income and expenditure. Another example, checking the accuracy of a respondent's report on a survey that no one in the family is working and that the family is very poor, which may be contradicted by observing the presence of a sewing machine or more food cooking on the stove than a poor family would normally consume, may suggest sources of income from dressmaking or selling food that the respondent did not mention. In cases such as this, the observer should find a tactful way to check whether, for example, the quantities of food are related to a source of income or signs of an upcoming family reunion.

Observational Protocols

Observational protocols provide a list of relevant aspects to be observed. When used in QUANT evaluations, the observations must be structured into categories so that they can be quantified. Here are some examples:

- *Using community stores as an indicator of the economic status of a community:* The range and quality of goods on sale in local stores are a good indicator of the economic status of a community. For example, in many parts of Latin America, the sale of whisky (compared with beer) is usually an indicator that at least a few families are doing well. The number and types of electrical appliances such as radios, video players, and TVs are another good indicator. The types of vegetables on offer and the types of footwear are other indicators. An exploratory study is required to identify the types of products that are the best indicators, and once they have been identified a checklist can be developed to record the presence or absence of different products in the local stores in different communities. These indicators are particularly useful for observing changes in the economic status of the community as storekeepers rapidly respond to changes in the purchasing power of their customers.

- *Families subletting part of their house:* In many low-income communities, subletting part of one's house is one of the few possibilities for earning money. Families are often reluctant to admit they are subletting, and in some housing projects, this is also forbidden. In some developing countries, an easily observable indicator is the number of doors that have numbers or letters painted on them; this usually indicates there are tenants.

- *Time use:* The amount of time (minutes, hours) that different categories of people spend on different activities (collecting water and fuel, preparing food, nonpaid agricultural work, self-employment, etc.) can be an indicator of constraints on the ability of different groups to participate in community activities or to seek new sources of income, and changes in time use can be an indicator of the impacts of certain types of projects. Changes in the amount of time that household members spend collecting water or fuel are often a good and easily observable indicator of the impact of a project to provide families with economical means of transport (bicycles, ox carts, etc.).

Unobtrusive Measures in Observation

It is sometimes possible to collect data using unobtrusive measures that have little or no effect on the situation being observed. Unobtrusiveness is a continuum, with some methods producing almost no effect on the situation being observed, but with other relatively unobtrusive methods producing some effects on the situation being observed. The degree of unobtrusiveness also depends on how conspicuous the observer is in a particular setting. Following are some examples of unobtrusive methods:

- Automatic counters to record the number of people entering or leaving a building or the number of vehicles using a road

- Natural accretion, such as the volume of waste accumulating in certain parts of a community or city

- Observation of types of housing materials (as an indicator of the wealth of the household), physical condition of roads and pathways, and maintenance of projects such as drainage channels or minor irrigation
- Observation of the types of goods on sale in community stores as an indicator of the economic conditions of the community
- Taking of photographs every year from the same locations in a community as a way to measure changes in the conditions of buildings or other infrastructure
- Secondary sources (discussed later in this chapter). Requesting documents from public agencies, registrars of births and deaths, or libraries offers opportunity for introducing observer effects, so these are not always unobtrusive.
- With the rapid increase in electronic communication, it is now possible to use the number of "hits" on a Web site as a measure of use. It is also possible to monitor chat rooms and e-mail traffic to identify issues and attitudes of a particular group.

Focus Groups

A focus group is "a small group of people involved in a research interviewing process specifically designed to uncover insights regarding the research focus. The group interview is distinctive in that it uses a set of questions deliberately sequenced or focused to move the discussion toward concepts of interest to the researcher" (Krueger and Casey 2005:158). Focus groups are discussed in Chapter 12 because they are normally considered a qualitative data collection method. However, it is possible to conduct quantitative analysis of the findings, particularly if a number of focus groups representing the different categories covered in a sample survey are selected as an in-depth follow-up to a quantitative method such as a structured questionnaire. This strategy is discussed as one of the mixed-method approaches in Chapter 13. For example, in a study of factors affecting women's use of public transport in Lima, Peru, 10 focus groups were organized with men and women of different age groups and different economic levels. Responses to questions such as mode of transport used to travel to school or work and the reasons for using or not using public transport were recorded into precoded categories and compared for different groups (Gomez 2000).

Self-Reporting Methods

Subjects can be asked to keep records of quantitative data such as income and expenditures, time use, or travel patterns. Diaries have been widely used for collecting data on household consumption and, when adequately supervised, can significantly reduce the costs of data collection. Even in countries where adult literacy rates are low, it may be possible to arrange for one of the children in a household to record the data (Deaton and Grosh 2000:119–22). Although there are sometimes problems with increasing nonresponse rates when families are requested to continue reporting over a long period of time, when families are motivated to participate, it has sometimes proved possible to achieve almost 100% response rates for daily reports over periods as long as one year (Valadez and Bamberger 1994:256–58). Participant self-reporting using standardized psychological and attitudinal assessments can also be used to measure needs and to assess outcomes (W. K. Kellogg Foundation 1998:82).

Knowledge and Achievement Tests

These can be used to test participants' knowledge and behavior with respect to the effects the project seeks to achieve. Tests can also be used to measure intervening (mediator) variables that explain variations in project effects. For example, people with more knowledge of business practices might use small business loans more effectively. Knowledge or achievement can also be tested through observation—for example, observing how well a mother follows instructions for giving her child medicine, or improvements in an elderly person's mobility (W. K. Kellogg Foundation 1998:81–82). When tests are used to compare changes over the life of a project, standardized indices must be used (see Klugman 2002, vol. 2, chaps. 18 and 19, for a discussion of indicators in the fields of health, nutrition, and education).

Standardized test scores are sometimes considered an objective and easily analyzed way to measure changes in performance associated with different kinds of educational programming. However, many argue that standardized tests are not, in fact, objective. Every step in the process of creating and scoring tests involves subjective judgments and the intrusion of measurement error. While test scores are increasingly used in education research and evaluation as impact indicators, they are a highly controversial type of data. Michael Kane (1994) has analyzed standard-setting procedure in current use and has found them all to be seriously flawed. The quality of the test, the reliability of scores, and the validity of inferences and decisions based on the scores should be scrutinized rather than accepted as objective and precise indicators of outcomes.

Anthropometric and Other Physiological Health Status Measures

Anthropometric measures of the height and weight of children under the age of five years are regularly used to assess the frequency and severity of malnutrition as well as to evaluate the impacts of poverty and health-related interventions, since many accept nutritional status as a proxy of poverty in a community (Alderman 2000). In countries with effective maternal and child care health programs, anthropometric measurements are relatively economical and easy to administer, and the data are usually reliable. Norms for average weight for height and weight for age have been developed for most countries, so it is also possible to estimate and assess **effect sizes** produced by different interventions.

A number of basic medical tests are also widely used in program evaluation. Probably the cheapest and most common are stool tests used for evaluating the effects of improved water quality and sanitation and of the incidence of infectious diseases. Blood tests, although more expensive and difficult to administer, are also used to assess the incidence of malaria and, of course, more recently for HIV/AIDS testing. Simpler cognitive tests can also be used to assess the cognitive functioning of adults and the cognitive development of children (Glewwe 2000).[6]

Using Secondary (Documentary) Data

QUANT and QUAL researchers tend to use secondary data—documents directly or indirectly informative about the program—differently. While documentary analysis is a major QUAL data collection technique (see Chapter 12) with a well-developed methodology, QUANT evaluators frequently only use many kinds of secondary data either to fill in gaps where there are no data but information is needed, or as a consistency check of data already collected to ascertain its accuracy. The analysis of many kinds of secondary data is a potentially important, but often underutilized, source of information for QUANT evaluations. The types of secondary data most widely employed in QUANT research are household surveys and national census data that are used extensively for impact evaluations, particularly posttest comparisons of project and comparison groups (see for example Box 5.7, p. **105**).

Table 11.2 summarizes some of the main types of secondary data used in QUANT evaluations. Sources include national surveys, including household and longitudinal student surveys; data from social sector ministries and governmental departments; records from institutions and facilities (e.g., schools, health centers); reports from international development agencies (e.g., UNICEF, U.S. Agency for International Development, the World Bank); reports from studies and evaluations conducted by universities, research institutions, and governmental and other agencies; and administrative records and monitoring data from the project itself. Care is needed in the interpretation and use of these data sources; most were not designed for evaluation purposes, and the quality of the data collection may be poor. The reader is referred to Chapter 5 for a discussion of how to assess the strengths and weaknesses for evaluation purposes of different types of secondary data.

Secondary data can be used both in an exploratory stage of the evaluation and also, where appropriate, as a substitute for primary data collection. For example, if all schools or local health facilities keep good records on students and patients, it may not be necessary to conduct new surveys to obtain information on how many children attend school or how many patients use local health services. It is, of course, necessary to check the quality and completeness of the records, for example, by visits to a sample of schools or health clinics. Similarly, periodic household socioeconomic surveys conducted by a central statistics bureau may provide required information on household expenditures or labor force participation rates.

Many of the following ways in which secondary data can be used are equally applicable to both QUANT and QUAL evaluation studies:

- In exploratory studies, to obtain initial estimates of the magnitude and characteristics of the program population and how they compare with the overall characteristics of the broader population
- To obtain information on comparison areas when surveys do not cover these areas
- To reconstruct baseline data and obtain information on different points in time
- As a substitute for collection of primary data
- To reduce the costs and time of data collection
- As a form of triangulation to compare evaluation survey estimates with other independent estimates

Common Problems with Secondary Data for Evaluation Purposes

Because most secondary data sources were collected for purposes quite distinct from those of a project evaluation, data may have serious limitations for evaluation purposes. In many cases, where data is collected for administrative purposes, quality control may have had relatively low priority. The following are some of the common problems of using secondary data for evaluation purposes:

Table 11.2   Useful Sources of Secondary Data

Source	Types of Data	Comments
National household surveys	• Income, expenditure, and consumption data • Access to public services (education, health) • Educational enrollment and performance • Poverty • Household demographic characteristics	• In some countries, these have been conducted several times a year for a number of years. • The National Center for Education statistics (NCES) in the United States has been surveying and making longitudinal data available for decades. • These normally use sound sampling techniques but may not cover all the informal sector population (which often represents an important part of the project population) or may not be disaggregated to the population targeted by a particular project.
Social sector ministries and departments (health, education, water, transport) in developed countries such as in North America and Europe, and in some developing countries	• Use of services (school attendance, use of health facilities) • Amount paid by users	• Some data sources are comprehensive and well designed, but the reliability and coverage of some studies, particularly in some developing countries, can vary. • Many surveys focus only on quantitative indicators such as access to services (e.g., water, education, and health) but do not include much information on the quality of these services.
Social service facilities (schools, health centers)	• Attendance and utilization rates • Common diseases and their incidence	• Data can be good and comprehensive, but quality varies greatly. • May be problems of under- or misreporting.
Bilateral and multilateral donor agencies (USAID,[a] World Bank, U.S. foundations)	• Extensive information on the programs and geographical areas where they operate	• Donors have promoted some of the most comprehensive socioeconomic databases (examples include the World Bank's Living Standards Measurement Studies and USAID's Demographic and Health Surveys).

Source	Types of Data	Comments
		• Data sometimes criticized for being too narrowly quantitative (e.g., the definition of poverty). • Sample often drawn for national statistics; not statistically significant for a smaller target population.
Universities and research institutions	• In many countries, these are the technically best studies available. • Often include both QUANT and QUAL approaches	• Although some university studies, particularly in countries such as the United States and Europe, may cover large populations, in developing countries, many such studies cover only relatively small areas and samples. For example, many graduate dissertations contain valuable information on the topics of interest to an evaluation but often they study only relatively small populations.
Government-, donor-, and foundations-supported programs and reports	• Detailed information on the characteristics of the target population, their access to the program, and program performance	• Many studies cover only program beneficiaries and do not include a comparison group. • In other cases, target population is not clearly defined.
Nongovernment organizations (NGOs)	• In-depth information on populations covered by the agency	• Often covers only relatively small populations and may be more qualitative. • There may be questions on the representativity of the data, particularly for organizations conducting studies on a small budget.
Cooperatives and microfinance programs	• Information on the size and use of loans and repayment rates • Sometimes information on the socioeconomic characteristics of program participants	• Quality of the data quite variable

a. U.S. Agency for International Development.

- The data may cover a different population (e.g., farmers producing for export but not those producing for local markets; only government or only private schools).
- The data may ask different questions (e.g., data may cover income but not expenditures, whereas the evaluation is measuring expenditures).
- Even if the same questions are addressed, different definitions and measurement techniques may be used. Concepts or variables such as poverty, vulnerability, well-being, sick/healthy, and employed/unemployed can be defined and measured in many different ways.
- The data may cover a time period not relevant for the evaluation.
- The data may include intentional or unintentional biases (e.g., may highlight the positive features of a program and downplay criticism).
- Coverage may not be complete.
- The quality of the data collection and reporting may be poor (e.g., coding instructions often get lost; old data on cards or tape may be difficult to access; and marginal notes on photocopied questionnaires may be difficult to read).
- The data may be recorded in a way that is difficult to analyze.
- Certain sectors of the target population may be underrepresented (e.g., only the "household head" may have been surveyed, leaving out women and other household members. In the United States and other countries, groups such as illegal immigrants may be insufficiently represented).
- Data may have been falsified, incomplete, inaccurate, or reflective of the perspective of the person producing the document (e.g., test scores inflated by a teacher paid per successful examinee).

Chapter 5 gives a number of criteria for assessing the quality and utility for evaluation of secondary data available within the organization and from outside sources. In both cases, it is important to understand why the information was collected, by whom, and by what methods. Also try to determine whether there were procedures to check the accuracy of the data (e.g., was there any quality control or follow-up) and what organizational incentive may there have been to distort or conceal the findings. The fact that an organization claimed to place a high value on accuracy does not guarantee that this was necessarily achieved. For example, a police department may have a greater incentive to report crimes that have been solved than those that have not. On the other hand, an agency that is trying to convince funding sources of the magnitude of a problem (e.g., prostitution, homelessness, drug abuse) might have an incentive to overestimate the number of potential clients (Best 2001, 2004).

The Management of Data Collection for Quantitative Studies

The management of the data collection process is often as critical to the success of an evaluation as the research design. Table 11.3 summarizes the requirements for a well-designed QUANT evaluation and also indicates the chapter in this volume where each requirement is discussed. Points 1 through 8 of this table (planning and design, implementation and management of data collection, and data analysis) are discussed in this chapter; reporting and communication of findings are discussed in Chapters 8 and 15.

Table 11.3   Features of Well-Designed Quantitative Evaluations

	Chapters in This Volume Where These Aspects Are Discussed
A. Planning and Design	
1. Clear definition of objectives	2 and 3
2. Definition in consultation with clients of a program theory model	2 and 9
3. Measurable indicators	2, 9, and 10
4. Sound research design	4–7 and 10
B. Implementation and Management of Data Collection	
5. Sound sampling	14
6. Recruitment, training, and supervision of interviewers	14 and 16
7. Reliable and valid instruments that have been tested in the field	2, 11, and 12
C. Data Analysis and Communication of Findings	
8. Appropriate analysis	6, 11, 12, and 14
9. Accurate reporting	15
10. Effective communication of findings to all key audiences	8 and 15

SOURCE: Adapted from Fink (2003a).

Survey Planning and Design

Planning should begin with a clear definition of objectives. Is this an exploratory study? Is the purpose to define and test quantitative hypotheses? Will the evaluation report be used by decision makers to decide whether the project should continue or be replicated on a much larger scale? The definition of objectives often has significant implications for the evaluation design and the required level of **precision**—which in turn can affect the sample size and design. For example, if the purpose is to provide the implementing agency with an initial assessment of whether the program has been successful in attracting and retaining the different sectors of the target population, a simpler and more economical design can probably be used than if outcomes and impacts have to be compared with competing programs. The objectives will also determine whether or not a comparison group is required (see Chapter 10). In the previous example, the second alternative—to compare outcomes with competing programs—might justify the selection of a comparison group, whereas the first option probably would not.

The incorporation of a program theory model can also contribute to the evaluation design (see Chapter 9). Once the objectives and the program theory are defined, it is then possible to identify and define the indicators that will be used to measure **inputs**, processes, **outputs**, outcomes, and impacts, as well as contextual factors. For RWE, the budget, time, data, and political constraints affecting data collection must be identified and their implications assessed. Based on all the above, a draft evaluation design is developed and the appropriate data collection methods are selected and tested, and the evaluation design is then finalized.

It should be noted that although all these steps are presented sequentially, the development of the evaluation design is actually an iterative process. For example, the constraints on data collection may lead the evaluator and the client to reconsider the evaluation objectives, state less ambitious objectives in the light of the types of information available, adjust data collection methods, and refocus analysis or reporting.

Implementation and Management of Data Collection

Once the evaluation design and the data collection methods have been defined, a data collection management plan is developed together with a plan to ensure the sound implementation of the proposed sample design. Even when the sample design is theoretically sound, problems often arise during implementation because of lack of attention to the construction of the sampling frame or inadequate monitoring and treatment of nonresponse in the sample selection. It is also critical to ensure that data collection instruments have been well formulated and adequately tested in the field. Many survey instruments go through a number of revisions before they are finalized. Investment of time and resources in interviewer selection, training, and supervision usually pays dividends. Training should include field experience for interviewers in the administration of the survey instrument. Experience shows that insufficient or poor quality supervision or training will often result in a significant proportion of the surveys being incomplete or wrongly completed or, in some cases, falsified. If the survey instrument has to be translated into the local language, it is also necessary to conduct a separate field test in the local language to be sure that people in the community understand what is being asked and that the evaluation team knows how to interpret possible answers in the way people are likely to express them.

RealWorld Constraints on the Management of Data Collection

A critical but often ignored component of the evaluation is the management of data collection. Many evaluations have rigorous design, clearly defined data collection procedures, and significant resources and effort to support data analysis, but the quality of the final product can be seriously affected by lack of attention to the management of data collection. The following are examples of common problems arising during data collection that can be addressed through careful management of the data collection process[7]:

- The sampling frame (the list or map that includes all units—individuals, schools, communities—in the population) does not adequately cover the target population. For example, if the sample of schools does not include private or religious schools a well-managed survey will detect this and take measures to include these two categories of schools in the sample.

- The actual sample selected does not conform to the sample design because of lack of supervision of the interviewers. For example, in cases where the person who should be interviewed is not at home, the interviewer may be instructed to return again at a time when the intended respondent is likely to be at home. However, some interviewers, to save time, may proceed directly to interview another family member, thus changing the composition of the selected sample. Again, a well-managed survey should monitor the respondent selection process and take appropriate actions if there are systematic deviations from the planned selection procedure.
- There is an unnecessarily high nonresponse rate and lack of supervision of how non-respondents are replaced.
- The interviewers do not have the necessary qualifications or experience to administer the data collection instruments.
- The interviewers are not well trained.
- Interviewers do not speak the local language or do not speak it well.
- The age, sex, ethnicity, and other characteristics of the interview team are not appropriate. A frequent problem is that only male interviewers are used, and there may be cultural constraints on their ability to interview female respondents.
- The data may be falsified by some interviewers who never conduct the interview but fill out the questionnaire sitting in the cafeteria.
- Interviews are conducted in the presence of other people (other family members, neighbors, community leaders, supervisors, or employers) who may inhibit respondents ability to talk freely.
- There is no immediate checking of completed interviews and there is no standard procedure for returning incomplete surveys to the **enumerators**.[8]

While some of these problems can be attributed to poor team management and could be corrected, in the real world a number of factors are difficult for the evaluator to control. For example, in many cultural contexts, it may be extremely difficult to contract female enumerators to conduct interviews in remote rural areas or to ensure that interviews are conducted without the presence of other people. Leaving aside cultural constraints, in crowded or confined spaces, such as a one- or two-room house or a bustling and brimming hospital, there may be no private place to talk.

Other issues concern the relationship with the client and program sponsors. Clients may expect to have choice in the selection or assignment of evaluation team members, expecting, for example, that top program administrators will be interviewed by the evaluation director. In many cases of evaluation in developing countries, enumerators are provided or recommended by the client or a government agency, and the evaluator may have little choice over the selection of the team. When enumerators are paid, the client agency may be particularly interested in deciding who should be provided the additional income, which may be quite substantial compared with government salaries. The political dynamics of enumerator selection may also limit the possibilities for close supervision, also making it impossible to dismiss enumerators who do not perform.

The following guidelines can help improve the efficiency and quality of the management of data collection in the real world:

- *Anticipate client concerns or constraints that might affect data collection.* The scoping exercise (RWE Step 1) can be used to identify client concerns or constraints that might potentially affect data collection. Sometimes clients may indicate a preference for certain data collection methods or reluctance to use other kinds of data collection. Although it is perfectly reasonable for the client to express views and preferences on data collection methods, in some cases, the evaluator may feel that client refusal to accept certain methods may prejudice the validity of the evaluation. In other cases, the client may be reluctant to allocate scarce budget resources to rigorous enumerator selection, training, and supervision. The evaluator should anticipate potential issues and should make sure that questions such as data collection methods, enumerator selection, training, and supervision are brought up early on. Some of the possible strategies that can be used to address the issues mentioned in this section include the following:
  - Set up a national steering committee to oversee the evaluation—but don't have too high expectations of the extent to which the committee will wish to get involved in sensitive management issues.
  - Consider the option of contracting a professional research agency to conduct the data collection rather than selecting and training a new interview team. This option may not in fact be more expensive than the selection and training of a new team. However, if **evaluation capacity building** is an objective, then it may be necessary to invest the time and resources in developing the new research team.
  - Be aware that when working on a tight budget there are trade-offs between the costs of selection, training, and supervision of enumerators and investment in other quality improvement activities, such as improving the sampling frame or trying to reduce nonresponse rates. There is no point in having a brilliant interview team if the sampling frame excludes major sections of the target population or if the nonresponse rate is extremely high.

- *Recruit the best available supervision/training team.* Even if resources are scarce, it is always a good idea to invest in the best available supervisors. The performance of even the best enumerators will seriously decline if there is not good supervision, whereas a good supervision team can do a great deal to improve the performance of inexperienced enumerators. Ensure also that there are sufficient numbers of supervisors. Particularly during the early stages of interviewing, there should be enough supervisors to be able to review all the completed surveys and to meet on a daily basis with the enumerators to detect problems and *to send them back to correct the interviews the next day.*

- *Develop a strategy for enumerator recruitment.* Define the type of enumerators required, including the sex, age, and other characteristics, and develop a strategy for contacting potential enumerators. Prepare a checklist that will be used in the selection.

- *Conduct pilot interviews.* This is a critical part of the enumerator training and also provides feedback on any unanticipated issues concerning the selection of respondents or how to complete the different sections of the questionnaire.

- *Prepare interview supervision guidelines and make sure that the enumerators fully understand them.* This strategy should include careful monitoring of how the sampling strategy is actually applied in the field and documentation of the procedures to follow when the desired subject (e.g., "household head") is not available or when the target family/individual cannot be identified or interviewed. In many cases, the enumerator will not receive part of his or her payment until the interview is satisfactorily completed, and it may be useful to get the enumerators to sign a document stating that they fully understand this procedure. Evaluators who have participated in heated meetings with enumerators late into the night about how this strict supervision shows a lack of trust or professional respect will appreciate the need to clarify the rules of the game well in advance.

- *Hold periodic debriefing meetings with the interview teams.* The only people who really know what happened during the interviews are the enumerators. Much of their experience and impressions will not be captured in the interview report, so it is important to have regular debriefing meetings to capture these impressions. Their impressions may cover questions that subjects did not understand or that were ambiguous, additional questions that should have been asked, significant information from observations or things respondents said that were not in the questionnaire, information that people were reluctant to provide, or factors inhibiting the respondent's ability to talk freely.

- *Prepare a report on the interview process.* This should identify issues affecting the quality of the data as well as the insights obtained from the enumerator debriefings.

Data Analysis

Steps in Data Analysis

An important but often underappreciated part of data analysis is the design and implementation of a data management plan. The purpose of the plan is to spell out the objectives of the analysis, the key questions to be addressed, and the hypotheses to be tested. The plan should refer to the scoping phase during which the client's information needs were defined. The analysis plan is particularly important for RWE to ensure that the limited resources and time are focused on the critical issues and questions of concern to clients. The data analysis plan involves the following stages:

- *Drafting an analysis plan* (see Table 11.4).
- *Developing and testing the codebook.* If there are open-ended questions, the responses must be reviewed in the preliminary stage of the analysis to define the categories that will be used in the final analysis[9]. If any of the numerical data have been classified into categories ("More than once a week," "Once a week," etc.), the responses should be reviewed to identify any problems or inconsistencies and to ensure responses are distributed across all categories and not just concentrated in one or two.
- *Ensuring reliable coding.* This involves both ensuring that the codebook is comprehensive and logically consistent and monitoring the data coding process to ensure accuracy and consistency between coders.
- *Reviewing surveys for missing data and deciding how to treat missing data.* In some cases, it will be possible to return to the field or mail the questionnaires back to respondents, but in most cases, this will not be practical. Missing data are often not random, so the treatment of these cases is important to avoid bias in the analysis. For example, there may be differences between sexes, age, economic status, or levels of education of respondents in their willingness to respond to certain questions. There may also be

Table 11.4   Example of an Analysis Plan for an Evaluation of the Impacts of Microcredit on Female Borrowers

---

Evaluation Objective 1: To assess the impacts of the program on women's earned income

Hypothesis: Women who participate in the program will have higher earned income than those who do not.

Variables: Women who have received loans and women who have not, earned income, age, education, prior experience in running a business.

Analysis 1: Comparing the mean earned income of women who have and have not received loans through the project (*t*-test for difference of means).

Analysis 2: Multiple regression analysis testing whether there is a difference in earned income for participants and nonparticipants after controlling for age, education, and prior experience in running a business.

Evaluation Objective 2: To assess the impact of the program on women's feeling of personal empowerment

Hypothesis: Women who have participated in the program will have a stronger feeling of personal empowerment than women who have not participated.

Variables: Women who have participated in the program and those who have not (note: Participation will be defined both as dichotomous Yes/No variables and also in terms of the number of different services received—loans, training courses, technical support, group meetings, etc.), scale of personal empowerment.

Analysis 1: Two-way table comparing participation/nonparticipation with the score on a 5-point empowerment scale. Chi-square or similar contingency test will be used.

Analysis 2: Two-way table comparing two ordinal variables: the score on the 5-point empowerment scale and the number of services received from the program (1 to 5). A contingency test for comparing two ordinal variables (e.g., Goodman and Kruksal's Gamma) will be used.

SOURCE: Adapted from Fink (2003c, ex. 1.1).

differences between ethnic or religious groups or between landowners and squatters. One of the first steps in the analysis should be to prepare frequency distributions to determine the frequency of missing data for key variables. For variables with significant levels of missing data, an exploratory analysis should be conducted to determine whether there are significant differences in missing data rates for the key population groups mentioned above.

- *Entering the data into the computer or manual data analysis system*
- *Cleaning the data.* This involves the following:
  - Doing exploratory data analysis to identify missing data and to identify potential problems such as outliers
  - Deciding how to treat missing data and the application of missing data policies[10]
  - Identifying any variables that may require recoding
- Full documentation of how data were cleaned, how missing data were treated, and how any indices were created[11]

Descriptive Data Analysis

Descriptive data analysis describes important characteristics of the populations studied through measures of central tendency—means, modes, and medians (discussed below)—or the distribution (spread) of the data. The purpose is to obtain an initial understanding of the characteristics of the population studied and to identify important similarities and differences between different sectors of the population. These kinds of analysis are almost always conducted before planning more detailed analysis. The types of analysis to be conducted and the statistics to be used will depend on what kind of variable is appropriate:

- *Nominal variables:* For these types of variable, the frequencies of each category can be counted, but the categories do not have any numerical order (i.e., one category is not greater or lesser than another on a scale). Examples: economic sectors in which persons work, regions of birth, reasons for migrating to a city, favorite subjects in school. While the distribution of responses among the different categories can be described, it is not possible with a nominal variable to calculate, for example, a mean or average.
- *Ordinal variables:* The values of these variables have an inherent order and can be ranked from lesser to greater. Examples: Relative satisfaction with local schools or health facilities can be ranked by asking respondents to indicate their satisfaction levels on a Likert scale (i.e., one that offers response choices such as *strongly agree, agree, disagree, strongly disagree*). However, because the intervals between the different categories (e.g., strongly agree and agree compared with disagree and strongly disagree) cannot be assumed to be equal, it is not possible to calculate the means and **standard deviations** (see below). Sometimes, to simplify the analysis, interval variables such as income or age may be transformed into ordinal variables by creating categories such as "Under 5 years of age," "5–10 years," "11–20 years," "over 20 years." This reclassification results in a considerable loss of data but may be justified due to budget and time constraints and to make the findings easier to understand for readers with no background in statistics.
- *Interval (numerical) variables:* These are variables such as weight, age, income, time traveling to work, and number of children that can be measured on a scale where the distance between each category is equal. Numerical ordering from largest, most frequent, or longest, for example, to smallest, rarest, or shortest is possible—and the distances between each two numbers is the same on an arithmetic number line. With interval variables, a much wider range of statistical indicators and tests can be used (e.g., mean, standard deviation, statistical significance tests).[12]

The analysis will often begin by presenting measures of central tendency and distribution and will then compare these values for different groups to identify similarities and differences. Let us take the example of household income. The analysis might begin by presenting one or more of the following indicators of central tendency:

- *The mean (average) income of all households:* For example, the mean household income may be 350 pesos per month.
- *A frequency distribution in which income is classified into groups:* The preliminary frequency distribution would give the frequency of each value, for example: "less than 50 pesos," "51–100 pesos," "101–150 pesos," and so on, and the number of families in each category is shown in a table.

- *The mode*: This is the category with the highest frequency. For example, "150–200 pesos."
- *The median:* Assume there were 150 interviews. If these are arranged in a frequency distribution from lowest to highest, the median with be the 75th value, for example, 175 pesos. In most distributions, the mode and the median will be fairly close to each other. However, there are some distributions where they can be quite different. For example, a bimodal distribution may have many values concentrated at the lower end of the distribution (many poor households) and many near the top of the distribution (relatively wealthy households) and relatively few in the middle. In this case, the mode (or modes) would be quite different from the median.

The next stage will often be the analysis of dispersion—whether values are very similar for most subjects (e.g., most families have similar incomes) or widely dispersed (e.g., some families have very low incomes and others have much higher income). The following indicators of dispersion might be used:

- *Range:* This is the difference between the highest and lowest value. For example, the lowest income may be 75 pesos and the highest may be 1,025 pesos [range=950].
- *Standard deviation:* This is based on the average difference between each value and the mean. This average is divided by the mean, and the square root is calculated. This is defined as a standardized statistic so that the value of the standard deviation can be compared for populations with different means[13]. One of the great advantages of the standard deviation for many kinds of statistical analysis (such as the statistical significance tests discussed in Chapter 14) is that approximately 65% of the scores in any approximately normal population will be within one standard deviation of the mean and 95% will fall within two standard deviations. In our earlier example, the mean income was 350. If the standard deviation was 25, then we would expect that approximately two-thirds of families (65%) would have incomes between 325 pesos (one standard deviation below the mean) and 375 pesos (one standard deviation above the mean). Similarly around 95% of families would have incomes between 300 and 400 pesos.

Comparisons and Relationships between Groups

Once the characteristics of the population have been studied using the descriptive statistics described above, the next stage will usually be to examine similarities and differences between groups on the variables of interest to the evaluation. For example, boys and girls might be compared on school enrollment rates or school test scores, or fishermen and farmers may be compared on income. The main kinds of comparisons include the following:

- Stratified comparison—comparing groups such as men and women, different age and economic groups, on the key variables being studied. Most comparisons concern output, outcome, or impact variables (e.g., school enrollment, nutrition, percentage of the population obtaining loans), but **process evaluations** also look at differences in levels and types of participation or in access to program resources (e.g., numbers of participants who seek and receive information or credit).

- Project and comparison areas can also be compared on similar variables.
- Comparisons can also be made between scores on outcome/impact variables before and after the project (e.g., changes in income, school enrollment, difference between the proportion of men and women voting).

The simplest comparisons involve two-way tables. Table 11.5 shows a hypothetical two-way table comparing the frequency with which men and women attend community meetings. From the table, it appears that women attend meetings more frequently than men: 71.1% of women attend either once a week or at least once a month compared with only 27.3% of men. However, when the number of observations is small, a large percentage difference may not be statistically significant. As will be discussed in Chapter 14, a statistical significance test calculates the probability that the difference between the two groups (71.1% and 27.3%) could occur by chance if the two groups actually came from the same population. This is often expressed by saying there is a statistically significant difference between the two groups "beyond a reasonable doubt." One of the key topics in Chapter 14 will be to discuss what we mean by "beyond a reasonable doubt." The key point for RWE is that to increase the confidence that there is a real difference between the two groups a significant increase in the size of the sample (and cost of the survey) may be required. A number of statistical tests (such as chi-square and the t test) are available to assess the statistical significance of differences.[14] It is important to ensure that the correct statistical test is used to avoid arriving at incorrect conclusions as to whether or not there are statistically significant differences between groups. In our discussion of threats to validity in Chapter 7, the incorrect application of statistical tests was given as one of the main threats to **statistical conclusion validity**. It is always a good idea to consult with a statistical specialist if there is any doubt.

Comparisons between more than two variables may use more sophisticated statistical tests of association such as analysis of variance (ANOVA), simple and multiple correlation, and multiple regression.[15]

Table 11.5   Example of a Tallying Chart of the Frequency with Which Men and Women Attend Community Meetings

Frequency of attending community meetings	Men		Women		All Adults	
	Number	% All Men	Number	% All Women	Number	% All Adults
1. Every week	25	11.3	60	38.8	85	22.7
2. At least once a month	35	16.0	50	32.3	85	22.7
3. Several times a year	80	36.3	25	16.1	105	28.0
4. Once a year	70	31.9	10	6.4	80	21.3
5. Never	10	4.5	10	6.4	20	5.3
Total	**220**	**100**	**155**	**100**	**375**	**100**

Hypothesis Testing and Analytical Models

Most QUANT evaluations involve the testing of hypotheses to determine whether the predicted or desired program effects have been achieved and whether the magnitude of the observed change (effect size) shows beyond a reasonable doubt that the program intervention is associated with this outcome (effect). In some cases, the hypotheses to be tested are derived from a program theory model (see Chapter 9). In other cases, the *null hypothesis* (often represented as H_0)—that there is no difference between project and comparison groups—is tested. The reason for using a null hypothesis is that it is never possible to prove that a hypothesis is true or that a program has produced a certain effect. What a statistical significance test does is to indicate the probability that the observed difference between the project and comparison groups could have occurred if the project participants and comparison groups are drawn from the same population. For example, let us assume that the study finds that the average household income of farmers who have used the new seed varieties is 8% higher than the income of farmers who have not used the new seeds, and let us also assume that the analysis finds that there is only a 4 in 100 (4%) chance of a difference as large as 8% occurring if there really is no difference between the two groups. The conventional practice is to assume that if the probability is less than 5 in 100 (5%), it is assumed that there is a statistically significant difference between the two groups. In situations where it is important to avoid wrongly assuming that treatments are effective (e.g., the testing of new drugs) a higher level of precision (e.g., 1 in a 100 or 1 in a 1,000) may be used. These issues are discussed further in Chapter 14. For readers interested in statistical analysis, Table 11.6 summarizes some of the common statistical procedures for testing different types of hypotheses and models with nominal, ordinal, and interval variables.

Statistical Packages and Online Analysis Resources

A number of survey design toolkits are available free on the Internet. A few of the many available resources include these:

- Trochim, W. M. K. 2000. *The Research Methods Knowledge Base.* A textbook covering all major topics in social research. Available online at www.socialresearchmethods.net/kb
- University of California. 2000. *Statistics calculator.* Available online at http://calculators .stat.ucla.edu
- Creative Research Systems. Sample size calculator. Available online at: http://survey system.com/
- Vanderbilt University. Statistical power and sample size calculator. Available online at http://biostat.mc.vanderbilt.edu/twiki/bin/view/Main/PowerSampleSize

There are also a large number of statistical packages available for data analysis. Two of the best known are SPSS and SAS. For a comprehensive reference guide to the use of SPSS, see Weinberg and Abramowitz (2002).

Table 11.6   Examples of Statistical Procedures for Testing the Main Types of Evaluation Hypotheses

Test	Type of variable	Type of data	Reference
Contingency tables: chi-square	Nominal	Two-way tables comparing the distribution of two nominal variables. *Example*: comparing male and female frequency of attending meetings	Sirkin (1999, chap. 12)
Contingency tables: for example, Goodman and Kruskal's Gamma	Ordinal	Two-way tables comparing the distribution of two ordinal variables. *Example*: comparing high, medium, and low levels of income with high, medium, and low levels of participation	Sirkin (1999:358–62)
t test	Interval	Comparing two means. *Example*: comparing the average income of two groups	Sirkin (1999, chaps. 8 and 9)
z test	Dichotomous (proportions)	Comparing two proportions. *Example*: comparing proportion of girls attending school before and after the project	More advanced discussion: Moore and McCabe (1999, chap. 8)
Analysis of variance	Interval	Comparing differences between three or more means. *Example*: comparing the average income of farmers, self-employed, and wage earners	Aron and Aron (2002, chap. 10) and Sirkin (1999, chap. 10)
Multiple regression	Interval sometimes including dichotomous or nominal (dummy) variables	Estimating the magnitude (proportion of the variance) and statistical significance of the association between two variables after controlling for intervening variables. *Example*: Is the incidence of intestinal infection lower in projects areas that have received communal toilets than in comparison areas after controlling for household income and the number of years of education of the adults?	Brief introduction: Aron and Aron (2002, chap. 12) fuller discussion in Sirkin (1999, chaps. 13 and 14)
Path analysis	Interval	Estimating the correlations between project interventions, intermediate outcomes, and final outcomes. *Example*: The correlation coefficients between discipline styles, marital satisfaction, and hostility—home conduct problems—school conduct problems—peer social performance	Brief introduction: Aron and Aron (2002, chap. 12)

Summary

- QUANT and QUAL methodologies represent two distinct social science traditions. It is important for evaluation practitioners, clients, and users to have a basic understanding of the two approaches; most social scientists have a professional or personal preference for one or the other of the two traditions, and this will often affect their approach to evaluation research.

- It is also useful for clients to understand these differences because QUANT and QUAL oriented evaluators may adopt quite different approaches to the same evaluation.

- Some of the advantages of QUANT approaches are that findings can be generalized to broader populations, subjects are selected to ensure their statistical representativity, quantitative estimates can be obtained of project impacts, and the quantitative contribution of intervening variables can be assessed. The combination of clearly documented procedures and standard instruments means that the research can be replicated in other settings.

- Some of the limitations of QUANT approaches are (a) many types of information are difficult to express numerically, (b) some groups are particularly difficult to reach using structured data collection instruments, (c) contextual factors are often ignored, (d) research methods are expensive and difficult to adapt to changing circumstances, (e) statistical associations may be misleading if important explanatory variables are not included in the analysis.

- QUANT evaluators tend to use experimental (randomized) or quasi-experimental designs that rely on the application of structured data collection instruments that must be administered in exactly the same way at different points in the project to ensure comparability.

- Some of the principle data collection instruments include structured questionnaires, structured observation, physical measurements (height, weight), and knowledge and aptitude tests.

- Secondary data are an important, but often underutilized, source of data for QUANT evaluations.

- The management of the process of data collection is often as critical to the success of evaluation as the research design. Some of the common data management problems for RWE are (a) the best available sampling frame may not cover all the target population; (b) the actual sample selected may not correspond exactly to the sampling plan due to lack of enumerator supervision; (c) there may be high nonresponse rates; (d) enumerators may lack experience, may not speak the local language, or the team may not have the right ethnic, sex, or age composition; or (e) interviews may have to be conducted in the presence of other people, which may have affected the responses.

- QUANT data analysis may include descriptive data analysis, comparisons and relationships between groups, hypothesis testing, and analytical models.

Further Reading

Aron, A. and E. Aron. 2002. *Statistics for the Behavioral and Social Sciences.* 2d ed. Upper Saddle River, NJ: Prentice Hall.

A thorough and clearly presented introduction to data analysis and hypothesis testing.

Fink, A. 2003. *How to Manage, Analyze, and Interpret Survey Data.* Vol. 9, *The Survey Kit.* Thousand Oaks, CA: Sage.

A simple and well-documented introduction to the management and analysis of surveys with a brief description of the main methods of data analysis and hypothesis testing. Chapter 1 presents an overview of data management.

Fink, A. 2003. *How to Report on Surveys.* Vol. 10, *The Survey Kit.* Thousand Oaks, CA: Sage.

Chapter 1 presents some useful guidelines for the preparation of visual material for group presentations.

Gray, D. 2004. *Doing Research in the Real World.* Thousand Oaks, CA: Sage.

A very thorough explanation and critique of all the main quantitative data collection and analysis methods. Chapter 10 reviews observational techniques, and Chapter 12 presents an overview of data management.

Grosh, M. and P. Glewwe, eds. 2000. *Designing Household Survey Questionnaires for Developing Countries: Lessons from 15 Years of the Living Standards Measurement Study.* 3 vols. Washington, DC: World Bank.

Probably the most comprehensive reference work on the design of household surveys in developing countries. The three volumes report on a 15-year program of Living Standards Measurement Studies supported by the World Bank. The chapter by Deaton and Grosh (2000) presents a detailed discussion of the use of diaries to report on household consumption, and the chapter by Harvey and Taylor (2000) describes self-reporting methods for recording time use.

Moore, D. and G. McCabe. 1999. *Introduction to the Practice of Statistics.* New York: Freeman.

A clearly presented but more comprehensive and technical discussion of data analysis, covering many topics not included in the other statistics books given in this list.

Patton, M. Q. 2002. *Qualitative Research and Evaluation Methods.* Thousand Oaks, CA: Sage.

A comprehensive review of a wide range of qualitative data collection and analysis techniques, including interviewing and observational techniques and challenges and the use of focus groups.

Presser, P., M. Couper, J. Lessler, M. Martin, J. Martin, J. Rothgeb, and E. Singer. 2004. *Methods for Testing and Evaluating Survey Questionnaires.* New York: John Wiley.

Presser, P., M. Couper, J. Lessler, M. Martin, J. Martin, J. Rothgeb, and E. Singer. 2004. "Methods for Testing and Evaluating Survey Questions." *Public Opinion Quarterly* 68(1):109–30.

Explains how the choice of items and the way questions are asked can influence responses. The second reference is a summary of the book.

Shadish, W. R., D. Newman, M. Scheirer, and C. Wye. 1995. *Guiding Principles for Evaluators.* New Directions for Program Evaluation, No. 66. San Francisco: Jossey-Bass.

One of the most widely used reference sources on the recommended principles for the design, implementation, presentation, and use of evaluations.

Sirkin, R. M. 1999. *Statistics for the Social Sciences.* Thousand Oaks, CA: Sage.

A more comprehensive but not too technical coverage of the principal techniques of data analysis.

Weinberg, S. L. and S. K. Abramowitz. 2002. *Data Analysis for the Behavioral Sciences Using SPSS.* Cambridge, UK: Cambridge University Press.

Thorough and clearly presented review of how to conduct statistical analysis using one of the most popular statistical analysis packages.

Notes

1. Some QUANT researchers also share similar concerns. Perhaps Heisenberg (with his famous principle that many physical objects can never be measured precisely because the act of measuring will change what is being measured) is the best-known example.

2. Vygotsky (1978) is the seminal source for this concept.

3. Quasi-experimental designs are discussed in more detail in Chapter 10. See also Reichardt (2005) for a brief overview of alternative approaches to quasi-experimental designs and Shadish, Cook, and Campbell (2002) for a more in-depth discussion.

4. More than 60 social investment funds are now operating in South America, Africa, Asia, and the Newly Independent States of the Former Soviet Union. Communities are able to select a service such as the construction of a school, health center, well, or footbridge from a menu of options. The **social fund** is usually managed by an autonomous government agency, and the community is required to contribute a certain percentage of the cost of the project in labor, materials, or cash.

5. For a comprehensive review of issues concerning questionnaire design and particularly question wording, see Presser et al. (2004a, 2004b). This book demonstrates the importance of careful choice and testing of question wording; seemingly small changes can have a major influence on how people respond.

6. Glewwe's (2000) research was conducted in very poor parts of Africa and recommended the following, based on the correlation of these factors with test scores: feeding poor children snacks but not meals, teacher-pupil ratios of greater than 1:40+, and shared rather than individual textbooks. Clearly, a setting very different from those normally found in most U.S. education research.

7. The list was originally prepared for developing country evaluations, and some of the issues may be less common in the United States and other developed countries, but all these issues do occur in these latter countries—although perhaps less frequently.

8. We use the term *enumerator* to refer to people who are administering structured questionnaires and *interviewers* to refer to people conducting qualitative, unstructured, or semistructured interviews.

9. Although open-ended questions should technically be considered as QUAL, a few such questions are often included in structured questionnaires (e.g., as follow-up in case of people responding "Other"), so they are mentioned here.

10. One option is to code all missing data as, for example, 99 and not include it in the analysis. In other cases, the value of missing data is estimated and this estimated value is included in the analysis. The missing value may be estimated through multiple regression that calculated the average value of, for example, earned income, for people of the same age, sex, and education. It is extremely important to document the procedures used for each missing value because this can be a potential source of bias.

11. Sometimes an index is created by combining several variables or by a statistical transformation. For example, the variable *consumption* might be created as the sum of expenditures on food, housing, transport, education, and other payments. It is essential that the procedures for creating all indices are clearly documented and easily accessible to the reader.

12. Statistical significance tests are discussed in Chapter 14.

13. The calculation of the standard deviation is discussed in Chapter 14.

14. Space does not permit a detailed discussion of the use of different statistical significance tests although there is a brief overview in Chapter 14. The reader is referred to the recommended readings at the end of this chapter, which give both brief introductory texts and more advanced treatments.

15. The recommended readings at the end of this chapter include several introductions to these techniques as well as several more advanced textbooks.

CHAPTER 12

Qualitative Evaluation Methods

T his chapter discusses QUAL data collection and analysis. It begins with an overview of QUAL methodology and traditions together with the main reasons for using these approaches, then describes data collection through observation, interviews, and the analysis of documents and artifacts. A number of hybrid data collection techniques are also described. The question of how to ensure quality in QUAL enquiry is also discussed. The chapter concludes with a description of QUAL methods of data analysis.

Qualitative Methodology and Tradition

Interpretivism, the term preferred by many practitioners, is often referred to as *qualitative methodology*. In this chapter, qualitative methods will be considered as a related group of approaches for collecting and analyzing data, often used in partnership with quantitative methods for mixed-method **designs** (see Box 12.1).

Box 12.1   Qualitative Data

Qualitative data is the general term given to evidence that is text based rather than numeric in representation. These kinds of data result from interviews (group, individual, focus, and so on), observations (more typically unstructured but also structured), and documents (both formal, such as mission statements, as well as informal, such as letters) that may be analyzed from a variety of perspectives.

SOURCE: Greene and Henry (2005:345).

As described in the educational and evaluation research literature, qualitative methodology is a general approach to empirical inquiry. According to some, qualitative methods are now used more frequently than quantitative methods. Table 12.1 describes some specific types of qualitative studies, all of which share an interest in the meanings constructed by insiders and interactions in context. While any general approach to evaluation might include qualitative data, some especially rely on qualitative methods, including the following:

- *Fourth-generation evaluation*—evaluation involving sensitive, systematic attention to context and to stakeholders' perceptions and meanings, verified (or verifiable) by member checking and audit trails (Guba and Lincoln 1989)
- *Connoisseurship evaluation*—evaluation relying on the enlightened eye of the expert to recognize program quality, including subtleties not easily discerned (Eisner 1985)
- *Utilization-focused evaluation*—evaluation organized to respond to information needs and to promote the use of evaluation results by "primary intended users" (Patton 1997:21)
- *Responsive evaluation*—evaluation more attentive to emerging issues than to an initial design (Stake 1975)
- *Participatory evaluation*—evaluation intended not only to improve program understanding but also to transform program-related working relationships through participation in evaluation (Greene 1997)

Table 12.1   Some Types of Qualitative Studies

Methods	*Description*
Ethnography	Sustained field studies to understand the ethos or culture of a group or society
Critical ethnography	Ethnography focused on power structures and relationships for the purpose of revealing and redressing oppression
Feminist research	Research focused on power structures that oppress women and often, by extension, other groups
Ethnomethodology	Study of human perceptions, meanings, interactions, and how they maintain social structure
Phenomenology	Study of things as they are perceived, without regard for whether they are objectively real, to clarify people's perceptions and experiences and the meanings they give to events and concepts
Naturalistic case study	Study of a particular case because of its intrinsic interest or because it is an instance of a phenomenon of interest, focusing on ordinary events in natural settings described in ordinary language
Participant observation	Study in which data are collected while the researcher is a full or partial member of the group studied
Hermeneutics	Interpretive study seeking contextual understanding of human expression and intention while attentive to the relationship between the subject and the enquirer

- *Empowerment evaluation*—evaluation intended to improve not only program understanding but also to raise the efficacy of participants (Fetterman 1996)
- *Ideological evaluation*—evaluation intended to promote certain ideologies or values, such as social justice, deliberative democracy, or the rights of the historically disenfranchised (e.g., minorities, the disabled) (see House 1993; Mertens 1999)

These approaches share a focus on stakeholder perceptions and experiences as necessary for understanding and improving program quality. To document and appreciate the thinking and behavior of participants, practitioners share a commitment to staying in the field long enough to understand the perspectives of a variety of stakeholders. This is an important point to keep in mind when using qualitative methods for RealWorld Evaluation (**RWE**), where there are often significant constraints on the amount of time that the evaluators can spend in the field.

Qualitative Methodology: An Overview

Drawn from social sciences such as anthropology and sociology, qualitative methodology is a general term for a family of approaches that shares a view of a program (or other phenomenon of interest) as an intricate composite of stakeholders' perceptions and experiences. Qualitative practitioners seek an insider's **emic** rather than an outsider's **etic** understanding. Prolonged engagement in the field provides opportunity to recognize patterns of behavior, themes and variations, nuances and subtleties, articulated and inarticulable meanings. In a process known as *emergent design* or *progressive focusing,* qualitative research questions and plans are revised during data collection as stakeholder experiences are better understood.

Interpretivism's historical and philosophical roots lie in 18th-century German distinctions between natural science and social science. Focusing on human meaning making, interpretive research was intended to discover the meanings people give to what they see and experience. These efforts foreshadowed Erickson's (1986) 20th-century admonition to "put *mind* back in the picture, in the central place it now occupies in cognitive psychology" (127, emphasis in the original) rather than trying to eliminate researcher subjectivity through futile attempts to achieve objectivity. Guba and Lincoln (1985, 1989, 1994) incorporated these ideas into a proposal for a constructivist paradigm in research, featuring a vision of truth as individually constructed and therefore multiple. Inquiry within this paradigm is a search for understanding of the human meanings given to social phenomena.

- Qualitative practitioners view the world differently than do their quantitative colleagues and, as a result, regard their tasks and responsibilities differently. Quantitative and qualitative research are based on different paradigms and many, not all, qualitative researchers consider the divergence as representing fundamental differences of philosophy and approach that are difficult, if not impossible to reconcile. A **paradigm** is "an integrated set of theoretical presuppositions that lead the researcher to see the world of one's research interest in a particular way" (Erickson 1986:120, after Kuhn 1962). As a framework for understanding what knowledge is and how it may be sought, the research paradigm one prefers may determine the following:

- *What constitutes data.* For example, should unplanned conversations with program personnel be considered data? Or observations of ordinary program events? Or participants' statements about program quality that include obvious bias?
- *How data may appropriately be collected and analyzed.* For example, are numerical indicators needed to determine program **outcomes**? Can human experiences be recorded and analyzed to discover program quality? Is, for example, quantifiable survey data more useful than unquantifiable interview data?
- *What constitutes an appropriate research or evaluation product.* For example, is deep understanding of a program in context as important to **clients** as a written report with charts and recommendations?
- *How the quality of that product may be judged.* For example, to be credible, must an evaluation provide experimental group, control group, or pre-post-program comparisons? Are experiential narratives credible and useful?

Qualitative-quantitative differences are essentially epistemological (i.e., differences in understandings of what constitutes knowledge) but most easily seen in different approaches to design, data collection, data analysis, reporting, and use. Qualitative and quantitative inquiry have sometimes been described as *epistemologically incommensurable* or *methodologically incommensurable*—that is, so fundamentally different that there can be no agreement, no collaboration, no mixing of methods. In the 1980s and 1990s, disagreements within the research and evaluation communities were so heated they came to be called the "paradigm wars." The strife was ultimately declared over by some or seen as different points along a continuum of inquiry by others. However, despite significant progress, the underlying differences of approach have not been completely reconciled, as seen in the proposal by the U.S. government to prefer "scientifically based evidence" obtained through certain quantitative designs described as more scientific or rigorous (U.S. Department of Education 2003; see also American Evaluation Association 2003; Shavelson and Towne 2002; Viadero 2004).

Evaluators may have been among the first to move pragmatically beyond this disagreement. Recognizing the benefits of both quantitative and qualitative approaches, they found ways to combine them in **mixed-methods** designs (see Chapter 13). Sometimes, mixing methods works well. Other times, one paradigm or the other clearly dominates, limiting use or the advantages of the other. Major use of one approach and minor use of the other may be appropriate to the evaluation question or may be necessitated by constrained resources. For example, a quantitative evaluation may rely primarily on numerical data from surveys, tests, or demographics, using a qualitative pilot study only to facilitate the subsequent evaluation design or to provide a bit of qualitative **triangulation** for quantitative data. Or a qualitative evaluation may emphasize systematic observations and stakeholder interviews, using quantitative survey and demographic data only for an explanation of the larger context. In such cases, evaluators may be balancing methodological choices against RWE constraints or may believe they are using both qualitative and quantitative methods well, not recognizing the priority they are actually giving their personal preferences. Fortunately, mixed methods can be used effectively by evaluators or evaluation teams with training and experience in both approaches.

Stakeholders and Narratives in Naturalistic Inquiry

Interpretation of qualitative data for the purpose of *understanding* has been distinguished from analysis of quantitative data for the purpose of *explanation* (von Wright 1971). Qualitative inquirers seek representation of multiple vantage points simultaneously in detailed, contextual, holistic portrayals. With deep, contextual understanding of the particular as the goal, reporting program events as narrative accounts promotes deep understanding through *vicarious experience* so that understanding is not merely abstract but deeply, personally felt.

The effectiveness of narratives for complex understanding can be seen in the power of fables and parables, of legends preserved over centuries, of the ease with which we remember a character in a novel longer than our own experiences at the time of reading it. For example, we may have drawn important personal lessons and vividly remember *Don Quixote* by Miguel de Cervantes Saavedra (1615/1964), or Scout in *To Kill a Mockingbird* by Harper Lee (1960) or *Anna Karenina* by Leo Tolstoy (1889) but remember little or nothing of our lives as we read the book. Don't we all try to remember not to tilt at windmills, to do what we can to protect the vulnerable, not to ruin our lives over an infatuation?

Qualitative evaluators see a program as created by human perceptions and actions. In keeping with this understanding, qualitative inquiry is *phenomenological*, the study of the program as it is perceived and created by those who experience it. In an ongoing process, stakeholders' understandings of a program affect their behavior, which influences the evolving nature and meaning of the program. Thus, the program is dynamic, not fixed, more subjective than objective in character, the creation of participants more than the implementation of program designs or criteria.

In qualitative evaluation, program **impact** and quality cannot be determined without understanding the diverse experiences of stakeholders. The perceptions of many must be searched out—managers, personnel, beneficiaries, supporters, proponents, adversaries. The qualitative idea that diverse perceptions and experiences constitute the reality of programs has drawn general attention.

The importance of observing natural settings where stakeholders engage in program activities makes qualitative evaluation *naturalistic*. **Naturalistic inquiry** involves time on site and data collection *unobtrusive* enough to minimize interference with ordinary interactions (Lincoln and Guba 1985). An ethnographic style requires repeated fieldwork until patterns emerge and analytic *thick description* (Geertz 1973) can be developed.

Purposeful Sampling[1]

Qualitative designs and methods would be compromised by some of the procedures intended to provide rigor in quantitative studies. For example, the introduction of artificial variation to test the strength of correlations among variables would disturb natural processes; qualitative practitioners might instead study *negative cases* that differ from the ordinary in informative ways. Division of stakeholders into experimental and control groups might alter program practices or deny needed services to half the eligible population, although natural comparison groups (i.e., preexisting groups similar to program beneficiaries and personnel) might sometimes be available and studied. Similarly, random and randomized sampling, important to generalizability of quantitative **findings**, are not best for qualitative evaluation, where local understanding rather than broad generalizability is the goal.

Because time is limited in many evaluations, care must be taken to select implementation sites for study, subjects to be interviewed, and events to be observed. Selections must be made that will maximize the opportunity to understand. *Purposeful selection* rather than random or randomized selection is better for qualitative work because, when few sites or participants can be observed in the time available, random selection might skew results. For example, in sampling beneficiaries to interview, the random selection of a dozen program beneficiaries from a cast of thousands might net twelve members of the dominant ethnic group or twelve who are more (or less) satisfied with their benefits than beneficiaries as a whole are, introducing *sampling bias* into the data set.

In such a case, better information can be obtained by carefully choosing a *range sample* or a *quota sample* that includes, to continue the example, six beneficiaries who received full program benefits and six who received partial benefits, or six men and six women, or six members of the majority culture and six of the minority culture. Interviewing people who represent a range of program effects, especially when time is short, may give a sense of the general beneficiary experience within the program. Selection criteria can be combined; for example:

Six men

- One from the majority culture who received full benefits
- One from the majority culture who received partial benefits
- One from the minority culture who received full benefits
- One from the minority culture who received partial benefits
- One program worker at Site A
- One program manager or administrator

And six women

- One from the majority culture who received full benefits
- One from the majority culture who received partial benefits
- One from the minority culture who received full benefits
- One from the minority culture who received partial benefits
- One program worker at Site B
- One manager of an agency that supports the program

In some cases, it may be more important to know the impact on the most difficult-to-serve population than to know the general impact. A *critical sample* may be more useful, for example, selecting all interviewees from the minority culture and who received few, if any, program benefits. A *reputational sample* may be informative, for example, where the most outspoken proponents (or opponents) of the program are selected for interviewing. Purposeful selection criteria themselves must be selected according to information needs considering, for example, whether a range sample or a critical sample would likely provide the most useful data.

Contextuality and Case-to-Case Generalizations

Qualitative inquiry is *contextual,* recognizing that contexts include supports and barriers that shape programs. For each program, a unique array of contexts influences the program and its outcomes. For example:

- *The macrosystem*—the ideological environment, including whether or not people believe in what the program is trying to accomplish
- *The exosystem*—the policy and regulations (and the politics involved in enacting and maintaining them) that govern program implementation and procedures
- *The mesosystem*—the working relationships among providers of program services and others, including whether personnel are accessible and supportive of each other or antagonistic and obstructive
- *The microsystem*—the daily interactions and practices in the program and the manner in which program personnel and beneficiaries communicate and interact (Bronfenbrenner 1979)

Contextual effects may be decisive or subtle and may originate locally or remotely. Many types of contexts may affect a program, including physical, social, economic, organizational, political, legal, ethical, psychological, emotional, and intellectual contexts. Investigation of the particular contexts of a program promotes understanding of what the program is able to accomplish, under what circumstances, and why.

Particularities of context are considered to work against program replication and large-scale case-to-population generalizations[2]. More appropriate and justifiable in qualitative work are *petite generalizations* (Erickson 1986) limited to the program at hand or *case-to-case generalizations* (Firestone 1993) made by readers to cases of personal interest to themselves. Experimental conditions that promote broad generalizations are often unavailable in naturalistic qualitative studies. However, deep experiential understanding of one program promotes understanding of similar programs and cumulative improvement over time within a sector or field of endeavor.

Emergent Design, Progressive Focusing, and Constant-Comparative Method

In quantitative studies, quality largely rests in following designs intended to protect against sampling bias and other confounding factors. In qualitative studies, *emergent design* is purposefully open to adjustment. As evaluators learn about the program, they are expected to refine the design, focus, and methods. The preordinate designs, where methods and sources are stated in advance and followed throughout data collection, typical of quantitative studies are considered too restrictive, limiting the possibility of recognizing and investigating unanticipated issues. Qualitative evaluators try to maximize opportunity to learn about critical program aspects that may not have been recognized initially. Questions and issues are to be revised or replaced by more sophisticated ones as the evaluator becomes better acquainted with the program as part of a process called *progressive focusing*.

Qualitative methods are also purposely open to capitalize on unanticipated interpretations or findings. *Constant-comparative method* (Glaser and Strauss 1967) describes the ongoing interplay between design, data collection, and data analysis. What is learned in the field contributes to the design, increasingly refining its focus through preliminary interpretations. Comparing preliminary interpretations with the data motivates additional, more focused data collection.

Box 12.2 Examples of the Importance of Context in Understanding Program Outcomes

Arts Education in a High-stakes Achievement Testing Context in the United States

In the 1990s, the Chicago Arts Partnership in Education (CAPE) funded 14 partnerships of schools and arts agencies. One of these, the Lakeview Education and Arts Partnership (LEAP) paired artists and teachers for the development of curricula the team taught so that students gained knowledge and skills in the academics and the arts simultaneously. The program was so successful that it was named by Harvard *ARTS Survive!* as one of only 14 thriving arts education programs in the United States. Program planners and managers were invited to help others nationally and internationally to implement new instantiations of the program.

LEAP's achievements and sustainability cannot be fully appreciated without understanding of the sociopolitical context. The four LEAP schools, three elementary and one high school, were located in high-poverty areas of the city of Chicago and enrolled high proportions of minority students and English language learners (ELL). In fact, more than 90% of the enrollment of the participating high school was Latino/a, including many recent immigrants from Mexico and Central and South America. These high-risk students did not perform well on standardized tests required by an incoming chief executive officer of the Chicago Public Schools, who put low-scoring schools on "warning" and "watch lists," threatening these schools with wholesale faculty and administrator firings if scores did not improve. LEAP teachers were consequently reassigned, some to teach test preparation courses, which resulted in the loss of the program—although indicators other than test scores (such as teacher's assessments of their students' and graduates' enrollment in college preparatory courses) showed student achievement gains. This context is critical to understanding the failure of sustainability of LEAP.

SOURCE: Mabry (1997).

A Slum Upgrading Project in the Philippines

In the 1960s, the World Bank funded a slum upgrading project in the Tondo Foreshore in Manila, the Philippines. Residents participated in the installation of water, sanitation, and footpaths and also invested their own money in improving the housing—often rebuilding a provisional dwelling with more permanent materials. A longitudinal impact evaluation was conducted in which the project area was compared with comparison communities to assess the impacts of the project on the social and economic conditions of the Tondo families. The evaluation found significant improvements in economic conditions but also in health. A contextual analysis revealed that one of the reasons for the significant improvements in health was that the municipal government was anxious to demonstrate that the project was a success because they wished to obtain another loan from the World Bank to continue and expand the program. Consequently, a number of health centers that were to be constructed in other areas of the city were instead constructed in Tondo and staffed with medical personnel. The provision of these health facilities, which were not part of the original project, contributed to the significant improvements in health conditions, particularly in comparison with other communities—many of which lost the health centers that had originally been planned. This illustrates the importance of contextual analysis when assessing the replicability of a pilot project (i.e., would it be likely to have the same effects in other locations?).

Holism, Expansionism, and Utility

Research in the quantitative paradigm is *reductionist,* reducing data to numbers to measure outcomes and support correlations, comparisons, trends, and probabilities. But qualitative data cannot be reduced to numbers without unacceptable loss of meaning. Because the qualitative view of a program involves interdependent aspects, too many and too dynamic to isolate meaningfully, qualitative practitioners attempt complex overall or *holistic* views. As new data reveal ever more complexity, the inquiry is *expansionist.* Theoretical triangulation in analysis increases the expansion as evaluators consider the data from different conceptual or theoretical frameworks and surface competing findings and rival explanations.

The Program Evaluation Standards (Joint Committee on Standards for Educational Evaluation 1994) strongly emphasize utility. However, although both quantitative and qualitative evaluations have influenced public policy, failure to use evaluation results is a chronic complaint in the field. Some evaluators have devised strategies and approaches specifically to promote evaluation use (see especially Patton 1997). Problematic issues regarding utility have been raised concerning qualitative methods: Can subjective, nonreplicable data and reporting be trusted? Can diverse interests be accurately represented? Are narrative reports too long and too late? Does focus on the particular, rather than on the generalizable, limit utility? Qualitative evaluators are likely to treat these issues as trade-offs and to point out compensatory strategies. For example, subjective accounts may enhance personal understanding even as they raise concern about bias, and the evaluator's subjectivity may be offset by triangulation, validation, and the critique of colleagues.

Reporting and Use of Evaluation Results

The effectiveness of qualitative reports comes from deep understanding by readers and stakeholders that promotes use of evaluation results for program improvement. On the other hand, narratives and complexity may increase the length of reports unhelpfully, and representation of diverse viewpoints may encourage conflict as to how evaluation results should be used.

To offset length, qualitative practitioners try to select for reporting those narratives that are most informative and interesting and that best convey complex implications that numbers may only suggest. Their experiential narratives help readers gain *tacit knowledge* (Polanyi 1958), considered more likely to influence behavior than the *declarative knowledge* of findings or recommendations, with positive effects regarding use of evaluation results. On the other hand, the promotion of personal understandings may encourage divergent views of a program rather than help generate consensual action plans.

Programs have many stakeholders, so representing their divergent positions introduces complexity in reports. Qualitative practitioners take particular care to share results with many stakeholder groups, and their nontechnical narrative reports improve access to information by many groups. However, wide access and the representation of diverse perspectives may discourage rather than promote consensus about use of evaluation findings. Stakeholders may see more clearly the issues that divide them and may be more empowered to press conflicting agendas.

Natural disagreement among competing stakeholder groups is not easily resolved or reconciled. The interests and interpretations of program managers may suggest uses far different from those of program personnel or beneficiaries. The more diverse a program's stakeholders, the more likely that qualitative promotion of individual interpretations may clarify divisions and entrench dissensus. The qualitative evaluator may need to work harder to help clients not only understand their programs from **multiple perspectives** but also to help them find enough working agreement to be able to use evaluation results. Perhaps the evaluators who have most strongly encouraged assisting stakeholders to use evaluation results have been qualitative practitioners urging **utilization** (Patton 1997) and **empowerment** (Fetterman 1996).

Different Reasons for Using Different Methodologies

Both quantitative and qualitative methods carry advantages and easily recognized disadvantages (see Tables 11.1 and 12.2). For example, the "QUANTs" sometimes still demean the approaches of the "QUALs" (Rossi 1994) as nonscientific and nonrigorous. Campbell and Stanley (1963) famously disapproved naturalistic research in which "a single group is studied only once" by means of "tedious collection of specific detail, careful observation, testing, and the like," claiming that "such studies have such a total absence of control as to be of almost no scientific value" (pp. 6–7). Forty years later, in *Scientific Research in Education* (Shavelson and Towne 2002), the U.S. National Research Council promoted qualitative methods but with cautions that continued to rankle qualitative folk: "Almost all of the qualitative research mentioned in the report is treated as 'descriptive,' . . . identified as a lower category . . . [and] described as appropriate only when theory is weak" (Maxwell 2004:8).

Similarly, qualitative methodologists still criticize their quantitative counterparts for numerical representations that describe complex social entities superficially and, consequently, misleadingly. Qualitative practitioners are skeptical about quantitative reduction of complex data to numerical indicators, about claims of objectivity and elimination of bias, and about priority for statistical significance over real or practical significance. Believing that context can significantly influence program implementation and outcomes, they are doubtful about insistence on the generalizability or replicability of a program in unstudied contexts.

The limitations of each methodology underlie the realization that using mixed-method designs can capitalize on the strengths of both qualitative and quantitative strategies, and each can help compensate for the weaknesses of the other (see Table 13.1). In mixed-method designs, quantitative measurements may explain how many, how much, and in what proportions while qualitative narratives may illuminate why, for whom, and under what conditions.

Reasons for Combining Qualitative with Quantitative Methodology in Mixed-Method Designs

As we discuss in more detail in the next chapter, qualitative and quantitative ways of knowing feature different strengths. Combining them offers what is sometimes called *binocular vision*. Used in combination as *mixed methods*, quantitative data provide breadth of understanding, while qualitative data provide depth. For example, quantitative data—counts, statistics—might indicate how many people own motorcycles, purchase helmets, and die annually in accidents, while qualitative data—observations of motorcycle riding, interviews with cyclists—might indicate why, despite accident reports, some riders choose not to wear helmets and the actual impact of accidents on riders and their families.

The benefits of both depth and breadth can significantly improve most evaluation studies. As a result, most evaluations do include both qualitative and quantitative data collection.

Table 12.2   Strengths and Weaknesses of Qualitative Methods in Evaluation

QUAL Features	Strengths	Weaknesses
Emergent design and progressive focusing	Evaluators are not bound by initial designs but, rather, are expected to improve them as they learn more about the program.	Designs cannot be fully articulated at the outset, which can be off-putting for clients who want to know what they're getting. QUAL evaluations are not usually replicable partly because of continuous adjustments.
Purposeful sampling	Stakeholders with experience or information related to specific aspects of the program are identified as data sources.	Samples are not random or large enough for reliability or generalizability in the quantitative sense.
Contextuality and generalizations	Qualitative evaluations support understanding of the program in its actual setting and also case-to-case generalizations by readers to settings relevant to them.	Qualitative evaluations do not usually support case-to-population generalizations or wide applicability to other populations and settings.
Stakeholder orientation	Emphasis on the experiences and perceptions of multiple stakeholders helps reveal program processes as experienced and their human impact.	Revealing many points of view tends not to lead to easy consensus, including consensus about use of findings for program decisions.
Holism	Big picture views that include many aspects and influences help convey the actual dynamics and complexity of programs.	Specific factors are not isolated, measured, and correlated, although their relationships and effects are documented and portrayed.
Expansionism	Proliferation of data and meanings contribute to complex understanding and improve the validity of program representations and findings.	Qualitative reports tend to be lengthy. Most findings are contextualized and conditional rather than clear and absolute.
Narrative reporting	Narrative reports are accessible to nontechnical audiences, including many evaluation stakeholders and users. Narratives promote readers' deep understanding through vicarious experience, which enhances use of findings.	Narrative reports tend to be lengthy and may not offer clear bottom-line results.
Validity of findings	Detailed data and triangulation support valid findings.	Interpretivist methods are considered by some to be too subjective to be credible.

However, some practitioners find it difficult to use mixed methods well because their prefer-ence or better understanding of either qualitative or quantitative methodology creates an imbalance. For example, an evaluator trying qualitative methods for the first time might limit the actual use of qualitative data to mere illustration by tacking onto a report a case study or vignette, or by sprinkling a report with a few interview excerpts. Or an evaluator trying to incorporate quantitative methods into a design that is essentially qualitative might tack on a table or two of survey results to suggest context or frequency without analyzing the survey data along with the qualitative data. However, the advantages of using both approaches in the same evaluation can be gained if both are well understood and appreciated, which sometimes requires teaming methodologists of different persuasions.

Qualitative Data Collection

Advance planning—the evaluation questions and design—provides initial focus without foreclosing on unanticipated opportunities to gather information. Qualitative evaluators are responsible for making flexible adjustments as appropriate. The emergent character of qualitative data collection is part of what makes interpretivist work expansionist, uncovering or generating new questions and data sources during the process of data collection. To avoid drifting off course as new information leads are followed, ongoing adaptation must be balanced with attention to the main focus or overarching question(s) of the inquiry. For example:

- Is this program providing the intended benefits to the intended beneficiaries without unintended harm?
- Do positive program effects justify resource allocations?
- Are procedures focused, supported, and efficient enough to ensure program **sustainability**?

Analysis occurs both during data collection and after data have been collected. The ongoing constant-comparative part of data analysis supports emergent design and progressive focusing, allowing the focus, methods, and the manner in which the methods are practiced to be refined in process. Focusing on the experiences of stakeholders, qualitative evaluators search for multiple perspectives from which they generate complex representations and interpretations sensitive to a program's culture.

Focus on stakeholders brings qualitative evaluators into closer personal contact with them than is typical with their quantitative counterparts, who are often working from surveys and test data. Close contact fosters understanding of intricate nuances and implications, but it also means that qualitative evaluators must work harder to maintain rapport so that informants will be willing to be observed and interviewed, will feel comfortable enough to behave in ordinary ways, and will respond honestly and fully to questions. This level of contact carries significant ethical obligations. Trust may lead informants to treat evaluators as friends and to fail to be appropriately self-protective. Qualitative data collection should begin with determination to avoid unnecessary risk to respondents.

Close proximity may also threaten accuracy—for example, if the evaluator produces overly sympathetic accounts of hard-working or well-meaning stakeholders, resulting in positive bias in findings. Qualitative designs may include safeguards for validity such as triangulation, validation, review panels, and meta-evaluation. To this repertoire of validity safeguards, qualitative evaluators should add personal discipline as they observe and interview, monitoring how their values and preferences may influence what they see and record.

Hallmark Qualitative Data Collection Methods

Traditionally, three ways of collecting information have been hallmarks in qualitative inquiry: observation, interview, and the review of documents or artifacts. These methods systematize ordinary human ways of learning or knowing: looking, listening, reading. There are many variations on the three qualitative data collection themes, suggesting many possibilities for adaptation sensitive to particular contexts and to specific programs, populations, and evaluation questions.

Observation

Often, qualitative data collection begins with observations, systematically repeated, of ordinary program events until enough redundancy in the data set is achieved to facilitate identification of themes, patterns, and issues. Viewing and documenting interactions is key to understanding what happens in programs and where, when, how, how frequently, how well, by whom, for whom, and why. Qualitative evaluators need to determine what should be observed and how frequently to be sure of seeing ordinary events, not behaviors intended to impress an observer.

The product of most qualitative observation is the **experiential narrative**, written with a storylike quality that promotes vicarious experience for the reader, giving the impression almost of having been there. So the qualitative observer must be skilled at recording fine details—what was done, in response to what, with what implications; what was said, in what tone or manner, with what accompanying nonverbal communication. And the observer must be skilled at conveying interactions in text that reveal the norms and expectations of the group and their culture.

Observation notes are typically taken by hand, often hurriedly to keep up with the dynamic flow of events. Notes need to capture detail for analysis and for narratives. The write-up must transform pages of scribbling into storylike experiential vignettes and narratives with evocative word choice, highlighting details, presenting word-for-word conversations where relevant and summarizing where less relevant, clarifying meanings and relating them coherently to larger themes. Crafting text takes time, sensitivity, and skill.

Because a level of detail that includes direct quotations, tones of voice, gestures, attitudes, and immediate contexts is difficult to capture in real-time notes, observation notes need to be written up as narratives as soon as possible after data collection. Laptop computers or video-taping may help, although video-taping can introduce an artificial element into the situation by creating self-consciousness in participants and undermining accuracy. Audiotape recorders and other handheld recording devices may help capture details if the observer can speak into the equipment without excessive obtrusiveness.

Cultural and Phenomenological Sensitivity. Being observed, especially by evaluators, often creates anxiety for those observed, even when assurances are given that it is the program, not those observed, being evaluated. Nervousness can interfere with naturalness, introducing inaccuracies—observer effects—into the data set. This may be especially true where there are cultural differences or perceived power differentials between observers and those observed, as is often the case in evaluation. Where natural behavior cannot be ensured, for example, by observations over a long term, qualitative evaluators must take this into account when analyzing and presenting data.

Cultural competence is increasingly recognized as vital as evaluation grows in its understanding of the importance of local customs, values, and norms. Qualitative emphasis on stakeholders and contexts positions this methodology well because cultural sensitivity is necessary to maintain the rapport and trust necessary for collecting accurate qualitative data. Close observation aids recognition of sensitive issues and how they may be approached. In unfamiliar contexts, qualitative practitioners may need to rely on key local informants or translators or to include local personnel as members of the evaluation team.

Participant Observation. One way to differentiate types of observation is by the role of the observer. The proverbial fly on the wall is an *external observer* and, at the opposite end of a continuum, a *program participant* may document activities while being fully engaged in them. In between is the *participant-observer,* someone who both observes and participates to some degree. To increase cultural sensitivity and to address time and budget constraints, people involved in the program may be asked to serve as participant-observers, documenting activities, perhaps in logs or journals, or recording observations after a program-related event.

At least initially, an external observer brings less understanding to the task than an insider can. More ignorant about the meaning of what is observed, the external observer may also be more impartial in interpreting what is seen. An internal evaluator or participant observer will have a very rich knowledge base for interpreting significance and implications and, consequently, a basis for judging appropriateness and effectiveness but will seem less impartial because of a personal connection to the program. The need for credibility is often the criterion on which the selection of an external or internal evaluator is based.

Conducting observations is more difficult for participant-observers than for external observers because simultaneous participation and observation compete for attention. It is difficult to take notes detailed enough to capture dialogue, nuance, nonverbal communication, and context while at work on some aspect of program delivery or procedure. Writing up the observation immediately after the event may be especially important for participant-observers.

Structured Observation. Another way to differentiate types of observation is by the degree of structure involved. The vast majority of qualitative observation data is unstructured, with the observer taking detailed notes initially on everything observed. Gradually, over time, observations tend to become more focused. For example:

- Moving from general observations to focus on how personnel determine which applicants are granted and which are denied program benefits and whether these determinations are fair
- Moving from general observations of how students progress through an educational process to specific observations of how students are selected for high-expectation and low-expectation academic tracks, and the outcomes for students in each track

Unstructured observation avoids *instrumentation bias*—misdirection of attention based on categories decided in advance and indicated on observation protocols. Structured observation protocols may be used to document (perhaps to quantify) specific program aspects. For example, specific types of activities may need to be counted to show the proportions of certain specified procedures or behaviors. For the two examples above, the more focused observations

---

Box 12.3 Participant Observation in a Peer Mediation Program

Hoping to decrease the incidence of harassment and violence on school grounds, a school district in Indiana approved pilot implementation of a peer mediation program at one of its elementary schools. Student volunteers were trained to listen to complainants accuse their alleged tormentors and to facilitate discussion and resolution of altercations to the satisfaction of each party. Peer mediators were trained in facilitation techniques, all students were directed to turn to the mediators (rather than to adults) when they encountered difficulties, and teachers and other adults were trained regarding the support and expectations of mediators.

A doctoral student at Indiana University was engaged to study the peer mediation program from its outset and to provide formative feedback. Presentations of data served essentially as formative feedback and, on the basis of the data and interpretations shared with stakeholders, targets for the program and for the study were revised. In addition, observation data revealed where additional or refresher training was needed for peer mediators and for adults involved with the program and the type of information—often data—needed in the additional training.

In the study of the program, the doctoral student was an observer (and interviewer and documents analyst) and, in providing feedback, participating in decisions about next steps for the program, and assisting with additional training, was also a participant. Because of her dual role in the study of the program and also in its implementation, evolving design, and delivery, the student was fully both a participant and an observer.

SOURCE: Mahoney (1998).

---

might ultimately include structuring through *observation protocols* (see Figures 12.1 and 12.2) to answer specific evaluation questions such as, "Are ethnic minorities excluded from program benefits?" or "Are low-tracked students inappropriately prevented from moving to high tracks?"

Date and Time	Applicant's Name	Applicant's Ethnicity	Application Examiner	Determination of Eligibility

Figure 12.1 Observation Protocol: Are Ethnic Minorities Excluded from Program Benefits?

Student	Student's Original Track	Length of Time in Original Track	Evidence of Achievement or Progress	Highest Track Reached

Figure 12.2   Observation Protocol: Are Low-Tracked Students Inappropriately Prevented from Moving to High Tracks?

The protocol in Figure 12.1 could be used to record observations of the application process, noting who applied for program benefits, their ethnicity, and determinations of their eligibility. Such data would support interpretations of which, if any, ethnic groups were obtaining program benefits in greater or lesser proportions. It would also help identify which, if any, application examiners were exercising preference based on the ethnicity of applicants. Systematic recording of such data, tallied over time, would allow an observer to make well-warranted interpretations of the influence of ethnicity and prejudice in delivery of program benefits. The protocol in Figure 12.2 could be used to observe and document how long students remain in different tracks and whether any evidence of achievement or progress that might have justified promotion to a higher track was ignored.

In a more complex example, based on unstructured observations in the first year of an evaluation, a highly detailed observation protocol (see Figure 12.3) was developed for the second year of data collection in a study of *Kidtech,* an educational program providing laptop computers to high-risk elementary students.

Perception and interpretation are entwined. It is impossible to see and recognize without judging. A visitor to a classroom, including a *Kidtech* classroom, would notice more than the number of students present. The visitor would also notice the relaxed or tense atmosphere, the level of student engagement, or whether the work is demanding or unchallenging. Assigning multiple observers to the same or similar events may help check the subjective bias in the judgments of each.

If multiple observers are to use the same observation protocol, *reliability testing* is needed to ensure that all observers record information similarly. The question for reliability testing is this: If Observer 1 judges a student's performance as exceeding class expectations (i.e., that the student should be promoted to a higher track), would Observer 2 make the same judgment in observing the same scene? Training, practice, and **moderation** (i.e., discussion of interpretive criteria to bring consensus) help ensure reliability or the consistent recording of activities.

Observation protocols with fewer categories require more judgment calls. As a case in point, in Figure 12.1, there may be many gradations of ethnicity, such as the many variations within the category "Hispanic," each of which may display distinguishable patterns of

*School:*___Riverdale   Hillside   Treetop   *Observer:*___L. Mabry   J. Snow

*Teacher:*_____   *Date and time of observation:*_____

*Grade level:*__ *Challenge:*__yes __no   *Number of students present:*_____

Classroom layout: __Rows of separate desks
                        __Rows/lines of adjacent desks
                        __Desks grouped as tables
                        __Desks in pairs __Other:_____

Teacher-student interaction:

__Teacher working 1:1 with students   __Teacher working with small groups   __Whole class

Subject: __Literacy __Math __Science __Social Studies __Other:_____

Check if clear to students: __directions __lesson purpose __assessment criteria, standards, process

Brief description of content/subject/activity observed:

Number of computers in use by students: __   *In use by teacher:* __yes __no

Student use of personal computers: __none __individual __pairs __small groups

Technology in evidence *as part of the culture of the learning environment*   __yes __no

Other technology in use, if any, and its purpose:

Criticality of computers (check 1 or none)   *Motivational effect of computers (check 1 or none)*

__Necessary for this activity to occur   __Enhances student motivation/on-taskness
__Enhances learning/the activity   __Distraction from content learning
__Not needed for this activity

Computers as support (check all that apply)

__Transparency/skill/automaticity in use of technology *as a tool*

__Computer as information source/provider

__Computer as logistical support—e.g., word processing, spreadsheets, PowerPoint

Rigor	Above Grade Level	Grade-Appropriate	Below Grade Level	Babysitting	Not applicable/ Not Appropriate
Discourse – content					
Discourse – vocab.					
Test/Assgmt – content					
Test/Assgmt – vocab.					

Describe:

Figure 12.3   Observation Protocol: *Kidtech* Program Evaluation, Year 2

Engagement	*Consistently/ Strongly/ Most Students*	*Often/ Moderately/ About Half of Students*	*Seldom/ Little/Few Students*	*None/No Evidence/No Students*	*Not Applicable/ Not Appropriate*
Motivation					
Time on task					
Smoothness of operations					
Efficiency of transitions					

Describe:

Personalization	*Teacher Directed*	*Student Chosen*	*None/Can't Tell*
Learning goals			
Learning activity (e.g., research report)			
Topics or tasks (e.g., report subject, report format)			
Modifications to assignments in progress			

Describe:

---

prejudice. On the other hand, instruments with more categories, such as the protocol in Figure 12.3, may become so complicated that it is difficult for an observer to make quick, consistent decisions in each required category.

For most qualitative observation, unstructured observation is practiced because the need for experiential data generally outweighs the need for tallies related to subquestions. Also, the openness of emergent design works against advance construction of categories. Nevertheless, structured observation is sometimes a useful application of observation methods.

Photography and Video Recording. After struggling to capture the details that make experiential observation narratives possible, qualitative practitioners often yearn for surer ways to record all they see. Photography and, even more, videography offer visual means of recording observation data. Whether such means are advisable and appropriate requires consideration not only of the accuracy of the recording of data but also of the possibility of intrusive observer effects: Will program participants behave differently than they otherwise would if they are being photographed or video-recorded? If the answer to this question is affirmative, would it be ethical or appropriate to use photography or videography surreptitiously? If the answer to this question is negative, as it is sure to be, these means of recording observations may be precluded.

If, however, photography and videography are available, not too intrusive in the naturalistic setting, and not involving (or not prohibited because of) ethical complications, then video offers the observer formidable assistance in capturing experiential detail. If photographs or video recordings may be taken but, because of confidentiality, not reported or published, the observer may review the visual data recording to capture details in subsequent text. If photographs or video recordings may be shared, reports and presentations can be made very experiential.

Rarely does audio-taping produce useful documentation of observations. In natural settings, conversations are often overlapping and simultaneous, obscuring parts of the dialogue and the identity of speakers, some of whom may be far from the recorder and unintelligible in the audio data. However, audio-taping may work when there are only one or two participants if the presence of the recording equipment does not interfere with natural behavior.

Observation often supports later interviews and analysis by promoting the development of specific interview questions that probe for explanations of what was seen, and by identifying documents and artifacts that can be requested for further analysis.

Interview

Interviews elicit information about stakeholders' experiences, perceptions, and meanings, critical to qualitative approaches to understanding. Because interview data incorporate interviewees' personal perspectives, confirmation of the data through direct observation or from other stakeholders is needed. Coupled with observation, interview data can help explain why participants act as they do, and observations can confirm the extent to which their behavior coheres with their statements of intent and personal meaning.

Structuring of Interviews. Interviews are often characterized as *structured, semistructured,* and *unstructured.* In structured interviewing, each informant is asked the same prepared questions in the same order. In semistructured interviewing, the questions and their order are varied according to the interviewer's judgment as to how to obtain the most useful information. In unstructured interviewing, there is no reference to interview protocols.

Qualitative interviewing is typically semistructured to allow for flexible use of prepared protocols, maximizing opportunity for both focused and emergent information gathering. Structured interviews are generally too limiting for progressive focusing, and unstructured interviews are usually reserved for situations where preparation of a protocol in advance is not possible. While semistructured interviewing is the most useful because it offers both focus and flexibility, it may also be the most demanding. The semistructured interviewer must record data while adjusting the wording and order of questions, maintaining rapport, preserving focus, and assessing and following up on conversational leads that may yield unexpected information by developing new questions on the spot.

Questions should be devised that call for explanations rather than simple answers, that are not leading, that are clear, and that are focused on information needs. For maximum informational value, different *interview protocols,* or lists of questions to be asked, are needed for different groups; for example, different questions for program managers and program beneficiaries, for students and teachers, for dam engineers and homeowners displace by damming.

To be sure that questions are comprehensible and answerable, protocols need to be carefully developed and field-tested in advance by trying out interview questions with groups similar to the interviewees, then refining questions before the evaluation interviewing begins in earnest.

Focus Groups, Group Interviews. Interviews may be conducted as individual or group sessions, the latter sometimes borrowing the term **focus groups** from marketing. More information may be gained in a shorter time with group interviews, especially as members of the group respond to each other as well as to an interviewer's questions. Participants may sharpen the focus or may take it in highly informative and unanticipated directions. In responding to each other as well as to the interviewer, they may deepen the discussion, add helpful detail, and correct each other in a manner that improves the accuracy of the data set.

However, group interviews are more difficult to arrange and manage. In some cases, the intended focus may be lost unless the interviewer is insistently directive, which can undermine rapport. Candor may be more difficult to elicit or assess with group interviews than with individual interviews, where concentration on a single individual allows appreciation of tone and nonverbal signals. In group situations, there may be social status or power issues unknown to the interviewer but clear to the interviewees, inhibiting some speakers and encouraging others. Loquacious participants may monopolize discussion, while others are silenced. Reticence is difficult to decipher; it may suggest restrained personalities, cultural conditions, the sensitivity of the issues being discussed, or status differentials.

Audio Recording. As with observation, detailed data are needed from interviews. Exact quotations must be recorded to support experientiality and exactness in reports. An interviewer may choose to take notes and write them up immediately afterward or to audiotape an interview

---

Box 12.4   Using Focus Groups to Analyze Factors Affecting Women's Use of Public Transport in Lima, Peru

---

As part of an international program to promote pilot projects and studies to increase women's access to transport, an evaluation was conducted in Lima, Peru, on women's experience with different types of transport, including buses, taxis, and bicycles. A series of focus groups was combined with participant observation in buses and taxis. In some focus groups, all participants were of the same sex and age group, whereas others mixed the sexes. Focus groups with women revealed that sexual harassment on buses was one of the main reasons that women did not like to use public transport and why some parents would not allow their daughters to attend university. When young men participated in an all-male group, they tended to downplay the importance of sexual harassment, but when they participated in mixed groups, they recognized the seriousness of harassment. Participant observation proved an effective way to obtain material that was used to stimulate discussion in the focus groups.

SOURCE: http://siteresources.worldbank.org/INTGENDERTRANSPORT/Resources/G_T_ReportMain.pdf

and transcribe the tape. Video recording of interviews may be too complicated and intrusive. Both taping and note taking introduce artificiality into a conversation, necessitating careful efforts to build and maintain rapport. Taping is also subject to technical difficulties and may be more likely to elicit cautious or stilted responses. For ethical reasons, interviewees should be offered opportunity to decline audio-taping.

Recording group interview data is particularly demanding. Because verbal interchanges overlap, note taking demands greater haste. If tape recording, identification of speakers may be obscured. An evaluator may find it helpful to take notes and also tape-record discussion. It may be even more helpful to have a colleague take notes and operate a tape recorder as the interviewer asks questions from the protocol and devises follow-up questions.

Cultural Competence and Sensitivity. Interviewing may require more cultural sensitivity and competence than observations because the interviewer must interact with the participant. A number of cautions apply. Where language is a significant barrier, translators may be required. Unfortunately, there may be no way to ensure exact translations either because of differences between languages or because of the translator's judgment about phrasing and about what is appropriate to convey. Even where language is not a barrier, cultural differences may prevent the evaluator from fully comprehending the nuances and implications of the information from an interviewee. Access to reliable key informants or teaming with a local participant, with whom the evaluator can later debrief, can help ensure (but not guarantee) accuracy in documentation and analysis.

Analysis of Documents and Artifacts

Documentary and artifactual data include texts, photographs, and other tangible items from the site that are collected and analyzed as data. Review of documents and other artifacts of material culture provides a relatively unobtrusive method for gaining information and may offer information unavailable from other types of data sources. For example, documents such as meeting minutes or journals and artifacts such as photographs and artworks may provide information about occurrences prior to the arrival of the evaluator. In some instances, documents and artifacts may offer better or more data than other sources or may do so more easily, unobtrusively, quickly, or cheaply.

As with other types of qualitative data, documents and artifacts include the perspectives and bias of their human creators. Each item must be considered for its **authenticity**, accuracy, and informativeness—which may be difficult to determine or verify—and treated accordingly. In some cases, the relevance, representativeness, completeness, or the meaning of a document may make it more informative than an observation or interview; in other cases, relevance or authenticity may be uncertain. Documents provided in response to evaluator requests may be selected such that only the most favorable are offered. Confirmation of accuracy should be checked against information collected from other sources and by other methods (see also Chapter 11, p. 246, on assessing the usefulness of documents).

Indicators, Statistics, Preexisting and Unobtrusive Measures. Analysis of documents and artifacts allows the evaluator to take advantage of existing information, improving the efficiency of the evaluation and reducing cost and effort. Available documentary sources vary by programs and types of programs. For example:

Educational program documents and artifacts

- Content and performance standards
- Curricula
- Lesson plans
- Samples of student work, including academic and artwork
- Student test scores
- Individual education plans (IEPs) or learning contracts
- Proportions of student populations regarding ethnicity and gender
- Student disciplinary and adjudication records
- Student poverty and free lunch eligibility
- Statements of purpose and mission
- Minutes of meetings
- Educational attainment of personnel
- Personnel allocations and distributions
- School accreditation and evaluation
- Funding levels, sources, and expenditures
- Laws and regulations pertaining to education

Social program documents and artifacts

- Statements of purposes, goals, and objectives
- Reports to funding agencies, government agencies, stakeholders, communities
- Documentation of program changes over time
- Databases and records
- Indicators of program accessibility and use
- Frequency of types of goods or services provided and to whom
- Procedural requirements
- Personnel schematics, records, allocations, and compensation
- Ethnicity of personnel, beneficiaries, and other stakeholders
- Indicators of affluence and poverty
- Minutes of meetings
- Training records
- Funding sources, budgets, and expenditures
- Professional standards for programs of the same type
- Legal and regulatory requirements
- Relevant judicial proceedings

Not all documents and artifacts are equally accessible. Some documents are legally protected against invasions of privacy, and others are restricted because they are classified or proprietary. The existence of some documents or artifacts may not be readily perceived or, even if they are, readily provided. Repeated requests may be required.

Journals and Other Self-Report Documents. Although all data should be analyzed critically, self-report documents especially require a healthy skepticism. Participants naturally want to present themselves and their work favorably. Their self-presentations and their choices of what to share should be checked against other data to take into account any inaccurately rosy glows. Caution applies both to self-initiated records and those that an evaluator may request participants to keep and submit.

Documents such as students' Individualized Educational Plans (IEPs) are legally protected to ensure privacy. Some other documents require special sensitivity because they may contain personal or confidential information. Participants sharing documents such as personal expense accounts, travel records, and training logs are not always aware that their cooperativeness may expose them to risk. Diaries and personal journals are particularly likely to expose vulnerabilities. It is sometimes ethically necessary for an evaluator to be more protective of participants than they themselves are.

Hybrid Qualitative Data Collection Methods

Qualitative data collection methods are amenable to an endless variety of adaptations. Purposeful modifications suited to particular program and evaluation circumstances help ensure the completeness and accuracy of the data. For example, the analysis of documents and artifacts may include **bibliometrics** to indicate the scholarly impact of a program by documenting the number of citations and publications of program products and descriptions. Technology also opens new data collection opportunities, as do hybrid amalgams of familiar methods and other innovative techniques.

Video-Stimulated Interviews

One type of hybrid technique is the video-stimulated interview. With the permission of those observed, a montage of video clips may stimulate focus group discussion of critical, typical, or ambiguous program events. Development of protocols for semistructured interviewing, at least as backup conversation starters, may be useful accompaniments. As participants are asked to describe or interpret the activities they view on the screen, differences in their reactions can surface the diversity of personnel or stakeholder views and aims. When used with focus groups, video-stimulated interviews may elicit deep discussion of different perspectives and meanings.

For example, imagine the analytic usefulness of having program directors, then service providers, then beneficiaries separately view and discuss video clips of interactive program processes. The beneficiaries might comment on the adequacy and real availability of services, service providers might explain difficulties in delivering services and ongoing problem solving, and program directors might discuss the relationship between overall goals and progress to date. These different perspectives might be very helpful for evaluators working to understand and interpret program outcomes.

Other purposes and types of understanding might be gained. Video clips of activities at different program sites might inform program managers about consistencies (or inconsistencies) in procedures and the effects of different contexts. Before-and-after scenes might clarify program progress and accomplishment for evaluators and stakeholders. A videotape from program sites and nonprogram or control sites might do the same, although viewers from nonprogram sites might become demoralized by seeing benefits not available to themselves or galvanized to demand similar services.

Video-stimulated interviews blur the distinction between observation and interview. Interviewees become co-observers, in a sense. Video-stimulated interviews also blur the distinction between data collection and analysis. While the comments and responses of interviewees constitute interview data, they also constitute participants' analyses of the interactions they observe on video.

Think-Aloud Interviews

Think-aloud or cognitive interviews similarly blend observation and interview. This technique calls for a subject to vocalize his or her thoughts while engaged in a task, such as using a computer to process or record program information, and for these vocalizations to be documented by a data collector. The evaluator could be seen as conducting an observation focused on a participant at task, or he or she could be seen as conducting an interview with one question: "Can you tell me what you are thinking as you do that?"

Think-aloud interviews provide insight into an individual's cognitive and metacognitive processing, decision making, and rationales. However, a caution is needed: Vocalizing while at task is not natural, ordinary behavior, which analysis of think-aloud data should take into account.

Arts-Based Research Methods

Qualitative methodology is useful for penetrating the tacit knowledge drawn from experience and existing at a subliminal level, things participants know but find difficult to articulate. Arts activities also elicit personal understandings not easily shared otherwise and manifest them. This conceptual linkage between qualitative methods and arts processes suggests opportunities for adapting arts processes in data collection, even for evaluations of non-arts programs.

Arts-based data collection procedures include use of images, drawing, music, metaphors, and other expressive modes to capture tacit knowledge. Participants might be asked to draw, select photographs, or mold clay and then to explain the meaning—relative to the program being evaluated—of their creations or selections. For example:

- Students might be asked to act out taking a high-stakes test (e.g., drinking coffee to stay alert, snoring).
- Personnel might be asked to sing a song that describes working relationships (e.g., "I get by with a little help from my friends" by the Beatles, "I can't get no satisfaction" by the Rolling Stones).
- Beneficiaries might be asked to select pictures or cartoons that indicate relative access to program goods or services (e.g., a long queue extending from a doorway, a whites-only drinking fountain).
- Managers might be asked to represent their experiences by drawing (e.g., a faucet that barely drips, an unscalable castle).

Subsequent discussion may get at experiences and perceptions not otherwise available to researchers and may reveal deep personal meanings relevant to the program.

Technology in Data Collection

Technology opens new data collection opportunities such as observation of interactions in virtual space, interviews by phone, videoconference, or e-mail, or on Web-based surveys, online documents, and asynchronous discussion.

Observation in Virtual Reality. In contrast to observation of ordinary events, interactions in virtual space occur by typing messages into a computer keyboard and transmitting them electronically. Messages in discussion threads document word-for-word the transmissions themselves. The online observer reads the text and simultaneously captures the activities as they happen.

This type of data collection may be especially important when the programs to be evaluated are online, such as distance education, Web-based training programs, and electronic referral and service delivery. As these programs proliferate, especially where potential participants are geographically dispersed but have access to computers and the Internet, program managers and consumers increasingly want to know about their quality.

Interview by Electronic Mail. Where face-to-face interviews cannot be conducted and electronic means are available, telephone or e-mail interviews may be useful. Both come with caveats. Telephone interviews, in contrast to in-person interviews, deprive the interviewer of opportunities to develop rapport, critical for gaining enough trust to ensure honest answers, and eliminate opportunities to observe nonverbal indications of meaning. Even more, e-mail interviews, convenient because the data are written up by the interviewee at the time they are collected, lack spontaneity. Because they allow the interviewee to revise responses, the data may be skewed by overediting, posturing, obfuscation, or other distortions. On the other hand, assuming that the respondent initiates the phone call (which is often not the case), phone interviews do give the interviewee the opportunity to respond when he or she feels ready to, with less real-time pressure and the possibility to more carefully craft his or her reply than might be the case with a spontaneous verbal response. This is somewhat similar to a respondent filling out a questionnaire.

Quality in Qualitative Data Collection

In an important sense, the quality of an evaluation rests on the validity of the findings—whether reports support adequate and appropriate inferences and actions regarding the program and participants (adapted from Messick 1989). Quality in qualitative evaluation is primarily about whether findings are empirically warranted, not about whether the evaluator has strictly adhered to prescribed procedures. In emergent design, procedures cannot be fully prescribed at the outset. Lacking procedural guarantees of quality, qualitative practitioners seek substantive assurances. Using evidence drawn from multiple subjective data sources and perspectives, these assurances are rarely clear and unequivocal, especially since the evaluator's subjectivity tends to work against credibility. Unfortunately, even when an evaluation supports valid inferences of program quality, it may not be credible to stakeholders. Both validity and credibility are needed to promote use of findings.

As stakeholders do, evaluators construct unique, irreplicable interpretations of program quality. The diversity of interpretive possibilities raises not only problems of consensus and closure but also of validity and credibility. Even to recognize critical program aspects and outcomes involves subjective filtering through prior experience and personal values. The obvious emphasis on human judgment in qualitative inquiry, which is less obvious but also operating in quantitative inquiry (Johnson and Onwuegbuzie 2004), opens possibilities not only for understanding but also for misunderstanding and for misinterpretation and misrepresentation. Practices that help ensure quality include triangulation, validation, peer review, and meta-evaluation.

Traditional science, with its search for value-free objective knowledge, implies a challenge as to whether valid inferences of program quality can be founded on such subjective ways of knowing. It is less subjectivity itself and more its implications for accuracy and bias that generate concern about the potential mischief of subjective judgment. Qualitative practitioners are likely to respond that human ways of knowing are necessarily subjective, that a subjective mind is all anyone has, that what is important in evaluation is **trustworthiness** (Lincoln and Guba 1985) with emphasis on *descriptive validity, interpretive validity,* and *evaluative validity* (Maxwell 1992). Appendix 1 includes an "Integrated Checklist for Assessing the Adequacy and Validity of Quantitative, Qualitative, and Mixed-Method Designs." Drawing on the work of Lincoln and Guba (1985) as well as later work in the same tradition (Miles and Huberman 1994; Yin 2003), the checklist includes five categories for assessing the validity and adequacy of QUAL evaluation designs: (a) confirmability and objectivity; (b) reliability and dependability; (c) internal validity, credibility, and authenticity; (d) external validity, transferability, and fittingness; and (e) utilization, application, and action orientation. The application of the checklist is discussed in Chapter 7.

While qualitative practitioners are more frequently subject to challenge, both qualitative and quantitative methods are susceptible to certain kinds of inaccuracies. *Methodological bias* is always a concern because "there are no procedures that will regularly (or always) yield either sound data or true conclusions" (Phillips 1987:21). All data sets are biased by decisions about what to observe or count, how to categorize, what to record, and how to interpret. Both QUAL and QUANT evaluations are susceptible to **clientism,** the positive skewing of evaluation results to secure the professional and financial rewards bestowed by happy clients. Qualitative reports may be especially endangered by the more personal interactions between data collectors and data providers.

Triangulation

Program quality should not, of course, be based on unsubstantiated opinion or a few site visits where the evaluator may observe nonrepresentative interactions, either innocent or planned. Triangulation, crucial to protecting against invalidity, involves deliberate attempts to confirm, elaborate, and disconfirm facts and interpretations through reference to the following:

- Multiple data sources
- Multiple methods of data collection
- Multiple evaluators or data collectors
- Repeated observations over time
- Multiple analytic perspectives

For example, the qualitative evaluator will need to confirm information from an interview through direct observation of the events noted by the interviewee, through interviews of others, and through documentary evidence of the events and the pattern of their occurrence. In this way, the descriptive validity of the data from the interview may be determined.

Triangulation tends not merely to confirm or disconfirm information but also to elaborate and complicate a data set. Imagine that an evaluator interviewed a teacher who reported that the training she received regarding a new reading program piloted in her school was working well in helping her encourage students to read. Data from her interview might corroborate interview data collected from the trainer and principal, who had previously attested to the success of the reading program. This would be an example of triangulation by data source, showing an effort to elicit multiple perspectives regarding the program and confirmation of information from one source through information from another. Imagine that, triangulating by method, the evaluator also observed the teacher's classroom each Tuesday morning for a month, where he saw that some students consistently selected reading as a voluntary activity but that others did not, even that some increasingly resisted the teacher's encouragements to read. The observation data documenting some students reading more would tend to confirm the interview data from the teacher and others, but the observation data documenting the increasing resistance of some students would disconfirm the interview reports suggesting the general effectiveness of the reading program. Imagine that observations in the classrooms of the 30 teachers participating in the pilot program showed a range of student willingness to read and that 2 teachers of 30 reported dissatisfaction with the program and suspicion that their colleagues spoke glowingly of the program in the hope of continuing to receive free books.

In this example and in the real world, the evaluator cannot merely consider the preponderance of the evidence. If he or she did in this case, the 2 less positive teachers' interview data would be far outweighed by that of the 28 other teachers, principal, and trainer. Consideration of the possibility of vested interests and the mixed evidence of the observations might convincingly suggest a lower level of program success than did the interview data. The evaluator should also consider that observations at regularly scheduled times might have elicited uncharacteristically pro-reading behaviors (recorded as inaccurately positive data) than if observations had occurred on an unannounced, drop-in basis. In this analysis, triangulation would support the evaluator in navigating through data that might ultimately contribute to a finding that the reading program was less successful than most informants indicated, counteracting positive bias in one part of the data set.

Validation

Validation involves checking with informants about the accuracy of the recorded data and the reasonableness of the interpretations drawn from it (see Box 12.5). The most common validation techniques are member checking and comprehensive individual validation. *Member checking* is the review of data and interpretations by a gathering of persons representing relevant stakeholders (Lincoln and Guba 1985). A more comprehensive process involves validation by each informant, first of relatively uninterpreted data that he or she has provided (such as an interview transcript or an observation write-up) and later of a draft of the report that includes the selected presentation and interpretation of data (Mabry 1998).

Drafts of reports may be submitted to diverse audiences, selected on the bases of expertise and confidentiality, to try to ensure "getting it right" (Geertz 1973:29). The scope of distribution of the draft should reflect sensitivity to ethics and politics, including matters such as possible need to protect informants' identities or to avoid premature distribution of tentative interpretations subject to change. Also, validation may occur informally by opening conversational opportunities for participants to react to some data or to ideas about its meaning.

Peer Review and Meta-Evaluation

In addition to review by program participants and internal review by the evaluation team, critical review by evaluation colleagues and external substantive experts, working either

---

Box 12.5   Examples of Requests for Comprehensive Validation

Example 1: Interview validation—a request included at the beginning of an interview data write-up sent to the interviewee:

Thank you for your participation in the evaluation. Please review for completeness and accuracy this write-up of your interview. Pseudonyms have been substituted for real names. If this narrative is used in future reports, additional care will be taken to avoid identification of you or anyone you named. Suggested corrections and additions would be welcome. Please contact (phone and e-mail listed here).

Example 2: Validation of state profile and narrative drawn from interview and documentary data—a cover letter:

Greetings!

As you know, we have been working to learn about state-mandated performance assessments from across the county for three years. We are now requesting a review of two brief summaries. We fully understand that state personnel are very busy, and we are working hard to limit to bare bones the amount of time we need from you. We have thoroughly reviewed all interview information and documents sent to us, and we have visited Web sites to minimize our data requests.

Enclosed please find a state performance assessment profile and a state narrative. Please check these for accuracy. If the profiles and narratives are accurate, please let us know via e-mail. If any corrections or updates are needed, please e-mail, fax, or mail corrections to us, or indicate corrections or new information on the profile. We respectfully request a response by May 13, at which time we will begin follow-up telephone calls.

---

individually or as professional panels, may be used to bolster validity and credibility. **Meta-evaluation,** the evaluation of an evaluation, is advisable, especially where evaluation findings may have substantial public impact. In situations where full-scale meta-evaluation would strain fiscal resources, other types of collegial review may not only counterbalance the subjectivity of the evaluator but also invigorate analysis. Technical advisory panels may monitor and assess an evaluation's quality, providing ongoing checks and critique during report drafting. Informally, too, colleagues may serve as critical friends as they listen, read, comment, argue, suggest, advise.

Qualitative Data Collection under RealWorld Constraints

Ideally, the ethnographic style of qualitative approaches requires more time and, consequently, larger budgets than evaluators are typically allocated in the real world. Moreover, these approaches put evaluators in closer contact with people serving as data sources, enlarging the possibility of political and cultural difficulties. Fortunately, these challenges are not insurmountable.

Data and Political Constraints

By nature, much qualitative data are more sensitive and personal than quantitative data. While surveys can be administered to more people in a shorter time (breadth), interviews probe for more information from fewer individuals (depth). Interviewees are more exposed to the evaluator and may feel uncomfortable for a variety of reasons, including cultural, linguistic, age-related, gender-related, and political reasons. Interviewees who are less than fully forthcoming, even with good or understandable justification, obstruct data collection. Following are suggested ways of approaching data and political constraints, common in the real-world settings of evaluation (see also Chapters 5 and 6 for further discussion):

- *Interpreters, translators, or guides* as members of the local community may help smooth access, helping ensure that data can be collected and that the data collected represent the actual intents or experiences of informants. If familiar or native-speaking persons have—or can be trained to have—interviewing skills, budget constraints may be simultaneously addressed. However, interpreters, especially those arranged or recommended by clients or community groups, may have ties to stakeholders that potentially complicate their role as impartial intermediaries. Also, without an evaluator's awareness, a community-based interpreter may explain what he or she thinks rather than simply translating the questions and answers. An evaluator should be aware of these openings for inaccuracy in the data set and attempt, to the extent possible, to detect them.
- *Authority figures,* either program officers or funding officers, may help ensure quality of information by directing personnel (and perhaps beneficiaries) to provide full access to data, even data that may have potential for embarrassment. On the other hand, passive resistance may nonetheless persist and may be difficult to detect. Especially with informants who may have something to lose from negative evaluation findings, an evaluator should be alert for subtle obstruction.
- *Conditions for collecting data from individuals,* especially interviewees, may be arranged to maximize their comfort and willingness to share information. For example, teachers might be interviewed away from school, persons seeking loans for cottage industries in locations where loan officers are not present, irrigation workers out of sight of their supervisors. Discomfort cannot always be dispelled, but sensitivity to reticence and unease may help an evaluator frame more successful questions or realize the usefulness of an offer to turn off a tape recorder.
- *Repeated observations* may help those observed to see the observer as unthreatening, an ordinary part of the scene, or may overwhelm the ability of those observed to maintain unnatural behaviors over time. Obtaining permission for unannounced, drop-in observations helps to minimize observer effects clouding data and findings.

An evaluator alert to signs of discomfort or unnatural behavior that might indicate political pressures may be better able to obtain and analyze the meaning of data.

Time and Budget Constraints

Two RWE constraints dog most qualitative work: time and budget. Spending enough time in the field to develop deep understanding is expensive. The travel, lodging, meals, and supplies necessary for fieldwork cost real money in the real world. Some strategies for conserving time add to budget woes, and some strategies for saving money require finding more time. When an evaluator's time is limited, others can be hired to collect data or, when budget is limited, fewer but longer trips can be made to the evaluation site or sites. To deal with both limited time and limited budget, which often occur together, the evaluator may find the following strategies helpful:

- *Request documents in advance.* Documents indicating program goals, such as program proposals and mission statements, and documents indicating progress to date, such as progress reports and newspaper accounts, may save interview time on site. The same is true for documentation of budgets, expenditures, and beneficiaries. Lists of personnel with contact information may help identify the most important data sources for prioritization.
- *Check electronic resources.* Increasingly, information is available online. Many programs have informative Web sites publicly available on the Internet. These may provide useful orientation that allows the evaluator to ask more focused questions in interviews on site or to identify the essential program activities to be observed.
- *Interview in advance using mail, telephone, or electronic mail.* Time on site and travel expenses may be reduced if some information can be obtained prior to the site visit using mail, telephone, or electronic mail. Triangulation and confirmation after arrival may be less time-consuming than beginning data collection from scratch on-site. Key informants and important events to be observed may be identified in advance, again saving time in situ.
- *Develop a site visit protocol.* From information gathered in advance, progressive focusing may occur before arrival. It may be possible to state hypotheses or preliminary interpretations that can be checked out on site. Site protocols that optimize data collection time may be developed.
- *Use assistants.* Less costly personnel, provided they have needed skills, may help with budget constraints. Local personnel may be especially helpful because of their experience of the context, although identifying them and their skills may be more difficult to do in advance.
- *Follow-up off-site.* Triangulation of some data may be completed after returning from the evaluation site. For example, in reviewing or analyzing some interview or observation data after a site visit, confirmatory telephone calls or electronic mail may be useful.

As the processes of triangulation and validation suggest, all data should be treated with skepticism until confirmed. This is certainly true of advance information that the evaluator will need to check against other data sources, especially his or her own first-hand observations.

Qualitative methods have been adapted as rapid assessment, rapid appraisal, quick **ethnography,** and rapid rural appraisal (see Chapters 3 and 5) for use in developing countries to address budget and time constraints. Unfortunately, most of these approaches give too little consideration to questions of validity to satisfy RWE validity criteria. There are many evaluations scenarios where time is of the essence and the assessment of the trade-offs between time, quality, and validity is an area requiring further research. Emergency situations such as civil war, epidemics, and natural disasters sometimes require evaluations conducted under considerable time pressure and severely limited access to data[3] (Roche 1999).

Qualitative Data Analysis

Qualitative findings are developed *inductively* from data. Nonnumeric qualitative data preclude statistical analysis. Rather, qualitative analysis is substantive, involving identification of patterns in the data from which understandings must be developed and interpretations constructed. Expansionist qualitative data are often both voluminous and ambiguous, sometimes overwhelmingly so. Moreover, the best descriptions of the interpretive process are rather nebulous, not a clear series of steps. Gaining understanding has been compared with reading and interpreting a complicated text, an intuitive process of grasping complexities and searching for meaning.

Qualitative interpretation is also *holistic*. Little attention is devoted to isolating and measuring decontextualized variables because the program is viewed as a complex tapestry of interwoven, interdependent threads, too many and too embedded to extract meaningfully. Numerical indicators are seen as merely indicating and, without care and triangulation, possibly distorting more than they reveal.

Qualitative analysis involves *intuitive* understanding. Noting that "judgments often involve multidimensional criteria and conflicting interests," House (1994), among others, has advised, "The evaluator should strive to reduce biases in making such judgments" (p. 15). But one's own biases can be difficult to recognize, much less reduce. Having accepted that objectivity is unattainable, qualitative practitioners use their subjective capacity to understand and also try hard to discipline their subjectivity so that it does not undermine accuracy. In this effort, triangulation, validation, and meta-evaluation are strong allies.

Thematic Content Analysis

Thematic analysis involves macro- and micro-examination of the data and identification of emergent patterns and themes, both broad-brush and fine-grained. Microreview of data promotes recognition of the importance of details that may have been barely noticed during data collection, identification of relationships between data and themes, and discovery of patterns and consistencies. Data are reorganized by emergent themes. Interpretations, triangulated across methods, and sources to enhance validity are derived from detailed data, layers, and patterns of lived and reported experience.

The process of thematic analysis often involves reading and rereading the entire data set several times, each time marking points of interest and gradually grouping them into themes. An abbreviated example is shown here:

Observation Data

- Grade 3 math lesson, Sept. 10
- Grade 3 math lesson, Oct. 15
- Grade 3 math lesson, Nov. 8
- Grade 3 math lesson, Dec. 12
- Grade 4 reading lesson, Sept. 14
- Grade 4 reading lesson, Oct. 10

Interview Data

- School principal, individual interview, Oct. 5
- Grade 3 math teachers, focus group, Dec. 4
- Grade 4 reading teachers, focus group, Dec. 5
- Grade 3 math students, focus group 1, Nov. 14
- Grade 3 math students, focus group 2, Nov. 14

Documentary Data

- State math curriculum
- State reading curriculum
- District math standards
- School math achievement test scores
- Grade records for each teacher
- Math lesson plans, Grade 3, Teacher 1 . . .

In rereading, the identification and articulation of themes is refined. More rereading is needed to identify all data related to each theme that emerges as an important strand for analysis and reporting. Data organized chronologically by method is reorganized by themes recognized through reading and rereading the data. For example:

Theme 1: Alignment of teaching with state math curriculum

State math curriculum: major and minor emphases

District math standards: similarities and disparities with state emphases

Grade 3 math lesson, Sept. 10: similarities and disparities with standards

Grade 3 math lesson, Oct. 15: similarities and disparities with standards

Grade 3 math lesson, Nov. 8: similarities and disparities with standards

Grade 3 math lesson, Dec. 12: similarities and disparities with standards

Math lesson plans, Grade 3, Teacher 1 . . .

Theme 2: Differential student achievement in math and reading

School math achievement test scores: compared with external expectations

School reading achievement test scores: compared with math scores

Grade records for each teacher

Theme 3: Local resistance to state mandate

State math curriculum: major and minor emphases

District math standards: similarities and disparities with state emphases

School principal, individual interview, Oct. 5: attitudes and justifications

Grade 3 math teachers, focus group, Dec. 4: attitudes and justifications

Grade 4 reading teachers, focus group, Dec. 5: attitudes and justifications

Grade 3 math lesson, Sept. 10: similarities and disparities with expectations

Grade 3 math lesson, Oct. 15: similarities and disparities with expectations

Grade 3 math lesson, Nov. 8: similarities and disparities with expectations

Grade 3 math lesson, Dec. 12: similarities and disparities with expectations

Math lesson plans, Grade 3, Teacher 1 . . .

Thematic analysis requires minute attention to both detail and holistic implications in the data. The reading and rereading is not just a coding or categorization activity; it is inductive minds-on analysis. Careful thematic analysis of content in qualitative data, often voluminous and sometimes ambiguous in meaning, requires complex thinking and substantial time. It is often complicated but improved by discussion with engaged colleagues whose interpretive judgments are likely to refine as well as expand the interpretive possibilities.

Constant-Comparative Method

In constant-comparative method (Glaser and Strauss 1967), data and preliminary interpretations are constantly compared with each other. Each preliminary interpretation requires confirmation, disconfirmation, and further warranting. New data are compared with preliminary interpretations, then revised, and the process repeats. The process is like an ongoing dialogue between incoming data and preliminary interpretations, a cycle that discovers many meanings and gradually closes in on accurate descriptions and valid interpretations.

Constant-comparative method was originally considered a process of inductive analysis of data for developing theory grounded in data. In practice, qualitative practitioners rarely begin with a plan to develop theory or grand generalizations. Local understandings are more relevant and desirable. For qualitative evaluators, the goal is grounded interpretations of program quality.

Program Theory and Theoretical Triangulation

Qualitative inquiry is not generally undertaken for the purpose of developing theory, but theory may emerge inductively, or existing theory may be extended or challenged by qualitative findings. Data are not considered illustrations or confirmations of external theories but may serve as building blocks for them. *Theoretical triangulation* (Denzin 1989), or examining the program through different theoretical lenses, may spur deeper understanding and may surface rival interpretations of quality. For example, the interpretation of the quality of an educational program might be quite different if the program were viewed from a standards-based perspective, where implementation of content standards and achievement of performance standards were important, or from a Deweyan (Dewey 1916) progressive education perspective, where student motivation and engagement in meaningful, real-world activities were more important.

Although in general, external theories are not the a priori impetus for qualitative study, not focal but instrumental to interpretation, program theory is an exception. Not external to programs, program theories are models (or **logic models**) describing how programs are expected to produce intended outcomes. Program theories, usually offered in diagrams, identify program goals and components, showing the expected contribution of each. The program theory, which may be developed with clients and perhaps other stakeholders, helps focus data collection and may, in constant-comparative fashion, be refined by it. Qualitative evaluation may involve program theory built from (or grounded in) data or concentrate on deep understanding without explicit reference to theory.

Rival lenses for interpreting data from different theoretical vantage points compound the expansionist tendencies of qualitative data collection and contrast with the data reduction strategies common to quantitative analysis. For example, a program might be considered in terms of its program theory, looking to see whether procedures and components actually do generate intended outcomes and whether there are also any negative unintended outcomes. The program might also be considered in terms of Stufflebeam's (1987) CIPP model, examining *c*ontext, *i*nput, *p*rocess, and *p*roduct. Finally, it might also be considered in terms of Bronfenbrenner's (1979) ecological analysis, scrutinizing the reciprocal effects of the ideological exosystem, policy macrosystem, mesosystem of working relationships, and microsystem of practices and interactions. Analysis from each perspective would emphasize and reveal different aspects about the program and different interpretations that, when juxtaposed, could deepen understanding.

Criteriality (Judging Programs against Criteria)

In some evaluations, programs are judged against criteria. The criteria may be prespecified and external—for example, in accreditation reviews where programs are judged against the criteria of the accrediting body—or the criteria may be prespecified but created specifically for the program to be evaluated—for example, by evaluators in consultation with clients. In other cases, the criteria may emerge during the course of the evaluation, as evaluators recognize critical components or performance requirements. In still other evaluations, program quality may be determined without reference to formal or articulated criteria and explained in terms of processes and outcomes.

One often-stated purpose of criterial strategies, the juxtaposition of program outcomes against explicit standards or criteria, is the avoidance of subjective bias. However, the objectivity conferred by standards and criteria is illusory, because they themselves manifest the subjective biases of their developers. Qualitative practitioners tend to recognize this. They also tend to be skeptical of presumptions that all relevant criteria can be identified in advance and to be concerned that preordinate criteria will skew focus away from actual program aspects and contexts. When preordinate criteria focus an evaluation, data collection and analysis will emphasize them, ensuring attention to some program aspects at the expense of others. In this way, rather than eliminating bias, a criterial approach to analysis will inject bias systematically during the evaluation process.

The qualitative perspective is that each program is complex, too intricate and contextual to be accurately rendered by comparison with a few criteria, and unique, so singular that superimposing common criteria amounts to fitting the proverbial square pegs into round holes. Instead, programs are generally evaluated on the basis of their discernible merits and shortcomings.

Time-Sensitive Data Analysis

Prioritizing among data analysis strategies can help the RealWorld evaluator working under time constraints. Following are some ideas for incorporating data analysis into the data collection timeline.

Ongoing Analysis

Constant-comparative methods (Glaser and Strauss 1967; Strauss and Corbin 1990, 1994) suggest a means of ongoing data analysis that can be augmented to save postdata collection time. Constructing data summaries at regular intervals during data collection is one way of ensuring and recording ongoing data analysis. Summaries might take the form of periodic (e.g., weekly or monthly) reflections. Where evaluation teams are deployed, summaries can be written by team members individually for central collation and sharing or recorded during discussion at end-of-day/week debriefings or end-of-week/month analytic discussions.

Where program theory is used to focus an evaluation and represent the program, it may be possible to conserve time by hypothesizing a program theory in advance and using it as a stimulus for interviews. After offering the tentative program theory to interviewees, their ideas and experiences can be used to modify it, making it more reflective of the actual program. This ongoing development of what might be called *evolving grounded program theory* would function as a type of analysis folded into data collection.

Report-and-Respond Forms

Another type of ongoing data analysis is available through report-and-respond forms (Stronach, Allan, and Morris 1996), a technique that offers simultaneous opportunity for data collection, multivocal analysis, and validation of preliminary interpretations. In a report-and-respond form, the evaluator offers brief data summaries and statements of preliminary interpretation to selected stakeholders for their input. Respondents revise or rewrite the statements to better represent their experiences and understandings of the program being evaluated.

Because the interpretations stated on report-and-respond forms are tentative, broad dissemination of premature statements should be avoided. Evaluators should select respondents carefully, perhaps in consultation with clients, and should clearly identify information on the forms as an intermediate rather than final stage in the development of findings.

Summary

- *Qualitative methodology* is a general term for a family of approaches that shares a view of a program as an intricate composite of stakeholders' perceptions and experiences. QUAL practitioners seek an insiders (*emic*) understanding rather than an outsiders (*etic*) understanding. Prolonged engagement in the field provides opportunities to recognize patterns of behavior, themes, and meanings.

- In a process known as *emergent design*, qualitative research questions and plans are revised during data collection as stakeholder experiences are documented and better understood.

- The main methods of data collection include observation, interview, and analysis of documents and artifacts. Variations of these basic methods include video-simulated interviews, think-aloud interviews, and arts-based research methods.

- A number of methods are used to ensure quality and validity. These include triangulation, validation (checking with informants on the accuracy of the data and the reasonableness of the interpretation of findings), peer review, and meta-evaluation.

- Ideally, qualitative methods require more time and budget than may be available in real-world circumstances. However, there are strategies that may be helpful in addressing these constraints.

Further Reading

Beebe, J. 2001. *Rapid Assessment Process: An Introduction.* Walnut Creek, CA: Altamira Press.

A clear overview of how to reduce the time required to conduct ethnographic studies of communities, programs, or organizations. Many of the techniques are also useful for reducing costs.

Carter, K. 1993. "The Place of Story in the Study of Teaching and Teacher Education." *Educational Researcher* 22(1):5–12, 18.

This article offers a compelling argument for the complex understandings carried and elicited by narratives in reporting.

Denzin, N. K. 1989. *The Research Act: A Theoretical Introduction to Sociological Methods.* 3d ed. Englewood Cliffs, NJ: Prentice Hall.
Denzin, N. K. 1997. *Interpretive Ethnography: Ethnographic Practices for the 21st Century.* Thousand Oaks, CA: Sage.

These texts explain the use of qualitative methods in the fields of sociology and ethnography in a manner that is readily extrapolated for evaluation. The 1989 text offers a strong presentation on triangulation.

Denzin, N. K. and Y. S. Lincoln. 2000. *Handbook of Qualitative Research.* 2d ed. Thousand Oaks, CA: Sage.

Perhaps the most comprehensive single source on qualitative methodology. Chapters by a wide variety of authors offer detail about many important aspects of qualitative research.

Erickson, F. 1986. "Qualitative Methods in Research on Teaching." Pp. 119–61 in *Handbook of Research on Teaching.* 3d ed., edited by M. C. Wittrock. New York: Macmillan.

An outstanding description of the epistemology, purpose, and methods of qualitative research, this chapter is significant in the field historically as well as substantively. It introduced *petite generalizations,* among other seminal concepts.

Firestone, W. A. 1993. "Alternative Arguments for Generalizing from Data as Applied to Qualitative Research." *Educational Researcher* 22(4):16–23.

This article distinguishes between case-to-population and case-to-case generalizations—the former an expectation in quantitative inquiry, the latter an expectation in qualitative inquiry.

Guba, E. G. and Y. S. Lincoln. 1989. *Fourth Generation Evaluation*. Newbury Park, CA: Sage.

One of the most important textbooks explaining the use of qualitative methodology in evaluation, extending the authors' earlier work on naturalistic inquiry in research.

Handwerker, W. P. 2001. *Quick Ethnography*. Walnut Creek, CA: Altamira Press.

Another clear overview of rapid ethnographic methods with applications to cost reduction.

Lincoln, Y. S. and E. G. Guba. 1985. *Naturalistic Inquiry*. Beverly Hills, CA: Sage.

A landmark in qualitative research and research generally, this text has been influential in a variety of disciplines, including business and education. The authors present a number of terms and ideas that have remained foundational, including *trustworthiness* as preferable to *validity* in understanding quality in qualitative work.

Maxwell, J. A. 1992. "Understanding and Validity in Qualitative Research." *Harvard Educational Review* 62(3):279–300.

This article presents a typology of *descriptive validity, interpretive validity,* and *evaluative validity,* explaining the importance of each.

Maxwell, J. A. 2004. "Causal Explanation, Qualitative Research, and Scientific Inquiry in Education." *Educational Researcher* 33(2):3–11.

Roche, C. 1999. *Impact Assessment for Development Agencies: Learning to Value Change*. Oxford, UK: OXFAM.

An explanation of how qualitative impact evaluation techniques are applied in the field in developing countries. Includes numerous case studies illustrating the application of the different tools and techniques.

Rossman, G. B. and S. F. Rallis. 1998. *Learning in the Field: An Introduction to Qualitative Research*. Thousand Oaks, CA: Sage.

A practical step-by-step guide conducting qualitative research.

Wolcott, H. F. 1994. *Transforming Qualitative Data: Description, Analysis, and Interpretation*. Thousand Oaks, CA: Sage.

Notes

1. See also Chapter 14.

2. In contrast, in QUANT analysis, **contextual variables** such as the economic, political, and institutional environment are sometimes coded as a set of **dummy variables** (e.g., *the local economy is growing* = 1; *the economy is not growing* = 0) that are then incorporated into multivariate analysis to help explain variations in project performance (see Chapter 10).

3. The Active Learning Network for Accountability and Performance (ALNAP) Web site (www.ALNAP.org) is a useful source for many other resources related to the evaluation of humanitarian/emergency response.

CHAPTER 13

Mixed-Method Evaluation

T his chapter reviews **mixed-method designs** that combine quantitative (**QUANT**) and qualitative (**QUAL**) approaches and methods to take advantage of the strengths of each approach and overcome their respective weaknesses when applied separately. We begin by describing the essential characteristics of mixed-method designs and consider when and why they are used. The two main mixed-method designs are then discussed: The first and more widely used is sequential, where QUANT and QUAL approaches are used one after the other; and the second is concurrent, where both approaches are applied at the same time. Distinctions are also made between (a) mixed-method designs in which either a QUAL or QUANT approach is dominant and the other approach is used to complement it and (b) **designs** in which both QUANT and QUAL are given equal weight. The chapter concludes with a discussion of strategies for using mixed-method designs, emphasizing that this requires an integrated approach at all stages of the evaluation, more complex than simply mixing and matching QUANT and QUAL data collection methods.

The Mixed-Method Approach

Mixed-method evaluation involves the planned use of two or more methods of data collection and analysis. Normally, the term is used to refer to designs that combine elements of both QUANT and QUAL approaches. Although many evaluators now routinely use a variety of methods because the field has come to accept the legitimacy of various methodological traditions, "What distinguishes mixed-method evaluation is the intentional or planned use of diverse methods for particular mixed-method purposes using particular mixed-method designs" (Greene 2005:255). Most commonly what are combined are methods of data collection, but it is also possible to combine conceptual frameworks, hypotheses, methods of data analysis, or frameworks for the interpretation of the evaluation **findings**. There are no uniquely mixed-method data collection methods. Instead, what characterizes mixed-method designs is the integration of elements from both QUANT and QUAL approaches.

Because both QUANT and QUAL methodologies, when used alone (*monomethod* approach) are prone to "methods-induced bias" (Johnson and Onwuegbuzie 2004:15), evaluators recognize that mixed-method designs generally produce more comprehensive coverage and more valid findings than either QUANT or QUAL alone. In evaluation, an applied social science, appreciation of mixed methods came early, even before formal articulation and documentation of the methodology. Now, "It is time that methodologists catch up with practicing researchers" (Johnson and Onwuegbuzie 2004:22) and evaluators.

Often, mixed-method evaluation designs have exhibited a dominant QUANT or QUAL orientation, with methods or approaches from the other orientation used to complement, strengthen, or corroborate data and findings. Lincoln and Guba (1985) introduced the notion of **incommensurability,** which has influenced subsequent discussion of the difficulties of trying to integrate different research methods. A number of other authors (e.g., Creswell et al. 2003; Morse 2003) have also cautioned against trying to work with two different evaluation approaches simultaneously:

> Recall that methodological strategies are tools for enquiry and that methods are cohesive collections of strategies that fit a particular perspective. To incorporate a different strategy into a study is risky and should be done with care, lest the core assumptions of the project be violated. Maintaining balance between respecting these assumptions and respecting the assumptions underlying your supplementary strategies is delicate, for they may often clash. (Morse 2003:192)

However, mixed-method designs need not feature a dominant and a secondary or subservient approach. The most powerful application of an integrated, mixed-method approach may well occur when both QUAL and QUANT approaches are used fully and appropriately (Bamberger 2000b; Greene and Caracelli 2003; Mertens 2003).

Rationale for Mixed-Method Approaches

In the two previous chapters, we mentioned what are frequently considered to be the main strengths and weaknesses of QUANT and QUAL approaches (see Table 11.1 for QUANT designs and Table 12.2 for QUAL designs). One of the main reasons for using mixed-method designs is to combine the strengths of QUANT and QUAL while at the same time addressing some of the inherent weaknesses of either monomethod approach. Mixed methods can be applied at any stage of the design, implementation or analysis of an evaluation.

Let us take the example of an evaluation of the effectiveness of rural health centers in reaching low-income and minority sectors of the community, and let us assume that the evaluation will adopt a predominantly QUAL approach. The evaluation team wishes their evaluation to influence national health policies by identifying some of the reasons why poor and minority families do not use the health centers, and they are aware that the Ministry of Health has criticized earlier evaluations for having focused on communities with particular problems so that the findings are not representative of the whole country. Although the evaluators are aware that the ministry has sometimes found this to be a convenient excuse for ignoring valid criticisms, the evaluators want to ensure that their study will not be dismissed on these grounds. Consequently, the evaluation team meets with the National Institute of Statistics and uses their national household sample frame to ensure that the sample of communities they select is broadly representative of the whole country (or the region where the study is conducted). The evaluation uses the same QUAL methods, but it is now possible to indicate that the sample of communities was selected in consultation with the National Institute of Statistics and is considered broadly representative of all communities (in the country or region).

Let us now assume that the same evaluation was to be conducted by a different team that was planning to use a QUANT approach based on a nationally representative household sample survey. They are concerned that although a well-designed survey may obtain reasonably reliable estimates of the proportion of the population using the health centers (although even then there is a potential problem of misreporting), they are fully aware that the survey will not provide a good understanding of why some groups use the health centers and others do not. Consequently, they invite an ethnographer to join their team and conduct in-depth studies in a small number of communities. The ethnographic studies will explore health-related attitudes and beliefs of different ethnographic groups and the factors influencing their decision to use or not use the health centers. The studies will also examine the economic, political, organizational, cultural, and ecological factors affecting the operation of the health centers in different communities. The first part of the analysis will address broad cultural differences likely to affect all health centers, and the latter part (the contextual analysis) will help to explain factors affecting the performance of different centers. The evaluation director is aware that mixed-method designs work well only when there is respect and understanding and a feeling of equality among team members from different professions, so the ethnographer was invited to join the team from the time of the first planning meeting. The following are some of the ways in which the QUANT and QUAL approaches will be integrated into this evaluation:

- Rapid ethnographic studies will be conducted in a small number of communities to identify some of the issues that must be addressed in the study and to help identify the best way to phrase the questions to be included in the questionnaire.
- Once the sample has been selected for the household survey, a number of communities will be selected from the same sample frame for conducting ethnographic studies of families and health services and for preparing contextual analysis.
- To compare information obtained by different methods, QUAL interviews and case studies may be conducted with a small number of families included in the sample survey.
- **Triangulation** procedures will be built into the evaluation design so that independent QUANT and QUAL estimates can be obtained for key variables (such as use of health facilities and attitudes toward these facilities).
- Separate QUANT and QUAL reports will be prepared, and the team will then meet to compare the two and to identify areas where the findings support each other as well as questions on which there are apparent differences of facts or interpretation.
- Follow-up fieldwork will be conducted to check on inconsistencies and also to prepare additional cases to illustrate and explain some of the key issues and conclusions.

Greene (2005:255–56) suggests five reasons for using mixed-method designs:

- *Triangulation,* or enhancing the validity or **credibility** of evaluation findings through results from the different methods that converge and agree, one with the other
- *Development,* or using the results of one method to help develop the sample or instrumentation for another
- *Complementarity,* or extending the comprehensiveness of evaluation findings through results from different methods that broaden and deepen the understanding reached

- *Initiation,* or generating new insights into evaluation findings through results from the different methods that diverge and thus call for reconciliation via further analysis, reframing, or some other shift in perspective
- *Value diversity,* or incorporating a wider diversity of values and thus greater consciousness about the value dimensions of evaluation through the use of different methods that themselves advance difference values

Table 13.1 describes some of the typical ways that QUANT and QUAL approaches are used in the different stages of an evaluation. Mixed methods seek to strengthen some or all stages of the evaluation by combining these different approaches.

- *Conceptual framework and formulation of hypotheses.* QUANT evaluations often derive hypotheses deductively from existing theories or literature reviews. In contrast, many QUAL evaluations emphasize the uniqueness of each situation and frequently do not identify hypotheses. When hypotheses are used by QUAL evaluators, they will often be developed inductively as the study evolves. Mixed methods can combine both approaches. For example, a QUANT evaluator may develop hypotheses deductively from a review of the literature, and the QUAL colleague can then explore and refine the ideas through, for example, interviews or observation. In contrast, the initial stages of QUAL data collection may identify and describe processes and issues that the QUANT team members may then define in such a way that they can be tested through data collected in a sample survey.
- *Selection of subjects or units of analysis.* QUAL evaluations typically, but not always, use a relatively small number of subjects, and a variety of procedures is used for selecting the sample. Often, subjects are selected purposively (theoretical sampling) to ensure that all important groups are included in the relatively small number of cases to be studied. In contrast, QUANT evaluations normally use a relatively large, randomly selected sample. The aim is to permit generalizability to larger populations and also to have a large enough sample to permit the statistical comparison of differences between groups (e.g., the **project** and **comparison groups**). The previous example of the health center evaluation illustrates how the QUANT and QUAL approaches to sampling can complement each other.
- *Evaluation design.* Most QUANT evaluations use one of a small number of clearly defined randomized or quasi-experimental designs (see Chapter 10). Where possible, representative samples of the project and comparison groups will be interviewed at two or more points during the life of the project to measure relative changes in **outcome** or impact indicators. In contrast, the QUAL evaluator normally becomes immersed in the community over a long period of time and seeks to understand the **program** through holistic analysis of the interrelationships among many different elements of the community and of the social, economic, political, and cultural setting in which the program operates. Normally, QUAL evaluations do not seek to establish a direct cause and effect or linear relationship between project interventions and outcomes, and the study may or may not involve a comparison group. One of the many ways in which the two approaches can be combined is to use QUAL methods to study the project **implementation process** and the influence of **contextual variables** (**contextuality**) on project performance in some of the communities where a QUANT survey of project participants is being conducted.

Table 13.1   Characteristics of Quantitative and Qualitative Approaches to Different Stages of the Evaluation Process

Evaluation Activity	Quantitative Approach	Qualitative Approach
The conceptual framework and the formulation of hypotheses	• Evaluations are usually, but not always, based on a theoretical framework derived from a review of the literature and usually involve testable hypotheses • Hypotheses are often *deductive* (based on testable hypotheses derived from theory) • Hypotheses are usually quantitative and can be evaluated with statistical significance tests • The framework often starts from the macro, rather than the micro level	• While some evaluations define and test hypotheses, many do not. • Many evaluations emphasize the uniqueness of each situation and the conceptual framework may be defined through a process of iteration with the framework being continuously updated as new information is obtained. • Hypotheses, if used, are often *inductive* (derived from information gathered during the course of the study).
Selection of subjects or units of analysis	• Random sampling so that findings can be generalized, and to permit statistical testing of differences between groups • Requires a sampling frame that lists all the members of the target population(s) to be studied. • Selection methods are usually defined in advance, clearly documented, and unchanging throughout the study • Typically a fairly large sample is selected from which to collect a finite set of quantitative data	• Choice of selection procedures varies according to the purpose of the study. • Purposive sampling used to collect the most useful and interesting data related to the purpose of the study. • While this is not usually done for QUAL evaluations, sometimes for mixed-method approaches, the sample may be selected using the same master sampling frame as for the QUANT component of the research. For example, a subsample of the villages in which samples of households (or other units) are selected for the QUANT survey may be selected for the QUAL analysis (although the types of data collection and the subjects, groups, or organizations to be studied in the QUAL analysis will usually be different). • Usually a smaller number of people are interviewed in more depth.
Evaluation design	• Normally one of the quasi-experimental designs described in Chapter 10 is used. A randomly selected sample that represents the project participants, and possibly a control or comparison group, is interviewed at one or more points of time during the project • Where possible, outcomes and impacts are estimated by comparing data collected before and after (and possibly during) the implementation of the project	• The researcher(s) become immersed in the community over a long period of time. • The effects of the program are studied through collecting information on the many different elements of the community and its economic, political, cultural, ecological, and psychological setting. • Normally the evaluation does not try to establish a direct cause and effect or linear relationship.

(Continued)

Table 13.1 (Continued)

Evaluation Activity	Quantitative Approach	Qualitative Approach
Data collection and recording methods	• Data are usually recorded in structured questionnaires that are administered consistently throughout the study • There is extensive use of precoded, closed-ended questions • The study mainly uses numerical values (integer variables) or closed-ended (ordinal or nominal) variables that can be subjected to statistical analysis • Observational checklists with precoded responses may be used	• Interview protocols are the most common instrument, often semistructured. • The data collection instrument may be modified during the course of the study as understanding grows. • Interview data are sometimes recorded verbatim (audiotape, videotape) and sometimes in written notes. • Study may use analysis of existing documents. Textual data from documents are often highlighted in a copy of the original, which is kept as part of the data set. • Study may use focus groups (usually fewer than 10 people) and meetings with larger community groups. • Study may use participant and nonparticipant observation. • Study may use photography.
Triangulation	• Consistency checks are built into questionnaires to provide independent estimates of key variables (e.g., data on income may be compared with data on expenditures) • Direct observation (a QUAL technique) can be used as a consistency check on answers given by the respondent (e.g., information on income can be compared with evidence of the number and quality of consumer durables in evidence inside or outside the house) • Information from earlier surveys with the same respondents is sometimes used as a consistency check on information given in a later survey • Secondary data (census data, national household surveys, information from government agencies) can be used to check estimates from the evaluation survey	• Several qualitative methods are used for multiple perspectives and triangulation. • Triangulation by observation: A monitor can observe a focus group or group meeting both to identify any potential bias resulting from how the session was conducted and also to provide an independent perspective (e.g., reporting on the interactions between group members, observing how certain people respond to the comments or behavior of others).

- *Data collection and recording methods.* Whereas QUANT evaluations seek the collection of standardized, numerical data (see Chapter 11), QUAL evaluations usually use less structured data collection methods that provide greater flexibility and that seek to describe and understand the complexities and holistic nature of a situation (see Chapter 12). QUAL evaluators draw on a wide range of data collection and recording methods. Semistructured data collection instruments are often used in interviews or observation. The instruments will often be modified as the evaluation progresses. Data from the interview may be recorded in the form of notes or with audio- or videotapes. Group interviews are also commonly used. These may involve unstructured or semistructured conversations with small groups, such as families, gangs, school staff, or police, or in more structured group meetings such as **focus groups** or community meetings. Participant and nonparticipant observation are also used to collect data on individuals, groups, communities, or organizations. Document analysis (e.g., organization documents, different kinds of records, meeting reports) is also widely used. Photography is another common method. In contrast, QUANT evaluations rely heavily on structured questionnaires applied in exactly the same way throughout the study and where most of the information is recorded in numerical form or precoded categories. Precoded checklists, performance tests, and physical measurement such as anthropometric tests are also used.
- *Triangulation.* Both QUAL and QUANT evaluators use triangulation to obtain two or more independent estimates of key variables concerning program outcomes and the factors affecting these outcomes. QUANT evaluators combine consistency checks built into the survey instruments with the use of secondary data (previous surveys and published reports) and the use of direct observation to compare with information provided by survey respondents. QUAL evaluations are often less concerned with consistency checks than with deepening and broadening understanding through multiple perspectives obtained from different sources of information. Triangulation is one of the most frequently used mixed-method approaches. For example, different methods of data collection can be used to validate data and to provide different perspectives and interpretations.
- *Data analysis.* QUAL evaluators use a wide range of data analysis methods. The purpose of many of these methods is to identify broad patterns and interrelations and to obtain a holistic overview of the complex interactions between a project and the setting within which it is embedded. The purpose of QUANT analysis, on the other hand, is to describe the statistical characteristics of the key variables, to determine statistical differences between project and comparison groups, and to identify factors contributing to the magnitude and direction of change. QUAL analysis can be used to help understand the meaning that different subjects or groups give to the statistical associations found in the QUANT analysis and to provide cases and examples to illuminate the findings. On the other hand, QUANT analysis can be used to assess how well the cases included in the QUAL studies represent the total population of interest and which if any sectors have not been covered. This complementarity is an important feature of mixed methods in situations where the evaluators are asked to generalize their findings.

While the methods, foci, and areas of concern of QUAL and QUANT approaches may seem to be heading in different directions and while adherents of each camp often criticize what they perceive as methodological or philosophical weakness of the other, in fact, the two can potentially complement each other. The purpose of mixed-method approaches is to draw on the strengths of each approach to overcome the weaknesses of the other when used in isolation. The rest of this chapter is devoted to discussing how the mixed-method approaches have developed and how they can be used to help evaluators to mitigate the budget, time, data, and, possibly, political constraints under which RealWorld Evaluations (**RWE**) must be conducted.

Different Applications of Mixed Methods When the Dominant Design Is Quantitative or Qualitative

Mixed-method designs are used differently, and produce different benefits, depending on whether the dominant design is QUANT or QUAL. For example, when the predominant design is QUANT, incorporating QUAL methods can provide the contextual analysis to help explain how project implementation and outcomes are affected by the economic, political, institutional, environmental, cultural, and other unique aspects of the project setting. Mixed methods also help QUANT evaluators to use triangulation to provide independent estimates of key information collected through surveys and help provide a broader framework for the interpretation of the statistical data. Methods can also be triangulated so that different approaches to data collection and analysis can also be compared.

In contrast, when the predominant design is QUAL, a mixed-method design can potentially strengthen the evaluation in a number of different ways. For example, what can the in-depth evaluation findings from a small number of schools, agricultural extension centers, village banks, or community development groups tell policymakers about the potential of these programs? How and why the programs work or don't work is often more important to planners and policymakers than the statistical significance of the findings. QUANT approaches can contribute either by helping with the selection of the sample (see earlier discussion) or by using secondary data from censuses and surveys to contextualize the sample against the wider population. One of the areas of strength of QUAL evaluations is the presentation of a holistic analysis of the many contextual factors affecting the performance of a program. This helps explain variations in outcomes among different project sites found in the QUANT analysis. When the program being evaluated is operating on a large scale (throughout a city or state or at the national level), it may be necessary to assess how these different contextual factors (e.g., economic, social, political, institutional, cultural) interact and how they affect program performance. Contextual factors can be analyzed either qualitatively through cross-case analysis (see Miles and Huberman 1994), or quantitatively by incorporating contextual variables into multiple regression and other forms of statistical analysis.[1] Rapid QUANT surveys can also be used to provide a project-wide backdrop for the interpretation of QUAL data by indicating the representativeness of the subjects or units studied within the project (cf. Erickson 1986, "petite generalizations").

Finally, statistical analysis can be used to present a broader context for assessing possible explanations of a phenomenon. For example, statistical analysis might identify household characteristics (e.g., household composition, educational level, economic status) associated with project outcomes, and this might identify some issues to be explored through in-depth QUAL analysis.

The following are examples of some of the ways in which mixed-method approaches can potentially strengthen evaluations conducted with budget, time, and data constraints:

- Judicious combinations of QUAL and QUANT methods enhance triangulation, helping confirm and elaborate the information in data.

- Different perspectives can be obtained by combining in-depth analysis of a small number of cases, holistic analysis of the project context, and broader QUANT analysis of relationships between, say, household characteristics and project outcomes. For example, a QUANT evaluation may have initially assumed income or consumption to be the key indicators of household welfare. However, ethnographic studies may reveal that women are more concerned about vulnerability (defined as the lack of access to social support systems in times of crises), powerlessness, or exposure to violence. This may encourage the QUANT evaluators either to include additional indicators in the survey or to commission case studies to help readers understand the multidimensionality of poverty. Similarly, a QUAL evaluation that had studied the impacts of government budget cuts on access to health services in a number of villages might benefit from the findings of a longitudinal statistical analysis showing that many of the reductions in health services had already started before the current rounds of budget cuts.[2] Comprehensive data of both types help pinpoint and explain critical aspects of a program.

- QUAL and QUANT methods typically adopt different approaches to multilevel analysis, and both can benefit from combining or sharing their approaches. For example, QUAL method-by-method analysis (e.g., analyze all the surveys first, then all the observations) combined with cross-method thematic analysis provides a useful framework for the interpretation of data from a range of mixed-method approaches. QUANT analysis can also contribute different approaches to multilevel analysis. For example, the analysis of surveys conducted at the level of the household, school, or farm can identify statistically significant differences in behavior or outcomes in different locations that cannot be fully explained in terms of the subject's socioeconomic characteristics (e.g., household members, students, or teachers). These differences can then be explored at a higher aggregate level (e.g., community, school district, local district of the ministry of agriculture). These higher levels of analysis can combine QUANT and QUAL approaches in ways that can contribute new perspectives to both.

- Preliminary evaluation reports frequently identify apparent inconsistencies in findings or interesting differences between communities or groups that cannot be explained by the currently available data. Mixed methods can widen the range of approaches available to understand these questions. In the case of QUANT evaluations, it is often the case that once the data collection phase is completed, it is not possible to return to the field to check on such questions. However, if planned ahead of time, it is sometimes possible to conduct a rapid QUAL follow-up to help understand some of these questions. For example, in a QUANT evaluation of village water supply programs in Indonesia, the survey found that in all villages except one, the women were responsible for water management. In the case of the single village where it was reported that men managed the water supply, the researchers were not certain if this was a reporting error or if this was an example of a different pattern of social organization that should be investigated. A rapid follow-up QUAL study found that in fact water was managed by men in this village because in this area women were involved in dairy farming and because this was a very profitable activity that in this culture could only be managed by women, the men were willing to take over water management to free up time for their wives to manage the dairy cattle (Brown 2000). In the case of a QUAL study, a mixed-method approach might permit a QUANT analysis of secondary data sources to compare the characteristics of the sample subjects or communities with the broader population, hence contributing to an assessment of the generalizability of the evaluation findings.

Mixed-Method Strategies

Mixed-method designs can be categorized along three key dimensions. One is whether the different methods are used concurrently or sequentially. A second is whether the different methods are considered to have relatively equal importance or one methodology is considered dominant and the others are used to complement it. A third dimension deals with the stages of the evaluation at which the methods are integrated. The options range from integration during a single stage to complete integration throughout all stages of the evaluation. In the next two sections, we discuss various sequential and concurrent mixed-method designs (see also Creswell et al. 2003).

Sequential Mixed-Method Designs

In sequential designs, the QUANT and QUAL data collection and/or analysis are conducted sequentially (in either order), with one method being used to identify issues or hypotheses to be studied in depth (often by the other method) to assess how findings can be generalized or to help interpret the findings. One method (either QUANT or QUAL) is generally, perhaps always, dominant (see Creswell et al. 2003). To the best of our knowledge, no analysis has been conducted on this point.

The advantage of sequential designs compared with concurrent designs (discussed in the next section) is that the logistics of sequential designs are often easier to organize. Data collection through structured questionnaires often involves having a relatively large team of **enumerators** in the field at the same time and following a precisely defined schedule of household selection and number of interviews to be conducted each day. The field supervisors need to know where all the enumerators are working each day because quality control often involves repeat visits to a subsample of subjects; also, the supervisor must be on hand to answer questions from any of the enumerators. In contrast, ethnographic and many other kinds of QUAL methods often have a much more flexible schedule both in terms of duration and where the researchers will be at any given time. For this and other reasons, concurrent mixed-method designs can often be more difficult to manage, particularly for evaluation teams with only a few experienced supervisors. On the other hand, a potential disadvantage of sequential designs for RWE evaluations is that the duration of the evaluation is likely to increase if one stage cannot begin until the previous stage is completed and analyzed.

Figure 13.1 presents an example of a sequential design with a dominant QUANT approach. This is a study of interhousehold transfers of money and goods among poor urban households in Colombia (Wansbrough, Jones, and Kappaz 2000). A common coping strategy among poor families is the transfer of money and goods from households that are doing relatively well at a particular point in time to their poorer and more needy relatives and friends. It is expected that when fortunes change, the transfer will be reciprocated or that other forms of assistance may be provided (e.g., labor to help build a house or having a child coming to live while attending high school). The purpose of the study was to describe the patterns of transfers and to estimate whether the transfers were sufficiently large to act as an informal social safety net to help

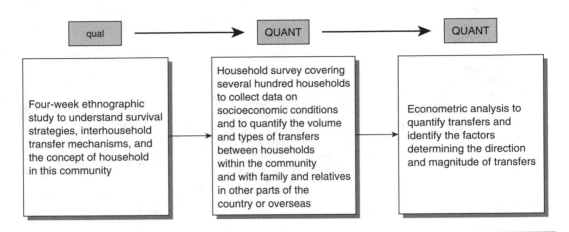

Figure 13.1   Sequential Mixed Methods with a Dominant Quantitative Design: Studying Interhousehold Transfers of Money and Goods in Cartagena, Colombia

the poorest sectors of the community in times of need. These kinds of interhousehold transfers are difficult to identify and measure, so an anthropologist spent a month living in the community prior to the design of the sample survey to study the patterns of transfers and to help design the questionnaire. A QUANT survey was then administered to several hundred households. The data were analyzed using QUANT economic analysis (econometrics).

Figure 13.2 illustrates a sequential design with a dominant QUAL approach. This describes a hypothetical evaluation to assess the adoption of new varieties of seed by different types of rural families. The principal data collection methods are qualitative: interviews, focus groups, observation, and case studies of individual households and small farming communities. The principal methods of analysis are also qualitative: within- and cross-case analysis and the constant comparative method. However, to obtain information on the ethnic distribution of households, household economic conditions, and agricultural production, the evaluation begins with a rapid QUANT household survey covering a sample of households in all the villages covered by the agricultural extension project. The findings of this study were used to help identify the types of households to be studied in more depth through the QUAL data collection methods.

Either of the two evaluation designs described above could have been modified to give equal weight to both QUANT and QUAL approaches with neither being dominant. In the case of the interhousehold transfer study, it would have been possible to complement the household survey with QUAL case studies on families or informal transfer networks. These could then have been integrated into the analysis to compare the description and interpretation of the functions and operation of the transfer networks obtained from the QUAL studies with the findings of the econometric analysis. In the second example, the QUANT data collection could have been complemented by an exploratory ethnographic study conducted in the planning phase to help design the structured questionnaire to be administered to a sample of families in all project communities to obtain more detailed QUANT data on the impacts of the seed distribution program. A QUAL or QUANT study of marketing outlets could also have been conducted to estimate the changes in sales of agricultural produce from the project areas and, possibly, the changes in the purchase of consumer goods by project area families.

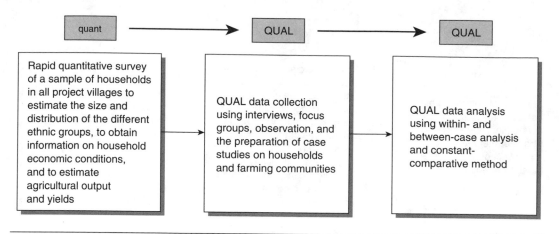

Figure 13.2   Sequential Mixed Methods with a Dominant Qualitative Design: Evaluating the Adoption of New Seed Varieties by Different Types of Rural Families

Concurrent Designs

In concurrent designs, the QUANT and QUAL approaches are used at the same time. An example of a concurrent design is where QUANT and QUAL data are collected simultaneously, using triangulation to compare information on outcomes, impacts, and other key indicators from different independent sources. Another example is when QUAL methods are used to conduct a contextual analysis of a project site (or the surrounding areas) at the same time that a QUANT sample survey of households or individuals is being carried out. This provides the opportunity for a very rich but more complicated analysis in which the interactions between the setting (context) and the project implementation process are analyzed.

Concurrent methods have the advantage for RWE in that data collection and analysis can be completed more quickly than for sequential designs. However, concurrent designs tend to be more difficult to manage, both because there are two sets of activities going on simultaneously and because QUANT and QUAL data collection methods typically have a different dynamic and timing, so that they can be difficult to conduct at the same time. This can be a particular problem in areas where logistical planning (e.g., travel to sites, places to stay, security) can become difficult to coordinate. Concurrent methods also make it more difficult to handle feedback from one method that may suggest changes required in other parts of the study. Decisions and actions will often have to be taken under greater time pressure than for sequential designs. For example, QUANT data collection has to be planned with a tight timetable so that a team of enumerators can be managed and perhaps transported to and from data collection sites. If QUAL observers, **interviewers**, and case study specialists are at a variety of different sites at the same time, this greatly complicates coordination of data and preliminary findings. It is sometimes easier to absorb incoming information with a sequential design, but this must be balanced against the longer period over which data are collected—a concern for most RWE evaluations.

Concurrent Triangulation Design

This is one of the most frequently used mixed-method designs. Two or more methods are used to confirm, cross-validate, or corroborate findings within a single study. Either the

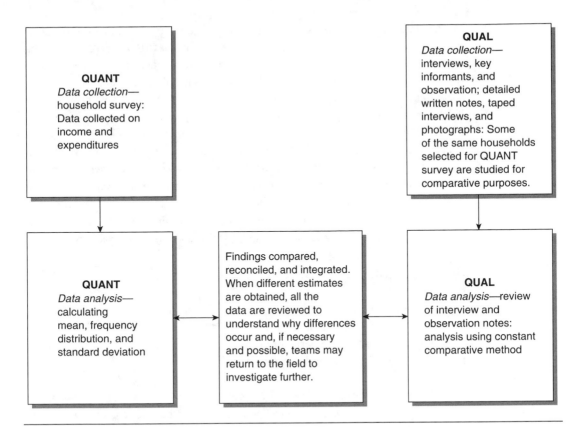

Figure 13.3   Concurrent Triangulation Design: Comparing and Integrating Different Data Sources on Poverty and Household Income

SOURCE: Model adapted from Creswell et al. (2005:226, Figure 8.5a). Example developed by present authors.

QUANT or QUAL design may be dominant or the two may be fully integrated and given equal weight. Figure 13.3 illustrates how this design could be used to obtain and triangulate different estimates of poverty and household income. The QUANT study uses household income as the primary indicator of poverty. A household questionnaire is administered to a sample of households, and a number of questions are included on household income and expenditures. Statistical analysis is conducted to calculate means, frequency distributions, and **standard deviations** of household income. Internal consistency checks are also used in which income is compared with expenditures. At the same time, a number of QUAL data collection techniques, including interviews with household members and key informants and observation, are used.

While the QUAL researchers look at household income and expenditures, they also try to understand how people in the community think about poverty, well-being, and security. Detailed notes are taken on the interviews and observation, and some interviews are taped. Photographs are also taken to illustrate the economic conditions of individual households and the community in general. A few of the households included in the QUANT household sample survey are also covered in the QUAL survey to permit direct comparisons. The notes are analyzed using the constant-comparative method, and some preliminary conclusions are drawn on how families think about well-being and economic security as well as describing their income and expenditure patterns.

The QUANT and QUAL teams then meet to present and compare their findings. For example, the QUAL team reports that although it may be true (from the QUANT data coming in) that many families have very low incomes and very modest consumption, there are some families (hard to know how many), particularly female-headed households, that are equally concerned about *vulnerability* and how well families will be able to survive crises such as unemployment, illness, or death. Crime and physical security are also major concerns expressed by those whom the QUAL team interviewed. The two teams also compare information obtained on the families that were included in both the QUANT household survey and interviewed and observed by the QUAL team. If specific inconsistencies arise, such as different estimates of income or expenditures for particular families, the two teams compare their notes to try to explain the differences. In some cases, resources and time permitting, one or more researchers might return to the field to check on some of these issues. The final report will integrate findings from all the different sources of QUAL and QUANT data collection and analysis.

Concurrent Nested Design

In this design, one method is dominant and the other method is *nested* within it (Creswell et al. 2005). The less-dominant method may be used to explore a particular aspect in more detail, to provide illustrative material, or to quantify different findings or processes. The following are examples of how this design can be used:

- Different methods can be used to study different groups. For example, if the dominant design is quantitative, a structured questionnaire may be used to interview all household heads, but a more open interview may be used to interview a subset of the population, such as spouses, children, and other household members. Similarly, a structured questionnaire may be used with a sample of employees, and focus groups may be used for more in-depth analysis of groups of particular interest, such as members of work groups with a particularly low or high level of work satisfaction.
- QUAL methods may be used to prepare in-depth case studies to describe the behavior, attitudes, or social and economic conditions of typical members of different subgroups covered by a QUANT survey.
- Rapid QUANT surveys can be used to estimate the prevalence of some of the behavior revealed in the QUAL studies. For example, if case studies reveal that the poorest families depend for their survival on receipts of money or food from relatives living outside the community, a rapid survey could try to assess what proportion of poor families receives these kinds of support.

Using Mixed Methods at Different Stages of the Evaluation

Mixed methods can be used at any stage of the evaluation. Although a fully integrated mixed-method design would require full integration of QUAL and QUANT approaches at all stages of the evaluation, in practice, mixed-method designs are usually applied at only one or two stages of an evaluation. This is usually the case for RWE where time and cost are likely to be constraints. The following are some of the ways in which mixed methods can be used at different stages of the evaluation:

- *During the formulation of hypotheses and research questions.* Exploratory QUAL studies can be used to better understand and refine the hypothesis to be tested in the dominant QUANT evaluation design. Similarly, rapid QUANT studies can be conducted to help refine the evaluation question by indicating some population characteristics, such as ethnic composition or principal economic activities, that should be explored.

- *During data collection.* Mixed data collection methods are often used as a component of triangulation to confirm, elaborate, or disconfirm data collected from various sources, by various methods, and by various evaluation team members. Mixed methods are also used to simultaneously collect information in different ways. For example, a QUANT structured questionnaire may be administered to a sample of school children and their parents while QUAL methods are used to document the culture and quality of schools and the behavior of teachers.

- *During data analysis and follow-up.* If triangulation has been used to obtain two or more independent sources of data on important indicators or topics, a key part of the analysis phase is to compare and reconcile the different sources. In many QUAL studies, much of this reconciliation and follow-up will be done during the data collection phase, but when QUANT and QUAL approaches are combined, the comparison and reconciliation will often not occur until after the preliminary analysis of the QUANT data has been conducted. Sometimes the reasons for inconsistencies among the different data sources are clear, as when observation indicates that families have informal sources of income such as dressmaking and beer brewing that were not captured by the structured questionnaire. However, in other cases, the explanation may not be evident, and if resources and time permit, follow-up fieldwork can greatly enhance the quality and depth of the analysis.

- *Presentation and dissemination of the findings.* The findings of QUANT evaluations are often presented in the form of written reports, including tables of QUANT data, supported by briefings of key **stakeholders** in which PowerPoint or other forms of graphical presentations are used. Often, there is very little feedback to the communities studied. In contrast, findings of QUAL evaluations are more likely to include presentations to a wider range of stakeholders, but the written reports may be more qualitative and descriptive. The presentation of mixed-method evaluations can draw on both approaches, both broadening the range of presentation techniques as well as reaching out to a wider range of stakeholders.

Implementing a Mixed-Method Design

Although some applications of mixed-method designs involve only adding additional data collection methods to a dominant QUANT or QUAL design, a fully integrated mixed-method evaluation strategy involves much more than this. To enjoy the full benefit of combining QUANT and QUAL orientations, methodologies, and methods, it is necessary to implement from the first day of the evaluation a mixed-method evaluation strategy involving the following aspects (see Box 13.1):

Composition of the Research Team. The effective design and application of fully integrated designs often require that the research team include principal researchers from two or more disciplines (e.g., anthropology, medicine, law, sociology, economics). It is important to allow

Box 13.1   Elements of an Integrated, Multidisciplinary Research Approach

Composition of the Research Team

- Include primary researchers from different disciplines. Allow time for researchers to develop an understanding and respect for each other's disciplines and work. Each should be familiar with the basic literature and current debates in the other field.
- Ensure similar linkages between local researchers from the city, state, country, or region where the project is being implemented.

Integrated Approaches during the Evaluation Design

- Ensure that the evaluation framework draws on theories and approaches from all the disciplinary teams involved in the evaluation (e.g., anthropology, medicine, law, sociology, economics, demography) and frameworks from predominantly qualitative and quantitative perspectives, with each being used to enrich and broaden the other.
- Ensure that hypotheses and research approaches draw from all disciplines.
- The research framework should formulate linkages between different levels of analysis (e.g., both quantitative survey and qualitative interviews of households, students, farmers; qualitative holistic analysis of the program setting).
- Ensure that concepts and methods are not taken out of context but draw on the intellectual debates and approaches within the respective disciplines.
- Consider using behavioral models that combine economic and other quantitative modeling with in-depth understanding of the cultural context within which the study is being conducted.

Data Collection and the Use of Triangulation

- Conduct exploratory analysis to assist in hypothesis development and definition of indicators.
- Select quantitative and qualitative data collection methods designed to complement each other, and specify the complementarities and how they will be used in the fieldwork and analysis.
- Select at least two independent estimating methods for key indicators and hypotheses.
- Ensure full documentation of all sample selection, data collection, and analysis methods.

Data Analysis and Interpretation and Possible Field Follow-Up

- Conduct and present separate analyses of quantitative and qualitative findings to highlight different interpretations and findings from different methods and then prepare an integrated report drawing on all of the data.
- Use systematic triangulation procedures to check on inconsistencies or differing interpretations. Follow up on differences, where necessary, with a return to the field.

- Budget resources and time for follow-up visits to the field.
- Highlight different interpretations and findings from different methods and discuss how these enrich the interpretation of the study. Different, and seemingly contradictory, outcomes should be considered a major strength of the integrated approach rather than an annoyance.
- Present cases and qualitative material to illustrate or test quantitative findings.

Presentation and Dissemination of Findings

- Combine conventional forms of presentation with written reports complemented by PowerPoint presentations with some of the more participatory presentation methods used in some qualitative evaluations. Recognizing lack of receptivity by many stakeholders to long technical reports, the team may also develop more innovative and user-friendly reports.
- Broaden the range of stakeholders invited to the presentation and review of findings to include some of the community and civil society groups that qualitative evaluators often work with but many of whom may not be consulted in many quantitative evaluations.

---

time and opportunities for each researcher to become familiar with the methodology of the others and to develop mutual respect and trust among the members of the team. Allowing sufficient time is even more important when the evaluation team comprises specialists from different countries as well as from different disciplines.

Integrated Approaches during the Evaluation Design. It is important to develop an evaluation framework that draws on all the involved disciplines and to ensure that the research questions and issues incorporate each of these methodologies. This will encourage the development of an evaluation design that draws on the literature and skills/benefits of each methodology. Integration will require careful sharing and joint planning by equal partners.

As discussed earlier in this chapter, project outcomes are affected significantly by the social, economic, political, institutional, and cultural context within which the project is implemented. One very valuable contribution that QUAL research can make to strengthen QUANT designs is to help understand these different contexts or processes, to evaluate which elements are likely to influence project outcomes, and to propose ways to study them. Hentschel (1999) discusses how contextual variables can be built into the research design and how they can be used to interpret findings. On the other hand, there are cases where QUANT sampling procedures and numerical analysis can contribute to QUAL designs by helping assess how widely opinions or behavior of the individuals or groups that have been studied in depth are shared by other sectors of the community or to assess the relative quantitative importance of different problems and issues identified in focus groups. Many evaluation **clients** want to know whether the groups studied are broadly representative of the total population or in what ways they differ. For example, if people who attend community meetings or focus groups differ in some important ways from the groups who do not attend, it is important to know this and, possibly, to conduct some follow-up interviews with the under-represented groups.[3]

Integrated Approaches during Data Collection. Although many QUAL data collection methods are designed to study and document in depth a limited number of individuals, cases, or settings and to provide a holistic understanding of the setting, QUANT data collection methods are designed to obtain precisely defined, comparable measures of a limited number of questions from a large and representative sample. Consequently, the goal of mixed methods is to combine depth and a holistic focus with quantification and generalizability. This is particularly important when a large, complex, and geographically dispersed program is being evaluated. The triangulation of data from a number of different QUAL and QUANT sources, as well as the triangulation of different methods, are both goals of using mixed methods. Mixed methods can be used both as a consistency check on key estimates or information and to provide different perspectives for interpreting and understanding a complex phenomenon.

Integrated Approaches during Data Analysis and Interpretation. With a dominant QUANT design, data analysis normally does not begin until all, or most, of the data have been collected. The preliminary stages of the analysis will normally try to determine whether there are statistically significant associations between participation in the project and the **outputs** or effects that the project is trying to achieve. Multivariate analysis may then be used to identify socioeconomic characteristics of the subjects, groups, or communities that contribute to variations in the project outcomes (see Chapter 11). QUAL analysis may then be used to enrich the interpretation of the findings, to examine some of the contextual factors that affect outcomes, or to help explain some of the unexpected statistical results.

In contrast, with a dominant QUAL design, analysis is an iterative process continuing throughout the data collection process. Consequently, the preliminary analysis and interpretation of findings will already be well advanced by the end of the data collection period. Data analysis can combine both descriptive textual analysis as well as matrices, tables, and charts (Miles and Huberman 1994). If survey data were collected, they can be used to generalize the findings to the population of concern to the evaluation. Because many QUAL evaluations do not seek to generalize their findings, or only do so to a limited extent, this is one of the areas in which QUANT analytical methods can contribute.

When both approaches are given equal weight, the general methods for integrating QUANT and QUAL analysis are similar to the above discussion. The main difference is that more complete integration offers more opportunities to enrich and deepen the analysis.

Summary

- Mixed-method designs involve the planned use of two or more QUANT and QUAL methods of data collection and analysis.

- Building on the strengths of both QUANT and QUAL approaches, mixed methods can combine more comprehensive coverage with in-depth analysis of individual cases and a holistic understanding of the context within which each project is implemented.

- There are at least five reasons for using mixed-method designs: (a) strengthening validity through triangulation, (b) using the results of one method to help develop the sample or instrumentation of the other, (c) extending the comprehensiveness of findings, (d) generating new insights, and (e) incorporating a wider diversity of values.

- Mixed methods can be used at any stage of an evaluation.

- Mixed methods can either be used where one approach (either QUANT or QUAL) is *dominant* and the other approach is used as a complement, or both approaches can have equal weight. Mixed methods are used differently and bring different benefits depending on which approach is dominant.

- Mixed methods can be used either *sequentially,* when one approach is used after the other, or *concurrently* when both approaches are used at the same time. The sequential approach is more widely used because it is simpler to manage.

- Although mixed-method approaches can be used at just one stage of the evaluation, a fully integrated mixed-method design involves more than simply combining data collection methods. A fully integrated approach involves (a) attention to the composition of the research team and allowing sufficient time to build relations between members from different professions; (b) integrating different conceptual frameworks and planning approaches during the design phase; (c) integrated data collection methods; (d) systematic use of triangulation during data collection; (e) integrating different approaches during data analysis, including the possibility of returning to the field to verify or elaborate on initial findings; and (f) combining different methods for the presentation of findings.

Further Reading

Bamberger, M. ed. 2000. *Integrating Quantitative and Qualitative Research in Development Projects.* Directions in Development. Washington, DC: World Bank.

Case studies on how integrated mixed-method evaluations have been conducted on education, health, poverty, and water supply projects in different parts of the world.

Creswell, J. 2003. *Research Design: Qualitative, Quantitative and Mixed-Methods Approaches.* Thousand Oaks, CA: Sage.

Chapter 11 provides an overview of the main stages in the design and implementation of a mixed-method evaluation and of six mixed-method designs.

Greene, J. C. and V. J. Caracelli. 2003. "Making Paradigmatic Sense of Mixed Methods Practice." Pp. 91–110 in *Handbook of Mixed Methods in Social & Behavioral Research,* edited by A. Tashakkori and C. Teddlie. Thousand Oaks, CA: Sage.

The authors argue that research decisions are rarely consciously rooted in philosophical assumptions or beliefs. They recommend that more attention should be paid to understanding the philosophical and methodological distinctions between QUANT and QUAL while at the same time balancing this with practical and political considerations relevant to the context of each study.

Greene, J. C., V. Caracelli, and W. F. Graham. 1989. "Toward a Conceptual Framework for Multimethod Evaluation Designs." *Educational Evaluation and Policy Analysis* 11:255–74.

Johnson, R. B. and A. J. Onwuegbuzie. 2004. "Mixed Methods Research: A Research Paradigm Whose Time Has Come." *Educational Researcher* 33(7):14–26.

Mertens, D. M. 2003. "Mixed Methods and the Politics of Human Research: The Transformatory-Emancipatory Perspective." Pp. 135–66 in *Handbook of Mixed Methods in Social & Behavioral Research,* edited by A. Tashakkori and C. Teddlie Thousand Oaks, CA: Sage.

The author argues that mixed methods are a powerful tool for contributing to the transformatory-emanicipatory perspective that recommends the adoption of an explicit goal for research to serve the ends of creating a more just and democratic society that permeates the entire research process, from the problem formulation to the drawing of conclusions and the use of results. Readers will find this provides a very different perspective than do some of the other more methodologically focused references.

Tashakkori, A. and C. Teddlie, eds. 2003. *Handbook of Mixed Methods in Social & Behavioral Research.* Thousand Oaks, CA: Sage.

Provides a comprehensive but technically more difficult selection of readings on these questions.

Notes

1. One of the ways to do this is through the transformation of contextual variables into a set of **dummy variables** that can then be incorporated into the regression analysis (see Chapter 11). For example, if the activities of a particular government agency support the project in a particular location, this could be coded "1"; if they do not, this could be coded "0." If the economy is growing, this could be coded "1," and if it is static or declining, this could be coded "0." Assume that a regression analysis is conducted with "proportion of farmers adopting the new type of seed" as the dependent variable. If the analysis finds that the regression coefficient of some of the dummy variables is statistically significant, this suggests that the particular factor (e.g., support of a particular government agency) contributes to the program outcome. This is a highly simplified example, and it would often be necessary to include a number of dummy variables to describe each contextual factor; also, a number of exploratory analyses would be conducted to refine the definition of the contextual variables—often, to combine several into a composite index.

2. There is an ongoing debate in Africa and other developing regions on the impacts of structural adjustment and other policy reforms involving budget cutbacks on the poor, particularly on poor women. Many QUAL studies report that families are convinced that the lack of access to public services is due to policy reforms supported by international development agencies. Another body of QUANT research suggests that it is more difficult to identify the causes of poor services. Both sides in the debate have benefited from the different perspectives provided by the other approach.

3. In some university or market research studies, it may be possible to carefully select and monitor participants in focus groups, but in many real-world contexts, the evaluator may have only a limited degree of control over who attends the groups.

CHAPTER 14

Sampling for RealWorld Evaluation

This chapter discusses the application of sample **design** principles to RealWorld Evaluation (**RWE**). The chapter begins by emphasizing the importance of sampling for both qualitative (**QUAL**) and quantitative (**QUANT**) evaluations while showing that the approach to sampling is quite different in each case. Most QUAL evaluations use **purposive sampling** in which a small number of carefully selected cases or individuals are studied in depth, and these sampling strategies are described. The next section discusses the use of **probability** (random) **sampling** for QUANT evaluations. Different sample selection procedures are discussed, and some of the key decisions at the presampling, sample design, and postsampling stages are considered. The concepts of power analysis and effect size are introduced, and their importance for estimating sample size is explained. The concept of **Type I** (wrongly concluding that a program has a significant effect) and **Type II errors** (wrongly concluding that a program does not have a significant effect) are introduced. A worked example is given to illustrate the different steps in estimating sample size. We then show how meta-analysis can be used to help estimate in advance the likely effect size that can be expected from any new program. The chapter ends with a discussion of sampling design issues for RWE.

The Importance of Sampling for RealWorld Evaluation

The approach to sampling varies according to the evaluation methodology and the purposes of a particular evaluation. Two concerns of most QUANT evaluations are to ensure that the selected sample is representative of the total population and to determine whether the **findings** can be generalized to a wider population (e.g., other school districts, other rural communities in the province or surrounding area). In QUANT evaluations, a *representative* sample is defined in statistical terms and has to do with whether the sample was selected randomly and is large enough to test for the statistical significance of differences between, for example, the project population and a **comparison group** or between the project group before and after the project has been implemented. It is, of course, possible to have an evaluation that uses a large and randomly selected sample but that produces misleading conclusions because the data collection instruments were poorly designed, respondents did not wish to provide some of the information, or because the study design ignored important contextual factors affecting program **outcomes**.

Although most QUANT evaluators broadly agree on the principles and uses of sampling in research and evaluation, QUAL evaluators have different approaches to sampling. QUAL evaluators often, but not always, work with a smaller number of organizations or communities (e.g., schools, factories, drug treatment centers, villages) or subjects (e.g., families, individuals, gangs). The relevant categories will often be determined and refined through a process of iteration. In most cases, the selection does not use **random sampling**, both because this will not work well for a very small sample (the sampling error would be too large to produce reliable estimates) and because most QUAL evaluators think about *representation* in terms of the care taken to ensure that the sample covers all important issues and types of subjects, not in terms of statistical procedures. The purpose of many evaluations is to understand a particular program rather than to make generalizations to broader populations. Some evaluators would also argue that each situation is so unique that it is very difficult (or even inappropriate) to try to generalize.

While some evaluations are looking at programs affecting only a few districts, communities, or subjects, others are undertaken to determine the **impacts** of a **project** or **program** on hundreds or sometimes hundreds of thousands of subjects (e.g., individuals, families, schools, water user associations). The numbers become even larger for evaluations—usually, but not always, quantitative—that include a comparison group. For all but the smallest program populations, it is not possible to interview all the affected subjects and **stakeholders** and, consequently, evaluation findings are normally based on generalizations from a sample of subjects.

Sampling is critical to evaluation for two reasons. First, the way in which the sample is designed and implemented partially determines the validity of the conclusions. Second, decisions about the type and size of the sample (the number of subjects to be interviewed or studied) is one of the major determinants of the cost and duration of the evaluation. The issue is how to ensure that the sample is appropriate for the type of findings based on it. Addressing this issue takes different forms in QUANT and QUAL evaluation.

Crystallizing the issue for QUANT evaluation, where *probabilistic sampling* is based on large numbers, Henry (1990) states:

> The sampling dilemma is simple. Time and cost prohibit a researcher from collecting data on the entire group or population that is of interest to a particular study. However, researchers and the consumers of research are usually interested in the population rather than a subset of the population. Extending the study findings from a subset of the population, or "sample" to the entire population is critically important to overcome the dilemma between cost and time on the one hand and information needs on the other. Knowledge of basic sampling logic and methods is fundamental to ascertain if study findings reasonably apply to the population represented by the study participants or the study respondents. (p. 9)

For QUAL evaluation, where time-intensive methods decree smaller numbers of subjects, groups, or organizations, the issue of appropriate selection is addressed through

---

Box 14.1   Small Samples May Overlook Real Project Effects

In a meta-analysis assessing the findings of large numbers of evaluations of programs to reduce juvenile delinquency, Lipsey estimated that when programs had small but operationally important effects, perhaps as many as 75% of the evaluations were not able to detect the effects because the sample was too small (the **power of the test** was too small) and it was wrongly concluded that the program had no effect.

SOURCE: Lipsey (1990, chap. 3) and Rossi, Lipsey, and Freeman (2004, chap. 10).

---

subject-by-subject choices according to specified criteria. Selecting subjects to be maximally informative about evaluation questions is called **purposive** or **purposeful sampling**.

An understanding of the basic principles of sampling is particularly critical for RWE because the size of the sample has a major impact on the cost and duration of the evaluation. If the size of the sample is reduced without serious danger to the validity of the findings, a significant saving in cost and time may be gained. The key question is, How can the size of the sample be reduced without affecting the validity of the conclusions and recommendations? On the one hand, if the sample is larger than necessary, money and time are wasted; on the other hand, if the sample is too small, or otherwise inappropriate, the validity of the conclusions and recommendations will be compromised (see Box 14.1).

Purposive Sampling

Because the QUAL methods used to obtain data from human subjects—observation and interview—take time, there is almost always a limit to the number of persons who can be observed or interviewed during the data collection period. Appropriate selection of persons to observe and interview helps to ensure the richest and most meaningful information and understanding of the program and its impact. What is learned about some individuals will support findings about the program and stakeholders as a whole. These *petite generalizations* (Erickson 1986), like any findings, need to be warranted by adequate and appropriate data. Questions of concern include the following: What kinds of findings will be made from the data? Will the subjects selected be able to provide adequate and appropriate information to support these findings?

Random or randomized selection is not appropriate where the number of respondents selected for data collection is small. A small random sample is very likely to result in a skewed or distorted data set and in the findings based on it. For example, random selection with a very small sample might by chance result in a lopsided sample of all or mostly men, mostly advocates of a particular cause, or residents of mostly one region served by the program. Sample selection procedures are needed that ensure the inclusion of participants who can inform understanding of the program. Instead, when the sample is small, subjects should be chosen carefully and deliberately, based on criteria related to the purpose and questions of the evaluation. This type of sampling is purposeful or purposive.

Purposive Sampling Strategies

Many strategies or selection criteria may be used for purposive sampling. Defining the selection criteria is as important as selecting the respondents. The goal is identifying persons with knowledge and experience relevant to and sufficient for the evaluation purpose(s) or question(s) to be addressed. Except for *comprehensive samples* in which every member of the population is selected, to some extent, all samples (both purposive and probabilistic and in both qualitative and quantitative evaluations) are *convenience samples.* In this context, convenience is a broad concept and includes not only persons who are readily at hand and agreeable to interviewing or surveying, for example, but also persons who are willing to provide information. No survey or interview schedule can obtain information from persons who refuse to respond[1]. Still, some of the willing are easier to reach than others, who may be so remote that evaluation resources exclude them on feasibility grounds.

Among the willing, researchers or evaluators may define what is convenient in a given project and, within the boundaries of their definition, find a convenience sample. *Typical case samples* are drawn when it is important to know how the program has affected typical stakeholders. *Representative samples* are drawn when it is important for the sample to reflect or represent an entire group of stakeholders. Either of these types of samples might be used in pursuit of evaluation questions like these: How does this program affect participants? If an average person accesses this program, what will he or she experience? In general, are most participants satisfied or dissatisfied with this program (or an aspect of it)?

Range samples, maximum variation samples, and *quota samples* involve identifying characteristics of interest and some or all the variations found in the population of interest; respondents are then selected such that each characteristic is proportionally represented in the sample. Because a range sample is often intended to be representative of the range of variations within a population, it can be similar to a typical case sample. A quota sample is one in which each group of interest is allocated proportional representation in the sample. An example: It may be important to include a number or proportion (exact or approximate) of men and women, young and old, working and unemployed, and different ethnic groups in order to understand the impact across a range of stakeholders and the perspectives and experiences of each.

Unique case samples are sometimes as informative or more informative than typical case samples. Many programs will have some personnel or beneficiaries who differ in unique ways from the group as a whole. Understanding their experiences and perspectives may be particularly helpful. A comparison example: An efficiency expert might choose to watch the fastest bricklayer in order to understand how he or she approaches the laying of brick and to train others. The different or unique cases, the *outliers* if graphed, may offer special insights unavailable in typical, range, or quota samples.

Snowball samples involve the identification of likely sources of information by the evaluators, perhaps in collaboration with **clients**, followed by the identification of other sources of information by the contacted informants themselves. For example, the final question to an interviewee might be, "Who else knows about this subject and might be willing to speak with me?" This strategy has the characteristic of capitalizing on insiders' knowledge of local sources of information and may identify data sources the evaluator might otherwise neglect.

Critical case samples are drawn when there is a particularly challenging subgroup within a program's stakeholders—for example, the chronically homeless, the lowest academic achievers, or the intended beneficiaries who live farthest from service delivery outlets. When evaluators feel that if these groups are well served, all groups are likely to be well served, and their interest in such critical cases suggests special attention to them during data collection. Critical case sampling may also be the selection criterion of choice when particularly challenging subgroups claim disproportionate program services or benefits, create the greatest disruption to program processes, or are the most likely to be overlooked. Learning from these groups may be recognized as particularly informative for program decision makers and other personnel.

Extreme case samples, negative case samples, and *deviant case samples* help evaluators and clients understand atypical experiences, some of which may be especially important. Among the atypical samples that might be drawn, extreme case samples obtain information about stakeholders at one end or another of the continuum of program experiences—for example, the most positive or negative or those receiving the most or fewest benefits. Negative case samples are not samples of those whose experiences are negative but of those whose experiences, like the negative of a photograph, are very different—even opposite—from those of most program participants. Finding out why their experiences or outcomes are so different from the mainstream can be helpful for understanding and improving a program. Deviant case samples are not samples of those whose behavior is legally or socially deviant but of those whose experiences deviate from the norm in the program, a concept similar to negative case samples.

Reputational samples are drawn from those who are recognized as having perspectives that might provide especially helpful information. A comparison example: The *American Journal of Evaluation* recently began publishing a series of interviews with nationally recognized evaluators, chosen on the basis of their reputations. In a program, stakeholders who might be known by reputation might be the most outspoken proponents or opponents of the program, the personnel most or least successful at dispensing services at the lowest cost, the community in the program that has improved the most or least, or the school with the highest or lowest test scores. As some of these examples show, some reputational samples are also extreme case samples.

Comparable case samples are drawn in order to allow for a comparison of some type. For example, a sample of men might be compared with a sample of women; a sample of urban beneficiaries might be compared with a sample of rural beneficiaries; a sample of teachers of high-risk students might be compared with a sample of teachers of college-bound students. Following the logic (but not the size) of samples common to experimental and quasi-experimental designs, a sample of nonparticipants might be drawn to compare with participants in a program. Thus, both within-program comparisons and a small-scale variation of experimental group and comparison group comparisons can be purposefully included in a qualitative evaluation.

Purposive Sampling for Different Types of Qualitative Data Collection and Use

Sampling for Data Collection

Sampling is often a decision point for more than one type of data collection. An evaluator must consider who and how many to sample in interviewing, which and how many sites and events to observe, and which and how many program documents and records to review when it is not possible to collect and study each potential datum. The different types or strategies for purposive sampling described above apply to each of these data collection types. For example:

Sampling interviewees (individual or **focus group** interviews)

- *Range sample,* including a member of each ethnic subgroup
- *Extreme case sample* of participants receiving the fewest benefits
- *Reputational sample* of local activists promoting the program

Sampling observations

- *Typical sample* of day-to-day program operations
- *Comparable case sample* of day-to-day activities outside the program
- *Critical case sample* of activities personnel find most difficult

Sampling documents

- *Quota sample* with a proportion of each of several types of documents
- *Comprehensive sample* of all prior evaluations of the program
- *Negative case sample* of all applications that were denied

More than one purposeful sampling strategy is often useful in an evaluation where many things must be understood—for example, both typical cases and extreme cases, both ordinary events and periodic ceremonies, both program plans and working documents such as beneficiary records.

Some evaluations (qualitative, quantitative, or mixed-method) include case studies in their designs. Although each evaluation could be considered a case study, with the program constituting the case, minicase studies within an evaluation might be employed to illuminate specific aspects of the program. For example, in a multisite study, evaluators might include a case study of each of three program implementation sites, perhaps choosing a thriving site, a failing site, and struggling site. This selection of sites could be considered a range sample, showing a range of implementation success, or it could be considered a typical case sample and two extreme case samples. This shows how the selection criteria can be applied to case selection and site selection as well as to specific data collection choices.

Sampling from Data for Reporting

Related to the concept and strategies of sampling for data collection is the sampling of data for qualitative reporting. From the many observation vignettes and interviews recorded, for example, which should be included in a report to provide a reader with a vicarious experience of the program to deepen his or her understanding of its workings and effects? Not merely the most interesting or most vivid snippets should be chosen; the point is not the entertainment of the reader. For understanding, a range sample of interviewees' experiences might be drawn from the interview data, and a typical sample juxtaposed against a deviant case sample from among the observation data documenting interactions between personnel and beneficiaries. The sample of data included in the report should be as purposeful as the sampling itself, revealing the basis on which findings were generated and warranting them. The purpose of sharing the selected samples should be explained along with the data presentation so the reader understands, for example, that an extreme case is not typical.

Considerations in Planning Purposive Sampling

Sampling can support or undermine the validity of evaluation findings about a program's merits and shortcomings, depending on the appropriateness of the sampling criteria for the purpose of the evaluation. An insufficient or skewed sample, one in which some aspect is exaggerated, is unlikely to lead to valid findings or real program improvement. Planning a sample larger than can be accomplished with evaluation resources (time, personnel, funds) may lead to truncation at the end, with no assurance that the data collected early would have been confirmed by the data lost. The particular question to be addressed may suggest the type of sample or samples that would be most appropriate. For example:

For interviewing (individual and focus group): Are new students benefiting from the school's peer-mentoring program?

- *Range sample* of mentees matching each ethnic group in the school
- *Extreme case samples* of mentees succeeding (and not) academically
- *Typical sample* of peer mentors
- *Reputational sample* of supportive and nonsupportive teachers

Is the new **microcredit** program helping beneficiaries establish sustainable businesses?

- *Quota sample* of each type of business begun by borrowers
- *Snowball sample* of the clients of (and identified by) these borrowers
- *Comprehensive sample* of the managers of the program
- *Negative case sample* of applicants denied loans

Again, these considerations hold not only for developing a sampling plan for data collection but also for sampling data to support findings in reports, where the sampling criteria should be documented and justified.

Probability (Random) Sampling

Key Questions in Designing a Random Sample

For QUANT evaluation, one of the most serious dangers of a sample too small is that the program may appear not to have produced its desired effects when, in fact, it did but the sample was too small to detect the effects (see Box 14.1). An understanding of the concepts of **effect size** and the **power of the test** and their influence on the determination of sample size is critical for all evaluation designs but particularly for RWE. In addition to questions of sample size, the following questions must usually be addressed for policy evaluations:

- Is the **target population** of concern to policymakers defined in the same way as the population in the study?
- Have the sampling procedures biased the estimates of project effects?
- Are the estimates of project effects and the influence of **intervening variables** on these effects precise enough for the policy purpose?

Although the estimation of sample size is important, it is only one of the factors affecting the choice of the appropriate sample design. Kraemer and Thiemann (1987, chap. 10) warn that quantitative researchers often become so involved with the statistical refinements of sample design and analysis that they tend to overlook some basic principles of sample planning. Making a mistake in planning a study as to what data to collect and how many subjects to study is irrevocable in quantitative studies. No amount of statistical analysis can overcome, for example, the use of a sampling plan that excludes critical parts of the target population. Box 14.2 points out that when consulting with statisticians on questions such as sample size, it is important to try to find a statistician who also has some familiarity with the specific subject area.

Box 14.2   Be Cautious about Advice from Statisticians Not Familiar with the Field of the Evaluation

---

When seeking statistical consultation, issues of particular and specific relevance in their own fields of research may never be brought to the attention of the consulting statistician. A consulting statistician (not versed in a particular field) may not know that there are several extant valid and reliable scales. . . . The researcher is then informed that 500 patients might be needed and never realizes that 50 might otherwise have sufficed. As a result, the most cost-effective decisions are not necessarily the ones made, even with expert advice.

SOURCE: Kraemer and Thiemann (1987:99).

Initial exploratory studies and careful review of the literature will often be required before finalizing the sample design and administering the data collection instrument. Statistical tests based on poorly prepared sample plans can often be misleading. For example, in the previously mentioned study of survival strategies of low-income families in Colombia (see Chapter 13), the exploratory participant observer study found that poor families relied heavily on the transfers of money, food, and even household members between family groups living in different parts of the country or even overseas. This preliminary observation modified the sample design because it became clear that it would be misleading to define the basic economic and social unit as people living in one particular house.

Researchers should think in terms of cost-efficiency to a much greater extent when defining the sampling strategy. For example, it probably does not make sense to invest too many resources in refining the **sampling frame** (the list or map from which the sample is to be selected) if this means that there is not enough money to hire a sufficient number of supervisors to ensure that **interviewers** follow the sample selection procedures.

There are at least five critical choices in sample design. These choices are mentioned below and then discussed in more detail in the following sections:

1. *Deciding whether a sample should be used.* In quantitative evaluation, when the population is large, there is often no choice but to select a sample, but there are several circumstances in which it may be better to cover the whole population. When the population is small, it is possible to consider collecting data on the whole population, and sometimes the **credibility** of the conclusions may require that all the population is studied. The concept of sampling is not

universally understood or accepted, and where it is important to convince key decision makers as to the validity of the findings, it may be necessary to go beyond normal sampling procedures (e.g., by surveying all the population, even though this may not be considered necessary by the evaluation team).

2. *Defining the population from which the sample will be drawn.* Frequently, the quantitative evaluator does not have access to a sampling frame (e.g., directory, list, or map listing all schools, households, or communities to be covered by the sample) that corresponds exactly to the target population. For example, the directory of schools may not include certain types of small private schools, or the map of urban communities may not include houses built within the past three years. An assessment must be made of the magnitude and importance of the discrepancies between the sampling frame and the program population, how these might affect the validity of the conclusions, and what if anything could be done to improve the coverage of the sampling frame. Assuming that the sampling frame could be improved (e.g., by finding ways to include small private schools excluded from the schools directory or updating community maps to include houses constructed since the map was prepared three years ago), a decision must be made on the potential trade-offs between investing resources to make these improvements, versus, for example, increasing the size of the sample or reducing the nonresponse rate.

For example, in communities where all adults have two or three different jobs, it may be very difficult to find people at home to interview. To get a representative sample, it may be necessary to revisit many houses two or three times. On the other hand, if the decision is made to interview any adult found at home on the first visit (rather than the household head, for example), the sample would be biased toward people who are unemployed or who are elderly or otherwise not working. Thus, ensuring a representative sample would significantly increase the costs of data collection (if on average two or three visits were required to complete each interview). In this case, the evaluator might have to decide whether it would be more useful to invest scarce resources to improve the sample frame or to increase the time and budget for data collection (to permit revisits to reduce the nonresponse rate).

3. *Choice of sampling methods.* Often, a number of different sampling methods are available, and a decision must be made as to which method will be most reliable and at the same time cost-effective for the purposes of this evaluation.

4. *Defining the precision of the estimates.* It is essential to agree with the client on the required level of **precision** and then to determine the size and type of sample that can best approximate this level within the available resources. We continually remind evaluators that decisions on precision must be made in consultation with the client—this is a policy decision and not just a "technical" issue that is better left to the experts, as many clients assume.

5. *Nonprobability (purposive) or probability sampling.* A critical decision is whether to use nonprobability or probability (random) sampling. Although the use of probability (random) sampling has the great advantage that it is possible to estimate the statistical precision of the findings, there are many circumstances in which random sampling is either not possible or not necessary. In the previous section, we discussed the wide range of purposive (nonrandom) sampling procedures available, and for many types of evaluation, these may be more appropriate than random sampling.

Selection Procedures in Probability (Random) Sampling

In probability (random) sampling, each unit (person, family, school) has a known, nonzero probability of being selected. Although some texts state that all units have an *equal* probability of selection, this is not correct because there are many types of stratified samples in which the probabilities of selection may be different. For example, small groups such as ethnic minorities or female-headed households may be deliberately oversampled to ensure sufficient appreciation of outcomes for them derived from the sample. The important point is that the probability of selection for each group is known, and weighting procedures can be used in the estimations. Henry (1990:26) points out that it is possible for some units to have a probability of 1 or certainty of being selected. He cites the example of an election study in Illinois where, because of its size and critical importance, Cook County would always be included in the sample. During the estimation process, adjustments would be made to compensate for the different probabilities of selection[2]. The following are the most common types of **probability samples**:

- *Simple random sample.* Every unit has an equal chance of being selected.
- *Stratified random sample.* The study population is divided into easily identifiable strata such as geographical regions, general health status (on a scale that has already been administered to the whole sample population), or sex and age groups. The strata must be easy to administer, cover the whole survey population, and categorize the population into groups directly related to the purpose of the study. An indicator of a good stratification design is that the within-strata variance of key variables should be significantly smaller than between-strata variation.
- *Systematic sample.* All subjects are listed and assigned sequential numbers from 1 to N (where N is the total number of subjects—for example, 1,000). The required sample size n (for example 100) is then determined (see later in the chapter) and a sampling fraction (f) is calculated by dividing the total population by n. In this case, $f = 1,000/100 = 10$, and every 10th subject is then selected from the list.
- *Random route.* This is a type of systematic sample that can be used when no listing of the total population is available. A sketch map of the community is drawn and the approximate number of families to be included in the sample is estimated. A random route is generated by selecting a starting point on the map and then instructing the interviewer to turn left or right or continue straight ahead at each intersection. The sampling fraction is then calculated, and the interviewer must interview each nth house encountered on this random route.[3]
- *Cluster sampling.* The sample population is divided into naturally occurring clusters such as geographical areas, schools, or places of employment. All the clusters are listed, and a sample of clusters is randomly selected. All subjects in each cluster, or a randomly selected sample of clusters, are then interviewed.
- *Multistage sampling.* The selection of subjects with stratified or cluster samples may involve several stages. For example, a sample of villages may be selected, then a sample of schools in each village, and then a sample of classes in each school. Finally, a sample of students may be selected within these classes (see Figure 14.1).

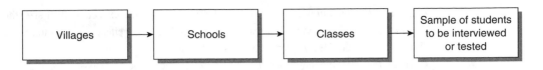

Figure 14.1   A Multistage Sample for Selecting a Sample of Students

Sample Design Decisions at Different Stages of the Survey

When designing a sample, a number of decisions must be made before deciding on the best sample design, others must be made during the process of sample design, and yet others must be made after data collection has been completed (Henry 1990). These three types of decisions are summarized next.

Presampling Questions

Before deciding on the best type of sample, it is necessary to consider the following:

- *What is the nature of the study?* Is it exploratory, descriptive, or analytical? Normally, larger samples and more precise estimates are required for analytical studies than for exploratory and descriptive ones.
- *What are the variables and hypotheses of greatest interest?* The characteristics of the key variables (including the size of **standard deviation**) and the nature of the hypotheses to be tested can affect the type of evaluation design and the size and type of sample. For example, the required sample size will be significantly smaller (by as much as 40%) if a **one-tailed** rather than a **two-tailed** significance test can be used (see p. 343, this chapter).
- *What is the target population?* How easily and economically can a good sampling frame (that closely approximates the total target population) be obtained or created?
- *Are subpopulations or special groups of importance to the study?* When subpopulations must be compared, this will normally increase the sample size.
- *How will the data be collected?* There are significant differences in the cost and time required to administer different data collection instruments.
- *Is sampling appropriate?* There are some situations when sampling is not possible or appropriate (see earlier discussion, p. 330, this chapter).

Questions and Choices during the Sample Design Process

Once the best type of sample design for this evaluation has been decided, there are a number of questions and choices on how to finalize and implement the design:

- *What listing can be used for the sampling frame?* How comprehensive and reliable is this? Could the sampling frame be improved and would it be worth investing (scarce) resources to improve it?

- *What is the minimum acceptable effect size?* The smaller the expected effect size, the larger the required sample. Is it reasonable to specify a larger effect size so as to reduce the required sample size (see p. 339, this chapter)?
- *What type of sampling technique will be used* (see earlier discussion, p. 332, this chapter)?
- *Will the probability of selection be equal or unequal if different strata or clusters are used in the sample?*
- *How many participants or units will be selected for the sample?* Is this number affordable, and if not would it be acceptable to reduce the sample size?
- *For longitudinal studies, what is the expected rate of population change?* Many longitudinal evaluations involve either panel studies where the sample subjects are reinterviewed or where the same sampling frame is used to select a new sample. In many areas, population size and composition can change dramatically as new families move in or others leave. It is not uncommon in informal urban settlements for the number of families or physical structures to increase by 10% to 20% per year. In these cases, it may be necessary to adjust the sample design to ensure that the samples at later points in time are still representative of the total population. The likely sample dropout rate should be estimated, and in some cases, the size of the original sample should be increased to compensate for dropouts or turnover. Another practical question concerns the feasibility of locating the same families again for the repeat survey (see Box 14.3).

Postsampling Questions and Choices

Once the data collection has been completed, there are often a number of questions and choices concerning how the sample should be analyzed. Some of these choices concern how to

---

Box 14.3   Longitudinal Panel Studies Are Great—But What If You Can't Find the Families Two Years Later?

An evaluation of a self-help housing program in informal settlements in El Salvador planned to use a panel study in which the same households would be reinterviewed two years later. Detailed demographic information was collected on each family, and a map was drawn to make sure that all the houses could be correctly identified two years later. Even with all these precautions, it was found that in 10% to 20% of the cases, the researchers were not sure if the same family had been found again. What had previously been two separate buildings had sometimes been combined into one; the front door of some houses had been moved from one street to another; families had decided to change the number of their house. Furthermore, women may have three or four different family names, and they may change from one year to another. Reported ages can also change depending on how the respondent is feeling. So how does the evaluator know if Maria Rodriguez Martinez who was 42 years old in 2000 and lived in a single-story house with its entrance on Calle Las Flores is the same person as 38-year-old Ana Maria Sanchez who in 2002 lives in a two-story house with its entrance on Calle Los Robles?

correct any problems that arose during the administration of the sample, whereas others concern statistical estimations from the sample.

- *How can nonresponse be evaluated?* If the nonresponse rate is relatively high, how might this affect the validity of the conclusions? Are there any adjustments that can be made (such as a rapid follow-up study to fill in some of the gaps)?
- *Is weighting necessary?* Weighting is the process of adjusting the proportion of certain groups included in the sample to their true proportion in the total population. If some small groups were deliberately oversampled (a higher proportion included in the sample than there are in the population) because of their importance to the evaluation, it might be necessary to make an adjustment in the analysis when estimates are being made for the total population. Sometimes weighting is necessary because of a deliberate sampling strategy to over- or underrepresent certain groups. In other cases, weighting is used to adjust for the low response rates of certain groups. For example, it might have proved difficult to interview men who are long-distance truck drivers or deep-sea fishermen because they are away from home for extended periods of time and difficult to contact. If, for example, it is estimated that about 20% of men are deep-sea fishermen but only about 10% of men interviewed were fishermen, then the evaluation team might decide to use a statistical weight to adjust the sample proportion to their true proportion of the population. However, a decision to weight the findings for certain groups is not automatic and always needs careful consideration because weighting can itself introduce a bias. For example, it may be that the fishermen who were interviewed were not typical of all fishermen (perhaps they were older and spend less time at sea), so giving a higher value to those who were interviewed on the assumption that they represented all fisherman could introduce a bias. In this example, the average age of fishermen who were interviewed would be higher than those who were not interviewed.

Sources of Error in Probabilistic Sample Design

There are two main sources of error affecting the reliability of sample estimates: sampling bias and nonsampling bias (Henry 1990, chap. 3). When samples have to be designed under budget and time constraints, there are often choices to be made about how to address each of these sources of bias. For example, it may not make sense to invest a lot of resources in trying to reduce nonresponse rates if there are some fundamental weaknesses in the sampling frame that cause important sectors of the target population to be excluded from the study.

Assume that an evaluation is being planned to assess the impacts of improved housing on the employment patterns of low-income urban families, many of whom work in small, largely unregistered businesses in the informal sector. The possibility is being considered of using as the sampling frame the list of enterprises compiled by the Ministry of Industry for its periodic employment surveys. The list is very current and easy to use, and it is believed to include almost all registered businesses employing 10 or more workers. However, the evaluation team estimates that the list does not cover at least 25% of the target population working in the informal sector. Two sampling options are being considered: The first is to use the Ministry of Industry sampling frame and to then use statistical techniques to extrapolate from this sample to estimate the characteristics of the smaller businesses not covered by the sample. The second option is to complement the Ministry of Industry sample with a cluster or quota sample covering some of the areas where the target population works. This second sample would be expensive to select and might have a lower level of statistical precision. Clearly, there are trade-offs of cost and accuracy between these options.

Nonsampling Bias

Samples can never be guaranteed to indicate the true value of the variables covered (e.g., average household income, average absentee rates from third-grade classes, the proportion of families earning over 500 pesos per month). Samples produce *estimates* that indicate the probability that the true value (of mean income, absentee rates) will lie within a certain range. This range, which depends on the size of the sample and the standard deviation of the statistic being estimated, is the *sampling error*. This error can be easily estimated because it is determined by the sample size and the standard deviation of the variable being estimated. However, sampling error is not the only source of bias of estimates from surveys. Some of the important *nonsampling biases* include the following:

- *The coverage of the sampling frame and the adequacy of listing of subjects.* Some sampling frames approximate the target population quite well, but the quality and comprehensiveness of the listings are questionable. For example, the Ministry of Education may have a complete listing of all schools, but there may be overreporting of children who actually attend.
- *Nonresponse.* Subjects who cannot be located or who refuse to be interviewed usually have different characteristics from willing respondents, so a significant nonresponse rate is likely to introduce important biases in the sample. For example, respondents may on average be younger, include more women, be better educated, or be from a higher income group.
- *Measurement error.* Information may be systematically misreported (people understate their income, women do not report domestic violence or that their husband has deserted them) or it may be misrecorded or misinterpreted by the interviewer. For example, the interviewer may assume that the respondent does not know how to read or write, so the question is not asked.

Sampling Bias

Certain kinds of biases are also due to the procedures used for sample selection:

- *Selection bias* occurs when not all sectors of the target population have an equal chance of being selected. For example, if one adult is randomly selected from each household, the probability of a particular adult being selected is greater in households with few adults than those with many adults.
- *Estimation bias* occurs when the average calculated from the sample provides a biased estimate of the true population mean. For example, the use of the median will provide a biased estimate of the population mean (Henry 1990:38). It is possible to adjust for most estimation biases during the statistical analysis *as long as the evaluator is aware that a bias exists.*

Using Power Analysis and Effect Size for Estimating the Appropriate Sample Size

The Importance of Power Analysis for Determining Sample Size for Probability Sampling

Power analysis is a tool for determining the relationship between sample size and the level of statistical precision in a survey or evaluation. It can be used to estimate the sample size required to achieve a specified level of statistical precision or to estimate the level of statistical precision that can be achieved with a given sample size.

Power analysis is particularly useful for RWE because reducing the sample size is usually one of the most important options for reducing costs. However, overzealous reductions in sample size can be fatal. Many programs, even if well managed, can expect to achieve only relatively small improvements (effect size), and if the sample is too small, the statistical significance tests may commit a Type II error (see p. 340) and fail to detect what was in fact a statistically significant project effect. The smaller the effect size, the larger the sample required to detect it. Power analysis is an essential tool for the RealWorld evaluator providing precise estimates of the sample size required to achieve the objectives of the evaluation. When the effect size is small, power analysis helps avoid selecting a sample that is too small, and conversely, when the effect size is relatively large, it can avoid wasting time and money through selecting a sample that is larger than necessary.

This is not just an academic concern. It has been estimated that when the effect size of many different types of social programs is less than about 0.3, in perhaps as many as 75% of the evaluation studies, the sample was too small to have been able to detect the effect even if it did exist (Rossi, Lipsey, and Freeman 2004, chap. 10). In other words, these evaluation studies were doomed to failure simply because the sample was too small to detect the effect being studied. Table 14.3 (p. 348, this chapter) shows that with conventional assumptions about significance levels and accepting a power level of 0.8, an estimated effect size of 0.3 could be detected with a total sample size of 132[4] (66 in both the project and comparison groups). However, a total sample of 304 (152 in both the project and comparison groups) would be required to identify an effect size of 0.2, and with an effect size as small as 0.1, the total sample size would increase to 1,232.

Although a full understanding of the logic of power analysis requires a solid grounding in statistics, the basic principles are easy to understand. For more complicated evaluation designs, or where high levels of statistical precision are required, it is advisable to consult with a statistical specialist[5]. However, it is important to understand the basic principles of power analysis to know what questions to ask the statistician and to make sure these questions are addressed.

Estimating Effect Size

The effect size is the size of the change or effect that a program produces or is expected to produce. Technically this is "*the difference between the outcome measured on program targets receiving the intervention and an estimate of what the outcome for those targets would have been had they not received the intervention*" [italics added] (Rossi et al. 2004:302). The larger the difference between the means (or other measures) of the two groups being compared (pretest-posttest project group or project and comparison group), the greater the effect size. Where possible, a **standardized effect size** is used so that comparisons can be made across programs or even across different kinds of effects (see next section). However, it is sometimes necessary to use less precise measures, such as the number of points increase on a behavior scale or aptitude test, where the meaning of the change can be difficult to interpret. For binary variables, an odds ratio is often used (see Rossi et al. 2004, chap. 10).

To obtain a standardized measure that can be used to compare the findings of different studies, the difference of means is divided by the standard deviation of the population. Thus:

$$\text{Standardized effect size} = \frac{\bar{x}_1 - \bar{x}_2}{\sigma x}$$

Where:

$\bar{x}_1 =$ the mean score for the project group

$\bar{x}_2 =$ the mean score for the total population (estimated from the comparison group)

$\sigma x =$ the standard deviation of the total population

For example, assume that after a microcredit program had been operating for two years, the average income of all adult women in the community was 300 pesos, whereas the average for women who had received loans was 350 pesos, and that the standard deviation for the total population was 100 pesos. The effect size would be calculated as follows:

$$\text{Standardized effect size} = (350 - 300)/100 = 0.5.$$

However, if the standard deviation had been only 75 pesos, then the effect size would have been (0.66).

Defining Minimum Acceptable Effect Size (MAES)

The minimum acceptable effect size (**MAES**), also called the *critical effect size,* is the minimum level of change that the evaluation design must be able to detect. The smaller the effect size that must be detected, the larger the required sample. Table 14.1 describes different criteria that can be used to define the MAES. In some cases, the MAES is defined in comparison with an accepted norm or target (e.g., average test scores for a particular school grade); in others, this is based on a comparison with other similar programs; and in yet other cases, policymakers determine what is a perceived by politicians and other stakeholders to be the minimum acceptable increase. Alternatively, the MAES may be based on cost-effectiveness calculations. The MAES is normally population specific so that the acceptable effect size for a group of young men may be quite different to the acceptable effect for a group of young women or a group of older people of either sex.

The choice of effect size is a key determinant of the required sample size. Where very small effect sizes must be detected, large samples will be required. Obviously, the MAES cannot be arbitrarily increased just to reduce the sample size. If it is believed that a 10% increase in

Table 14.1   Criteria for Determining the Minimum Acceptable Effect Size (MAES)

Criterion	Examples
1. Difference in the original measurement scale	When the outcome measure has a clearly understood meaning, the MAES may be stated directly in terms of this unit—for example, the dollar value of health services after the introduction of a new program or the reduced recidivism rate for juvenile offenders.
2. Comparison with test norms or performance of a normative population	For a literacy program, MAES may be defined as reducing the gap between the average grade score (for the city or state) and the target group score.
3. Differences between criterion groups	Comparison of school with national grade scores
4. Proportion over a diagnostic or other success threshold	A mental health program might use a well-known test of clinical depression such as the Beck Depression Inventory, which defines a score of 17 to 20 as borderline clinical depression. The MAES could be defined as the proportion with scores below 17.
5. Proportion over an arbitrary success threshold	Proportion of families in an employment program with incomes above the federal poverty level.
6. Comparison with the effects of similar programs	One of the goals of local irrigation programs is the proportion of farmers paying the water service charges required to maintain the system. MAES could be defined as the average repayment rate found in similar projects.
7. Conventional guidelines	Cohen (1988) proposed conventional guidelines, based on meta-evaluations conducted in different sectors of small effects (0.2), medium effects (0.50), and large effects (0.80)
8. Cost-effectiveness	The average unit cost of delivering services is compared with alternative programs or what is considered by stakeholders to be a "reasonable" unit cost.

SOURCE: Adapted by the authors from Rossi, Lipsey, and Freeman (2004:318–19). Criterion 8 was added by the authors.

school enrollment is the most optimistic estimate, it clearly does not make any sense to say, "Let us assume there will be a 25% increase." However, once clients understand the trade-offs between effect size and cost of the evaluation (i.e., sample size), there are sometimes ways to increase effect size. For example, if it is anticipated that enrollment is likely to increase more for girls than for boys, then it would be possible in the first evaluation to study program impact only on girls. Obviously, it should be made completely clear to clients and readers that the evaluation does not cover the whole population. Another way to increase effect size is to improve the program design and delivery of services. Assume there is evidence from earlier programs that student math skills increase more when new textbooks are complemented by orientation sessions for teachers. Providing these orientation sessions might improve student performance and hence the effect size. Clearly, there are trade-offs, and the client would have to decide whether the additional cost and effort of organizing the orientation sessions were justified.

Type I and Type II Errors

One of the challenges of sample design is to try, within available resources, to reduce two types of error (see Table 14.2):

- **Type I error**. Wrongly concluding that a program has a significant effect on the target variable when in fact it does not. [error of inclusion]
- **Type II error**. Wrongly concluding that a program does not have a significant effect on the target variable when in fact it does. [error of exclusion]

The relative importance of these two types of error varies according to the research context and the policy objectives. For example, in testing new drugs, the first priority is to ensure that all drugs that do *not* have a positive effect are detected (Type I error). The financial and human costs of wrong decisions are very high. However, for many types of development programs, the primary concern may be to ensure that small but potentially important effects are not overlooked (Type II error). Meta-analysis studies in many sectors have found that the effect size of even the most successful programs is quite small, and consequently, it is important to ensure that these are not overlooked by setting too rigorous criteria for accepting a statistically significant effect. We will see in the next section that β, the accepted level for the Type II error, is equivalent to the statistical power of the test.

Table 14.2   Type I and Type II Errors in the Interpretation of Evaluation Findings

Results of significance test on sample data	*Population Circumstances*	
	Intervention and control means differ	*Intervention and control means do not differ*
Significant difference found	Correct conclusion (probability $= 1 - \beta$)	**Type 1 error.** Wrongly concluding the project does have a statistically significant impact (probability $= \alpha$)
No significant difference found	**Type II error.** Wrongly concluding the project did not have a statistically significant impact (probability $= \beta$). This is equivalent to the statistical power of the test.	Correct conclusion (probability $= 1 - \alpha$)

SOURCE: Rossi, Lipsey, and Freeman (2004:309).

The probability of making a Type I or Type II error is related to the size of the sample. Both kinds of error can be reduced but at the cost of increasing the sample size. Consequently, it is essential to determine the relative importance of the two types of error and to set the statistical confidence levels, and the resultant sample sizes, accordingly.

The Power of the Test

As indicated earlier, statistical power analysis is one of the key tools for estimating how large a sample is required to find a statistically significant project impact if one really does exist. In cases where a project is not expected to produce a very large impact (effect), many evaluation studies have wrongly assumed that a project did not have a statistically significant effect when in fact the sample was too small to detect the effect if it did exist (Lipsey 1990; Rossi et al. 2004). Statistical power is "the probability that an estimate will be statistically significant when, in fact, it represents a real effect of a given magnitude" (Rossi et al. 2004:309). The normal convention is to set power equal to 0.80, meaning that that there is an 80% chance that a particular sample will reject the **null hypothesis** (i.e., will find a statistically significant difference) if the program really does have an effect (see Box 14.4). Where it is particularly important to avoid Type II errors and to ensure that real program effects are not rejected, it is possible to set power equal to 0.90 or even 0.95 or 0.99. However, the reason these higher power levels are often not used is that the increase in power requires a significant increase in the sample size. For example, Table 14.3 shows that increasing power from 0.8 to 0.9 may require an increase of 30% in the sample size, whereas an increase to 0.95 may almost double the required sample size. Box 14.5 points out that when statistical advice is sought on power and effect size calculations, it is important to find a statistician who understands the subject area and particularly what are realistic assumptions about effect size.

Box 14.4   Conventions for Defining the Statistical Power of the Test

---

- The power of the test is conventionally set at 0.80 (an 80% probability that a sample will find a statistically significant result if the null hypothesis is false).
- Power analysis usually assumes that the 0.05 significance level is being used.

Where greater precision is required, power can be set at 0.90 or 0.05 (or even higher) and the significance level can be set at 0.01 (or even higher). However, increasing the precision level will significantly increase the required sample size.

Box 14.5   Sampling Specialists Are Often Not Familiar with the Fields of Application on Which Their Advice Is Sought

---

It is not a minor problem that those who are able to do power calculations readily are generally those who least know the fields of application, and those who best know the fields of application are least able to do power calculations.

SOURCE: Kraemer and Thiemann (1987:99).

An Example: The Statistical Power of an Evaluation of Special Instruction Programs on Aptitude Test Scores

A hypothetical study was conducted to assess the impact of special instruction programs on aptitude scores of fifth-grade students. It was known from previous studies that the mean score for fifth graders on this test was 200 (see Figure 14.2 lower distribution) and that the population standard deviation (*SD*) was 48. This means that for the null hypothesis (that special instruction did not raise aptitude test scores) to be rejected at the 0.05 level, the mean for the treatment group would have to be greater than 209.84 (the shaded area at the right end of the curve in the lower distribution).[6]

It was hypothesized, based on a review of the literature, that the treatment (special instruction) could be expected to raise the mean test score by 8 points, so that the mean of the treatment group would be 208 points[7]. The shaded area in the upper distribution shows the probability that a sample of the treatment group would have a mean score sufficiently high (i.e., above 209.84) to reject the null hypothesis, even when the treatment really does have an effect. In this case, the probability is only 40% that a sample from the treatment group would find a statistically significant difference. In other words, the risk of a Type II error is very high (60%).

Why is this so? Many people might assume that a carefully selected sample of the treatment group would always find a statistically significant difference (if, as in this case, the treatment really did have an effect). The reason can be seen by comparing the two distributions in Figure 14.2. It can be seen that the hypothesized increase in test scores (the effect size) is quite small (0.166) and that there is a considerable overlap between the two distributions. This means that if the null hypothesis was true and the treatment had no effect, many samples would by chance have means equal to or greater than the hypothesized treatment mean score of 208. Using the 0.05 confidence interval, the mean score would have to be greater than 209.84 to reject the null hypothesis—even when the treatment does have an effect.

Calculating Statistical Power

To calculate the statistical power of the test in a particular evaluation, it is necessary to know the effect size and the sample size. The statistical power can then be obtained from a power table (see Table 14.3 for a simplified power table). In our example, the effect size is 0.166, which is quite small. Our sample size is 67. Consulting a more complete power table than Table 14.3 (we have used Kraemer and Thiemann 1987:105) shows that for an effect size of 0.17 and a sample size of 67, the statistical power = 0.40.

If the predicted average increase in test score had been 16 instead of 8 (an effect size of 0.33), then the power of the test would increase to 0.85 (Aron and Aron 2002:134). In this case, the risk of wrongly rejecting a real project effect would drop from 60% in the earlier case to only 15%. Increasing effect size always increases the power of the test, so it is obviously desirable to have as large an effect size as possible. We saw earlier in this chapter that there are various ways in which the effect size and, consequently, the power of the test can be increased.

Deciding How to Set the Power Level

In the exploratory stage of an evaluation, the goal is often to determine whether there are potentially important effects that should be explored further. From this perspective, it may be worth defining a fairly low power level so as not to exclude potentially interesting but small

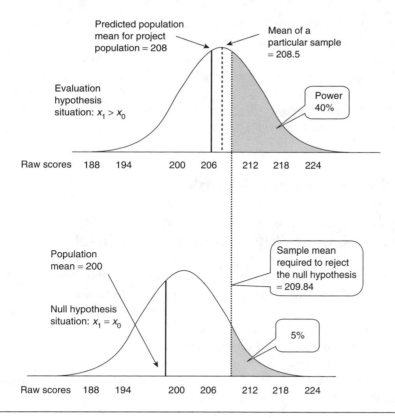

Figure 14.2   Statistical Power Analysis: Testing the Effect of a Program to Raise Mathematical Aptitude Test Scores

NOTE: The figure presents the distribution of mean test scores of 67 students on a standardized mathematical aptitude test in a fictional study. The lower curve is based on the known distribution of means for the total student population and has a mean of 200. The upper distribution is based on a predicted distribution, assuming that the evaluation hypothesis (that the treatment raises aptitude score) is correct. It is hypothesized that the mean for the project group is 208. Shaded sections of both curves indicate the areas in which the null hypothesis will be rejected. Power = 0.40, indicating that there is only a 40% probability that any particular sample will reject the null hypothesis, even though the project treatment did produce a statistically significant increase in test scores.

SOURCE: Adapted with permission from Aron, A., E. Aron, and E. Coups, *Statistics for the Behavioral and Social Sciences: A Brief Course, 3/e,* Copyright © 2005 by Pearson Education, Inc. Some of the figures have been slightly adjusted to make the results consistent with the Kraemer and Thiemann Power Table.

effects. Subsequent stages of the analysis—for example, the introduction of control variables (see below)—may raise the significance level by eliminating confounding factors or by showing that the program has significant effects for some groups but not for others (e.g., for women but not for men). In these later stages of the analysis, the power level will probably be raised.

One- and Two-Tailed Statistical Significance Tests

Most programs have a clearly defined objective to produce a positive outcome either by reducing a negative indicator (infant mortality, illiteracy, criminal behavior) or increasing a positive indicator (school attendance rates, household income, agricultural output). When the direction of the desired change is known (to increase school enrolment or reduce malnutrition), a "one-tailed" statistical test can be used[8]. Although this is much less common, the direction of the effect is sometimes not known, and it will be necessary to use a "two-tailed test." For example, introducing school fees might increase enrollment (because the quality of education and the maintenance of the facilities might improve), or it might decrease attendance if many poor families are not able to pay the fees. When a two-tailed test is required, the size of the sample will increase by about 40%.[9]

Determining the Size of the Sample

The Null Hypothesis, the Evaluation Hypothesis, and Deciding the Statistical Significance Level

To evaluate whether an intervention has had a statistically significant impact, it is necessary to start with a null hypothesis. We use a null hypothesis because it is never possible to prove statistically that a hypothesis is true, but only to estimate the probability that an effect size as large as the one observed could have occurred if there really was no difference between the project group and the total population. The null hypothesis states that there is no difference between the total population and the project group with respect to the outcome measure (aptitude test score, household income, proportion of girls attending secondary score, etc.). The null hypothesis (H_0) is specified as follows:

$$H_0 : x_0 = x_1$$

Where:
x_0 = mean or other outcome measure for the total population.
x_1 = mean or other outcome measure for the project population.

The purpose of the statistical significance test is to decide how big a difference would have to be found between the total population and the project group to reject "beyond a reasonable doubt" the null hypothesis. The normal convention is to state that the null hypothesis will be rejected if there is less than a 5% chance of a difference as large as that found in a survey having occurred by chance. This is called the 0.05 (or 95%) significance level. One of the key questions for the evaluation design is to determine the level of statistical significance that would satisfy the "beyond a reasonable doubt" requirement. By increasing the size of the sample, we can reduce the level of reasonable doubt from, say, a 1 in 20 chance of wrongly concluding that the program had an effect to a 1 in 100 or even a 1 in 1,000 chance (e.g., for testing new drugs). However, reducing the level of reasonable doubt involves significant increases in the size of the sample and the resulting cost and time required to conduct the study. In a real-world environment, the challenge is to satisfy the client's needs for acceptably precise estimates while remaining within the available budget and time. Consequently, defining "reasonable doubt" is a critical decision in evaluation design.

Evaluability Assessment

Many evaluators become overwhelmed by the statistical calculations required to estimate sample size, and it is often forgotten that there are several important preliminary steps in the evaluation before even thinking about testing and sample sizes. The first step involves a thorough review of the existing evidence from the research literature, reports of similar programs, and, if possible, discussions with experts. This will help determine whether the proposed program is likely to have an effect. An exploratory field study should then be conducted to understand the program and how it operates and to determine whether the program effects can be measured at this point in time, for this particular project, and with the available resources. This **evaluability assessment** may suggest various reasons why an evaluation may not be appropriate. The literature may suggest that the program model is unlikely to work, it may be considered too early in the **project cycle** to measure effects, the target population may be too small to permit the kinds of statistical analysis required, or the proposed effects may be too difficult to quantify and measure. Assuming that none of these problems is considered too serious, it is then possible to begin to plan the evaluation. Henry (1990, chap. 3) and Kraemer and Thieman (1987, chap. 2) provide useful overviews of these preparatory stages of the evaluation.

Estimating the Required Sample Size for Power Analysis[10]

The choice of sample size cannot be made in a vacuum; there are trade-offs concerning the most effective way to use the evaluation resources. For example, spending more to increase sample size may mean fewer resources and less time for following up on nonresponses to reduce this often important source of nonsampling bias.

Each step in the estimation of sample size is illustrated for a hypothetical example that estimates the sample size for evaluating the impact of special instructions on student performance on a standardized mathematical aptitude test. We use the previous example but change several details. In the present case, we assume the following:

- The mean aptitude test score for the total student population is again 200, and the population *SD*, based on previous studies, is again estimated to be 48.
- In this case, the survey will cover both students who received the special instruction and the comparison group of students, who did not.
- The total fifth-grade student population is over 20,000, and the number of students who have received the special instructions is 650.

The following steps must be followed for determining the efficient sample size:

Step 1: Determine the purpose of the evaluation. Smaller sample sizes are usually needed for exploratory studies than for testing hypotheses concerning project effects.

~ The more precise the required results, the greater the required sample size. ~

In the example, the Ministry of Education stated that the purpose of the evaluation is to determine whether the special instruction program is a cost-effective way to increase student mathematical skills. The ministry also needs to demonstrate that the program is more effective than other approaches. Many supporters of alternative mathematics teaching programs will try to challenge the findings, so the ministry requires "acceptable professional levels of significance testing." This is taken to mean that the 0.05 significance level will be used.

Step 2: Decide on using a one- or two-tailed test. In most cases, a one-tailed test will be used, but the evaluator should always check this.

~ Using a two-tailed test will increase the sample size by about 40%. ~

In the example, the purpose is to test for increased aptitude scores, so a one-tailed test is appropriate.

Step 3: Estimate the standard deviation (SD) of the population[11]. The size of the *SD* will affect the estimation of the effect size and consequently the sample size. Sometimes *SD* is known from previous studies. In other cases, it can be estimated from a small pilot study. Henry (1990:119) suggests that if no other source of information is available, a rough estimate can be obtained by dividing the range (the difference between the highest and lowest values of the variable) by 4. The situation is simple for proportions because the maximum variance, and hence the maximum required sample size, occurs when $p = 0.5$.

~ The larger the *SD* the larger the required sample size. ~

In the example, earlier studies have shown that the population mean for fifth-grade students is 200 and the *SD* is 48 (assumed similar for the project population)[12].

Step 4: Determine the minimum acceptable effect size (MAES)

~ The smaller the MAES the larger the required sample size. ~

In the example, a meta-analysis review of other programs to increase math skills has found that effect sizes range between 0.1 and 0.25. In addition, the ministry indicated that a 5% increase in test scores is the minimum effect that could justify funding to continue the program. This would require an increase of 10 points in the average population test score of 200. With a population *SD* of 48, this is equivalent to an effect size of

MAES = [210 – 200]/48 = 0.208 [this is rounded to 0.2 to simplify the calculations]

Step 5: Determine the required statistical significance level. Should the statistical significance of the findings be tested at the 0.01 level (when a high level of precision is required), at the 0.05 level (the normally accepted level), or at the 0.1 level (for exploratory studies)?

~ The higher the required confidence level the larger the required sample size. ~

In the example, it is agreed to use the 0.05 confidence level.

Step 6: Decide on the required power of the test.

~ The higher the required power the larger the sample. ~

In the example, the ministry agrees to use the conventional power = 0.8. They initially wished to use the 0.01 confidence level to achieve a level of statistical precision, but when they were advised that this would increase the sample size by almost 40% they decided to accept the conventional 0.05 level.

Step 7: Consult a master statistical power table to calculate the required sample size for a given effect size and power level. Table 14.3 is a simplified version of a power table that only covers the 0.05 confidence level and only a one-tailed test[13]. The use of the table involves the following steps:

- Decide the required confidence level and then consult the appropriate power table. In our example, Table 14.3 assumes that the confidence level is set at 0.05.
- Consult the column for the specified power.
- Consult the row for the effect size.
- Locate the intersecting cell to find the required sample size for each group.

Where the survey covers both the project and comparison groups, multiply the given sample size by two to estimate the total number of interviews required to cover both groups[14]. Note that in the previous aptitude test example, the sample covered only the treatment group because test score information was already available for the total school population.

In the example:

- The client indicated that normal standards of professional precision should be followed, so the 0.05 confidence level will be used.
- The power level is set at 0.80 (second column).
- The MAES is 0.2 (second row). The intersection of the power column and MAES row shows that 152 interviews would be required in each group or a total sample size of 304. Note that if the goal were to achieve a 7.5% increase in enrollment, the effect size would increase to 0.31 (rounded to 0.3 to simplify the calculations), then samples of only 66 would be required for each group, reducing the total sample size to 132.

Step 8: Find the finite population correction factor. The master tables assume that the sample will represent a very small proportion of the total target population. If in fact the sample represents more than, say, 5% of the population, then the sample size can be reduced through the application of the finite population correction factor (FPCF). This involves a very simple computation:

$$n = \tilde{n} \, (1 - \tilde{n}/N)$$

Where:
n = the adjusted sample size.
$\tilde{n}$ = the original sample size.
N = the total population size.

Table 14.3 Approximate Sample Size for the Project and Comparison Groups Needed to Attain Various Criterion Levels of Power for a Range of Effect Sizes with a One-Tailed Test (confidence level = 0.05)[a]

Effect Size	Power Criterion				
	0.90	0.80	0.60	0.40	0.20
0.10	852	616	359	194	66
0.20	210	152	89	49	17
0.30	91	66	39	22	—
0.40	49	36	21	14	—
0.50	30	22	13	—	—
0.60	19	14	—	—	—
0.70	13	10	—	—	—
0.80	—	—	—	—	—
0.90	—	—	—	—	—
1.00	—	—	—	—	—

SOURCE: Kraemer and Thiemann (1987). Summarized from master power analysis table for one-tailed test and 0.05 significance level. Other tables are given for two-tailed tests and 0.01 confidence level.

NOTES: The numbers in the table refer to the required sample size for different combinations of effect size and power. The sample sizes refer only to the project or the comparison group. If the sample will cover both groups, the total sample size must be doubled (assuming both samples are the same size).

a. The table assumes a one-tailed test at the 0.05 confidence level. The required sample size increases by approximately 40% if a two-tailed test is used. Required sample sizes increase if the 0.01 confidence level is used. When the sample size is more than, say, 5% of the total population, the use of the finite population correction factor will produce a significant reduction in the required sample size. If the sample is 5% of the total population, the required sample size can be reduced by 5%; if the sample is 10% of the population, then the sample size can be reduced by 10%; and so on.

In the example, the total fifth-grade student population is more than 20,000, so the sample proportion is too small to require a finite population correction. However, the project sample represents slightly over 10% of the total project population (650), so it is worth using the finite population correction. The adjusted sample size n_1 for the project group is estimated to be as follows:

$$n_1 = \tilde{n}_1 \, (1 - \tilde{n}_1/N_1) = 66 \, (1 - 66/650) = 59$$

So the project sample size can be reduced by 7. Given the small sample size, this does not make much difference, but where the sample sizes are much larger, this reduction of 10% in the required number of interviews could represent a significant cost saving.

Factors Affecting the Sample Size

In addition to the factors discussed earlier, the required sample size is also affected by the following:

- *The reliability of the instrument used to measure effect.* In cases where effects cannot be reliably measured, the variance of the estimates increases and the sample size required to achieve a certain power also increases.
- *The evaluation design.* More sophisticated evaluation designs that include intervening (mediator) variables can reduce the variance and, consequently, the required sample size to achieve a certain statistical power.
- *The estimated sample dropout rate* (for panel studies).
- *Changes in the size and characteristics of the total study population* (for longitudinal studies).
- *Effect size.* If effect size can be increased, this will automatically increase statistical power and/or permit the sample size to be reduced. As indicated earlier, it may be possible to increase effect size by improving the design and administration of the treatment (special instruction) or by limiting the study to those groups where the effect is expected to be greatest.

The Contribution of Meta-Analysis

Meta-analysis is the review and synthesis of all research or evaluation studies that have been conducted in a particular field. Meta-analysis has proved particularly helpful in estimating the range of effect sizes that have been produced by programs in a particular sector. This provides a reference point for defining the effect size that can reasonably be expected for the program being evaluated and, consequently, is a valuable guide for estimating the required sample size. Table 14.4 summarizes some of the average effect sizes found in a meta-analysis of 221 programs addressing aggressive behavior in schools. None of the average effect sizes for any of the five types of intervention exceeds 0.33, and for multimodal approaches, the average is only 0.15. If an evaluation of a new social competence program using techniques other than cognitive behavior was being planned, it would seem reasonable to assume that even a very successful intervention would probably not have an effect size greater than 0.3, so the total sample size for the two groups (with power = 0.90) would be around 182. Using power = 0.8, the required sample size for the two groups would be reduced to 132.

Another very important finding from this study was that for many programs with an effect size less than 0.3, the sample size was too small to detect a statistically significant effect. The authors conclude that greater attention must be given to estimating the power of the test for

Table 14.4   Mean Effect Sizes for Different Interventions Addressing Aggressive Behavior in Schools

Therapy or counseling services	0.33
Social competence training using cognitive-behavioral approaches	0.27
Behavioral and classroom management techniques	0.22
Social competence training using techniques other than cognitive-behavioral approaches	0.20
Multimodal programs	0.15

SOURCE: Rossi, Lipsey, and Freeman (2004, Exhibit 10-G, p. 326).

small effect sizes to avoid many Type II errors whereby it was incorrectly concluded that programs had no effect.

Sampling Issues for Mixed-Method Evaluations

As discussed in the previous chapter, the purpose of using **mixed-method** designs is to combine the complementary strengths of QUAL and QUANT methods and to overcome some of the limitations of either approach when used on its own. Very often, QUAL data collection and analysis methods are used to provide depth and richness of interpretation and a holistic perspective on the context within which the project is being implemented, whereas QUANT methods are used to ensure representativity of the findings and to permit generalizations to the total populations from which the samples are drawn.

As we discussed earlier in this chapter, most QUAL evaluations do not seek to generalize their findings (except perhaps through petite generalizations), and a relatively small number of subjects are selected purposively to ensure the maximum richness of data and that all important evaluation questions are adequately covered. However, when QUAL methods are incorporated into a mixed-method evaluation design, it often becomes important to make certain that QUANT and QUAL data and analysis are referring to comparable populations.

One way to ensure comparability is to use the QUANT sampling frame to select the communities or subjects where QUAL case studies or observations will be conducted. Another approach is to assume that quantitative and qualitative data collection are studying different levels of the same context. For example, a QUANT survey may interview individuals on their use of health, education, or other social services, while the QUAL studies may describe the quality of the services or may examine **contextual variables** that affect the way the program operates or that may influence **utilization** rates among different sectors of the target population. Box 14.6 illustrates how a rapid QUANT survey was used by Oscar Lewis in his seminal 1965 study of Puerto Rican families in New York to show that the families included in his in-depth anthropological study had characteristics similar to other families in the same neighborhoods.

Sampling Issues for RealWorld Evaluation

Sample Design Trade-Offs between Cost, Time, and Validity

Data collection is usually one of the largest budget items for an evaluation, so reducing sample size is usually one of the easiest ways to save costs and time. However, if the sample is inappropriate, the validity of evaluation findings will be jeopardized. In probabilistic sampling, if the sample size becomes too small, there is the danger of committing Type II errors and rejecting real project effects. As discussed earlier, this is a particular problem when the expected effect size is small. The potential benefits and dangers involved in sampling show the importance of the scoping phase (Step 1) of the RWE approach. The evaluator should

---

Box 14.6   Using Rapid Sample Surveys to Place Case Studies in a Broader
Socioeconomic Context: Oscar Lewis's Study of Puerto Rican
Families in New York

In 1961, Oscar Lewis published *The Children of Sanchez,* a very influential anthropological study describing the "culture of poverty" in Mexico City. The study had an
important effect on policy discussions on ways to address poverty in Latin America
and the United States. At the same time, the study was widely criticized by left-wing
political scientists for placing the blame for poverty on the individual rather than on
the inequities of the capitalist system. It was claimed that Lewis had deliberately
selected the Sanchez family, which was not typical, to support his arguments. When
Lewis conducted his follow-up study, *La Vida: A Puerto Rican Family in the Culture of
Poverty in San Juan and New York*, he was careful to include a randomly selected sample of 100 families in order to place the Rios family in a broader context. The study
combined a sample survey, interviews, **participant observation**, review of secondary
data, and a small number of in-depth studies. The study covered family structure, an
inventory of household goods, a history of mobility and employment, and the history
of migration from San Juan to New York.

SOURCE: Lewis (1961, 1965).

understand the purposes of the evaluation, how the results will be used, and the types of
decisions to which the evaluation will contribute. There are two challenges: (a) to avoid using
a larger sample than is required for the purposes of the study and (b) to ensure that the sample is appropriate and sufficiently large for the types of analysis and findings desired.

Comparison Groups

One important sampling decision is whether a comparison group is required. In QUANT
experimental and quasi-experimental designs, a comparison group is required for both the
baseline and the posttest surveying or testing. Complete elimination of the pre- and posttest
comparison group would probably reduce the cost of data collection significantly, but the lack
of a comparison group would also significantly weaken the validity of the evaluation results.
In QUAL and mixed-method designs, comparison groups may also be useful for fully understanding program effects, although, in some cases, they may not be of critical importance for
detailing program merits and shortcomings.

When time, personnel, and budget are severe constraints, various options may be worth
considering. For example, a QUANT evaluator might choose to use documentary or secondary
data rather than to survey or test a comparison group. This may be a way to produce significant cost savings, but again, the trade-offs with respect to validity should be considered. The
guidelines in Chapter 5 are designed to help to assess the strengths and weaknesses of a variety of decisions and alternatives concerning the use of documentary data.

Summary

- Sampling issues are important for both QUAL and QUANT evaluations, but the approaches to sampling tend to be quite different in each case.

- QUAL evaluations tend to use *purposive sampling* to carefully select a small number of cases that represent all the main categories of interest to the study. Although random sampling would not be appropriate with these kinds of small samples, each sample is selected to ensure that the maximum amount of information is obtained.

- In contrast, QUANT evaluations normally use random sampling procedures to ensure that the selected sample is statistically representative of the total population so that generalizations can be made from the sample to this population with a measurable level of statistical precision.

- For QUANT evaluations, questionnaire administration and other forms of data collection usually represent one of the largest cost items in an evaluation; therefore, when RWE constraints require cost reductions, reducing the size of the sample is always a tempting option.

- However, if the sample is too small (as is often the case when there are budget and time constraints), it will not be possible to identify statistically significant relations between the project interventions and the production of the desired outcomes and impacts—even when they do exist.

- Consequently, deciding what is the appropriate sample size to achieve the desired levels of precision of the evaluation findings is one of the critical evaluation design decisions.

- Two key factors in the estimation of sample size are the estimated *effect size* (how large a change the project is expected to produce if it is successful) and statistical *power analysis* (the required level of confidence that the project effect will be detected if it really exists). The smaller the expected effect size, the larger the sample needed to detect the effect. The higher the required level of confidence (power), the larger the required sample size.

- Estimating the effect size and adjusting the power of the test are two of the key factors in estimating sample size.

- When there are cost pressures to reduce sample size, this can be achieved either by accepting a lower power (a higher risk that a real project effect will not be detected) or by finding ways to increase the effect size (e.g., studying only those groups where the project is expected to have a larger effect).

Further Reading

Aron, A. and E. Aron. 2002. *Statistics for the Behavioral and Social Sciences: A Brief Course.* 2d ed. Upper Saddle River, NJ: Prentice Hall.

This is a thorough, clear review of all the statistical concepts discussed in the present text. Chapter 7 provides a good overview of statistical power analysis and effect size. There is also a companion study guide and workbook.

Fink, A. 2003. *How to Sample in Surveys.* Vol. 7, *The Survey Kit.* 2d ed. Thousand Oaks, CA: Sage.

A useful introduction to sample design.

Henry, G. 1990. *Practical Sampling.* Thousand Oaks, CA: Sage.

A thorough, clear review of sample design and power analysis.

Kraemer, H. C. and S. Thiemann. 1987. *How Many Subjects? Statistical Power Analysis in Research.* Thousand Oaks, CA: Sage.

A comprehensive and quite technical discussion of the estimation of sample sizes with different kinds of statistical tests. Chapters 1 and 10 provide a useful summary of key issues in sample size estimation. This book also contains master tables for estimating sample size with different levels of confidence and for one- and two-tailed tests.

Lohr, S. 1999. *Sampling Design and Analysis.* New York: Duxbury Press.

Covers all the methods and procedures for sample design and analysis, including a chapter on the treatment of nonresponse. Also includes a CD with a comprehensive data set (including survey instruments and complete information on the sampling frame) and a set of exercises that can be used to practice all the different sampling designs. A useful feature for RWE is that the database also includes cost data so that the impact of different sample designs on the evaluation budget can be tested.

Rossi, P., M. Lipsey, and H. Freeman. 2004. *Evaluation: A Systematic Approach.* 7th ed. Thousand Oaks, CA: Sage.

Chapter 10 presents an overview of power analysis and the estimation of sample size.

Sirken, R. 1999. *Statistics for the Social Sciences.* Thousand Oaks, CA: Sage.

Comprehensive and clear coverage of the application of statistics in the social sciences, which pertains to the statistical techniques discussed in this chapter.

Notes

1. Although this is true to some extent, many QUANT samples do aim to cover all the population and not only those willing to be interviewed. In these cases, procedures are used to obtain information on subjects who cannot be located or who are not willing to respond so that their characteristics can be compared with people willing to be interviewed. A well-known example is voting surveys where it is important to cover all the electorate, not only those willing to be interviewed. When face-to-face interviews are conducted, it is possible to note the sex, age, and ethnicity of nonrespondents. If the interviewer visits homes, it is also possible to note characteristics of the house and the neighborhood.

2. When strata have different probabilities of selection, weighting is used in the analysis to readjust the numbers from each stratum to their true proportions in the total population. For example, if Stratum X is particularly important for the study, twice as many subjects from Stratum X might be included in the sample. In the analysis, a weighting factor of 0.5 would then be used for Stratum X when making estimates for the total population.

3. The procedure is slightly more complicated if the sample unit is a certain type of individual in the household (e.g., student attending the local school), but the same general principle applies.

4. It is assumed in this example that the conventional power level of 0.8 is used (see Box 14.6). The table also shows that the sample size increases dramatically if higher power levels (0.90 or 0.95) are specified.

5. Readers wishing for a fuller understanding of power analysis are recommended to consult Lipsey (1990), *Design Sensitivity: Statistical Power for Experimental Research,* or Kraemer and Thiemann (1987), *How Many Subjects? Statistical Power Analysis in Research.*

6. This is equivalent to a Z score of 1.64 (see Aron and Aron 2002, chap. 2). The Z score is defined as (sample mean – population mean)/standard deviation of the population mean. In this case (209.84 – 200)/6.

7. It was assumed, as is usually done unless other information is available, that the SD of the treatment group would be the same as for the total population.

8. For an explanation of use of the normal distribution in statistical significance testing, see Aron and Aron (2002, chaps. 2 and 4).

9. Kraemer and Thiemann (1987) include master tables for both one- and two-tailed tests.

10. For a more detailed discussion on the estimation of sample size, see Henry (1990, chap. 7).

11. It is usually assumed that the project group will have the same standard deviation as the total population. However, in **nonequivalent control group** designs, it is possible that the project group could have a different standard deviation. Where sample precision is important, it would be useful to consult with a statistician as to whether an adjustment should be made. For most RWE purposes, this is probably not a major concern.

12. It is important to check that estimates of the SD from previous studies are applicable. If different populations were studied or different questions were asked, earlier studies may not provide a good estimate of the SD for the present study.

13. For more comprehensive master tables covering both one- and two-tailed tests and 0.5 and 0.1 confidence levels, see Kraemer and Thiemann (1987:105–12). A number of free Web sites also provide tools for estimating sample size and the power of the test. See, for example, the site developed by Vanderbilt University at http://biostat.mc.vanderbilt.edu/twiki/bin/view/Main/PowerSampleSize. The reader should be aware that a certain level of statistical knowledge is required to use this Web site. Fink (2003b) cites a number of other Web sites (not all free) providing similar software.

14. In the simplest case, we assume that the same number of interviews will be conducted in the project and comparison areas. See Lipsey (1990, chap. 6) for a discussion of the required adjustments when sample sizes are not equal.

PART IV

Pulling It All Together

CHAPTER 15

Learning Together

Building Capacity for RealWorld Evaluation

RealWorld Evaluation (**RWE**) approaches can never be sustainable in an organization or a country unless capacity is developed to plan for, implement, use, and teach about evaluation. This chapter discusses the elements of a RWE capacity building strategy. We begin by defining capacity building and discuss what capacities and skills must be developed for evaluation practitioners and evaluation users. We discuss how to design and deliver evaluation capacity building for different audiences, including policymakers, the agencies that commission evaluation, the consultants and agencies that conduct evaluations, and community-level organizations. Capacity-building approaches include both structured training programs and interaction with stakeholders during the implementation of the evaluation.

Defining Evaluation Capacity Building

Evaluation capacity building involves strengthening the ability and willingness to commission, conduct, understand, and use studies evaluating development **projects, programs,** or policies. Capacity building covers (a) strengthening the required evaluation skills and knowledge; (b) developing an understanding of the value of evaluation as a planning, management, policy, and political tool; and (c) encouraging willingness to use evaluations to achieve these objectives. Creating understanding and willingness to use evaluation is at least as important as strengthening technical skills; many managers, planners, and policymakers are either not convinced of the utility of evaluation or consider it more an inconvenience or a threat than a useful tool.

Two of the major challenges in evaluation capacity building are to demonstrate to potential users that evaluation can help solve their problems while at the same time increasing the willingness and capacity of professional evaluators to conduct and present evaluations in a way that increases the likelihood of their being used. Although decision makers want objective information at a time when social science is aware that all "facts" and data are value laden, they do not want information billed as "objective" when it is simply the personal opinion of the researcher. What they want is information that is scientifically valid and packaged for use by decision makers (Vaughn and Buss 1998:xii).

Vaughan and Buss (1998) also argue that one of the main reasons for the lack of enthusiasm of many policymakers for research studies is the major divide between the purpose and style of academic research and the very practical and immediate needs of the policymaker. While this divide is often less pronounced for program evaluation compared with research, it does still exist, particularly among researchers who see evaluation as a potential source of funding to further their research interests.

RealWorld Evaluation Capacity Building

RWE capacity building addresses the added challenge of showing that useful and technically sound evaluations can be conducted under real-world constraints. Many government departments and funding agencies are skeptical that rapid evaluations can be "professional." RealWorld evaluators, like all evaluators, need to be able to explain and justify their approaches. It is particularly important to explain that, when properly applied, RWE adhere to expectations of professional rigor—despite budget, time, and other constraints.

RWE capacity building may involve (but is not limited to) strengthening evaluation capacity at the community and local level, developing an evaluation culture among government and nongovernmental organization (**NGO**) agencies and budget committees, and introducing evaluation practitioners and users already familiar with conventional evaluation methods to the RWE approach (see Box 15.1).

Box 15.1   RealWorld Evaluation Capacity-Building Scenarios

The following four examples illustrate the many different levels and modalities of evaluation capacity building:

World Neighbors has been working for many years in rural and marginalized areas to help local organizations develop their capacity to analyze and resolve community problems through rapid assessment and participatory evaluation techniques (Gubbels and Koss 2000; Rugh 1986).

The Ministry of Finance of Chile has been developing over the past five years a system to evaluate the performance of government-funded programs. The goal is to develop an evaluation culture, and the **findings** and recommendations of the evaluations are presented to the Parliamentary Budget Committee to guide decisions on future financing of these programs. Although the goal is to introduce the highest possible standards of methodological rigor, in practice, there is a strong reliance on RWE approaches, particularly with respect to data and time constraints (www.dipres. cl/fr_control.html).

The International Program for Development Evaluation Training (IPDET) provides a comprehensive program of evaluation training for new and experienced evaluation practitioners, managers, and planners from around the world. The program includes a three-day workshop on RWE (www.ipdet.org).

American Evaluation Association (AEA) professional development presession workshops in RWE have been offered for a number of years by the authors of this book and other colleagues. Many new, intermediate, and experienced evaluation professionals have shown interest in these workshops.

While the main concern of most RealWorld evaluators is to *increase* interest in the use of evaluations, particularly those conducted with time constraints, it is not uncommon to also have to face the opposite problem: convincing policymakers, managers, and fund-raising departments not to make unfounded claims about the success of their programs on the basis of evaluations that lack adequate rigor and validity. In these cases, evaluators may find themselves in the paradoxical situation of having to dampen the enthusiasm of stakeholders interested in using exploratory evaluation findings to bolster **evidence** in support of the success of their programs (Box 15.2).

Although discussions of evaluation capacity building often focus on strengthening the technical skills of the **evaluation practitioners** who design and implement evaluations, the success of most evaluations also depends on the support and understanding of at least five distinct **client** and **stakeholder** groups, each of whom have different roles in the evaluation process and each of whom require different sets of skills or knowledge. An evaluation capacity-building strategy that defines ways to strengthen the evaluation skills of each of the following groups may be helpful:

1. *Agencies that commission and fund evaluations.* These include donor agencies, foundations, government budget and finance departments, and national and international NGOs.

2. *Evaluation practitioners who design, implement, analyze, and disseminate evaluations.* These include evaluation units of governmental departments or ministries, planning and finance units or agencies, national and international NGOs, foundations and donor agencies, evaluation consultants, and university research groups.

3. *Evaluation users.* These include government, foundation, donor, and civil society organizations that use the results of evaluations to help formulate policies, allocate resources, and design and implement programs and projects.

Box 15.2   The RealWorld Evaluation Dilemma: Convincing Some Clients to Make More Use of Evaluation Findings While Convincing Others to Not Overstate the Findings of Exploratory Studies!

While the major concern of most RealWorld evaluators (as well as their mainstream evaluation colleagues) is to increase interest in the use of evaluation findings; evaluators can also face the need to discourage enthusiastic clients from making exaggerated claims on the basis of the findings from small exploratory studies. In a recent workshop titled "Making Sure Your Evaluation Findings Are Used," it was observed that the fundraising departments of many voluntary agencies are always looking for evidence that contributors' funds are producing significant impacts at the community level. Consequently, the evaluators often have to discourage their management from using promising findings from a single exploratory case study on a program to reduce teenage pregnancy, school dropout rates, or gang violence to claim that "every X dollars you send us will mean one less teen pregnancy or school dropout."

SOURCE: Karry Gillespie and Suzanne McDonald. "Making Sure Your Evaluation Is Used." Oregon Program Evaluators Network Technical Assistance Exchange. June 4, 2004.

4. *Groups affected by the programs or policies being evaluated.* These can include community organizations, farmers organizations, trade associations and business groups, trade unions and workers organizations, and many other stakeholder groups affected directly or indirectly by the programs and policies being evaluated.

5. *Public opinion.* This includes broad categories such as the general public, the academic community, and civil society. The media are also an extremely important sector of civil society, particularly for large evaluations that are likely to influence policy.

Capacity-building programs need to target different groups for developing the knowledge and skill needed by each group. For example, a capacity-building program for small community organizations would logically have a very different focus from that for a program sponsored by a ministry of finance that targets national agencies in a variety of sectors. The level of education and professional experience must also be taken into account.

RealWorld Evaluation Skills to Be Developed

Each target group is concerned with different aspects of the evaluation process, and each requires some basic and some differentiated skills and knowledge. Some of the broad or basic categories of skills and knowledge include the following:

Defining evaluation needs and commissioning evaluations

- Knowing when evaluations are required
- Understanding what evaluations can and cannot achieve and knowing what questions to ask (**evaluability assessment**)
- Defining evaluation questions, topics, and issues
- Commissioning or financing evaluations
- Assessing the cost, time, and technical requirements for an evaluation

Designing evaluations

- Articulating client concerns as research questions or testable hypotheses and/or **program theories** whose components and links can be examined as pathways to intended **outcomes**
- Identifying contextual factors influencing the program and needing study
- Developing evaluation **terms of reference** (ToR), including defining data collection and analysis methods, data sources, personnel, deliverables, timelines, and resources

Implementing the evaluation

- Involving stakeholders
- Data collection
- Managing the evaluation

Data analysis

- Managing data analysis
- Qualitative and quantitative data analysis

Disseminating and using evaluations

- Communicating and promoting clarity of presentation and usability of evaluation findings for key stakeholders
- Building in evaluation reporting that supports **utilization**

Conducting evaluations under real-world constraints

- Identifying the special challenges or real-world constraints that apply
- Adapting evaluation methodology to real-world constraints
- Assessing the quality, validity, and utility of evaluations **designs**

Table 15.1 summarizes the types of evaluation skills typically required by each of the five target groups. Although there is some overlap, the evaluation capacity needs are significantly different for each group. For example, the *agencies that fund evaluations* (Capacity Building Target Group 1) require skills in these areas:

- *How to identify evaluation needs.* When are evaluations needed and what questions should they address? This also addresses how to specify the purpose of the evaluation in a request for proposals.
- *Evaluating and selecting firms and individual consultants.* Balancing evaluation expertise with knowledge of the sector or subject area. Balancing academic status with operational experience. Ensuring the right composition of the team (e.g., gender balance, local language skills and knowledge of the community, professional mix).
- *Assessing evaluation proposals.* Developing an objective rating assessment system so that different members of the evaluation proposal review panel are using the same criteria for rating each proposal. Clarifying how much time each member of the proposed team will actually devote to the evaluation (consulting firms sometimes include names of prestigious people who will have only a token involvement in the evaluation once the proposal is approved).
- *Estimating evaluation resource requirements* (e.g., funds, human resources, time, access to computers, transportation). Managers, particularly people relatively new to the field of evaluation, will often significantly underestimate the resource needed to conduct, analyze, and disseminate the evaluation[1].
- *Understanding what questions an evaluation can and cannot answer.* The concept of **evaluability assessment** will be further discussed later in this chapter. This is important because many agencies overestimate what an evaluation can reasonably be expected to produce.

On the other hand, *the groups affected by programs and policies* (Target Group 4) must be able to do the following:

- *Define when and for what purposes evaluations are required.* Different kinds of evaluations are useful at different stages of a project or program. However, it will often be possible to lobby for only a single evaluation to be done for a small or medium-sized project, so it is important to understand when it will be most useful.

- *Negotiate with evaluators and funding agencies on the content, purpose, use, and dissemination of evaluations.* Funding and executing agencies will usually have different interests from the groups affected by the project, so it is important to ensure that the evaluation will also cover the concerns of the affected populations.
- *Ensure that the right questions are asked, information is collected from the right people, and the questions are formulated so as to avoid bias.* In addition, ensure that sufficient (but not excessive) rigor will be used so that the questions are answered with the requisite degree of precision and credibility.
- *Understand, use, and disseminate the evaluation findings.* Unless actions are taken, the evaluation findings will often be disseminated to only a limited audience, and often the report will not be easily accessible to the affected populations. In some cases, it may be necessary to ensure that the report is available in the local language and that a user-friendly and nontechnical version is available.
- *Conduct an independent evaluation if it is necessary to challenge the findings of the "official" evaluation.*

Designing and Delivering Evaluation Capacity Building

In this section, we have tried to select examples of evaluation capacity-building approaches used by community groups and NGOs, governments, and international development agencies to illustrate the wide variety of approaches available. The examples are only a very small sampling and certainly do not claim to represent all the many types of capacity-building programs being organized in the United States and around the world. See also Appendix 4 for additional evaluation capacity-building resources.

RWE capacity can be developed through either formal or informal training programs or through interaction with different stakeholder groups during the design, implementation, dissemination, and use of evaluation studies. We call these two approaches *structured training* and *interactive capacity development*. Often, the process of interactive capacity development will help raise awareness of the utility of RWE and will lead to a later request to develop structured training programs aimed at specific target audiences. In practice, the distinction between the two approaches is often not very clear, and most successful evaluation capacity development programs involve a combination of the two approaches. While all the approaches discussed in the following paragraphs are standard capacity-building tools, they are all directly applicable to the needs of agencies involved in RWEs. Some of the activities can be completed in a few days, whereas others can be incorporated into regular longer-duration training programs organized by donor agencies, governments, universities, and NGOs.

RealWorld Evaluation Capacity Development through Structured Training Programs

Structured evaluation capacity building can be delivered in many different ways, formally and informally, as a component of semester-long university or training institution programs, or through workshops lasting a few days or weeks. Some of the common evaluation capacity-building approaches include the following:

- As components of formal university or training institute programs—ranging from an academic semester to seminars lasting from several days to several weeks
- Workshops lasting one to several days
- Distance learning and other online programs
- Mentoring
- On-the-job training where evaluation skills are learned as part of a package of work skills
- As part of a community development program
- As part of a community or group empowerment program

Table 15.2 illustrates different methods for evaluation capacity development and how they can be applied to different audiences. For example, **evaluation users** will strengthen their capacity to understand and use evaluation findings through briefings and short workshops, often with additional documentation available on Web sites. Examples of briefing or debriefing workshops include the following:

- Beneficiary assessment studies conducted for government sector ministries to assess the attitudes and experiences of intended beneficiaries (community groups, local government agencies, etc.) with public service delivery programs such as housing, health, education, and **microcredit**
- Workshops to disseminate the findings of studies related to national Millennium Development Goals, health status (such as the Demographic and Health Surveys), the UNDP's Human Development Reports, or the national poverty assessments conducted by many development funding agencies

An example of distance learning is the Brazilian *Interlegis* program organized by the Brazilian Senate to train municipal government functionaries on how to use social development indicators and evaluation studies to help identify priority areas for action.[2] A particularly important function is helping mayors and other elected officials use social indicators to compare their municipality with neighboring municipalities on key indicators such as school attendance, infant mortality, unemployment, and crime. This is useful both to identify priority areas and to evaluate performance. For functionaries at this level, it is much more meaningful to compare progress with neighboring municipalities than to try to understand and use the overwhelming amounts of information available from national Millennium Development Goals or Human Development Reports.

Box 15.3 gives an example of a possible three- to five-week evaluation capacity-building course for evaluation practitioners from central government agencies. An important part of the program is the inclusion of field visits in which participants test out the different evaluation tools and also conduct rapid assessment studies on completed or ongoing projects. Methods for conducting evaluations under budget, time, and data constraints would be only one of the topics covered, but RWE issues would probably receive a lot of attention in many countries because many agencies continually face these constraints in their research and evaluation work.

Evaluation Capacity Building for Community Organizations

An increasingly important area of evaluation capacity building involves developing the capacity of community and local-level organizations to design, conduct, and use planning and

Table 15.1   Evaluation Skills Required by Different Groups

Group	Examples	Evaluation Skills Needed
1. Agencies that fund and commission evaluations	• Donor agencies • Ministry of Finance and finance and planning departments of sector ministries • Foundations • International NGOs (nongovernmental organizations)	• Defining when evaluations are required • Evaluating consulting firms and individual consultants • Assessing proposals • Estimating evaluation resource requirements (budget, time, human resources) • Negotiating the most effective evaluation design under real-world constraints • Assessing the adequacy and validity of RWE proposals
2. Evaluation practitioners	• Evaluation units of line ministries • Evaluation departments of ministries of planning and finance • Evaluation units of NGOs • Evaluation consultants • Universities	• Defining client needs • Adapting methodologically sound designs to real-world budget, time, data, and political constraints • Understanding and selecting among different evaluation designs • Data collection and analysis • Sampling • Supervision • Institutional development • Adapting evaluation methodologies to the real world
3. Evaluation users	• Central government agencies (finance, planning, etc.) • Line ministries • NGOs • Foundations • Donor agencies	• Assessing the validity of quantitative evaluation designs and findings • Assessing the adequacy and validity of qualitative evaluation designs and findings • Assessing the adequacy and validity of mixed-method evaluation designs and findings

(Continued)

Table 15.1 (Continued)

Group	Examples	Evaluation Skills Needed
4. Groups affected by the programs or policies being evaluated	• Community organizations • Farmers organizations • Trade associations and business groups • Trade unions and workers organizations • Parent-teacher associations	• Defining when evaluations are required • Negotiating with evaluators and funding agencies on the content, purpose, use, and dissemination of evaluations • Asking the right questions • Participating in evaluations • Understanding and using evaluation findings
5. Public opinion and the mass media	• The general public • The academic community • Civil society • The media (both mass media and professional media)	• Knowing how to get evaluations commissioned • Making sure the right questions get asked • Basic understanding of evaluation methodologies • Understanding and using evaluation findings.

Table 15.2 Examples of Capacity-Building Approaches Customized for Different Audiences

Audience	Type of training	Duration	Example
Funding agencies	Workshops and seminars	½ – 3 days	• IPDET 3-day workshop on RealWorld Evaluation. How to assess the validity and adequacy of evaluation designs and how to estimate budget, time, and human resources to conduct the evaluation.[a] • Chile: briefings to Ministry of Finance and Parliamentary Budget Committee on the findings and recommendations of the evaluations of government programs[b]
Evaluation practitioners	Short courses combining theory and practice in evaluation tools and techniques	1 day – 2 weeks	• IPDET 2-week course: Review of evaluation methods and approaches • Workshops at conferences of evaluation professionals such as AEA
Evaluation users	• Debriefing workshop presenting the findings of an evaluation • Distance learning • Case studies and other short publications on how evaluations are used	½ – 1 day Short sessions once a week over a period of months	• Beneficiary assessment studies[c] • National Millennium Development Goals[d] workshops: These workshops have been organized in many developing countries by United Nations organizations, often in coordination with mass media campaigns, publications, and Web sites. • Brazil: InterLegis distance learning program for municipal governments on how to use social development indicators and research findings to identify priority areas of action[e] • "Influential Evaluations": Eight case studies of evaluations from around the world where there is convincing evidence that the results influenced policy formulation or program design[f]
Affected populations	Participatory assessment and community consultations	½ day to 1 week	"Building Community Capacity with Evaluation Activities That Empower" (Mayer 1996)[g]

(Continued)

Table 15.2 (Continued)

Audience	Type of training	Duration	Example
Public opinion	Mass media campaigns to disseminate citizen scorecards	Intensive campaigns over several weeks combining short workshops, briefings, and mass media coverage	• "Holding the State to Account": Citizen Report Card study in Bangalore, India. Mass media reporting on citizen attitudes to the quality of public services supported by workshops organized by NGOs.[h]

a. International Program for Development Evaluation Training. This program, organized by the World Bank in cooperation with Carleton University in Ottawa and with support from a number of multilateral and bilateral development agencies, is one of the most comprehensive training programs available to evaluators working in developing countries. There is a two-week core program followed by two weeks of optional modules. For more information, go to www.worldbank.org/oed/ipdet/modules.html. The course modules are also available on this Web site.

b. For more information on the Chile program of impact evaluations and evaluations of government programs (in Spanish), go to www.dipres.cl/fr_control.html

c. Beneficiary assessment studies are used by many international development agencies, including the United Nations Development Program and the World Bank, among others, to obtain feedback from project beneficiaries on how they feel about a project. As part of the methodology, workshops and briefings are organized with implementing agencies and other stakeholders to provide feedback on the opinions and experiences of beneficiaries (Salmen 1992; World Bank 1996).

d. The MDGs, as they are widely known, are the eight sets of development goals (e.g., halving world poverty, increasing school enrollment, increasing access to safe water, combating HIV/AIDS and other killer diseases) that most developing countries and development agencies are committed to achieving by 2015 or 2025.

e. For more information about the InterLegis program (in Portuguese), go to www.interlegis.gov.br

f. *Influential Evaluations: Evaluations that Improved Performance and Impacts of Development Programs* (World Bank 2004 and 2005). Available at www.worldbank.org/oed/ecd.

g. Examples of how the Rainbow Coalition uses empowerment evaluation to strengthen community capacity in areas such as drug abuse, women's empowerment, and leadership development.

h. A summary of this study is included in *Influential Evaluations* (World Bank 2004). For a more detailed assessment, see *An Assessment of the Impact of the Bangalore Citizen Report Cards on the Performance of Public Agencies* (Ravindra 2004). Also available at www.worldbank.org/oed/ecd

Table 15.3   Agenda Used for One-Day RealWorld Evaluation Professional
Development Presession at American Evaluation Association (AEA)
Conferences[a]

Session 1. Introduction
- Workshop objectives
- Introducing participants
- Feedback from participant survey

Session 2. RWE an overview
- Presentation
- Discussion

Session 3. Steps 2 and 3: Strategies for addressing budget and time constraints
- Presentation
- Discussion

Session 4. Step 4: Addressing data constraints
- Presentation
- Discussion

BREAK

Session 5: Plenary discussion

Session 6. Identifying and addressing threats to validity and adequacy
- Presentation
- Discussion

Session 7. Plenary discussion and overview of the four case studies to be given to participants as reference documents.

LUNCH: Resource people available to have lunch with those participants wishing to continue discussion

Session 8. Integrating quantitative/qualitative approaches
- Presentation
- Discussion

Session 9. Group discussion/exercise: Each group discusses a case applying a RWE design
- Group 1: Models 2: Pretest-posttest with control
- Group 2: Model 5: Posttest with control
- Group 3: Model 7: Posttest without control: budget and time constraints
- Group 4: Model 7: Posttest without control: no major budget constraints

Session 10. Wrap up and workshop evaluation

a. One-day professional development workshops on RealWorld Evaluation have been organized at the AEA annual conference every year since 2001. Similar workshops, lasting from one to three days, have been organized in Canada, Japan, and a number of countries in Asia and Africa, and the Ukraine.

evaluation studies rather than relying on outside organizations to guide communities in the definition of their priorities and how to achieve them. This is associated with the growing importance of empowerment evaluation (Fetterman 1996; Narayan 2002; Patton 2002). Gubbels and Koss (2000:3) describe three views of community capacity building:

> **Box 15.3** Example of an Evaluation Capacity-Building Course for Central Monitoring and Evaluation (M&E) Agencies
>
> This is one of a number of model courses recommended for different evaluation stakeholders in Asia.
>
> **Audience**: State agencies—central government agencies and, possibly, major NGOs
>
> **Duration**: Three- to five-week basic course, possibly followed by shorter, specialized workshops
>
> **Objectives**: To provide M&E staff with the technical skills to carry out their work and help them understand how their work at the center is linked to evaluation activities at the provincial and project levels
>
> **Content**
>
> - The organization and functions of the different elements of the national M&E system
> - The importance of government/NGO coordination on M&E
> - The contribution of M&E to national development planning
> - M&E and the **project cycle** for government and donor-funded programs
> - Design and use of different kinds of studies
> - Methods for data collection and analysis
> - Principles of sample design
> - Research designs for estimating project **impacts**
> - Creation and use of M&E databases (meta-analysis, sector reviews, and prospective evaluation)
> - Management of databases: quality control, ensuring feedback, and rapid utilization
>
> **Methodology**
>
> - Reading assignments followed by lectures and discussion
> - Small-group exercises and discussion
> - Preparation and use of case studies
> - Field exercises to gain practical experience with different data collection methods and to conduct rapid assessments of completed or ongoing projects
>
> SOURCE: Valadez and Bamberger (1994, chap. 13).

1. Capacity building as a *means:* to strengthen the organization's ability to carry out specific activities

2. Capacity building as a *process:* to enable the organization to continually reflect and adapt its purpose in response to change and learning; to connect its evolving purpose and vision on the one hand and its structure and development activities on the other

3. Capacity building as an *end:* to strengthen an organization's ability to survive, become self-sustaining, and fulfill its purpose

Some of the key capacity areas to be developed at the community level include the following:

- Legitimacy and recognition
- Governance and leadership

Table 15.4   Program for a Five-Day Community Capacity-Building Workshop

Date	Time	Subgroup 1: Mission	Subgroup 2: History	Subgroup 3: Women
Sunday	Morning	Travel		
	Afternoon	Opening meetings		
Monday	Morning	Purpose mapping	Organizational	Strengths and weaknesses
	Afternoon	Organizational structure	timeline	Information flow
			Timeline analysis	
	Evening	Meeting with facilitators		
Tuesday	Morning	Information flow	Strengths and weaknesses	Evolution of organizational capacities
	Afternoon	Viability assessment and threats to viability	Autonomy assessment	Trend analysis: women's well-being
	Evening	Meeting with facilitators		
Wednesday	Morning	Evolution of organizational capacities	Transfer of responsibilities	Program results: health Trend analysis: health
	Afternoon	Trend analysis: food security	Program results: agriculture	
	Evening	Meeting with facilitators		
Thursday	Morning	Class villages by capacity	Impact: food security	Impact: health
	Afternoon	Activity matrix and support/self-reliance matrix	Impact: food security (continued)	Motivation of female leaders
	Evening	Meeting with facilitators		
Friday	All day	Synthesis and analysis		

SOURCE: Reprinted with permission from Gubbels and Koss (2000:43).

- Identify and vision
- Resource mobilization
- Systems and procedures
- Relationships
- Performance and results
- Advocacy (Gubbels and Koss 2000:14)

Indicators can be developed through a *guided self-assessment strategy* to assess the current status of an organization on each of these dimensions and to evaluate progress. Table 15.4 describes a typical one-week, community-level training program organized by World Neighbors. This would normally be preceded by a one-week training program for the staff of the local partner organization that would review the concepts of community and organizational capacity building, describe the different exercises and techniques to be used in the community training program, and discuss the strategy for the transfer of responsibilities to the community.

The following is a list of the participatory self-assessment exercises that can be used in these workshops.[3] A typical application is given for each exercise:

- *Listing and brainstorming.* What are the characteristics of a viable organization?
- *Key words.* List some key words describing your organization's purpose with respect to healthy children and mothers.
- *Grouping and categorizing.* List areas where the community is BETTER than before; the SAME as before; WORSE OFF than before.
- *Scoring.* Participants are asked to rate characteristics of their organization, such as effective leadership and level of participation on a five-point scale where 1 = *embryonic;* 2 = *emerging;* 3 = *growing;* 4 = *well developed;* and 5 = *mature.*
- *Ranking.* Rank women's priority needs.
- *Weighting.* Participants are given a certain number of stones or beans and are asked to distribute them among different activities or needs according to their importance.
- *Matrices.* A matrix can be constructed to compare different community groups—such as men's and women's groups—on the level of support they receive and their level of self-reliance.
- *Diagrams.* Venn diagrams, organizational charts, and so on are used to show relationships between actors or structures.
- *Maps.* Groups are asked to construct social maps, physical maps, or mobility maps to help understand relationships between different sectors of the community or to identify constraints (such as areas of the community that women or other groups are not able to visit).
- *Calendars.* Groups construct calendars to help understand cyclical patterns such as periods of stress during the year.
- *Timelines.* These show sequences of activities such as the evolution of a community or changing economic activities.
- *Graphs and charts.* These provide a simple visual way to present information in bar charts, pie charts, and the like.
- *Direct observation.* This can be used to record activities such as travel and transport at different times of the day, use of community facilities, and attendance at community meetings.
- *Minisurveys.* Rapid surveys can be used to collect information on topics such as use of clinics, school attendance, adoption of new seed varieties, use of public transport, and so on.
- *Analogies and metaphors.* Pictures of trees or the human body can be used to help explain complex ideas such as the stages of evolution of a community organization or the interdependency of different sectors of the community.
- *Dialogue and semistructured interviews.* This is one of the principal tools used in both group meetings and individual interviews to permit maximum participation while ensuring that key issues are covered.

Interactive Evaluation Capacity Development

As discussed earlier, one of the most important ways in which RWE capacity is developed is through interaction among evaluation practitioners, sponsors, and users during the planning, implementation, interpretation, and use of evaluations. In many cases, there is no formal capacity-building program, although there will usually be a series of meetings and perhaps workshops during the different stages of the evaluation. As we discussed in Chapter 8, it is important in all evaluations to maintain constant communication with clients and to ensure there are "no surprises" when the main evaluation reports are presented and discussed. Maintaining this interaction with clients is particularly important for many RWEs for several reasons. First, many of the evaluations are implemented and finalized very rapidly so that the reports are likely to be ready for discussion much more rapidly than is the case for many other types of evaluation. Second, many organizations that commission RWEs are very short of staff so that it may be more difficult for staff to find time to attend briefing meetings. Finally, many clients may have a concern that RWE approaches, with their many cost- and time-saving strategies, are not "professional" or "scientific" evaluation. Consequently, the evaluation team must convince the client that the most rigorous evaluation methods possible are being used within the resource constraints under which the evaluation is conducted.

Summary

- Evaluation capacity building involves strengthening the ability and willingness of clients, evaluation practitioners, and other stakeholders to commission, conduct, understand, and use studies evaluating development projects, programs, and policies.

- RWE has the added challenge of showing that useful and technically sound evaluations can be conducted under budget, time, and other constraints.

- Evaluation capacity building is targeted to at least five groups: agencies that commission and fund evaluations, evaluation practitioners, evaluation users, groups affected by the programs or policies being evaluated, and those who shape public opinion.

- The main types of evaluation skills and knowledge to be developed include (a) defining evaluation needs and commissioning evaluations, (b) designing evaluations, (c) for people working with RWE **scenarios**, conducting evaluations under real-world constraints, and (d) disseminating and using evaluations.

- Capacity building must be customized to the specific skills and knowledge required by different groups as well as their level of education and professional expertise.

- The first way to deliver capacity building is through structured training programs, including formal university training, short workshops and seminars, distance learning and online training, on-the-job training, mentoring, and as part of community development programs.

- The second way to deliver capacity building is by interactive evaluation capacity development by involving sponsors, program participants, and other stakeholders during the planning, implementation, dissemination, and use of an evaluation. This can include planning sessions, workshops, briefing meetings, dissemination of progress reports, site visits, and informal conversations with stakeholders. Where the goal is to reach a wider public, it may also involve contacts and cooperation with the media.

- A number of techniques are recommended for promoting the involvement of community participants in the process of evaluating their own development process.

Further Reading

Chambers, R. 2002. *Participatory Workshops: A Sourcebook of 21 Sets of Ideas and Activities.* Sterling, VA: Earthscan.

Practical guidelines from a veteran participatory evaluation trainer on how to plan and organize participatory workshops. Includes an amusing but insightful section on all the things that can go wrong when organizing workshops in typical real-world scenarios.

Gubbels, P. and C. Koss. 2000. *From the Roots Up: Strengthening Organizational Capacity through Guided Self-Assessment.* Oklahoma City, OK: World Neighbors.

Comprehensive and systematic guidelines for community-level evaluation capacity building. Also provides detailed descriptions of how to use the most common PRA (participatory appraisal) techniques (see www.wn.org).

Kumar, S. 2002. *Methods for Community Participation: A Complete Guide for Practitioners.* London: ITDG.

Detailed guidelines for the use of all the most common participatory evaluation research and community capacity-building techniques (including PRA and similar approaches).

Rugh, J. 1986. *Self-Evaluation: Ideas for Participatory Evaluation of Rural Community Development Projects.* Oklahoma City, OK: World Neighbors.

Manual of basic evaluation concepts addressed to community-based program staff and drawing on experiences from many different countries.

Salmen, L. F. 1992. *Beneficiary Assessment: An Approach Described.* Washington, DC: World Bank.

Explains, with extensive examples from Africa, Latin America, and Asia, the use of beneficiary assessment as a tool for interactive evaluation capacity development (although it does not use this term).

Valadez, J. and M. Bamberger. 1994. *Monitoring and Evaluating Social Programs in Developing Countries: A Handbook for Policymakers, Managers and Researchers.* Washington, DC: World Bank.

Review of the organization of structured evaluation capacity-building programs for each of the major stakeholder groups.

Vaughan, R. and T.F. Buss. 1998. *Communicating Social Science Research to Policy Makers.* Thousand Oaks, CA: Sage.

A comprehensive and clearly written discussion of the eight steps for formulating, conducting, and presenting social science research and program evaluations to policymakers. Each chapter contains a set of practical rules and guidelines. Includes a wide selection of cases and examples from many areas of policy research in the United States.

Notes

1. The W. K. Kellogg Foundation (1998) in its *Evaluation Handbook,* published as a resource for community organizations and other grantees, specifically recognizes that many organizations and evaluators will underestimate the cost of conducting an evaluation and encourages grantees to come back for additional funds to complete the evaluation if this proves necessary. (The handbook is available at www.wkkf.org/Pubs/Tools/Evaluation/Pub770.pdf. See Chapter 3, "Not Enough Money: Addressing Budget Constraints.")

2. For more information about the Interlegis program (in Portuguese), go to www.interlegis.gov.br.

3. The list is adapted from Gubbels and Koss (2000, chap. 4). See also Dayal, Van Wijk, and Mukherjee (2000); Rietberger-McKracken and Narayan (1997); Patton (2002); Kumar (2002); Salmen (1987); and Rugh (1986) for discussions of other techniques.

CHAPTER 16

Bringing It All Together

Applying RealWorld Evaluation Approaches to Each Stage of the Evaluation Process

I n this chapter, we discuss how RealWorld Evaluation (**RWE**) approaches can be applied at each stage of the **design** and implementation of a typical evaluation. We identify RWE issues that can come up—that is, where there are constraints related to funding, time, availability of data, and clients' preconceptions—and suggest how the RWE approach can help to address those constraints. Readers new to the evaluation field might also find this chapter useful as a general introduction to the planning, design, implementation, dissemination, and use of any evaluation.

A reader who does not have time to read the whole book might find this chapter a useful condensation. There are references to other chapters where more detailed coverage of particular issues can be found. If you have read the rest of this book, we hope you will find this chapter a useful review of the main points relevant to planning and conducting RWEs. Consequently, this chapter is intentionally somewhat longer and more detailed than a typical summary.

Scoping the Evaluation

It is important that those charged with conducting an evaluation gain a clear understanding of what those asking for the evaluation (the **clients**[1] and **stakeholders**) are expecting—that is, the political setting within which the **project** and the evaluation will be implemented. It is also important to understand the policy and operational decisions to which the evaluation will contribute and the level of **precision** required in providing the information that will inform those decisions (see Chapter 2).

Understanding the Client's Needs

An essential first step in preparing for any evaluation is to obtain a clear understanding of the priorities and information needs of the client (the agency or agencies commissioning the evaluation) and the key stakeholders (persons interested in or affected by the project). The timing, focus, and level of detail of the evaluation should be determined by the client information needs and the types of decisions to which the evaluation must contribute.

The process of clarifying what questions need to be answered can help those planning the evaluation to identify ways to eliminate unnecessary data collection and analysis, hence reducing cost and time. The RealWorld evaluator must distinguish between (a) information that is essential to answer the key questions driving the evaluation and (b) additional questions that would be interesting to ask, if there were adequate time and resources, but that may have to be omitted given the limitations faced by the evaluation.

An additional decision relating to cost and time may concern who should be involved in data collection and review of the evaluation reports. Many development projects have a philosophy of promoting the empowerment of community members and other stakeholders, such as school administrators and teachers, health center staff members, local government agencies, and nongovernmental agencies (**NGOs**), which includes inviting their participation in monitoring and evaluation activities. A question that can arise in the face of RWE constraints is, "How important is it to include participatory methods and adequate representation of project participants and other stakeholders in the evaluation?" Participatory data collection methods tend to be more expensive and time-consuming, because sufficient time must be allowed to develop rapport with the community and other stakeholders and to build trust. The cost-conscious RealWorld evaluator must determine whether the client and key stakeholders place a sufficiently high value on participatory approaches to allow for the time and budget required *to do them well.*

Another challenge for RWE is that it is often more time-consuming and expensive to reach the poorest and most vulnerable groups, so when time and budgets are constrained, there will often be pressures to drop these groups from the consultations. "It would be really great to consult with the squatters who do not have land title, but unfortunately . . . we just don't have the money and/or the time."

An important function of the scoping phase is to understand whether the lack of consultation with the groups affected by the project, including the poorest and most vulnerable groups, is due to a lack of resources or to the low priority that the client assigns to their involvement. Often, lack of time and money may be used as an excuse, so it is important for the evaluator to fully understand the perspective of the client before deciding what approach to adopt.

Understanding the Political Environment

The political environment includes the priorities and perspectives of the client and other key stakeholders, the dynamics of power and relationships between them and the key players in the project being evaluated, and even the philosophical or methodological biases or preferences of those conducting the evaluation (see Chapter 6).

It is important to avoid the assumption that political influence is bad and that evaluators should be allowed to conduct the evaluation in the way that they know is "best" without interference from politicians and other "narrow-minded" stakeholders trying to make sure that their concerns are introduced into the evaluation. The whole purpose of evaluation is to contribute to a better understanding of policies and **programs** about which people have strong and, often, opposed views. If an evaluation is not subject to any political pressures or influences, this probably means either that the topic being studied is of no consequence to anyone or that the evaluation is designed in such a way that the concerned groups are not able to express their views. Evaluators should never assume that they are right and that stakeholders who hold different views on the key issues, appropriate methodology, or interpretation of the **findings** are biased, misinformed, or just plain wrong. In the "Integrated Checklist for Assessing the Adequacy and Validity of Quantitative, Qualitative, and Mixed-Method Designs" (Appendix 1), assessment Criteria C has to do with the **internal validity** and **authenticity** of the evaluation findings: "Are the findings credible to the people studied and to readers, and do we have an authentic portrait of what we are studying?"

If key groups do not find the analysis credible, then the evaluator may need to go back and check carefully on the methodology and underlying assumptions. It is never an appropriate response to sigh and think how difficult it is to get the client to "understand" the findings and recommendations.

One of the dimensions of **contextual analysis** used in developing the **program theory model** (see following section) is to examine the influence of political factors. Many of the contextual dimensions—economic, institutional, environmental, and sociocultural—influence the way that politically concerned groups will view the project and its evaluation. A full understanding of these contextual factors is essential to understanding the attitudes of key stakeholders to the program and to its evaluation. Once these concerns are understood, it may become easier to identify ways to address the pressures placed by these stakeholders on the evaluation.

Not surprisingly, many program evaluations are commissioned with political motives in mind. A client may plan to use the evaluation to bolster support for the program and may consequently resist the inclusion of anything but positive findings. On the other hand, the real but undisclosed purpose the client may have had for commissioning the evaluation may be to provide ammunition for firing a manager or closing down a project or a department. Seldom if ever are such purposes made explicit. Different stakeholders may also hold strongly divergent opinions about a program, its execution, its motives, its leaders, and how it is to be evaluated. Persons who are opposed to the evaluation's being conducted may be able to preempt an evaluation or obstruct access to data, acceptance of evaluation results, or continuation of an evaluation contract.

Before the evaluation begins, the evaluator should anticipate these different kinds of potential political issues and try to explore them, directly or indirectly, with the client and key stakeholders. Chapter 6, Table 6.1, illustrates some of the many ways that the political context can affect how an evaluation is designed, implemented, disseminated, and used.

Political dimensions include not only clients and other stakeholders. They also include individual evaluators who have preferred approaches that resonate with their personal and professional views as to what constitutes competent, appropriate practice. Different evaluators, even those who have chosen to work together on a project, may take different stances regarding their public and ethical responsibilities. Evaluators, like everyone else, have their own personal values. However, for many evaluators, it may be more comfortable to think of the work of evaluation not as an imposition of the evaluator's values but, rather, as an impartial or objective data-based judgment about program merit, shortcomings, effectiveness, efficiency, and goal achievement. The evaluators must be aware of their own perspectives (and biases) and seek to ensure that these are acknowledged and taken into consideration. (See Section A of the Integrated Checklist in Appendix 1.)

Clients may base their selection of evaluators on their reputations for uncompromising honesty, counting on those reputations to ensure the **credibility** and acceptance of findings. Or the choice of evaluator may be based on ideological stances the evaluator has taken that are in agreement with the client's. These decisions may be so understated as to initially go unnoticed in friendly negotiations and enthusiastic statements about the strategic importance of the proposed evaluation. Chapter 6 discusses some of the options available to the evaluator when it is felt that some of the pressures from clients are ethically or professionally unacceptable.

Evaluators should also be alert to the fact that political orientations of clients and stakeholders can influence how evaluation findings are disseminated and used. Clients can sometimes ignore findings they do not like and can suppress distribution by circulating reports only to carefully selected readers, by sharing only abbreviated and softened summaries, and by taking responsibility for presenting reports to boards or funding agencies and then acting on that responsibility in manipulative ways. Clients have been known to give oral presentations and even testimony that distorted evaluation findings, to take follow-up activities not suggested and even contraindicated by evaluation reports, and to discredit evaluations and evaluators who threaten their programs and prestige.

The wise evaluator should be aware of such realities and be prepared to deal with them in appropriate ways. Chapter 6 suggests some RWE strategies for addressing political constraints such as these, as well as others, during the evaluation design, the implementation of the evaluation and in the presentation, and use of the evaluation findings.

Defining the Program Theory

Before an evaluation can be conducted, it is necessary to identify the explicit or implicit theory or **logic model** that underlies the design on which a project was based (see Chapter 9). An important function of an impact evaluation is to test the hypothesis that the project's interventions and **outputs** contributed to the desired **outcomes**, which, along with external factors that the project assumed would prevail, were to have led to sustainable **impact**.

Defining the program theory or logic model is good practice for any evaluation. It is especially useful in RWE, where, due to budget, time, and other constraints, it is necessary to prioritize what the evaluation needs to focus on. An initial review of what a project did in light of its logic model could reveal missing data or information that is needed to verify whether the logic was sound and whether the project was able to do what was needed to achieve the desired impact.

If the logic model was clearly articulated in the project plan, it can be used to guide the evaluation. If not, the evaluator needs to construct it based on reviews of project documents and discussions with the project implementing agency, project participants, and other stakeholders (see Chapter 9). In many cases, this requires an iterative process in which the design of the logic model evolves as more is learned during the course of the evaluation.

In addition to articulating the internal cause-effect theory on which a project was designed, a logic model should also identify the socioeconomic characteristics of the affected population groups, as well as contextual factors such as the economic, political, organizational, psychological, and environmental conditions that affect the target community.

The key phases or levels of a simple logic model can be summarized as follows (see Figure 16.1 and Chapter 2):

1. **Design**[1]. How was the project designed? Who designed this project? Was it only a few staff members of the donor or implementing agency or a consultant, or was there extensive participation by a mixture of stakeholders, including the intended beneficiaries? Was the design based on a holistic diagnostic assessment of the conditions in the target communities? And was the design informed by lessons learned from evaluations of previous projects using similar approaches under similar conditions?

2. **Inputs**. Inputs represent the financial, human, material, technological, and information resources used for the development intervention.

3. **Implementation process**. This includes actions taken or work performed through which **inputs** such as funds, technical assistance, and other types of resources are mobilized to produce specific outputs. One of the critical factors is whether, and how, intended beneficiaries and other stakeholders were involved in the implementation process.

4. **Outputs**. Outputs include the products and services that result from the completion of activities within a development intervention. Note that project implementers have direct control over outputs—although not over the external contextual factors that may affect the timely delivery or quality of the outputs.

5. **Outcomes**. Outcomes are the intended or achieved short-term and medium-term effects of an intervention's outputs. Note that project implementers do not have direct control over outcomes. Outcomes are what others do on their own, albeit influenced by the project's outputs.

6. **Impacts**. Impacts are the positive and negative long-term effects on identifiable population groups produced by a development intervention, directly or indirectly, intended or unintended. These impacts can be economic, sociocultural, institutional, environmental, technological, or of other types.

7. **Sustainability**. Sustainability refers to the continuation of benefits from a development intervention after major external assistance has been completed; it is the resilience to risk of net benefit flows over time. Many people either do not think about this at all, or they assume that impacts will be sustained. However, impacts may not be sustained for a number of reasons: The project may receive subsidies that will not continue; external conditions such as weather or political or economic conditions may change and thus threaten the stability of the project's outcomes; the underlying causes of the problem may not have been addressed so that the project interventions will not resolve *these* problems and will not be sustainable; and the project may introduce techniques or technologies that people or organizations are unable to continue implementing on their own.

Every project is designed and implemented within a unique *setting* or *context* that includes local and regional economic, political, institutional, and environmental factors as well as the sociocultural characteristics of the communities or groups affected by the project. The program theory must incorporate all these factors through a *contextual analysis*. Where a project is implemented in a number of different locations, it will often be the case that performance and outcomes will differ significantly from one site to another because of the different configurations of **contextual variables**.

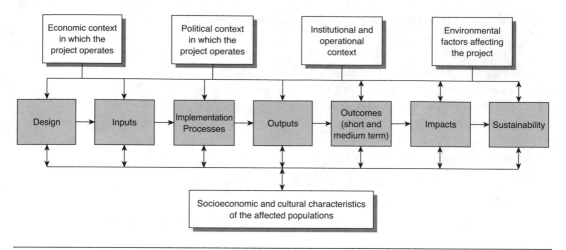

Figure 16.1   A Simple Program Theory Model

Customizing Plans for Evaluation

Those commissioning an evaluation need to consider a number of factors that should be included in the **terms of reference** (ToR). The client, and an evaluator being contracted to undertake this assignment, might find the following set of questions helpful to be sure these factors are taken into consideration as plans are made for conducting an evaluation. The answers to these questions can help to focus on important issues to be addressed by the evaluation, including ways to deal with RWE constraints.

- Who asked for the evaluation? Who are the key stakeholders? Do they have preconceived ideas regarding the purpose for the evaluation and expected findings?
- Who should be involved in planning/implementing the evaluation?
- What are the key questions to be answered?
- Will this be a **formative** or **summative evaluation**? Is its purpose primarily for learning and improving, accountability, or a combination of both?
- Will there be a next phase, or will other projects be designed based on the findings of this evaluation?
- What decisions will be made in response to the findings of this evaluation? By whom?
- What is the appropriate level of rigor needed to inform those decisions?
- What is the scope/scale of the evaluation?
- How much time will be needed/available?
- What financial resources are needed/available?
- What evaluation design would be required/is possible under the circumstances?
- Should the evaluation rely mainly on quantitative (QUANT) methods, qualitative (QUAL) methods, or a combination of the two?
- Should participatory methods be used?
- Can/should there be a survey of individuals, households, or other entities?
- Who should be interviewed?
- What sample design and size are required/feasible?

- What form of analysis will best answer the key questions?
- Who are the audiences for the report(s)? How will the findings be communicated to each audience?

Choosing the Best Design from the Available Options

Chapter 10, Table 10.1, summarizes seven widely used RWE designs. The first two of these designs are methodologically the most robust (subject to the fewest threats to conclusion validity) and are recommended when budget and time are not major constraints and when the evaluation can begin at the start of the project. Designs 3 through 6 all have important methodological limitations but can provide reasonably robust estimates of program impacts and can also be more flexible concerning when they begin. Design 7, which begins only when the project is nearing completion and only covers the project group, is the weakest methodologically. However, given the constraints under which many evaluations are conducted, this is, unfortunately, the situation faced by many evaluators. When designed creatively—using the **mixed-method** designs that draw on all the available QUANT and QUAL design, data collection, and analysis approaches (see Chapter 14)—even Design 7 can provide operationally useful estimates of the extent to which the project contributes to the desired effects. However, given the many threats to the validity of conclusions, it is important to review carefully the limitations on the kinds of conclusions that can be drawn from the analysis. Chapter 10 describes each of the evaluation designs, gives a case study illustrating how the design has been applied in the field, and assesses the major threats to validity and adequacy. Table 10.4 summarizes the conditions under which each design does and does not work well. This should be consulted at an early stage in the evaluation planning to help narrow down the options.

We describe below a number of strategies that can be used to strengthen most RWEs. Evaluators are strongly encouraged to consider using some of these strategies whenever appropriate and feasible. The choice of the most appropriate RWE design is determined by a number of factors, including the following:

- *When did the evaluation begin?* At the start of the project, while the project was being implemented, or after the project had ended?
- *When will the evaluation end?* Will this be a one-time evaluation conducted while the project is being implemented (most commonly for the midterm review), will it end at approximately the same time as the project (end-of-project evaluation and report), or will it continue after the project ends (longitudinal or ex-post evaluation)?
- *What type of comparison will be used?* There are three main options: (a) a randomized design in which individuals, families, groups, or communities are randomly assigned to the project and **control groups**; (b) a **comparison group** selected to match as closely as possible the characteristics of the project group; or (c) no type of control or comparison group.
- *Does the design include process evaluation?* Even if an evaluation is focused on measuring sustainable changes in the conditions of the **target population**, it needs to identify what most likely led to those changes. That includes an assessment of the quality of a

project's implementation process and whether it made a plausible contribution to any
measured impact.
- *Are there preferences for the use of QUANT, QUAL, or mixed-method approaches?* See
Chapters 11, 12, and 13.

Paring Down the Evaluation Design

RWE approaches are used because time, resources, the available data, and possibly, the political setting do not permit the use of stronger evaluation designs. Under these circumstances, the
evaluator must work with the client to agree on how the resource and time requirements as well
as the data needs can be pared down while still ensuring an acceptable level of precision.
Chapters 3 and 4 discuss options for working within a tight budget or under time constraints,
and Chapter 5 describes ways to make the most effective use of the available data. The following
are recommended steps in defining the best and most acceptable design under given constraints:

- Spend the time needed to fully understand the client's priority information needs and
  the political and other constraints under which they are operating:
  - What does the client really need from the evaluation?
  - Is it essential to have rigorous QUANT analysis to ensure the credibility of the eval-
    uation, or is an in-depth QUAL analysis more important and credible to clients?
  - What is the nonnegotiable "bottom line" in terms of the minimum information
    needs and the real deadlines for producing a first draft and a final report?
  - Who are the stakeholders to whom the evaluation is directed and whose opinions
    are critical?
- Review the options for reducing costs (Chapter 3) and time (Chapter 4) and for
  strengthening the available database (Chapter 5).
- Use these options to prepare several possible **scenarios** for achieving the evaluation
  objectives within the resource constraints. Review the "Integrated Checklist for Assess-
  ing the Adequacy and Validity of Quantitative, Qualitative, and Mixed-Method Designs"
  (Appendix 1) and assess strengths and weaknesses of each option from the perspective
  of the client(s) and other key stakeholders.
- If none of the available scenarios can satisfy the client's bottom line, prepare two addi-
  tional scenarios:
  - Scenario 1: Estimate what would be the additional budget or time requirements to
    satisfy the bottom line (e.g., an extra $25,000 would be required to include a com-
    parison group in the evaluation design or the deadline for the submission of the
    draft report would need to be extended by three months).
  - Scenario 2: Indicate what modifications would be required in the evaluation design
    to stay within the available resources.

Under Scenario 2, it might be possible to produce aggregate estimates of project impact at the
national level but not to provide the requested disaggregated estimates of the impact of different
combinations of services or the impact at different project sites or on different socioeconomic
groups (e.g., men and women, wage earners and the self-employed, different ethnic groups).

Alternatively, or in addition, it might be necessary to lower the statistical confidence
level (see Chapter 14) so that statistically significant differences between the project and

comparison groups might be assessed at only the 0.10 (10%) confidence level rather than the conventional 0.05 (5%) level.

Some of the information might have to be obtained from, for example, **focus group** interviews and **PRA** (the term is now used to refer to a wide range of participatory appraisal methods, although it originally meant participatory rural appraisal) group techniques rather than from a household sample survey.

All the options should be discussed with the client as well as the implications of each option in terms of the level of precision, the types of analysis that can be conducted, and the credibility of the findings to different stakeholders. It is essential to ensure that the client fully understands the options and trade-offs before a decision is made on how to proceed. Sometimes the client will ask the evaluator, "What would you advise is the best approach, because you are the expert." If asked this question, the evaluator must explain that this is a policy decision to be made in consultation with the client and that the role of the evaluator is simply to provide advice on the technical implications of each option with respect to precision, types of analysis, and professional credibility.

Identify the Kinds of Analysis and Comparisons That Are Critical to the Evaluation

A key factor in the choice of the evaluation design, and for determining the size and structure of the sample, has to do with the kinds of analysis required and the levels of statistical precision needed. It is useful to think of three kinds of evaluation:

1. *Exploratory or research evaluations* in which the purpose is to assess whether the basic project concept and approach "works." This is often used when a new type of service is being piloted or when an existing service is to be provided in a new way or to reach new target groups. Examples of the key evaluation questions include the following:
   a. Are farmers willing to experiment with new kinds of seed?
   b. Do the new teaching methods get a positive response from the schools, students, and parents; and is there initial **evidence** of improved performance?
   c. If poor women are given loans, are they able to use the money to start or expand a small business?
   d. Which groups benefit most and least, and why?

2. *Small-scale* QUANT *or* QUAL *designs* to assess whether there is evidence that the project is producing significant effects on the target population. Some designs include a comparison group, whereas others use a more general comparison with similar communities through PRA techniques or focus groups. Questions of attribution (what would have been the condition of the project group if the project had not taken place?) are addressed but in a less rigorous way than for large-scale impact assessments (see below). Some of the critical questions might include the following:
   a. Are the intended project beneficiaries (e.g., individuals, families, schools, communities) better off as a result of the project?
   b. How confident are we that the observed changes were caused by the project and not be external factors such as improvements in the local economy?
   c. Would the project be likely to have similar effects in other areas if it were replicated? Where would it work well and less well, and why?

d. Which contextual factors (economic, political, institutional, environmental, and cultural) affect success? (See Chapter 9 for a discussion of contextual factors and mediator variables.)

e. Who did and who did not benefit from the project?

3. *Large-scale impact assessment* where the purpose is to assess, with greater statistical rigor, how large an effect (defined numerically in terms of percentage or quantitative change) has been produced, and who does and does not benefit. Ideally, the evaluation should use a mixed-method approach integrating QUANT and QUAL methods. Critical questions might include the following:

a. What QUANT impacts (high-level sustainable effects) has the project produced? The emphasis is on "how much" and not just "what."

b. What is the quality of the services (compared with other programs, to expected standards, and in the opinion of the target groups)?

c. Are the project effects statistically significant "beyond a reasonable doubt"?

d. Who has benefited most and least, and are there any groups that have not benefited at all or who are worse off?

e. What are the **intervening variables** (e.g., socioeconomic characteristics of the project groups, cultural factors affecting participation) that influence the magnitude of impacts?

For *exploratory evaluations,* a descriptive analysis using techniques such as observation, interviews of at least a few selected members of the target population, key informant interviews, and perhaps focus groups would probably suffice. A simple and rapid survey might also be used to collect basic information on the project population. It would probably not be necessary to use a formal comparison group, although similar communities or areas might be visited to assess how similar or different they are to the project areas.

For *small-scale QUANT and QUAL evaluations of outcomes and impacts* it is useful, although not always possible, to identify a comparison group to help estimate what the situation of the project group would have been in the absence of the project (the **counterfactual**). Ideally, a mixed-method approach is used, assessing both quality and quantity of services and impacts. The design is also much stronger if baseline data (in whatever form available) can be obtained. Simple statistical comparisons such as difference of means or proportions should be made between the project and comparison groups.

For *large-scale impact assessments,* relatively large samples (often requiring hundreds of observations in both project and comparison groups) are required so that multivariate analysis can be used to statistically control for differences between the project and comparison groups and estimate the quantitative influence of the intervening variables. Again a mixed-method approach should be used so that QUANT estimates are complemented by QUAL descriptions of the project context, the process of project implementation, the quality of services, and the opinions and experiences of beneficiaries and agencies and staff responsible for project implementation.

Assessing Threats to Validity and Adequacy of Different Designs

The RWE approach assesses the strengths and weaknesses of the different stages of the evaluation design to identify factors affecting the validity of the conclusions and recommendations.

This is important for any evaluation, but particularly so for RWE where conventional methodological procedures often have to be relaxed due to time or budget constraints or because some of the required data are not available. Several factors affect the adequacy of the evaluation design and findings (see Chapter 7, Table 7.2), including the following:

- The appropriateness of the evaluation focus, approach, and methods for obtaining the types of information required
- The availability of data and data sources
- How well the data collected will support interpretations about program performance and impacts
- The qualifications of the evaluation team in terms of both evaluation methodology and the specific fields of the program

For QUANT evaluations, four sets of generally accepted "threats to validity" were established by Cook and Campbell in the 1960s (see Shadish, Cook, and Campbell 2002 for an updated version). Appendix 1 (Sections F, G, H, and I, respectively) describes and explains the different types of threats to QUANT evaluation designs under each of the four categories described below:

- *Threats to statistical conclusion validity* (Appendix 1, Section F)—incorrect inferences/conclusions about the effects of project interventions on the intended outcomes and impacts: The problems may result from the incorrect application of a statistical test or because of limitations of the sample (e.g., the sample may not cover all the population). Another common problem is that because of the small sample size (usually due to budget or time constraints), the analysis may conclude that the project did not have a statistically significant effect, when in fact the sample was too small to have found this effect, even if it did exist. There is often a trade-off between reducing sample size to cut costs and the need to ensure the sample is large enough to find the effects if they do exist. Also, many well-designed and -executed projects can expect to produce only small effects, which makes it more difficult to detect the effects. The issues of Type II errors (wrongly concluding there was no effect), the **power of the test**, **effect size,** and the estimation of sample size are discussed in Chapter 14.
- *Threats to internal validity* (Appendix 1, Section G)—incorrectly inferring that the project intervention "caused" or contributed to a particular outcome or impact: Many internal validity problems arise from the way in which project participants were selected (they are different in important ways from the comparison group), because the characteristics of the project group changes over the life of the project because of people dropping out or because experiences during the project influence the way people respond.
- *Threats to construct validity* (Appendix 1, Section H)—refers to the degree to which inferences can legitimately be made from the theoretical constructs (definition of key concepts) on which the program theory is based: Many of the key constructs are difficult to define (e.g., poverty, vulnerability, well-being, hostile work environment) and even harder to measure. A lack of precision and clarity in the definition and measurement of these key constructs will undermine the ability of the evaluation to understand and interpret how the project has operated and what it has achieved.

- *Threats to external validity* (Appendix 1, Section I)—incorrect inferences about whether evaluation findings would apply to different persons, times, or settings: Most QUANT evaluations are intended to determine the extent to which the evaluation findings can be generalized to a broader population (e.g., all low-income communities, all unskilled women workers, all secondary schoolchildren). There are a number of ways in which the characteristics of the project population may not be typical of the broader population so that generalization of findings may be misleading. For example, an adult literacy program may have been successful, at least in part, because of the enthusiastic support of the local chamber of commerce, which provided transport, free exercise books, and snacks for participants. Consequently, the program's success might not justify the conclusion that it would be similarly successful in other cities where it did not enjoy this strong local support.

The threats to validity checklist can be used to identify and assess potential weaknesses in all the seven most frequently used QUANT RWE designs (see Chapters 7 and 10). Readers who are not specialists in statistical analysis and QUANT evaluation may find sections F through I of the Integrated Checklist difficult to follow. While it is worth glancing through the categories to get an idea of the wide range of factors that can affect the validity of QUANT evaluation designs, it is always possible to ask the advice of a specialist when rigorous QUANT evaluations must be designed and assessed.

For nonspecialist readers, Parts A through E of Appendix 1 (see below) provide sufficient guidance for assessing the validity of most evaluations. These are normally used to assess the validity (often called adequacy) of QUAL and mixed-method evaluation designs, but they also complement categories F thru I in the assessment of QUANT evaluation designs.

- *Confirmability and objectivity* (Appendix 1, Section A): Are the conclusions drawn from the available evidence, and is the research relatively free of researcher bias? There are five subcategories concerning how well the methods and procedures are described, whether data are presented to support conclusions, whether potential researcher biases are recognized and addressed, and whether competing hypotheses were considered.
- *Reliability and dependability* (Appendix 1, Section B): Is the process of the study consistent, coherent, and reasonably stable over time and across researchers and methods? There are eight subcategories concerning the clarity of research questions, the application of the data collection methods, and the procedures for checking and validating the methods. Whereas QUANT evaluations seek to ensure uniformity and standardization, many QUAL evaluations use *emergent designs* where the data collection methods and interpretation evolve and change as the evaluation progresses. The challenge is to assess whether the emergent processes are adequately documented and assessed so that the reader can understand the basis of evidence on which conclusions were based.
- *Internal validity, credibility, and authenticity* (Appendix 1, Section C): Are findings credible to the people studied and to readers, and do they provide an authentic portrait of what is being studied? The eight subcategories address the depth and richness of data collection and analysis, how different groups feel about the credibility of the analysis, the consistency of the findings with existing theory and hypotheses, and how well the findings are supported by the data.

- *External validity, transferability, and fittingness* (Appendix 1, Section D): Do the conclusions fit other contexts and how widely can they be generalized? The 11 subcategories assess how widely and to what other groups or populations the findings can be generalized.
- *Utilization, application, and action orientation* (Appendix 1, Section E): How useful were the findings to the client, researchers, and the communities studied? The seven subcategories provide indicators for assessing utility.

When and How to Use the Threats to Validity and Adequacy Checklist

The checklist should be referred to throughout the evaluation to ensure that things are on the right track and to rapidly identify and address problems affecting the validity of the methodology and the conclusions. The most important times to use the checklist are these:

- *When the evaluation is being designed and data collection and analysis methods are being planned.* The checklist can be used to identify potential problems and to consider ways to address them. It is particularly useful in RWE for identifying the potential threats to validity resulting from the methods proposed to reduce costs and time and to work with limited databases. For example, what additional threats to validity arise if the baseline comparison group is eliminated or if income data are collected through focus groups rather than through household sample surveys?
- *When most of the data collection has been completed.* The checklist can help identify any potential threats that have arisen during data collection (e.g., unexpectedly high nonresponse rates or confusion about the concept of unemployment). It should be applied as soon as possible after data collection is completed (or even when it is still underway) so that there is still time to take corrective measures.
- *When the draft evaluation report has been completed.* Ideally, there may still be time to take some corrective measures, but if this is no longer possible, the evaluation report should use the checklist to identify and clearly state the potential threats to validity and how these might affect the conclusions and recommendations.

Appendix 2 presents an "RWE Project Worksheet for Identifying and Addressing Threats to Validity and Adequacy" that can be used at any stage of the evaluation to identify threats to validity and adequacy, to assess the seriousness of each threat for the purposes of the evaluation, and to identify actions that can be taken to correct or at least address the most important threats. Appendix 3 gives a worked example illustrating how the worksheet could be applied to the assessment of an evaluation of a housing project.

Determining Appropriate Methodologies

QUANT and QUAL approaches and methods are, by and large, designed for different purposes. Chapter 11 and 12 discuss the strengths and potential weaknesses of QUANT and QUAL approaches, respectively. Recognizing these strengths and weaknesses, the RWE approach considers that in most situations the strongest and most robust evaluation design will probably combine both QUANT and QUAL approaches. Chapter 13 is devoted to a detailed discussion of how mixed methods, systematically combining QUANT and QUAL approaches, can be useful in RWEs. It is argued that mixed-method approaches are particularly valuable for RWEs because the combination of different data collection and analysis methods can detect and overcome, or at least reduce, some of the threats to validity resulting from the compromises that have to be made in the light of budget, time, and data constraints. For example, reducing sample size increases the sampling error, making it more difficult to detect significant differences. If PRA and other QUAL techniques are used to obtain independent estimates of project impacts and if the findings are consistent with the statistical analysis of the sample surveys, then confidence in the findings may be increased.

Many authors argue that when mixed-method approaches are used, every evaluation has either a predominant QUANT or QUAL focus ("theoretical drive") and the other approach is used to complement this. The theoretical drive will be determined by the professional orientation of the researcher or the preference of the client. However, other authors propose an integrated approach that does not give primacy to either approach. Whichever position is taken on this issue, some programs lend themselves more naturally to QUANT evaluation methods (e.g., very large programs affecting many thousands of people), whereas in other cases QUAL methods may seem better suited (e.g., a program whose goal is to improve the quality of teaching practices or one that is trying to introduce vegetable growing into several fairly small villages). However, in all cases, the choice of methods will also be influenced by the preferences of the evaluators and the clients.

Throughout this book, we strongly urge evaluators to select the data collection and analysis tools best suited to the needs of the client and the nature of the program being evaluated and to avoid selecting methods simply because they are qualitative or because they are quantitative.

Ways to Strengthen RealWorld Evaluation Designs

Because of the contexts within which RWEs are implemented, the conventional quasi-experimental QUANT designs, when used in isolation, are subject to a number of threats to validity that are likely to weaken the quality of the data and the validity of the conclusions. (This is why RWE strongly encourages the use of mixed-method designs.) These issues are addressed in more detail in Chapter 10. The limitations of the conventional QUANT designs include the following:

- Problems can arise concerning the reliability of measurement of key indicators, particularly when these relate to sensitive issues such as illegal drug use, control of resources, domestic violence, and social constraints on women's economic activities or mobility.
- There can be difficulties in capturing variations in project implementation, the quality of services, and the access of different groups to the services and benefits.
- Conventional designs do not analyze contextual factors affecting the outcomes and impacts of the project in different locations.
- Important differences (nonequivalency) between the project and comparison groups, particularly those that are difficult to quantify (e.g., motivation, community organization), are difficult to capture.

The following are a number of procedures that can be used to strengthen these designs (see also Box 7.2, p. 144, for examples of ways to address common threats to **statistical**, **internal**, **construct**, and **external validity**). Evaluators should consider incorporating some of the following procedures into RWE designs where appropriate.

Basing the Evaluation Design on a Program Theory Model

As we saw earlier in this chapter, the formulation of a program theory model helps identify the key issues and hypotheses on which the limited evaluation resources should focus (see Chapters 2 and 9). A theory model can also be used to complement a quasi-experimental design by describing the project **implementation process** and analyzing the contextual factors that affect implementation and outcomes, and it helps interpret the evaluation findings and the assessment of whether a project should continue or be replicated.

Complementing the Quantitative (Summative) Evaluation with Process Evaluation

A **process evaluation** uses QUANT, QUAL, and mixed methods to observe and assess the process of project implementation and to make recommendations for ways to strengthen subsequent phases of an ongoing program. It addresses questions such as these:

- How were the different components of the project implemented, and how closely did implementation on the ground conform to the project plan or operational manual?
- For ongoing projects, how could the quality of the services be assessed and be improved? Is there evidence that they are leading to desired outcomes?
- Who has access to and/or uses the services and who does not? Why do certain groups not use the services?
- Was the design and organization of the project participatory, managed by a small group, or top-down? Who is involved in decision making during implementation?
- What proportion of the community (intended beneficiaries) know about the project? Is their information correct? What do they think about the project?
- What are the relations between the project organizers and the community?
- What do governmental and other organizations know about this project, and what impressions do they have of the quality of services and effectiveness of this project?

Incorporating Contextual Analysis

Contextual analysis assesses the influence of economic, political, organizational, and environmental factors on the implementation and outcome of projects. These are defined in program theory models as **mediators** (see Chapter 9). It also examines the influence of the preexisting sociocultural characteristics of the target populations on how different groups respond to the project.

Most contextual analysis is qualitative (e.g., interviews with key informants, review of project documents, and **participant observation**), but it may also include QUANT analysis of data from household surveys. **Contextual variables** can also be transformed into numerical variables (e.g., **dummy variables**) and incorporated into multivariate analysis (see Chapter 13, endnote 1).

Reconstructing Baseline Conditions

Many evaluations do not begin until the project has been underway for some time or perhaps is even nearing completion. It is very common under these circumstances to find that no baseline data have been collected at the beginning of the project. This is most commonly the case for the comparison group, but it is also often true for the project group. The absence of baseline data is usually one of the most serious threats to validity, and therefore, RWE proposes a number of different ways to *reconstruct* baseline data. Some of these approaches, described in Chapter 5, Table 5.1, include the following:

- Using secondary data (see following section)
- Using individual **recall** (respondents are asked to recall the situation of their family or community at around the time the project began)
- Using PRA and other participatory group techniques to *reconstruct* the history of the community and to assess the changes that have been produced by the project
- Interviews with key informants, preferably persons who know the target community, as well as other communities, and therefore have a perspective on relative changes occurring over time

Although all these methods provide potentially valuable information, there are significant threats to validity inherent in any recall method. These result from lack of precise memory, the tendency to confuse the precise time period (so that events that took place earlier may be reported as having occurred since the project began or vice versa), and in some cases, deliberate distortion. Consequently, it is important to treat all recall data with caution and to always use mixed-method approaches to triangulate independent estimates of the reported information from different sources.

Using Secondary Data

Administrative planning and monitoring data collected by the organization being evaluated. Data collected as part of the preproject diagnostic assessment and data collected by the project implementers' monitoring system during the life of a project are important but often underutilized sources for reconstructing baseline conditions (see Chapter 5). Most projects collect a lot of data for administrative and monitoring purposes, and frequently these records contain information that can be useful for reconstructing information on the conditions of the project population at the time the project started (baseline data). Some of the kinds of data typically collected include the following:

- Planning and feasibility studies before the project began
- Socioeconomic characteristics of individuals or families who apply for or receive services

- Attendance at community meetings and, possibly, reports on the meetings (e.g., minutes)
- Activity reports by the agency staff or others involved in the implementation of the project. At a minimum, these provide information on the implementation process; ideally, they also mention changes observed in clients' knowledge, attitude, and practices.

Although these kinds of administrative data can be extremely useful as surrogate baseline data, it is important to be aware that the data were not collected for the purpose of evaluation and they may have some limitations (such as being incomplete or poorly kept or not including all the information required for the purposes of evaluation). The second section of Chapter 5 (pp. 90–100) lists some of the questions that should be asked when assessing the quality and utility of this information for the reconstruction of baseline data.

Records from outside the organization. Records from other programs or projects in the same area can often provide information on conditions before the current project began. For example, surveys are often conducted to estimate the number of children not attending school, sources and costs of water supply, or availability of **microcredit**. More general statistical data may also be available on, for example, school enrollment rates, infant mortality, agricultural prices, microcredit lending, and transport patterns. It is important to assess the strengths and weaknesses of these records with respect to the following:

- Time differences between the start of the project (when data are required for the baseline) and the time when the secondary data were collected. Time differences are particularly critical when general economic conditions may have changed between the survey date and the project launch.
- Differences in the population covered. For example, did the surveys include employment in the informal as well as the formal sectors? Did it cover pedestrian as well as vehicular means of transport?
- Was information collected on key project variables and potential impacts? Are the secondary data statistically valid for the particular target population addressed by the project being evaluated?
- Does information cover both men and women? Or was all information obtained from a single person (usually the "household head") and aggregated for all household members (see Box 5.2)?

The Use of Mixed-Method Approaches to Strengthen Validity of Indicators and to Improve Interpretation of Findings

Each of the seven evaluation designs described in Chapter 10 can be strengthened using mixed-method designs (see Chapter 13) that combine QUANT and QUAL approaches in one of the following ways:

- Exploratory studies to understand the context and to identify key issues and hypotheses to be tested. This is particularly important in the construction of the program theory model (see Chapter 9).

- Analysis of the quality of the services provided by the project
- Analysis of the accessibility of the project to different sectors of the target population
- Analysis of the contextual factors (the economic, political, organizational, and natural environmental conditions) within which each project site operates
- Understanding the cultural characteristics of the affected populations and how these influence project implementation and outcomes
- Using **triangulation** to provide two or more independent estimates of key process and outcome indicators (see below). Estimates are always stronger if they can be independently confirmed from two or more independent sources. This can be done by the following:
  - Using independent estimates of change in impact variables obtained from surveys through the use of observation, focus groups, and secondary data. Compare the estimates through triangulation. If estimates from different sources are consistent, greater confidence can be given to the findings.
  - If estimates are inconsistent, there should be a follow-up strategy to determine reasons and make adjustments to estimates.

Chapter 10 (p. 207) illustrates the use of triangulation to compare three independent estimates (survey, observation, and key informants) of household income. In one example, the three estimates are *converging* (consistent), whereas in the second example, the estimates are *diverging* (inconsistent). In this second case, it is necessary to follow up to determine the reason for the inconsistencies and to decide how to select the most credible value (or values) to use in the analysis. Ideally, the evaluation design should allow time and resources to return to the field to follow up, either during the interview supervision phase or during the analysis phase (when the discrepancies tend to be discovered). Unfortunately, this is usually not possible, particularly on the RWE budget, so other options should be considered:

- **Enumerators** should be instructed to note inconsistencies between reported information and their direct observation. They should indicate how they interpret the discrepancies and possibly what they think is the best estimate. They may also be instructed to ask some follow-up questions (see Chapter 11).
- Inconsistencies should be identified during the interview supervision phase and follow-up should be carried out through postinterview discussion with **interviewer**s and possibly by revisits to a sample of respondents.
- Rules for survey instrument coding and analysis of how to address inconsistencies should be defined (e.g., should more weight be given to one source of data, should QUANT estimates be adjusted in a certain defined way).
- For critical variables, it is possible to create two different indicators giving upper and lower estimates (e.g., income, school enrollment, unemployment), one in which the survey information is not adjusted and the other in which it is adjusted through triangulation. Both estimates will be presented separately in the analysis.

Adjusting for Differences between the Project and Comparison Groups

Multivariate Analysis

When large sample surveys are conducted, multivariate analysis is often used to statistically control for differences between the project and comparison groups to improve the estimates of project impact (see Chapters 10 and 11). The analysis statistically matches subjects (e.g., individuals, households) on variables such as age, education, and income and determines whether there is still a significant difference between the project and comparison groups on the impact variable (e.g., proportion of children attending school, number of adults unemployed). If there is still a significant difference after this statistical matching, this gives greater confidence that the project is really contributing to the difference. However, if there is no longer a difference, this suggests that school attendance or unemployment may be determined more by, for example, household characteristics than by participation in the project.

Using Qualitative Methods to Analyze Differences between Project and Comparison Groups

Key informants, focus groups, and participant observation are some of the methods that can be used to identify potentially important differences between project and comparison groups and to assess how they might affect project outcomes and the estimation of project impacts. (See Chapter 5 on collecting data from difficult-to-reach groups and rapid methods for comparing project and comparison groups.)

Staffing the Evaluation Economically

In this section, we address issues concerning external experts (either from another country or from a different part of the country), content area specialists, and locally available data collectors. The ideal is to compose an evaluation team that includes a good combination of persons with different experiences, skill sets, and perspectives. Where RWE constraints are faced, especially funding, compromises may have to be made in the composition of the evaluation team. Although we address each of these categories of persons separately, it is important to consider the overall combination and the effectiveness of the full evaluation team in meeting the requirements of an evaluation.

Use External Consultants Wisely

External consultants are usually contracted (a) because of lack of local technical expertise (inside the organization or in the local research community), (b) to build up local capacity, (c) to save time, (d) to ensure independence and objectivity, (e) to ensure expert credibility, or (f) because of a requirement by the funding agency. While, if well selected and used, external consultants can significantly improve the quality of the present and future evaluations, they are also expensive and sometimes disruptive, so they should be selected and used wisely. Under RWE constraints, the goal should be to limit the use of external consultants to those areas where they are essential. Although many of the following points refer to the use of national or international evaluation consultants in developing countries, the same general principles apply in developed countries. For example, the cost and time implications of a consultant flying from Washington, DC, to work on an evaluation on the West Coast of the United States (a distance of almost 3,000 miles) are similar to someone flying from England to Nigeria. Similarly, there are many situations in the United States where English is not the first language in the project areas, so language and cultural competence and sensitivity are similarly important.

Here are a few general rules for selecting and using consultants:

- Ensure that local agencies and the client are actively involved in defining the requirements for the external consultant and in the selection process.
- Consider carefully the merits of an international as opposed to a national consultant. There is often a trade-off between greater technical expertise of the international consultant and the local knowledge (and of course language ability) of the national consultant. Not using any national consultants can also antagonize the local professional community, who may be reluctant to cooperate with the international expert.
- If an international consultant is used, give priority to candidates who have experience in the particular country and with local language skills (if required).
- For evaluations with an operational focus, avoid selecting consultants with impressive academic credentials but limited field experience in conducting program evaluations. The requirements are different from those for an academically oriented research project.

External consultants are often not used in the most cost-effective way, either because they are doing many things that could be done as well or better by local staff or because they are brought in at the wrong time. Here are some suggestions on ways to ensure the effective use of external consultants:

- Define carefully what the consultant is being asked to do and consider whether all these activities are necessary.
- Even when the budget is tight, try to plan sufficient time for the consultant to become familiar with the organization, the project, and settings in which it is being implemented. A consultant who does not understand the project, has not spent some time in the communities, or has not built up rapport with project staff, clients, and other stakeholders will be of very little use.
- Plan carefully at what points the consultant should be involved and coordinate ahead of time to ensure that he or she will be available when required. Get tough with consultants who wish to change the timing, particularly at short notice, to suit their own convenience. Some of the critical times to involve a consultant are these:
  - During the scoping phase when critical decisions are being made on objectives, design, and data collection methods and when agreement is being reached with the client on options for addressing time, budget, and data constraints
  - When decisions are being made on sample size and design
  - When the results of the initial round of data collection are being reviewed
  - When the draft evaluation report is being prepared
  - When the findings of the evaluation are being presented to the different stakeholders
- Arrange for a briefing document (preparatory study) to be prepared, by agency staff or local consultants, before the external consultant starts work. This should summarize important information about the project (including compilation of key documents), key partner agencies, and the settings where the project is located. The document, which should be prepared in coordination with the consultant (e.g., through an exchange of e-mail or phone calls), might also include rapid diagnostic studies in a few communities. A well-prepared document of this kind can save a great deal of time for the consultant and can initiate dialogue on key issues and priorities among clients, local researchers and stakeholders before the consultant even arrives.

- Consider the use of video or phone conferences so that the consultant can maintain more frequent contact with others involved in planning and implementing the evaluation. This enables the consultant to contribute at critical stages of the evaluation without having to always be physically present. In this way, the consultant can make suggestions about the sample or other stages of the design at a sufficiently early stage for it to be possible to make changes based on these recommendations. Video and phone conferences also have the advantage of flexibility, thus avoiding the extremely costly situation where, for example, a consultant flies from Europe to West Africa to participate in the project design phase, only to discover that everything has been delayed for several weeks.

Think about Content Area Specialists

In addition to expertise in the relevant evaluation areas (e.g., qualitative interviewing, questionnaire construction, sample design, and data analysis), it is also essential to include at least one team member with the necessary experience in the content area of the evaluation (e.g., agricultural extension, secondary education, microcredit). Ideally, if resources permit, the team should include both a sector expert with experience in many different countries or programs as well as someone with local knowledge. The school or health system in Chicago or Dhaka will probably have many unique features (cultural, organizational, and political) that it is important to incorporate into the evaluation.

Chapter 14 makes the same point with respect to sample design and statistical analysis. The effectiveness of sample design or the application of the appropriate statistical tests is often compromised because the statistician is not familiar with the literature on practices in a particular area (such as educational testing or a branch of psychological research).

Be Creative about Data Collectors

Creative options are sometimes available for reducing the cost of contracting data collectors. In a health evaluation, it may be possible to contract student nurses; in an agricultural evaluation, to contract agricultural extension workers; and for many types of evaluation, to contract graduate students as interviewers or enumerators. Arrangements can often be made with the teaching hospital, the ministry of agriculture, or a university professor to contract students or staff at a rate of pay that is satisfactory to them but well below the market rate. Although these options can be attractive in terms of potential cost savings or for the opportunity to develop local evaluation capacity, there are obvious dangers from the perspective of quality. The interviewers may not take the assignment very seriously; it may be politically difficult to select only the most promising interviewers or to take action against people producing poor-quality work. Supervision and training costs may also be high, and the time required to complete data collection may increase. However, experience shows that these kinds of cooperation can work very well if there is a serious commitment on the part of the agency or university faculty.

Another creative option is to employ data collectors from the community. Sometimes a local high school can conduct a community needs assessment study, or a community organization can conduct baseline studies or monitor project progress. A number of self-reporting techniques can also be used. For example, individuals or families can keep diaries of income and expenditures, daily time use, or time, mode, and destination of travel. Community groups can be given cameras, tape recorders, or video cameras and asked to make recordings on issues such as problems facing young people, community needs, or the state of community infra-structure. Although all these techniques pose potential validity questions, they are valuable ways to understand the perspective of the community on the issues being studied.

Collect Data Efficiently

Simplifying the Plans to Collect Data

Data collection tends to be one of the most expensive and time-consuming items in an evaluation. Consequently, any efforts to reduce costs or time will almost inevitably involve sim-plifying plans for data collection. This involves three main approaches:

1. Discuss with the client what information is really required for the evaluation and elim-inate other information in the ToR or mentioned in subsequent discussions that is not essential in answering the key questions driving this evaluation.

2. Review data collection instruments to eliminate unnecessary information. Data collec-tion instruments tend to grow in length as different people suggest additional items that it would be "interesting" to include, even though not directly related to the purpose of the evaluation.

3. Streamline the process of data collection to reduce costs and time. Chapter 3, Table 3.1, summarizes a number of different strategies to reduce the costs of data collection. These include the following:
   - Simplifying the evaluation design (e.g., eliminating the collection of baseline data or cutting out the comparison group)
   - Clarifying client information needs (discussed above)
   - Look for reliable secondary data (discussed above)
   - Reducing sample size (see Chapter 14)
   - Reducing the costs of data collection, input, and analysis (e.g., use of self-administered questionnaires, using direct observation instead of surveys, using focus groups and community forums instead of household surveys, and finding cheaper data collectors)

Commission Preparatory Studies

It is sometimes possible to achieve considerable cost and time savings by commissioning an agency staff person or local consultant to prepare a preparatory study. This can cover these points:

- A description of the different components of the project being evaluated and how they are organized
- Basic information on the implementing agency
- Rapid diagnostic studies of the project communities and possible comparison communities
- Information on government agencies, NGOs, and other organizations involved in or familiar with the project
- Recommendations on community leaders and other key informants with whom the inter-national consultant should meet and preparation of background information on them

Look for Reliable Secondary Data

A great deal of time and expense can be saved if reliable and relevant secondary data can be obtained. Depending on the country and subjects, it may be possible to find records maintained by government statistical agencies or planning departments, university or other research organizations, schools, commercial banks or credit programs, mass media, and many sectors of civil society. Indeed, the evaluator should make use of any relevant records such as monitoring data and annual reports produced by the implementing agency itself. These records may be produced for planning purposes, administrative and financial control, assessing progress, or communicating with the different groups whose authorization, financial support, or general approval are critical to the success of the organization and its activities. Some of the important points to check when assessing the strengths and weaknesses of various kinds of secondary data were discussed earlier in this chapter (pp. 388–389).

Caution: never accept secondary data at face value without checking its reliability.

While many problems with secondary data concern differences in the time period covered, inadequate coverage of some sectors of the target population, or poor quality of data collection and reporting, there are sometimes more fundamental weaknesses in the data. When the quality of supervision is poor, a significant number of interviews may have been completely falsified by the interviewers or important sections may have been left out or poorly recorded.

Collect Only the Necessary Data

It is important to ensure that only essential information is collected. The collection of unnecessary information increases costs and time and also reduces the quality of the information required because respondents become tired if they have to answer large numbers of questions. Therefore, we recommend that all data collection instruments be carefully scrutinized to cut out information that is not relevant and essential to the purpose of the evaluation and that will never be analyzed or used.

Similarly, the data analysis plan should be reviewed to determine what kinds of disaggregated data analysis are actually required. If it is found that certain kinds of proposed disaggregation are not needed (e.g., comparing the impacts of the project on participants in different locations), then it will often be possible to reduce the size of the sample.

Find Simple Ways to Collect Data on Sensitive Topics and from Difficult-to-Reach Populations

Another challenge to evaluators, although not unique to RWE, regards the collection of data on sensitive topics such as domestic violence, contraceptive usage, or teenage violence or from difficult-to-reach groups such as commercial sex workers, drug users, ethnic minorities, migrants, the homeless, or, in some cultures, women. A number of methods can help to address such topics and reach such groups. However, RWE constraints such as budget, time, or political prejudices could create pressures to ignore these sensitive topics or leave out groups of people who are difficult to reach. There are at least three strategies for addressing sensitive topics:

1. Identify a wide range of informants who can provide different perspectives.

2. Select a number of culturally appropriate strategies for studying sensitive topics.

3. Systematically triangulate.

Some of the culturally appropriate methodologies that can be used include the following:

- Participant observation
- Nonparticipant observation (observation of persons or groups as an outsider without being involved in their activities)
- Focus groups
- Case studies
- Key informants
- PRA techniques

Difficult-to-reach groups include commercial sex workers, drug or alcohol users, criminals, informal and unregistered small businesses, squatters and illegal residents, ethnic or religious minorities, boyfriends or absent fathers, indentured laborers and slaves, informal water sellers, girls attending boys' schools, migrant workers, and persons with HIV/AIDS, particularly those who have not been tested.

The evaluator may face one of two scenarios. In the first scenario, the groups may be known to exist, but members are difficult to find and reach. In the second scenario, the clients and, at least initially, the evaluator may not even be aware of the existence of such marginalized or "invisible" groups. The techniques for identifying and studying difficult-to-reach groups are similar to those used for addressing sensitive topics and include the following:

- *Participant observation.* This is one of the most common ways to become familiar with and accepted into the milieu where the groups operate or are believed to operate. Often, initial contacts or introductions will be made through friends, family, clients, or in some cases, the official organizations with whom the groups interact.
- *Key informants.* Schedule interviews with persons who are particularly familiar with and well informed about the target groups.
- *Tracer studies.* Neighbors, relatives, friends, work colleagues, and so on are used to help locate people who have moved.
- *Snowball samples.* With this technique, efforts are made to locate a few members of the difficult-to-locate group by whatever means are available. These members are then asked to identify other members of the group so that if the approach is successful, the size of the sample will increase. This technique is often used in the study of sexually transmitted diseases.
- *Sociometric techniques.* Respondents are asked to identify to whom they go for advice or help on particular topics (e.g., advice on family planning, traditional medicine, or for the purchase of illegal substances). A sociometric map is then drawn with arrows linking informants to the opinion leaders, informants, or resource persons.

Analyze the Data Efficiently

Look for Ways to Manage the Data Efficiently

Before data can be analyzed, they must be input into an electronic or manually-coded format. If this is not done properly, the quality and reliability of the data can be compromised or time, money, or both can be wasted. Furthermore, if data are not properly managed, there is the risk that significant amounts of information will be lost. The following are some of the main steps in the development and implementation of an analysis plan:

- *Drafting an analysis plan* (see Table 11.4, Chapter 11). This must specify for each proposed type of analysis the objectives of the analysis, the hypothesis to be tested, the variables included in the analysis, and the types of analysis to be conducted.
- *Developing and testing the codebook.* If there are open-ended questions, the responses must be reviewed to define the categories that will be used. If any of the numerical data have been classified into categories ("More than once a week," "Once a week," etc.), the responses should be reviewed to identify any problems or inconsistencies.
- *Ensuring reliable coding.* This involves both ensuring that the codebook is comprehensive and logically consistent and also monitoring the data-coding process to ensure accuracy and consistency between coders.
- *Reviewing surveys for missing data and deciding how to treat missing data* (see Chapter 14). In some cases, it will be possible to return to the field or mail the questionnaires back to respondents, but in most cases, this will not be practical. Missing data are often not random, so the treatment of these cases is important to avoid bias. For example, there may be differences between sexes, age, and economic or education groups in their willingness to respond to certain questions. There may also be differences between ethnic or religious groups or between landowners and squatters. One of the first steps in the analysis should be to prepare frequency distributions of missing data for key variables and, when necessary, to conduct an exploratory analysis to determine whether there are significant differences in missing data rates for the key population groups mentioned above.
- *Entering the data into the computer or manual data analysis system.*
- *Cleaning the data.* This involves the following:
  - Doing exploratory data analysis to identify missing data and to identify potential problems such as outliers. These are survey variables where a few scores on a particular variable fall far above or below the normal range. A few outliers can seriously affect the analysis by making it much more difficult to find statistically significant results (because the **standard deviation** is dramatically increased). Consequently, the data cleaning process must include clear rules on how to treat outliers (see Chapter 11).
  - Deciding how to treat missing data and the application of the policies
  - Identifying any variables that may require recoding

- *Providing full documentation of how data were cleaned, how missing data were treated, and how any indices were created.*[2]

While RWE follows most of the standard data analysis procedures, a number of special approaches may be required when time or budget is a constraint. When *time* is the main constraint and where additional resources may be available to speed up the process, the following approaches can be considered:

- Direct inputting of survey data into handheld computers
- Use of electronic scanning to read questionnaires
- Subcontracting data analysis to a university or commercial research organization
- Hiring more, or more experienced, data coders and analysts

When *money* is the main constraint, one or more of the following options can be considered:

- Limiting the kinds of statistical analysis to reduce expensive computer time
- Consider acquiring and using popular statistical packages such as SPSS or SAS so that the analysis can be conducted in-house rather than subcontracting. Needless to say, this option requires the availability of statistical expertise in-house.

Focus Analysis on Answering Key Questions

It is sage advice for any evaluation to focus on the key questions that relate to the main purpose of undertaking an assessment. This is especially important for RWE, because choices need to be made as to what can be dropped as a consequence of limitations of time and funding. By being reminded of what the major questions are and what is required to adequately answer them, those planning a RWE can be sure to focus on those issues and not others. Typically, the clients and stakeholders, as well as the evaluators themselves, would like to collect additional information. However, when faced with RWE constraints, what would be "interesting to find out" must be culled from "what is essential" to respond to those key questions that drive the evaluation.

As we saw in Chapter 2 and earlier in this chapter, examples of typical key evaluative questions include the following:

- Is there evidence that the project achieved (or will achieve) its objectives? Are there measurable changes in the characteristics of the target population with respect to the impacts the project was trying to produce? Which objectives were (and were not) achieved? Why? Is it reasonable to assume that the changes were due in a significant measure to the project rather than to external factors (not controlled by the project implementers)?
- Did the project aim for the right objectives? Was it based on an adequate diagnosis of the underlying causes of the problem(s) to be addressed?
- What impact has the project had on different sectors of the target population—including the poorest and most vulnerable groups? Are there different impacts on men and women? Are there ethnic, religious, or similar groups who do not benefit or who are affected negatively?
- Are the outcomes sustainable and are benefits likely to continue? Were the target communities or groups reasonably typical of broader populations (such as all poor farmers or all urban slum dwellers), and is it likely that the same impacts could be achieved if the project were replicated on a larger scale?
- What are the contextual and external factors determining the degree of success or failure of the project?

The RealWorld evaluator must understand which are the critical issues that must be explored in depth and which are less critical and can be studied less intensively or eliminated completely. It is also essential to understand when the client needs rigorous (and expensive) statistical analysis to legitimize the evaluation findings to members of congress or parliament, or to funding agencies critical of the program, and when more general analysis and findings would be acceptable. The answer to these questions can have a major impact on the evaluation budget and time required, particularly on the required sample design and size.

Report Findings Efficiently and Effectively

As we mentioned in the section above titled "Customizing Plans for Evaluation," an evaluation should focus on the key questions that relate to the main purpose of its being undertaken. This is especially important for RWE, because choices need to be made about what can be dropped as a consequence of limitations of time and funding. Those key questions need to be kept in mind not only during the planning for the evaluation, data collection, and analysis but also when the report(s) are being written. There is a temptation to report on all sorts of "interesting findings," but the evaluator(s) need to keep the report focused on answering the key questions that the client(s) and stakeholders wanted answered.

One of the most effective ways to increase the likelihood that evaluation findings are used is to ensure that they are of direct practical utility to the different stakeholders. Some of the factors affecting **utilization** include the following:

- Timing of the evaluation
- Recognizing that the evaluation is only one of several sources of information and influence on decision makers and ensuring that the evaluation complements these other sources
- Building an ongoing relationship with key stakeholders, listening carefully to their needs, understanding their perception of the political context, and keeping them informed of the progress of the evaluation. There should be "no surprises" when the evaluation report is presented (Operations Evaluation Department 2005; Patton 1997).

Some steps in the presentation of evaluation findings include these:

- Understand the evaluation stakeholders and how they like to receive information.
- Use visual presentation to complement written reports or verbal presentations. Where appropriate and feasible, make use of presentation tools such as PowerPoint, but do not become a slave to the technology and be prepared to work without this if the logistics become too complicated. Visual presentations are particularly useful when the presentation is not made in the first language of many people in the audience.
- Share the evaluation results through oral presentations. Many stakeholders are not comfortable with written reports or slide presentations, so talking about the findings can be important.
- Plan the written report to make it simple, attractive, and user-friendly. Consider presenting different version of findings in ways that are most understandable and useful to different audiences. (We'll say more about this below.)
- Involve the mass media. When a goal is to reach and influence a wide audience (e.g., public opinion, all parents of secondary-school-age children, lawmakers), the press can be a valuable ally. However, working with the media requires time and preparation and if their involvement is important, it may be worth hiring a consultant who "knows the ropes."

Succinct Report to Primary Clients

The impact of many evaluations is reduced because the findings and recommendations do not reach the primary clients in a form they like and understand. There is no one best way to report evaluation findings, which depends on the clients and the nature of the evaluation. A good starting point is to ask clients which previous reports they found most useful and why.

A general rule, particularly for RWE where time tends to be a constraint, is to keep the presentation short and succinct. It is a good idea to have a physically short document that can be widely distributed; although the executive summary at the start of a large report may be well written, some clients and stakeholders may be intimidated by the size of the document and may not get round to opening the summary.

Vaughan and Buss (1998) present some useful guidelines for figuring out what to say to busy policymakers and how to say it. They point out that many policymakers have the intellectual capacity to read and understand complicated analysis, but most do not have the time. Consequently, many will want to be given a flavor of the complexities of the analysis (they do not wish to be talked down to) but without getting lost in details. Other policymakers may not have the technical background and will want a simpler presentation. So there is a delicate balance between keeping the respect and interest of the more technical while not losing the less technical. However, everyone is short of time. Therefore the presentation must be short, even if not necessarily simple. Vaughan and Buss's rules for figuring out what to say are the following:

- Analyze policy but not politics. Evaluators are hired to provide technical expertise, not to advise on political strategies.
- Keep it simple.
- Communicate reasoning as well as bottom lines. Many policymakers will want to know how the evaluator arrived at the conclusions so that they can assess how much weight to give to the findings.
- Use numbers sparingly.
- Elucidate, don't advocate. If evaluators advocate particular policies, they risk losing the trust of the policymaker.
- Identify winners and losers. Decision makers are concerned with how policies affect their constituencies, particularly in the short run. Consequently, if evaluators and analysts want policymakers to listen to them, they must identify winners and losers. For example, one of the most effective selling points of the study on why the very expensive but politically sensitive wheat flour ration program in Pakistan should be terminated was the analysis of who were the potential losers (the distributors of wheat flour and the retail store owners) and how their losses could be mitigated (Operations Evaluation Department 2005, chap. 6).
- Don't overlook unintended consequences. People will often respond to new policies and programs in unexpected ways, particularly to take advantage of new resources or opportunities. Sometimes, unexpected reactions can destroy a potentially good program, and in other cases, unanticipated outcomes may add to the program's success. Policymakers are sensitive to the unexpected because they understand the potentially high political or economic costs. Consequently, if the evaluation can identify some important consequences of which policymakers were not aware, this will catch the attention of the audience and raise the credibility of the evaluation.

Practical, Understandable, and Useful Reports to Other Audiences

In addition to the client and other primary stakeholders (e.g., concerned government ministries and the funding agency), there are often other stakeholders who are interested in the evaluation for different reasons. Some groups, such as members of the target population, are directly affected by the evaluation; others are involved in advocacy and either wish to use the findings to support their arguments or to criticize the report because it does not support them; and others are interested in the practical applications of the findings. Often, the client does not wish to have the evaluation findings too widely disseminated, particularly if they are critical or might raise sensitive issues. In these cases, evaluators may face sensitive ethical and professional concerns about whether they have the ethical and perhaps professional obligation to disseminate the evaluation findings to all groups affected by the project, despite the instruction of the client to limit distribution. These ethical issues are discussed in Chapters 6 and 7.

Assuming that these ethical issues are satisfactorily resolved, a dissemination strategy has to be defined to reach groups with different areas of interest, levels of expertise in reading evaluation reports, and preferences in terms of how they like to receive information. In some cases, different groups may also require the report in different languages. The evaluation team must decide which stakeholders are sufficiently important to merit the preparation of a different version of the report (perhaps even translation into a different language) or the organization of separate presentations and discussions.

These issues are particularly important for RWE because reaching the different audiences, particularly the poorest, least educated, and least accessible, has significant cost and time implications. There is a danger that when there are budget or time constraints, the evaluation will reach only the principle clients, and many of the groups whose lives are most affected (such as the indigenous groups whose way of life is threatened, the urban squatters who may be forcibly relocated, or the low-income communities who may or may not benefit from the new water and sanitation technology) may never see the evaluation and may never be consulted on the conclusions and recommendations.

An important purpose of the scoping exercise (Step 1 of the RWE approach) is to agree with the client who will receive and have the opportunity to express opinions about the evaluation report. If the client shows little interest in wider dissemination, but is not actively opposed, then the evaluator can propose cost-effective strategies for reaching a wider audience. If, on the other hand, the client is actively opposed to wider consultation or dissemination, then the evaluator must consider the options—one of which would be to not accept the evaluation contract.

Assuming the main constraints to wider dissemination are time and budget, the following are some of the options:

- Enlist the support of the mass media. It will often be necessary to invest considerable time in cultivating relationships with television, radio, and print journalists. They can be invited to join in field visits or community meetings and they can be sent interesting news stories from time to time.
- Enlist the support of NGOs and civil society organizations. They will often be willing to help disseminate but may wish to present the findings from their own perspective (which might be quite different from the evaluation team's findings), so it is important to get to know different organizations before inviting them to help with dissemination.
- Meetings can be arranged with organizations in the target communities to present the findings and obtain feedback. It is important that these meetings are organized sufficiently early in the report preparation process so that the opinions and additional information can be incorporated into the final report.

Help Clients Use the Findings Well

Unfortunately, it is all too common for an evaluation to be completed, a formal report written and handed over to the client, and then nothing more done about it. Following the above advice, including involving the client and other key stakeholders throughout the evaluation process, one would hope that the findings of an evaluation are relevant and taken seriously. However, if there is no follow-up, one can be left with the impression that the evaluation had no value. There are examples where major donor agencies, noting the limited use of evaluation reports, have decided to simply stop commissioning routine evaluations. Wouldn't it be better for more effort to be put into making sure evaluations are focused on answering key questions, well done, and then more fully utilized?

A major purpose of RWE is to help those involved focus on what is most important and to be as efficient as possible in conducting evaluations that add value and are useful. The final step—utilization—must be a part of that efficiency formula. If information is not used to inform decisions that lead to improved program quality and effectiveness, it is wasted. The point here is that those conducting evaluations need to see that the follow-through is an important part of the evaluation process.

One way to do this is to help the client develop an action plan that outlines steps that will be taken in response to the recommendations of an evaluation and then to monitor implementation of that action plan. Doing this is obvious if this was a **formative evaluation**, where the findings are used to improve subsequent implementation of an ongoing project. Even in the case of a summative evaluation (where the purpose was to estimate the degree to which project outcomes and impacts had been achieved) or where the project that was evaluated has now ended, follow-up should include helping to utilize the lessons learned to inform future strategy and in the design of future projects. At a minimum, those responsible for an evaluation need to do whatever can be done to be sure that the findings and recommendations are documented and communicated in helpful ways to present and future decision makers.

Further Reading

Readers should consult the reading list at the end of each chapter and the references at the end of the book. Appendix 4 also presents electronic resources covering many of the issues discussed in this chapter.

Notes

1. Many of these definitions are based on the OECD glossary (Organization for Economic Cooperation and Development 2002). See also the glossary at the end of this book for definitions of words in bold.

2. Sometimes an index is created by combining several variables or by a statistical transformation. For example, the variable *consumption* might be created as the sum of expenditures on food, housing, transport, education, and other payments. It is essential that the procedures for creating all indices are clearly documented and easily accessible to the reader.

Appendix 1

Integrated Checklist for Assessing the Adequacy and Validity of Quantitative, Qualitative, and Mixed-Method Designs[1]

A. Confirmability (and objectivity)[3]	v^2
Are the conclusions drawn from the available evidence, and is the research relatively free of researcher bias?	
1. Are the study's methods and procedures adequately described? Are study data retained and available for reanalysis?*	
2. Are data presented to support the conclusions?*	
3. Has the researcher been as explicit and self-aware as possible about personal assumptions, values, and biases?*	
4. Were the methods used to control for bias adequate?*	
5. Were competing hypotheses or rival conclusions considered?	
B. Reliability and Dependability	
Is the process of the study consistent, coherent, and reasonably stable over time and across researchers and methods? If emergent designs are used, are the processes through which the design evolves clearly documented?	
1. Are findings trustworthy, consistent, and replicable across data sources and over time?	
2. Were data collected across the full range of appropriate settings, times, respondents, etc.?	
3. Did all fieldworkers have comparable data collection protocols?	
4. Were coding and quality checks made, and did they show adequate agreement?	
5. Do the accounts of different observers converge? If they do not (which is often the case in QUAL studies), is this recognized and addressed?[4]**	
6. Were peer or colleague reviews used?	
7. Are the conclusions subject to "Threats to Construct Validity" (See Section H)? If so, were these adequately addressed?**	
8. Were the rules used for confirmation of propositions, hypotheses, etc., made explicit?	
C. Internal Validity, Credibility, and Authenticity	
Are the findings credible to the people studied and to readers, and do we have an authentic portrait of what we are studying?	
1. How context rich and meaningful ("thick") are the descriptions? Is there sufficient information to provide a credible/valid description of the subjects or the situation being studied?**	
2. Does the account ring true, make sense, seem convincing? Does it reflect the local context?	

3. Did triangulation among complementary methods and data sources produce generally converging conclusions? If expansionist QL methods are used where interpretations do not necessarily converge, are the differences in interpretations and conclusions noted and discussed?**	
4. Are the presented data well linked to the categories of prior or emerging theory? Are the findings internally coherent, and are the concepts systematically related?	
5. Are areas of uncertainty identified? Was negative evidence sought, found? How was it used? Have rival explanations been actively considered?	
6. Were conclusions considered accurate by the researchers responsible for data collection?	
7. Are the findings subject to "Threats to Internal Validity" (see Section G)? If so, were these addressed?**	
8. Are the findings subject to "Threats to Statistical Conclusion Validity" (see Section F)? If so, were these adequately addressed?**	
D. External Validity, Transferability, and Fittingness	
Do the conclusions fit other contexts and how widely can they be generalized?	
1. Are the characteristics of the sample of persons, settings, processes, etc., described in enough detail to permit comparisons with other samples?	
2. Does the sample design theoretically permit generalization to other populations?	
3. Does the researcher define the scope and boundaries of reasonable generalization from the study?	
4. Do the findings include enough "thick description" for readers to assess the potential transferability?	
5. Does a range of readers report the findings to be consistent with their own experience?	
6. Do the findings confirm or are they congruent with existing theory? Is the transferable theory made explicit?	
7. Are the processes and findings generic enough to be applicable in other settings?	
8. Have narrative sequences been peserved? Has a general cross-case theory using the sequences been developed?	
9. Does the report suggest settings where the findings could fruitfully be tested further?	
10. Have the findings been replicated in other studies to assess their robustness. If not, could replication efforts be mounted easily?	
11. Are the findings subject to "Threats to External Validity" (see Section I)? If so, were these addressed?	

E. Use/Application/Action Orientation	
How useful were the findings to clients, researchers, and the communities studied?	
1. Are the findings intellectually and physically accessible to potential users?	
2. Were any predictions made in the study and, if so, how accurate were they?	
3. Do the findings provide guidance for future action?	
4. Do the findings have a catalyzing effect leading to specific actions?	
5. Do the actions taken actually help solve local problems?	
6. Have users of the findings experienced any sense of empowerment or increased control over their lives? Have they developed new capacities?	
7. Are value-based or ethical concerns raised explicitly in the report? If not, do some exist that the researcher is not attending to?	
F. Threats to Statistical Conclusion Validity.[5] *Reasons why inferences about covariation between two variables may be incorrect*	
1. *The sample is too small to detect program effects (low statistical power).*[6] The sample is too small for it to be possible to detect statistically significant differences between groups even if they do exist.	
2. *Violated assumptions of statistical tests.* Many statistical tests require that observations are independent of each other. If this assumption is violated— for example, by studying children in the same classroom or patients in the same clinic who may be more similar to each other than the population in general—this can increase the risk of Type I error (see Chapter 14) and wrongly conclude that the project had an effect.	
3. *Fishing for statistically significant results:* A certain percentage of statistical tests will show "significant" results by chance (1 in 20 results if the 0.05 significance level is used). "Fishing" through large numbers of statistical tables will always find some of these spurious results.	
4. *Unreliability of measures of change of outcome indicators.* Unreliable measures of, for example, rates of change in income, literacy, or infant mortality always reduce the likelihood of finding a significant effect.	
5. *Restriction of range.* If only similar groups are compared, the power of the test is reduced and the likelihood of finding a significant effect is also reduced.	
6. *Unreliability of treatment implementation.* If the treatment is not administered in an identical way to all subjects, the probability of finding a significant effect is reduced.	
7. *External events influence outcomes (extraneous variance in the experimental setting).* External events or pressures (electrical power failure, community violence, election campaigns) may distract subjects and affect behavior and program outcomes.	
8. *Diversity of the population (heterogeneity of units).* If subjects have widely different characteristics, this may increase the variance of results and make it more difficult to detect significant effects.	

9. *Inaccurate effect size estimation.* A few outliers (extreme values) can significantly reduce effect size (see Chapter 14) and make it less likely that significant differences will be found.	
10. *Extrapolation from a truncated or incomplete database.*** If the sample covers only part of the population (e.g., only the poorest families or only people working in the formal sector), this can affect the conclusions of the analysis and can bias generalizations to the total population.	
11. *Project and comparison group samples do not cover the same populations.*** It is often the case that the comparison group sample is not drawn from exactly the same population as the project sample. In these cases, differences in outcomes may be due to the differences in the characteristics of the two samples and not to the effects of the project.	
12. *Information is not collected from the right people, or some categories of informants are not interviewed.*** Sometimes information is collected only from, and about, certain sectors of the target population (men but not women, teachers but not students), in which case estimates for the total population may be biased.	
G. Threats to Internal Validity. *Reasons why inferences that the relationships between two variables is causal may be incorrect*	
1. *Unclear whether project intervention actually occurs before presumed effect (ambiguous temporal precedence).* A cause must precede its effect. However, it is often difficult to know the order of events in a project. Many projects (for example, urban development programs) do not have a precise starting date but get going over periods of months or even years.	
2. *Selection.* Project participants are often different from comparison groups either because they are self-selected or because the project selects people with certain characteristics (the poorest farmers or the best-organized communities).	
3. *History.* Participation in a project may produce other experiences unrelated to the project treatment that might distinguish the project and control groups. For example, entrepreneurs who are known to have received loans may be more likely to be robbed or pressured by politicians to make donations, or girls enrolled in high school may be more likely to get pregnant.	
4. *Maturation.* Maturation produces many natural changes in behavior, knowledge, and exposure to new experiences. It is often difficult to separate changes due to maturation from those due to the project.	
5. *Regression toward the mean.* If subjects are selected because of their extreme scores (weight, physical development), there is a natural tendency to move closer to the mean over time, thus diminishing or distorting the effects of the program.	
6. *Attrition.* Even when project participants originally had characteristics similar to the total population, selective dropout over time may change the characteristics of the project population (e.g., the poorest or least educated might drop out).	

7. *Testing*. Being interviewed or tested may affect behavior or responses. For example, being asked about expenditures may encourage people to cut down on socially disapproved expenditures (e.g., cigarettes and alcohol) and spend more on acceptable items.	
8. *Researchers may alter how they describe/interpret data as they gain more experience (instrumentation)*. As interviewers or observers become more experienced, they may change the way they interpret the rating scales, observation checklists, and so on.	
9. *Respondent distortion when using recall*.** Respondents may deliberately or unintentionally distort their recall of past events. Opposition politicians may exaggerate community problems and community elders may romanticize the past.	
10. *Use of less rigorous designs due to budget and time constraints*.** RWE evaluations are particularly vulnerable to many kinds of internal validity problems because of the need to cut costs and save time.	
H. Threats to Construct Validity. *Reasons why inferences about the constructs that characterize study operations may be incorrect*	
1. *Inadequate explanation of constructs*. Constructs (the effects/outcomes) being studied are defined in terms that are too general or are confusing or ambiguous, thus making it impossible to have precise measurement (examples of potentially ambiguous constructs include unemployed, hostile work environment, participation in community affairs, empowerment, sex discrimination)	
2. *Indicators do not adequately measure constructs (construct confounding)*. The operational definition may not adequately capture the desired construct. For example, defining the unemployed as those who have registered with an employment center will ignore the many people who are unemployed but do not use these centers. Similarly, defining domestic violence as cases reported to the police significantly underrepresents the real number of incidents.	
3. *Use of single indicator to measure a complex construct (mono-operation bias)*. A single indicator (operation) of a complex construct (such as poverty, well-being, domestic violence) will usually produce bias.	
4. *Use of a single method to measure a construct (monomethod bias)*. If only one method is used to measure a construct, this will produce a narrow and often biased measure (e.g., observing communities in formal meetings will produce different results than observing social events or communal work projects).	
5. *Only one level of the treatment is studied (confounding constructs with levels of constructs)*. Often, a treatment is administered only at one level of intensity, and this is often quite low (only small business loans, only a short training program for community leaders, only a small number of computers given to a school), and the results are used to make general conclusions about the effectiveness (or lack of effectiveness) of the construct. This is misleading because a higher level of treatment might have produced a more significant effect.	

6. *Program participants and comparison group respond differently to some questions (treatment-sensitive factorial structure).* Program participants may respond in a more nuanced way to questions. For example, they may distinguish between different types and intensities of domestic violence or racial prejudice, whereas the comparison group may have broader, less discriminated responses.	
7. *Participants assess themselves and their situation differently than comparison group (reactive self-report changes).* People selected for programs may self-report differently from those not selected even before the program begins. They may wish to make themselves more needy of the program (poorer, sicker), or they may wish to appear more meritorious if that is a criterion for selection.	
8. *Reactivity to the experimental situation.* Project participants try to interpret the project situation, and this may affect their behavior. If they believe the program is being run by a religious organization or a political group, they may respond differently.	
9. *Experimenter expectancies.* Experimenters also have expectations about how men and women or different socioeconomic groups will react to the program, and this may affect how they react to different groups.	
10. *Novelty and disruption effects.* Novel programs can generate excitement and produce a big effect. If a similar program is introduced later, the effect may be less as novelty has worn off.	
11. *Compensatory effects and rivalry.* Programs create a dynamic that can affect outcomes in different ways. There may be pressures (political or otherwise) to provide benefits to nonparticipants; rivalry may be created with comparison groups who may try to show what they can achieve on their own, or those receiving no treatment or a less attractive treatment may become demoralized.	
12. *Using indicators and constructs developed in other countries without pretesting in the local context.*** Many evaluations import theories and constructs from other countries, and these may not adequately capture the local project situation. For example, many evaluations of the impacts of microcredit on women's empowerment in countries such as Bangladesh and India have used definitions of empowerment that may not be appropriate for South Asian women.	
I. Threats to External Validity. *Reasons why inferences about how study results would hold over variations in persons, settings, treatments, and outcomes may be incorrect*	
1. *Sample does not cover the whole population of interest.* Subjects may come from one sex or from certain ethnic or economic groups, or they may have certain personality characteristics (e.g., depressed, self-confident). Consequently, it may be difficult to generalize from the study findings to the whole population.	
2. *Different settings affect program outcomes (interaction of the causal relationship over treatment variations).* Treatments may be implemented in different settings that may affect outcomes. If pressure to reduce class size forces schools to construct extra temporary and inadequate classrooms, the outcomes may be very different from having smaller classes in suitable classroom settings.	

3. *Different outcome measures give different assessments of project effectiveness (interaction of the causal relationship with outcomes).* Different outcome measures can produce different conclusions on project effectiveness. Microcredit programs for women may increase household income, and expenditure on children's education but may not increase women's political empowerment.	
4. *Program outcomes vary in different settings (interactions of the causal relationships with settings).* Program success may be different in rural and urban settings or in different kinds of communities. So it may not be appropriate to generalize findings from one setting to different settings.	
5. *Programs operate differently in different settings (context-dependent mediation).* Programs may operate in different ways and have different intermediate and final outcomes in different settings. The implementation of community-managed schools may operate very differently and have different outcomes when managed by religious organizations, government agencies, or nongovernmental organizations.	
6. *The attitude of policymakers and politicians to the program.*** Identical programs will operate differently and have different outcomes in situations where they have the active support of policymakers or politicians than in situations where they face opposition or indifference. When the party in power or the agency head changes, it is common to find that support for programs can vanish or be increased.	
7. *Seasonal and other cycles.*** Many projects will operate differently in different seasons, at different stages of the business cycle, or according to the international terms of trade for key exports and imports. Attempts to generalize or extrapolate findings from pilot programs must take these cycles into consideration.	

1. Sections A through E are adapted from Miles and Huberman (1994), Chapter 10 Section C (see also Guba and Lincoln 1989). Sections F through I are adapted from Shadish, Cook, and Campbell (2002), Tables 2.2, 2.4, 3.1, and 3.2, respectively.

2. The checkmark can be used to indicate if this question has been addressed. The authors decided not to recommend any system of rating (e.g., good, adequate, poor) for each item because ratings are difficult to apply in an objective and consistent manner.

3. Miles and Huberman (1994) consider that all these are indicators of both confirmability and objectivity. However, the present authors consider that several categories support confirmability but not objectivity. These are indicated with an *.

4. The items indicated by ** have been added or modified by the present authors as being of particular relevance to RWE evaluations.

5. Some of the technical terminology has been simplified. The original titles are given in parenthesis.

6. See Chapter 14 for a discussion of effect size, power of the tests, and other sampling terminology.

Appendix 2

RWE Project Worksheet for Identifying and Addressing Threats to Validity and Adequacy

---

RealWorld Evaluation (RWE) Project Evaluation Worksheet

Part I: Description of the Evaluation

Name of Evaluation:

1. **Stage of the study at which the worksheet was prepared**

   o Evaluation design stage
   o Pilot testing of instruments
   o During data collection
   o Data analysis
   o Report writing

2. **Objectives of the evaluation**

   a. Why was the evaluation commissioned?
   b. Purpose of the evaluation:

      o Exploratory study to provide initial indications on whether the project model "works"
      o Assessing the efficiency and potential impacts of a small pilot project to recommend whether it is worth replicating on a larger scale
      o Rigorous multivariate statistical analysis of a large-scale, multicomponent project to compare costs and benefits with alternative investment options

   c. What are the specific decisions or actions that will be taken on the basis of the findings?
   d. Key stakeholders and their expectations

      o *Donor agency*
      o *Project executing agency*
      o *Government funding or planning agency*

3. **Evaluation design**

   o RWE quasi-experimental design
   o Other quantitative design
   o Qualitative design
   o Mixed-method design

Describe briefly, indicating modifications to the basic design.

Page 1

4. <u>**RWE constraints addressed in the evaluation design**</u>

   a. Budget
   b. Time
   d. Data
   e. Political

5. <u>**Options for addressing time and resource constraints.**</u>

   o There is a very tight deadline and no possibility of additional resources.
   o There is a tight deadline but additional resources could be obtained for use within this deadline.
   o The priority is to produce a high-quality product with a solid methodology that can withstand scrutiny from the critics of the project.

6. <u>**Major threats to the validity and adequacy of the evaluation design and conclusions**</u>
   [explained in Part III]

   o Baseline data
   o Control group
   o Data collection methods and quality of data
   o Analysis of contextual factors
   o Other: _____

7. <u>**Recommended actions**</u>

Note: Complete a Question 14 sheet for each important threat to validity or adequacy

Page 2

Part II: Assessment of the Five Dimensions of Adequacy of the Evaluation Design

8. <u>Objectivity/confirmability</u> [*Checklist Section A*]
Are the conclusions drawn from the available evidence, and is the research relatively free of researcher bias?

9. <u>Reliability/dependability</u> [*Checklist Section B*]
Is the process of the study consistent and reasonably stable over time and across researchers and methods?

10. <u>Internal validity/credibility/authenticity</u> [*Checklist Section C*]
Are the findings credible to the people studied and to readers? Do we have an authentic portrait of what we are studying?

11. <u>External validity/transferability/fittingness</u> [*Checklist Section D*]
Do the conclusions fit other contexts and how widely can they be generalized?

12. <u>Utilization/application/action orientation</u> [*Checklist Section E*]
How useful were the findings to clients, researchers, and the communities studied?

Page 3

Part III: [For Quasi-Experimental Designs]

13. **Strength of design with respect to four types of threat to validity**
    a. **Statistical conclusion validity**
       o Good
       o Satisfactory
       o Poor
    Comments:

    b. **Internal validity**
       o Good
       o Satisfactory
       o Poor
    Comments:

    c. **Construct validity**
       o Good
       o Satisfactory
       o Poor
    Comments:

    d. **External validity**
       o Good
       o Satisfactory
       o Poor
    Comments:

Part IV: Analysis and Discussion of Each Threat to Validity

14: Threat (give name and number): _____

A. How is this threat manifested in the evaluation?

B. Potential effects on the study findings and generalizations.

C. How big a problem is this for the evaluation?

D. Proposed actions

E. How adequate are the proposed actions?

> Complete a separate page for each important threat

Page 5

Appendix 3

*Example of a Completed RealWorld
Evaluation Project Evaluation Worksheet*

Using the Worksheet to Assess an Already Completed
Evaluation of a Low-Cost Housing Project

This example illustrates the use of the worksheet for a fictitious but fairly typical housing project in Central America. The three-year low-cost housing project began in June 2000 and closed in December 2003. A baseline study was conducted with project beneficiaries at the start of the project and about six months before the project closing date. It was originally intended to include a comparison group, but this was cut out both because of budget constraints and because the Ministry of Housing did not wish to raise expectations that comparison families would become eligible to obtain houses in a second phase of the project. There were delays in commissioning consultants to conduct the posttest interviews, so the evaluation had to be completed with considerable time pressure and with a tight budget.

RealWorld Evaluation [RWE] Project Evaluation Worksheet

Part I: Description of the Evaluation

Name of Evaluation: *Central America Low-Cost Housing Project*

1. **Stage of the study at which the worksheet was prepared**
   - ○ Evaluation design stage
   - ○ Pilot testing of instruments
   - ○ During data collection
   - ○ Data analysis
   - • **Report writing**

2. **Objectives of the evaluation**
   a. Why was the evaluation commissioned?
      To assess the impacts of low-cost housing on poverty reduction and household income.
   b. Purpose of the evaluation:
      - ○ Exploratory study to provide initial indications on whether the project model "works"
      - • **Assessing the efficiency and potential impacts of a small pilot project to recommend whether it is worth replicating on a larger scale**
      - ○ Rigorous multivariate statistical analysis of a large-scale, multicomponent project to compare costs and benefits with alternative investment options
   c. What are the specific decisions or actions that will be taken on the basis of the findings?
      Decide if the project should be replicated on a larger scale.
   d. Key stakeholders and their expectations
      - ○ *Donor agency: Assessing economic impacts and contribution to poverty reduction. Should the project be replicated?*
      - ○ *Project executing agency: Community development and empowerment impacts of the project. Accessibility to low-income groups and female-headed households.*
      - ○ *Ministry of Finance: Comply with obligation to complete evaluation and provide justification for requesting final loan disbursement.*

3. **Evaluation design**
   - • **RWE quasi-experimental design:** *Model No. 2*
   - ○ Other quantitative design
   - ○ Qualitative design
   - ○ Mixed-method design

Describe briefly, indicating modifications to the basic design.

Random sample of project families interviewed at start and end of project. All information obtained from household head. No comparison group used.

Page 1

4. <u>RWE constraints addressed in the evaluation design</u>

    a. Budget: *The evaluation consultants considered the budget was less than required to conduct a methodologically sound study.*

    b. Time: *The posttest survey had to be completed and analyzed and the report prepared in about six months.*

    c. Data: No comparison group. *Information obtained only from the household head. Information obtained only on wages and income from own business, but no information collected on interhousehold transfer income.*

    d. Political: *Evaluators not allowed to include a control group. Pressures from the Ministry of Finance to produce a positive evaluation.*

5. <u>Options for addressing time and resource constraints</u>

    o   There is a very tight deadline and no possibility of additional resources.

    •   **There is a tight deadline but additional resources could be obtained for use within this deadline.** *Some additional resources might be available, but the deadline for report presentation could not be extended.*

    o   The priority is to produce a high-quality product with a solid methodology that can withstand scrutiny from the critics of the project.

6. <u>Major threats to the validity and adequacy of the evaluation design and conclusions</u>
    [explain in Part III]

    o   Baseline data

    •   **Comparison group**: *No comparison group. This is a serious problem as project participants are highly motivated and many have previous experience with house construction—so they are not typical of the low-income population.*

    •   **Data collection methods and quality of data**: *Information obtained only from the household head. Information obtained only on wages and income from own business, but no information collected on interhousehold transfer income.*

    o   Analysis of contextual factors

    o   Other: _____

7. <u>Recommended actions</u>

    o   *Compare socioeconomic characteristics of project population with available data on the low-income population.*

    o   *Conduct rapid-assessment study in comparable comparison areas to determine what, if any, housing improvements have occurred in these areas and to compare characteristics of project and comparison populations.*

Note: Complete a Question 14 sheet for each important threat to validity or adequacy.

Part II Assessment of the Five Dimensions of Adequacy of the Evaluation Design

8. <u>Objectivity/confirmability</u> [*Checklist Section A*]

   Are the conclusions drawn from the available evidence, and is the research relatively free of researcher bias?

   Study methodology is clear and well documented. The problems arising from the lack of a comparison group are clearly identified.

9. <u>Reliability/dependability</u> [*Checklist Section B*]

   Is the process of the study consistent and reasonably stable over time and across researchers and methods?

   Research questions clearly defined and consistently measured. The definition of household income is not satisfactory because interhousehold transfers, one of the most important sources of income for poor and particularly female-headed households, are not included. Data were not collected across all settings because only household head interviewed and there was no comparison group.

10. <u>Internal validity/credibility/authenticity</u> [*Checklist Section C*]

    Are the findings credible to the people studied and to readers? Do we have an authentic portrait of what we are studying?

    Most key informants and stakeholders agree with the finding that improved housing contributes to poverty reduction. However, NGOs and informants in comparison areas believe that project participants were not typical of the low-income population, and that part of the impact is due to these differences. Some informants also believed the Ministry of Housing provided free services and other support not recorded in the evaluation report because they wish the project to succeed so that more donor funding could be obtained.

11. <u>External validity/transferability/fittingness</u> [*Checklist Section D*]

    Do the conclusions fit other contexts and how widely can they be generalized?

    The lack of comparison group and supposed special characteristics of the project group make it difficult to generalize. Also some question about whether the positive impacts may have been overestimated due to unreported support from the Ministry of Housing.

12. <u>Utilization/application/action orientation</u> [*Checklist Section E*]

    How useful were the findings to clients, researchers, and the communities studied?

    The report was too long and technical to be easily accessible to many stakeholders. The report was only presented in a workshop with the government and implementing agency, and little effort was made to disseminate the findings to other stakeholders.

Part III: [For Quasi-Experimental Designs]

13. <u>Strength of design with respect to four types of threat to validity</u>

 a. **Statistical conclusion validity**

  o Good

  o Satisfactory

  • **Poor**

Comments:

Lack of comparison group and no attempt to check for differences between social and economic characteristics of project participants and low-income population.

---

 b. **Internal validity**

  o Good

  o Satisfactory

  • **Poor**

Comments:

Lack of comparison group. No comparison for history. Household head cannot provide reliable information on income and attitudes of other household members.

---

 c. **Construct validity**

  o Good

  o Satisfactory

  • **Poor**

Comments:

Unsatisfactory definition of household income.

---

 d. **External validity**

  o Good

  o Satisfactory

  • **Poor**

Comments:

Lack of comparison group limits generalizability. Possible political influence/support from Ministry of Housing may have contributed to some of the positive outcomes.

Part IV: Analysis and Discussion of Each Threat to Validity

14 (1): Threat: *H.3: History*

A. **How is this threat manifested in the evaluation?**
The evaluation estimates the project produced a 70% increase in household income. But no comparison group used to define the counterfactual and estimate how income might have changed if there had been no project.

B. **Potential effects on the study findings and generalizations**
The study findings may be completely wrong because the impact of the project on income may be much less than estimated due to external factors such as improved economic conditions in the city.

C. **How big a problem is this for the evaluation?**
Potentially a very serious problem.

D. **Proposed actions**
Reconstruct comparison group through
- *Secondary data*
- *Key informants [Chamber of Commerce, Ministry of Planning, local industries, community leaders, NGOs]*

Select comparison area and use the following data collection methods:

- *Rapid survey of current economic conditions and recall of past conditions*
- *Focus groups*
- *Observation*

E. **How adequate are the proposed actions?**
The procedures can identify potentially important external factors and can provide a rough estimate of their importance. This will significantly reduce, but not eliminate, the threat to validity.

> Complete a separate page for each important threat.

Page 5

14 (2) Threat: *F.4. Unreliability of measures for estimating change in outcome indicators*

A. <u>How is this threat manifested in the evaluation?</u>
- *Earnings of other household members may be underestimated or ignored.*
- *Informal earnings may be underestimated.*
- *Transfer income is ignored.*

B. <u>Potential effects on the study findings and generalizations</u>.
- *Household earning and total income likely to be significantly underestimated.*

C. <u>How big a problem is this for the evaluation?</u>
- *Potentially very serious.*

D. <u>Proposed actions</u>
- *Rapid resurvey of subsample of project households to*
  - *Interview other household members about their income*
  - *Estimate transfer income*
  - *Estimate informal earnings*
- *Focus groups and PRA to obtain independent estimates of income*
- *Direct observation of economic conditions*

E. <u>How adequate are the proposed actions?</u>
- *Improved estimates of household earnings and total income*
- *Harder to obtain reliable estimates of income before the project but proposed actions improve estimates*
- *The proposed methods will significantly improve the estimates but will only partially correct potential errors.*

Appendix 4

Resources for Evaluation Capacity Building

This section lists some of the many resources that are available electronically to individuals or organizations wishing to strengthen their evaluation capacities. The list is certainly not comprehensive, but for readers with time and patience these links will lead to many other sources. The information given here was current as of October 2005, but this is a dynamic and changing field, so readers may find that some Web sites have changed and that some information requires updating. Recognizing that our readers come from all parts of the world, we have included links to resources in Danish, Dutch, Finnish, French, German, Italian, Japanese, Polish, Portuguese, Russian, Spanish, and Swedish.

National and International Evaluation Organizations

In recent years, there has been a rapid expansion of national and international evaluation associations and organizations operating in at least the following countries and regions (our apologies to any organizations we have missed). The Web sites of many of these associations contain extensive material on conferences, publications, and, usually, links to other evaluation Web sites.

International

IOCE: International Organization for Cooperation in Evaluation. There are 60 national associations affiliated with IOCE of whom 27 have Web sites—in English with some material in French and Spanish (www.ioce.net).

IDEAS: The International Development Evaluation Association. A worldwide, nonprofit, membership organization seeking to advance and extend the practice of development evaluation by refining methods, strengthening capacity, and expanding ownership (www.ideas-int.org).

Africa

Regional Association. The African Evaluation Association (www.afrea.org)

African National Associations and Networks. Evaluation associations or networks (all listed on the African Evaluation Association Web site) now operate in the following countries (and more are being created). At the time of publication, most of these associations did not have Web sites.

- Benin
- Cameroon
- Cape Verde
- Comoros
- Ghana
- Kenya
- Madagascar
- Malawi
- Mauritania
- Niger (www.pnud.ne/rense)
- Nigeria
- Rwanda
- Senegal
- South Africa (http://66.201.99.156/afrea/webs/southafrica/home/index.cfm?navID=1 &itemID=1)
- Uganda (http://www.ueas.org)
- Zambia
- Zimbabwe

Asia

At the time of publication, most of these associations did not have Web sites.

- Australasian Evaluation Association (www.aes.asn.au)
- Bangladesh
- Korea
- Japan Evaluation Society—in Japanese (www.idcj.or.jp)
- Malaysian Evaluation Society (www.mes.org.my)
- Nepal
- Sri Lankan Evaluation Association
- Thailand

Europe and the Middle East

Regional *Association.* The European Evaluation Society (www.europeanevaluation.org)

National European Associations

- Danish Evaluation Society—in Danish with some material in English (www.danskeval ueringsselskab.dk)
- Dutch Evaluation Society—in Dutch (www.videnet.nl)

- Finnish Evaluation Society—in Finnish and English (www.finnishevaluationsociety .net)
- French Evaluation Society—in French (www.sfe.asso.fr)
- German Evaluation Society—in German (www.degeval.de)
- Irish Evaluation Network
- Israeli Association for Program Evaluation—in Hebrew and English (http://ayelet.net firms.com)
- Italian Evaluation Society—in Italian (www.valutazione.it)
- Newly Independent States: International Program Evaluation Network—in Russian with English link (http://ipen21.org/ipen/en)
- Polish Evaluation Society—in Polish with some material in English (www.valu tazione.it)
- Spanish Public Policy Evaluation Society—in Spanish (http://www.sociedadevaluacion.org)
- Swiss Evaluation Society—English, German, and French (www.seval.ch/en/index.cfm)
- United Kingdom Evaluation Society (http://www.evaluation.org.uk)
- Swedish Evaluation Society (Utvärderana)—in Swedish with English link (http:// www.statskontoret.se/utvarderarna/english.html)
- Walloon Evaluation Society—in French (www.prospeval.org)

The Americas

At the time of publication, several of these associations did not have Web sites.

- American Evaluation Association. Information is also given on their Web site (www.eval.org) on local affiliates in different parts of the country.
- Brasilian Evaluation Association—in Portuguese and English (www.avaliabrasil.org.br)
- Canadian Evaluation Society—in French and English (www.evaluationcanada.ca)
- Colombia
- Peru
- PREVAL (program for strengthening monitoring and evaluation capacity in Latin America and the Caribbean)—in Spanish (www.preval.org)
- Quebec Society for Program Evaluation (www.sqep.ca)

Electronic Reference Material on Evaluation Methods

Collections

Table 1 of this appendix lists some of the collections of evaluation reference material compiled by the American Evaluation Association and published on their Web site. This is just a small sampling of the very extensive reference material now available on the internet.

Appendix 4, Table 1   Collections of Evaluation Reference Material

---

Site: Ericae.net

Sponsor: ERIC Clearinghouse on Assessment and Evaluation

Scope: Very extensive comprehensive list of educational evaluation resources; includes broad-ranging searchable test review and test/instrument locator with 10,000 instruments indexed (although not available online).

Organization: Highly organized, indexed, searchable

Link: http://ericae.net

Site: Online Evaluation Resource Library

Sponsor: National Science Foundation's (NSF) Directorate for Education and Human Resources (EHR)

Scope: Extensive list of evaluation plans, instruments, and reports developed for NSF/EHR funded projects; uses specific quality criteria for inclusion.

Organization: Excellent, broken down by project type and resource type

Link: http://oerl.sri.com

Site: Resources for Methods in Evaluation and Social Research

Sponsor: Private site compiled by Ya-Lin Liu and Gene Shackman

Scope: Extensive list of free evaluation-related sites, organized with annotation

Organization: Good, broken down by topics; can be difficult to find specific types of links.

Link: http://gsociology.icaap.org/methods

Site: WWW Virtual Library: Evaluation

Sponsor: Confederation of volunteers

Scope: Extensive list of evaluation-related sites, many international

Organization: Good, broken down by topics; can be difficult to find specific types of links.

Link: www.policy-evaluation.org

SOURCE: American Evaluation Association Web site (www.eval.org).

Many of the Web sites of the national evaluation associations listed earlier in this Appendix include links to reference material, often in the national language (although in most cases, the majority of the material cited is in English).

The World Bank Operations Evaluation Department Web site contains hundreds of evaluation reports on World Bank country strategies, programs, and projects (www.worldbank.org/oed).

Electronic Resources on Particular Topics

Statistical Software, Texts Online

- http://members.aol.com/johnp71/javastat.html#TOC. This selection of Electronic Resources for Evaluators was compiled in coordination with the American Evaluation Association lists statistical software and textbooks available online.
- http://biostat.mc.vanderbilt.edu/twiki/bin/view/Main/PowerSampleSize. Free Web site developed by Vanderbilt University for estimating power of the test and sample size

Randomized Experimental Designs

- www.povertyactionlab.com. Reports on all of the randomized evaluation designs conducted by the MIT Poverty Action Lab

Mixed-Methods Evaluation

- www.ehr.nsf.gov/EHR/REC/pubs/NSF97-153/start.htm

Preparing Terms of Reference for Evaluation Consultants

- www.ausaid.gov.au/ausguide/ausguidelines (see section 2 for terms of reference)

Conferences and Events

Many of the Web sites of the national and international evaluation associations include information on conferences, events, and, sometimes, training activities within particular countries or regions or internationally. A few of the many useful calendars of conferences and training activities are the following:

- American Evaluation Association: http://eval.org/meetings.html
- Canadian Evaluation Society: http://www.evaluationcanada.ca
- PREVAL: Conferences and courses mainly in Latin America: www.preval.org/pagina.php?secCodigo=7&idioma=7
- European Evaluation Association: Conferences in Europe: www.europeanevaluation.org/conferences/index.html
- IDEAS (www.ideas-int.org)

Evaluation Training Programs

The Electronic Resources for Evaluators database compiled in cooperation with the American Evaluation Association is a very extensive reference source for evaluators. It also includes a list of universities offering evaluation training programs: www.tandl.leon.k12.fl.us/programme/Electronic%20Resources%20for%20Evaluators.htm

Many of the national and international evaluation organizations listed above also provide information on training programs.

One of the most comprehensive training programs for international development evaluation is the International Program for Development Evaluation Training (IPDET) at Carleton University in Ottawa. It offers a two-week core course designed to cover development evaluation basics, followed by two weeks of 26 free-standing workshops on specific development evaluation topics. For general information and to review the curriculum, go to www.ipdet.org/curriculum.aspx

All the modules (both text and PowerPoint presentations) for the two-week IPDET core training program are available at www.worldbank.org/oed/ipdet/modules.html

Glossary of Terms and Acronyms

Authenticity: The fidelity of the work to the real world. In education and educational testing, authentic tasks refer to those that simulate professional or nonacademic work outside classrooms. In evaluation, accurate presentation of stakeholder perspectives and experiences may be considered to give an evaluation an air of authenticity. See Chapter 7 and Appendix 1.

Bibliometrics: Methods for documenting the number of citations and publications of program products and descriptions. See Chapter 12.

Black box evaluation: A term used to describe evaluation designs that do not articulate a program theory about how the project is expected to operate or to achieve the intended outcomes and impacts. It also refers to evaluations that measure indicators of outcomes without examining the process (quality of project interventions) that supposedly led to changes in those outcome indicators. The term is frequently used to describe and critique many randomized and quasi-experimental designs where pretest-posttest comparisons are made of the project population but where the project itself is a "black box" about which no information is obtained. See Chapter 10.

Clientism: Providing overly positive evaluation findings to avoid conflict with clients and ensure future work. See Chapter 6.

Clients/evaluation clients: Those for whom an evaluation is conducted—for example, those who commission the evaluation and sign the contract, and sponsoring or funding agencies of the project to be evaluated. These are the groups to whom the evaluators are directly accountable.

Cohort analysis: The analysis of data about a particular group. Cohort analysis may involve comparing successive groups passing through a cycle of activity (e.g., third-grade students, medical trainees, families who receive public services). One variant is using subjects scheduled to receive services or benefits in later phases of a project as a control or comparison group for subjects who received services in an earlier phase (sometimes referred to as "pipeline comparison"). See Chapter 10.

Comparison group/nonequivalent control group or matched control group: A group selected to match as closely as possible the project (experimental) group with respect to relevant internal and external characteristics, except that the comparison group did not receive the interventions of the project being evaluated. A comparison group is used when it is not possible to randomly assign subjects (individuals, communities, groups) to the project and control situations as would be done in randomized experimental design. See Chapters 10 and 14.

Confirmability: The extent to which the conclusions drawn can be confirmed by the available evidence. See Chapter 7 and Appendix 1.

Construct validity: Incorrect inferences about the constructs identifying what a project is intended to achieve. Because constructs tend to be intangible (e.g., student knowledge acquisition, improved quality of life), there may be some ambiguity regarding operational definitions or exactly what is being scrutinized or measured. See Chapter 7 and Appendix 1.

Contextual variables (or factors): Factors in the community or region that can affect how a project is implemented, how—and how successfully—it achieves its outcomes and impacts, and which sectors of the target population do and do not benefit. Contextual variables may include economic, political, institutional, environmental, security, and sociopsychological factors and the sociocultural environment. See Chapters 2, 9, and 10.

Contextuality: The extent to which aspects of a program's setting are considered in the evaluation. Qualitative inquiry is *contextual*, recognizing that a unique array of contexts influences the program and its outcomes, such as policy and political contexts, ideological and value contexts, organizational and sociological contexts. See Chapter 12.

Control group: When experimental evaluation designs are used with random assignment of subjects to treatment and nontreatment groups, the control group consists of subjects who will not receive the experimental treatment (project services) and with whom the experimental group that does receive services will be compared. Where large groups are available, random assignment of persons to experimental and control groups is considered to result in comparable or equivalent groups, differing only in their participation (or not) in the project. When it is not possible to randomly assign subjects to the experimental and control groups, as is the case with most quasi-experimental designs, a matched *comparison group* is used. When sufficiently detailed secondary data are available, it may be possible to use statistical matching techniques such as propensity scores, but in most real-world contexts judgmental matching must be used. When the number of persons available is too small for random assignment or quasi-experimental designs, to ensure that the two groups will be equivalent, matched groups may be formed and designated as experimental and comparison groups. See Chapters 10, 12, and 14.

Counterfactual: What would have happened to a population if it had not participated in the program or received its services or benefits. For quantitative evaluations, a control or comparison group may serve as a counterfactual. However, in many cases, a counterfactual may be constructed based on documentary data or interviews asking respondents to reconstruct what they think would have happened without the project.

Credibility: The extent to which the data and findings from an evaluation are accepted as true by audiences. All types of evaluations, evaluation data, and evaluation findings are vulnerable to being considered to lack credibility, even when evaluators have attempted to collect appropriate and sufficient data and to base findings on the data (cf. *validity*) and to include stakeholder perspectives and consideration of contexts. See Chapter 7 and Appendix 1.

Criteriality: Judging programs against explicit criteria. The criteria may be prespecified and external (e.g., an accreditation review), or they may be prespecified but created specifically for this program. See Chapter 12.

Critical ethnography: Ethnography focused on power structures and relationships for the purpose of revealing and redressing oppression. See Chapter 12.

Dependability: The degree to which data are stable. This term, from Lincoln and Guba (1985), is often preferred by interpretivists to the term *reliability*, which refers to replicability, a related concept. See Chapter 7 and Appendix 1.

Design/evaluation design: We use design in two ways. The first is the plan for conducting an evaluation, including methods and sources of data collection, deliverables, methods of analysis, and a timeline. The evaluation design is distinct from the project design or theory. Design also refers to the first stage in the model of the project cycle. See Chapters 2, 9, and 10.

Disaggregated analysis: Breaking down the analysis of overall findings on project outcomes or impacts into more detailed comparative analysis for subcategories such as sex, age, social class, different project sites or regions of the country, or types of services received. Determining whether and what types of disaggregated analysis of outcomes and impacts are required is critical when operating under budget constraints because disaggregated analysis usually requires increasing sample size and hence the cost of the evaluation.

Dummy variables: A technique used in multivariate analysis to transform information such as whether a household is participating in the project, or whether a family owns its own house, into a variable with values of 1 (e.g., participates in the project) and 0 (e.g., does not participate in the project). The purpose of these transformations is to permit statistical analysis of this information. A common use of dummy variables in impact evaluation is to determine the effect of project participation on an outcome variable such as household income or education test scores. The coefficient of the dummy variable indicates the proportion of the variance (in household income for example) explained by project participation. In RWE, dummy variables can also be used to transform contextual information (local government does/does not support the project; the local economy is growing/is not growing) into variables that can be subjected to statistical analysis.

Effect size: The size of the change or effect that a project produces or is expected to produce. In quantitative approaches to evaluation, the effect size is calculated as the measurable difference between the outcome measured on the project group receiving the intervention or treatment and outcomes for control or comparison groups. The *standardized effect size* is the difference between the sample and population means divided by the population standard deviation, permitting comparison of effect sizes for different projects. The *minimum acceptable effect size* [MAES], or critical effect size, is the minimum level of change that the evaluation design must be able to detect. In quantitative studies, the smaller the effect size that must be detected, the larger the required sample. See Chapter 14.

Emic: The perspective of interest in qualitative approaches that seek to obtain the insider's understanding and meanings rather than an *etic* or outsider's perspective. See Chapter 12.

Enumerators: Research staff who administer structured questionnaires or survey instruments. This is contrasted with interviewers who administer less structured data collection instruments or who conduct interviews without a questionnaire. Interviewers normally require a higher level of training and more field experience.

Ethnography: Sustained field studies to understand the ethos or culture of a group or society. See Chapter 12.

Ethnomethodology: The study of human perceptions, meanings, interactions, and how they maintain social structure. See Chapter 12.

Etic: Evaluation approaches based on an outsider's perspectives rather than an *emic* or insider's perspective. See Chapter 12.

Evaluability assessment: A determination as to whether a program can be evaluated using the type of evaluation planned with the available resources and within the proposed time frame. See Chapter 2.

Evaluand: The project or program being evaluated.

Evaluation capacity building/evaluation capacity development: Strengthening the capacity of stakeholders to commission, design, implement, interpret, and use evaluations. This may be achieved through formal training or through interactive evaluation capacity development. See Chapter 15.

Evaluation designs: Different approaches to evaluation that prioritize different elements such as purposes, stakeholders, and procedures. Stufflebeam (2001) identifies 22 evaluation designs (see also Mathison 2005:256–58).

Evaluation practitioners: People who conduct evaluations, including staff of government and funding agencies, NGOs, consulting firms, academics, independent consultants, and external evaluators.

Evaluation users: All those who may potentially use the evaluation findings. These include funding agencies, government planning and finance ministries, agencies implementing the project being evaluated, intended project beneficiaries and groups that may be affected by the project, academics, evaluation consultants, and civil society.

Evidence: The information used to support conclusions. This can include data from surveys, observation, documents, and interviews.

Evidence-based evaluation (evidence-based practice): A treatment practice or service delivery system based on consistent scientific evidence showing that it improves client/participant outcomes in both clinically (scientifically) controlled and everyday settings. Although widely used, the approach has proved difficult to apply in fields such as education due to disagreement concerning what are the acceptable evaluation methods and standards of evidence.

Experimental designs: See *randomization*. A research design in which subjects are randomly assigned (allocated) to the experimental (treatment) group and the control (nontreatment) group. Both groups are tested or measured through a survey or other instrument before the experiment begins. The experimental treatment is then applied to the experimental group but not to the control group. The conditions of the two groups are then carefully regulated during the period of the experiment to eliminate any external factors that might influence outcomes. The test or survey is then administered again to the two groups. Any significant difference in the change in the mean value of the outcome variable between the experimental and control groups is interpreted as initial indication of potential treatment effect. The experiment should be repeated several times to test for consistency of the findings. For the purposes of RealWorld Evaluation, it is important to distinguish between *true experimental designs* that combine randomization with careful regulation of the conditions of the two groups through the period required for the treatment to take effect, and *randomized (randomization) designs* where in most RWE evaluations the conditions of the two groups cannot be regulated or held constant.

External validity: The generalizability of study results to other groups, settings, treatments, and outcomes. See Chapters 7 and 10 and Appendix 1.

Findings: Stated judgments and interpretations regarding program quality and impacts. Warranted findings are adequately and appropriately based on relevant and comprehensive data. See Chapter 7.

Focus group: A group of people, usually between six and eight, interviewed regarding the research focus. A set of questions is often used that is deliberately sequenced or focused to move the discussion toward concepts of interest to the researcher. A number of sessions with different groups sharing characteristics (e.g., age, sex, socioeconomic status, type of project participation) may be of interest to the purposes of the evaluation. See Chapters 5, 11, and 12.

Formative evaluation: An evaluation intended to help improve the implementation and outcomes of the ongoing project or program being evaluated. By contrast, a *summative evaluation* is intended to assess the impacts or effects of a completed program but not usually to improve its implementation.

Hermeneutics: Interpretive study of human expression and intention often attentive to the relationship between the subject and the enquirer.

Impact: The long-term effects on identifiable populations or groups produced by a project or program. Impacts may be direct or indirect, intended or unintended, economic, sociocultural, institutional, environmental, technological, or other. See Chapters 3 and 10.

Implementation process: The running or putting into effect of a program. Also the third stage of the project cycle: the operational procedures used to transform project inputs into project outputs. See Chapters 3 and 9.

Incommensurability: The belief that two perspectives are so fundamentally different that there can be no mutual understanding, agreement, or collaboration. See Chapter 12.

Inputs: The money, materials, equipment, staff, consultants, and other resources available to a project. The project implementation process is intended to transform *inputs* into *outputs*. See Chapters 2 and 9.

Instrumental variable (IV): A statistical technique used in quasi-experimental designs to control for project participant *selection bias* due to variables not measured in the survey instrument (*unobservables*). These variables influence program participation (for example geographical differences in program availability), but do not affect outcomes once someone is selected. IVs model the participant selection process to separate the effect of the selection process on outcomes from the effects of the project intervention. IV analysis is often combined with **propensity scores** (see separate entry).

Integrated checklist: RWE's nine categories for assessing the threats to the adequacy and validity of quantitative, qualitative, and mixed-method evaluation designs. The five categories for assessing qualitative and mixed-method designs are adapted from the work of Guba and Lincoln (1989) and Miles and Huberman (1994), and the four categories for evaluating quantitative designs are adapted from Shadish, Cook, and Campbell (2002). See Chapter 7 and Appendix 1.

Internal validity: The accuracy of the data in reflecting the reality of the program. See Chapters 7 and 10.

Intervening variables: See also *moderators* and *mediators*. Factors that may explain differences in the level or direction of project outcomes from the anticipated outcomes or for different groups. See Chapters 9 and 10.

Interviewer: Research staff members who collect information from subjects either in an informal context without any survey instrument or using an unstructured data collection instrument. This is contrasted with *enumerators* who administer structured questionnaires or survey instruments. Being an interviewer normally requires a higher professional level and more experience than being an enumerator.

Logical framework analysis/LFA, logframe, logic modeling: A matrix, flowchart, or graphic that translates program theory into a series of indicators facilitating the monitoring and assessing of factors related to achievement or nonachievement of program goals. Logframes or other forms of logic models, including results-based monitoring, are widely used as program monitoring and evaluation tools by international development agencies and also agencies such as the Department of Education and the Centers for Disease Control and Prevention in the United States. See Chapter 9.

Logic model: See *program theory model.*

MAES: The minimum acceptable effect size. See *effect size.*

Mediators: Intervening variables that influence program outcomes and that program interventions can modify. See Chapters 9 and 10.

Meta-evaluation: Evaluation of an evaluation. Meta-evaluation is particularly needed where evaluation results may influence critical or resource-consuming decisions. See Chapters 7 and 14.

Microcredit/microcredit program: Programs providing small-scale loans and technical assistance to low-income individuals to help promote the creation or expansion of small businesses. Many microcredit programs require the creation of small groups of families who form a "solidarity group," which in addition to reviewing and approving all loan proposals also creates community organizations and promotes other social and economic development activities. Microcredit is considered one of the most successful mechanisms for strengthening the economic conditions of the poorest sectors of society, and microcredit programs, organized by government, international agencies, or NGOs, are now operating in most developing countries.

Mixed-method designs: Designs involving the planned use of both quantitative and qualitative methods. See Chapter 13.

Moderators: Intervening variables that influence program outcomes and that a program cannot modify. See Chapter 9.

Naturalistic inquiry: Study focusing on ordinary events in natural settings described in ordinary language. Naturalistic inquiry, a term introduced by Lincoln and Guba (1985), involves time at the program's site or sites and data collection unobtrusive enough to minimize altering or interfering with ordinary activities. See Chapter 12.

NGO/nongovernmental organization (also known as PVOs/private voluntary organization): A group or institution entirely or largely independent of government with humanitarian rather than commercial objectives. International NGOs (INGOs) are private, not-for-profit agencies based mainly but not exclusively in industrial countries that support international relief and development. Local or national NGOs are indigenous groups organized regionally or nationally. In some cases, these may be membership-run groups in villages, although these are more commonly referred to as community-based organizations (CBOs). NGOs include charitable and religious associations that mobilize private funds for development, respond to emergencies, distribute food and family-planning services, promote community organization, and provide other forms of direct service or policy advocacy. These and other civil society organizations (CSOs) also include independent cooperatives, community associations, water-user societies, women's groups, and pastoral associations.

Nonequivalent control group: See *comparison group.*

Nonprobability sampling/purposive sampling: Sampling procedures involving relatively small samples. Each subject or case is selected individually to ensure that the maximum information is obtained. Sometimes all subjects or cases will be selected at the same time, but additional cases may be added as need and opportunity emerge. Purposive sampling strategies include typical case samples, range samples, maximum variation samples, quota samples, unique case samples, snowball samples, critical case samples, reputational samples, and comparable case samples. See Chapters 12 and 14.

Null hypothesis: A hypothesis in quantitative evaluations stating that there is no statistically significant difference between the experimental and control/comparison groups. According to statistical theory, it is never possible to prove that a hypothesis is true (i.e., that a project or intervention does have an effect), so proving a null hypothesis (or series of null hypotheses) false is taken as corroborative evidence of an intervention or project's effect. See Chapter 14.

Omitted variable problem: A variable not included in a study's design or analysis that may have influenced program results, for example, when important characteristics of experimental and comparison groups do not match. See Chapter 10.

One-tailed test: When testing for statistical significance, a one-tailed test is used when the direction of the expected change or difference is known (e.g., to test whether there has been a significant increase in a mathematical aptitude test score or whether the proportion of the project population with household income below the poverty line has decreased). The one-tailed test indicates the probability of finding a result as large as the test score if there really is no difference between the two groups being compared (e.g., the project and comparison groups). If the direction of the expected change is not known, then a *two-tailed test* must be used. See Chapter 14.

Outcomes: Short- and medium-term program effects, e.g. changes in what others do, as influenced by a project's outputs. Project staff have little direct control over outcomes. See Chapters 2 and 10.

Outputs: Products and services resulting directly from project activities; program effects over which project personnel have direct control. See Chapters 3, 9, and 10.

Paradigm: A perspective or point of view affecting what is recognized, known, valued, and done. For example, those who adhere to the positivist paradigm consider to be "true" only that which they can observe to be in one-to-one correspondence with an objective reality, while those who adhere to the interpretivist paradigm consider reality to be subjectively constructed and apprehended.

Participant observation: Study in which data are collected while the researcher is a full or partial member of the group studied. See Chapters 5 and 12.

Phenomenology: Study of stakeholder's perceptions and the meanings they give to events and concepts. See Chapter 12.

Power of the test/statistical power of the test: The probability that a statistical test of project impact will correctly identify that there is a statistically significant impact when the impact really does exist. The normal convention is to set power equal to 0.80, meaning that there is an 80% chance that a particular sample will correctly identify a project effect if the program really does have an effect. The power level can be set higher (reducing the risk of rejecting a statistically significant project effect but requiring a larger sample) or lower (reducing the sample size but increasing the risk of wrong rejecting a significant project effect). See Chapter 14.

PRA: Originally an abbreviation for participatory rural appraisal, PRA is now used as a generic term covering a range of participatory research methods, including RRA (rapid rural appraisal) and participatory learning and action (PLA). All these approaches are based on the principle of empowering the community to conduct its own analysis of its needs and priorities and translate these into a plan of action. All the approaches work through community groups rather than individuals, relying heavily on mapping and other graphical techniques that can be used with populations having low literacy rates. See Chapter 5.

Precision: The level of statistical significance used to accept that an observed project effect does not occur by chance. The convention is to accept a 95% confidence level (a 1 in 20 possibility that the apparent project effect is due to chance). If a higher level of precision is required, the confidence level can be increased to 99% (only a 1 in 100 possibility that the result is due to chance) or even higher. See Chapter 14.

Probability sample: See *random sampling*.

Process evaluation: An evaluation that studies and assesses the way in which a project is implemented and how it is affected by the context within which it operates. This may be a stand-alone evaluation or combined with an outcome-oriented evaluation that identifies project effects. See Chapters 2, 9, and 10.

Program: See *project*.

Program theory model/logic model: A program theory is a theory or model of how a program is expected to cause the intended or observed outcomes. Program theories identify program resources, activities, and intended outcomes and specify a chain of causal hypotheses linking program resources, activities, intermediate outcomes, and ultimate program goals. Many program theories also identify the contextual variables (economic, political, organizational, psychological, environmental, and cultural) that influence program implementation and outcomes in each site or location. See Chapter 9.

Project (development project): A time-bound intervention involving multiple activities intended to provide a defined set of services or to produce a defined set of outcomes or impacts usually for a specified population group. While the terms project and program are sometimes used interchangeably, a program is usually understood to include a number of different projects and is intended to produce broader and possibly longer-term outcomes and impacts. See Chapter 2.

Project cycle: The different stages through which a project intends to achieve its objectives. The project cycle usually comprises seven stages: design, inputs, implementation process, outputs, outcomes, impacts, and sustainability. See Chapters 2 and 9.

Propensity score: A technique used in quasi-experimental designs whereby each subject in the project sample is statistically matched (using logistical regression or a similar technique) to a group of non-participants ("nearest neighbors") on a set of relevant characteristics. The mean value of the outcome variable is calculated for the nearest neighbors and this is compared with the outcome score for the project participant to estimate the *gain score*. Propensity scores are often combined with **instrumental variable** analysis (see separate entry).

Pseudoevaluation: An evaluation undertaken to serve a public relations function. See Chapter 6.

Purposive sampling: See *nonprobability sampling*.

QED/quasi-experimental design: A set of quantitative evaluation designs used where randomized assignment of subjects to the experimental and control conditions is not possible. In this book, seven quasi-experimental designs are described that are widely used in RealWorld evaluation contexts. The strongest design uses a pretest-posttest project and comparison group design but without randomization. The other designs address budget, time, and data constraints by eliminating one or more of the four data collection points. See Chapter 10.

QUAL: Abbreviation for *qualitative*. The abbreviations QUAL and QUANT were introduced by Rossi (1994).

QUANT: Abbreviation for *quantitative*.

Random sampling/probability sampling: In simple random sampling, all units (e.g., individuals, schools, households) in the population have the same probability of being selected to participate in the study. Selection procedures may use random number tables, select every *n*th unit, or use other techniques ensuring equal probability of selection. Random selection helps to ensure the comparability of experimental and control groups, requiring that these groups be large enough to neutralize the unique characteristics of individuals in consideration of group trends. See Chapters 11 and 14.

Randomization/randomized trials: See also *experimental designs*. Research designs in which subjects are randomly assigned to experimental (treatment) and control groups. Both groups are tested or measured on an appropriate measure of the intended effect. The treatment is then administered to the experimental group, and the two groups are tested or measured again. Any significant difference in the change in the mean value of the outcome variable between the experimental and control groups is interpreted as a treatment effect. In most real-world evaluation contexts, randomized designs are not true experimental designs in that it is not possible to control the external influences to which the two groups are subjected during the period required for the treatment to take effect (which may be several years for some projects). Consequently, it is often necessary to assess whether apparent project effects may be partially explained by different influences on the two groups during the treatment period. See Chapters 10 and 11.

Recall: Techniques used to elicit information on, among other things, behavior (e.g., contraceptive use, time use), access to public services (e.g., water, education, health), economic status (e.g., income, employment, agricultural production), attitudes, knowledge, or beliefs (e.g., attitudes to child care, contraception, opinions about community or government agencies) at an earlier point in time—usually around the time the project began. Recall techniques include questionnaire items, in-depth interviews, and PRA techniques (see *PRA*). See Chapter 5.

Results chain: A diagram showing the sequence of steps linking the project design to the intended outcome. At each step, the results chain shows the desired outcome and the possible alternative negative or nondesired outcomes. The preparation of a results chain can be used in conjunction with logical framework analysis to identify the critical assumptions and the key indicators to be incorporated into the logframe. See Chapters 2 and 9.

RWE: RealWorld Evaluation. An approach developed for evaluations operating under budget, time, data, or political constraints intended to maximize the rigor of methods and the validity of findings.

Sampling frame/pool: A list of all of the units in the population to be sampled that is used to identify the units to be included in the sample. See Chapter 14.

Scenarios: Common situations that an evaluation may face. See Chapter 1.

Social funds/social investment funds: Funds used to support social infrastructure projects identified by local communities (e.g., water supply, schools, roads, health centers, etc.) and usually constructed by local government agencies with a high level of community involvement.

Stakeholder: Individuals, groups, or organizations having an interest in a program. Stakeholders may include funding agencies, policymakers, planners, advocacy groups, the communities, or groups that the program is intended to benefit and other groups that might be affected negatively or positively. See Chapters 2, 8, 15, and 16.

Standard deviation: A widely used statistical measure to describe how widely dispersed sample scores are around the sample mean. The more widely dispersed the scores, the greater the value of the standard deviation. An important characteristic of the standard deviation for most distributions is that approximately 65% of all observations will lie within one standard deviation of the mean and approximately 95% will lie within two standard deviations of the mean. For example, if the average household income is $200 per month with a standard deviation of $25, that means that approximately 65% of households would have a monthly income between $175 and $225 (within $25 of the mean), and 95% would have monthly incomes between $150 and $250. See Chapter 14.

Standardized effect size: See *effect size.*

Statistical conclusion validity: The analysis of evaluation findings may arrive at incorrect conclusions as to whether the project had an effect due to weaknesses in the sample design or to the incorrect application or interpretation of statistical tests. See Chapter 7 and Appendix 1.

Summative evaluation: An evaluation conducted to determine the quality, merit, worth, or shortcomings of a program. By contrast, *formative evaluation* is intended to provide information to help improve the program during its implementation. See Chapter 8.

Sustainability: Whether a project or its effect will continue over time. Sustainability can either be predicted prospectively to estimate future effects or determined retrospectively some time after the project has ended (ex-post evaluation). See Chapters 2 and 9.

Target population: The population eligible to receive program services or benefits.

Terms of reference (ToR): A document prepared by the evaluation client specifying the objectives, contents, organization, and timeline for the evaluation and defining the scope of work and responsibilities for the evaluation consultant(s).

Tracer study: The location and reinterviewing of subjects in an earlier study where records do not list their present location, often through knowledgeable people from the same community.

Transferability: In qualitative evaluations, a concept analogous to the quantitative concept of generalizability or external validity. See Chapter 7 and Appendix 1.

Triangulation: Improving the validity of evaluation findings by drawing information from different sources, through different methods of inquiry, by different investigators, or through analysis from different theoretical or conceptual frameworks. See Chapters 10 and 12.

Trustworthiness: A term used in qualitative evaluation with approximately the same meaning as validity in quantitative evaluation. See Chapter 12.

Two-tailed test: See *one-tailed test.*

Type I error/false positive: Wrongly concluding that a program had a statistically significant impact on the outcome variable when in fact it does not. See Chapter 14.

Type II error/false negative: Wrongly concluding that a program does *not* have a statistically significant impact on the outcome variable when in fact it does. See Chapter 14.

Utilization: Whether and how evaluation findings are used. See Chapters 8 and 15.

References

Alderman, H. 2000. "Anthropometry." Pp. 251–72 in *Designing Household Survey Questionnaires for Developing Countries: Lessons from 15 Years of the Living Standards Measurement Study,* vol. 1, edited by M. Grosh and P. Glewwe. Washington, DC: World Bank.

American Evaluation Association. 1995. "Guiding Principles for Evaluators." Pp. 19–26 in *Guiding Principles for Evaluators,* edited by W. R. Shadish, D. L. Newman, M. A. Scheirer, and C. Wye. New Directions for Program Evaluation, No. 66. San Francisco: Jossey-Bass.

American Evaluation Association. 2003. "Response to U.S. Department of Education notice of proposed priority, 'Scientifically Based Evaluation Methods.'" *Federal Register,* November 4, RIN 1890-ZA00. Retrieved October 3, 2005 (www.eval.org/doestatement.htm).

American Evaluation Associations. 2004. *Guiding Principles for Evaluators.* Retrieved November 15, 2005 (www.eval.org/Guiding%20Principles.htm).

Aron, A. and E. Aron. 2002. *Statistics for the Behavioral and Social Sciences. A Brief Course.* 2d ed. Upper Saddle River, NJ: Prentice Hall.

Atkinson, P. and A. Coffey. 2004. "Analyzing Documentary Realities." Pp. 45–62 in *Qualitative Research: Theory, Method and Practice.* 2d ed., edited by D. Silverman. Thousand Oaks, CA: Sage.

Baker, J. 2000. *Evaluating the Impacts of Development Projects on Poverty: A Handbook for Practitioners.* Directions in Development. Washington, DC: World Bank.

Bamberger, M. 2000a. "The Evaluation of International Development Programs: A View from the Front." *American Journal of Evaluation* 21(1):95–102.

Bamberger, M. ed. 2000b. *Integrating Quantitative and Qualitative Research in Development Projects.* Directions in Development. Washington, DC: World Bank.

Bamberger, M. 2000c. "Opportunities and Challenges for Integrating Quantitative and Qualitative Research." Pp. 3–36 in *Integrating Quantitative and Qualitative Research in Development Projects,* edited by M. Bamberger. Directions in Development. Washington, DC: World Bank.

Bamberger, M. 2001. "Evaluation in Developing Countries: Experience with Agricultural Research and Development and the Annotated Bibliography of International Program Evaluation." Book Review Article. *American Journal of Evaluation* 21(1):117–22.

Bamberger, M., J. Rugh, M. Church, and L. Fort. 2004. "Shoestring Evaluation: Designing Impact Evaluations under Budget, Time and Data Constraints." *American Journal of Evaluation* 25(1):5–37.

Beebe, J. 2001. *Rapid Assessment Process: An Introduction.* Walnut Creek, CA: Altamira Press.

Best, J. 2001. *Damned Lies and Statistics: Untangling Numbers from the Media, Politicians and Activists.* Los Angeles: University of California Press.

Best, J. 2004. *More Damned Lies and Statistics: How Numbers Confuse Public Issues.* Los Angeles: University of California Press.

Bickman, L. ed. 1987. *Using Program Theory in Evaluation.* New Directions for Program Evaluation, No. 33. San Francisco. Jossey-Bass.

Bickman, L., C. A. Heflinger, D. Northrup, S. Sonnichsen, and S. Schilling. 1998. "Long-Term Outcomes to Family Caregiver Empowerment." *Journal of Child and Family Studies* 7(3):269–82.

Bourgois, P. 2002. "Respect at Work: Going Legit." Pp. 15–35 in *Ethnographic Research: A Reader*, edited by S. Taylor. Thousand Oaks, CA: Sage.

Brandt, R. S., ed. 1981. *Applied Strategies for Curriculum Evaluation*. Alexandria, VA: Association for Supervision and Curriculum Development.

Bronfenbrenner, U. 1979. *The Ecology of Human Development*. Cambridge, MA: Harvard University Press.

Brown, G. 2000. "Evaluating the Impact of Water Supply Projects in Indonesia." Pp. 107–13 in *Integrating Quantitative and Qualitative Research in Development Projects*, edited by M. Bamberger. Directions in Development. Washington, DC: World Bank.

Caldwell, J. 1985. "Strengths and Limitations of the Survey Method Approach for Measuring and Understanding Fertility Change: Alternative Possibilities." Pp. 45–63 in *Reproductive Change in Developing Countries: Insights from the World Fertility Survey*, edited by J. Cleland and J. Hobcraft. Oxford, UK: Oxford University Press.

Campbell, D. T. 1966. "Pattern Matching as an Essential in Distal Knowing." Pp. 81–106 in *The Psychology of Egon Brunswick*, edited by K. R. Hammond. New York: Holt, Rinehart.

Campbell, D. T. and J. C. Stanley. 1963. *Experimental and Quasi-Experimental Designs for Research*. Boston: Houghton-Mifflin.

CARE International. 2003. *Program Standards Framework*. Available at www.globaldev.org/m&e

Carlsson, J., M. Eriksson-Baaz, A. M. Fallenius, and E. Lövgren. 1999. *Are Evaluations Useful? Cases from Swedish Development Cooperation*. Sida Studies in Evaluation, 99/1. Stockholm: Swedish International Development Agency. Retrieved September 1, 2005 (www.sida.se/Sida/articles/5400-5499/5452/STUD99-1.PDF).

Carter, K. 1993. "The Place of Story in the Study of Teaching and Teacher Education." *Educational Researcher* 22(1):5–12, 18.

Carvalho, S. and H. White. 2004. "Theory Based Evaluation: The Case of Social Funds." *American Journal of Evaluation* 25(2):141–60.

Centers for Disease Control and Prevention. 1999. Summary of the Framework for Program Evaluation in Public Health. *Morbidity and Mortality Weekly Report* 48(No. RR-11):1–43. Retrieved August 10, 2005 (www.cdc.gov/eval/framework.htm).

Cervantes Saavedra, M. 1615/1964. *Don Quixote*. New York: Signet.

Chambers, R. 1983. *Rural Development: Putting the Last First*. Essex, UK: Longman.

Chambers, R. 2002. *Participatory Workshops: A Sourcebook of 21 Sets of Ideas and Activities*. Sterling, VA: Earthscan.

Chelimsky, E. 1994. "Evaluation: Where We Are." *Evaluation Practice* 15(3):339–45.

Chelimsky, E. 1997. "The Political Environment of Evaluation and What it Means for the Development of the Field." Pp. 53–68 in *Evaluation for the 21st Century*, edited by Chelimsky and Shadish. Thousand Oaks, CA: Sage.

Chelimsky, E. and W. R. Shadish, eds. 1997. *Evaluation for the 21st Century: A Handbook*. Thousand Oaks, CA: Sage.

Chen, H. T. 2005. *Practical Program Evaluation: Assessing and Improving Planning, Implementation, and Effectiveness*. Thousand Oaks, CA: Sage.

Cohen, J. 1988. *Statistical Power Analysis for the Behavioral Sciences*. 2d ed. Hillsdale, NJ: Lawrence Erlbaum.

Community Tool Box. 2005. *Developing a Framework or Model of Change: Part J. Evaluating Community Programs and Initiatives*. Available at http://ctb.ku.edu/tools/en/chapter_1036.htm

Cook, T. D. 2000. "The False Choice between Theory-Based Evaluation and Experimentation." Pp. 27–34 in *Program Theory in Evaluation: Challenges and Opportunities*, edited by P. Rogers, T. Hacsi, A. Petrosino, and T. Huebner. New Directions for Evaluation, No. 87. San Francisco: Jossey-Bass.

Cook, T. D. and D. T. Campbell. 1979. *Quasi-Experimentation: Design & Analysis Issues for Field Settings.* Chicago: Rand McNally.

Creswell, J. 2003. *Research Design: Qualitative, Quantitative and Mixed-Methods Approaches.* Thousand Oaks, CA: Sage.

Creswell, J. C., V. L. Clark, M. L. Gutmann, and W. Hanson. 2003. "Advanced Mixed Method Research Designs." Pp. 209–40 in *Handbook of Mixed Methods in Social & Behavioral Science,* edited by A. Tashakkori and C. Teddlie. Thousand Oaks, CA: Sage.

Davidson, J. 2000. "Ascertaining Causality in Theory-Based Evaluation." Pp. 17–26 in *Program Theory in Evaluation: Challenges and Opportunities,* edited by P. Rogers, T. Hacsi, A. Petrosino, and T. Huebner. New Directions for Evaluation, No. 87. San Francisco: Jossey-Bass.

Dayal, R., C. van Wijk, and N. Mukherjee. 2000. *Methodology for Participatory Assessments with Communities, Institutions and Policy Makers: Linking Sustainability with Demand, Gender and Poverty.* Washington, DC: World Bank, Water and Sanitation Program.

Deaton, A. 2005. "Measuring Poverty in a Growing World (or Measuring Growth in a Poor World)." *Review of Economics and Statistics* 87(1):1–19.

Deaton, A. and M. Grosh, 2000. "Consumption." Pp. 91–134 in *Designing Household Survey Questionnaires for Developing Countries: Lessons from 15 Years of the Living Standards Measurement Study,* vol. 1, edited by M. Grosh and P. Glewwe. Washington, DC: World Bank.

Denzin, N. K. 1989. *The Research Act: A Theoretical Introduction to Sociological Methods.* 3d ed. Englewood Cliffs, NJ: Prentice Hall.

Denzin, N. K. 1997. *Interpretive Ethnography: Ethnographic Practices for the 21st Century.* Thousand Oaks, CA: Sage.

Denzin, N. K. and Y. S. Lincoln. 2000. *Handbook of Qualitative Research.* 2d ed. Thousand Oaks, CA: Sage.

Dewey, J. 1916. *Democracy and Education: An Introduction to the Philosophy of Education.* New York: Macmillan.

Dimitrov, T. 2005. "Enhancing the Performance of a Major Environmental Project through a Focused Mid-Term Evaluation: The Kombinat za Cvetni Metali Environmental Improvement Project in Bulgaria." Pp. 50–57 in *Influential Evaluations: Evaluations That Improved Performance and Impacts of Development Programs.* Operations Evaluation Department. Washington, DC: World Bank. Available at http://worldbank.org/oed/ecd

Donaldson, S. 2003. "Theory Driven Program Evaluation in the New Millennium." Pp. 109–41 in *Evaluating Social Programs and Problems,* edited by S. Donaldson and M. Scriven, Mahwah, NJ: Lawrence Erlbaum.

Eisner, E. W. 1985. *The Art of Educational Evaluation: A Personal View.* London: Falmer.

Erickson, F. 1986. "Qualitative Methods in Research on Teaching." Pp. 119–61 in *Handbook of Research on Teaching.* 3d ed., edited by M. C. Wittrock. New York: Macmillan.

Fetterman, D. M. 1996. *Empowerment Evaluation: Knowledge and Tools for Self-Assessment and Accountability.* Thousand Oaks, CA: Sage.

Fink, A. 2003a. *How to Design Survey Studies.* Vol. 6, *The Survey Kit.* 2d ed. Thousand Oaks, CA: Sage.

Fink, A. 2003b. *How to Sample in Surveys.* Vol. 7, *The Survey Kit.* 2d ed. Thousand Oaks, CA: Sage.

Fink, A. 2003c. *How to Manage, Analyze, and Interpret Survey Data.* Vol. 9, *The Survey Kit.* 2d ed. Thousand Oaks, CA: Sage.

Fink, A. 2003d. *How to Report on Surveys.* Vol. 10, *The Survey Kit.* Thousand Oaks, CA: Sage.

Firestone, W. A. 1993. "Alternative Arguments for Generalizing from Data as Applied to Qualitative Research." *Educational Researcher* 22(4):16–23.

Funnell, S. 1997. "Program Logic: An Adaptable Tool." *Evaluation News and Comment* 6(1):5–17.

Funnell, S. 2000. "Developing and using a program theory matrix for program evaluation and performance monitoring." Pp. 91–102 in *Program Theory in Evaluation: Challenges and Opportunities,* edited by P. Rogers, T. Hacsi, A. Petrosino, and T. Huebner. New Directions for Evaluation, No. 87. San Francisco: Jossey-Bass.

Geertz, C. 1973. *The Interpretation of Cultures: Selected Essays.* New York: Basic Books.

General Accounting Office. 1995. *Program Evaluation: Improving the Flow of Information to the Congress.* GAO/PEMD-95-1. Washington, DC: GAO.

Glaser, B. G. and A. I. Strauss. 1967. *The Discovery of Grounded Theory.* Chicago: Aldine.

Glewwe, P. 2000. "Education." Pp. 143-76 in *Designing Household Survey Questionnaires for Developing Countries: Lessons from 15 years of the Living Standards Measurement Study.* Vol. 1, edited by M. Grosh and P. Glewwe. Washington, DC: World Bank.

Glewwe, P., M. Kremer, S. Moulin, and E. Zitzewitz, 2004. "Retrospective vs. Prospective Analyses of School Inputs: The Case of Flip Charts in Kenya." *Journal of Development Economics* 74:251-68. Retrieved October 3, 2005 (www.povertyactionlab.com/projects/project.php?pid=26).

Gomez, L. 2000. *Gender Analysis of Two Components of the World Bank Transport Projects in Lima, Peru: Bikepaths and Busways.* Available at http://web.worldbank.org/WBSITE/EXTERNAL/TOPICS/EXTGENDER/EXTGENDERTRANSPORT/0,,contentMDK:20202435~menuPK:522654~pagePK:148956~piPK:216618~theSitePK:338726,00.html#Peru_Bike

Gray, D. 2004. *Doing Research in the Real World.* Thousand Oaks, CA: Sage.

Greene, J. C. 1997. "Participatory Evaluation." Pp. 171-89 in *Evaluation and the Postmodern Dilemma,* edited by L. Mabry. Greenwich, CT: JAI Press.

Greene, J. C. 2005. "Mixed Methods." Pp. 255-56 in *Encyclopedia of Evaluation,* edited by S. Mathison. Thousand Oaks, CA: Sage.

Greene, J. C. and V. J. Caracelli. 2003. "Making Paradigmatic Sense of Mixed Methods Practice." Pp. 91-110 in *Handbook of Mixed Methods in Social & Behavioral Research,* edited by A. Tashakkori and C. Teddlie. Thousand Oaks, CA: Sage.

Greene, J. C., V. Caracelli, and W. F. Graham. 1989. "Toward a Conceptual Framework for Multimethod Evaluation Designs." *Educational Evaluation and Policy Analysis* 11:255-74.

Grosh, M. and P. Glewwe, eds. 2000. *Designing Household Survey Questionnaires for Developing Countries: Lessons from 15 Years of the Living Standards Measurement Study.* 3 vols. Washington, DC: World Bank.

Guba, E. G. and Lincoln, Y. S. 1989. *Fourth Generation Evaluation.* Newbury Park, CA: Sage.

Guba, E. G. and Y. S. Lincoln. 1994. "Competing Paradigms in Qualitative Research." Pp. 105-17 in *Handbook of Qualitative Research,* edited by N. K. Denzin and Y. S. Lincoln. Thousand Oaks, CA: Sage.

Gubbels, P. and C. Koss. 2000. *From the Roots Up: Strengthening Organizational Capacity through Guided Self-Assessment.* Oklahoma City, OK: World Neighbors.

Handwerker, W. P. 2001. *Quick Ethnography.* Walnut Creek, CA: Altamira Press.

Harvey, A. S. and M. E. Taylor. 2000. "Time Use." Pp. 249-74 in *Designing Household Survey Questionnaires for Developing Countries: Lessons from 15 Years of the Living Standards Measurement Study,* vol. 2, edited by M. Grosh and P. Glewwe. Washington, DC: World Bank.

Hashemi, S., S. R. Schuler, and A. P. Riley. 1996. "Rural Credit Programs and Women's Empowerment in Bangladesh." *World Development* 24(4):635-53.

Heath, C. 2004. "Analyzing Face to Face Interaction: Video and the Visual and Material." Pp. 283-304 in *Qualitative Research: Theory, Method and Practice*, edited by D. Silverman. Thousand Oaks, CA: Sage.

Henry, G. 1990. *Practical Sampling.* Applied Social Science Methods Series, Vol. 21. Thousand Oaks, CA: Sage.

Hentschel, J. 1999. "Contextuality and Data Collection Methods: A Framework and Application to Health Service Utilization." *Journal of Development Studies* 35(4):64-94.

Hochschild, A. 1998. *King Leopold's Ghost.* Boston: Houghton Mifflin.

Horton, D. and R. Mackay, eds. 1999. "Evaluation in Developing Countries: Experience with Agricultural Research and Development." *Knowledge, Technology and Policy* 11(4, Special issue).

House, E. 1972. "The Conscience of Educational Evaluation. *Teachers College Record* 73(3):405–14.

House, E. 1990. "Trends in Evaluation." *Educational Researcher* 19(3):24–28.

House, E. R. 1993. *Professional Evaluation: Social Impact and Political Consequences.* Newbury Park, CA: Sage.

House, E. R. 1994. "Integrating the Quantitative and Qualitative." Pp. 13–22 in *The Qualitative-Quantitative Debate: New Perspectives*, edited by C. S. Reichardt and S. F. Rallis. New Directions for Program Evaluation, No. 61. San Francisco: Jossey-Bass.

House, E. R., and K. R. Howe. 1999. *Values in Evaluation and Social Research.* Thousand Oaks, CA: Sage.

House, E. R., and K. R. Howe. 2000. "Deliberative Democratic Evaluation." Pp. 3–12 in *New Directions for Evaluation 85*, edited by K. Ryan and L. DeStefano. San Francisco: Jossey-Bass.

International Program for Development Evaluation Training. 2004. *Evaluation Models.* Retrieved August 10, 2005 (www.worldbank.org/oed/ipdet/Modules/M_02-na.pdf).

Johnson, R. B. and A. J. Onwuegbuzie. 2004. "Mixed Methods Research: A Research Paradigm Whose Time Has Come." *Educational Researcher* 33(7):14–26.

Joint Committee on Standards for Educational Evaluation. 1994. *The Program Evaluation Standards: How to Assess Evaluations of Educational Programs.* 2d ed. Thousand Oaks, CA: Sage.

Jolliffe, D. 2001. "Measuring Absolute and Relative Poverty: The Sensitivity of Estimated Household Consumption to Survey Design." *Journal of Economic and Social Measurement* 27(1):1–23.

Justice, J. 1986. *Policies, Plans and People: Culture and Health Development in Nepal.* Berkeley: University of California Press.

Kane, M. 1994. "Validating the Performance Standards Associated with Passing Scores." *Review of Educational Research* 64(3):425–561.

Khandker, S. 1998. *Fighting Poverty with MicroCredit: Experience in Bangladesh.* Oxford, UK: Oxford University Press.

Kim, J., H. Alderman, and P. Orazem, 1999. "Can Private School Subsidies Increase Schooling for the Poor? The Quetta Urban Fellowship Program." *World Bank Economic Review* 13(3):443–66.

Klugman, J. 2002. *A Sourcebook for Poverty Reduction Strategies.* 2 vols. Washington, DC: World Bank.

Kraemer, H. C. and S. Thiemann. 1987. *How Many Subjects? Statistical Power Analysis in Research.* Newbury Park, CA: Sage.

Krueger, R. A. 2005. "Focus Groups." Pp. 158–60 in *Encyclopedia of Evaluation*, edited by S. Mathison. Thousand Oaks, CA: Sage.

Krueger, R. A. and M. A. Casey. 2000. *Focus Groups: A Practical Guide for Applied Research.* 3d ed. Thousand Oaks, CA: Sage.

Kuhn, T. 1962. *The Structure of Scientific Revolutions.* Princeton, NJ: Princeton University Press.

Kumar, K. ed. 1993. *Rapid Appraisal Methods.* Regional and Sectoral Studies. Washington, DC: World Bank.

Kumar, S. 2002. *Methods for Community Participation: A Complete Guide for Practitioners.* London: ITDG.

Lee, H. 1960. *To Kill a Mockingbird.* Philadelphia: Lippincott.

Leeuw, F. 2003. "Reconstructing Program Theories: Methods Available and Problems to Be Solved." *American Journal of Evaluation* 24(1):5–20.

Lenne, B. and H. Cleland. 1987. *Describing Program Logic* (Program Evaluation Bulletin No. 2). Sydney: Public Service Board of New South Wales.

Lewis, O. 1961. *The Children of Sanchez.* New York: Random House.

Lewis, O. 1965. *La Vida: A Puerto Rican Family in the Culture of Poverty in San Juan and New York.* New York: Random House.

Lincoln, Y. S. and E. G. Guba. 1985. *Naturalistic Inquiry.* Beverly Hills, CA: Sage.

Lipsey, M. W. 1990. *Design Sensitivity: Statistical Power for Experimental Research.* Newbury Park, CA: Sage.

Lipsey, M. W. 1993. "Theory as Method: Small Theories of Treatment." Pp. 5–38 in *Understanding Causes and Generalizing About Them,* edited by L. Sechrest and A. Scott. New Directions for Program Evaluation, No. 57. San Francisco: Jossey-Bass.

Lohr, S. 1999. *Sampling Design and Analysis.* New York: Duxbury Press.

Mabry, L. 1997. "A Dramatic Difference in Education in Chicago." *Stage of the* 9(3):17–22.

Mabry, L. 1998. "Case Study Methods." Pp. 155–70 in *Evaluation Research for Educational Productivity,* edited by H. J. Walberg and A. J. Reynolds. Greenwich, CT: JAI Press.

Mabry, L. 1999. "Circumstantial Ethics." *American Journal of Evaluation* 20(2):199–212.

Mabry, L., D. Stufflebeam, R. Hambleton, C. Ovando, R. O'Sullivan, B. Page, M. Wakely, and C. Swartz. 2000. "Both sides now: Perspectives of evaluators and stakeholders in educational evaluations." Paper presented at the annual meeting of the American Educational Research Association. New Orleans.

Mabry, L. and J. Z. Snow. 2004. "Three Innovative Evaluation Methods: Online Surveys, Video-Stimulated Focus Groups, and Think-Aloud Interviews." Presentation to the Oregon Program Evaluators Network annual meeting, October, Portland, OR.

Mabry, L. and J. Z. Snow. 2005. "Individual Laptop Computers to Support Learning of High-Risk Elementary Students and Classroom Culture Change." Paper presented at the annual meeting of the American Educational Research Association, April 12, Montreal.

Madaus, G. F., M. S. Scriven, and D. L. Stufflebeam, eds. 1987. *Evaluation Models: Viewpoints on Educational and Human Services Evaluation.* Boston: Kluwer-Nijhoff.

Mahoney, K. K. 1999. "Peer Mediation: An Ethnographic Investigation of an Elementary School's Program." Ph.D. dissertation, Indiana University, Bloomington, IN.

Malone, D. L. 1997. "*Namel manmeri:* Language and Culture Maintenance and Mother Tongue Education in the Highlands of Papua New Guinea." Ph.D. dissertation, Indiana University, Bloomington, IN.

Mathison, S., ed. 2005. *Encyclopedia of Evaluation.* Thousand Oaks, CA: Sage.

Maxwell, J. A. 1992. "Understanding and Validity in Qualitative Research." *Harvard Educational Review* 62(3):279–300.

Maxwell, J. A. 2004. "Causal Explanation, Qualitative Research, and Scientific Inquiry in Education." *Educational Researcher* 33(2):3–11.

Mayer, S. 1996. "Building Community Capacity with Evaluation Activities That Empower." Pp. 332–75 in *Empowerment Evaluation: Knowledge and Tools for Self-Assessment and Accountability,* edited by D. Fetterman, S. Kaftarian, and A. Wandersman. Thousand Oaks, CA: Sage.

Mertens, D. M. 1999. "Inclusive Evaluation: Implications of Transformative Theory for Evaluation." *American Journal of Evaluation* 20(1), 1–14.

Mertens, D. M. 2003. "Mixed Methods and the Politics of Human Research: The Transformatory-Emancipatory Perspective." Pp. 135–66 in *Handbook of Mixed Methods in Social & Behavioral Research,* edited by A. Tashakkori and C. Teddlie. Thousand Oaks, CA: Sage.

Messick, S. 1989. "Validity." Pp. 13–103 in *Educational Measurement.* 3d ed., edited by Robert L. Linn. New York: Macmillan.

Miles, M. and Huberman, M. 1994. *Qualitative Data Analysis.* 2d ed. Thousand Oaks, CA: Sage.

Moore, D. and G. McCabe. 1999. *Introduction to the Practice of Statistics.* 3d ed. New York: Freeman.

Morse, J. M. 2003. "Principles of Mixed Methods and Multimethod Research Design." Pp. 189–208 in *Handbook of Mixed Methods in Social & Behavioral Research,* edited by A. Tashakkori and C. Teddlie. Thousand Oaks, CA: Sage.

Narayan, D. 2002. *Empowerment and Poverty Reduction: A Sourcebook.* Washington, DC: World Bank.

Newman, C. 2001. *Gender, Time Use, and Change: Impacts of Agricultural Export Employment in Ecuador* (Policy Research Report on Gender and Development, Working Paper Series No. 18). Washington, DC: World Bank, Poverty Reduction and Economic Management Network/ Development Research Group. Available at http://scholar.google.com/scholar?hl=en&lr=&q=cache:UOHVbCs-SRgJ:www.world bank.org/gender/prr/wp18.pdf+newman,+c.+2001+Gender,+time+use+and+change

Newman, D. L. and R. D. Brown. 1996. *Applied Ethics for Program Evaluation.* Thousand Oaks, CA: Sage.

Organization for Economic Cooperation and Development. 1986. *Methods and Procedures in Aid Evaluation.* Paris: OECD.

Organization for Economic Cooperation and Development/Development Advisory Committee. 2002. *Glossary of Key Terms in Evaluation.* Retrieved August 14, 2005 (www.oecd.org/findDocument/ 0,2350,en_2649_34435_1_119678_1_1_1,00.html).

Operations Evaluation Department. 2004. *Influential Evaluations: Evaluations That Improved Performance and Impacts of Development Programs.* Washington, DC: World Bank. Available at http:// worldbank.org/oed/ecd

Operations Evaluation Department. 2005. *Influential Evaluations: Evaluations That Improved Performance and Impacts of Development Programs.* Washington, DC: World Bank.

Patton, M. Q. 1997. *Utilization-Focused Evaluation.* 3d ed. Thousand Oaks, CA: Sage.

Patton, M. Q. 2002. *Qualitative Research and Evaluation Methods.* Thousand Oaks, CA: Sage.

Paul, S. 2002. *Holding the State to Account: Citizen Monitoring in Action.* Bangalore: Books for Change ActionAid.

Pebley, A., N. Noreen, and M. K. Choe, 1986. "Evaluation of Contraceptive History Data in the Republic of Korea." *Studies in Family Planning* 17(1):22–35.

Perlman, J. 1976. *The Myth of Marginality: Urban Poverty and Politics in Rio de Janeiro.* Berkley: University of California Press.

Perlman, J. 2002. *The Metamorphosis of Marginality: Rio's Favelas 1969–2002.* World Bank conference May 7, 2002. Retrieved August 8, 2005 (www.kas.de/upload/dokumente/megacities/janiceperl man.pdf).

Phillips, D. C. 1987. "Validity in Qualitative Research: Why the Worry about Warrant Will Not Wane." *Education and Urban Society* 20:9–24.

Picciotto, R. 2002. *Development Cooperation and Performance Evaluation: The Monterrey Challenge.* Washington, DC: World Bank, Operations Evaluation Department.

Polanyi, M. 1958. *Personal Knowledge: Towards a Post-Critical Philosophy.* Chicago: University of Chicago Press.

Pratt, C., W. McGuigan, and A. Katzev. 2002. "Measuring Program Outcomes: Using Retrospective Pretest Methodology." *American Journal of Evaluation* 21(5):341–50.

Presser, P., M. Couper, J. Lessler, M. Martin, J. Martin, J. Rothgeb, and E. Singer. 2004a. *Methods for Testing and Evaluating Survey Questionnaires.* New York: John Wiley.

Presser, P., M. Couper, J. Lessler, M. Martin, J. Martin, J. Rothgeb, and E. Singer. 2004b. "Methods for Testing and Evaluating Survey Questions." *Public Opinion Quarterly* 68(1):109–30.

Ravindra, A. 2004. *Assessment of the Impact of the Bangalore Citizen Report Cards on the Performance of Public Agencies.* Washington, DC: World Bank. Available at www.worldbank.org/oed/ecd

Reichardt, C. 2005. "Quasi-Experimental Designs." Pp. 351–55 in *Encyclopedia of Evaluation,* edited by S. Mathison. Thousand Oaks, CA: Sage.

Rietberger-McCracken, J. and D. Narayan 1997. Participatory Rural Appraisal. Module III of *Participatory Tools and Techniques: A Resource Kit for Participation and Social Assessment.* Washington, DC: World Bank. Environment Department.

Roche, C. 1999. *Impact Assessment for Development Agencies: Learning to Value Change.* Oxford, UK: OXFAM.

Rogers, P., T. Hacsi, A. Petrosino and T. Huebner eds. 2000. *Program Theory in Evaluation: Challenges and Opportunities.* New Directions for Evaluation, No. 87. San Francisco: Jossey-Bass.

Rogers, P., A. Petrosino, T. Huebner, and T. Hacsi. 2000. "Program Theory Evaluation: Practice, Promise and Problems." Pp. 5–13 in *Program Theory in Evaluation: Challenges and Opportunities,* edited by P. Rogers, T. Hacsi, A. Petrosino, and T. Huebner. New Directions for Evaluation, No. 87. San Francisco: Jossey-Bass.

Rosenbaum, P. R. 1995. "Design Sensitivity in Observational Studies." *Biometrika* 91(1):153–64.

Rossi, P. H. 1994. "The War between the Quals and the Quants: Is a Lasting Peace Possible?" Pp. 23–36 in *The Qualitative-Quantitative Debate: New Perspectives*, edited by C. S. Reichardt and S. F. Rallis. New Directions for Program Evaluation, No. 61. San Francisco: Jossey-Bass.

Rossi, P., M. Lipsey, and H. Freeman. 2004. *Evaluation: A Systematic Approach.* 7th ed. Thousand Oaks, CA: Sage.

Rossman, G. B. and S. F. Rallis. 1998. *Learning in the Field: An Introduction to Qualitative Research.* Thousand Oaks, CA: Sage.

Rugh, J. 1986. *Self-Evaluation: Ideas for Participatory Evaluation of Rural Community Development Projects.* Oklahoma City, OK: World Neighbors.

Russon, C. 2005. *The Mega 2004 Evaluation (Meta-Evaluation of Goal Achievement of CARE Projects).* Atlanta, GA: CARE International. Available at www.globaldev.org/m&e

Russon, C. and G. Russon, eds. 2005. *International Perspectives on Evaluation Standards.* New Directions for Evaluation, No. 104. San Francisco: Jossey-Bass.

Salmen, L. F. 1987. *Listen to the People: Participant Observer Evaluation of Development Projects.* New York: Oxford University Press.

Salmen, L. F. 1992. *Beneficiary Assessment: An Approach Described.* Washington, DC: World Bank.

Schwarz, N and D. Oyserman. 2001. "Asking Questions about Behavior: Cognition, Communication, and Questionnaire Construction." *American Journal of Evaluation* 22(2):127–60.

Scott, C. and B. Amenuvegbe. 1991. "Recall Loss and Recall Duration: An Experimental Study in Ghana." *Inter-Stat* 4(1):31–55.

Scott, K. and W. Okrasa. 1998. *Analysis of Latvia Diary Experiment.* Washington, DC: World Bank, Development Research Group.

Scrimshaw, S. and E. Hurtado. 1987. *RAP: Rapid Assessment Procedures for Nutrition and Primary Health Care.* Tokyo: United Nations University.

Scriven, M. 1972. "Pros and Cons About Goal-Free Evaluation." Evaluation comment. 3:1–7.

Scriven, M. 1991. *Evaluation Thesaurus.* 4th ed. Newbury Park, CA: Sage.

Scriven, M. 1997. "Truth and Objectivity in Evaluation." Pp. 477–500 in *Evaluation for the 21st Century: A Handbook,* edited by E. Chelimsky and W. R. Shadish. Thousand Oaks, CA: Sage.

Scriven, M. 1998. "An Evaluation Dilemma: Change Agent vs. Analyst." Paper presented at the annual meeting of the American Evaluation Association, November 6, Chicago.

Shadish, W., T. Cook, and D. Campbell. 2002. *Experimental and Quasi-Experimental Designs for Generalized Causal Inference.* Boston: Houghton Mifflin.

Shadish, W. R., D. Newman, M. Scheirer, and C. Wye. 1995. *Guiding Principles for Evaluators.* New Directions for Program Evaluation, No. 66. San Francisco: Jossey-Bass.

Shavelson, R. and L. Towne, eds. 2002. *Scientific Research in Education.* Committee on Scientific Principles for Educational Research. Washington, DC: National Academy Press.

Silverman, D. 2004. *Qualitative Research: Theory, Method and Practice.* 2d ed. Thousand Oaks, CA: Sage.

Sirken, R. 1999. *Statistics for the Social Sciences.* Thousand Oaks, CA: Sage.

Stack, C. 1996. *Call to Home: African Americans Reclaim the Rural South.* New York: Basic Books.

Stake, R. E. 1975. *Evaluating the Arts in Education: A Responsive Approach.* Columbus, OH: Merrill.

Stake, R. E. 1986. *Quieting Reform: Social Science and Social Action in an Urban Youth Program.* Urbana: University of Illinois Press.

Strauss, A. and J. Corbin. 1990. *Basics of Qualitative Research: Grounded Theory Procedures and Techniques.* Newbury Park, CA: Sage.

Strauss, A. and J. Corbin 1994. "Grounded Theory Methodology: An Overview." Pp. 273–85 in *Handbook of Qualitative Research,* edited by N. K. Denzin and Y. S. Lincoln. Thousand Oaks, CA: Sage.

Stronach, I., J. Allan, and B. Morris, 1996. "Can the Mothers of Invention Make Virtue Out of Necessity? An Optimistic Deconstruction of Research Compromises in Contract Research and Evaluation." *British Educational Research Journal* 22(4):493–509.

Stufflebeam, D. L. 1987. "The CIPP Model for Program Evaluation." Pp. 117–41 in *Evaluation Models: Viewpoints on Educational and Human Services Evaluation,* edited by G. F. Madaus, M. S. Scriven, and D. L Stufflebeam. Boston: Kluwer-Nijhoff.

Stufflebeam, D. L. 1994. "Empowerment Evaluation, Objectivist Evaluation, and Evaluation Standards: Where the Future of Evaluation Should Not Go and Where It Needs to Go." *Evaluation Practice* 15(3):321–38.

Stufflebeam, D. 2001a. *Evaluation Models.* New Directions for Evaluation, No. 89. San Francisco: Jossey-Boss.

Stufflebeam, D. L. 2001b. "The Metaevaluation Imperative." *American Journal of Evaluation* 22(2): 183–209.

Stufflebeam, D. L., M. Q. Patton, D. Fetterman, J. G. Greene, M. S. Scriven, and L. Mabry. 2001. "Theories of Action in Program Evaluation." Panel presentation at the annual meeting of the American Evaluation Association, November 9, St. Louis.

Tashakkori, A. and C. Teddlie, eds. 2003. *Handbook of Mixed Methods in Social & Behavioral Research.* Thousand Oaks, CA: Sage.

Theis, J. and H. Grady. 1991. *Participatory Rapid Appraisal for Community Development: A Training Manual Based on Experiences in the Middle-East and North Africa Region* London: Save the Children/International Institute for Environment and Development.

Tolstoy, L. 1889. *Anna Karenina.* New York: Crowell.

U.S. Department of Education. 2003, November 4. "Notice of Proposed Priority: Scientifically Based Evaluation Methods (RIN 1890-ZA00). *Federal Register* 68(213):62445–447.

United Way. 1999. *Achieving and Measuring Community Outcomes.* Retrieved September 2, 2005 (http://national.unitedway.org/files/pdf/outcomes/cmtyout1.pdf).

United Way. 2005. *Connecting Program Outcome Measurement to Community Impact.* Retrieved September 2, 2005 (http://national.unitedway.org/files/pdf/outcomes/ConnectingPOM_toCI%20Final.pdf).

Valadez, J. and M. Bamberger. 1994. *Monitoring and Evaluating Social Programs in Developing Countries: A Handbook for Policymakers, Managers and Researchers.* Washington, DC: World Bank.

Vaughan, R. J. and T. F. Buss. 1998. *Communicating Social Science Research to Policy Makers.* Applied Social Research Methods Series, No. 48. Thousand Oaks, CA: Sage.

Viadero, D. 2004. "'What Works Research Site Unveiled." *Education Week,* July 14, p. 33.

von Wright, G. H. 1971. *Explanation and Understanding.* London: Routledge and Kegan Paul.

Vygotsky, L. S. 1978. *Mind in Society: The Development of Higher Mental Process.* Cambridge, MA: Harvard University Press.

Wansbrough, G., D., Jones, and C. Kappaz, 2000. "Studying Interhousehold Transfers and Survival Strategies of the Poor in Cartagena, Colombia." Pp. 69–84 in *Integrating Quantitative and Qualitative Research in Development Projects*, edited by M. Bamberger. Directions in Development. Washington, DC: World Bank.

Weinberg, S. L. and S. K. Abramowitz. 2002. *Data Analysis for the Behavioral Sciences Using SPSS.* Cambridge, UK: Cambridge University Press.

Weiss, C. H. 1993. "Where Politics and Evaluation Research Meet." *Evaluation Practice* 14(1):93–106.

Weiss, C. H. 1995. "Nothing as Practical as Good Theory: Exploring Theory-Based Evaluation for Comprehensive Community Initiatives for Children and Families." Pp. 65–92 in *New Approaches to Evaluating Community Initiatives: Concepts, Methods and Contexts,* edited by J. P. Connell, A. C. Kubisch, L. B. Schorr, and C. H. Weiss. Washington, DC: Aspen Institute.

Weiss, C. H. 1997. "How Can Theory-based Evaluation Make Greater Headway?" *Evaluation Review* 21:501–24.

Weiss, C. H. 2000. "Which Links in Which Theories Shall We Evaluate?" Pp. 35–45 in *Program Theory in Evaluation: Challenges and Opportunities,* edited by P. J. Rogers, T. A. Hacsi, A. Petrosino, and T. A. Huebner. New Directions for Evaluation, No. 87. San Francisco: Jossey-Bass.

Weiss, C. H. 2001. "Theory-Based Evaluation: Theories of Change for Poverty Based Programs." Pp. 103–14 in *Evaluation and Poverty Reduction,* edited by O. Feinstein and R. Picciotto. New Brunswick, NJ: Transaction.

Weitzman, B., D. Silver, and K. N. Dillman. 2002. "Integrating a Comparison Group Design into a Theory of Change Evaluation: The Case of the Urban Health Initiative." *American Journal of Evaluation* 23(4):371–86.

Wholey, J. S. 1987. "Evaluability Assessment: Developing Program Theory." Pp. 35–46 in *Using Program Theory in Evaluation*, edited by L. Bickman. New Directions for Program Evaluation, No. 33. San Francisco: Jossey-Bass.

Wholey, J., J. Scanlon, H. Duffy, J. Fukumoto, and L. Vogt. 1970. *Federal Evaluation Policy: Analyzing the Effects of Public Programs.* Washington, DC: Urban Institute.

W. K. Kellogg Foundation. 1998. *Evaluation Handbook.* Retrieved September 5, 2005 (www.wkkf.org/Pubs/Tools/Evaluation/Pub770.pdf).

Wolcott, H. F. 1994. *Transforming Qualitative Data: Description, Analysis, and Interpretation.* Thousand Oaks, CA: Sage.

World Bank. 1993. *Early Experience with Involuntary Resettlement: Impact Evaluation on India: Maharashtra Irrigation Project.* Operations Evaluation Department. Washington, DC: World Bank.

World Bank. 1996. *Participation Sourcebook.* Washington, DC: World Bank. Available at www.worldbank.org/wbi/sourcebook/sbpdf.htm

World Bank. 2001. *Engendering Development: Through Gender Equality in Rights, Resources and Voice.* Oxford, UK: Oxford University Press.

World Bank. 2004. *Influential Evaluations: Evaluations that Improved Performance and Impacts of Development Programs.* Evaluation Capacity Development, Operations Evaluation Department. Washington, DC: World Bank. Available at www.worldbank.org/oed/ecd

Yin, R. 2003. *Case Study Research: Design and Methods.* 3d ed. Thousand Oaks, CA: Sage.

Index

About the Authors

Michael Bamberger has almost 40 years of experience in development evaluation, including a decade working with nongovernmental organizations in Latin America; almost 25 years working on evaluation with the World Bank in most of the social and economic sectors and in most regions of the world; and several years as an independent evaluation consultant. He has published two books and several monographs and handbooks on development evaluation, and numerous articles in professional journals. He has been active for 15 years with the American Evaluation Association, serving on the Board and as Chair of the International Committee. He is on the Editorial Advisory Board of *New Directions for Evaluation*, a regular reviewer for several professional evaluation journals, and Special Editor for international evaluation for the *American Journal of Evaluation.* He has taught program evaluation in different countries in Africa, Latin America, Asia, and the Middle East, and since 2002 has been on the Faculty of the International Program for Development Evaluation Training (IPDET) in Ottawa, Ontario, Canada, and since 2001 has lectured at the Foundation for Advanced Studies on International Development (FASID) in Tokyo.

Jim Rugh has had 41 years of professional involvement in rural community development in Africa, Asia, and Appalachia. He has specialized in evaluation for 25 years—the past 10 years as head of Design, Monitoring and Evaluation for CARE International, a large nongovernmental organization (**NGO**). His particular skills include promoting strategies for enhanced capacity for evaluation throughout this worldwide organization. He is a recognized leader in evaluation among colleagues in the international NGO community, including InterAction. He has been an active member of the American Evaluation Association since 1986, currently serving on the Nominations and Election Committee. He was a founding member of the Atlanta-area Evaluation Association. He has experience in promoting community development and evaluating and facilitating self-evaluation by participants in such programs. He has provided training for and/or evaluated many different international NGOs. He brings a perspective of the "big picture," including familiarity with a wide variety of community groups and assistance agencies in many countries, plus an eye to detail and a respect for inclusiveness and the participatory process.

Linda Mabry is an immediate past member of the Board of Directors of the American Evaluation Association and serves on the Public Affairs Committee and as chair of the task force to develop a public statement on Educational Accountability. She is also a member of the

Board of Trustees for the National Center for the Improvement of Educational Assessments and of the editorial board for *Studies in Educational Evaluation*. For six years, she served as leader of the evaluation course strand at Indiana University School of Education, teaching a variety of evaluation courses providing practical experiences for graduate students. She has conducted evaluations for the U.S. Department of Education, National Science Foundation, National Endowment for the Arts, the Jacob Javits Foundation, Hewlett-Packard Corporation, Ameritech Corporation, ATT-Comcast Corporation, the New York City Fund for Public Education, the Chicago Arts Partnerships in Education, the Chicago Teachers Academy of Mathematics and Science, and a variety of university, state, and school agencies. She has written several books, including *Evaluation and the Postmodern Dilemma* (1997).